Rail Guide

2014

Colin J. Marsden

First published 2010
Reprinted 2010, 2011, 2012, 2013
This Fourth Edition first published 2014

ISBN 978 0 7110 3771 7

Published by Ian Allan Publishing.

An imprint of Ian Allan Publishing Ltd, Hersham, Surrey KT12 4RG.
Printed in Bulgaria.

Visit the Ian Allan Publishing website at www.ianallanpublishing.com

Distributed in the United States of America and Canada by BookMasters Distribution Services.

Front Cover Top: *Newly painted in Freightliner Powerhaul colours Class 66 No. 66504 runs out of a thunderstorm passing Barham Sidings on 4 May 2013 powering the 22.00 Coatbridge to Felixstowe intermodal.* **Antony Guppy**

Front Cover Bottom: *The latest Welsh Government-sponsored two-tone turquoise livery is now being widely applied to Arriva Trains Wales stock. Class 158 No. 158835 shows the livery at Cardiff on 6 June 2013.* **CJM**

Back Cover Top: *Dual voltage Class 378 'Electrostar' No. 378225 operating with Transport for London arrives at West Brompton on 1 May 2013 with a Stratford to Clapham Junction service.* **CJM**

Back Cover Bottom: *East Coast-operated Mk3 HST buffet car No. 40750 is seen from its counter end corridor side at Doncaster on 16 April 2013.* **CJM**

Acknowledgement – The Author would like to record his thanks to the many railway staff who have provided invaluable information for the production of this book. Also to the many photographers, especially Nathan Williamson, Antony Christie, Stacey Thew and John Binch, for providing many of the images. I would also like to express my thanks to Keith Ewins and Antony Christie for reading the updated manuscript. **CJM**

The 2014 edition of the Ian Allan *ABC Rail Guide*, the only comprehensive listing of all locomotives, multiple-units, coaches and track machines provided by operator, reflects the huge number of changes made to the UK rail system in 2013.

The year saw more new locomotives and multiple units ordered, extra sets already ordered enter traffic and many extra details emerge on the InterCity Express project (IEP) to replace the HST fleet on main-line routes and the Thameslink Class 700s.

In terms of locomotives, GBRf ordered yet more Class 66s, with an order for eight locos made in mid-summer for delivery in 2014. Colas Rail Freight also placed its first order for new traction when nine Class 70s were ordered from General Electric, while the operator also took over the Class 70 demonstrator No. 70099, which was renumbered to 70801. Direct Rail Services also ordered new power, with an announcement that 10 dual-mode electro-diesel Class 88s would be built by Vossloh in Spain to operate alongside its new Class 68 diesels on delivery in early 2014.

The DB-Schenker 'Super 60' upgrade project reached the target figure of 21 locos by the end of 2013; while no others were immediately being overhauled, it is likely that another batch will follow in 2014. During 2013, DB-S sold 20 of its long out of service Class 60s to Wabtec.

Colas Rail Freight also extended its Class 56 fleet by returning more long-out-of-services locos to the core fleet.

On the multiple unit front, First TransPennine Express started to take delivery of 'Desiro' Class 350/4 sets, while additional Class 350/3s for London Midland were expected in early 2014.

During 2013 the Class 377/6 five-car 'Electrostar' sets entered service on Southern, and two further orders for 377/7s and 377/8s were placed for delivery in 2014-15.

One of the largest EMU rebuild projects of modern times, that of extending the Class 458 sets from four to five cars and building six extra 458s from the former Class 460 Gatwick Express stock, made huge advances with the first of the 'new' five-car sets emerging from Wabtec Doncaster. This project calls for the entire front end of new and overhauled stock to be replaced with a Class 450-style cab.

With the delivery of the Class 377/6s to Southern, a start was made to transfer the 24 two-car Class 456 sets to South West Trains allowing operation of ten-car suburban trains.

During 2013, the new Class 374 'Eurostar' stock started to emerge from the Siemens plant in Germany and commence testing in Belgium; the first sets are not scheduled to enter service from the UK until at least 2015.

The Editor of the *ABC Rail Guide* welcomes correspondence about omissions or corrections or suggestions for further items to be included.

We hope you enjoy following the UK rail scene in 2014, but please always remember to keep safe, do not trespass on the railway and keep an eye open around you and if you see anything suspicious please notify the British Transport Police or a railway official.

Colin J. Marsden
Dawlish, January 2014

Information in Rail Guide 2014 is correct to 15 January 2014

Still painted in Channel Tunnel 'Railfreight Grey' colours and carrying an EWS 'animal head' logo on the bodyside, applied after EWS took over the UK freight operations in 1996, DB-Schenker-operated Class 92 No. 92037 **Sullivan** *passes South Kenton on the West Coast Main Line on 3 July 2013 in charge of the 11.34 Willesden to Daventry.* **CJM**

Train Operators, The Association of Train Operating Companies, and Network Rail welcome rail enthusiasts and photographers, but in today's safety-led railway and with the continued concerns about possible transport terrorism, guidelines are very important and we encourage all to follow these published guidelines as much as possible. They are available to view and download from the National Rail and ATOC websites, but are reproduced in full below to assist you with this information. ■

The Official Railway Enthusiasts Guidelines

■ Network Rail welcomes rail enthusiasts to our stations.
■ The following guidelines are designed to help you to have a safe and enjoyable experience. Please keep them with you when you are at Network Rail-managed stations.
■ You may also wish to take a copy of the Railway by-laws which are available from the Office of Public Sector Information website.

Before you enter the platform

■ When you arrive at a station, please let the staff at the Network Rail Reception Desk know that you are on the station. This will help keep station staff informed so that they can go about their duties without concern as to your reasons for being there.
■ You may require a platform ticket to allow access to platforms.

While you are on the platform

■ You need to act safely and sensibly at all times.

- Stay clear of the platform edge and stay behind the yellow lines where they are provided.
- Be aware of your surroundings.

Please DO NOT:

- Trespass on to the tracks or any other part of the railway that is not available to passengers.
- Use flash photography because it can distract train drivers and train despatch staff and so is potentially very dangerous.
- Climb on any structure or interfere with platform equipment.
- Obstruct any signalling equipment or signs which are vital to the safe running of the railway.
- Wear anything which is similar in colour to safety clothing, such as high-visibility jackets, as this could cause confusion to drivers and other railway employees.
- Gather together in groups at busy areas of the platform (e.g. customer information points, departure screens, waiting areas, seating etc.) or where this may interfere with the duties of station staff.

■ If possible, please try to avoid peak hours which are Monday – Friday 6:00am (06.00) – 10:30am (10.30) and 3:30pm (15.30) – 7:30pm (19.30).

Extra eyes and ears

■ If you see anything suspicious or notice any unusual behaviour or activities, please tell a member of staff immediately.
■ For emergencies and serious incidents, either call:
The British Transport Police on 0800 40 50 40.
The Police on 999, or 101
■ Your presence at a station can be very helpful to us as extra "eyes and ears" and can have a positive security benefit.

Photography

■ You can take photographs at stations provided you do not sell them. However, you are not allowed to take photographs of security related equipment, such as CCTV cameras.
■ Flash photography on platforms is not allowed at any time. It can distract train drivers and train despatch staff and so is potentially very dangerous.

■ Tripod legs must be kept away from platform edges and behind the yellow lines. On busy stations, you may not be allowed to use a tripod because it could be a dangerous obstruction to passengers.

Railway By-laws

For safety and ease of travel on the railway system (which includes passengers, staff, property and equipment), the by-laws must be observed by everyone. A copy of the by-laws can be obtained at stations or downloaded from the Office of Public Sector Information website.

General

Train operators must put the safety of their passengers and staff first. You may very occasionally be asked by station staff to move to another part of the station or to leave the station altogether. Station staff should be happy to explain why this is necessary. If you are travelling by train, they may ask you to remain in the normal waiting areas with other passengers. If this occurs, please follow their instructions with goodwill as staff have many things to consider, including the safety and security of all passengers, and are authorised to use judgement in this regard.

Below: *In recent years the Class 56 fleet has seen a signifficant return to front-line use with both the smaller freight operators and loco hire providers. One of the largest users in 2014 is Colas Rail Freight, with a growing fleet based at Washwood Heath and deployed on a diverse selection of medium and long-distance freight and departmental traffic flows. One traffic the class has been seen regularly operating are the log flows for Kronospan based in Chirk, North Wales, with the class powering loaded log trains to their workshops from South Wales, The West Country, Cumbria and Scotland. On 31 July 2013, No. 56087 passes Hereford, powering train 6Z52, the 11.13 Chirk Kronospan to Teigngrace empty log service.* **CJM**

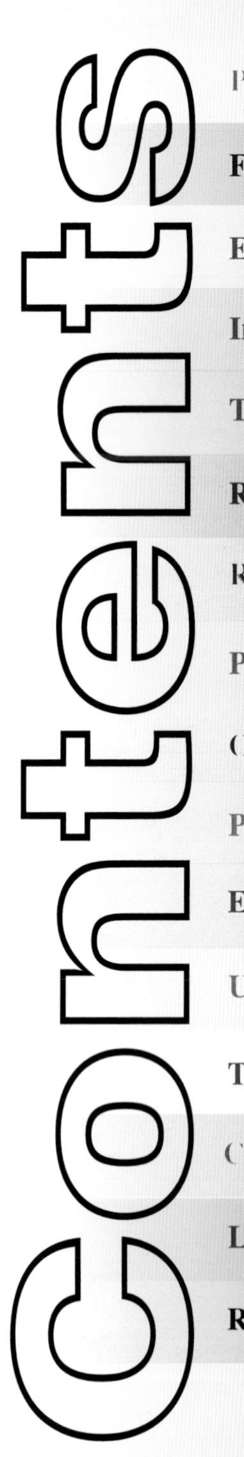

Contents

Arriva Trains Wales
Trenau Arriva Cymru

Address: ✉ St Mary's House, 47 Penarth Road, Cardiff, CF10 5DJ

customer.relations@arrivatrainswales.co.uk

✆ 0845 6061 660

ⓘ www.arrivatrainswales.co.uk

Managing Director: Ian Bullock

Franchise Dates: 7 December 2003 - October 2018

Principal Routes: Cardiff to Swansea and West Wales
Cardiff Valleys
Cardiff - Hereford - Shrewsbury - Crewe - Manchester Piccadilly
Cardiff - Hereford - Shrewsbury - Chester - Bangor - Holyhead
Manchester - Crewe - Bangor - Holyhead
Shrewsbury - Pwllheli / Aberystwyth
Swansea - Shrewsbury

Depots: Cardiff Canton (CF), Chester (CH), Holyhead* (HD)
Machynlleth (MN), Shrewsbury* (SX) * Stabling point

Parent Company: Deutsche Bahn AG (DB Regio)

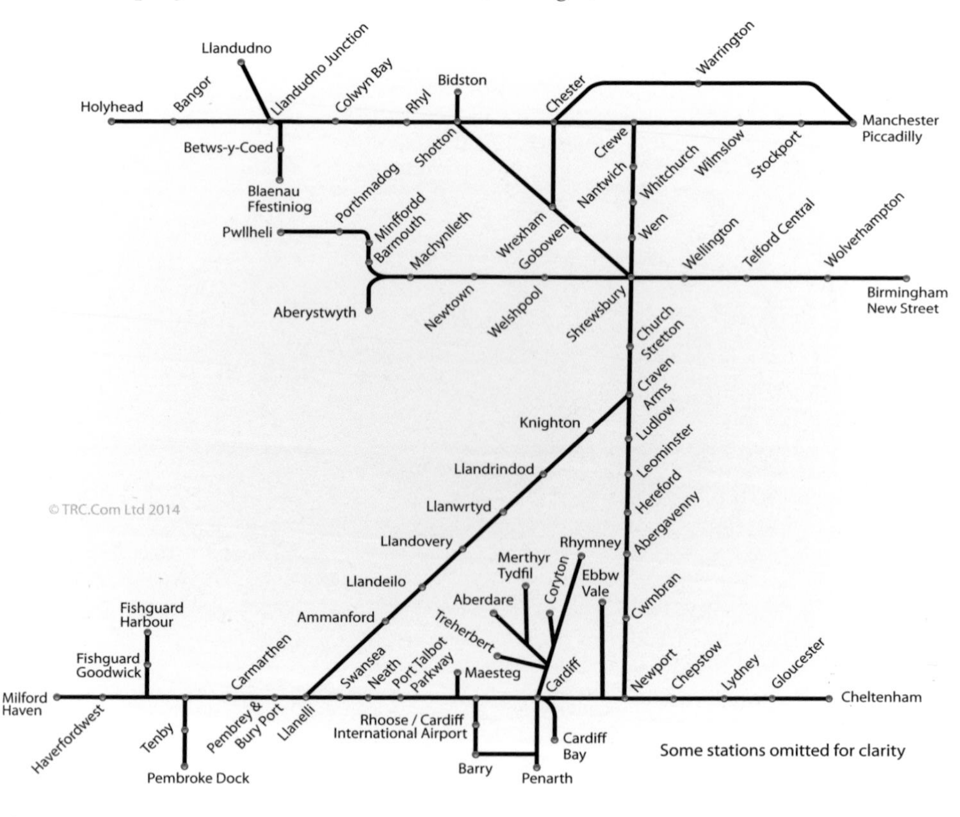

Class 67

Vehicle Length: 64ft 7in (19.68m)
Height: 12ft 9in (3.88m)
Width: 8ft 9in (2.66m)
Engine: EMD 12N-710G3B-EC
Horsepower: 2,980hp (2,223kW)
Electrical Equipment: EMD

Number	Depot	Pool	Livery	Owner	Operator
67001	CE	WATN	ATW	ANG	DBS/ATW
67002	CE	WATN	ATW	ANG	DBS/ATW
67003	CE	WATN	ATW	ANG	DBS/ATW

Right: *Three DB-Schenker Class 67s, Nos. 67001-67003, are dedicated to the ATW Cardiff-Holyhead route loco-hauled service. The three locos are painted in Arriva Trains mid blue with a light grey roof. No bodyside branding is carried. The locos power rakes of four or five refurbished Mk3 stock with a DVT forming one southbound train between Holyhead and Cardiff in the morning and a return service in the late afternoon. No. 67001 is seen at Newport on 6 June 2013, leading the 05.33 Holyhead to Cardiff service.* **CJM**

Class 142

Vehicle Length: 51ft 0½in (15.55m)
Height: 12ft 8in (3.86m)
Width: 9ft 2¼in (2.80m)
Engine: 1 x Cummins LTA10-R per vehicle
Horsepower: 460hp (343kW)
Seats (total/car): 90S, 46S/44S

Number	Formation DMS+DMSL	Depot	Livery	Owner	Operator
142002	55543+55593	CF	ATW	ANG	ATW
142006	55547+55597	CF	ATW	ANG	ATW
142010	55551+55601	CF	ATW	ANG	ATW
142069	55719+55765	CF	ATW	ANG	ATW
142072	55722+55768	CF	ATW	ANG	ATW
142073	55723+55769	CF	ATW	ANG	ATW
142074	55724+55770	CF	ATW	ANG	ATW
142075	55725+55771	CF	ATW	ANG	ATW
142076	55726+55772	CF	ATW	ANG	ATW
142077	55727+55773	CF	ATW	ANG	ATW
142080	55730+55776	CF	ATW	ANG	ATW
142081	55731+55777	CF	ATW	ANG	ATW
142082	55732+55778	CF	ATW	ANG	ATW
142083	55733+55779	CF	ATW	ANG	ATW
142085	55735+55781	CF	ATW	ANG	ATW

Name applied
142072 *Myfanwy*

Above: *A fleet of 15 Class 142s operates from Cardiff on Valley Line services, working alongside the Class 143 and 150 fleets, usually in pairs. On 6 June 2013, Nos. 142085 and 142082 are recorded at Taffs Well, forming the 13.47 Treherbert to Cardiff Central service. All the '142s' have 2+2 low-density seating.* **CJM**

Arriva Trains Wales

Class 143

Vehicle Length: 51ft 0½in (15.55m)
Height: 12ft 2¼in (3.73m)
Width: 8ft 10½in (2.70m)
Engine: 1 x Cummins LTA10-R per vehicle
Horsepower: 460hp (343kW)
Seats (total/car): 92S, 48S/44S

Number	Formation DMS+DMSL	Depot	Livery	Owner	Operator
143601	55642+55667	CF	ATW	BCC	ATW
143602	55651+55668	CF	ATW	PTR	ATW
143604	55645+55670	CF	ATW	PTR	ATW
143605	55646+55671	CF	ATT	PTR	ATW
143606	55647+55672	CF	ATW	PTR	ATW
143607	55648+55673	CF	ATW	PTR	ATW
143608	55649+55674	CF	ATW	PTR	ATW
143609	55650+55675	CF	ATW	CCC	ATW
143610	55643+55676	CF	ATW	BCC	ATW
143614	55655+55680	CF	ATW	BCC	ATW
143616	55657+55682	CF	ATW	PTR	ATW
143622	55663+55688	CF	ATW	PTR	ATW
143623	55664+55689	CF	ATW	PTR	ATW
143624	55665+55690	CF	ATT	PTR	ATW
143625	55666+55691	CF	ATW	PTR	ATW

Name applied

143609 ***Sir Tom Jones***

Below: *ATW has a fleet of 15 refurbished Class 143s with 2+2 seating allocated to Cardiff for Valley Line operation and usually operated in a mixed pool with the Class 142s. Set No. 143623 is seen with a Cardiff-bound service at Radyr in June 2013 coupled to a Class 150 set. These sets are likely to remain in the Cardiff area until replaced following electrification.* **CJM**

Class 150/2

Vehicle Length: 64ft 9¾in (19.74m)
Height: 12ft 4½in (3.77m)
Width: 9ft 3⅛in (2.82m)
Engine: 1 x NT855R5 of 285hp per vehicle
Horsepower: 570hp (425kW)
Seats (total/car): 128S, 60S/68S

Number	Formation DMSL+DMS	Depot	Livery	Owner	Operator
150208	52208+57208	CF	ATW	PTR	ATW
150213	52213+57213	CF	ATT	PTR	ATW
150217	52217+57217	CF	ATW	PTR	ATW
150227	52227+57227	CF	ATW	PTR	ATW
150229	52227+57227	CF	ATW	PTR	ATW
150230	52230+57230	CF	ATW	PTR	ATW
150231	52231+57231	CF	ATW	PTR	ATW
150235	52235+57235	CF	ATW	PTR	ATW
150236	52236+57236	CF	ATT	PTR	ATW
150237	52237+57237	CF	ATT	PTR	ATW
150240	52240+57240	CF	ATW	PTR	ATW
150241	52241+57241	CF	ATW	PTR	ATW
150242	52242+57242	CF	ATW	PTR	ATW
150245	52245+57245	CF	ATW	PTR	ATW
150250	52250+57250	CF	ATT	PTR	ATW
150251	52251+57251	CF	ATT	PTR	ATW
150252	52252+57252	CF	ATT	PTR	ATW
150253	52253+57253	CF	ATT	PTR	ATW
150254	52254+57254	CF	ATW	PTR	ATW
150255	52213+57255	CF	ATT	PTR	ATW
150256	52256+57256	CF	ATW	PTR	ATW
150257	52257+57257	CF	ATT	PTR	ATW

150258	52258+57258	CF	ATW	PTR	ATW
150259	52259+57259	CF	ATW	PTR	ATW
150260	52260+57260	CF	ATW	PTR	ATW
150262	52262+57262	CF	ATW	PTR	ATW
150264	52264+57264	CF	ATW	PTR	ATW
150267	52267+57267	CF	ATW	PTR	ATW
150278	52278+57278	CF	ATT	PTR	ATW
150279	52270+57279	CF	ATT	PTR	ATW
150280	52280+57280	CF	ATT	PTR	ATW
150281	52281+57281	CF	ATW	PTR	ATW
150282	52282+57282	CF	ATW	PTR	ATW
150283	52283+57283	CF	ATW	PTR	ATW
150284	52284+57284	CF	ATT	PTR	ATW
150285	52285+57280	CF	ATW	PTR	ATW

Right: *Refurbishment of the 36 Cardiff-allocated Class 150/2 sets has commenced with sets emerging from the LNWR Workshops at Crewe painted in the revised ATW two-tone turquoise livery, with bodyside branding showing rail support by the Welsh Assembly Government. Refurbished and re-liveried set No. 150236 departs from Taffs Well on 6 June 2013 forming the 13.38 Merthyr Tydfil to Bridgend service.* **CJM**

Class 153

Vehicle Length: 76ft 5in (23.29m)
Height: 12ft 3⅛in (3.75m)
Width: 8ft 10in (2.70m)
Engine: 1 x NT855R5 of 285hp
Horsepower: 285hp (213kW)
Seats (total/car): 72S

Number	*Formation DMSL*	*Depot*	*Livery*	*Owner*	*Operator*
153303	52303	CF	ATW	ANG	ATW
153312	52312	CF	ATT	ANG	ATW
153320	52320	CF	ATW	PTR	ATW
153323	52323	CF	ATT	PTR	ATW
153327	52327	CF	ATW	ANG	ATW
153353	57353	CF	ATT	ANG	ATW
153362	57362	CF	ATW	ANG	ATW
153367	57367	CF	ATW	PTR	ATW

Right: *Owned by both Angel Trains and Porterbrook Leasing, ATW operates a fleet of eight single-car Class 153 vehicles, based at Cardiff for use on lightly used services as well as on the Cardiff Queen Street to Cardiff Bay 'shuttle' service. The vehicles are painted in standard ATW livery and have 2+2 seating. These vehicles were adapted from Class 155 two-car sets many years ago to provide greater flexibility to operators. Set No. 153303 is seen at Cardiff Queen Street with a 'shuttle' service bound for Cardiff Bay.* **CJM**

Class 158

Vehicle Length: 76ft 1¾in (23.21m)
Height: 12ft 6in (3.81m)
Width: 9ft 3¼in (2.82m)
Engine: 1 x Perkins 2006-TWH of 350hp per vehicle
Horsepower: 700hp (522kW)
Seats (total/car): 134S, 66S/68S

Number	*Formation DMSL+DMSL*	*Depot*	*Livery*	*Owner*	*Operator*
158818	52818+57818	MN	ATT	ANG	ATW
158819	52819+57819	MN	ATT	ANG	ATW
158820	52820+57820	MN	ATT	ANG	ATW
158821	52821+57821	MN	ATT	ANG	ATW
158822	52822+57822	MN	ATT	ANG	ATW
158823	52823+57823	MN	ATT	ANG	ATW
158824	52824+57824	MN	ATT	ANG	ATW
158825	52825+57825	MN	ATT	ANG	ATW
158826	52826+57826	MN	ATT	ANG	ATW
158827	52827+57827	MN	ATT	ANG	ATW
158828	52828+57828	MN	ATT	ANG	ATW
158829	52829+57829	MN	ATT	ANG	ATW
158830	52830+57830	MN	ATT	ANG	ATW
158831	52831+57831	MN	ATT	ANG	ATW
158832	52832+57832	MN	ATT	ANG	ATW
158833	52833+57833	MN	ATT	ANG	ATW
158834	52834+57834	MN	ATT	ANG	ATW
158835	52835+57835	MN	ATT	ANG	ATW
158836	52836+57836	MN	ATT	ANG	ATW
158837	52837+57837	CF	ATT	ANG	ATW
158838	52838+57838	CF	ATT	ANG	ATW
158839	52839+57839	CF	ATT	ANG	ATW
158840	52840+57840	CF	ATT	ANG	ATW
158841	52841+57841	CF	ATT	ANG	ATW

Arriva Trains Wales

Left: *A fleet of 24 two-car Class 158s is allocated to ATW and maintained at Machynlleth and Cardiff depots, being owned by Angel Trains. All sets are fitted with ERTMS for use on the Cambrian Line. All sets are now refurbished and carry the latest Arriva Trains Wales two-tone turquoise livery. Set No. 158835 is seen at Cardiff Central with stock to form a Holyhead service.* **CJM**

Class 175/0
Coradia 1000

Vehicle Length: 75ft 7in (23.06m)
Height: 12ft 4in (3.75m)
Width: 9ft 2in (2.80m)
Engine: 1 x Cummins N14 of 450hp per vehicle
Horsepower: 900hp (671kW)
Seats (total/car): 118S, 54S/64S

Number	*Formation DMSL+DMSL*	*Depot*	*Livery*	*Owner*	*Operator*
175001	50701+79701	CH	ATW	ANG	ATW
175002	50702+79702	CH	ATW	ANG	ATW
175003	50703+79703	CH	ATW	ANG	ATW
175004	50704+79704	CH	ATW	ANG	ATW
175005	50705+79705	CH	ATW	ANG	ATW
175006	50706+79706	CH	ATW	ANG	ATW
175007	50707+79707	CH	ATW	ANG	ATW
175008	50708+79708	CH	ATW	ANG	ATW
175009	50709+79709	CH	ATW	ANG	ATW
175010	50710+79710	CH	ATW	ANG	ATW
175011	50711+79711	CH	ATW	ANG	ATW

Left: *A fleet of 27 long-distance Class 175 units is operated by Arriva Trains Wales, owned by Angel Trains. Eleven two-car sets are allocated to Chester and usually operate the north to south and west Wales services. Sets have 2+2 seating, in a mix or group and airline. All '175s' are painted in the standard Arriva Trains livery. Set No. 175010 is seen at Newport with a Manchester Piccadilly to Milford Haven service.* **CJM**

Class 175/1
Coradia 1000

Vehicle Length: 75ft 7in (23.06m)
Height: 12ft 4in (3.75m)
Width: 9ft 2in (2.80m)
Engine: 1 x Cummins N14 of 450hp per vehicle
Horsepower: 1,350hp (1,007kW)
Seats (total/car): 186S, 54S/68S/64S

Number	*Formation DMSL+MSL+DMSL*	*Depot*	*Livery*	*Owner*	*Op'r*
175101	50751+56751+79751	CH	ATW	ANG	ATW
175102	50752+56752+79752	CH	ATW	ANG	ATW
175103	50753+56753+79753	CH	ATW	ANG	ATW
175104	50754+56754+79754	CH	ATW	ANG	ATW
175105	50755+56755+79755	CH	ATW	ANG	ATW
175106	50756+56756+79756	CH	ATW	ANG	ATW
175107	50757+56757+79757	CH	ATW	ANG	ATW
175108	50758+56758+79758	CH	ATW	ANG	ATW
175109	50759+56759+79759	CH	ATW	ANG	ATW
175110	50760+56760+79760	CH	ATW	ANG	ATW
175111	50761+56761+79761	CH	ATW	ANG	ATW
175112	50762+56762+79762	CH	ATW	ANG	ATW
175113	50763+56763+79763	CH	ATW	ANG	ATW
175114	50764+56764+79764	CH	ATW	ANG	ATW
175115	50765+56765+79765	CH	ATW	ANG	ATW
175116	50766+56766+79766	CH	ATW	ANG	ATW

Left: *Sixteen members of the Class 175 fleet, classified as 175/1, are formed of three coaches, with an additional intermediate MSL vehicle seating 68 standard class passengers. These sets are usually rostered for the more heavily loaded services with a train capacity of 186 standard class passengers. Three-car set No. 175109 stands at Cardiff Central on 6 June 2013 with the 08.04 Fishguard Harbour to Manchester Piccadilly service.* **CJM**

Class AJ1G / RFM

Vehicle Length: 75ft 0in (22.86m) *Width: 8ft 11in (2.71m)*
Height: 12ft 9in (3.88m) *Bogie Type: BT10*

Number	Type	Depot	Livery	Owner	Operator
10249 (10012)	RFM	CF	ATT	DBR	ATW
10259 (10025)	RFM	CF	ATT	ATW	ATW

Above: *The present Arriva Trains Wales loco-hauled fleet consists of just eight Mk3 passenger and three non-passenger DVT vehicles. All are refurbished and allocated to Cardiff to operate exclusively on the one out-and-back daily service between Holyhead and Cardiff. First class and refreshment facilities are provided by two RFM vehicles, painted in the latest joint Arriva/Welsh Assembly Government livery. Vehicle No. 10259 is shown in a train consist at Newport.* **CJM**

Class AD1H / TSO

Vehicle Length: 75ft 0in (22.86m) *Width: 8ft 11in (2.71m)*
Height: 12ft 9in (3.88m) *Bogie Type: BT10*

Number	Type	Depot	Livery	Owner	Operator
12176 (11064)	TSO	CF	ATT	ATW	ATW
12177 (11065)	TSO	CF	ATT	ATW	ATW
12178 (11071)	TSO	CF	ATT	ATW	ATW
12179 (11083)	TSO	CF	ATT	ATW	ATW
12180 (11084)	TSO	CF	ATT	ATW	ATW
12181 (11086)	TSO	CF	ATT	ATW	ATW

Right: *Six heavily refurbished Mk3 TSOs form the main ATW loco-hauled passenger fleet, allocated to Cardiff. These coaches were rebuilt from Mk3a FO stock. Seating is now in the 2+2 style in a mix of airline and group. Car No. 12180 is illustrated.* **CJM**

Mk3 Hauled Stock (NPCCS)

Length: 75ft 0in (22.86m) *Width: 8ft 11in (2.71m)*
Height: 12ft 9in (3.88m) *Bogie Type: BT7*

NZAG - DVT

Number	Depot	Livery	Owner	Operator
82306 (82144)	CF	ATT	ATW	ATW
82307 (82131)	CF	ATT	ATW	ATW

Right: *Remote driving facilities for the ATW loco-hauled services are provided by a fleet of two Mk3 DVTs. These were heavily rebuilt by Brush Traction to allow operation with the Class 67s, and were renumbered into a new 823xx series (together with the Chiltern DVTs). Vehicle No. 82308 is illustrated which has now been transferred to Chiltern Railways.* **CJM**

c2c

Address: ✉ 10th Floor, 207 Old Street, London, EC1V 9NR
c2c.customerrelations@nationalexpress.com
✆ 0845 6014873
ⓘ www.c2c-online.co.uk

Managing Director: Julian Drury
Franchise Dates: 26 May 1996 - extension to 13 September 2014 §
Principal Routes: London Fenchurch Street - Shoeburyness
Barking - Pitsea via Purfleet
Ockendon branch
London Liverpool Street - Barking (limited service)
Depots: East Ham (EM), Shoeburyness*
* Stabling point
Parent Company: National Express

§ Likely to be extended, re-franchising placed on hold

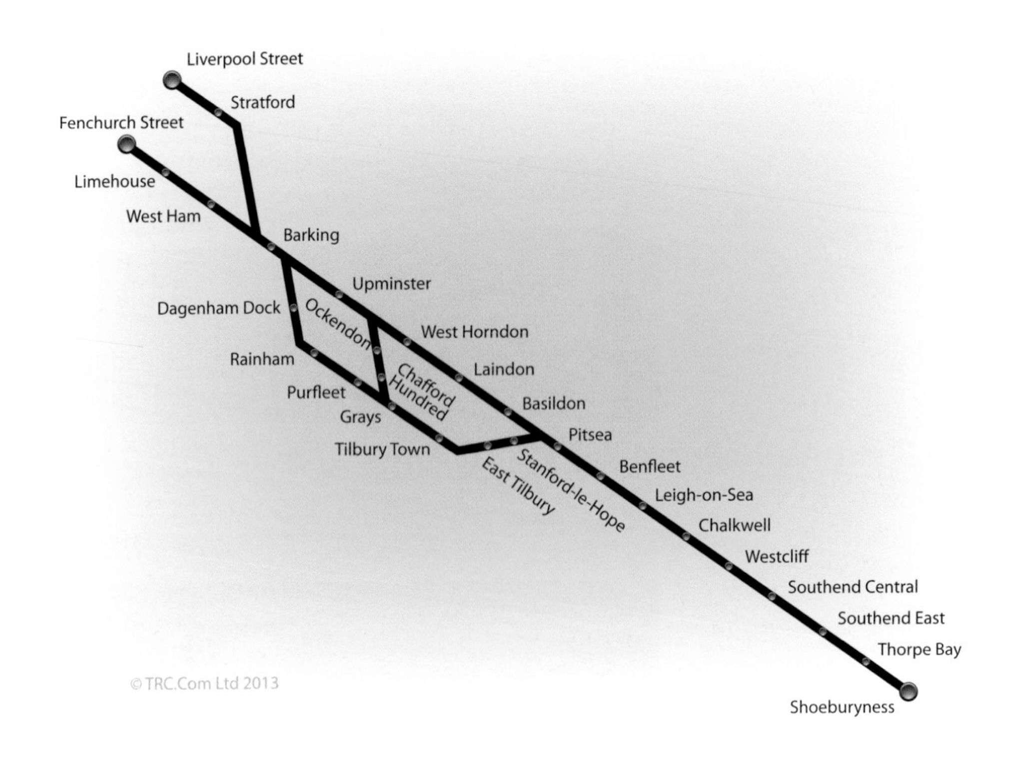

Class 357/0
Electrostar

Vehicle Length: (Driving) 68ft 1in (20.75m) *Width: 9ft 2½in (2.80m)*
(Inter) 65ft 11½in (20.10m) *Horsepower: 2,011hp (1,500kW)*
Height: 12ft 4½in (3.78m) *Seats (total/car): 282S, 71S/78S/62S/71S*

Number	*Formation* DMSO(A)+MSO+PTSO+DMSO(B)	*Depot*	*Livery*	*Owner*	*Op'r*	*Name*
357001	67651+74151+74051+67751	EM	NE2	PTR	c2c	*Barry Flaxman*
357002	67652+74152+74052+67752	EM	NE2	PTR	c2c	*Arthur Lewis Stride 1841-1922*
357003	67653+74153+74053+67753	EM	NE2	PTR	c2c	*Southend City on Sea*
357004	67654+74154+74054+67754	EM	NE2	PTR	c2c	*Tony Amos*
357005	67655+74155+74055+67755	EM	NE2	PTR	c2c	
357006	67656+74156+74056+67756	EM	NE2	PTR	c2c	*Diamond Jubilee 1952 - 2012*
357007	67657+74157+74057+67757	EM	NE2	PTR	c2c	
357008	67658+74158+74058+67758	EM	NE2	PTR	c2c	
357009	67659+74159+74059+67759	EM	NE2	PTR	c2c	
357010	67660+74160+74060+67760	EM	NE2	PTR	c2c	
357011	67661+74161+74061+67761	EM	NE2	PTR	c2c	*John Lowing*
357012	67662+74162+74062+67762	EM	NE2	PTR	c2c	
357013	67663+74163+74063+67763	EM	NE2	PTR	c2c	
357014	67664+74164+74064+67764	EM	NE2	PTR	c2c	
357015	67665+74165+74065+67765	EM	NE2	PTR	c2c	
357016	67666+74166+74066+67766	EM	NE2	PTR	c2c	
357017	67667+74167+74067+67767	EM	NE2	PTR	c2c	
357018	67668+74168+74068+67768	EM	NE2	PTR	c2c	
357019	67669+74169+74069+67769	EM	NE2	PTR	c2c	
357020	67670+74170+74070+67770	EM	NE2	PTR	c2c	
357021	67621+74171+74071+67771	EM	NE2	PTR	c2c	
357022	67672+74172+74072+67772	EM	NE2	PTR	c2c	
357023	67673+74173+74073+67773	EM	NE2	PTR	c2c	
357024	67674+74174+74074+67774	EM	NE2	PTR	c2c	
357025	67675+74175+74075+67775	EM	NE2	PTR	c2c	
357026	67676+74176+74076+67776	EM	NE2	PTR	c2c	
357027	67677+74177+74077+67777	EM	NE2	PTR	c2c	
357028	67678+74178+74078+67778	EM	NE2	PTR	c2c	*London, Tilbury & Southend Railway 1854-2004*
357029	67679+74179+74079+67779	EM	NE2	PTR	c2c	*Thomas Whitelegg 1840-1922*
357030	67680+74180+74080+67780	EM	NE2	PTR	c2c	*Robert Harben Whitelegg 1871-1957*
357031	67681+74181+74081+67781	EM	NE2	PTR	c2c	
357032	67682+74182+74082+67782	EM	NE2	PTR	c2c	
357033	67683+74183+74083+67783	EM	NE2	PTR	c2c	
357034	67684+74184+74084+67784	EM	NE2	PTR	c2c	
357035	67685+74185+74085+67785	EM	NE2	PTR	c2c	
357036	67686+74186+74086+67786	EM	NE2	PTR	c2c	
357037	67687+74187+74087+67787	EM	NE2	PTR	c2c	
357038	67688+74188+74088+67788	EM	NE2	PTR	c2c	
357039	67689+74189+74089+67789	EM	NE2	PTR	c2c	
357040	67690+74190+74090+67790	EM	NE2	PTR	c2c	
357041	67691+74191+74091+67791	EM	NE2	PTR	c2c	
357042	67692+74192+74092+67792	EM	NE2	PTR	c2c	
357043	67693+74193+74093+67793	EM	NE2	PTR	c2c	
357044	67694+74194+74094+67794	EM	NE2	PTR	c2c	
357045	67695+74195+74095+67795	EM	NE2	PTR	c2c	
357046	67696+74196+74096+67796	EM	NE2	PTR	c2c	

Right: *Two fleets of non-end-corridor-fitted 'Electrostar' stock form the c2c passenger fleet. The 46 Class 357/0 sets are owned by Porterbrook. All sets are allocated to East Ham and carry the standard c2c National Express white livery. Set No. 357036 is seen from its DMSO(B) end passing Shadwell. These units operate in a common pool with the Class 375/2 fleet.* **CJM**

c2c

Class 357/2
Electrostar

Vehicle Length: (Driving) 68ft 1in (20.75m)
(Inter) 65ft 11½in (20.10m)
Height: 12ft 4½in (3.78m)
Width: 9ft 2½in (2.80m)
Horsepower: 2,011hp (1,500kW)
Seats (total/car): 282S, 71S/78S/62S/71S

Number	*Formation* DMSO(A)+MSO+PTSO+DMSO(B)	*Depot*	*Livery*	*Owner*	*Operator*	*Name*
357201	68601+74701+74601+68701	EM	NE2	ANG	c2c	*Ken Bird*
357202	68602+74702+74602+68702	EM	NE2	ANG	c2c	*Kenny Mitchell*
357203	68603+74703+74603+68703	EM	NE2	ANG	c2c	*Henry Pumfrett*
357204	68604+74704+74604+68704	EM	NE2	ANG	c2c	*Derek Flowers*
357205	68605+74705+74605+68705	EM	NE2	ANG	c2c	*John D'Silva*
357206	68606+74706+74606+68706	EM	NE2	ANG	c2c	*Martin Aungier*
357207	68607+74707+74607+68707	EM	NE2	ANG	c2c	*John Page*
357208	68608+74708+74608+68708	EM	NE2	ANG	c2c	*Dave Davis*
357209	68609+74709+74609+68709	EM	NE2	ANG	c2c	*James Snelling*
357210	68610+74710+74610+68710	EM	NE2	ANG	c2c	
357211	68611+74711+74611+68711	EM	NE2	ANG	c2c	
357212	68612+74712+74612+68712	EM	NE2	ANG	c2c	
357213	68613+74713+74613+68713	EM	NE2	ANG	c2c	*Upminster IECC*
357214	68614+74714+74614+68714	EM	NE2	ANG	c2c	
357215	68615+74715+74615+68715	EM	NE2	ANG	c2c	
357216	68616+74716+74616+68716	EM	NE2	ANG	c2c	
357217	68617+74717+74617+68717	EM	NE2	ANG	c2c	*Allan Burnell*
357218	68618+74218+74618+68718	EM	NE2	ANG	c2c	
357219	68619+74719+74619+68719	EM	NE2	ANG	c2c	
357220	68620+74720+74620+68720	EM	NE2	ANG	c2c	
357221	68621+74721+74621+68721	EM	NE2	ANG	c2c	
357222	68622+74722+74622+68722	EM	NE2	ANG	c2c	
357223	68623+74723+74623+68723	EM	NE2	ANG	c2c	
357224	68624+74724+74624+68724	EM	NE2	ANG	c2c	
357225	68625+74725+74625+68725	EM	NE2	ANG	c2c	
357226	68626+74726+74626+68726	EM	NE2	ANG	c2c	
357227	68627+74727+74627+68727	EM	NE2	ANG	c2c	*Southend United*
357228	68628+74728+74628+68728	EM	NE2	ANG	c2c	

Below: *A follow-on fleet of 28 Class 357/2 sets was built, funded by Angel Trains and these are identical to the slightly earlier Class 357/0 fleet. With its DMSO(A) leading, set No. 357214 departs from Fenchurch Street and approaches Shadwell on 19 September 2013 forming the 13.30 Fenchurch Street to Shoeburyness service.* **CJM**

Chiltern Railways

Address: ✉ 2nd floor, Western House, Rickfords Hill, Aylesbury, Buckinghamshire, HP20 2RX
Via website (www.chilternrailways.co.uk)
✆ 08456 005165
ⓘ www.chilternrailways.co.uk

Managing Director: Rob Brighthouse
Franchise Dates: 21 July 1996 - 21 December 2021
Principal Routes: London Marylebone - Birmingham Snow Hill
London Marylebone - Aylesbury
London Marylebone - Stratford-upon-Avon
Depots: Aylesbury (AL), Wembley*
* Stabling point
Parent Company: Deutsche Bahn AG (DB Regio)

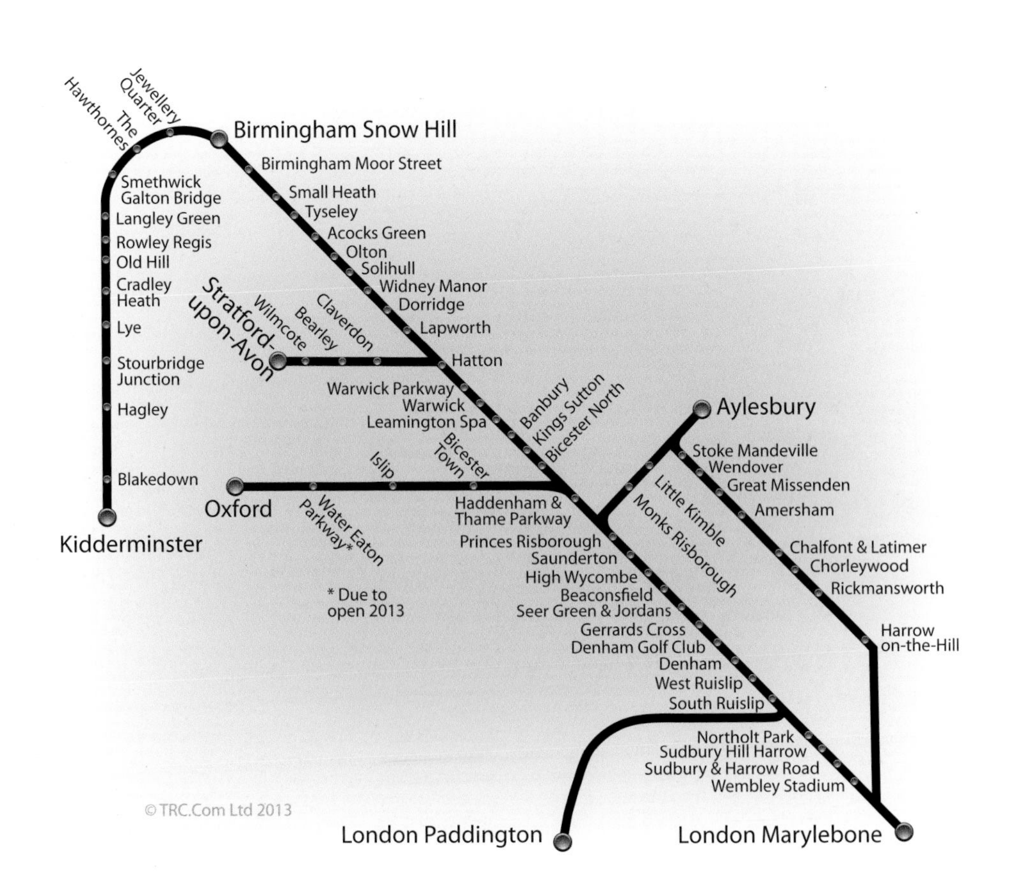

Chiltern Railways

Class 121

Length: 64ft 6in (19.66m)
Height: 12ft 8½in (3.87m)
Width: 9ft 3in (2.81m)
Engine: 2 x Leyland 150hp
Horsepower: 300hp (224kW)
Seats (total/car): 65S

Number	Formation DMBS	Depot	Livery	Owner	Operator
121020	55020	AY	BLU	CRW	CRW
121032(S)	55032	AY	ATW	CRW	-
121034	55034	AY	GRN	CRW	CRW

Left: *Three 'heritage' Class 121 'bubble-car' vehicles are on the books of Chiltern, allocated to Aylesbury for use on the Aylesbury to Princes Risborough line. Car No. 55032 recently obtained from ATW is to provide spares for the two operational vehicles. Green-liveried No. 55034 is illustrated. All vehicles have central door locking.* **Kim Fullbrook**

Class 165/0 (2-car)
Networker Turbo

Vehicle Length: (Driving) 75ft 2½in (22.91m), (Inter) 74ft 6½in (22.72m)
Height: 12ft 5¼in (3.79m)
Width: 9ft 2½in (2.81m)
Engine: 1 x Perkins 2006 TWH of 350hp per vehicle
Horsepower: 700hp (522kW)
Seats (total/car): 183S, 89S/94S

Number	Formation DMSL+DMS	Depot	Livery	Owner	Operator
165001	58801+58834	AL	CRW	ANG	CRW
165002	58802+58835	AL	CRW	ANG	CRW
165003	58803+58836	AL	CRW	ANG	CRW
165004	58804+58837	AL	CRW	ANG	CRW
165005	58805+58838	AL	CRW	ANG	CRW
165006	58806+58839	AL	CRW	ANG	CRW
165007	58807+58840	AL	CRW	ANG	CRW
165008	58808+58841	AL	CRW	ANG	CRW
165009	58809+58842	AL	CRW	ANG	CRW
165010	58810+58843	AL	CRW	ANG	CRW
165011	58811+58844	AL	CRW	ANG	CRW
165012	58812+58845	AL	CRW	ANG	CRW
165013	58813+58846	AL	CRW	ANG	CRW
165014	58814+58847	AL	CRW	ANG	CRW
165015	58815+58848	AL	CRW	ANG	CRW
165016	58816+58849	AL	CRW	ANG	CRW
165017	58817+58850	AL	CRW	ANG	CRW
165018	58818+58851	AL	CRW	ANG	CRW
165019	58819+58852	AL	CRW	ANG	CRW
165020	58820+58853	AL	CRW	ANG	CRW
165021	58821+58854	AL	CRW	ANG	CRW
165022	58822+58855	AL	CRW	ANG	CRW
165023	58873+58867	AL	CRW	ANG	CRW
165024	58874+58868	AL	CRW	ANG	CRW
165025	58874+58869	AL	CRW	ANG	CRW
165026	58876+58870	AL	CRW	ANG	CRW
165027	58877+58871	AL	CRW	ANG	CRW
165028	58878+58872	AL	CRW	ANG	CRW

Left: *Under Network SouthEast, in the final years of British Rail, the Chiltern route was modernised with the introduction of a fleet of Class 165 'Networker Turbo' sets, maintained at a new purpose-built depot located at Aylesbury. The sets came in both two-car and three-car formation. All have subsequently been refurbished with new one-class interiors and updated front ends. Two-car set No. 165020 is seen at Birmingham Moor Street displaying the standard Chiltern Railways livery.* **John Binch**

Class 165/0 (3-car)
Networker Turbo

Vehicle Length: (driving) 75ft 2½in (22.91m), (Inter) 74ft 6½in (22.72m)
Height: 12ft 5¼in (3.79m)
Width: 9ft 2½in (2.81m)
Engine: 1 x Perkins 2006 TWH of 350hp per vehicle
Horsepower: 1,050hp (783kW)
Seats (total/car): 289S, 89S/106S/94S

Number	Formation DMSL+MS+DMS	Depot	Livery	Owner	Operator
165029	58823+55404+58856	AL	CRW	ANG	CRW
165030	58824+55405+58857	AL	CRW	ANG	CRW
165031	58825+55406+58858	AL	CRW	ANG	CRW
165032	58826+55407+58859	AL	CRW	ANG	CRW
165033	58827+55408+58860	AL	CRW	ANG	CRW
165034	58828+55409+58861	AL	CRW	ANG	CRW
165035	58829+55410+58862	AL	CRW	ANG	CRW
165036	58830+55411+58863	AL	CRW	ANG	CRW
165037	58831+55412+58864	AL	CRW	ANG	CRW
165038	58832+55413+58865	AL	CRW	ANG	CRW
165039	58833+55414+58866	AL	CRW	ANG	CRW

Class 168/0
Turbostar

Vehicle Length: 77ft 6in (23.62m)
Height: 12ft 4½in (3.77m)
Width: 8ft 10in (2.69m)
Engine: 1 x MTU 6R 183TD13H 422hp per vehicle
Horsepower: 1,688hp (1,259kW)
Seats (total/car): 278S, 60S/73S/77S/68S

Number	Formation DMSL(A)+MSL+MS+DMSL(B)	Depot	Livery	Owner	Operator
168001	58151+58651+58451+58251	AL	CRW	PTR	CRW
168002	58152+58652+58452+58252	AL	CRG	PTR	CRW
168003	58153+58653+58453+58253	AL	CRW	PTR	CRW
168004	58154+58654+58454+58254	AL	CRG	PTR	CRW
168005	58155+58655+58455+58255	AL	CRW	PTR	CRW

Right: *Directly after privatisation, Chiltern Railways sought extra stock and ordered a fleet of Class 168/0s from Adtranz. Five four-car sets were built and were the first of the 'Turbostar' product line. Follow-on orders sported the revised and standard cab-end design. Set No. 168004 is seen at Banbury on 28 June 2013.* **Antony Christie**

Class 168/1
Turbostar

Vehicle Length: 77ft 6in (23.62m)
Height: 12ft 4½in (3.77m)
Width: 8ft 10in (2.69m)
Engine: 1 x MTU 6R 183TD13H of 422hp per vehicle
Horsepower: 3/4-car 1,266hp (944kW)/1,688hp (1,259kW)
Seats (total/car): 3-car - 208S, 59S/73S/76S, 4-car - 284S, 59S/73S/76S/76S

Number	Formation DMSL(A)+MS+MS+DMSL(B)	Depot	Livery	Owner	Operator	Notes
168106	58156+58756§+58456+58256	AL	CRW	PTR	CRW	§ is a MSL vehicle
168107	58157+58457+58757§+58257	AL	CRW	PTR	CRW	§ is a MSL vehicle
168108	58158+58458+58258	AL	CRW	PTR	CRW	
168109	58159+58459+58259	AL	CRW	PTR	CRW	
168110	58160+58460+58260	AL	CRW	PTR	CRW	
168111	58161+58461+58261	AL	CRW	EVL	CRW	58461 was originally 58661
168112	58162+58462+58262	AL	CRW	EVL	CRW	58462 was originally 58662
168113	58163+58463+58263	AL	CRW	EVL	CRW	58463 was originally 58663

Class 168/2
Turbostar

Vehicle Length: 77ft 6in (23.62m)
Height: 12ft 4½in (3.77m)
Width: 8ft 10in (2.69m)
Engine: 1 x MTU 6R 183TD13H of 422hp per vehicle
Horsepower: 3/4-car 1,266hp (944kW)/1,688hp (1,259kW)
Seats (total/car): 3-car - 204S, 59S/76S/69S, 4-car - 277S, 59S/73S/76S/696S

Number	Formation DMSL(A)+MS+MS+DMSL(B)	Depot	Livery	Owner	Operator
168214	58164+58464+58264	AL	CRW	PTR	CRW
168215	58165+58465+58365+58265	AL	CRG	PTR	CRW
168216	58166+58466+58366+58266	AL	CRG	PTR	CRW
168217	58167+58467+58367+58267	AL	CRG	PTR	CRW
168218	58168+58468+58268	AL	CRW	PTR	CRW
168219	58169+58469+58269	AL	CRG	PTR	CRW

Right: *In mid-2013 a start was made to refurbish the Chiltern Railways 'Turbostar' fleet with revised interiors and application of the new standard Chiltern grey livery, similar to that applied to its loco-hauled stock. Set No. 168216 is seen passing Dorridge on 29 September 2013.* **John Binch**

Chiltern Railways

Class 172/1

Vehicle Length: 73ft 4in (22.37m)
Height: 12ft 4½in (3.77m)
Width: 8ft 8in (2.69m)
Engine: MTU 6H1800 of 360kW
Horsepower: 965hp (720kW)
Seats (total/car): 121S, 53S/68S

Number	*Formation DMS+DMS*	*Depot*	*Livery*	*Owner*	*Operator*
172101	59111+59211	AL	CRW	ANG	CRW
172102	59112+59212	AL	CRW	ANG	CRW
172103	59113+59213	AL	CRW	ANG	CRW
172104	59114+59214	AL	CRW	ANG	CRW

Left: *Passenger growth on Chiltern Railways routes was such that extra stock was required and in 2011 four two-car Class 172 sets were ordered with funding from Angel Trains. The sets were a new design of DMMU. All four are allocated to Aylesbury and painted in Chiltern blue and white livery. Set No. 172101 is shown at London Marylebone.*
Antony Christie

Class 67

Vehicle Length: 64ft 7in (19.68m)
Height: 12ft 9in (3.88m)
Width: 8ft 9in (2.66m)
Engine: EMD 12N-710G3B-EC
Horsepower: 2,980hp (2,223kW)
Electrical Equipment: EMD

Number	*Depot*	*Pool*	*Livery*	*Owner*	*Operator*	*Name*
67010	CE	WNTR	CRG	ANG	DBS/CRW	
67012	CE	WAWN	CRG	ANG	DBS/CRW	*A Shropshire Lad*
67013	CE	WNTR	CRG	ANG	DBS/CRW	*Dyfrbont Pontcysyllte*
67014	CE	WAAN	CRG	ANG	DBS/CRW	*Thomas Telford*
67015	CE	WAWN	CRG	ANG	DBS/CRW	*David J. Lloyd*

Left: *Chiltern Railways took over the Class 67s previously used by Wrexham & Shropshire (W&S) Railways and now deploy these with upgraded Mk3 stock on main-line services between London Marylebone and Birmingham. The locos carry unbranded W&S livery with Chiltern branding and have retained their cast W&S nameplates. No. 67012* A Shropshire Lad *is seen passing Hatton on 15 August 2013.*
John Binch

Mk3 Hauled Stock (Passenger)

Vehicle Length: 75ft 0in (22.86m)
Height: 12ft 9in (3.88m) *Width: 8ft 11in (2.71m)*
Bogie Type: BT10

AJ1F - GFW *Seating 30F*

Number		*Depot*	*Livery*	*Owner*
10271	(10236/10018)	AL	CRG	DBR
10272	(10208/40517)	AL	CRG	DBR
10273	(10230/10021)	AL	CRG	DBR
10274	(10255/11010)	AL	CRG	DBR

AC2G - TSO/TSOL* *Seating 72S*

Number		*Depot*	*Livery*	*Owner*
12602	(12072)	AL	CRG	DBR
12603*	(12053)	AL	CRG	DBR
12604	(12131)	AL	CRG	DBR
12605*	(11040)	AL	CRG	DBR
12606	(12048)	AL	CRG	DBR
12607*	(12038)	AL	CRG	DBR
12608	(12069)	AL	CRG	DBR
12609*	(12014)	AL	CRG	DBR
12612	(12117)	AL	CRG	DBR
12613*	(12173/11042)	AL	CRG	DBR
12614	(12145)	AL	CRG	DBR

Number		Depot	Livery	Owner
12615*	(12059)	AL	CRG	DBR
12616	(12127)	AL	CRG	DBR
12617*	(12174/11050)	AL	CRG	DBR
12618	(12169)	AL	CRG	DBR
12619*	(12175/11052)	AL	CRG	DBR
12621	(11046)	AL	CRG	DBR
12623	(11019)	AL	CRG	DBR
12625	(11030)	AL	CRG	DBR
12627	(11054)	AL	CRG	DBR

Right: *A huge investment has been made by Chiltern Railways in its loco-hauled fleet, with power-operated plug doors installed. The only hinged doors to remain are the service doors of the GFW vehicles. GFW No. 10274 is shown; this was rebuilt from buffet vehicle 11010 (10225). All the loco-hauled stock is based at Aylesbury.* **Antony Christie**

Mk3 Hauled Stock (NPCCS)

Vehicle Length: 75ft 0in (22.86m)
Height: 12ft 9in (3.88m)
Width: 8ft 11in (2.71m)
Bogie Type: BT7

NZAG - DVT

Number	*Depot*	*Livery*	*Owner*
82301 (82117)	AL	CRG	DBR
82302 (82151)	AL	CRG	DBR
82303 (82135)	AL	CRG	DBR
82304 (82130)	AL	CRG	DBR
82305 (82134)	AL	CRG	DBR
82308 (82108)	AL	ATT	DBR
82309 (82104)	AL	CRG	DBR

Right: *The remote driving facility on the Chiltern Railways loco-hauled sets is provided by a fleet of five Mk3 DVTs, which have received major modification since their previous days with Virgin Trains. The vehicles are now fitted with an auxiliary Penta TAD1352GE diesel engine and alternator group; this is housed behind the driving cab with the near former luggage door replaced by a ventilation grille. An underslung fuel tank is also provided. Vehicle No. 82303 is illustrated.* **Antony Christie**

Class 960 – Service Units

Class 121
Length: 64ft 6in (19.66m)
Height: 12ft 8½in (3.87m)
Width: 9ft 3in (2.81m)
Engine: 2 x Leyland 150hp
Horsepower: 300hp (224kW)
Seats (total/car): None

Class 117
Length: 64ft 0in (19.50m)
Height: 12ft 8½in (3.87m)
Width: 9ft 3in (2.81m)
Engine: 2 x Leyland 150hp
Horsepower: 300hp (224kW)
Seats (total/car): None

Number	*Formation*	*Depot*	*Livery*	*Owner*	*Operator*	*Notes*
960014	977873	AL	BLG	CRW	CRW	Ex-Class 121 55022, Route Learning/Sandite
960301	977987+977992+977988	AL	GRN	CRW	CRW	Ex-Class 117, 51371/51375/51413 - used for water jetting

Class 01.5 (0-6-0)

Number	*Depot*	*Pool*	*Livery*	*Owner*	*Operator*	*Name*
01509 (433) RH468043	AL	MBDL	BLU	CRW	CRW	*Lesley*

CrossCountry Trains

Address: ✉ Cannon House, 18 The Priory, Queensway, Birmingham, B4 6BS
info@crosscountrytrains.co.uk
✆ 0870 0100084
ⓘ www.crosscountrytrains.co.uk

Managing Director: Andy Cooper

Franchise Dates: 11 November 2007 - 31 March 2016*

Principal Routes: Penzance/Paignton - Manchester/Edinburgh/Aberdeen
Bournemouth - Manchester/Edinburgh/Aberdeen
Birmingham - Stansted
Nottingham - Cardiff

Depots: Central Rivers (CZ), Tyseley (TS), Craigentinny (EC)

Parent Company: Deutsche Bahn AG (DB Regio) / Arriva

* Proposed extension to November 2019

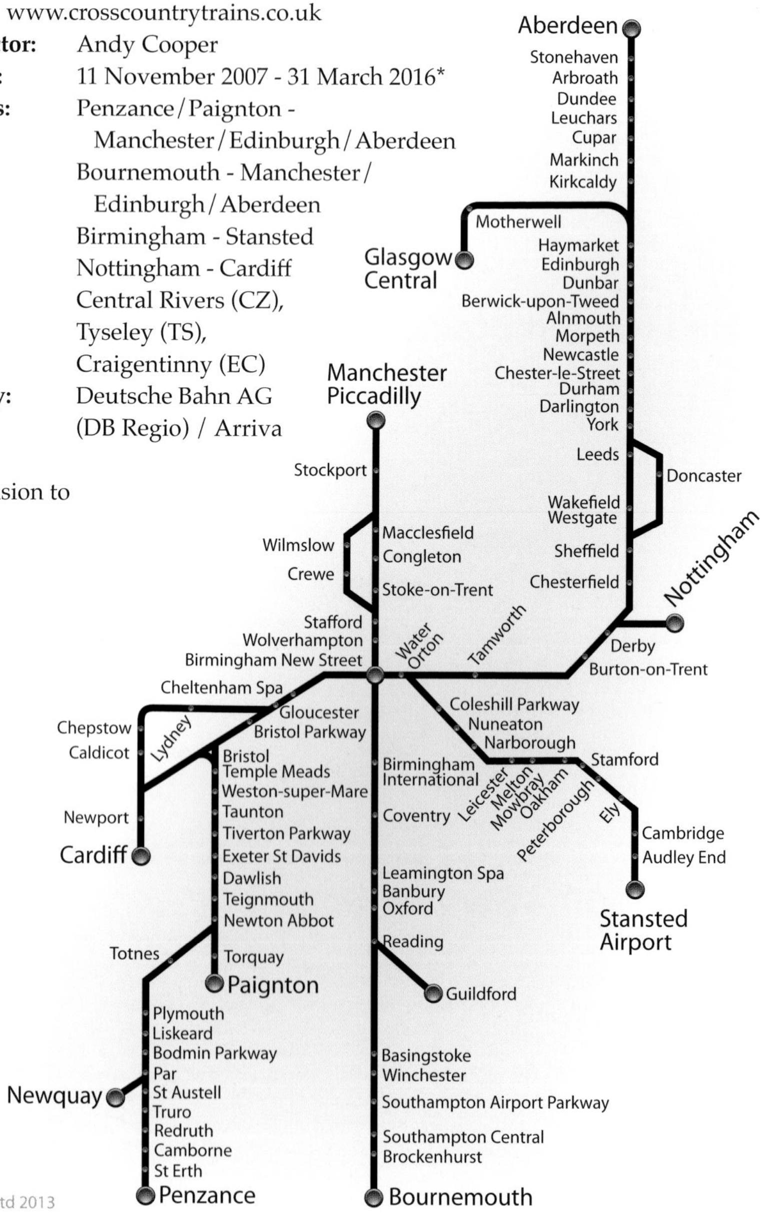

Aberdeen
Stonehaven
Arbroath
Dundee
Leuchars
Cupar
Markinch
Kirkcaldy
Motherwell
Glasgow Central
Haymarket
Edinburgh
Dunbar
Berwick-upon-Tweed
Alnmouth
Morpeth
Newcastle
Chester-le-Street
Durham
Darlington
York
Leeds
Doncaster
Wakefield Westgate
Sheffield
Chesterfield
Nottingham
Derby
Burton-on-Trent
Manchester Piccadilly
Stockport
Macclesfield
Wilmslow
Congleton
Crewe
Stoke-on-Trent
Stafford
Wolverhampton
Birmingham New Street
Water Orton
Tamworth
Cheltenham Spa
Gloucester
Bristol Parkway
Lydney
Chepstow
Caldicot
Newport
Cardiff
Coleshill Parkway
Nuneaton
Narborough
Leicester
Melton Mowbray
Oakham
Stamford
Peterborough
Ely
Cambridge
Audley End
Stansted Airport
Bristol Temple Meads
Weston-super-Mare
Taunton
Tiverton Parkway
Exeter St Davids
Dawlish
Teignmouth
Newton Abbot
Torquay
Paignton
Totnes
Plymouth
Liskeard
Bodmin Parkway
Par
Newquay
St Austell
Truro
Redruth
Camborne
St Erth
Penzance
Birmingham International
Coventry
Leamington Spa
Banbury
Oxford
Reading
Guildford
Basingstoke
Winchester
Southampton Airport Parkway
Southampton Central
Brockenhurst
Bournemouth

Class 43 – HST

Vehicle Length: 58ft 5in (18.80m)
Height: 12ft 10in (3.90m)
Width: 8ft 11in (2.73m)
Engine: MTU 16V4000 R41R
Horsepower: 2,250hp (1,680kW)
Electrical Equipment: Brush

Number	Depot	Pool	Livery	Owner	Operator
43207 (43007)	EC	EHPC	AXC	ANG	AXC
43285 (43085)	EC	EHPC	AXC	PTR	AXC
43301 (43101)	EC	EHPC	AXC	PTR	AXC
43303 (43103)	EC	EHPC	AXC	PTR	AXC
43304 (43104)	EC	EHPC	AXC	ANG	AXC
43321 (43121)	EC	EHPC	AXC	PTR	AXC
43357 (43157)	EC	EHPC	AXC	PTR	AXC
43366 (43166)	EC	EHPC	AXC	ANG	AXC
43378 (43178)	EC	EHPC	AXC	ANG	AXC
43384 (43184)	EC	EHPC	AXC	ANG	AXC

Right: *CrossCountry Trains operates a fleet of 10 Class 43 HST power cars, based at Craigentinny, Edinburgh. Usually a maximum of four HST sets are in operation at one time, usually working over the busy North East-South West corridor, providing extra accommodation than could be provided by using 'Voyager' train sets. All power cars are refurbished and now have MTU 16V4000 power units and fully overhauled electrical equipment. The 10 XC Class 43s are finished in CrossCourty grey/deep maroon livery, with XC CrossCountry bodyside branding. No vehicles are named. On 8 June 2013, No. 43357 passes Dawlish, leading the 06.01 Glasgow Central to Paignton service.* **CJM**

HST passenger fleet

Vehicle Length: 75ft 0in (22.86m)
Height: 12ft 9in (3.88m)
Width: 8ft 11in (2.71m)
Bogie Type: BT10

GH1G - TF *Seating 40F*

Number	Depot	Livery	Owner	
41026	EC	AXC	ANG	
41035	EC	AXC	ANG	
41193 (11060)	EC	AXC	PTR	
41194 (11016)	EC	AXC	PTR	
41195¤ (11020)	EC	AXC	PTR	¤ = TFD

GH2G - TS *Seating 82S*

Number	Depot	Livery	Owner	
42036	EC	AXC	ANG	
42037	EC	AXC	ANG	
42038	EC	AXC	ANG	
42051	EC	AXC	ANG	
42052	EC	AXC	ANG	
42053	EC	AXC	ANG	
42097	EC	AXC	ANG	
42234	EC	AXC	PTR	
42290	EC	AXC	PTR	
42342 (44082)	EC	AXC	ANG	
42366 (12007)	EC	AXC	PTR	
42367 (12025)	EC	AXC	PTR	
42368 (12028)	EC	AXC	PTR	
42369 (12050)	EC	AXC	PTR	
42370 (12086)	EC	AXC	PTR	
42371 (12052)	EC	AXC	PTR	
42372 (12055)	EC	AXC	PTR	
42373 (12071)	EC	AXC	PTR	
42374 (12075)	EC	AXC	PTR	
42375 (12113)	EC	AXC	PTR	
42376 (12085)	EC	AXC	PTR	
42377 (12102)	EC	AXC	PTR	
42378 (12123)	EC	AXC	PTR	
42379* (41036)	EC	AXC	ANG	*=TSD
42380* (41025)	EC	AXC	ANG	*=TSD

GJ2G - TGS *Seating 67S*

Number	Depot	Livery	Owner
44012	EC	AXC	ANG
44017	EC	AXC	ANG
44021	EC	AXC	ANG
44052	EC	AXC	PTR
44072	EC	AXC	PTR

GH3G - TCC *Seating 30F/10S*

Number	Depot	Livery	Owner
45001 (12004)	EC	AXC	PTR
45002 (12106)	EC	AXC	PTR
45003 (12076)	EC	AXC	PTR
45004 (12077)	EC	AXC	PTR
45005 (12080)	EC	AXC	PTR

CrossCountry Trains

Above: *A total of 40 HST trailer vehicles are operated by CrossCountry of four main types, Trailer First, Trailer Standard, Trailer Guards Standard and Trailer Composite Catering. All are finished in grey livery off-set by pink doors and pink/white bodyside branding. TS 42366 is illustrated, a converted loco-hauled vehicle.* **Antony Christie**

Class 170/1
Turbostar

Vehicle Length: 77ft 6in (23.62m)
Height: 12ft 4½in (3.77m)
Width: 8ft 10in (2.69m)
Engine: 1 x MTU 6R 183TD13H 422hp per vehicle
Horsepower: 1,266hp (944kW)
Seats (total/car): 9F/191S 52S/80S/9F-59S

Number	*Formation DMS+MS+DMCL*	*Depot*	*Livery*	*Owner*	*Operator*
170101	50101+55101+79101	TS	AXC	PTR	AXC
170102	50102+55102+79102	TS	AXC	PTR	AXC
170103	50103+55103+79103	TS	AXC	PTR	AXC
170104	50104+55104+79104	TS	AXC	PTR	AXC
170105	50105+55105+79105	TS	AXC	PTR	AXC
170106	50106+55106+79106	TS	AXC	PTR	AXC
170107	50107+55107+79107	TS	AXC	PTR	AXC
170108*	50108+55108+79108	TS	AXC	PTR	AXC
170109*	50109+55109+79109	TS	AXC	PTR	AXC
170110	50110+55110+79110	TS	AXC	PTR	AXC

Vehicle Length: 77ft 6in (23.62m)
Height: 12ft 4½in (3.77m)
Width: 8ft 10in (2.69m)
Engine: 1 x MTU 6R 183TD13H 422hp per vehicle
Horsepower: 844hp (629kW)
Seats (total/car): 9F-111S 59S/9F-52S

Number	*Formation DMS+DMCL*	*Depot*	*Livery*	*Owner*	*Operator*
170111*	50111+79111	TS	AXC	PTR	AXC
170112	50112+79112	TS	AXC	PTR	AXC
170113	50113+79113	TS	AXC	PTR	AXC
170114	50114+79114	TS	AXC	PTR	AXC
170115	50115+79115	TS	AXC	PTR	AXC
170116	50116+79116	TS	AXC	PTR	AXC
170117	50117+79117	TS	AXC	PTR	AXC

* Fitted with passenger counters

Left: *Four different breeds of Class 170 'Turbostar' now operate for CrossCountry, mainly operating the east-west services and those between the Midlands and South Wales. The 17 original Midland Mainline sets of Class 170/1 are now operated by CrossCountry; these come in both three-car (10 sets) and two-car (seven sets) formation and are based at Tyseley. All are internally refurbished and are painted in corporate CrossCountry livery. Most vehicles carry bodyside advertising in relation to the CrossCountry website. Set No. 170110 is illustrated at Newport with a Nottingham to Cardiff service.* **CJM**

Class 170/3
Turbostar

Vehicle Length: 77ft 6in (23.62m)
Height: 12ft 4½in (3.77m)
Width: 8ft 10in (2.69m)
Engine: 1 x MTU 6R 183TD13H 422hp per vehicle
Horsepower: 1,266hp (944kW)
Seats (total/car): 9F-191S 59S/80S/9F-52S

Number	Formation DMSL+MS+DMCL	Depot	Livery	Owner	Operator
170397	**50397+56397+79397**	**TS**	**AXC**	**PTR**	**AXC**
170398	**50398+56398+79398**	**TS**	**AXC**	**PTR**	**AXC**

Class 170/5
Turbostar

Vehicle Length: 77ft 6in (23.62m)
Height: 12ft 4½in (3.77m)
Width: 8ft 10in (2.69m)
Engine: 1 x MTU 6R 183TD13H 422hp per vehicle
Horsepower: 844hp (629kW)
Seats (total/car): 9F-111S 59S/9F-52S

Number	Formation DMSL+DMCL	Depot	Livery	Owner	Operator
170518	**50518+79518**	**TS**	**AXC**	**PTR**	**AXC**
170519	**50519+79519**	**TS**	**AXC**	**PTR**	**AXC**
170520	**50520+79520**	**TS**	**AXC**	**PTR**	**AXC**
170521	**50521+79521**	**TS**	**AXC**	**PTR**	**AXC**
170522	**50522+79522**	**TS**	**AXC**	**PTR**	**AXC**
170523	**50523+79523**	**TS**	**AXC**	**PTR**	**AXC**

Right: *A fleet of six two-car Class 170/5s is operated by CrossCountry, numbered in the 1705xx series. These sets have been given standard XC refurbishment, with first class seating located in the DMCL vehicle directly behind the driving cab. Unit No. 170522 is illustrated from the Driving Motor Composite vehicle.* **CJM**

Class 170/6
Turbostar

Vehicle Length: 77ft 6in (23.62m)
Height: 12ft 4½in (3.77m)
Width: 8ft 10in (2.69m)
Engine: 1 x MTU 6R 183TD13H 422hp per vehicle
Horsepower: 1,266hp (944kW)
Seats (total/car): 9F-191S 59S/80S/9F-52S

Number	Formation DMSL+MS+DMCL	Depot	Livery	Owner	Operator
170636	**50636+56636+79636**	**TS**	**AXC**	**PTR**	**AXC**
170637	**50637+56637+79637**	**TS**	**AXC**	**PTR**	**AXC**
170638	**50638+56638+79638**	**TS**	**AXC**	**PTR**	**AXC**
170639	**50639+56639+79639**	**TS**	**AXC**	**PTR**	**AXC**

Below: *Just four three-car Class 170/6s sets operate for CrossCountry, again allocated to Tyseley. Set No. 170637 is shown at Ely forming a Stansted Airport to Birmingham service.* **Antony Christie**

CrossCountry Trains

Class 220
Voyager

Vehicle Length: 77ft 6in (23.62m)
Height: 12ft 4in (3.75m)
Width: 8ft 11in (2.73m)
Engine: 1 x Cummins 750hp per vehicle
Horsepower: 3,000hp (2,237kW)
Seats (total/car): 26F/174S 42S/66S/66S/26F

Number	Formation DMS+MS+MS+DMF	Depot	Livery	Owner	Operator
220001	60301+60701+60201+60401	CZ	AXC	HBS	AXC
220002	60302+60702+60202+60402	CZ	AXC	HBS	AXC
220003	60303+60703+60203+60403	CZ	AXC	HBS	AXC
220004	60304+60704+60204+60404	CZ	AXC	HBS	AXC
220005	60305+60705+60205+60405	CZ	AXC	HBS	AXC
220006	60306+60706+60206+60406	CZ	AXC	HBS	AXC
220007	60307+60707+60207+60407	CZ	AXC	HBS	AXC
220008	60308+60708+60208+60408	CZ	AXC	HBS	AXC
220009	60309+60709+60209+60409	CZ	AXC	HBS	AXC
220010	60310+60710+60210+60410	CZ	AXC	HBS	AXC
220011	60311+60711+60211+60411	CZ	AXC	HBS	AXC
220012	60312+60712+60212+60412	CZ	AXC	HBS	AXC
220013	60313+60713+60213+60413	CZ	AXC	HBS	AXC
220014	60314+60714+60214+60414	CZ	AXC	HBS	AXC
220015	60315+60715+60215+60415	CZ	AXC	HBS	AXC
220016	60316+60716+60216+60416	CZ	AXC	HBS	AXC
220017	60317+60717+60217+60417	CZ	AXC	HBS	AXC
220018	60318+60718+60218+60418	CZ	AXC	HBS	AXC
220019	60319+60719+60219+60419	CZ	AXC	HBS	AXC
220020	60320+60720+60220+60420	CZ	AXC	HBS	AXC
220021	60321+60721+60221+60421	CZ	AXC	HBS	AXC
220022	60322+60722+60222+60422	CZ	AXC	HBS	AXC
220023	60323+60723+60223+60423	CZ	AXC	HBS	AXC
220024	60324+60724+60224+60424	CZ	AXC	HBS	AXC
220025	60325+60725+60225+60425	CZ	AXC	HBS	AXC
220026	60326+60726+60226+60426	CZ	AXC	HBS	AXC
220027	60327+60727+60227+60427	CZ	AXC	HBS	AXC
220028	60328+60728+60228+60428	CZ	AXC	HBS	AXC
220029	60329+60729+60229+60429	CZ	AXC	HBS	AXC
220030	60330+60730+60230+60430	CZ	AXC	HBS	AXC
220031	60331+60731+60231+60431	CZ	AXC	HBS	AXC
220032	60332+60732+60232+60432	CZ	AXC	HBS	AXC
220033	60333+60733+60233+60433	CZ	AXC	HBS	AXC
220034	60334+60734+60234+60434	CZ	AXC	HBS	AXC

Below: *The majority of long-distance CrossCountry services are formed of 'Voyager' four- or five-car sets, and 34 non-tilt four-car sets are allocated to Central Rivers. With its first class vehicle nearest the camera, identifiable by the yellow band on the coupling, set No. 220008 passes Clay Cross Junction near Chesterfield on 17 April 2013 forming the 07.40 Reading to Newcastle service.* **CJM**

Class 221 Super Voyager

Vehicle Length: 77ft 6in (23.62m)	*Engine: 1 x Cummins 750hp per vehicle*
Height: 12ft 4in (3.75m)	*Horsepower: 3,750hp (2,796kW)*
Width: 8ft 11in (2.73m)	*Seats (total/car): 26F/236S 42S/66S/66S/62S/26F*

Originally fitted with tilt system to allow higher speeds over curves. Equipment now isolated.

Number	*Formation* DMS+MS+MS+MS+DMF	*Depot*	*Livery*	*Owner*	*Operator*	
221119	60369+60769+60969+60869+60469	CZ	AXC	HBS	AXC	
221120	60370+60770+60970+60870+60470	CZ	AXC	HBS	AXC	
221121	60371+60771+60971+60871+60471	CZ	AXC	HBS	AXC	
221122	60372+60772+60972+60872+60472	CZ	AXC	HBS	AXC	
221123	60373+60773+60973+60873+60473	CZ	AXC	HBS	AXC	
221124	60374+60774+60974+60874+60474	CZ	AXC	HBS	AXC	
221125	60375+60775+60975+60875+60475	CZ	AXC	HBS	AXC	
221126	60376+60776+60976+60876+60476	CZ	AXC	HBS	AXC	
221127	60377+60777+60977+60877+60477	CZ	AXC	HBS	AXC	
221128	60378+60778+60978+60878+60478	CZ	AXC	HBS	AXC	
221129	60379+60779+60979+60879+60479	CZ	AXC	HBS	AXC	
221130	60380+60780+60980+60880+60480	CZ	AXC	HBS	AXC	
221131	60381+60781+60981+60881+60481	CZ	AXC	HBS	AXC	
221132	60382+60782+60982+60882+60482	CZ	AXC	HBS	AXC	
221133	60383+60783+60983+60883+60483	CZ	AXC	HBS	AXC	
221134	60384+60784+60984+60884+60484	CZ	AXC	HBS	AXC	
221135	60385+60785+60985+60885+60485	CZ	AXC	HBS	AXC	
221136	60386+60786+60986+60886+60486	CZ	AXC	HBS	AXC	
221137	60387+60787+60987+60887+60487	CZ	AXC	HBS	AXC	
221138	60388+60788+60988+60888+60488	CZ	AXC	HBS	AXC	
221139	60389+60789+60989+60889+60489	CZ	AXC	HBS	AXC	
221140	60390+60790+60990+60890+60490	CZ	AXC	HBS	AXC	
221141	60391+60791+60991+-+60491	CZ	AXC	HBS	AXC	*(Four-car set)*

Below: *A fleet of 23 tilting 'Voyager' sets is operated by CrossCountry; 22 are formed of five coaches and one as a four-car set. These have more sturdy bogies, being fitted with a tilting system. The sets operate in a common pool with the Class 220 stock, and are based at Central Rivers. Seating and internal layouts are the same on both classes of 'Voyager' stock. Set No. 221128 is seen at Basingstoke on 24 April 2013 forming the 13.45 Bournemouth to Manchester Piccadilly service.* **CJM**

East Coast

Address: ✉ East Coast House, 25 Skeldergate, York, YO1 6DH
customers@eastcoast.co.uk
✆ 08457 225225
ⓘ www.eastcoast.co.uk

Managing Director: Karen Boswell
Operation Started: 13 November 2009*
Principal Routes: London King's Cross - Aberdeen/ Inverness, Edinburgh, Glasgow Hull, Leeds, Bradford, Skipton and Harrogate
Depots: Bounds Green (BN), Craigentinny (EC)
Parent Company: InterCity East Coast (DfT) (Directly Operated Railways Ltd)

* The Government took over operation from 13 November 2009 and will continue to operate the franchise as a 'stopgap' measure using the in-place operational staff. A new franchise process was started in autumn 2013 and will commence operation in February 2015.

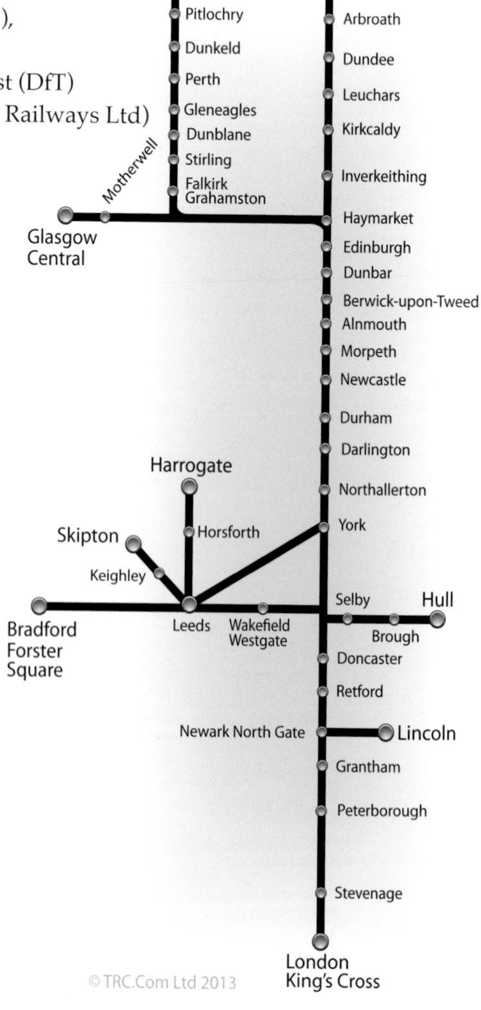

Class 43 – HST

Vehicle Length: 58ft 5in (18.80m)
Height: 12ft 10in (3.90m)
Width: 8ft 11in (2.73m)
Engine: MTU 16V4000 R41R
Horsepower: 2,250hp (1,680kW)
Electrical Equipment: Brush

Number		Depot	Pool	Livery	Owner	Operator	Name
43206	(43006)	EC	IECP	ECG	ANG	ICE	Kingdom of Fife
43208	(43008)	EC	IECP	NXE	ANG	ICE	Lincolnshire Echo
43238	(43038)	EC	IECP	ECG	ANG	ICE	
43239	(43039)	EC	IECP	ECG	ANG	ICE	
43251	(43051)	EC	IECP	ECG	PTR	ICE	
43257	(43057)	EC	IECP	ECG	PTR	ICE	
43272	(43072)	EC	IECP	ECG	PTR	ICE	
43274	(43074)	EC	IECP	ECG	PTR	ICE	
43277	(43077)	EC	IECP	ECG	PTR	ICE	
43290	(43090)	EC	IECP	NXE	PTR	ICE	MTU Fascination of Power
43295	(43095)	EC	IECP	ECG	ANG	ICE	
43296	(43096)	EC	IECP	ECG	PTR	ICE	
43299	(43099)	EC	IECP	ECG	PTR	ICE	
43300	(43100)	EC	IECP	ECG	PTR	ICE	Craigentinny
43302	(43102)	EC	IECP	ECG	PTR	ICE	
43305	(43105)	EC	IECP	NXE	ANG	ICE	
43306	(43106)	EC	IECP	NXE	ANG	ICE	
43307	(43107)	EC	IECP	ECG	ANG	ICE	
43308	(43108)	EC	IECP	ECG	ANG	ICE	
43309	(43109)	EC	IECP	ECG	ANG	ICE	
43310	(43110)	EC	IECP	ECG	ANG	ICE	
43311	(43111)	EC	IECP	ECG	ANG	ICE	
43312	(43112)	EC	IECP	ECT	ANG	ICE	
43313	(43113)	EC	IECP	ECT	ANG	ICE	
43314	(43114)	EC	IECP	ECG	ANG	ICE	
43315	(43115)	EC	IECP	ECG	ANG	ICE	
43316	(43116)	EC	IECP	ECG	ANG	ICE	
43317	(43117)	EC	IECP	ECG	ANG	ICE	
43318	(43118)	EC	IECP	ECT	ANG	ICE	
43319	(43119)	EC	IECP	ECG	ANG	ICE	
43320	(43120)	EC	IECP	NXE	ANG	ICE	
43367	(43167)	EC	IECP	ECG	ANG	ICE	Deltic 50 1955 - 2005 v

Right: *East Coast operates its main-line services from King's Cross to Scotland, Newcastle, Leeds and Harrogate with a mix of diesel HST sets and electric-powered Class 91s. The Class 43 power cars are owned by Porterbrook and Angel Trains and the majority sport East Coast grey livery with purple East Coast branding. All Class 43s are refurbished with MTU power units and are allocated to Edinburgh Craigentinny depot. No. 43299 is seen at Doncaster with a southbound service.* **CJM**

Class 91

Vehicle Length: 63ft 8in (19.40m)
Height: 12ft 4in (3.75m)
Width: 9ft 0in (2.74m)
Power Collection: 25kV ac overhead
Horsepower: 6,300hp (4,700kW)
Electrical Equipment: GEC

Number		Depot	Pool	Livery	Owner	Operator	Name
91101	(91001)	BN	IECA	ADV	EVL	ICE	Flying Scotsman (branding)
91102	(91002)	BN	IECA	ECG	EVL	ICE	City of York
91103	(91003)	BN	IECA	ECW	EVL	ICE	
91104	(91004)	BN	IECA	ECG	EVL	ICE	
91105	(91005)	BN	IECA	ECW	EVL	ICE	
91106	(91006)	BN	IECA	ECS	EVL	ICE	
91107	(91007)	BN	IECA	ECS	EVL	ICE	Skyfall

East Coast

91108	(91008)	BN	IECA	ECG	EVL	ICE	
91109	(91009)	BN	IECA	ECG	EVL	ICE	*Sir Bobby Robson*
91110	(91010)	BN	IECA	ADV	EVL	ICE	*Battle of Britain Memorial Flight - Spitfire Hurricane Lancaster Dakota*
91111	(91011)	BN	IECA	ECG	EVL	ICE	
91112	(91012)	BN	IECA	ECG	EVL	ICE	
91113	(91013)	BN	IECA	NXE	EVL	ICE	
91114	(91014)	BN	IECA	ECG	EVL	ICE	*Durham Cathedral*
91115	(91015)	BN	IECA	ECG	EVL	ICE	*Blaydon Races*
91116	(91016)	BN	IECA	ECG	EVL	ICE	
91117	(91017)	BN	IECA	ECG	EVL	ICE	*West Riding Limited*
91118	(91018)	BN	IECA	NXE	EVL	ICE	
91119	(91019)	BN	IECA	ECG	EVL	ICE	
91120	(91020)	BN	IECA	ECG	EVL	ICE	
91121	(91021)	BN	IECA	ECG	EVL	ICE	
91122	(91022)	BN	IECA	ECG	EVL	ICE	
91124	(91024)	BN	IECA	ECG	EVL	ICE	
91125	(91025)	BN	IECA	ADV	EVL	ICE	
91126	(91026)	BN	IECA	ECG	EVL	ICE	
91127	(91027)	BN	IECA	ECS	EVL	ICE	
91128	(91028)	BN	IECA	ECG	EVL	ICE	
91129	(91029)	BN	IECA	ECG	EVL	ICE	
91130	(91030)	BN	IECA	ECW	EVL	ICE	
91131	(91031)	BN	IECA	ECG	EVL	ICE	
91132	(91023)	BN	IECA	ECG	EVL	ICE	

Below: *The Class 91-powered Mk4 formations are the backbone of East Coast services. The locos and stock are allocated to Bounds Green depot in London and usually trains are operated with the Class 91 on the north end of the formation attached to the standard class carriages. No. 91105 painted in East Coast grey livery approaches Doncaster on 16 April 2013 with the 10.30 King's Cross to Newcastle service.* **CJM**

Class 800 and 801 'Super Express'

In summer 2012 Agility Trains signed a contract with the Department for Transport (DfT) to design, build, finance and maintain 596 state-of-the-art carriages for the East Coast Main Line and Great Western Main Line as part of the Intercity Express Programme to replace HST and IC225 trains.

Hitachi Rail Europe and John Laing are the main shareholders of Agility Trains and in summer 2013 the Secretary of State for Transport announced that an additional contract for the provision of an extra 270 carriages for the East Coast Main Line was to be placed, bringing the total number of vehicles ordered to 866.

East Coast will have between 2017 and 2019 13 nine-car Class 800 dual mode and 51 nine-car electric Class 801 train sets delivered. The first pre-production sets are to be built by Hitachi in Kasado, Japan, with the remainder built at a new Hitachi plant at Newton Aycliffe.

Mk3 HST Stock

Vehicle Length: 75ft 0in (22.86m) Width: 8ft 11in (2.71m)
Height: 12ft 9in (3.88m) Bogie Type: BT10

GK1G - TRFB *Seating 17F*

Number	Depot	Livery	Owner
40701	EC	NXE	PTR
40702	EC	NXE	PTR
40704	EC	NXE	ANG
40705	EC	NXE	ANG
40706	EC	NXE	ANG
40708	EC	ECT	PTR
40711	EC	NXE	ANG
40720	EC	NXE	ANG
40732	EC	ECG	PTR
40735	EC	NXE	ANG
40737	EC	NXE	ANG
40740	EC	NXE	ANG
40742	EC	NXE	ANG
40748	EC	NXE	ANG
40750	EC	NXE	ANG
40805	EC	NXG	ANG

GH1G - TF *Seating 48F*

Number	Depot	Livery	Owner
41039	EC	NXE	ANG
41040	EC	NXE	ANG
41043	EC	ECS	ANG
41044	EC	NXE	ANG
41058	EC	NXE	PTR
41062	EC	ECG	PTR
41066	EC	NXE	ANG
41083	EC	NXE	PTR
41087	EC	NXE	ANG
41088	EC	NXE	ANG
41090	EC	NXE	ANG
41091	EC	NXE	ANG
41092	EC	NXE	ANG
41095	EC	NXE	ANG
41097	EC	NXE	ANG
41098	EC	NXE	ANG
41099	EC	NXE	ANG
41100	EC	NXE	ANG
41115	EC	NXE	PTR
41118	EC	NXE	ANG
41120	EC	ECT	ANG
41150	EC	ECT	ANG
41151	EC	NXE	ANG
41152	EC	NXE	ANG
41154	EC	ECG	PTR
41159	EC	NXE	PTR
41164	EC	NXE	ANG
41165	EC	NXE	PTR
41170(41001)	EC	NXE	ANG
41185(42313	EC	NXE	PTR
41190(42088)	EC	NXG	PTR

GH2G - TS (*TSD) *Seating 76/62*S*

Number	Depot	Livery	Owner
42057	EC	NXE	ANG
42058	EC	NXE	ANG
42059	EC	NXE	ANG
42063	EC	NXE	ANG
42064	EC	NXE	ANG
42065	EC	NXE	ANG
42091*	EC	ECT	ANG
42106	EC	NXE	ANG
42109	EC	NXE	PTR
42110	EC	NXE	PTR
42116*	EC	NXE	ANG
42117	EC	NXE	PTR
42123	EC	ECG	PTR
42125	EC	ECG	PTR
42127*	EC	NXE	ANG
42128*	EC	NXE	ANG
42130	EC	NXE	PTR
42134	EC	NXE	ANG
42146	EC	ECT	ANG
42147	EC	NXE	PTR
42150	EC	ECT	ANG
42154	EC	ECT	ANG
42158	EC	NXE	ANG
42159*	EC	NXE	PTR
42160	EC	NXE	PTR
42161*	EC	NXE	PTR
42163	EC	NXE	PTR
42171	EC	NXE	ANG
42172	EC	NXE	ANG
42179	EC	NXE	ANG
42180	EC	NXE	ANG
42181	EC	NXE	ANG
42182	EC	NXE	ANG
42186	EC	ECT	ANG
42188*	EC	NXE	ANG
42189*	EC	NXE	ANG
42190	EC	NXE	ANG
42191	EC	NXE	ANG
42192	EC	NXE	ANG
42193	EC	NXE	ANG
42198	EC	NXE	ANG
42199	EC	NXE	ANG
42205	EC	ECG	PTR
42210	EC	ECG	PTR
42215	EC	ECT	ANG
42219	EC	NXE	ANG
42226	EC	NXE	ANG
42228	EC	ECT	PTR
42235	EC	NXE	ANG
42237	EC	NXE	PTR
42238*	EC	NXE	ANG
42239*	EC	NXE	ANG
42240	EC	NXE	ANG
42241	EC	NXE	ANG
42242	EC	NXE	ANG
42243	EC	NXE	ANG
42244	EC	NXE	ANG
42286	EC	ECT	PTR
42306	EC	NXE	PTR
42307	EC	NXE	PTR
42322	EC	ECT	PTR
42323	EC	NXE	ANG
42326	EC	NXE	PTR
42330	EC	NXE	PTR
42335	EC	ECG	PTR
42340	EC	NXE	ANG
42352(41176)	EC	NXE	PTR
42354(41175)	EC	ECT	ANG
42355(41172)	EC	NXE	ANG
42357(41174)	EC	NXE	ANG
42363(41082)	EC	NXE	ANG

GJ2G - TGS *Seating 65S*

Number	Depot	Livery	Owner
44019	EC	NXE	ANG
44031	EC	NXE	ANG
44045	EC	NXE	ANG
44050	EC	ECT	PTR
44056	EC	NXE	ANG
44057	EC	NXE	PTR
44058	EC	NXE	ANG
44061	EC	NXE	ANG
44063	EC	NXE	ANG
44073	EC	ECG	PTR
44075	EC	NXE	PTR
44077	EC	NXE	ANG
44080	EC	NXE	ANG
44094	EC	ECT	ANG
44098	EC	NXE	ANG

Above: *The HST trailer vehicles for the East Coast operation are based at Edinburgh Craigentinny, with the ability to form up to 15 train sets. Carrying the former National Express East Coast livery style, TRFB No. 40750 is illustrated from the corridor side at the buffet end.* **CJM**

Mk4 Stock

Vehicle Length: 75ft 5in (23m) Height: 12ft 5in (3.79m) Width: 8ft 11in (2.73m) Bogie Type: BT41

AJ2J - RSB *Seating 30S*

Number	Depot	Livery	Owner
10300	BN	ECS	EVL
10301	BN	ECG	EVL
10302	BN	ECS	EVL
10303	BN	ECS	EVL
10304	BN	ECG	EVL
10305	BN	ECG	EVL
10306	BN	ECG	EVL
10307	BN	ECS	EVL
10308	BN	ECS	EVL
10309	BN	ECG	EVL
10310	BN	ECG	EVL
10311	BN	ECG	EVL
10312	BN	ECG	EVL
10313	BN	ECG	EVL
10315	BN	ECG	EVL
10317	BN	ECG	EVL
10318	BN	ECG	EVL
10319	BN	ECG	EVL
10320	BN	ECS	EVL
10321	BN	ECG	EVL
10323	BN	ECS	EVL
10324	BN	ECG	EVL
10325	BN	ECG	EVL
10326	BN	ECS	EVL
10328	BN	ECG	EVL
10329	BN	ECG	EVL
10330	BN	ECG	EVL
10331	BN	ECS	EVL
10332	BN	ECG	EVL
10333	BN	ECG	EVL

AD1J - FO *Seating 46F*

Number	Depot	Livery	Owner
11201	BN	ECG	EVL
11219	BN	ECS	EVL
11229	BN	ECG	EVL
11237	BN	ECG	EVL
11241	BN	ECG	EVL
11244	BN	ECG	EVL
11273	BN	ECG	EVL
11277(12408)	BN	ECS	EVL
11278(12479)	BN	ECS	EVL
11279(12521)	BN	ECG	EVL
11280(12523)	BN	ECS	EVL
11281(12418)	BN	ECG	EVL
11282(12524)	BN	ECS	EVL
11283(12435)	BN	ECS	EVL
11284(12487)	BN	ECG	EVL
11285(12537)	BN	ECG	EVL
11286(12482)	BN	ECG	EVL
11287(12527)	BN	ECG	EVL
11288(12517)	BN	ECG	EVL
11289(12528)	BN	ECG	EVL
11290(12530)	BN	ECG	EVL
11291(12535)	BN	ECG	EVL
11292(12451)	BN	ECG	EVL
11293(12536)	BN	ECG	EVL
11294(12529)	BN	ECG	EVL
11295(12475)	BN	ECG	EVL
11298(12416)	BN	ECS	EVL
11299(12532)	BN	ECS	EVL

AL1J - FOD *Seating 42F*

Number	Depot	Livery	Owner
11301(11215)	BN	ECS	EVL
11302(11203)	BN	ECS	EVL
11303(11211)	BN	ECS	EVL
11304(11257)	BN	ECS	EVL
11305(11261)	BN	ECS	EVL
11306(11276)	BN	ECG	EVL
11307(11217)	BN	ECS	EVL
11308(11263)	BN	ECG	EVL
11309(11262)	BN	ECG	EVL
11310(11272)	BN	ECS	EVL
11311(11221)	BN	ECS	EVL
11312(11225)	BN	ECG	EVL
11313(11210)	BN	ECG	EVL
11314(11207)	BN	ECG	EVL
11315(11238)	BN	ECG	EVL
11316(11227)	BN	ECG	EVL
11317(11223)	BN	ECG	EVL
11318(11251)	BN	ECG	EVL
11319(11247)	BN	ECG	EVL
11320(11255)	BN	ECG	EVL
11321(11245)	BN	ECG	EVL
11322(11228)	BN	ECG	EVL
11323(11235)	BN	ECG	EVL
11324(11253)	BN	ECG	EVL
11325(11231)	BN	ECG	EVL
11326(11206)	BN	ECG	EVL
11327(11236)	BN	ECG	EVL
11328(11274)	BN	ECG	EVL
11329(11243)	BN	ECG	EVL
11330(11249)	BN	ECG	EVL

AD1J - FO *Seating 46F*

Number	Depot	Livery	Owner
11401(11214)	BN	ECS	EVL
11402(11216)	BN	ECS	EVL
11403(11258)	BN	ECS	EVL
11404(11202)	BN	ECS	EVL
11405(11204)	BN	ECS	EVL
11406(11205)	BN	ECG	EVL
11407(11256)	BN	ECS	EVL
11408(11218)	BN	ECG	EVL
11409(11259)	BN	ECG	EVL
11410(11260)	BN	ECG	EVL
11411(11240)	BN	ECS	EVL
11412(11209)	BN	ECG	EVL
11413(11212)	BN	ECG	EVL
11414(11246)	BN	ECG	EVL
11415(11208)	BN	ECG	EVL
11416(11254)	BN	ECG	EVL
11417(11226)	BN	ECG	EVL
11418(11222)	BN	ECG	EVL
11419(11250)	BN	ECG	EVL
11420(11242)	BN	ECG	EVL
11421(11220)	BN	ECG	EVL
11422(11232)	BN	ECG	EVL
11423(11230)	BN	ECG	EVL
11424(11239)	BN	ECG	EVL
11425(11234)	BN	ECG	EVL
11426(11252)	BN	ECG	EVL
11427(11200)	BN	ECG	EVL
11428(11233)	BN	ECG	EVL
11429(11275)	BN	ECG	EVL
11430(11248)	BN	ECG	EVL
11998(10314)	BN	ECG	EVL
11999(10316)	BN	ECG	EVL

AI2J - TSOE *Seating 76S*

Number	Depot	Livery	Owner
12200	BN	ECG	EVL
12201	BN	ECS	EVL
12202	BN	ECS	EVL
12203	BN	ECS	EVL
12204	BN	ECG	EVL
12205	BN	ECG	EVL
12207	BN	ECS	EVL
12208	BN	ECG	EVL
12209	BN	ECS	EVL
12210	BN	ECG	EVL
12211	BN	ECG	EVL
12212	BN	ECG	EVL
12213	BN	ECG	EVL
12214	BN	ECS	EVL
12215	BN	ECG	EVL
12216	BN	ECG	EVL
12217	BN	ECG	EVL
12218	BN	ECG	EVL
12219	BN	ECG	EVL
12220	BN	ECG	EVL
12222	BN	ECG	EVL
12223	BN	ECG	EVL
12224	BN	ECG	EVL
12225	BN	ECG	EVL
12226	BN	ECG	EVL
12227	BN	ECG	EVL
12228	BN	ECG	EVL
12229	BN	ECG	EVL
12230	BN	ECG	EVL
12231	BN	ECS	EVL
12232	BN	ECS	EVL

AL2J - TSOD *Seating 68S*

Number	Depot	Livery	Owner
12300	BN	ECS	EVL
12301	BN	ECS	EVL
12302	BN	ECS	EVL
12303	BN	ECG	EVL
12304	BN	ECG	EVL
12305	BN	ECS	EVL
12307	BN	ECS	EVL
12308	BN	ECG	EVL
12309	BN	ECG	EVL
12310	BN	ECG	EVL
12311	BN	ECG	EVL
12312	BN	ECG	EVL
12313	BN	ECG	EVL
12315	BN	ECS	EVL
12316	BN	ECG	EVL
12317	BN	ECG	EVL
12318	BN	ECG	EVL
12319	BN	ECG	EVL
12320	BN	ECG	EVL
12321	BN	ECG	EVL
12322	BN	ECG	EVL
12323	BN	ECG	EVL

Number	Depot	Livery	Owner
12324	BN	ECG	EVL
12325	BN	ECG	EVL
12326	BN	ECG	EVL
12327	BN	ECS	EVL
12328	BN	ECG	EVL
12329	BN	ECS	EVL
12330	BN	ECG	EVL
12331(12531)	BN	ECG	EVL

AC2J - TSO *Seating 76S*

Number	*Depot*	*Livery*	*Owner*
12400	BN	ECG	EVL
12401	BN	ECS	EVL
12402	BN	ECS	EVL
12403	BN	ECG	EVL
12404	BN	ECG	EVL
12405	BN	ECS	EVL
12406	BN	ECG	EVL
12407	BN	ECG	EVL
12409	BN	ECG	EVL
12410	BN	ECG	EVL
12411	BN	ECS	EVL
12414	BN	ECS	EVL
12415	BN	ECS	EVL
12417	BN	ECS	EVL
12419	BN	ECS	EVL
12420	BN	ECG	EVL
12421	BN	ECS	EVL
12422	BN	ECG	EVL
12423	BN	ECG	EVL
12424	BN	ECG	EVL
12425	BN	ECG	EVL
12426	BN	ECG	EVL
12427	BN	ECG	EVL
12428	BN	ECG	EVL
12429	BN	ECG	EVL
12430	BN	ECG	EVL
12431	BN	ECG	EVL
12432	BN	ECG	EVL
12433	BN	ECG	EVL
12434	BN	ECG	EVL
12436	BN	ECS	EVL
12437	BN	ECS	EVL
12438	BN	ECG	EVL
12439	BN	ECG	EVL
12440	BN	ECG	EVL
12441	BN	ECG	EVL
12442	BN	ECG	EVL
12443	BN	ECS	EVL
12444	BN	ECG	EVL
12445	BN	ECG	EVL
12446	BN	ECG	EVL
12447	BN	ECG	EVL
12448	BN	ECS	EVL
12449	BN	ECG	EVL
12450	BN	ECS	EVL
12452	BN	ECG	EVL
12453	BN	ECG	EVL
12454	BN	ECG	EVL
12455	BN	ECG	EVL
12456	BN	ECG	EVL
12457	BN	ECG	EVL
12458	BN	ECG	EVL
12459	BN	ECS	EVL
12460	BN	ECG	EVL
12461	BN	ECG	EVL
12462	BN	ECG	EVL
12463	BN	ECG	EVL
12464	BN	ECG	EVL
12465	BN	ECG	EVL
12466	BN	ECG	EVL
12467	BN	ECG	EVL
12468	BN	ECG	EVL
12469	BN	ECG	EVL
12470	BN	ECG	EVL
12471	BN	ECG	EVL
12472	BN	ECG	EVL
12473	BN	ECG	EVL
12474	BN	ECG	EVL
12476	BN	ECG	EVL
12477	BN	ECG	EVL
12478	BN	ECS	EVL
12480	BN	ECS	EVL
12481	BN	ECG	EVL
12483	BN	ECG	EVL
12484	BN	ECS	EVL
12485	BN	ECG	EVL
12486	BN	ECS	EVL
12488	BN	ECS	EVL
12489	BN	ECS	EVL
12513	BN	ECG	EVL
12514	BN	ECG	EVL
12515	BN	ECG	EVL
12518	BN	ECS	EVL
12519	BN	ECG	EVL
12520	BN	ECS	EVL
12522	BN	ECS	EVL
12526	BN	ECG	EVL
12533	BN	ECG	EVL
12534	BN	ECG	EVL
12538	BN	ECG	EVL

NZAJ - DVT

Number	*Depot*	*Livery*	*Owner*
82200	BN	ECG	EVL
82201	BN	ECG	EVL
82202	BN	ECS	EVL
82203	BN	ECG	EVL
82204	BN	ECW	EVL
82205	BN	ADV	EVL
82206	BN	ECG	EVL
82207	BN	ECS	EVL
82208	BN	ECG	EVL
82209	BN	ECG	EVL
82210	BN	ECS	EVL
82211	BN	ECS	EVL
82212	BN	ECG	EVL
82213	BN	ECG	EVL
82214	BN	ECG	EVL
82215	BN	ECG	EVL
82216	BN	ADV	EVL
82217	BN	ECG	EVL
82218	BN	ECS	EVL
82219	BN	ECW	EVL
82220	BN	ECG	EVL
82222	BN	ECG	EVL
82223	BN	ECG	EVL
82224	BN	ECG	EVL
82225	BN	ECG	EVL
82226	BN	ECG	EVL
82227	BN	ECG	EVL
82228	BN	ECG	EVL
82229	BN	ECG	EVL
82230	BN	ECG	EVL
82231	BN	ECG	EVL

82205 Flying Scotsman livery
82216 Sky TV livery

Below: *The Mk4 fleet is based at Bounds Green and operates in semi-permanent formations. RSB No. 10323 is illustrated from the catering end galley side. The non-passenger doors are finished in body colour.* **CJM**

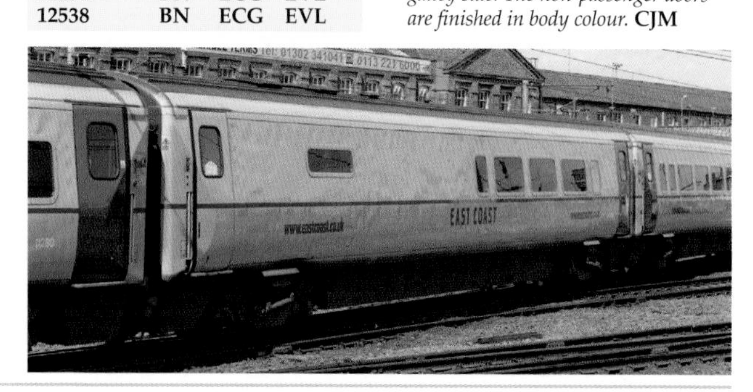

Service Stock

HST and Mk4 Barrier Vehicles

Number	*Depot*	*Livery*	*Owner*	*Former Identity*
6340	EC	NEG	ANG	BCK - 21251
6344	EC	NEG	ANG	BG - 92080
6346	EC	NEG	ANG	BSO - 9422
6352	BN	NEG	ANG	SK - 19465
6353	BN	NEG	ANG	SK - 19478
6354	BN	NEG	ANG	BSO - 9459
6355	BN	NEG	ANG	BSO - 9477
6358	BN	NEG	EVL	BSO - 9432
6359	BN	NEG	EVL	BSO - 9429
9393	EC	PTR	PTR	BG - 92196
9394	EC	PTR	PTR	BG - 92906

East Midlands Trains

Address: ✉ 1 Prospect Place, Millennium Way, Pride Park, Derby, DE24 8HG
getintouch@eastmidlandstrains.co.uk
✆ 08457 125678
ⓘ www.eastmidlandstrains.co.uk

Managing Director: David Horae
Franchise Dates: 11 November 2007 - 31 March 2015*
Principal Routes: St Pancras - Sheffield / York / Leeds / Nottingham
Norwich / Skegness / Cleethorpes - Nottingham / Crewe / Liverpool and Matlock
Depots: Derby (DY), Nottingham (NM), Neville Hill (NL)
Parent Company: Stagecoach Group

* Proposed extension to October 2017

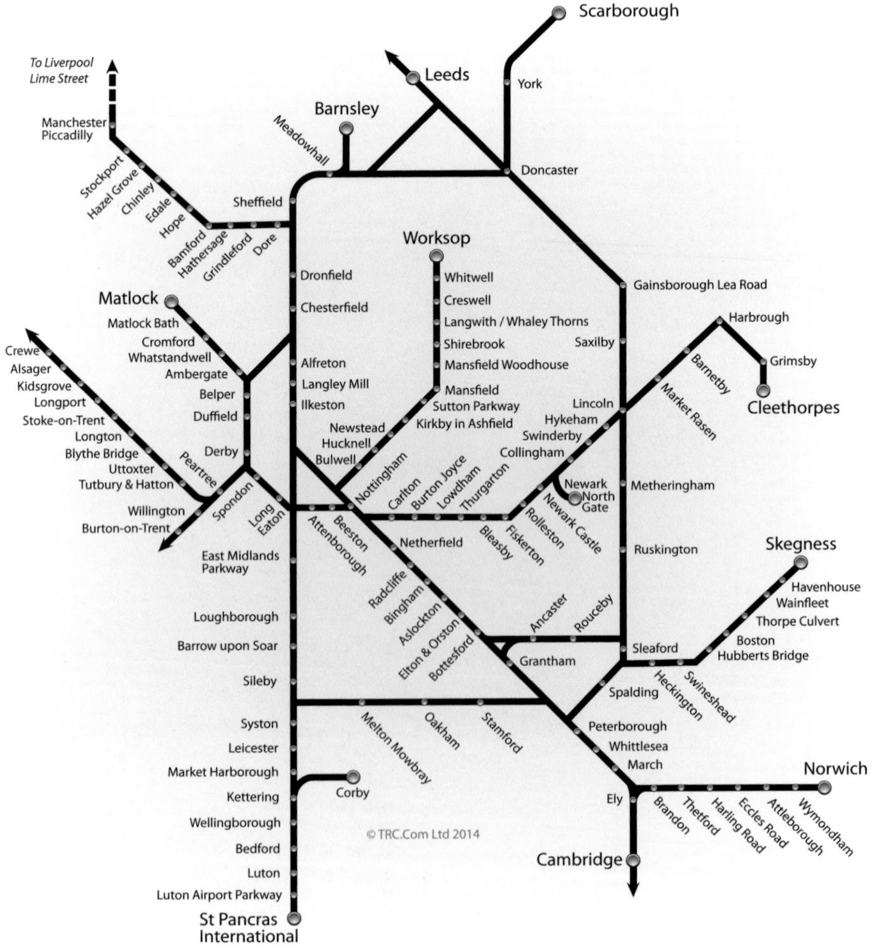

Class 08

Vehicle Length: 29ft 3in (8.91m)
Height: 12ft 8⅝in (3.87m)
Width: 8ft 6in (2.59m)
Engine: English Electric 6K
Horsepower: 400hp (298kW)
Electrical Equipment: English Electric

Number	Depot	Pool	Livery	Owner	Operator	Name
08525	NL	EMSL	EMT	EMT	EMT	*Duncan Bedford*
08690	NL	EMSL	EMT	EMT	EMT	*David Thirkill*
08899	DY	EMSL	BLU	EMT	EMT	
08908	DY	EMSL	EMT	EMT	EMT	*Ivan Stephenson*
08950	NL	EMSL	EMT	EMT	EMT	*David Lightfoot*

Right: *Like many of the long-distance operators, East Midlands Trains, part of the Stagecoach Group, has a need for shunting power at its main depots of Derby Etches Park and Leeds Neville Hill. This is provided by a small fleet of Class 08 0-6-0 diesel-electric shunting locos. Four of the five on the books of EMT are painted in full East Midlands Trains livery, as shown on No. 08690 inside Leeds Neville Hill depot.* **Ron Cover**

Class 43 – HST

Vehicle Length: 58ft 5in (18.80m)
Height: 12ft 10in (3.90m)
Width: 8ft 11in (2.73m)
Engine: Paxman VP185
Horsepower: 2,100hp (1,565kW)
Electrical Equipment: Brush

Number	Depot	Pool	Livery	Owner	Operator
43043	NL	EMPC	SCE	PTR	EMT
43044	NL	EMPC	SCE	PTR	EMT
43045	NL	EMPC	SCE	PTR	EMT
43046	NL	EMPC	SCE	PTR	EMT
43047	NL	EMPC	SCE	PTR	EMT
43048	NL	EMPC	SCE	PTR	EMT
43049	NL	EMPC	SCE	PTR	EMT
43050	NL	EMPC	SCE	PTR	EMT
43052	NL	EMPC	SCE	PTR	EMT
43054	NL	EMPC	SCE	PTR	EMT
43055	NL	EMPC	SCE	PTR	EMT
43058	NL	EMPC	SCE	PTR	EMT
43059	NL	EMPC	SCE	PTR	EMT
43060	NL	EMPC	SCE	PTR	EMT
43061	NL	EMPC	SCE	PTR	EMT
43064	NL	EMPC	SCE	PTR	EMT
43066	NL	EMPC	SCE	PTR	EMT
43073	NL	EMPC	SCE	PTR	EMT
43075	NL	EMPC	SCE	PTR	EMT
43076	NL	EMPC	SCE	PTR	EMT
43081	NL	EMPC	SCE	PTR	EMT
43082	NL	EMPC	SCE	PTR	EMT
43083	NL	EMPC	SCE	PTR	EMT
43089	NL	EMPC	SCE	PTR	EMT

Names applied

43048	*T. C. B Miller MBE*
43049	*Neville Hill*
43055	*The Sheffield Star 125 Years*
43076	*In Support of Help for Heroes*
43082	*Railway Children The Voice for Street Children Worldwide*

Right: *East Midlands Trains operates its long-distance services on the London St Pancras International to Derby, Sheffield and Nottingham routes with a mix of HST and Class 222 rolling stock. All offer a mix of first and standard class accommodation and a catering service appropriate for the time of day. In the main the Class 222 stock operates on the Sheffield route and the HSTs on Nottingham services, but this is not a hard rule. Trains are usually formed with their first class seating at the London end of the formation. Led by Class 43 HST power car No. 43058 the 14.28 Nottingham to St Pancras International service departs from East Midlands Parkway on 17 April 2013.* **CJM**

East Midlands Trains

Class 153

Vehicle Length: 76ft 5in (23.29m)
Height: 12ft 3⅛in (3.75m)
Width: 8ft 10in (2.70m)
Engine: 1 x NT855R5 of 285hp
Horsepower: 285hp (213kW)
Seats (total/car): 66S

Number	Formation DMSL	Depot	Livery	Owner	Operator
153302	52302	NM	EMT	ANG	EMT
153308	52308	NM	EMT	ANG	EMT
153310	52310	NM	EMT	PTR	EMT
153311	52311	NM	EMT	PTR	EMT
153313	52313	NM	EMT	PTR	EMT
153319	52319	NM	EMT	ANG	EMT
153321	52321	NM	EMT	PTR	EMT
153326	52326	NM	EMT	PTR	EMT
153355	57355	NM	EMT	ANG	EMT
153357	57357	NM	EMT	ANG	EMT
153374	57374	NM	EMT	ANG	EMT
153376	57376	NM	EMT	PTR	EMT
153379	57379	NM	EMT	PTR	EMT
153381	57381	NM	EMT	PTR	EMT
153383	57383	NM	EMT	PTR	EMT
153384	57384	NM	EMT	PTR	EMT
153385	57385	NM	EMT	PTR	EMT

Left: *Owned by both Angel Trains and Porterbrook, East Midlands Trains has a fleet of 17 single-car Class 153s, allocated to its prime multiple unit depot at Nottingham Eastcroft. The single cars, converted from Class 155s, seat 66 standard class passengers, have a toilet at one end and a luggage stack. Painted in standard EMT blue livery, the '153s' are deployed on lighter-used medium distance routes. Viewed from its small cab end (added during conversion from a Class 155, No. 153313 arrives at Doncaster with a service from Lincoln.* **CJM**

Class 156

Vehicle Length: 75ft 6in (23.03m)
Height: 12ft 6in (3.81m)
Width: 8ft 11in (2.73m)
Engine: 1 x Cummins NT855R5 of 285hp
Horsepower: 570hp (425kW)
Seats (total/car): 148S, 72S/76S

Number	Formation DMSL+DMS	Depot	Livery	Owner	Operator
156401	52401+57401	NM	EMT	PTR	EMT
156403	52403+57403	NM	EMT	PTR	EMT
156404	52404+57404	NM	EMT	PTR	EMT
156405	52405+57405	NM	EMT	PTR	EMT
156406	52406+57406	NM	EMT	PTR	EMT
156408	52408+57408	NM	EMT	PTR	EMT
156410	52410+57410	NM	EMT	PTR	EMT
156411	52411+57411	NM	EMT	PTR	EMT
156413	52413+57413	NM	EMT	PTR	EMT
156414	52414+57414	NM	EMT	PTR	EMT
156415§	52415+57415	NM	EMT	PTR	EMT
156470	52470+57470	NM	EMT	PTR	EMT
156473	52473+57473	NM	EMT	PTR	EMT
156497	52497+57497	NM	EMT	PTR	EMT
156498	52498+57498	NM	EMT	PTR	EMT

§ Lease to Greater Anglia

Below: *In 2014 East Midlands Trains operates a fleet of 15 Class 156 two-car main-line sets, painted in EMT/Stagecoach blue livery. The sets allocated to Nottingham Eastcroft are used on longer-distance domestic services and provide seating for 148 standard class passengers in the 2+2 mode. Set No. 156473 is seen near Cossington.* **Nathan Williamson**

Class 158

Vehicle Length: 76ft 1¾in (23.21m)
Height: 12ft 6in (3.81m)
Width: 9ft 3¼in (2.82m)
Engine: 158770-813 - 1 x Cummins NT855R5 of 350hp
Horsepower: 700hp (522kW)
Engine: 158846-862 - 1 x Perkins 2006TWH of 350hp
Horsepower: 700hp (522kW)
Engine: 158863-865 - 1 x Cummins NT855R5 of 400hp
Horsepower: 800hp (597kW)
Seats (total/car): 146S - 74S, 72S

Number	Formation DMSL+DMSL	Depot	Livery	Owner	Operator
158770	52770+57770	NM	SCE	PTR	EMT
158773	52773+57773	NM	SCE	PTR	EMT
158774	52774+57774	NM	SCE	PTR	EMT
158777	52777+57777	NM	SCE	PTR	EMT
158780	52780+57780	NM	SCE	ANG	EMT
158783	52783+57783	NM	SCE	ANG	EMT
158785	52785+57785	NM	SCE	ANG	EMT
158788	52788+57788	NM	SCE	ANG	EMT
158799	52799+57799	NM	SCE	PTR	EMT
158806	52806+57806	NM	SCE	PTR	EMT
158810	52810+57810	NM	SCE	PTR	EMT
158812	52812+57812	NM	SCE	PTR	EMT
158813	52813+57813	NM	SCE	PTR	EMT
158846	52846+57846	NM	SCE	ANG	EMT
158847	52847+57847	NM	SCE	ANG	EMT
158852	52852+57852	NM	SCE	ANG	EMT
158854	52854+57854	NM	SCE	ANG	EMT
158856	52856+57856	NM	SCE	ANG	EMT
158857	52857+57857	NM	SCE	ANG	EMT
158858	52858+57858	NM	SCE	ANG	EMT
158862	52862+57862	NM	SCE	ANG	EMT
158863	52863+57863	NM	SCE	ANG	EMT
158864	52864+57864	NM	SCE	ANG	EMT
158865	52865+57865	NM	SCE	ANG	EMT
158866	52866+57866	NM	SCE	ANG	EMT

Right: *A fleet of 25 longer-distance Class 158s are operated by East Midlands Trains, allocated to Nottingham Eastcroft. These sets are painted in the Stagecoach white main- line colours, but differ from those on South West Trains by having a ripple in the blue base colour, which is straight on the SWT sets. With a No. 2 applied to the front end to indicate the 52xxx vehicle, set No. 158783 approaches Clay Cross Junction on 17 April 2013 with a Liverpool to Norwich service.*
CJM

Class 222

Vehicle Length: 77ft 6in (23.62m)
Height: 12ft 4in (3.75m)
Width: 8ft 11in (2.73m)
Engine: 1 x Cummins OSK9R of 750hp per vehicle
Horsepower: 5,250hp (3,914kW)
Seats (total/car): 106F/236S
38S/68S/68S/62S/42F/42F/22F

Number	Formation DMS+MS+MS+MSRMB+MF+MF+DMRFO	Depot	Livery	Owner	Op'r	Name
222001	60161+60551+60561+60621+60341+60445+60241	DY	SCE	EVL	EMT	*The Entrepreneur Express*
222002	60162+60544+60562+60622+60342+60346+60242	DY	SCE	EVL	EMT	*The Cutlers' Company*
222003	60163+60553+60563+60623+60343+60446+60243	DY	SCE	EVL	EMT	*Tornado*
222004	60164+60554+60564+60624+60344+60345+60244	DY	SCE	EVL	EMT	*Childrens Hospital Sheffield*
222005	60165+60555+60565+60625+60443+60347+60245	DY	SCE	EVL	EMT	
222006	60166+60556+60566+60626+60441+60447+60246	DY	SCE	EVL	EMT	*The Carbon Cutter*

Vehicle Length: 77ft 6in (23.62m)
Height: 12ft 4in (3.75m)
Width: 8ft 11in (2.73m)
Engine: 1 x Cummins OSK9R of 750hp per vehicle
Horsepower: 3,750hp (2,796kW)
Seats (total/car): 50F/190S
38S/68S/62S/28F-22S/22F

Number	Formation DMS+MS+MSRMB+MC+DMRFO	Depot	Livery	Owner	Operator	Name
222007	60167+60567+60627+60442+60247	DY	SCE	EVL	EMT	
222008	60168+60545+60628+60918+60248	DY	SCE	EVL	EMT	
222009	60169+60557+60629+60919+60249	DY	SCE	EVL	EMT	
222010	60170+60546+60630+60920+60250	DY	SCE	EVL	EMT	
222011	60171+60531+60631+60921+60251	DY	SCE	EVL	EMT	

East Midlands Trains

222012	60172+60532+60632+60922+60252	DY	SCE	EVL	EMT	
222013	60173+60536+60633+60923+60253	DY	SCE	EVL	EMT	
222014	60174+60534+60634+60924+60254	DY	SCE	EVL	EMT	
222015	60175+60535+60635+60925+60255	DY	SCE	EVL	EMT	
222016	60176+60533+60636+60926+60256	DY	SCE	EVL	EMT	
222017	60177+60537+60637+60927+60257	DY	SCE	EVL	EMT	
222018	60178+60444+60638+60928+60258	DY	SCE	EVL	EMT	
222019	60179+60547+60639+60929+60259	DY	SCE	EVL	EMT	
222020	60180+60543+60640+60930+60260	DY	SCE	EVL	EMT	
222021	60181+60552+60641+60931+60261	DY	SCE	EVL	EMT	
222022	60182+60542+60642+60932+60262	DY	SCE	EVL	EMT	*Invest in Nottingham*
222023	60183+60541+60643+60933+60263	DY	SCE	EVL	EMT	

Left: *Long-distance non-HST services on EMT are operated by Class 222 DMUs in formations of seven, five or four vehicles. Allocated to Derby Etches Park, the sets offer standard class seating in the 2+2 style and first in the 2+1 layout. Five-car set No. 222011 is illustrated passing Clay Cross bound for Sheffield. The row of red dots above the passenger windows indicate, the first class seating area.* **CJM**

Class 222/1

Vehicle Length: 77ft 6in (23.62m)
Height: 12ft 4in (3.75m)
Width: 8ft 11in (2.73m)
Engine: 1 x Cummins OSK9R of 750hp per vehicle
Horsepower: 3,000hp (2,237kW)
Seats (total/car): 33F/148S 22F/11F-46S/62S/40S

Number	*Formation* DMF+MC+MSRMB+DMS	*Depot*	*Livery*	*Owner*	*Operator*
222101	60271+60571+60681+60191	DY	SCE	EVL	EMT
222102	60272+60572+60682+60192	DY	SCE	EVL	EMT
222103	60273+60573+60683+60193	DY	SCE	EVL	EMT
222104	60274+60574+60684+60194	DY	SCE	EVL	EMT

Left: *The Class 222/1 sub-class (four units) were originally introduced for First Hull Trains to operate on its open access King's Cross-Hull route. When these were replaced by Class 180s, the spare Class 222s were transferred to East Midlands Trains and brought up to the same standard in terms of interior decor and external branding as the existing Class 222/0 sets. Owned by Eversholt Leasing, these sets tend to operate the lighter-used services, such as the St Pancras to Corby corridor. On 16 July 2013, set No. 222103 passes Langham Junction between Melton Mowbray and Oakham with a diverted Derby to St Pancras working.* **Kim Fullbrook**

HST Passenger Fleet

Vehicle Length: 75ft 0in (22.86m) Width: 8ft 11in (2.71m)
Height: 12ft 9in (3.88m) Bogie Type: BT10

GK1G - TRFB *Seating 17F*

Number	Depot	Livery	Owner
40700	NL	SCE	PTR
40728	NL	SCE	PTR
40730	NL	SCE	PTR
40741	NL	SCE	PTR
40746	NL	SCE	PTR
40749	NL	SCE	PTR
40751	NL	SCE	PTR
40753	NL	SCE	PTR
40754	NL	SCE	PTR
40756	NL	SCE	PTR

GH1G - TF *Seating 46F*

Number	Depot	Livery	Owner
41041	NL	SCE	PTR
41046	NL	SCE	PTR
41057	NL	SCE	PTR
41061	NL	SCE	PTR
41063	NL	SCE	PTR
41064	NL	SCE	PTR
41067	NL	SCE	PTR
41068	NL	SCE	PTR
41069	NL	SCE	PTR
41070	NL	SCE	PTR
41071	NL	SCE	PTR
41072	NL	SCE	PTR
41075	NL	SCE	PTR
41076	NL	SCE	PTR
41077	NL	SCE	PTR
41079	NL	SCE	PTR
41084	NL	SCE	PTR
41111	NL	SCE	PTR
41112	NL	SCE	PTR
41113	NL	SCE	PTR
41117	NL	SCE	PTR
41156	NL	SCE	PTR

GH2G - TS *Seating 74S*

Number	Depot	Livery	Owner
42100	NL	SCE	PTR
42111	NL	SCE	PTR
42112	NL	SCE	PTR
42113	NL	SCE	PTR
42119	NL	SCE	PTR
42120	NL	SCE	PTR
42121	NL	SCE	PTR
42124	NL	SCE	PTR
42131	NL	SCE	PTR
42132	NL	SCE	PTR
42133	NL	SCE	PTR
42135	NL	SCE	PTR
42136	NL	SCE	PTR
42137	NL	SCE	PTR
42139	NL	SCE	PTR
42140	NL	SCE	PTR
42141	NL	SCE	PTR
42148	NL	SCE	PTR
42149	NL	SCE	PTR
42151	NL	SCE	PTR
42152	NL	SCE	PTR
42153	NL	SCE	PTR
42155	NL	SCE	PTR
42156	NL	SCE	PTR
42157	NL	SCE	PTR
42164	NL	SCE	PTR
42165	NL	SCE	PTR
42194	NL	SCE	PTR
42220	NL	SCE	PTR
42225	NL	SCE	PTR
42227	NL	SCE	PTR
42229	NL	SCE	PTR
42230	NL	SCE	PTR
42327	NL	SCE	PTR
42328	NL	SCE	PTR
42329	NL	SCE	PTR
42331	NL	SCE	PTR
42337	NL	SCE	PTR
42339	NL	SCE	PTR
42341	NL	SCE	PTR
42384¤	NL	SCE	PTR

¤ Modified from 41078

GJ2G - TGS *Seating 63S*

Number	Depot	Livery	Owner
44027	NL	SCE	PTR
44041	NL	SCE	PTR
44044	NL	SCE	PTR
44046	NL	SCE	PTR
44047	NL	SCE	PTR
44048	NL	SCE	PTR
44051	NL	SCE	PTR
44054	NL	SCE	PTR
44070	NL	SCE	PTR
44071	NL	SCE	PTR
44085	NL	SCE	PTR

Below: *At the start of 2014, East Midlands Trains operated a fleet of 84 HST trailer vehicles of four main types. All vehicles are allocated to Leeds Neville Hill, have been refurbished and carry the latest East Midlands Trains/Stagecoach white main-line livery. TS No. 42133 is illustrated.* **Nathan Williamson**

Service Stock

HST Barrier Vehicles

Number	Depot	Livery	Owner	Former Identity
6392	NL	PTR	PTR	BG - 81588/92183
6395	NL	PTR	EMT	BG - 81506/92148
6397	NL	PTR	PTR	BG - 81600/92190
6398	NL	MAI	EMT	BG - 81471/92126
6399	NL	MAI	EMT	BG - 81367/92994

Eurostar

Address: ✉ Eurostar, Times House, Bravingtons Walk, Regent Quarter, London, N1 9AW

new.comments@eurostar.com

✆ 08701 606 600

ⓘ www.eurostar.com

Managing Director: Nicolas Petrovic / Richard Brown

Principal Routes: St Pancras International - Brussels and Paris, also serving Disneyland Paris, Avignon and winter sport service to Bourg St Maurice

Owned Stations: St Pancras International, Stratford International, Ebbsfleet

Depots: Temple Mills [UK] (TI), Forest [Belgium] (FF), Le Landy [France] (LY)

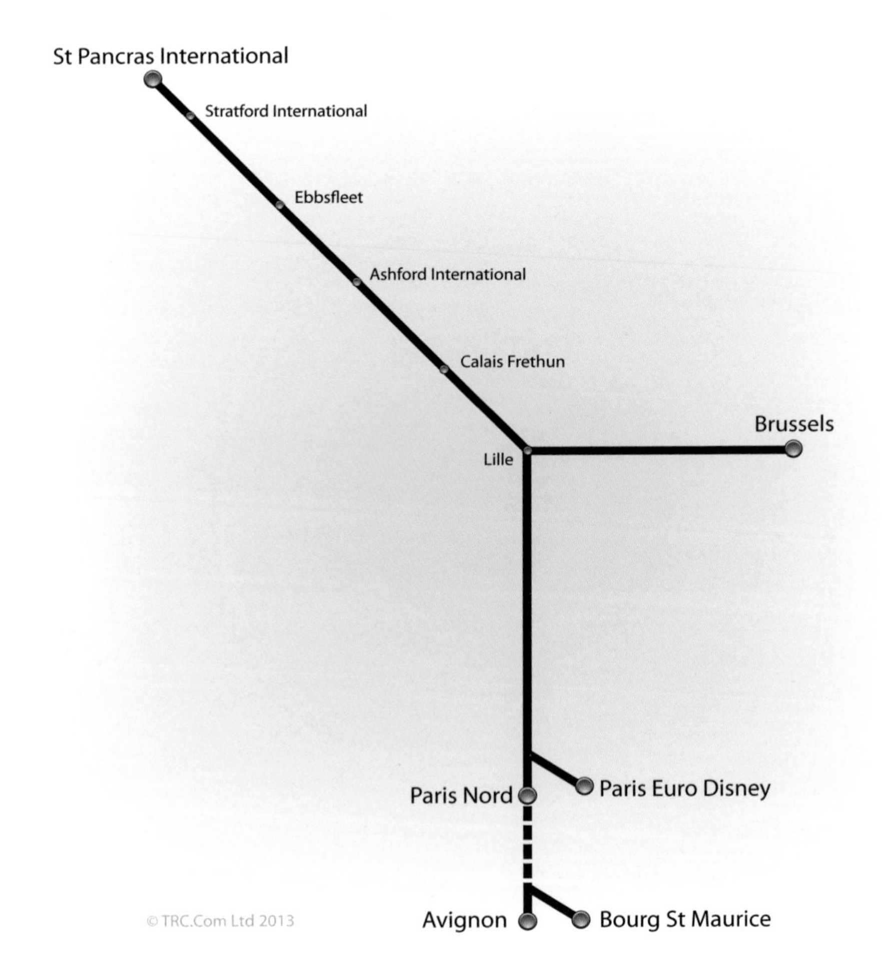

Class 373

Vehicle Length: (DM) 72ft 8in (22.15m), (MS) 71ft 8in (21.84m)
(TS, TBK, TF, TBF) 61ft 4in (18.70m)
Height: 12ft 4½in (3.77m)
Width: 9ft 3in (2.81m)
Horsepower: 16,400hp (12,249kW)
Seats (total/car): 102F/272S, 0/48S/56S/56S/56S/56S/0/39F/39F/24F

Number	*Formation* DM+MSO+TSO+TSO+TSO+TSO+RB+TFO+TFO+TBFO	*Depot*	*Livery*	*Owner*	*Operator*	*Name*
UK sets (Class 373/0)						
373001	3730010+3730011+3730012+3730013+3730014+3730015+3730016+3730017+3730018+3730019	TI	EUS	EUS	EUS	*Tread Lightly*
373002	3730020+3730021+3730022+3730023+3730024+3730025+3730026+3730027+3730028+3730029	TI	EUS	EUS	EUS	*Voyage Vert*
373003	3730030+3730031+3730032+3730033+3730034+3730035+3730036+3730037+3730038+3730039	TI	EUS	EUS	EUS	*Tri City Athlon 2010*
373004	3730040+3730041+3730042+3730043+3730044+3730045+3730046+3730047+3730048+3730049	TI	EUS	EUS	EUS	*Tri City Athlon 2010*
373005	3730050+3730051+3730052+3730053+3730054+3730055+3730056+3730057+3730058+3730059	TI	EUS	EUS	EUS	
373006	3730060+3730061+3730062+3730063+3730064+3730065+3730066+3730067+3730068+3730069	TI	EUS	EUS	EUS	
373007	3730070+3730071+3730072+3730073+3730074+3730075+3730076+3730077+3730078+3730079	TI	EUS	EUS	EUS	*Waterloo Sunset*
373008	3730080+3730081+3730082+3730083+3730084+3730085+3730086+3730087+3730088+3730089	TI	EUS	EUS	EUS	*Waterloo Sunset*
373009	3730090+3730091+3730092+3730093+3730094+3730095+3730096+3730097+3730098+3730099	TI	EUS	EUS	EUS	*Remembering Fromelles*
373010	3730100+3730101+3730102+3730103+3730104+3730105+3730106+3730107+3730108+3730109	TI	EUS	EUS	EUS	*Remembering Fromelles*
373011	3730110+3730111+3730112+3730113+3730114+3730115+3730116+3730117+3730118+3730119	TI	EUS	EUS	EUS	
373012	3730120+3730121+3730122+3730123+3730124+3730125+3730126+3730127+3730128+3730129	TI	EUS	EUS	EUS	
373013	3730130+3730131+3730132+3730133+3730134+3730135+3730136+3730137+3730138+3730139	TI	EUS	EUS	EUS	*London 2012*
373014	3730140+3730141+3730142+3730143+3730144+3730145+3730146+3730147+3730148+3730149	TI	EUS	EUS	EUS	*London 2012*
373015	3730150+3730151+3730152+3730153+3730154+3730155+3730156+3730157+3730158+3730159	TI	EUS	EUS	EUS	
373016	3730160+3730161+3730162+3730163+3730164+3730165+3730166+3730167+3730168+3730169	TI	EUS	EUS	EUS	
373017	3730170+3730171+3730172+3730173+3730174+3730175+3730176+3730177+3730178+3730179	TI	EUS	EUS	EUS	
373018	3730180+3730181+3730182+3730183+3730184+3730185+3730186+3730187+3730188+3730189	TI	EUS‡	EUS	EUS	
373019	3730190+3730191+3730192+3730193+3730194+3730195+3730196+3730197+3730198+3730199	TI	EUS	EUS	EUS	
373020	3730200+3730201+3730202+3730203+3730204+3730205+3730206+3730207+3730208+3730209	TI	EUS	EUS	EUS	
373021	3730210+3730211+3730212+3730213+3730214+3730215+3730216+3730217+3730218+3730219	TI	EUS	EUS	EUS	
373022	3730220+3730221+3730222+3730223+3730224+3730225+3730226+3730227+3730228+3730229	TI	EUS	EUS	EUS	
Belgian sets (Class 373/1)						
373101	3731010+3731011+3731012+3731013+3731014+3731015+3731016+3731017+3731018+3731019	FF[S]	EUS	SNB	EUS	
373102	3731020+3731021+3731022+3731023+3731024+3731025+3731026+3731027+3731028+3731029	FF[S]	EUS	SNB	EUS	
373103	3731030+3731031+3731032+3731033+3731034+3731035+3731036+3731037+3731038+3731039	FF	EUS	SNB	EUS	
373104	3731040+3731041+3731042+3731043+3731044+3731045+3731046+3731047+3731048+3731049	FF	EUS	SNB	EUS	
373105	3731050+3731051+3731052+3731053+3731054+3731055+3731056+3731057+3731058+3731059	FF	EUS	SNB	EUS	
373106	3731060+3731061+3731062+3731063+3731064+3731065+3731066+3731067+3731068+3731069	FF	EUS	SNB	EUS	
373107	3731070+3731071+3731072+3731073+3731074+3731075+3731076+3731077+3731078+3731079	FF	EUS	SNB	EUS	
373108	3731080+3731081+3731082+3731083+3731084+3731085+3731086+3731087+3731088+3731089	FF	EUS	SNB	EUS	
French sets (Class 373/2)						
373201	3732010+3732011+3732012+3732013+3732014+3732015+3732016+3732017+3732018+3732019	LY	EUS	SNF	EUS	
373202	3732020+3732021+3732022+3732023+3732024+3732025+3732026+3732027+3732028+3732029	LY	EUS	SNF	EUS	
373203¤	3732030+3732031+3732032+3732033+3732034+3732035+3732036+3732037+3732038+3732039	LY	SNT	SNF	EUS	
373204¤	3732040+3732041+3732042+3732043+3732044+3732045+3732046+3732047+3732048+3732049	LY	SNT	SNF	EUS	
373205	3732050+3732051+3732052+3732053+3732054+3732055+3732056+3732057+3732058+3732059	LY	EUS	SNF	EUS	
373206	3732060+3732061+3732062+3732063+3732064+3732065+3732066+3732067+3732068+3732069	LY	EUS	SNF	EUS	

Eurostar

Number	Formation	Depot	Livery	Owner	Operator	Name
373207	3732070+3732071+3732072+3732073+3732074+3732075+3732076+3732077+3732078+3732079	LY	EUS	SNF	EUS	*Michel Hollard*
373208	3732080+3732081+3732082+3732083+3732084+3732085+3732086+3732087+3732088+3732089	LY	EUS	SNF	EUS	*Michel Hollard*
373209	3732090+3732091+3732092+3732093+3732094+3732095+3732096+3732097+3732098+3732099	LY	EUS	SNF	EUS	*The Da Vinci Code*
373210	3732100+3732101+3732102+3732103+3732104+3732105+3732106+3732107+3732108+3732109	LY	EUS	SNF	EUS	*The Da Vinci Code*
373211	3732110+3732111+3732112+3732113+3732114+3732115+3732116+3732117+3732118+3732119	LY	EUS	SNF	EUS	
373212	3732120+3732121+3732122+3732123+3732124+3732125+3732126+3732127+3732128+3732129	LY	EUS	SNF	EUS	
373213	3732130+3732131+3732132+3732133+3732134+3732135+3732136+3732137+3732138+3732139	LY	EUS	SNF	EUS	
373214	3732140+3732141+3732142+3732143+3732144+3732145+3732146+3732147+3732148+3732149	LY	EUS	SNF	EUS	
373215	3732150+3732151+3732152+3732153+3732154+3732155+3732156+3732157+3732158+3732159	LY	EUS	SNF	EUS	
373216	3732160+3732161+3732162+3732163+3732164+3732165+3732166+3732167+3732168+3732169	LY	EUS	SNF	EUS	
373217	3732170+3732171+3732172+3732173+3732174+3732175+3732176+3732177+3732178+3732179	LY	EUS	SNF	EUS	
373218	3732180+3732181+3732182+3732183+3732184+3732185+3732186+3732187+3732188+3732189	LY	EUS	SNF	EUS	
373219	3732190+3732191+3732192+3732193+3732194+3732195+3732196+3732197+3732198+3732199	LY	EUS	SNF	EUS	
373220	3732200+3732201+3732202+3732203+3732204+3732205+3732206+3732207+3732208+3732209	LY	EUS	SNF	EUS	
373221	3732210+3732211+3732212+3732213+3732214+3732215+3732216+3732217+3732218+3732219	LY	EUS	SNF	EUS	
373222	3732220+3732221+3732222+3732223+3732224+3732225+3732226+3732227+3732228+3732229	LY	EUS	SNF	EUS	
373223	3732230+3732231+3732232+3732233+3732234+3732235+3732236+3732237+3732238+3732239	LY	EUS	SNF	EUS	
373224	3732240+3732241+3732242+3732243+3732244+3732245+3732246+3732247+3732248+3732249	LY	EUS	SNF	EUS	
373225¤	3732250+3732251+3732252+3732253+3732254+3732255+3732256+3732257+3732258+3732259	LY	SNT	SNF	EUS	
373226¤	3732260+3732261+3732262+3732263+3732264+3732265+3732266+3732267+3732268+3732269	LY	SNT	SNF	EUS	
373227¤	3732270+3732271+3732272+3732273+3732274+3732275+3732276+3732277+3732278+3732279	LY	SNT	SNF	EUS	
373228¤	3732280+3732281+3732282+3732283+3732284+3732285+3732286+3732287+3732288+3732289	LY	SNT	SNF	EUS	
373229	3732290+3732291+3732292+3732293+3732294+3732295+3732296+3732297+3732298+3732299	LY	EUS	SNF	EUS	
373230	3732300+3732301+3732302+3732303+3732304+3732305+3732306+3732307+3732308+3732309	LY	EUS	SNF	EUS	
373231	3732310+3732311+3732312+3732313+3732314+3732315+3732316+3732317+3732318+3732319	LY	EUS	SNF	EUS	
373232	3732320+3732321+3732322+3732313+3732324+3732325+3732326+3732327+3732328+3732329	LY	EUS	SNF	EUS	

¤ Operated in France on domestic services.

Vehicle Length: (DM) 72ft 8in (22.15m), (MS) 71ft 8in (21.84m)
(TS, TBK, TF, TBF) 61ft 4in (18.70m)
Height: 12ft 4½in (3.77m)
Width: 9ft 3in (2.81m)
Horsepower: 16,400hp (12,249kW)
Seats (total/car): 102F/272S, 0/48S/56S/56S/56S/56S/0/39F/39F/24F

Number	*Formation* DM+MSO+TSO+TSO+TSO+RB+TFO+TBFO	*Depot*	*Livery*	*Owner*	*Operator*
Regional sets (373/3)					
373301	3733010+3733011+3733012+3733013+3733015+3733016+3733017+3733019	LY	EUS	EUS	SNF
373302	3733020+3733021+3733022+3733023+3733025+3733026+3733027+3733029	LY	EUS	EUS	SNF
373303(S)	3733030+3733031+3733032+3733033+3733035+3733036+3733037+3733039	LY	EUS	EUS	SNF
373304(S)	3733040+3733041+3733042+3733043+3733045+3733046+3733047+3733049	LY	EUS	EUS	SNF
373305	3733050+3733051+3733052+3733053+3733055+3733056+3733057+3733059	LY	EUS	EUS	SNF
373306	3733060+3733061+3733062+3733063+3733065+3733066+3733067+3733069	LY	EUS	EUS	SNF
373307(S)	3733070+3733071+3733072+3733073+3733075+3733076+3733077+3733079	LY	EUS	EUS	SNF
373308(S)	3733080+3733081+3733082+3733083+3733085+3733086+3733087+3733089	LY	EUS	EUS	SNF
373309	3733090+3733091+3733092+3733093+3733095+3733096+3733097+3733099	LY	EUS	EUS	SNF
373310	3733100+3733101+3733102+3733103+3733105+3733106+3733107+3733109	LY	EUS	EUS	SNF
373311	3733110+3733111+3733112+3733113+3733115+3733116+3733117+3733119	LY	EUS	EUS	SNF
373312	3733120+3733121+3733122+3733123+3733125+3733126+3733127+3733129	LY	EUS	EUS	SNF
373313	3733130+3733131+3733132+3733133+3733135+3733136+3733137+3733139	LY	EUS	EUS	SNF
373314	3733140+3733141+3733142+3733143+3733145+3733146+3733147+3733149	LY	EUS	EUS	SNF

■ *These 14 short half-sets are loaned to SNCF for domestic duties until 2013.*

Spare DM

Number		*Depot*	*Livery*	*Owner*	*Operator*
3999	(Spare vehicle used as required to cover for maintenance)	**TI**	**EUS**	**EUS**	**EUS**

Right: *At present the Class 373 'Eurostar' sets operated by Eurostar UK, SNCF and SNCB are the sole operators of passenger services through the Channel Tunnel. Soon German ICE sets and new Eurostar train sets will be introduced, widening the operating range to provide timetabled services to Germany and other European countries. UK Eurostar sets Nos. 373004 and 373003 passes Tutthill on HS1 forming train No. 9O31, the 13.08 Paris Nord to St Pancras International, captured on the 10th anniversary of the CTRL stage one opening on 28 September 2013.* **Brian Stephenson**

Class 374 (e320)

Vehicle Length: DM, T, M, T, T, M, T, M
Height: Details awaited *Width: Details awaited*
Horsepower: 25kV ac operation - 21,000hp (16,000kW)
15kV, 3,000V dc, 1,500V dc tba
Seats (total/car): 450 (half train) *Electrical Equipment: Siemens*

● Twenty new Eurostar e320 eight-car Class 374 sets are on order from Siemens for delivery in 2015; these will have a 200mph (320km/h) top speed capability and two half-sets will seat around 900. The 374s sets will have the ability to operate throughout Europe. Length: 400m, Power: 16,000kW from 25kV ac and 1.5/3kV dc. Driving cars will be 25.7m, and Intermediate cars 14.2m in length.

Set Number	*Formation eight vehicles [half-set] DM, T, M, T, T, M, T, M*	*Depot*	*Livery*	*Owner*	*Operator*
374001	**93-70-3740-011 GB-EIL – 93-70-3740-018 GB-EIL** *(under test on SNCB)*	**TI**	**EUN**	**EUS**	**EUS**
374002	**93-70-3740-021 GB-EIL – 93-70-3740-028 GB-EIL** *(under test on SNCB)*	**TI**	**EUN**	**EUS**	**EUS**
374003	**93-70-3740-031 GB-EIL – 93-70-3740-038 GB-EIL** *(on order)*	**TI**	**EUN**	**EUS**	**EUS**
374004	**93-70-3740-041 GB-EIL – 93-70-3740-048 GB-EIL** *(on order)*	**TI**	**EUN**	**EUS**	**EUS**
374005	**93-70-3740-051 GB-EIL – 93-70-3740-058 GB-EIL** *(on order)*	**TI**	**EUN**	**EUS**	**EUS**
374006	**93-70-3740-061 GB-EIL – 93-70-3740-068 GB-EIL** *(on order)*	**TI**	**EUN**	**EUS**	**EUS**
374007	**93-70-3740-071 GB-EIL – 93-70-3740-078 GB-EIL** *(on order)*	**TI**	**EUN**	**EUS**	**EUS**
374008	**93-70-3740-081 GB-EIL – 93-70-3740-088 GB-EIL** *(on order)*	**TI**	**EUN**	**EUS**	**EUS**
374009	**93-70-3740-091 GB-EIL – 93-70-3740-098 GB-EIL** *(on order)*	**TI**	**EUN**	**EUS**	**EUS**
374010	**93-70-3740-101 GB-EIL – 93-70-3740-108 GB-EIL** *(on order)*	**TI**	**EUN**	**EUS**	**EUS**
374011	**93-70-3740-111 GB-EIL – 93-70-3740-118 GB-EIL** *(on order)*	**TI**	**EUN**	**EUS**	**EUS**
374012	**93-70-3740-121 GB-EIL – 93-70-3740-128 GB-EIL** *(on order)*	**TI**	**EUN**	**EUS**	**EUS**
374013	**93-70-3740-131 GB-EIL – 93-70-3740-138 GB-EIL** *(on order)*	**TI**	**EUN**	**EUS**	**EUS**
374014	**93-70-3740-141 GB-EIL – 93-70-3740-148 GB-EIL** *(on order)*	**TI**	**EUN**	**EUS**	**EUS**
374015	**93-70-3740-151 GB-EIL – 93-70-3740-158 GB-EIL** *(on order)*	**TI**	**EUN**	**EUS**	**EUS**
374016	**93-70-3740-161 GB-EIL – 93-70-3740-168 GB-EIL** *(on order)*	**TI**	**EUN**	**EUS**	**EUS**
374017	**93-70-3740-171 GB-EIL – 93-70-3740-178 GB-EIL** *(on order)*	**TI**	**EUN**	**EUS**	**EUS**
374018	**93-70-3740-181 GB-EIL – 93-70-3740-188 GB-EIL** *(on order)*	**TI**	**EUN**	**EUS**	**EUS**
374019	**93-70-3740-191 GB-EIL – 93-70-3740-198 GB-EIL** *(on order)*	**TI**	**EUN**	**EUS**	**EUS**
374020	**93-70-3740-201 GB-EIL – 93-70-3740-208 GB-EIL** *(on order)*	**TI**	**EUN**	**EUS**	**EUS**

Class 08

Vehicle Length: 29ft 3in (8.91m)
Height: 12ft 8⅝in (3.87m)
Width: 8ft 6in (2.59m)
Engine: English Electric 6K
Horsepower: 400hp (298kW)
Electrical Equipment: English Electric

Number	*Depot*	*Pool*	*Livery*	*Owner*	*Op'r*
08948	TI	GPSS	TTG	EUS	EUS

First Capital Connect

Address: ✉ Hertford House, 1 Cranwood Street, London, EC1V 9QS
customer.relations.fcc@firstgroup.com
✆ 0845 026 4700
ⓘ www.firstcapitalconnect.co.uk

Managing Director: David Statham

Franchise Dates: 1 April 2006 - 14 September 2013§

Principal Routes: London King's Cross - King's Lynn, Peterborough / Cambridge
Moorgate - Hertford Loop and Letchworth
Bedford - Brighton (Thameslink)
Luton - Wimbledon / Sutton (Thameslink)

Depots: Bedford Cauldwell Walk (BF), Hornsey (HE), Brighton (BI)*
* Stabling point

Parent Company: First Group PLC

§ Might be extended, re-franchising suspended

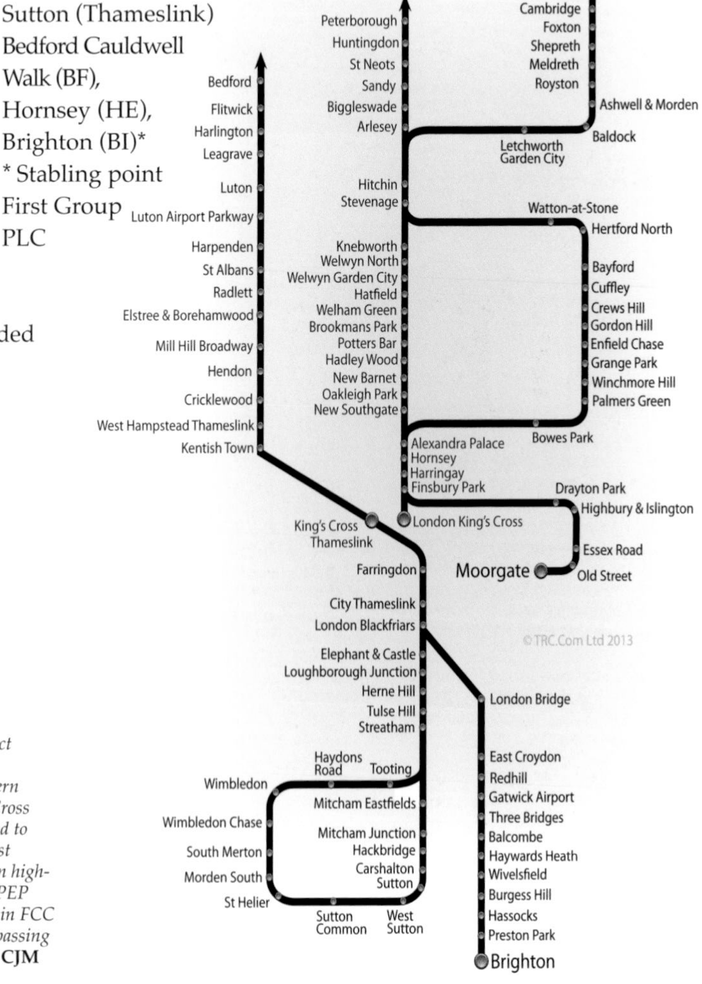

Far right: *First Capital Connect currently operate a fleet of 44 Class 313s on the Great Northern suburban routes from King's Cross and Moorgate. Sets are allocated to Hornsey depot and were the first production build of 1972-design high-density stock derived from the PEP prototype. The sets are painted in FCC livery. Set No. 313053 is seen passing Harringay in September 2013.* **CJM**

Class 313/0 & 313/1

Vehicle Length: (Driving) 64ft 11½in (20.75m) (Inter) 65ft 4¼in (19.92m)
Height: 11ft 9in (3.58m)
Width: 9ft 3in (2.82m)
Horsepower: 880hp (656kW)
Seats (total/car): 231S, 74S/83S/74S

Number	Formation DMSO+PTSO+BDMSO	Depot	Livery	Owner	Operator	Name
313018	62546+71230+62160	HE	FCC	EVL	FCC	
313024	62552+71236+62616	HE	FCC	EVL	FCC	
313025	62553+71237+62617	HE	FCC	EVL	FCC	
313026	62554+71238+62618	HE	FCC	EVL	FCC	
313027	62555+71239+62619	HE	FCC	EVL	FCC	
313028	62556+71240+62620	HE	FCC	EVL	FCC	
313029	62557+71241+62621	HE	FCC	EVL	FCC	
313030	62558+71242+62622	HE	FCC	EVL	FCC	
313031	62559+71243+62623	HE	FCC	EVL	FCC	
313032	62560+71244+62643	HE	FCC	EVL	FCC	
313033	62561+71245+62625	HE	FCC	EVL	FCC	
313035	62563+71247+62627	HE	FCC	EVL	FCC	
313036	62564+71248+62628	HE	FCC	EVL	FCC	
313037	62565+71249+62629	HE	FCC	EVL	FCC	
313038	62566+71250+62630	HE	FCC	EVL	FCC	
313039	62567+71251+62631	HE	FCC	EVL	FCC	
313040	62568+71252+62632	HE	FCC	EVL	FCC	
313041	62569+71253+62633	HE	FCC	EVL	FCC	
313042	62570+71254+62634	HE	FCC	EVL	FCC	
313043	62571+71255+62635	HE	FCC	EVL	FCC	
313044	62572+71256+62636	HE	FCC	EVL	FCC	
313045	62573+71257+62637	HE	FCC	EVL	FCC	
313046	62574+71258+62638	HE	FCC	EVL	FCC	
313047	62575+71259+62639	HE	FCC	EVL	FCC	
313048	62576+71260+62640	HE	FCC	EVL	FCC	
313049	62577+71261+62641	HE	FCC	EVL	FCC	
313050	62578+71262+62649	HE	FCC	EVL	FCC	
313051	62579+71263+62624	HE	FCC	EVL	FCC	
313052	62580+71264+62644	HE	FCC	EVL	FCC	
313053	62581+71265+62645	HE	FCC	EVL	FCC	
313054	62582+71266+62646	HE	FCC	EVL	FCC	*Captain William Leefe Robinson VC*
313055	62583+71267+62647	HE	FCC	EVL	FCC	
313056	62584+71268+62648	HE	FCC	EVL	FCC	
313057	62585+71269+62642	HE	FCC	EVL	FCC	
313058	62586+71270+62650	HE	FCC	EVL	FCC	
313059	62587+71271+62651	HE	FCC	EVL	FCC	
313060	62588+71272+62652	HE	FCC	EVL	FCC	
313061	62589+71273+62653	HE	FCC	EVL	FCC	
313062	62590+71274+62654	HE	FCC	EVL	FCC	
313063	62591+71275+62655	HE	FCC	EVL	FCC	
313064	62592+71276+62656	HE	FCC	EVL	FCC	
313122	62550+71234+62614	HE	FCC	EVL	FCC	*Eric Roberts 1946-2012 'The Flying Nottsman'*
313123	62551+71235+62615	HE	FCC	EVL	FCC	
313134	62562+71246+62626	HE	FCC	EVL	FCC	*City of London*

First Capital Connect

Class 317/3

Vehicle Length: (Driving) 65ft 0¾in (19.83m) (Inter) 65ft 4¼in (19.92m) Height: 12ft 1½in (3.58m) Width: 9ft 3in (2.82m) Horsepower: 1,000hp (746kW) Seats (total/car): 22F/269S, 74S/79S/22F-46S/70S

Number	Formation DTSO+MSO+TCO+DTSO	Depot	Livery	Owner	Operator	Name
317337	77036+62671+71613+77084	HE	FCC	ANG	FCC	
317338	77037+62698+71614+77085	HE	FCC	ANG	FCC	
317339	77038+62699+71615+77086	HE	FCC	ANG	FCC	
317340	77039+62700+71616+77087	HE	FCC	ANG	FCC	
317341	77040+62701+71617+77088	HE	FCC	ANG	FCC	
317342	77041+62702+71618+77089	HE	FCC	ANG	FCC	
317343	77042+62703+71619+77090	HE	FCC	ANG	FCC	
317344	77029+62690+71620+77091	HE	FCC	ANG	FCC	
317345	77044+62705+71621+77092	HE	FCC	ANG	FCC	*Driver John Webb*
317346	77045+62706+71622+77093	HE	FCC	ANG	FCC	
317347	77046+62707+71623+77094	HE	FCC	ANG	FCC	
317348	77047+62708+71624+77095	HE	FCC	ANG	FCC	*Richard A. Jenner*

Left: *A small fleet of 12 Class 317/3s are operated by First Capital Connect and operate alongside the Class 365s on longer-distance outer suburban services. The fleet is based at Hornsey depot and all are painted in FCC corporate livery. This view recorded at Harringay shows the comparison between the Class 317 on the right and the more modern Class 365 on the left. The Class 317 is set No. 317345.* **CJM**

Class 319/0

Vehicle Length: (Driving) 65ft 0¾in (19.83m) (Inter) 65ft 4¼in (19.92m) Height: 11ft 9in (3.58m) Width: 9ft 3in (2.82m) Horsepower: 1,326hp (990kW) Seats (total/car): 319S, 82S/82S/77S/78S

Number	Formation DTSO(A)+MSO+TSO+DTSO(B)	Depot	Livery	Owner	Operator	Name
319001	77291+62891+71772+77290	SU	FCC	PTR	FCC	*Driver Mick Winnett*
319002	77293+62892+71773+77292	SU	FCC	PTR	FCC	
319003	77295+62893+71774+77294	SU	FCC	PTR	FCC	
319004	77297+62894+71775+77296	SU	FCC	PTR	FCC	
319005	77299+62895+71776+77298	SU	FCC	PTR	FCC	
319006	77301+62896+71777+77300	SU	FCC	PTR	FCC	
319007	77303+62897+71778+77302	SU	FCC	PTR	FCC	
319008	77305+62898+71779+77304	SU	SOU	PTR	FCC	*Cheriton*
319009	77307+62899+71780+77306	SU	SOU	PTR	FCC	*Coquelles*
319010	77309+62900+71781+77308	SU	FCC	PTR	FCC	
319011	77311+62901+71782+77310	SU	SOU	PTR	FCC	*John Ruskin College*
319012	77313+62902+71783+77312	SU	SOU	PTR	FCC	
319013	77315+62903+71784+77314	SU	SOU	PTR	FCC	*The Surrey Hills*

Class 319/2

Vehicle Length: (Driving) 65ft 0¾in (19.83m) (Inter) 65ft 4¼in (19.92m) Height: 11ft 9in (3.58m) Width: 9ft 3in (2.82m) Horsepower: 1,326hp (990kW) Seats (total/car): 18F/212S, 64S/60S/52S/18F-36S

Number	Formation DTSO+MSO+TSO+DTCO	Depot	Livery	Owner	Operator	Name/Notes
319214	77317+62904+71785+77316	SU	SOU	PTR	FCC	
319215	77319+62905+71786+77318	SU	ADV	PTR	FCC	(Visit Switzerland livery)
319216	77321+62906+71787+77320	SU	SOU	PTR	FCC	
319217	77323+62907+71788+77322	BF	SOU	PTR	FCC	*Brighton*
319218	77325+62908+71789+77324	BF	ADV	PTR	FCC	*Croydon*
319219	77327+62909+71790+77326	BF	SOU	PTR	FCC	
319220	77329+62910+71791+77328	BF	SOU	PTR	FCC	

Class 319/3

Vehicle Length: (Driving) 65ft 0¾in (19.83m) Width: 9ft 3in (2.82m)
(Inter) 65ft 4¼in (19.92m) Horsepower: 1,326hp (990kW)
Height: 11ft 9in (3.58m) Seats (total/car): 300S, 70S/78S/74S/78S

Number	Formation DTSO(A)+MSO+TSO+DTSO(B)	Depot	Livery	Owner	Operator	Name
319361	77459+63043+71929+77458	BF	FCC	PTR	FCC	
319362	77461+63044+71930+77460	BF	FCC	PTR	FCC	
319363	77463+63045+71931+77462	BF	FCC	PTR	FCC	
319364	77465+63046+71932+77464	BF	FCC	PTR	FCC	*Transforming Blackfriars*
319365	77467+63047+71933+77466	BF	FCC	PTR	FCC	*Transforming Farringdon*
319366	77469+63048+71934+77468	BF	FCC	PTR	FCC	
319367	77471+63049+71935+77470	BF	FCC	PTR	FCC	
319368	77473+63050+71936+77472	BF	FCC	PTR	FCC	
319369	77475+63051+71937+77474	BF	FCC	PTR	FCC	
317370	77477+63052+71938+77476	BF	FCC	PTR	FCC	
319371	77479+63053+71939+77478	BF	FCC	PTR	FCC	
319372	77481+63054+71940+77480	BF	FCC	PTR	FCC	
319373	77483+63055+71941+77482	BF	FCC	PTR	FCC	
319374	77485+63056+71942+77484	BF	FCC	PTR	FCC	*Bedford Cauldwell Walk TMD*
319375	77487+63057+71943+77486	BF	FCC	PTR	FCC	
319376	77489+63058+71944+77488	BF	FCC	PTR	FCC	
319377	77491+63059+71945+77490	BF	FCC	PTR	FCC	
319378	77493+63060+71946+77492	BF	FCC	PTR	FCC	
319379	77495+63061+71947+77494	BF	FCC	PTR	FCC	
319380	77497+63062+71948+77496	BF	FCC	PTR	FCC	
319381	77973+63093+71979+77974	BF	FCC	PTR	FCC	
319382	77975+63094+71980+77976	BF	FCC	PTR	FCC	
319383	77977+63096+71981+77978	BF	FCC	PTR	FCC	
319384	77979+63096+71982+77980	BF	FCC	PTR	FCC	
319385	77981+63097+71983+77982	BF	FCC	PTR	FCC	
319386	77983+63098+71984+77984	BF	FCC	PTR	FCC	

Right: *The First Capital Connect Thameslink operation will be drastically altered in the next few years with introduction of new stock which will see the Class 319s cascaded to new routes. At present the Class 319 fleets operate the core Bedford-Brighton service. Four different sub-classes are to be found. The majority of sets sport First standard livery. Set No. 319421 is seen passing Honor Oak Park with a Bedford to Brighton service.* **CJM**

Class 319/4

Vehicle Length: (Driving) 65ft 0¾in (19.83m) Width: 9ft 3in (2.82m)
(Inter) 65ft 4¼in (19.92m) Horsepower: 1,326hp (990kW)
Height: 11ft 9in (3.58m) Seats (total/car): 12F/277S, 12F-54S/77S/72S/74S

Number	Formation DTCO+MSO+TSO+DTSO	Depot	Livery	Owner	Operator	Name
319421	77331+62911+71792+77330	BF	FCC	PTR	FCC	
319422	77333+62912+71793+77332	BF	FCC	PTR	FCC	
319423	77335+62913+71794+77334	BF	FCC	PTR	FCC	
319424	77337+62914+71795+77336	BF	FCC	PTR	FCC	
319425	77339+62915+71796+77338	BF	FCC	PTR	FCC	*Transforming Travel*
319426	77341+62916+71797+77340	BF	FCC	PTR	FCC	
319427	77343+62917+71798+77342	BF	FCC	PTR	FCC	
319428	77345+62918+71799+77344	BF	FCC	PTR	FCC	
319429	77347+62919+71800+77346	BF	FCC	PTR	FCC	
319430	77349+62920+71801+77348	BF	FCC	PTR	FCC	
319431	77351+62921+71802+77350	BF	FCC	PTR	FCC	
319432	77353+62922+71803+77352	BF	FCC	PTR	FCC	
319433	77355+62923+71804+77354	BF	FCC	PTR	FCC	

First Capital Connect

Number	Formation	Depot	Livery	Owner	Operator	Name
319434	77357+62924+71805+77356	BF	FCC	PTR	FCC	
319435	77359+62925+71806+77358	BF	FCC	PTR	FCC	*Adrian Jackson-Robbins Chairman 1987-2007 Association of Public Transport Users*
319436	77361+62926+71807+77360	BF	FCC	PTR	FCC	
319437	77363+62927+71808+77362	BF	FCC	PTR	FCC	
319438	77365+62928+71809+77364	BF	FCC	PTR	FCC	
319439	77367+62929+71810+77366	BF	FCC	PTR	FCC	
319440	77369+62930+71811+77368	BF	FCC	PTR	FCC	
319441	77371+62931+71812+77370	BF	FCC	PTR	FCC	
319442	77373+62932+71813+77372	BF	FCC	PTR	FCC	
319443	77375+62933+71814+77374	BF	FCC	PTR	FCC	
319444	77377+62934+71815+77376	BF	FCC	PTR	FCC	
319445	77379+62935+71816+77378	BF	FCC	PTR	FCC	
319446	77381+62936+71817+77380	BF	FCC	PTR	FCC	
319447	77431+62961+71866+77430	BF	FCC	PTR	FCC	
319448	77433+62962+71867+77432	BF	FCC	PTR	FCC	
319449	77435+62963+71868+77434	BF	FCC	PTR	FCC	
319450	77437+62964+71869+77436	BF	FCC	PTR	FCC	
319451	77439+62965+71870+77438	BF	FCC	PTR	FCC	
319452	77441+62966+71871+77440	BF	FCC	PTR	FCC	
319453	77443+62967+71872+77442	BF	FCC	PTR	FCC	
319454	77445+62968+71873+77444	BF	FCC	PTR	FCC	
319455	77447+62969+71874+77446	BF	FCC	PTR	FCC	
319456	77449+62970+71875+77448	BF	FCC	PTR	FCC	
319457	77451+62971+71876+77450	BF	FCC	PTR	FCC	
319458	77453+62972+71877+77452	BF	FCC	PTR	FCC	
319459	77455+62973+71878+77454	BF	FCC	PTR	FCC	
319460	77457+62974+71879+77456	BF	FCC	PTR	FCC	

Class 321/4

Vehicle Length: (Driving) 65ft 0¾in (19.83m)
(Inter) 65ft 4¼in (19.92m)
Height: 12ft 4¾in (3.78m)
Width: 9ft 3in (2.82m)
Horsepower: 1,328hp (996kW)
Seats (total/car): 28F/271S, 28F-40S/79S/74S/78S

Number	*Formation* DMCO+MSO+TSO+DMSO	*Depot*	*Livery*	*Owner*	*Operator*	*Name*
321401	78095+63063+71949+77943	HE	FCC	EVL	FCC	
321402	78096+63064+71950+77944	HE	FCC	EVL	FCC	
321403	78097+63065+71951+77945	HE	FCC	EVL	FCC	*Stewart Fleming Signalman King's Cross*
321404	78098+63066+71952+77946	HE	FCC	EVL	FCC	
321405	78099+63067+71953+77947	HE	FCC	EVL	FCC	
321406	78100+63068+71954+77948	HE	FCC	EVL	FCC	
321407	78101+63069+71955+77949	HE	FCC	EVL	FCC	
321408	78102+63070+71956+77959	HE	FCC	EVL	FCC	
321409	78103+63071+71957+77960	HE	FCC	EVL	FCC	*Dame Alice Owen's School 400 years of Learning*
321410	78104+63072+71958+77961	HE	FCC	EVL	FCC	
321418	78112+63080+71968+77962	HE	FCC	EVL	FCC	*The Poppy Express - Supporting The British Legion*
321419	78113+63081+71969+77963	HE	FCC	EVL	FCC	
321420	78114+63082+71970+77964	HE	FCC	EVL	FCC	*We are proud supporters of Movember*

Left: *To help offset chronic overcrowding on peak hour Great Northern services, FCC took over 13 Class 321/4 sets when these became spare from West Coast services. The Class 321s are based at Hornsey and all carry standard First corporate livery. The units tend to be used in pairs on peak hour services. Set No. 321403 is illustrated from its Motor Standard Open vehicle. Three sets are named, with a 'stick-on' names applied to the TSO vehicle.* **CJM**

Class 365
Networker Express

Vehicle Length: (Driving) 68ft 6½in (20.89m) (Inter) 65ft 9¼in (20.89m)
Height: 12ft 4½in (3.77m)
Width: 9ft 2½in (2.81m)
Horsepower: 1,684hp (1,256kW)
Seats (total/car): 24F/239S, 12F-56S/59S/68S/12F-56S

Number	Formation DMCO(A)+TSO+PTSO+DMCO(B)	Depot	Livery	Owner	Operator	Name
365501	65894+72241+72240+65935	HE	FCC	EVL	FCC	
365502	65895+72243+72242+65936	HE	FCC	EVL	FCC	
365503	65896+72245+72244+65937	HE	FCC	EVL	FCC	
365504	65897+72247+72246+65938	HE	FCC	EVL	FCC	
365505	65898+72249+72248+65939	HE	FCC	EVL	FCC	
365506	65899+72251+72250+65940	HE	FCC	EVL	FCC	The Royston Express
365507	65900+72253+72252+65941	HE	FCC	EVL	FCC	
365508	65901+72255+72254+65942	HE	FCC	EVL	FCC	
365509	65902+72257+72256+65943	HE	FCC	EVL	FCC	
365510	65903+72259+72258+65944	HE	FCC	EVL	FCC	
365511	65904+72261+72260+65945	HE	FCC	EVL	FCC	
365512	65905+72263+72262+65946	HE	FCC	EVL	FCC	
365513	65906+72265+72264+65947	HE	FCC	EVL	FCC	Hornsey Depot
365514	65907+72267+72266+65948	HE	FCC	EVL	FCC	Captain George Vancouver
365515	65908+72269+72268+65949	HE	FCC	EVL	FCC	
365516	65909+72271+72270+65950	HE	FCC	EVL	FCC	
365517	65910+72273+72272+65951	HE	SPL	EVL	FCC	
365518	65911+72275+72274+65952	HE	FCC	EVL	FCC	The Fenman
365519	65912+72277+72276+65953	HE	FCC	EVL	FCC	
365520	65913+72279+72278+65954	HE	FCC	EVL	FCC	
365521	65914+72281+72280+65955	HE	FCC	EVL	FCC	
365522	65915+72283+72282+65956	HE	FCC	EVL	FCC	
365523	65916+72285+72284+65957	HE	FCC	EVL	FCC	
365524	65917+72287+72286+65958	HE	FCC	EVL	FCC	
365525	65918+72289+72288+65959	HE	FCC	EVL	FCC	
365527	65920+72293+72292+65961	HE	FCC	EVL	FCC	Robert Stripe Passengers' Champion
365528	65921+72296+72294+65962	HE	FCC	EVL	FCC	
365529	65922+72297+72296+65963	HE	FCC	EVL	FCC	
365530	65923+72299+72298+65964	HE	FCC	EVL	FCC	The Interlink Partnership Promoting Integrated Transport Since 1999
365531	65924+72301+72300+65965	HE	FCC	EVL	FCC	
365532	65925+72303+72302+65966	HE	FCC	EVL	FCC	
365533	65926+72305+72304+65967	HE	FCC	EVL	FCC	
365534	65927+72307+72306+65968	HE	FCC	EVL	FCC	
365535	65928+72309+72308+65969	HE	FCC	EVL	FCC	
365536	65929+72311+72310+65970	HE	FCC	EVL	FCC	
365537	65930+72313+72312+65971	HE	FCC	EVL	FCC	Daniel Edwards (1974-2010) Cambridge Driver
365538	65931+72315+72314+65972	HE	FCC	EVL	FCC	
365539	65932+72317+72316+65973	HE	FCC	EVL	FCC	
365540	65933+72319+72318+65974	HE	FCC	EVL	FCC	
365541	65934+72321+72320+65975	HE	FCC	EVL	FCC	

Right: *Today, a fleet of 40 Class 365 'Networker Express' sets operate for FCC, based at Hornsey and used on outer-suburban services to locations such as Peterborough, King's Lynn and Cambridge. When introduced the sets had standard 'Networker' front ends, similar to those applied to the Class 465s, but new 'happy face' front ends have now been applied. Most sets display corporate First livery, with a small number carrying route specific advertising branding. Set No. 365527 is illustrated. Originally these sets were built for dual ac/dc operation, but the dc equipment has now been isolated.* **CJM**

First Capital Connect

Class 377/5
Electrostar

Vehicle Length: (Driving) 66ft 9in (20.40m)
(Inter) 65ft 6in (19.99m)
Height: 12ft 4in (3.77m)
Width: 9ft 2in (2.80m)
Horsepower: 2,012hp (1,500kW) (ac), dual voltage sets
Seats (total/car): 20F-221S, 10F-48S/69S/56S/10F-48S

Number	*Formation* DMCO(A)+MSO+PTSO+DMCO(B)	*Depot*	*Livery*	*Owner*	*Operator*
377501	73501+75901+74901+73601	BF	FCC	PTR	FCC *(Sub-lease from Southern)*
377502	73502+75902+74902+73602	BF	FCC	PTR	FCC *(Sub-lease from Southern)*
377503	73503+75903+74903+73603	BF	FCC	PTR	FCC *(Sub-lease from Southern)*
377504	73504+75904+74904+73604	BF	FCC	PTR	FCC *(Sub-lease from Southern)*
377505	73505+75905+74905+73605	BF	FCC	PTR	FCC *(Sub-lease from Southern)*
377506	73506+75906+74906+73606	BF	FCC	PTR	FCC *(Sub-lease from Southern)*
377507	73507+75907+74907+73607	BF	FCC	PTR	FCC *(Sub-lease from Southern)*
377508	73508+75908+74908+73608	BF	FCC	PTR	FCC *(Sub-lease from Southern)*
377509	73509+75909+74909+73609	BF	FCC	PTR	FCC *(Sub-lease from Southern)*
377510	73510+75910+74910+73610	BF	FCC	PTR	FCC *(Sub-lease from Southern)*
377511	73511+75911+74911+73611	BF	FCC	PTR	FCC *(Sub-lease from Southern)*
377512	73512+75912+74912+73612	BF	FCC	PTR	FCC *(Sub-lease from Southern)*
377513	73513+75913+74913+73613	BF	FCC	PTR	FCC *(Sub-lease from Southern)*
377514	73514+75914+74914+73614	BF	FCC	PTR	FCC *(Sub-lease from Southern)*
377515	73515+75915+74915+73615	BF	FCC	PTR	FCC *(Sub-lease from Southern)*
377516	73516+75916+74916+73616	BF	FCC	PTR	FCC *(Sub-lease from Southern)*
377517	73517+75917+74917+73617	BF	FCC	PTR	FCC *(Sub-lease from Southern)*
377518	73518+75918+74918+73618	BF	FCC	PTR	FCC *(Sub-lease from Southern)*
377519	73519+75919+74919+73619	BF	FCC	PTR	FCC *(Sub-lease from Southern)*
377520	73520+75920+74920+73620	BF	FCC	PTR	FCC *(Sub-lease from Southern)*
377521	73521+75921+74921+73621	BF	FCC	PTR	FCC *(Sub-lease from Southern)*
377522	73522+75922+74922+73622	BF	FCC	PTR	FCC *(Sub-lease from Southern)*
377523	73523+75923+74923+73623	BF	FCC	PTR	FCC *(Sub-lease from Southern)*

At present the most modern rolling stock operated by First Capital Connect is a fleet of 23 four-car Class 377/5 'Electrostar' sets, allocated to Bedford and used on Thameslink services between Bedford and Brighton. These sets were originally ordered for Southern, but due to late progression of the Thameslink project and huge passenger growth the sets were sub-leased to FCC. All carry FCC livery. Set No. 377505 leads an eight-car set through Honor Oak Park bound for Bedford . **CJM**

Thameslink

New rolling stock is now under design and construction for the revised Thameslink franchise, which by 2016 will see a much wider route covered, including the present Southern franchise, and new Siemens 'Desiro City' rolling stock introduced.

In summer 2013 more details of this huge 1,140-vehicle order, the largest in Siemens history, emerged. The stock will be classified as Class 700, built at the Siemens factory in Krefeld, Germany, and shipped to the UK as fully operational train sets hauled via the Channel Tunnel.

The vehicles will be formed into 60 eight-car sets classified as 700/0 and numbered 700001-700060, and 55 12-car sets classified 700/1 and numbered 700101-700155. It has also been confirmed that the sets will be finished in a mid-grey livery with blue doors and receive branding on arrival with the Thameslink operation.

First Great Western

Address: ✉ Milford House, 1 Milford Street, Swindon, SN1 1HL

fgwfeedback@firstgroup.com

✆ 08457 000125 ⓘ www.firstgreatwestern.co.uk

Managing Director: Mark Hopwood

Franchise Dates: 1 April 2006 - Extension to July 2016

Principal Routes: Paddington - Penzance / Paignton, Bristol, Swansea
Thames Valley local lines
Local lines in Bristol, Exeter, Plymouth and Cornwall
Bristol - Weymouth, Portsmouth / Brighton

Depots: Exeter (EX), Old Oak Common (OO), Laira (LA), Landore (LE), St Philip's Marsh (PM), Penzance (PZ), Reading (RG)

Parent Company: First Group PLC

Class 08

Vehicle Length: 29ft 3in (8.91m)
Height: 12ft 8⅝in (3.87m)
Width: 8ft 6in (2.59m)
Engine: English Electric 6K
Horsepower: 400hp (298kW)
Electrical Equipment: English Electric

Number	*Depot*	*Pool*	*Livery*	*Owner*	*Operator*
08410	LA	EFSH	FGB	FGP	FGW
08483	OO	EFSH	GWG	FGP	FGW
08641	LA	EFSH	FGB	FGP	FGW
08644	PZ	EFSH	BLU	FGP	FGW
08645	LA	EFSH	GWG	FGP	FGW
08663	PM	EFSH	FGB	FGP	FGW
08795	LE	EFSH	BLK	FGP	FGW
08822	LE	EFSH	FGB	FGP	FGW
08836	OC	EFSH	GWG	FGP	FGW

Names applied

08483	*Dusty - Driver David Miller*
08645	*Mike Baggott*
08663	*Jack,*
08822	*John*

Below: *Like many main-line operators First Great Western operates a small fleet of traditional 0-6-0 Class 08 shunting locos, mainly to undertake depot shunting duties, especially the formation of HST trains and sleeper formations. In addition a number of First Great Western locos are fitted for limited main-line use to power empty sleeper trains from carriage sheds to either Paddington or Penzance stations. These are fitted with headlights and OTMR equipment. Painted in First Group blue livery, No. 08410 is seen under the roof at Penzance station.* **Antony Christie**

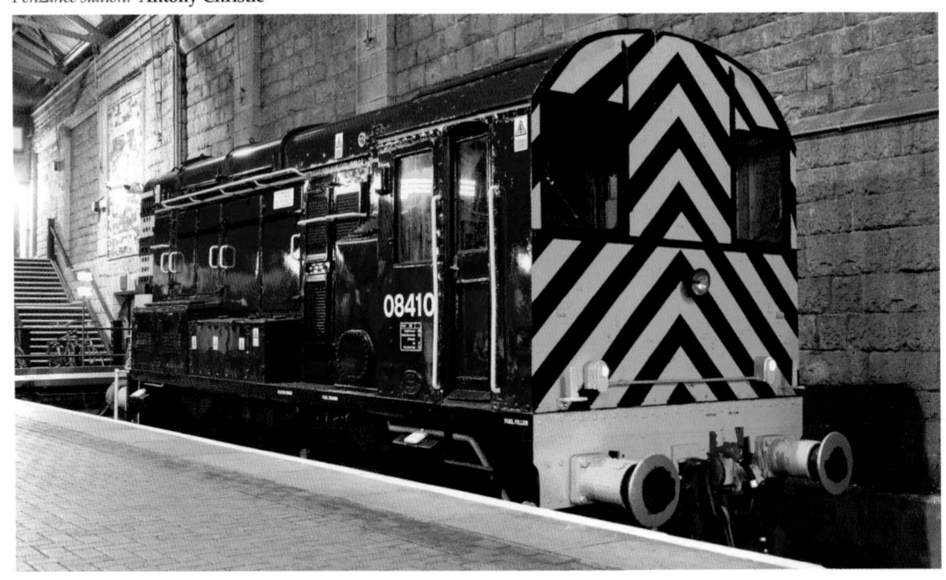

First Great Western

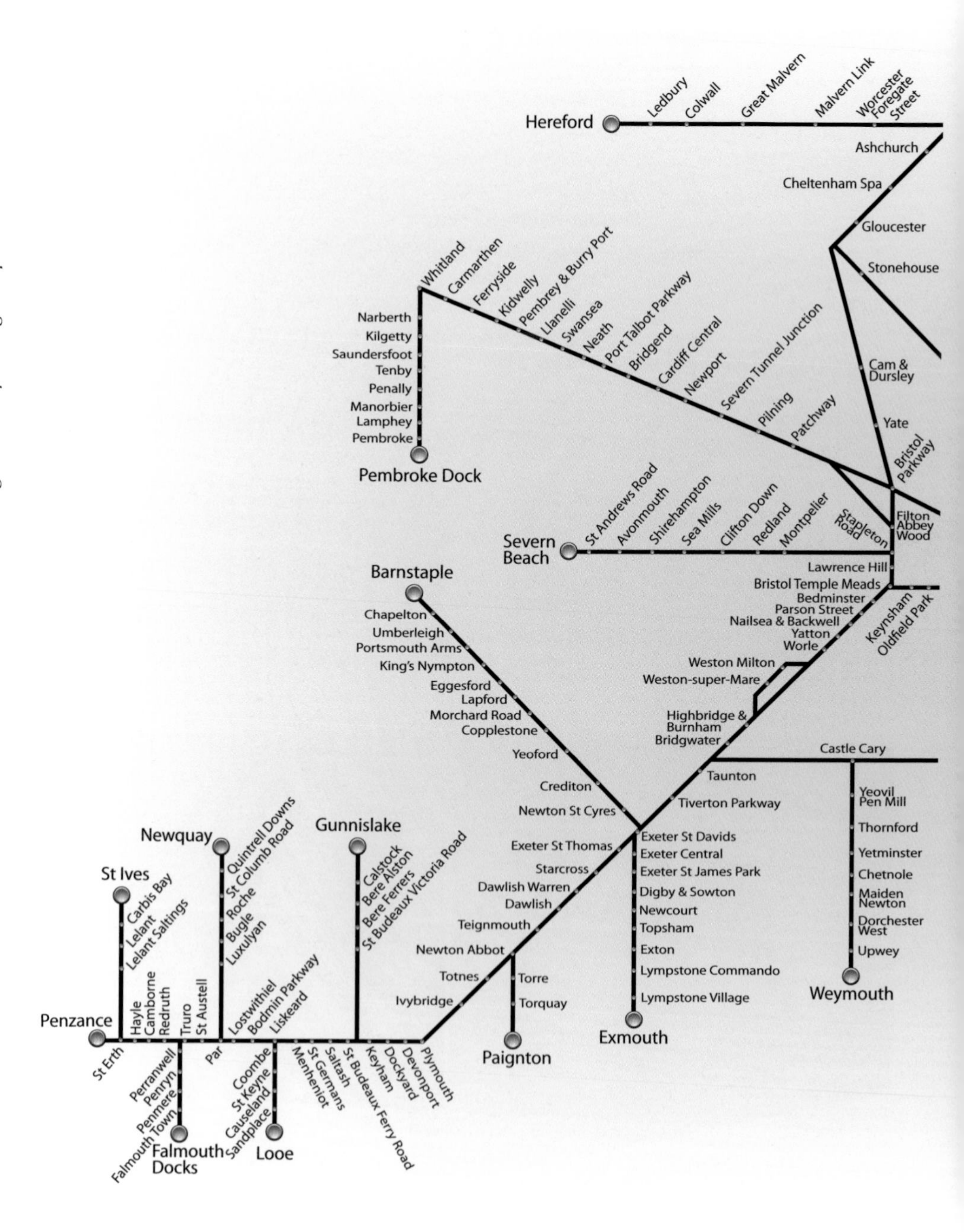

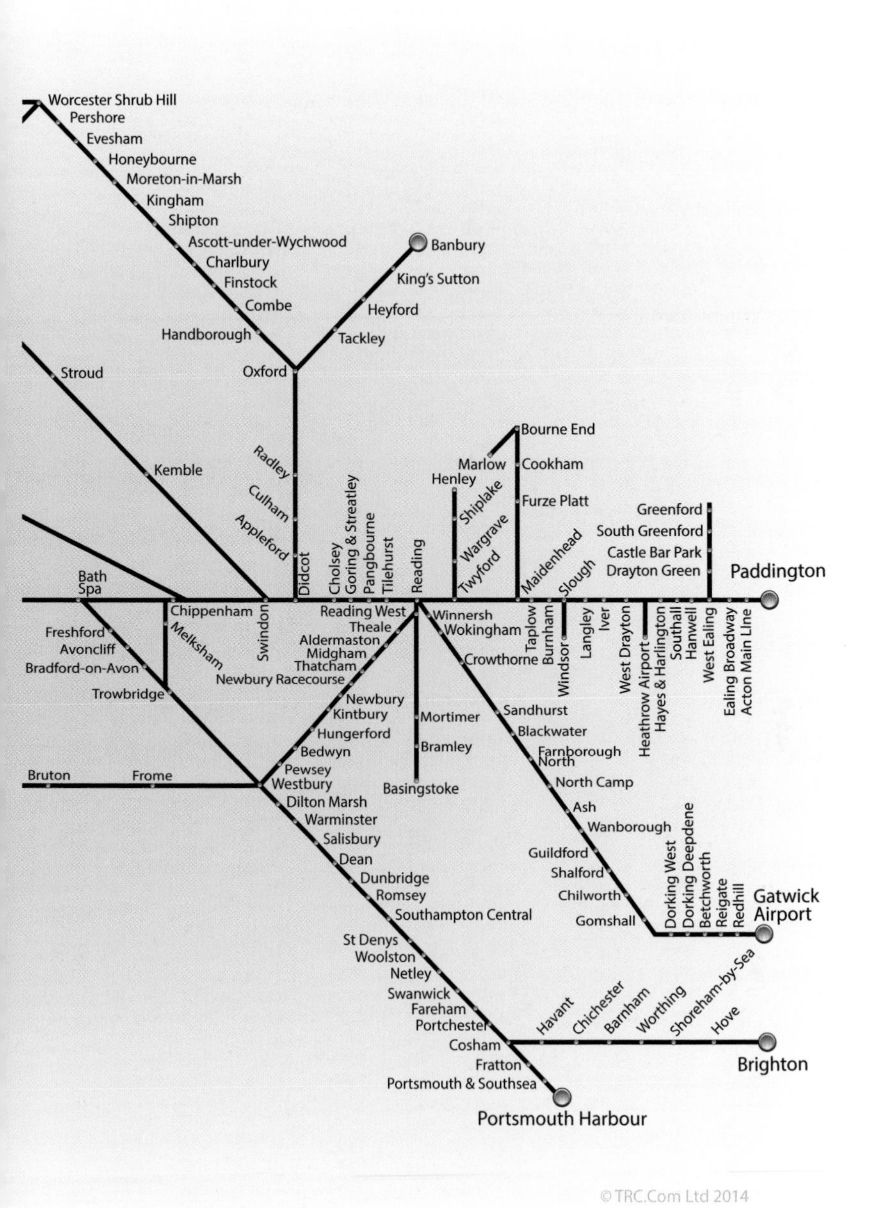
Worcester Shrub Hill
Pershore
Evesham
Honeybourne
Moreton-in-Marsh
Kingham
Shipton
Ascott-under-Wychwood
Charlbury
Finstock
Combe
Handborough
Oxford
Banbury
King's Sutton
Heyford
Tackley
Stroud
Kemble
Radley
Culham
Appleford
Didcot
Cholsey
Goring & Streatley
Pangbourne
Tilehurst
Reading
Bourne End
Marlow
Cookham
Henley
Shiplake
Wargrave
Twyford
Furze Platt
Maidenhead
Slough
Greenford
South Greenford
Castle Bar Park
Drayton Green
Paddington
Bath Spa
Chippenham
Swindon
Melksham
Freshford
Avoncliff
Bradford-on-Avon
Trowbridge
Reading West
Theale
Aldermaston
Midgham
Thatcham
Newbury Racecourse
Newbury
Kintbury
Hungerford
Bedwyn
Pewsey
Westbury
Bruton
Frome
Dilton Marsh
Warminster
Salisbury
Dean
Dunbridge
Romsey
Southampton Central
St Denys
Woolston
Netley
Swanwick
Fareham
Portchester
Cosham
Fratton
Portsmouth & Southsea
Portsmouth Harbour
Mortimer
Bramley
Basingstoke
Winnersh
Wokingham
Crowthorne
Sandhurst
Blackwater
Farnborough North
North Camp
Ash
Wanborough
Guildford
Shalford
Chilworth
Gomshall
Dorking West
Dorking Deepdene
Betchworth
Reigate
Redhill
Gatwick Airport
Taplow
Burnham
Windsor
Langley
Iver
West Drayton
Heathrow Airport
Hayes & Harlington
Southall
Hanwell
West Ealing
Ealing Broadway
Acton Main Line
Havant
Chichester
Barnham
Worthing
Shoreham-by-Sea
Hove
Brighton

First Great Western

Class 43 – HST

Vehicle Length: 58ft 5in (18.80m)
Height: 12ft 10in (3.90m)
Width: 8ft 11in (2.73m)
Engine: MTU 16V4000 R41R
Horsepower: 2,250hp (1,680kW)
Electrical Equipment: Brush

Number	*Depot*	*Pool*	*Livery*	*Owner*	*Operator*
43002	LA	EFPC	FGB	ANG	FGW
43003	LA	EFPC	FGB	ANG	FGW
43004	LA	EFPC	FGB	ANG	FGW
43005	LA	EFPC	FGB	ANG	FGW
43009	LA	EFPC	FGB	ANG	FGW
43010	LA	EFPC	FGB	ANG	FGW
43012	LA	EFPC	FGB	ANG	FGW
43015	LA	EFPC	FGB	ANG	FGW
43016	LA	EFPC	FGB	ANG	FGW
43017	LA	EFPC	FGB	ANG	FGW
43018	LA	EFPC	FGB	ANG	FGW
43020	LA	EFPC	FGB	ANG	FGW
43021	LA	EFPC	FGB	ANG	FGW
43022	LA	EFPC	FGB	ANG	FGW
43023	LA	EFPC	FGB	ANG	FGW
43024	LA	EFPC	FGB	ANG	FGW
43025	LA	EFPC	FGB	ANG	FGW
43026	LA	EFPC	FGB	ANG	FGW
43027	LA	EFPC	FGB	ANG	FGW
43028	LA	EFPC	FGB	ANG	FGW
43029	LA	EFPC	FGB	ANG	FGW
43030	LA	EFPC	FGB	ANG	FGW
43031	LA	EFPC	FGB	ANG	FGW
43032	LA	EFPC	FGB	ANG	FGW
43033	LA	EFPC	FGB	ANG	FGW
43034	LA	EFPC	FGB	ANG	FGW
43035	LA	EFPC	FGB	ANG	FGW
43036	LA	EFPC	FGB	ANG	FGW
43037	LA	EFPC	FGB	ANG	FGW
43040	LA	EFPC	FGB	ANG	FGW
43041	OO	EFPC	FGB	ANG	FGW
43042	OO	EFPC	FGB	ANG	FGW
43053	LE	EFPC	FGB	PTR	FGW
43056	LE	EFPC	FGB	PTR	FGW
43063	OO	EFPC	FGB	PTR	FGW
43069	OO	EFPC	FGB	PTR	FGW
43070	OO	EFPC	FGB	PTR	FGW
43071	OO	EFPC	FGB	PTR	FGW
43078	OO	EFPC	FGB	PTR	FGW
43079	OO	EFPC	FGB	PTR	FGW
43086	OO	EFPC	FGB	PTR	FGW
43087	OO	EFPC	FGB	PTR	FGW
43088	OO	EFPC	FGB	PTR	FGW
43091	OO	EFPC	FGB	PTR	FGW
43092	OO	EFPC	FGB	PTR	FGW
43093	OO	EFPC	FGB	PTR	FGW
43094	OO	EFPC	FGB	PTR	FGW
43097	OO	EFPC	FGB	PTR	FGW
43098	OO	EFPC	FGB	PTR	FGW
43122	OO	EFPC	FGB	FGP	FGW
43124	LE	EFPC	FGB	ANG	FGW
43125	LE	EFPC	FGB	ANG	FGW
43126	LE	EFPC	FGB	ANG	FGW
43127	LE	EFPC	FGB	ANG	FGW
43128	LE	EFPC	FGB	ANG	FGW
43129	LE	EFPC	FGB	ANG	FGW
43130	LE	EFPC	FGB	ANG	FGW
43131	LE	EFPC	FGB	ANG	FGW
43132	LE	EFPC	FGB	ANG	FGW
43133	LE	EFPC	FGB	ANG	FGW
43134	LE	EFPC	FGB	ANG	FGW
43135	LE	EFPC	FGB	ANG	FGW
43136	LE	EFPC	FGB	ANG	FGW
43137	LE	EFPC	FGB	ANG	FGW
43138	LE	EFPC	FGB	ANG	FGW
43139	LE	EFPC	FGB	ANG	FGW
43140	LE	EFPC	FGB	ANG	FGW
43141	LE	EFPC	FGB	ANG	FGW
43142	LE	EFPC	FGB	ANG	FGW
43143	LE	EFPC	FGB	ANG	FGW
43144	LE	EFPC	FGB	ANG	FGW
43145	LE	EFPC	FGB	ANG	FGW
43146	LE	EFPC	FGB	ANG	FGW
43147	LE	EFPC	FGB	ANG	FGW
43148	LE	EFPC	FGB	ANG	FGW
43149	LE	EFPC	FGB	ANG	FGW
43150	LE	EFPC	FGB	ANG	FGW
43151	LE	EFPC	FGB	ANG	FGW
43152	LE	EFPC	FGB	ANG	FGW
43153	OO	EFPC	FGB	FGP	FGW
43154	OO	EFPC	FGB	FGP	FGW
43155	OO	EFPC	FGB	FGP	FGW
43156	OO	EFPC	FGB	PTR	FGW
43158	OO	EFPC	FGB	FGP	FGW
43159	OO	EFPC	FGB	PTR	FGW
43160	OO	EFPC	FGB	PTR	FGW
43161	OO	EFPC	FGB	PTR	FGW
43162	OO	EFPC	FGB	ANG	FGW
43163	OO	EFPC	FGB	ANG	FGW
43164	OO	EFPC	FGB	ANG	FGW
43165	OO	EFPC	FGB	ANG	FGW
43168	OO	EFPC	FGB	ANG	FGW
43169	OO	EFPC	FGB	ANG	FGW
43170	OO	EFPC	FGB	ANG	FGW
43171	OO	EFPC	FGB	ANG	FGW
43172	OO	EFPC	FGB	ANG	FGW
43174	OO	EFPC	FGB	ANG	FGW
43175	OO	EFPC	FGB	ANG	FGW
43176	OO	EFPC	FGB	ANG	FGW
43177	OO	EFPC	FGB	ANG	FGW
43179	OO	EFPC	FGB	ANG	FGW
43180	OO	EFPC	FGB	PTR	FGW
43181	OO	EFPC	FGB	ANG	FGW
43182	OO	EFPC	FGB	ANG	FGW
43183	OO	EFPC	FGB	ANG	FGW
43185	OO	EFPC	FGB	ANG	FGW
43186	OO	EFPC	FGB	ANG	FGW
43187	OO	EFPC	FGB	ANG	FGW
43188	OO	EFPC	FGB	ANG	FGW
43189	OO	EFPC	FGB	ANG	FGW
43190	OO	EFPC	FGB	ANG	FGW
43191	OO	EFPC	FGB	ANG	FGW
43192	OO	EFPC	FGB	ANG	FGW
43193	OO	EFPC	FGB	PTR	FGW
43194	OO	EFPC	FGB	FGP	FGW
43195	OO	EFPC	FGB	PTR	FGW
43196	OO	EFPC	FGB	PTR	FGW
43197	OO	EFPC	FGB	PTR	FGW
43198	OO	EFPC	FGB	FGP	FGW

Names applied

43003	*Isambard Kingdom Brunel*
43004	*First for the Future / First ar gyfer y dyfodol*
43009	*First Transforming Travel*
43020	*MTU Power Passion Partnership*
43021	*David Austin – Cartoonist*
43024	*Great Western Society 1961-2011 Didcot Railway Centre*
43025	*The Institution of Railway Operators*
43027	*Glorious Devon*
43030	*Christian Lewis Trust*
43033	*Driver Brian Cooper 15 June 1947 – 5 October 1999*
43037	*Penydarren*
43040	*Bristol St Philip's Marsh*
43041	*Meningitis Trust Support for Life*
43053	*University of Worcester*
43056	*The Royal British Legion*
43070	*The Corps of Royal Electrical and Mechanical Engineers*
43087	*11 Explosive Ordnance Disposal Regiment Royal Logistic Corps*
43097	*Environment Agency*
43127	*Sir Peter Parker 1924-2002 – Cotswold Line 150*
43132	*We Save the Children - Will You?*
43137	*Newton Abbot 150*
43139	*Driver Stan Martin 25 June 1960 – 6 November 2004*
43140	*Depo Diesel Glandŵr 1963 Dathlu 50 Mlynedd 2013 Landore Diesel Depot 1963 Celebrating 50 Years 2013*
43142	*Reading Panel Signal Box 1965 - 2010*
43143	*Stroud 700*
43149	*University of Plymouth*
43156	*Dartington International Summer School*
43160	*Sir Moir Lockhead OBE*
43163	*Exeter Panel Signal Box 21st Anniversary 2009*
43165	*Prince Michael of Kent*
43169	*The National Trust*
43175	*GWR 175th Anniversary*
43179	*Pride of Laira*
43185	*Great Western*
43189	*Railway Heritage Trust*
43198	*Oxfordshire 2007*

Right: *First Great Western operates the largest number of Class 43 HST power cars, with some 95% of main line services HST formed. All are painted in First Group corporate blue, and are based at Laira, Old Oak Common and Landore depots. The FGW HST fleet will be reduced following introduction of the new generation of High Speed Train in 2017. No. 43150 is seen passing Dawlish.* **CJM**

Class 57/6

Vehicle Length: 63ft 6in (19.38m)
Height: 12ft 10⅛in (3.91m)
Width: 9ft 2in (2.79m)
Engine: EMD 645-12E3
Horsepower: 2,500hp (1,860kW)
Electrical Equipment: Brush

Number	*Depot*	*Pool*	*Livery*	*Owner*	*Operator*	*Name*
57602 (47337)	OO	EFOO	FGB	PTR	FGW	*Restormel Castle*
57603 (47349)	OO	EFOO	FGB	PTR	FGW	*Tintagel Castle*
57604 (47209)	OO	EFOO	GWR	PTR	FGW	*Pendennis Castle*
57605 (47206)	OO	EFOO	FGB	PTR	FGW	*Totnes Castle*

Right: *As First Great Western is required under the terms of its franchise to operate the overnight sleeper service between Penzance and Paddington, a fleet of four Class 57/6s are on its books. These are used to power the overnight service, its associated stock moves and any loco-hauled stock movements. Three locos carry FGW blue livery, while one (No. 57604) in painted in Great Western green livery. The green loco is seen passing Dawlish Warren with a daytime empty sleeper stock movement from Penzance to London.* **CJM**

HST Passenger Fleet

Vehicle Length: 75ft 0in (22.86m) Width: 8ft 11in (2.71m)
Height: 12ft 9in (3.88m) Bogie Type: BT10

GN2G - TSRMB *Seating 70S*

Number	Depot	Livery	Owner
40101 (42170)	LA	FGW	PTR
40102 (42223)	LA	FGW	PTR
40103 (42316)	LA	FGW	PTR
40104 (42254)	LA	FGW	PTR
40105 (42084)	LA	FGW	PTR
40106 (42162)	LA	FGW	PTR
40107 (42334)	LA	FGW	PTR
40108 (42314)	LA	FGW	PTR
40109 (42262)	LA	FGW	PTR
40110 (42187)	LA	FGW	PTR
40111 (42248)	LA	FGW	PTR
40112 (42336)	LA	FGW	PTR
40113 (42309)	LA	FGW	PTR
40114 (42086)	LA	FGW	PTR
40115 (42320)	LA	FGW	PTR
40116 (42147)	LA	FGW	PTR
40117 (42249)	LA	FGW	PTR
40118 (42338)	LA	FGW	PTR
40119 (42090)	LA	FGW	PTR

GN1G - TRFB *Seating 23F*

Number	Depot	Livery	Owner
40204	LA	FGW	ANG
40205	LA	FGW	ANG
40207	LA	FGW	ANG
40210	LA	FGW	ANG
40221	LA	FGW	ANG
40231	LA	FGW	ANG

GK1G - TRFB *Seating 17F*

Number	Depot	Livery	Owner
40703	LA	FGW	ANG
40707	LA	FGW	ANG
40710	LA	FGW	ANG
40713	LA	FGW	ANG
40715	LA	FGW	ANG
40716	LA	FGW	ANG
40718	OO	FGW	ANG
40721	LA	FGW	ANG
40722	LA	FGW	ANG
40727	LA	FGW	ANG
40733	LA	FGW	ANG
40734	LA	FGW	ANG
40739	LA	FGW	ANG
40743	LA	FGW	ANG
40752	LA	FGW	ANG
40755	LA	FGW	ANG
40757	LA	FGW	ANG

GL1G - TRFB *Seating 17F*

Number	Depot	Livery	Owner
40801	OO	FGW	PTR
40802	OO	FGW	PTR
40803	OO	FGW	PTR
40806	OO	FGW	PTR
40807	OO	FGW	PTR
40808	OO	FGW	PTR
40809	OO	FGW	PTR
40810	OO	FGW	PTR
40811	OO	FGW	PTR

GN1G - TRB *Seating 23F*

Number	Depot	Livery	Owner
40900	LA	FGW	FGP
40901	LA	FGW	FGP
40902	LA	FGW	FGP
40903	LA	FGW	FGP
40904	LA	FGW	FGP

GH1G - TF *Seating 48F*

Number	Depot	Livery	Owner
41003	LA	FGW	ANG
41004	OO	FGW	ANG
41005	OO	FGW	ANG
41006	OO	FGW	ANG
41007	OO	FGW	ANG
41008	OO	FGW	ANG
41009	LA	FGW	ANG
41010	LA	FGW	ANG
41011	LA	FGW	ANG
41012	LA	FGW	ANG
41015	LA	FGW	ANG
41016	LA	FGW	ANG
41017	OO	FGW	ANG
41018	OO	FGW	ANG
41019	LA	FGW	ANG
41020	LA	FGW	ANG
41021	LA	FGW	ANG
41022	LA	FGW	ANG
41023	LA	FGW	ANG
41024	LA	FGW	ANG
41027	OO	FGW	ANG
41028	OO	FGW	ANG
41029	OO	FGW	ANG
41030	OO	FGW	ANG
41031	LA	FGW	ANG
41032	LA	FGW	ANG
41033	OO	FGW	ANG
41034	OO	FGW	ANG
41037	LA	FGW	ANG
41038	LA	FGW	ANG
41045	LA	FGW	FGP
41051	LA	FGW	ANG
41052	LA	FGW	ANG
41055	OO	FGW	ANG
41056	OO	FGW	ANG
41059	LA	FGW	FGP
41065	OO	FGW	ANG
41081	OO	FGW	PTR
41085	LA	FGW	FGP
41086	LA	FGW	FGP
41089	OO	FGW	ANG
41093	LA	FGW	ANG
41094	LA	FGW	ANG
41096	LA	FGW	PTR
41101	OO	FGW	ANG
41102	OO	FGW	ANG
41103	LA	FGW	ANG
41104	LA	FGW	ANG
41105	OO	FGW	ANG
41106	OO	FGW	ANG
41108	OO	FGW	PTR
41109	OO	FGW	PTR
41110	OO	FGW	ANG
41114	LA	FGW	FGP
41116	LA	FGW	ANG
41119	OO	FGW	PTR
41121	LA	FGW	ANG
41122	LA	FGW	ANG
41123	LA	FGW	ANG
41124	LA	FGW	ANG
41125	OO	FGW	ANG
41126	OO	FGW	ANG
41127	OO	FGW	ANG
41128	OO	FGW	ANG
41129	LA	FGW	ANG
41130	LA	FGW	ANG
41131	OO	FGW	ANG
41132	OO	FGW	ANG
41133	LA	FGW	ANG
41134	LA	FGW	ANG
41135	LA	FGW	ANG
41136	LA	FGW	ANG
41137	OO	FGW	ANG
41138	OO	FGW	ANG
41139	OO	FGW	ANG
41140	OO	FGW	ANG
41141	LA	FGW	ANG
41142	LA	FGW	ANG
41143	LA	FGW	ANG
41144	LA	FGW	ANG
41145	LA	FGW	ANG
41146	LA	FGW	ANG
41147	OO	FGW	PTR
41148	OO	FGW	PTR
41149	OO	FGW	PTR
41155	OO	FGW	PTR
41157	LA	FGW	ANG
41158	LA	FGW	ANG
41160	LA	FGW	FGP
41161	OO	FGW	PTR
41162	LA	FGW	FGP
41163	LA	FGW	FGP
41166	LA	FGW	FGP
41167	LA	FGW	FGP
41168	OO	FGW	PTR
41169	OO	FGW	PTR
41176	OO	FGW	PTR
41179	OO	FGW	ANG
41180	OO	FGW	ANG
41181	OO	FGW	PTR
41182	OO	FGW	PTR
41183	OO	FGW	PTR
41184	OO	FGW	PTR
41186	OO	FGW	PTR
41187	OO	FGW	PTR
41189	OO	FGW	PTR
41191	OO	FGW	PTR
41192	OO	FGW	PTR

GH2G - TS *Seating 68-84S*

Number	Depot	Livery	Owner
42003	OO	FGW	ANG
42004	LA	FGW	ANG
42005 •	LA	FGW	ANG
42006	LA	FGW	ANG
42007	LA	FGW	ANG
42008	OO	FGW	ANG
42009	LA	FGW	ANG
42010 •	LA	FGW	ANG
42012	LA	FGW	ANG
42013	LA	FGW	ANG
42014	LA	FGW	ANG
42015	LA	FGW	ANG
42016	LA	FGW	ANG
42019 •	LA	FGW	ANG

42021	LA	FGW	ANG
42023	LA	FGW	ANG
42024	OO	FGW	ANG
42025	OO	FGW	ANG
42026	OO	FGW	ANG
42027	OO	FGW	ANG
42028	LA	FGW	ANG
42029	LA	FGW	ANG
42030	LA	FGW	ANG
42031	LA	FGW	ANG
42032	LA	FGW	ANG
42033 ●	LA	FGW	ANG
42034	LA	FGW	ANG
42035	LA	FGW	ANG
42039 ●	OO	FGW	ANG
42040	OO	FGW	ANG
42041	OO	FGW	ANG
42042 ●	OO	FGW	ANG
42043	OO	FGW	ANG
42044	OO	FGW	ANG
42045 ●	LA	FGW	ANG
42046	LA	FGW	ANG
42047	LA	FGW	ANG
42048 ●	OO	FGW	ANG
42049	OO	FGW	ANG
42050	OO	FGW	ANG
42054 ●	LA	FGW	ANG
42055	LA	FGW	ANG
42056	LA	FGW	ANG
42060	OO	FGW	ANG
42061	OO	FGW	ANG
42062	OO	FGW	ANG
42066	OO	FGW	ANG
42067	OO	FGW	ANG
42068	OO	FGW	ANG
42069	OO	FGW	ANG
42070 ●	OO	FGW	ANG
42071	OO	FGW	ANG
42072	LA	FGW	ANG
42073 ●	OO	FGW	ANG
42074 ●	OO	FGW	ANG
42075 ●	LA	FGW	ANG
42076 ●	LA	FGW	ANG
42077	LA	FGW	ANG
42078	LA	FGW	ANG
42079	OO	FGW	ANG
42080	OO	FGW	ANG
42081	OO	FGW	ANG
42083	OO	FGW	ANG
42085 ●	OO	FGW	ANG
42087	OO	FGW	ANG
42089	OO	FGW	ANG
42092	LA	FGW	FGP
42093	LA	FGW	FGP
42094	LA	FGW	FGP
42095	LA	FGW	FGP
42096 ●	LA	FGW	ANG
42098 ●	OO	FGW	ANG
42099	OO	FGW	ANG
42101	OO	FGW	PTR
42102	OO	FGW	PTR
42103	LA	FGW	FGP
42105	LA	FGW	FGP
42107	LA	FGW	ANG
42108	LA	FGW	FGP
42115 ●	OO	FGW	PTR
42118	OO	FGW	ANG
42126	OO	FGW	ANG

42129 ●	LA	FGW	ANG
42138	OO	FGW	ANG
42143	LA	FGW	ANG
42144	LA	FGW	ANG
42145	LA	FGW	ANG
42166 ●	OO	FGW	PTR
42167	LA	FGW	FGP
42168 ●	LA	FGW	FGP
42169	LA	FGW	FGP
42173	OO	FGW	PTR
42174	OO	FGW	PTR
42175	LA	FGW	FGP
42176 ●	LA	FGW	FGP
42177	LA	FGW	FGP
42178 ●	OO	FGW	PTR
42183	LA	FGW	ANG
42184 ●	LA	FGW	ANG
42185	LA	FGW	ANG
42195	OO	FGW	PTR
42196	OO	FGW	ANG
42197 ●	OO	FGW	ANG
42200	LA	FGW	ANG
42201	OO	FGW	ANG
42202	OO	FGW	ANG
42203	OO	FGW	ANG
42204	OO	FGW	ANG
42206	LA	FGW	ANG
42207	LA	FGW	ANG
42208	LA	FGW	ANG
42209	LA	FGW	ANG
42211	OO	FGW	ANG
42212 ●	OO	FGW	ANG
42213	OO	FGW	ANG
42214	OO	FGW	ANG
42216 ●	OO	FGW	ANG
42217	OO	FGW	PTR
42218	OO	FGW	PTR
42221 ●	OO	FGW	ANG
42222 ●	OO	FGW	PTR
42224	OO	FGW	PTR
42231	LA	FGW	FGP
42232 ●	LA	FGW	FGP
42233	LA	FGW	FGP
42236 ●	OO	FGW	ANG
42245	LA	FGW	ANG
42247 ●	OO	FGW	PTR
42250	LA	FGW	ANG
42251	OO	FGW	ANG
42252	LA	FGW	ANG
42253	LA	FGW	ANG
42255	LA	FGW	ANG
42256	LA	FGW	ANG
42257	LA	FGW	ANG
42258 ●	OO	FGW	PTR
42259	LA	FGW	ANG
42260	OO	FGW	ANG
42261	OO	FGW	ANG
42263 ●	LA	FGW	ANG
42264	OO	FGW	ANG
42265 ●	LA	FGW	ANG
42266	OO	FGW	PTR
42267	LA	FGW	ANG
42268	LA	FGW	ANG
42269	LA	FGW	ANG
42271	OO	FGW	ANG
42272	OO	FGW	ANG
42273	OO	FGW	ANG
42275	LA	FGW	ANG

42276	LA	FGW	ANG
42277	LA	FGW	ANG
42279	LA	FGW	ANG
42280	LA	FGW	ANG
42281	LA	FGW	ANG
42283	OO	FGW	ANG
42284	OO	FGW	ANG
42285	OO	FGW	ANG
42287	OO	FGW	ANG
42288	OO	FGW	ANG
42289	OO	FGW	ANG
42291	LA	FGW	ANG
42292	LA	FGW	ANG
42293	LA	FGW	ANG
42294	OO	FGW	PTR
42295	LA	FGW	ANG
42296	LA	FGW	ANG
42297	LA	FGW	ANG
42299	LA	FGW	ANG
42300	LA	FGW	ANG
42301	LA	FGW	ANG
42302	LA	FGW	FGP
42303 ●	LA	FGW	FGP
42304	LA	FGW	FGP
42305	LA	FGW	FGP
42308 ●	OO	FGW	PTR
42310	OO	FGW	PTR
42315 ●	OO	FGW	PTR
42317	OO	FGW	PTR
42319 ●	OO	FGW	PTR
42321	OO	FGW	PTR
42325 ●	LA	FGW	ANG
42332 ●	LA	FGW	ANG
42333	LA	FGW	ANG
42343 ●	LA	FGW	ANG
42344	OO	FGW	ANG
42345	LA	FGW	ANG
42346	OO	FGW	ANG
42347	OO	FGW	ANG
42348	OO	FGW	ANG
42349 ●	OO	FGW	ANG
42350 ●	LA	FGW	ANG
42351 ●	LA	FGW	ANG
42353	LA	FGW	FGP
42356	OO	FGW	ANG
42360 ●	LA	FGW	ANG
42361	LA	FGW	ANG
42362 ●	OO	FGW	ANG
42364	OO	FGW	PTR
42365	OO	FGW	PTR
42381 (41058)	OO	FGW	PTR
42382 (12128)	OO	FGW	PTR
42383 (12172)	OO	FGW	PTR
42385 (41153)	OO	FGW	PTR
42501 (40744)	OO	FGW	ANG
42502 (40731)	OO	FGW	ANG
42503 (40712)	OO	FGW	ANG
42504 (40714)	OO	FGW	ANG
42505 (40228)	OO	FGW	ANG
42506 (40724)	OO	FGW	ANG
42507 (40209)	OO	FGW	ANG
42508 (40725)	OO	FGW	ANG
42509 (40736)	OO	FGW	ANG
42510 (40717)	OO	FGW	ANG
42511 (40709)	OO	FGW	ANG
42512 (40208)	OO	FGW	ANG
42513 (40738)	OO	FGW	ANG
42514 (40726)	OO	FGW	ANG

First Great Western

42515 (40747) OO FGW ANG
42516 (40723) to be converted 2014
42517 (40745) to be converted 2014
42518 (40403) to be converted 2014
42519 (40416) to be converted 2014
42520 (40434) to be converted 2014
● Volo Television fitted

GJ2G - TGS *Seating 67-71S*

Number	*Depot*	*Livery*	*Owner*
44000	OO	FGW	PTR
44001	LA	FGW	ANG
44002	OO	FGW	ANG
44003	OO	FGW	ANG
44004	LA	FGW	ANG
44005	LA	FGW	ANG
44007	LA	FGW	ANG
44008	OO	FGW	ANG
44009	LA	FGW	ANG
44010	LA	FGW	ANG
44011	LA	FGW	ANG
44013	OO	FGW	ANG
44014	OO	FGW	ANG
44015	LA	FGW	ANG
44016	OO	FGW	ANG
44018	LA	FGW	ANG
44020	OO	FGW	ANG
44022	OO	FGW	ANG
44023	OO	FGW	ANG
44024	OO	FGW	ANG
44025	LA	FGW	ANG
44026	OO	FGW	ANG
44028	LA	FGW	ANG
44029	LA	FGW	ANG
44030	OO	FGW	ANG
44032	LA	FGW	ANG
44033	OO	FGW	ANG
44034	LA	FGW	ANG
44035	LA	FGW	ANG
44036	OO	FGW	ANG
44037	OO	FGW	ANG
44038	LA	FGW	ANG
44039	LA	FGW	ANG
44040	LA	FGW	ANG
44042	OO	FGW	PTR
44043	OO	FGW	ANG
44049	LA	FGW	ANG
44055	LA	FGW	FGP
44059	LA	FGW	ANG
44060	OO	FGW	PTR
44064	OO	FGW	ANG
44066	LA	FGW	ANG
44067	OO	FGW	ANG
44068	LA	FGW	FGP
44069	OO	FGW	PTR
44074	LA	FGW	FGP
44076	LA	FGW	FGP
44078	OO	FGW	PTR
44079	OO	FGW	PTR
44081	LA	FGW	FGP
44083	OO	FGW	PTR
44086	LA	FGW	ANG
44090	OO	FGW	PTR
44091	OO	FGW	PTR
44093	OO	FGW	ANG
44097	OO	FGW	PTR
44100	LA	FGW	FGP
44101	OO	FGW	PTR

Left: *The huge fleet of FGW HST passenger stock is allocated to Laira and Old Oak Common depots, with vehicles owned by Angel Trains, Porterbrook and First Group. Trailer Standard with disabled access toilet No. 42173 is illustrated from the large toilet compartment end.* **CJM**

Class 143
Pacer

Vehicle Length: 51ft 0½in (15.55m)
Height: 12ft 2¼in (3.73m)
Width: 8ft 10½in (2.70m)
Engine: 1 x Cummins LTA10-R per vehicle
Horsepower: 460hp (343kW)
Seats (total/car): 92S, 48S/44S

Number	*Formation DMS+DMSL*	*Depot*	*Livery*	*Owner*	*Operator*
143603	55658+55689	EX	FGL	PTR	FGW
143611	55652+55677	EX	FGL	PTR	FGW
143612	55653+55678	EX	FGL	PTR	FGW
143617	55644+55683	EX	FGL	PTR	FGW
143618	55659+55684	EX	FGL	PTR	FGW
143619	55660+55685	EX	FGL	PTR	FGW
143620	55661+55686	EX	FGL	PTR	FGW
143621	55662+55687	EX	FGL	PTR	FGW

Left: *Eight Class 143 'Pacer' sets are based at Exeter depot for Devon branch-line operations, working services to Barnstaple, Exmouth and Paignton. Frequently sets operate in pairs, but due to stock shortages some sets operate alone, or in multiple with Class 150 sets. Class 143 No. 143618 departs from Dawlish with a Paignton service while a Class 143/153 combination heads towards Exeter. All sets are painted in FGW Local Lines livery.* **CJM**

Class 150/0

Vehicle Length: (Driving) 65ft 9¾in (20.05m), (Inter) 66ft 2½in (20.18m)
Height: 12ft 4½in (3.77m)
Width: 9ft 3⅛in (2.82m)
Engine: 1 x Cummins NT855R4 of 285hp per car
Horsepower: 855hp (638kW)
Seats (total/car): 240S, 72S/92S/76S

Number	*Formation DMSL+MS+DMS*	*Depot*	*Livery*	*Owner*	*Op'r*
150001	55200+55400+55300	RG	FGB	ANG	FGW
150002	55201+55401+55301	RG	FGB	ANG	FGW

Class 150/1

Vehicle Length: 64ft 9¾in (19.74m)
Height: 12ft 4½in (3.77m)
Width: 9ft 3⅛in (2.82m)
Engine: 1 x NT855R5 of 285hp per vehicle
Horsepower: 570hp (425kW)
Seats (total/car): 141S, 71S/70S

Two-car sets

Number	*Formation DMSL+DMS*	*Depot*	*Livery*	*Owner*	*Operator*
150101	52101+57101	PM	FGB	PTR	FGW
150102	52102+57102	PM	FGB	PTR	FGW
150104	52104+57104	PM	FGB	PTR	FGW
150106	52106+57106	PM	FGB	PTR	FGW
150108	52108+57108	PM	FGB	PTR	FGW
150120	52120+57120	EX	FGB	PTR	FGW
150122	52122+57122	EX	FGB	PTR	FGW
150123	52123+57123	EX	FGB	PTR	FGW
150124	52124+57124	EX	FGB	PTR	FGW
150125	52125+57125	EX	FGB	PTR	FGW
150126	52126+57126	EX	FGB	PTR	FGW
150128	52128+57128	EX	FGB	PTR	FGW
150129	52129+57129	EX	FGB	PTR	FGW
150130	52130+57130	EX	FGB	PTR	FGW
150131	52130+57130	EX	FGB	PTR	FGW

Three-car sets - Class 150/9

150921	52121+57212+57121	PM	FGB	PTR	FGW
150927	52127+57209+57127	PM	FGB	PTR	FGW

Names applied

150125 ***The Heart of Wessex Line***
150129 ***Devon & Cornwall Rail Partnership***
150130 ***Severnside Community Rail Partnership***

Right: *The FGW depots at Exeter and Bristol St Philip's Marsh operate fleets of Class 150/1 two-car sets, with Bristol having an additional two three-car Class 150/9 units. All sets are painted in First Great Western blue livery with pink doors. The sets are owned by Porterbrook Leasing. These sets are usually deployed on Bristol local area duties as well as services in Devon and Cornwall. Set No. 150128 passes along the Dawlish sea wall on 22 April 2013 with a Penzance to Exeter St Davids service.* **CJM**

Class 150/2

Vehicle Length: 64ft 9¾in (19.74m)
Height: 12ft 4½in (3.77m)
Width: 9ft 3⅛in (2.82m)
Engine: 1 x NT855R5 of 285hp per vehicle
Horsepower: 570hp (425kW)
Seats (total/car): 116S, 60S/56S

Number	*Formation DMSL+DMS*	*Depot*	*Livery*	*Owner*	*Operator*
150202	52202+57202	PM	FGB	ANG	FGW
150216	52216+57216	PM	FGB	ANG	FGW
150219	52219+57219	PM	FGL	PTR	FGW
150221	52221+57221	PM	FGL	PTR	FGW
150232	52232+57232	PM	FGL	PTR	FGW
150233	52233+57233	PM	FGL	PTR	FGW
150234	52234+57234	PM	FGL	PTR	FGW
150238	52238+57238	PM	FGL	PTR	FGW
150239	52239+57239	PM	FGL	PTR	FGW
150243	52243+57243	PM	FGL	PTR	FGW
150244	52244+57244	PM	FGL	PTR	FGW
150246	52246+57246	PM	FGL	PTR	FGW
150247	52247+57247	PM	FGL	PTR	FGW
150248	52248+57248	PM	FGL	PTR	FGW
150249	52249+57249	PM	FGL	PTR	FGW
150261	52261+57261	PM	FGL	PTR	FGW
150263	52263+57263	PM	FGL	PTR	FGW
150265	52265+57265	PM	FGL	PTR	FGW
150266	52266+57266	PM	FGL	PTR	FGW

Right: *A fleet of 19 corridor-fitted Class 150/2 sets is operated by First Great Western, based at Bristol St Philip's Marsh depot, but operate throughout the Bristol and West of England areas, including the Devon and Cornish branch lines. Two sets, Nos. 150202/216, are painted in all-over blue, with the remainder in FGW Local Lines colours. Set No. 150221 is seen at St Erth with a service bound for St Ives.* **CJM**

First Great Western

Class 153

Vehicle Length: 76ft 5in (23.29m)
Height: 12ft 3⅛in (3.75m)
Width: 8ft 10in (2.70m)
Engine: 1 x NT855R5 of 285hp
Horsepower: 285hp (213kW)
Seats (total/car): 72S

Number	Formation DMSL	Depot	Livery	Owner	Operator
153305	52305	EX	FGL	ANG	FGW
153318	52318	EX	FGL	ANG	FGW
153325	52325	EX	LMI	PTR	FGW
153329	52329	EX	FGB	ANG	FGW
153333	52333	EX	LMI	PTR	FGW
153361	57361	EX	FGB	ANG	FGW
153368	57368	EX	FGL	ANG	FGW
153369	57369	EX	FGB	ANG	FGW
153370	57370	EX	FGL	ANG	FGW
153372	57372	EX	FGL	ANG	FGW
153373	57373	EX	FGB	ANG	FGW
153377	57377	EX	FGL	ANG	FGW
153380	57380	EX	FGB	ANG	FGW
153382	57382	EX	FGL	ANG	FGW

Left: *A fleet of 14 single-car Class 153s is allocated to Exeter depot to operate branch-line services and to strengthen two-car formations to three to reduce overcrowding. Some services are booked to be operated by a single Class 153, while frequently two Class 153s will be coupled together to substitute for a non-available two-car set. Many passengers prefer to travel in the '153s' as these have 2+2 seating with carpeted floors. Vehicles were all painted in FGW Local Lines livery, but in 2013 a start was made to repaint sets in FGW all-over blue colours to reduce vehicle corrosion from water penetrating behind the vinyl branding. Car No. 153369 is illustrated.* **CJM**

Class 158/0 (2-car)

Vehicle Length: 76ft 1¾in (23.21m)
Height: 12ft 6in (3.81m)
Width: 9ft 3¼in (2.82m)
Engine: 1 x Cummins NTA855R of 350hp per vehicle
Horsepower: 700hp (522kW)
Seats (total/car): 134S, 66S/68S

Number	Formation DMSL+DMSL	Depot	Livery	Owner	Operator
158763	52763+57763	PM	FGL	PTR	FGW
158766	52766+57766	PM	FGL	PTR	FGW

Class 158/0 (3-car)

158798
Vehicle Length: 76ft 1¾in (23.21m)
Height: 12ft 6in (3.81m)
Width: 9ft 3¼in (2.82m)
Engine: 1 x Cummins NTA855R of 350hp per vehicle
Horsepower: 1,050hp (783kW)
Seats (total/car): 200S, 66S/66S/68S

158950 - 158959
Vehicle Length: 76ft 1¾in (23.21m)
Height: 12ft 6in (3.81m)
Width: 9ft 3¼in (2.82m)
Engine: 1 x Cummins NTA855R of 350hp per vehicle
Horsepower: 1,050hp (783kW)
Seats (total/car): 204S, 66S/70S/68S

Number	Formation DMSL+MSL+DMSL	Depot	Livery	Owner	Operator
158798	52798+58715+57798	PM	FGL	PTR	FGW

Number		Formation DMSL+DMSL+DMSL	Depot	Livery	Owner	Operator
158950	(158751/761)	57751+52761+57761	PM	FGL	PTR	FGW
158951	(158751/764)	52751+52764+57764	PM	FGL	PTR	FGW
158952	(158745/762)	57745+52762+57762	PM	FGL	PTR	FGW
158953	(158745/750)	52745+52750+57750	PM	FGL	PTR	FGW
158954	(158747/760)	57747+52760+57760	PM	FGL	PTR	FGW
158955	(158747/765)	52747+52765+57765	PM	FGL	PTR	FGW
158956	(158748/768)	57748+52768+57768	PM	FGL	PTR	FGW
158957	(158748/771)	52748+52771+57771	PM	FGL	PTR	FGW
158958	(158746/776)	57746+52776+57776	PM	FGL	PTR	FGW
158959	(158746/778)	52746+52778+57778	PM	FGL	PTR	FGW
158960	(158769/749)	57769+52769+57749	PM	FGL	PTR	FGW
158961	(158767/749)	57767+52767+52749	PM	FGL	PTR	FGW

Right: *Operated on longer-distance local services in the Bristol/Cardiff area to locations such as Portsmouth and Weymouth is a fleet of Class 158 sets, either formed as two- or three- car formations. A number of these are ex-Scottish sets and have modified obstacle deflector plates formed as small snowploughs. Many of the three-car sets are formed with three driving cars - a conventional two-car sets with an additional vehicle on one end. Set No. 158956 is seen at Bristol Temple Meads, formed of set No. 158768 plus one vehicle from set No. 158748.* **CJM**

Class 165/1 (3-car)
Networker Turbo

Vehicle Length: (Driving) 75ft 2½in (22.91m), (Inter) 74ft 6½in (22.72m)
Height: 12ft 5¼in (3.79m)
Width: 9ft 5½in (2.81m)
Engine: 1 x Perkins 2006TWH of 350hp
Horsepower: 1,050hp (783kW)
Seats (total/car): 16F/270S, 16F-66S/106S/98S

Number	Formation DMCL+MS+DMS	Depot	Livery	Owner	Operator
165101	58953+55415+58916	RG	FGT	ANG	FGW
165102	58954+55416+58917	RG	FGT	ANG	FGW
165103	58955+55417+58918	RG	FGT	ANG	FGW
165104	58956+55418+58919	RG	FGT	ANG	FGW
165105	58957+55419+58920	RG	FGT	ANG	FGW
165106	58958+55420+58921	RG	FGT	ANG	FGW
165107	58959+55421+58922	RG	FGT	ANG	FGW
165108	58960+55422+58923	RG	FGT	ANG	FGW
165109	58961+55423+58924	RG	FGT	ANG	FGW
165110	58962+55424+58925	RG	FGT	ANG	FGW
165111	58963+55425+58926	RG	FGT	ANG	FGW
165112	58964+55426+58927	RG	FGT	ANG	FGW
165113	58965+55427+58928	RG	FGT	ANG	FGW
165114	58966+55428+58929	RG	FGT	ANG	FGW
165116	58968+55430+58931	RG	FGT	ANG	FGW
165117	58969+55431+58932	RG	FGT	ANG	FGW

Right: *The Network SouthEast modernisation of the Thames and Chiltern routes saw a fleet of Class 165 sets introduced; known as 'Networker Turbo', these came in both two- and three- car formations. Sets operated on First Great Western are classified as 165/1 and allocated to Reading, being deployed alongside the Class 166s on all Thames local services. These sets will be largely displaced following the opening of the electrified CrossRail routes. Two-car set No. 165137 is seen at West Ealing with a Greenford to Paddington service.* **CJM**

Class 165/1 (2-car)
Networker Turbo

Vehicle Length: 75ft 2½in (22.91m)
Height: 12ft 5¼in (3.79m)
Width: 9ft 5½in (2.81m)
Engine: 1 x Perkins 2006TWH of 350hp per car
Horsepower: 700hp (522kW)
Seats (total/car): 16F/170S, 16F-72S/98S

Number	Formation DMCL+DMS	Depot	Livery	Owner	Operator
165118	58879+58933	RG	FGT	ANG	FGW
165119	58880+58934	RG	FGT	ANG	FGW
165120	58881+58935	RG	FGT	ANG	FGW
165121	58882+58936	RG	FGT	ANG	FGW
165122	58883+58937	RG	FGT	ANG	FGW
165123	58884+58938	RG	FGT	ANG	FGW
165124	58885+58939	RG	FGT	ANG	FGW
165125	58886+58940	RG	FGT	ANG	FGW
165126	58887+58941	RG	FGT	ANG	FGW
165127	58888+58942	RG	FGT	ANG	FGW

165128	58889+58943	RG	FGT	ANG	FGW
165129	58890+58944	RG	FGT	ANG	FGW
165130	58891+58945	RG	FGT	ANG	FGW
165131	58892+58946	RG	FGT	ANG	FGW
165132	58893+58947	RG	FGT	ANG	FGW
165133	58894+58948	RG	FGT	ANG	FGW
165134	58895+58949	RG	FGT	ANG	FGW
165135	58896+58950	RG	FGT	ANG	FGW
165136	58897+58951	RG	FGT	ANG	FGW
165137	58898+58952	RG	FGT	ANG	FGW

Class 166
Networker Turbo Express

Vehicle Length: (Driving) 75ft 2½in (22.91m), (Inter) 74ft 6½in (22.72m)
Height: 12ft 5¼in (3.79m)
Width: 9ft 5½in (2.81m)
Engine: 1 x Perkins 2006TWH of 350hp per car
Horsepower: 1,050hp (783kW)
Seats (total/car): 16F/259S, 90S/96S/16F-72S

Number	Formation DMSL+MS+DMCL	Depot	Livery	Owner	Operator
166201	58101+58601+58122	RG	FGT	ANG	FGW
166202	58102+58602+58123	RG	FGT	ANG	FGW
166203	58103+58603+58124	RG	FGT	ANG	FGW
166204	58104+58604+58125	RG	FGT	ANG	FGW
166205	58105+58605+58126	RG	FGT	ANG	FGW
166206	58106+58606+58127	RG	FGT	ANG	FGW
166207	58107+58607+58128	RG	FGT	ANG	FGW
166208	58108+58608+58129	RG	FGT	ANG	FGW
166209	58109+58609+58130	RG	FGT	ANG	FGW
166210	58110+58610+58131	RG	FGT	ANG	FGW
166211	58111+58611+58132	RG	FGT	ANG	FGW
166212	58112+58612+58133	RG	FGT	ANG	FGW
166213	58113+58613+58134	RG	FGT	ANG	FGW
166214	58114+58614+58135	RG	FGT	ANG	FGW
166215	58115+58615+58136	RG	FGT	ANG	FGW
166216	58116+58616+58137	RG	FGT	ANG	FGW
166217	58117+58617+58138	RG	FGT	ANG	FGW
166218	58118+58618+58139	RG	FGT	ANG	FGW
166219	58119+58619+58140	RG	FGT	ANG	FGW
166220	58120+58620+58141	RG	FGT	ANG	FGW
166221	58121+58621+58142	RG	FGT	ANG	FGW

Left: *For outer-suburban Thames route services, a fleet of 'Networker Turbo Express' sets was built, of a like design to the Class 165s, but with air conditioning and slightly lower-density interior layout. First class seating was provided in both driving cars, behind the driving cab, but in 2013 first class was removed from one vehicle. The three-car sets are allocated to Reading depot and operate alongside the Class 165 stock. These sets will also be displaced for redeployment to other parts of the FGW network after CrossRail electrification is launched. Set No. 166206 is illustrated on the route between Reading and Didcot.* **Antony Christie**

Class 180
Adelante

Vehicle Length: (Driving) 75ft 7in (23.71m), (Inter) 75ft 5in (23.03m)
Height: 12ft 4in (3.75m)
Width: 9ft 2in (2.80m)
Engine: 1 x Cummins OSK19 of 750hp per car
Horsepower: 3,750hp (2,796kW)
Seats (total/car): 42F/226S, 46S/42F/68S/56S/56S

Number	Formation DMSL(A)+MFL+MSL+MSLRB+DMSL(B)	Depot	Livery	Owner	Operator
180102	50902+54902+55902+56902+59902	OO	FGW	ANG	FGW
180103	50903+54903+55903+56903+59903	OO	FGW	ANG	FGW
180104	50904+54904+55904+56904+59904	OO	FGW	ANG	FGW
180106	50906+54906+55906+56906+59906	OO	FGW	ANG	FGW
180108	50908+54908+55908+56908+59908	OO	FGW	ANG	FGW

Right: *As part of the modernisation of Great Western under privatisation came a fleet of 14 five-car Class 180 'Adelante' sets to operate alongside the HST fleet on more lightly used services. After a time of technical issues the sets were withdrawn from FGW use and redeployed in other areas. A batch of five sets has subsequently returned to FGW use, based at Old Oak Common and predominantly used on the Paddington-Oxford-Worcester corridor. Set No. 180103 is illustrated from its DMSL(A) end.* **Nathan Williamson**

Mk3 Hauled Stock

Vehicle Length: 75ft 0in (22.86m)
Height: 12ft 9in (3.88m)
Width: 8ft 11in (2.71m)
Bogie Type: BT10

AJ1G - RFB *Seating 18F*

Number	*Depot*	*Livery*	*Owner*
10219	PZ	FGW	PTR
10225	PZ	FGW	PTR
10232	PZ	FGW	PTR

AU4G - SLEP *Comps 12*

Number	*Depot*	*Livery*	*Owner*
10532	PZ	FGW	PTR
10534	PZ	FGW	PTR
10563	PZ	FGW	PTR
10584	PZ	FGW	PTR
10589	PZ	FGW	PTR
10590	PZ	FGW	PTR
10594	PZ	FGW	PTR
10596	(PZ	FGW	PTR)§
10601	PZ	FGW	PTR
10612	PZ	FGW	PTR
10616	PZ	FGW	PTR

AC2G - TSO *Seating 45S*

Number	*Depot*	*Livery*	*Owner*
12100	PZ	FGW	PTR
12142	(PZ	FGW	PTE)§
12161	PZ	FGW	PTR

AE1H - BFO *Seating 36F*

Number	*Depot*	*Livery*	*Owner*
17173	PZ	FGW	PTR
17174	PZ	FGW	PTR
17175	PZ	FGW	PTR

§ to be added to fleet in 2014

Right: *Twenty loco-hauled Mk3 vehicles are operated by FGW, and allocated to Penzance for use on the overnight sleeper services between Penzance and London Paddington. Refreshment services are provided by three RFBs, while seating is provided by TSOs and BFO stock. Overnight sleeping accommodation is provided in 11 SLEP vehicles. Brake First Open (BFO) No. 17175 is illustrated at Plymouth on a daytime stock movement.* **Antony Christie**

Class 800 and 801 'Super Express'

In summer 2012 Agility Trains signed a contract with the Department for Transport (DfT) to design, build, finance and maintain 596 state-of-the-art carriages for the Great Western Main Line and East Coast Main Line as part of the Intercity Express Programme to replace HST and IC225 trains.

Hitachi Rail Europe and John Laing are the main shareholders of Agility Trains and in summer 2013 the Secretary of State for Transport announced that an additional contract for the provision of an extra 270 carriages for the East Coast Main Line was to be placed, bringing the total number of vehicles ordered to 866.

Great Western will have between 2016 and 2019 46 five-car Class 800 dual mode and 12 nine-car electric Class 801 trains sets delivered. The first pre-production sets are to be built by Hitachi in Kasado, Japan, with the remainder built at a new Hitachi plant at Newton Aycliffe.

Service Stock

HST Barrier Vehicles

Number	*Depot*	*Livery*	*Owner*	*Former Identity*
6330	PM	FGB	ANG	BFK - 14084
6336	LA	FGB	ANG	BG - 81591/92185
6338	LA	FGB	ANG	BG - 81581/92180
6348	PM	FGB	ANG	BG - 81233/92963

First Hull Trains

Address: ✉ Europa House, 184 Ferensway, Kingston-upon-Hull, HU1 3UT
customer.services@hulltrains.co.uk
✆ 0845 676 9905
ⓘ www.hulltrains.co.uk

Managing Director: Will Dunnett **General Manager:** Cath Bellamy
Franchise Dates: Private Open Access Operator, agreement to December 2016
Principal Route: London King's Cross - Hull
Depots: Old Oak Common (OO) [Operated by FGW], Crofton (XW)
Parent Company: First Group PLC

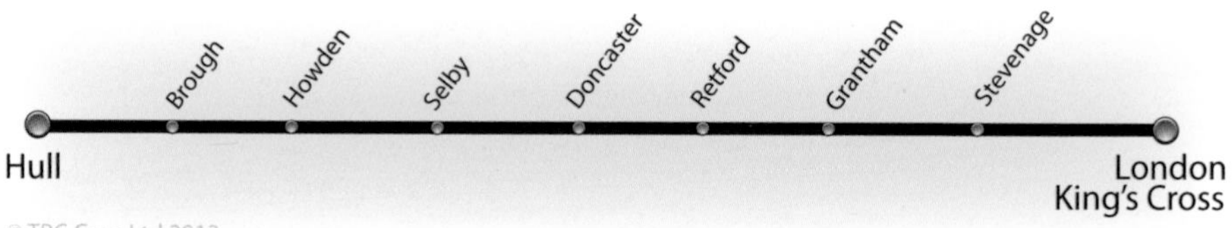

Class 180
Adelante

Vehicle Length: (Driving) 75ft 7in (23.71m), (Inter) 75ft 5in (23.03m)
Height: 12ft 4in (3.75m)
Width: 9ft 2in (2.80m)
Engine: 1 x Cummins OSK19 of 750hp per car
Horsepower: 3,750hp (2,796kW)
Seats (total/car): 42F/226S, 46S/42F/68S/56S/56S

Number	*Formation* DMSL(A)+MFL+MSF+MSLRB+DMSL(B)	*Depot*	*Livery*	*Owner*	*Operator*
180109	50909+54909+55909+56909+59909	OO/XW	FHT	ANG	FHT
180110	50910+54910+55910+56910+59910	OO/XW	FHT	ANG	FHT
180111	50911+54911+55911+56911+59911	OO/XW	FHT	ANG	FHT
180113	50913+54913+55913+56913+59913	OO/XW	FHT	ANG	FHT

Below: *Under an Open Access agreement First Hull Trains operates a limited service between London King's Cross and Hull, using Class 180 stock originally displaced from First Great Western. Prior to '180s' being used, Class 222/1s were deployed, which replaced Class 170s hired from Anglia. The FHT fleet is maintained jointly at Crofton and Old Oak Common. All four sets carry First Group livery. Sadly sets have lost their original coupling cover doors. Set No. 180109 is illustrated at Harringay.* **CJM**

First ScotRail

Address: ✉ Atrium Court, 50 Waterloo Street, Glasgow, G2 6HQ
scotrail.enquiries@firstgroup.com
✆ 08700 005151
ⓘ www.firstscotrail.com

Managing Director: Steve Montgomery
Franchise Dates: 17 October 2004 - March 2015
Principal Routes: All Scottish services, plus ScotRail sleeper services
Depots: Corkerhill (CK), Glasgow Shields Road (GW), Haymarket (HA), Inverness (IS)
Parent Company: First Group PLC

Class 156

Vehicle Length: 75ft 6in (23.03m)
Height: 12ft 6in (3.81m)
Width: 8ft 11in (2.73m)
Engine: 1 x Cummins NT855R5 of 285hp
Horsepower: 570hp (425kW)
Seats (total/car): 142S, 70 or 72S

Number	*Formation DMSL+DMS*	*Depot*	*Livery*	*Owner*	*Operator*
156430	52430+57430	CK	FSS	ANG	FSR
156431	52431+57431	CK	FSS	ANG	FSR
156432	52432+57432	CK	FSS	ANG	FSR
156433	52433+57433	CK	FSS	ANG	FSR
156434	52434+57434	CK	FSS	ANG	FSR
156435	52435+57435	CK	FSS	ANG	FSR
156436	52436+57436	CK	FSS	ANG	FSR
156437	52437+57437	CK	FSS	ANG	FSR
156439	52439+57439	CK	FSS	ANG	FSR
156442	52442+57442	CK	FSS	ANG	FSR
156445	52445+57445	CK	FSS	ANG	FSR
156446	52446+57446	CK	FSR	ANG	FSR
156447	52447+57447	CK	FSR	ANG	FSR
156449	52449+57449	CK	FSR	ANG	FSR
156450	52450+57450	CK	FSR	ANG	FSR
156453	52453+57453	CK	FSR	ANG	FSR
156456	52456+57456	CK	FSR	ANG	FSR
156457	52457+57457	CK	FSR	ANG	FSR
156458	52458+57458	CK	FSR	ANG	FSR
156462	52462+57462	CK	FSR	ANG	FSR
156465	52465+57465	CK	FSR	ANG	FSR
156467	52467+57467	CK	FSR	ANG	FSR
156474	52474+57474	CK	FSR	ANG	FSR
156476	52476+57476	CK	FSR	ANG	FSR
156477	52477+57477	CK	FSR	ANG	FSR
156478	52478+57478	CK	FSR	ANG	FSR
156485	52485+57485	CK	FSR	ANG	FSR
156492	52492+57492	CK	FSS	ANG	FSR
156493	52493+57493	CK	FSR	ANG	FSR
156494	52494+57494	CK	FSS	ANG	FSR
156495	52495+57495	CK	FSS	ANG	FSR
156496	52496+57496	CK	FSS	ANG	FSR
156499	52499+57499	CK	FSR	ANG	FSR
156500	52500+57500	CK	FSS	ANG	FSR
156501	52501+57501	CK	FSS	ANG	FSR
156502	52502+57502	CK	FSS	ANG	FSR
156503	52503+57503	CK	FSS	ANG	FSR
156504	52504+57504	CK	FSS	ANG	FSR
156505	52505+57505	CK	FSS	ANG	FSR
156506	52506+57506	CK	FSS	ANG	FSR
156507	52507+57507	CK	FSS	ANG	FSR
156508	52508+57508	CK	FSS	ANG	FSR
156509	52509+57509	CK	FSS	ANG	FSR
156510	52510+57510	CK	FSS	ANG	FSR
156511	52511+57511	CK	FSS	ANG	FSR
156512	52512+57512	CK	FSS	ANG	FSR
156513	52513+57513	CK	FSS	ANG	FSR
156514	52514+57514	CK	FSS	ANG	FSR

Right: *First ScotRail is the largest Class 156 operator, with a total of 48 sets on its books based at Corkerhill depot near Glasgow. The 2+2 low-density units are deployed on longer-distance domestic services and are currently in a transition from First ScotRail to Saltire livery. Set No. 156435 is recorded in First Saltire livery at Crossmyloof with an East Kilbride to Glasgow service.* **Murdock Currie**

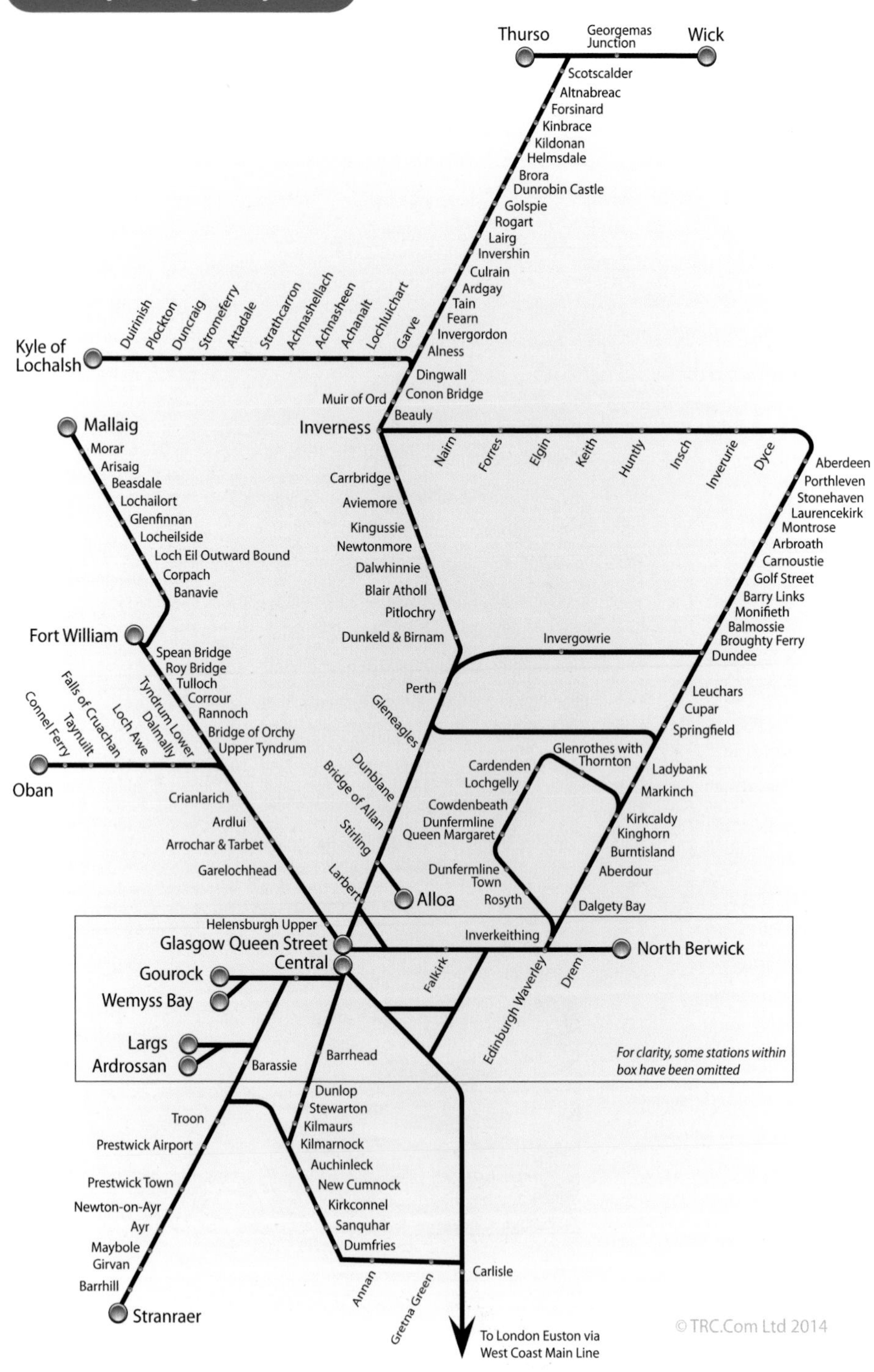
Thurso
Georgemas Junction
Wick
Scotscalder
Altnabreac
Forsinard
Kinbrace
Kildonan
Helmsdale
Brora
Dunrobin Castle
Golspie
Rogart
Lairg
Invershin
Culrain
Ardgay
Tain
Fearn
Invergordon
Alness
Dingwall
Conon Bridge
Muir of Ord
Beauly
Kyle of Lochalsh
Duirinish
Plockton
Duncraig
Stromeferry
Attadale
Strathcarron
Achnashellach
Achnasheen
Achanalt
Lochluichart
Garve
Inverness
Nairn
Forres
Elgin
Keith
Huntly
Insch
Inverurie
Dyce
Aberdeen
Porthleven
Stonehaven
Laurencekirk
Montrose
Arbroath
Carnoustie
Golf Street
Barry Links
Monifieth
Balmossie
Broughty Ferry
Dundee
Mallaig
Morar
Arisaig
Beasdale
Lochailort
Glenfinnan
Locheilside
Loch Eil Outward Bound
Corpach
Banavie
Fort William
Spean Bridge
Roy Bridge
Tulloch
Corrour
Rannoch
Bridge of Orchy
Upper Tyndrum
Tyndrum Lower
Dalmally
Loch Awe
Falls of Cruachan
Taynuilt
Connel Ferry
Oban
Crianlarich
Ardlui
Arrochar & Tarbet
Garelochhead
Helensburgh Upper
Carrbridge
Aviemore
Kingussie
Newtonmore
Dalwhinnie
Blair Atholl
Pitlochry
Dunkeld & Birnam
Invergowrie
Perth
Gleneagles
Dunblane
Bridge of Allan
Stirling
Larbert
Alloa
Leuchars
Cupar
Springfield
Ladybank
Markinch
Glenrothes with Thornton
Cardenden
Lochgelly
Cowdenbeath
Dunfermline Queen Margaret
Dunfermline Town
Rosyth
Kirkcaldy
Kinghorn
Burntisland
Aberdour
Dalgety Bay
Inverkeithing
Glasgow Queen Street
Central
North Berwick
Gourock
Wemyss Bay
Largs
Ardrossan
Falkirk
Edinburgh Waverley
Drem
Barrhead
Barassie
For clarity, some stations within box have been omitted
Troon
Prestwick Airport
Prestwick Town
Newton-on-Ayr
Ayr
Maybole
Girvan
Barrhill
Stranraer
Dunlop
Stewarton
Kilmaurs
Kilmarnock
Auchinleck
New Cumnock
Kirkconnel
Sanquhar
Dumfries
Annan
Gretna Green
Carlisle
To London Euston via West Coast Main Line
© TRC.Com Ltd 2014

Class 158

Vehicle Length: 76ft 1¾in (23.21m)
Height: 12ft 6in (3.81m)
Width: 9ft 3¼in (2.82m)
Engine: 1 x Cummins NTA855R of 350hp per vehicle
Horsepower: 700hp (522kW)
*Seats (total/car): 14F/116S, 14F-46S/70S, * 138S, 68S/70S*

Number	Formation DMCL/DMSL*+DMS	Depot	Livery	Owner	Operator
158701	52701+57701	IS	FSR	PTR	FSR
158702	52702+57702	IS	FSR	PTR	FSR
158703	52703+57703	IS	FSR	PTR	FSR
158704	52704+57704	IS	FSR	PTR	FSR
158705	52705+57705	IS	FSR	PTR	FSR
158706	52706+57706	IS	FSR	PTR	FSR
158707	52707+57707	IS	FSR	PTR	FSR
158708	52708+57708	IS	FSR	PTR	FSR
158709	52709+57709	IS	FSR	PTR	FSR
158710	52710+57710	IS	FSR	PTR	FSR
158711	52711+57711	IS	FSR	PTR	FSR
158712	52712+57712	IS	FSR	PTR	FSR
158713	52713+57713	IS	FSR	PTR	FSR
158714	52714+57714	IS	FSR	PTR	FSR
158715	52715+57715	IS	FSR	PTR	FSR
158716	52716+57716	IS	FSR	PTR	FSR
158717	52717+57717	IS	FSR	PTR	FSR
158718	52718+57718	IS	FSR	PTR	FSR
158719	52719+57719	IS	FSR	PTR	FSR
158720	52720+57720	IS	FSR	PTR	FSR
158721	52721+57721	IS	FSR	PTR	FSR
158722	52722+57722	IS	FSR	PTR	FSR
158723	52723+57723	IS	FSR	PTR	FSR
158724	52724+57724	IS	FSR	PTR	FSR
158725	52725+57725	IS	FSR	PTR	FSR
158726	52726+57726	HA	FSR	PTR	FSR
158727	52727+57727	IS	FSR	PTR	FSR
158728	52728+57728	IS	FSR	PTR	FSR
158729	52729+57729	HA	FSR	PTR	FSR
158730	52730+57730	HA	FSR	PTR	FSR
158731	52731+57731	HA	FSR	PTR	FSR
158732	52732+57732	HA	FSR	PTR	FSR
158733	52733+57733	HA	FSR	PTR	FSR
158734	52734+57734	HA	FSR	PTR	FSR
158735	52735+57735	HA	FSR	PTR	FSR
158736	52736+57736	HA	FSR	PTR	FSR
158737	52737+57737	HA	FSR	PTR	FSR
158738	52738+57738	HA	FSR	PTR	FSR
158739	52739+57739	HA	FSR	PTR	FSR
158740	52740+57740	HA	FSR	PTR	FSR
158741	52741+57741	HA	FSR	PTR	FSR
158782	52782*+57782	HA	FSS	ANG	FSR
158786	52786*+57786	HA	FSS	ANG	FSR
158789	52789*+57789	HA	FSS	ANG	FSR
158867	52867*+57867	HA	FSS	ANG	FSR
158868	52868*+57868	HA	FSS	ANG	FSR
158869	52869*+57869	HA	FSS	ANG	FSR
158870	52870*+57870	HA	FSS	ANG	FSR
158871	52871*+57871	HA	FSS	ANG	FSR

Name applied
158707 - *Far North Line*

Right: *Showing the First ScotRail style modified front light cluster design, Saltire-liveried Class 158 No. 158786 forms an Edinburgh to Dunblane service at Falkirk Grahamston station. A total of 49 two-car Class 158s are operated by First ScotRail, allocated to Inverness and Haymarket depots.* **Murdoch Currie**

Class 170/3
Turbostar

Vehicle Length: 77ft 6in (23.62m)
Height: 12ft 4½in (3.77m)
Width: 8ft 10in (2.69m)
Engine: 1 x MTU 6R 183TD13H 422hp per vehicle
Horsepower: 1,266hp (944kW)
Seats (total/car): 164S, 57S/43S/64S

Number	Formation DMSL+MS+DMSL	Depot	Livery	Owner	Operator
170393	50393+56393+79393	HA	FSS	PTR	FSR
170394+	50394+56394+79394	HA	FSS	PTR	FSR
170395+	50395+56395+79395	HA	FSS	PTR	FSR
170396	50396+56396+79396	HA	FSR	PTR	FSR

+ Standard class only

Class 170/4
Turbostar

Vehicle Length: 77ft 6in (23.62m)
Height: 12ft 4½in (3.77m)
Width: 8ft 10in (2.69m)
Engine: 1 x MTU 6R 183TD13H 422hp per vehicle
Horsepower: 1,266hp (944kW)
(170431/432 have 3 x 483hp engines giving 1,449hp)
Seats (total/car): 18F/168S 9F-43S/76S/9F-49S

Number	Formation DMCL+MS+DMCL	Depot	Livery	Owner	Operator	Name
170401	50401+56401+79401	HA	FSR	PTR	FSR	*Sir Moir Lockhead OBE*
170402	50402+56402+79402	HA	FSS	PTR	FSR	
170403	50403+56403+79403	HA	FSR	PTR	FSR	
170404	50404+56404+79404	HA	FSR	PTR	FSR	

First ScotRail

170405	50405+56405+79405	HA	FSR	PTR	FSR	*Riverside Museum*
170406	50406+56406+79406	HA	FSR	PTR	FSR	
170407	50407+56407+79407	HA	FSR	PTR	FSR	*University of Aberdeen*
170408	50408+56408+79408	HA	FSR	PTR	FSR	
170409	50409+56409+79409	HA	FSR	PTR	FSR	
170410	50410+56410+79410	HA	FSR	PTR	FSR	
170411	50411+56411+79411	HA	FSR	PTR	FSR	
170412	50412+56412+79412	HA	FSS	PTR	FSR	
170413	50413+56413+79413	HA	FSR	PTR	FSR	
170414	50414+56414+79414	HA	FSR	PTR	FSR	
170415	50415+56415+79415	HA	FSS	PTR	FSR	
170416	50416+56416+79416	HA	FSR	EVL	FSR	
170417	50417+56417+79417	HA	FSR	EVL	FSR	
170418	50418+56418+79418	HA	FSS	EVL	FSR	
170419	50419+56419+79419	HA	FSR	EVL	FSR	
170420	50420+56420+79420	HA	FSR	EVL	FSR	
170421	50421+56421+79421	HA	FSR	EVL	FSR	
170422	50422+56422+79422	HA	FSR	EVL	FSR	
170423	50423+56423+79423	HA	FSR	EVL	FSR	
170424	50424+56424+79424	HA	FSR	EVL	FSR	
170425	50425+56425+79425	HA	FSS	PTR	FSR	
170426	50426+56426+79426	HA	FSS	PTR	FSR	
170427	50427+56427+79427	HA	FSS	PTR	FSR	
170428	50428+56428+79428	HA	FSS	PTR	FSR	
170429	50429+56429+79429	HA	FSS	PTR	FSR	
170430	50430+56430+79430	HA	FSS	PTR	FSR	
170431	50431+56431+79431	HA	FSS	PTR	FSR	
170432	50432+56432+79432	HA	FSS	PTR	FSR	
170433	50433+56433+79433	HA	FSR	PTR	FSR	*Investor in People*
170434	50434+56434+79434	HA	FSS	PTR	FSR	

Class 170/4
Turbostar

Vehicle Length: 77ft 6in (23.62m)
Height: 12ft 4½in (3.77m)
Width: 8ft 10in (2.69m)

Engine: 1 x MTU 6R 183TD13H 422hp per vehicle
Horsepower: 1,266hp (944kW)
Seats: 170450-170471 (total/car) 198S, 55S/76S/67S
170472-170478 (total/car) 200S, 57S/76S/67S

Number	*Formation DMSL+MS+DMSL*	*Depot*	*Livery*	*Owner*	*Op'r*
170450	50450+56450+79450	HA	FSS	PTR	FSR
170451	50451+56451+79451	HA	FSS	PTR	FSR
170452	50452+56452+79452	HA	FSS	PTR	FSR
170453	50453+56453+79453	HA	FSS	PTR	FSR
170454	50454+56454+79454	HA	FSS	PTR	FSR
170455	50455+56455+79455	HA	FSS	PTR	FSR
170456	50456+56456+79456	HA	FSS	PTR	FSR
170457	50457+56457+79457	HA	FSS	PTR	FSR
170458	50458+56458+79458	HA	FSS	PTR	FSR
170459	50459+56459+79459	HA	FSS	PTR	FSR
170460	50460+56460+79460	HA	FSR	PTR	FSR
170461	50461+56461+79461	HA	FSR	PTR	FSR
170470	50470+56470+79470	HA	FSS	PTR	FSR
170471	50471+56471+79471	HA	FSS	PTR	FSR
170472	50472+56472+79472	HA	FSS	PTR	FSR
170473	50473+56473+79473	HA	FSS	PTR	FSR
170474	50474+56474+79474	HA	FSS	PTR	FSR
170475	50475+56475+79475	HA	FSS	PTR	FSR
170476	50476+56476+79476	HA	FSS	PTR	FSR
170477	50477+56477+79477	HA	FSS	PTR	FSR
170478	50478+56478+79478	HA	FSP	PTR	FSR

Left: *Longer-distance domestic First ScotRail services are in the hands of a fleet of three-car Class 170 'Turbostar' units, First ScotRail being the largest user of this class in the UK. Three different sub-classes exist, all with slightly different interior layouts, but all are built to the same design. One of the standard-class-only Class 170/3 sets No. 170393 is recorded at Glasgow Queen Street with a service bound for Alloa. The Class 170 units are all allocated to Edinburgh Haymarket depot.* **Murdoch Currie**

Class 314

Vehicle Length: (Driving) 64ft 11½in (19.80m) (Inter) 65ft 4¼in (19.92m)
Height: 11ft 6½in (3.58m)
Width: 9ft 3in (2.82m)
Horsepower: 880hp (656kW)
Seats (total/car): 212S, 68S/76S/68S

Number	Formation DMSO(A)+PTSO+DMSO(B)	Depot	Livery	Owner	Operator	Name
314201	64583+71450+64584	GW	FSP	ANG	FSR	
314202	64585+71451+64586	GW	FSP	ANG	FSR	
314203	64587+71452+64588*	GW	FSS	ANG	FSR	
314204	64589+71453+64590	GW	FSS	ANG	FSR	
314205	64591+71454+64592	GW	FSS	ANG	FSR	
314206	64593+71455+64594	GW	FSP	ANG	FSR	
314207	64595+71456+64596	GW	FSP	ANG	FSR	
314208	64597+71457+64598	GW	FSS	ANG	FSR	
314209	64599+71458+64600	GW	FSP	ANG	FSR	
314210	64601+71459+64602	GW	FSP	ANG	FSR	
314211	64603+71460+64604	GW	FSS	ANG	FSR	
314212	64604+71461+64606	GW	FSS	ANG	FSR	
314213	64607+71462+64608	GW	FSP	ANG	FSR	
314214	64609+71463+64610	GW	FSS	ANG	FSR	
314215	64611+71464+64612	GW	FSP	ANG	FSR	
314216	64613+71465+64614	GW	FSP	ANG	FSR	

* 64588 was rebuilt from Class 507 car No. 64426 and seats 74S

Right: *A fleet of 16 Class 314s of 1970s BREL design is allocated to Glasgow Shields depot for suburban services in and around Glasgow. The sets have recently undergone a face-lift including a repaint into the latest Saltire blue and white livery. Set No. 314208 is seen at Glasgow Central station with a service to Newton.* **Murdoch Currie**

Class 318

Vehicle Length: (Driving) 65ft 0¾in (19.83m) (Inter) 65ft 4¼in (19.92m)
Height: 12ft 1½in (3.70m)
Width: 9ft 3in (2.82m)
Horsepower: 1,328hp (996kW)
Seats (total/car): 216S, 66S/79S/71S

Number	Formation DTSO(A)+MSO+DTSO(B)	Depot	Livery	Owner	Operator	Name
318250	77240+62866+77260	GW	FSP	EVL	FSR	
318251	77241+62867+77261	GW	FSS	EVL	FSR	
318252	77242+62868+77262	GW	FSP	EVL	FSR	
318253	77243+62869+77263	GW	FSP	EVL	FSR	
318254	77244+62870+77264	GW	FSP	EVL	FSR	
318255	77245+62871+77265	GW	FSP	EVL	FSR	
318256	77246+62872+77266	GW	FSP	EVL	FSR	
318257	77247+62873+77267	GW	FSP	EVL	FSR	
318258	77248+62874+77268	GW	FSP	EVL	FSR	
318259	77249+62875+77269	GW	FSP	EVL	FSR	*Citizens' Network*
318260	77250+62876+77270	GW	FSP	EVL	FSR	
318261	77251+62877+77271	GW	FSP	EVL	FSR	
318262	77252+62878+77272	GW	FSP	EVL	FSR	
318263	77253+62879+77273	GW	FSP	EVL	FSR	
318264	77254+62880+77274	GW	FSP	EVL	FSR	
318265	77255+62881+77275	GW	FSP	EVL	FSR	
318266	77256+62882+77276	GW	FSP	EVL	FSR	*Strathclyder*
318267	77257+62883+77277	GW	FSP	EVL	FSR	
318268	77258+62884+77278	GW	FSP	EVL	FSR	
318269	77259+62885+77279	GW	FSP	EVL	FSR	
318270	77288+62890+77289	GW	FSP	EVL	FSR	

First ScotRail

Left: *A fleet of 21 three-car Class 318s is allocated to Glasgow Shields and they usually operate on the Argyle line. When introduced, these units were fitted with end gangways, but during refurbishment in recent years these have been removed, changing the appearance of the sets. All sets are currently painted in ScotRail carmine and cream livery, as shown on set No. 318263 at Carluke forming a Dalmuir to Lanark service.* **Robin Ralston**

Class 320

Vehicle Length: (Driving) 65ft 0¾in (19.83m)
(Inter) 65ft 4¼in (19.92m)
Height: 12ft 4¾in (3.78m)
Width: 9ft 3in (2.82m)
Horsepower: 1,328hp (996kW)
Seats (total/car): 227S, 76S/76S/75S

Number	*Formation* DTSO(A)+MSO+DTSO(B)	*Depot*	*Livery*	*Owner*	*Operator*
320301	77899+63021+77921	GW	FSS	EVL	FSR
320302	77900+63022+77922	GW	FSS	EVL	FSR
320303	77901+63023+77923	GW	FSS	EVL	FSR
320304	77902+63024+77924	GW	FSS	EVL	FSR
320305	77903+63025+77925	GW	FSS	EVL	FSR
320306	77904+63026+77926	GW	FSS	EVL	FSR
320307	77905+63027+77927	GW	FSS	EVL	FSR
320308	77906+63028+77928	GW	FSS	EVL	FSR
320309	77907+63029+77929	GW	FSS	EVL	FSR
320310	77908+63030+77930	GW	FSS	EVL	FSR
320311	77909+63031+77931	GW	FSS	EVL	FSR
320312	77910+63032+77932	GW	FSS	EVL	FSR
320313	77911+63033+77933	GW	FSS	EVL	FSR
320314	77912+63034+77934	GW	FSS	EVL	FSR
320315	77913+63035+77935	GW	FSS	EVL	FSR
320316	77914+63036+77936	GW	FSS	EVL	FSR
320317	77915+63037+77937	GW	FSS	EVL	FSR
320318	77916+63038+77938	GW	FSS	EVL	FSR
320319	77917+63039+77939	GW	FSS	EVL	FSR
320320	77918+63040+77940	GW	FSS	EVL	FSR
320321	77919+63041+77941	GW	FSS	EVL	FSR
320322	77920+63042+77942	GW	FSS	EVL	FSR

Left: *All 22 members of the Class 320 ScotRail fleet are now painted in the blue Saltire livery. Allocated to Glasgow Shields depot, these sets operate outer-suburban Glasgow routes. Each three-car set seats 227 standard class passengers. On 24 April 2013 No. 320311 forms the 15.19 Springburn to Dalmuir service at Barnhill.* **Robin Ralston**

Class 334
Juniper

Vehicle Length: (Driving) 69ft 0¾in (21.04m)
(Inter) 65ft 4½in (19.93m)
Height: 12ft 3in (3.77m)
Width: 9ft 2¾in (2.80m)
Horsepower: 1,448hp (1,080kW)
Seats (total/car): 183S, 64S/55S/64S

Number	Formation DMSO(A)+PTSO+DMSO(B)	Depot	Livery	Owner	Operator	Name
334001	64101+74301+65101	GW	FSP	EVL	FSR	*Donald Dewar*
334002	64102+74302+65102	GW	FSS	EVL	FSR	
334003	64103+74303+65103	GW	FSS	EVL	FSR	
334004	64104+74304+65104	GW	FSP	EVL	FSR	
334005	64105+74305+65105	GW	FSP	EVL	FSR	
334006	64106+74306+65106	GW	FSS	EVL	FSR	
334007	64107+74307+65107	GW	FSP	EVL	FSR	
334008	64108+74308+65108	GW	FSP	EVL	FSR	
334009	64109+74309+65109	GW	FSS	EVL	FSR	
334010	64110+74310+65110	GW	FSP	EVL	FSR	
334011	64111+74311+65111	GW	FSP	EVL	FSR	
334012	64112+74312+65112	GW	FSS	EVL	FSR	
334013	64113+74313+65113	GW	FSS	EVL	FSR	
334014	64114+74314+65114	GW	FSS	EVL	FSR	
334015	64115+74315+65115	GW	FSS	EVL	FSR	
334016	64116+74316+65116	GW	FSP	EVL	FSR	
334017	64117+74317+65117	GW	FSS	EVL	FSR	
334018	64118+74318+65118	GW	FSS	EVL	FSR	
334019	64119+74319+65119	GW	FSP	EVL	FSR	
334020	64120+74320+65120	GW	FSS	EVL	FSR	
334021	64121+74321+65121	GW	FSS	EVL	FSR	
334022	64122+74322+65122	GW	FSS	EVL	FSR	
334023	64123+74323+65123	GW	FSS	EVL	FSR	
334024	64124+74324+65124	GW	FSS	EVL	FSR	
334025	64125+74325+65125	GW	FSS	EVL	FSR	
334026	64126+74326+65126	GW	FSP	EVL	FSR	
334027	64127+74327+65127	GW	FSS	EVL	FSR	
334028	64128+74328+65128	GW	FSS	EVL	FSR	
334029	64129+74329+65129	GW	FSS	EVL	FSR	
334030	64130+74330+65130	GW	FSS	EVL	FSR	
334031	64131+74331+65131	GW	FSS	EVL	FSR	
334032	64132+74332+65132	GW	FSP	EVL	FSR	
334033	64133+74333+65133	GW	FSS	EVL	FSR	
334034	64134+74334+65134	GW	FSP	EVL	FSR	
334035	64135+74335+65135	GW	FSS	EVL	FSR	
334036	64136+74336+65136	GW	FSS	EVL	FSR	
334037	64137+74337+65137	GW	FSS	EVL	FSR	
334038	64138+74338+65138	GW	FSS	EVL	FSR	
334039	64139+74339+65139	GW	FSS	EVL	FSR	
334040	64140+74340+65140	GW	FSS	EVL	FSR	

Right: *As part of the post-privatisation modernisation of Glasgow area suburban and outer-suburban services, a fleet of 40 three-car Alstom 'Juniper' sets was built. These are allocated to Shields depot, Glasgow, and operate North Clyde services. Set No. 334020 leads the 10.10 Helensburgh Central to Edinburgh service at Hillend Loch on 30 April 2013. All '334s' are now painted in blue Saltire livery.*
Robin Ralston

Class 380/0
Desiro

Vehicle Length: 77ft 3in (23.57m)
Height: 12ft 1½in (3.7m)
Width: 9ft 2in (2.7m)
Horsepower: 1,341hp (1,000kW)
Seats (total/car): 191S, 70S/57S/64S

Number	*Formation* DMSO(A)+PTSO+DMSO(B)	*Depot*	*Livery*	*Owner*	*Operator*
380001	38501+38601+38701	GW	FSS	EVL	FSR
380002	38502+38602+38702	GW	FSS	EVL	FSR
380003	38503+38603+38703	GW	FSS	EVL	FSR
380004	38504+38604+38704	GW	FSS	EVL	FSR
380005	38505+38605+38705	GW	FSS	EVL	FSR
380006	38506+38606+38706	GW	FSS	EVL	FSR
380007	38507+38607+38707	GW	FSS	EVL	FSR
380008	38508+38608+38708	GW	FSS	EVL	FSR
380009	38509+38609+38709	GW	FSS	EVL	FSR
380010	38510+38610+38710	GW	FSS	EVL	FSR
380011	38511+38611+38711	GW	FSS	EVL	FSR
380012	38512+38612+38712	GW	FSS	EVL	FSR
380013	38513+38613+38713	GW	FSS	EVL	FSR
380014	38514+38614+38714	GW	FSS	EVL	FSR
380015	38515+38615+38715	GW	FSS	EVL	FSR
380016	38516+38616+38716	GW	FSS	EVL	FSR
380017	38517+38617+38717	GW	FSS	EVL	FSR
380018	38518+38618+38718	GW	FSS	EVL	FSR
380019	38519+38619+38719	GW	FSS	EVL	FSR
380020	38520+38620+38720	GW	FSS	EVL	FSR
380021	38521+38621+38721	GW	FSS	EVL	FSR
380022	38522+38622+38722	GW	FSS	EVL	FSR

Class 380/1
Desiro

Vehicle Length: 77ft 3in (23.57m)
Height: 12ft 1½in (3.7m)
Width: 9ft 2in (2.7m)
Horsepower: 1,341hp (1,000kW)
Seats (total/car): 265S, 70S/57S/74S/64S

Number	*Formation* DMSO(A)+PTSO+MSO+DMSO(B)	*Depot*	*Livery*	*Owner*	*Operator*
380101	38551+38651+38851+38751	GW	FSS	EVL	FSR
380102	38552+38652+38852+38752	GW	FSS	EVL	FSR
380103	38553+38653+38853+38753	GW	FSS	EVL	FSR
380104	38554+38654+38854+38754	GW	FSS	EVL	FSR
380105	38555+38655+38855+38755	GW	FSS	EVL	FSR
380106	38556+38656+38856+38756	GW	FSS	EVL	FSR
380107	38557+38657+38857+38757	GW	FSS	EVL	FSR
380108	38558+38658+38858+38758	GW	FSS	EVL	FSR
380109	38559+38659+38859+38759	GW	FSS	EVL	FSR
380110	38560+38660+38860+38760	GW	FSS	EVL	FSR
380111	38561+38661+38861+38761	GW	FSS	EVL	FSR
380112	38562+38662+38862+38762	GW	FSS	EVL	FSR
380113	38563+38663+38863+38763	GW	FSS	EVL	FSR
380114	38564+38664+38864+38764	GW	FSS	EVL	FSR
380115	38565+38665+38865+38765	GW	FSS	EVL	FSR
380116	38566+38666+38866+38766	GW	FSS	EVL	FSR

Left: *The most modern EMUs operating on the First ScotRail franchise are a fleet of 38 Siemens-built 'Desiro' units, which are formed into three- and four-car sets, classified as 380/0 and 380/1 respectively. Built in Germany, the sets sport the latest blue Saltire livery and are allocated to Shields depot operating Ayrshire and Inverclyde services. Class 380/1 set No. 380101 passes Craigenhill on 18 February 2013 forming an Edinburgh to Glasgow via Carstairs service.* **Robin Ralston**

Mk2 & Mk3 Hauled Stock

Mk2
Vehicle Length: 66ft 0in (20.11m) *Width: 9ft 3in (2.81m)*
Height: 12ft 9½in (3.89m) *Seats (total/car): 60S*

Mk3
Vehicle Length: 75ft 0in (22.86m) *Width: 8ft 11in (2.71m)*
Height: 12ft 9in (3.88m) *Bogie Type: BT10*

AN1F (Mk2) - RLO *Seating 28-30F*

Number	Depot	Livery	Owner
6700 (3347)	IS	FSS	EVL
6701 (3346)	IS	FSR	EVL
6702 (3421)	IS	FSR	EVL
6703 (3308)	IS	FSR	EVL
6704 (3341)	IS	FSR	EVL
6705 (3310)	IS	FSR	EVL
6706 (3283)	IS	FSR	EVL
6707 (3276)	IS	FSR	EVL
6708 (3370)	IS	FSR	EVL

AN1F (Mk2) - BUO *Seating 31U*

Number	Depot	Livery	Owner
9800 (5751)	IS	FSR	EVL
9801 (5760)	IS	FSR	EVL
9802 (5772)	IS	FSR	EVL
9803 (5799)	IS	FSR	EVL
9804 (5826)	IS	FSR	EVL
9805 (5833)	IS	FSR	EVL
9806 (5840)	IS	FSR	EVL
9807 (5851)	IS	FSS	EVL
9808 (5871)	IS	FSS	EVL
9809 (5890)	IS	FSR	EVL
9810 (5892)	IS	FSR	EVL

AU4G (Mk3) - SLEP *Comps 12*

Number	Depot	Livery	Owner
10501	IS	FSR	PTR
10502	IS	FSR	PTR
10504	IS	FSR	PTR
10506	IS	FSR	PTR
10507	IS	FSR	PTR
10508	IS	FSR	PTR
10513	IS	FSR	PTR
10516	IS	FSS	PTR
10519	IS	FSR	PTR
10520	IS	FSR	PTR
10522	IS	FSR	PTR
10523	IS	FSR	PTR
10526	IS	FSR	PTR
10527	IS	FSR	PTR
10529	IS	FSR	PTR
10531	IS	FSR	PTR
10542	IS	FSR	PTR
10543	IS	FSR	PTR
10544	IS	FSR	PTR
10548	IS	FSR	PTR
10551	IS	FSR	PTR
10553	IS	FSR	PTR
10561	IS	FSR	PTR
10562	IS	FSS	PTR
10565	IS	FSR	PTR
10580	IS	FSR	PTR
10597	IS	FSR	PTR
10598	IS	FSR	PTR
10600	IS	FSR	PTR
10605	IS	FSR	PTR
10607	IS	FSR	PTR
10610	IS	FSR	PTR
10613	IS	FSR	PTR
10614	IS	FSR	PTR
10617	IS	FSR	PTR

AS4G (MK3) - SLE *Comps 13*

Number	Depot	Livery	Owner
10675	IS	FSR	PTR
10683	IS	FSR	PTR
10688	IS	FSR	PTR
10690	IS	FSR	PTR
10693	IS	FSR	PTR
10703	IS	FSR	PTR

AQ4G (Mk3) - SLED *Comps 11*

Number	Depot	Livery	Owner
10648	IS	FSR	PTR
10650	IS	FSR	PTR
10666	IS	FSR	PTR
10680	IS	FSR	PTR
10689	IS	FSR	PTR
10699	IS	FSR	PTR
10706	IS	FSR	PTR
10714	IS	FSR	PTR
10718	IS	FSR	PTR
10719	IS	FSR	PTR
10722	IS	FSR	PTR
10723	IS	FSR	PTR

Right: *At present the Scottish sleeper services are operated as part of the First ScotRail franchise, but in the future they are likely to be operated as a separate franchise. In 2014 73 Mk2 and Mk3 loco-hauled vehicles were operated by ScotRail for sleeper services, being allocated to Inverness depot. The sleeper vehicles are all of the Mk3 design, while the support coaches are of Mk2 design. These two views show a Mk3 sleeper vehicle; the above view is seen from the long corridor side with just five windows, while the view below shows the sleeper compartment side with 12 windows, one for each compartment, plus a toilet compartment at each end.*
Robin Ralston / Nathan Williamson

First TransPennine Express

Address: ✉ Floor 7, Bridgewater House, 60 Whitworth Street, Manchester, M1 6LT
tpecustomer.relations@firstgroup.com
✆ 0845 600 1671
ⓘ www.tpexpress.co.uk

Managing Director: Nick Donovan
Franchise Dates: 1 February 2004 - Extension proposed to February 2016
Principal Routes: Newcastle, Middlesbrough, Scarborough, Hull, Cleethorpes to Manchester, Liverpool, Barrow, Carlisle, Edinburgh and Glasgow
Depots: Ardwick (AK) - Siemens-operated, York (YK), Crofton (XW)
Parent Company: First Group, Keolis

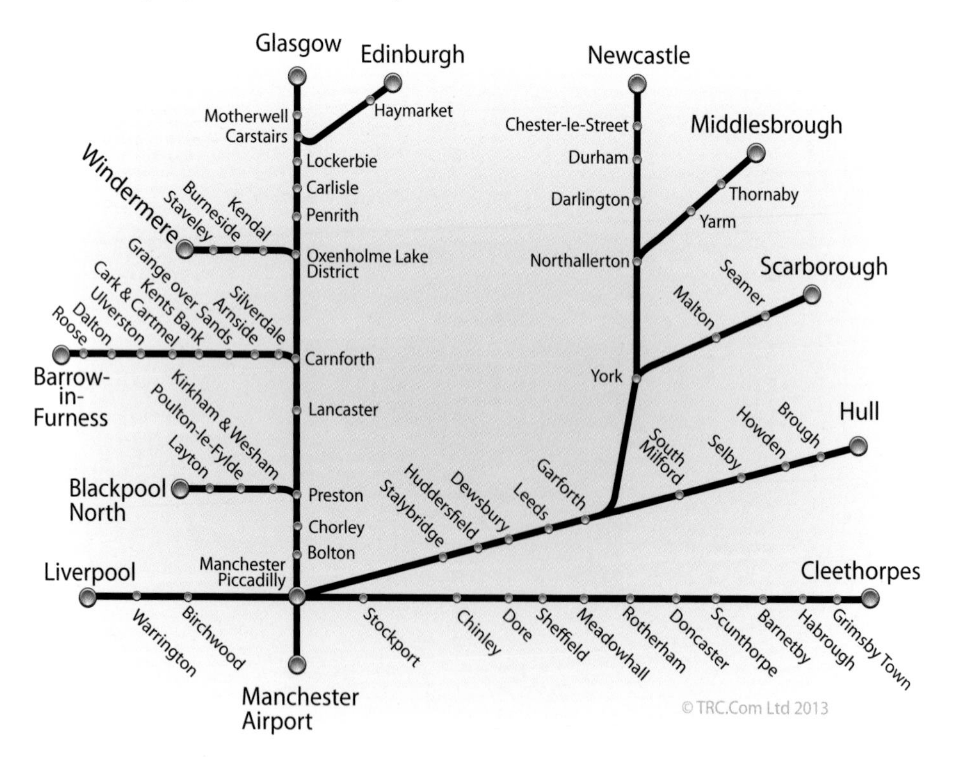

Class 350/4
Desiro

Vehicle Length: 66ft 9in (20.4m)
Height: 12ft 1½in (3.78m)
Width: 9ft 2in (2.7m)
Horsepower: 1,341hp (1,000kW)
Seats (total/car): 19F/178S

Number	Formation DMSO(A)+TCO+PTSO+DMSO(B)	Depot	Livery
350401	60691+60901+60941+60671	AK	GRY
350402	60692+60902+60942+60672	AK	GRY
350403	60693+60903+60943+60673	AK	GRY
350404	60694+60904+60944+60674	AK	GRY
350405	60695+60905+60945+60675	AK	GRY
350406	60696+60906+60946+60676	AK	GRY
350407	60697+60907+60947+60677	AK	GRY
350408	60698+60908+60948+60678	AK	GRY
350409	60699+60909+60949+60679	AK	GRY
350410	60700+60910+60950+60680	AK	GRY

Class 170/3
Turbostar

Vehicle Length: 77ft 6in (23.62m)
Height: 12ft 4½in (3.77m)
Width: 8ft 10in (2.69m)
Engine: 1 x MTU 6R 183TD13H 422hp per vehicle
Horsepower: 844hp (629kW)
Seats (total/car): 8F/108S 8F-43S/65S

Number	*Formation DMCL+DMS*	*Depot*	*Livery*	*Owner*	*Operator*
170301	50301+79301	XW	FTP	PTR	FTP
170302	50302+79302	XW	FTP	PTR	FTP
170303	50303+79303	XW	FTP	PTR	FTP
170304	50304+79304	XW	FTP	PTR	FTP
170305	50305+79305	XW	FTP	PTR	FTP
170306	50306+79306	XW	FTP	PTR	FTP
170307	50307+79307	XW	FTP	PTR	FTP
170308	50308+79308	XW	FTP	PTR	FTP
170309	50399+79399	XW	FTP	PTR	FTP

Right: *First TransPennine Express operates a fleet of nine two-car Class 170/3 sets, mainly on the Manchester to East Coast corridor. These sets were previously used by South West Trains. All 170/3s are painted in FTPE Dynamic Lines livery and are allocated to Crofton depot near Wakefield. Set No. 170305 is captured near Melton Ross.* **Antony Christie**

Class 185
Desiro

Vehicle Length: (Driving) 77ft 11in (23.76m), (Inter) 77ft 10in (23.75m)
Height: 12ft 4in (3.75m)
Width: 9ft 3in (2.81m)
Engine: 1 x Cummins OSK19 of 750hp per car
Horsepower: 2,250hp (1,680kW)
Seats (total/car): 15F/154S, 15F-18S/72S/64S

Number	*Formation DMCL+MSL+DMS*	*Depot*	*Livery*	*Owner*	*Op'r*
185101	51101+53101+54101	AK	FTP	EVL	FTP
185102	51102+53102+54102	AK	FTP	EVL	FTP
185103	51103+53103+54103	AK	FTP	EVL	FTP
185104	51104+53104+54104	AK	FTP	EVL	FTP
185105	51105+53105+54105	AK	FTP	EVL	FTP
185106	51106+53106+54106	AK	FTP	EVL	FTP
185107	51107+53107+54107	AK	FTP	EVL	FTP
185108	51108+53108+54108	AK	FTP	EVL	FTP
185109	51109+53109+54109	AK	FTP	EVL	FTP
185110	51110+53110+54110	AK	FTP	EVL	FTP
185111	51111+53111+54111	AK	FTP	EVL	FTP
185112	51112+53112+54112	AK	FTP	EVL	FTP
185113	51113+53113+54113	AK	FTP	EVL	FTP
185114	51114+53114+54114	AK	FTP	EVL	FTP
185115	51115+53115+54115	AK	FTP	EVL	FTP
185116	51116+53116+54116	AK	FTP	EVL	FTP
185117	51117+53117+54117	AK	FTP	EVL	FTP
185118	51118+53118+54118	AK	FTP	EVL	FTP
185119	51119+53119+54119	AK	FTP	EVL	FTP
185120	51120+53120+54120	AK	FTP	EVL	FTP
185121	51121+53121+54121	AK	FTP	EVL	FTP
185122	51122+53122+54122	AK	FTP	EVL	FTP
185123	51123+53123+54123	AK	FTP	EVL	FTP
185124	51124+53124+54124	AK	FTP	EVL	FTP
185125	51125+53125+54125	AK	FTP	EVL	FTP
185126	51126+53126+54126	AK	FTP	EVL	FTP
185127	51127+53127+54127	AK	FTP	EVL	FTP
185128	51128+53128+54128	AK	FTP	EVL	FTP
185129	51129+53129+54129	AK	FTP	EVL	FTP
185130	51130+53130+54130	AK	FTP	EVL	FTP
185131	51131+53131+54131	AK	FTP	EVL	FTP
185132	51132+53132+54132	AK	FTP	EVL	FTP
185133	51133+53133+54133	AK	FTP	EVL	FTP
185134	51134+53134+54134	AK	FTP	EVL	FTP
185135	51135+53135+54135	AK	FTP	EVL	FTP
185136	51136+53136+54136	AK	FTP	EVL	FTP
185137	51137+53137+54137	AK	FTP	EVL	FTP
185138	51138+53138+54138	AK	FTP	EVL	FTP
185139	51139+53139+54139	AK	FTP	EVL	FTP
185140	51140+53140+54140	AK	FTP	EVL	FTP
185141	51141+53141+54141	AK	FTP	EVL	FTP
185142	51142+53142+54142	AK	FTP	EVL	FTP
185143	51143+53143+54143	AK	FTP	EVL	FTP
185144	51144+53144+54144	AK	FTP	EVL	FTP
185145	51145+53145+54145	AK	FTP	EVL	FTP
185146	51146+53146+54146	AK	FTP	EVL	FTP
185147	51147+53147+54147	AK	FTP	EVL	FTP
185148	51148+53148+54148	AK	FTP	EVL	FTP
185149	51149+53149+54149	AK	FTP	EVL	FTP
185150	51150+53150+54150	AK	FTP	EVL	FTP
185151	51151+53151+54151	AK	FTP	EVL	FTP

Below: *The main FTPE fleet consists of 51 three-car diesel Siemens 'Desiro' units, based in Manchester and operating all long-distance services. The sets are finished in First Dynamic Lines livery. Set No. 185113 is seen approaching Doncaster, with a service from Manchester.* **CJM**

Grand Central

Address: River House, 17 Museum Street, York, YO1 7DJ
info@grandcentral.com
0845 603 4852
www.grandcentral.co.uk

Managing Director: Richard McLean
Franchise Dates: Private Open Access Operator, to December 2016
Principal Routes: London King's Cross - Sunderland / Bradford
Depots: Heaton (HT)
Parent Company: Arriva PLC

Sunderland
Hartlepool
Eaglescliffe
Northallerton
Thirsk
York
Bradford Interchange
Halifax
Brighouse
Wakefield Kirkgate
Pontefract Monkhill
Doncaster
London King's Cross

Below: *Six Class 43 HST power cars are operated by Grand Central, allocated to Heaton depot. They are used on the King's Cross-Sunderland route, usually operated in 2+6 formations. A London-bound train is seen south of York on 21 August 2013 led by power car No. 43467.* **Antony Christie**

Class 43 – HST

Vehicle Length: 58ft 5in (18.80m)
Height: 12ft 10in (3.90m)
Width: 8ft 11in (2.73m)
Engine: MTU 16V4000 R41R
Horsepower: 2,250hp (1,680kW)
Electrical Equipment: Brush

Number	Depot	Pool	Livery	Owner	Operator
43423 (43123)	HT	GCHP	GTO	ANG	GTL
43465 (43065)	HT	GCHP	GTO	ANG	GTL
43467 (43067)	HT	GCHP	GTO	ANG	GTL
43468 (43068)	HT	GCHP	GTO	ANG	GTL
43480 (43080)	HT	GCHP	GTO	ANG	GTL
43484 (43084)	HT	GCHP	GTO	ANG	GTL

Names applied

43423 *'Valenta' 1972 - 2010*
43484 *Peter Fox 1942 - 2011*

Class 180

Zephyrs

Vehicle Length: (Driving) 75ft 7in (23.71m), (Inter) 75ft 5in (23.03m)
Height: 12ft 4in (3.75m)
Width: 9ft 2in (2.80m)
Engine: 1 x Cummins QSK19 of 750hp per car
Horsepower: 3,750hp (2,796kW)
Seats (total/car): 42F/226S, 46S/42F/68S/56S/56S

Number	Formation DMSL(A)+MFL+MSL+MSLRB+DMSL(B)	Depot	Livery	Owner	Operator	Name
180101	50901+54901+55901+56901+59901	HT	GTL	ANG	GTL	
180105	50905+54905+55905+56905+59905	HT	GTL	ANG	GTL	*The Yorkshire Artist Ashley Jackson*
180107	50907+54907+55907+56907+59907	HT	GTL	ANG	GTL	*Hart of the North*
180112	50912+54912+55912+56912+59912	HT	GTL	ANG	GTL	*James Herriot*
180114	50914+54914+55914+56914+59914	HT	GTL	ANG	GTL	

Above: *The five former First Great Western Class 180s allocated to Heaton for GC use are classified as 'Zephyrs'. The sets are internally refurbished to a GC theme and painted in GC black and orange livery. Standard class passenger doors are painted silver and first class doors in gold. Devoid of its original nose-end coupling doors, set No. 180105 is seen approaching Doncaster from the south .* **CJM**

Mk3 HST stock

Vehicle Length: 75ft 0in (22.86m) *Width: 8ft 11in (2.71m)*
Height: 12ft 9in (3.88m) *Bogie Type: BT10*

GK2G - TRSB *Seating 33S*

Number		Depot	Livery	Owner
40424	(40024)	HT	GTO	ANG
40426	(40026)	HT	GTL	ANG
40433	(40033)	HT	GTL	ANG

GH1G - TF *Seating 48F*

Number		Depot	Livery	Owner
41201	(11045)	HT	GTO	ANG
41202	(11017)	HT	GTL	ANG
41203	(11038)	HT	GTL	ANG
41204	(11023)	HT	GTL	ANG
41205	(11036)	HT	GTL	ANG
41206	(11055)	HT	GTL	ANG

GH2G - TS *Seating 64S *TSD Seating 60S*

Number		Depot	Livery	Owner
42401	(12149)	HT	GTO	ANG
42402	(12155)	HT	GTO	ANG
42403*	(12033)	HT	GTO	ANG
42404	(12152)	HT	GTL	ANG
42405	(12136)	HT	GTL	ANG
42406*	(12112)	HT	GTL	ANG
42407	(12044)	HT	GTL	ANG
42408	(12121)	HT	GTL	ANG
42409*	(12088)	HT	GTL	ANG

GJ2G - TGS *Seating 67S*

Number	Depot	Livery	Owner
44065 (S)	HT/LM	GTL	GTL
44088 (S)	HT/LM	GTL	GTL
44089 (S)	HT/LM	GTL	GTL

Right: *The Grand Central HST passenger fleet consists of 18 operational and three stored vehicles. Based at Heaton, Newcastle, the stock is usually formed into two operational sets and one spare set each day. All TS and TF vehicles were rebuilt from Mk3 loco-hauled stock. All vehicles including the HST power cars are owned by Angel and leased to GC. Carriages are painted in black and orange livery and retain their traditional 2+2 standard and 2+1 first class seating layouts. TS vehicle No. 42404 is shown, a rebuild from hauled vehicle No. 12152.* **Antony Christie**

Greater Anglia

Address: ✉ 2nd Floor, East Anglia House, 12-34 Great Eastern Street, London, EC2A 3EH
contactcentre@greateranglia.co.uk
✆ 0845 600 7245
ⓘ www.greateranglia.co.uk

Managing Director: Jamie Burles
Franchise Dates: 1 February 2012 - 19 July 2014
Principal Routes: London Liverpool Street to Norwich, Cambridge, Enfield Town, Hertford East, Upminster, Southend Victoria, Southminster, Braintree, Sudbury, Clacton, Walton, Harwich Town, Felixstowe, Lowestoft, Great Yarmouth, Sheringham, Stansted Airport and Peterborough
Depots: Ilford (IL), Norwich (NC), Clacton (CC)
Parent Company: Abellio

Class 90/0

Vehicle Length: 61ft 6in (18.74m)
Height: 13ft 0¼in (3.96m)
Width: 9ft 0in (2.74m)
Power Collection: 25kV ac overhead
Horsepower: 7,860hp (5,860kW)
Electrical Equipment: GEC

Number	Depot	Pool	Livery	Owner	Operator	Name
90001	NC	IANA	ORA	PTR	GAR	
90002	NC	IANA	ORA	PTR	GAR	*Eastern Daily Press 1870-2010 Serving Norfolk for 140 years*
90003	NC	IANA	GAR	PTR	GAR	*Raedwald of East Anglia*
90004	NC	IANA	ORA	PTR	GAR	*City of Chelmsford*
90005	NC	IANA	AWT	PTR	GAR	
90006	NC	IANA	ORA	PTR	GAR	*Roger Ford / Modern Railways Magazine*
90007	NC	IANA	ORA	PTR	GAR	*Sir John Betjeman*
90008	NC	IANA	GAR	PTR	GAR	*The East Anglian*
90009	NC	IANA	ORA	PTR	GAR	*Diamond Jubilee*
90010	NC	IANA	ORA	PTR	GAR	*Bressingham Steam and Gardens*
90011	NC	IANA	ORA	PTR	GAR	*Let's Go - East of England*
90012	NC	IANA	ORA	PTR	GAR	*Royal Anglian Regiment*
90013	NC	IANA	ORA	PTR	GAR	*The Evening Star*
90014	NC	IANA	ORA	PTR	GAR	*Norfolk and Norwich Festival*
90015	NC	IANA	GAR	PTR	GAR	*Colchester Castle*

Below: *Operated by Abellio, the Greater Anglia franchise uses a fleet of 15 Class 90/0s for its core London Liverpool Street to Norwich route, powering rakes of Mk3 stock and DVTs, which are normally attached to the London end of formations. Locos are painted in a mix of older route liveries with Greater Anglia branding. Franchise changes in the near future are likely to see orders placed for high-quality EMUs to replace this loco-hauled fleet. No. 90002* Eastern Daily Press *is seen heading towards London Liverpool Street at Stratford.* **CJM**

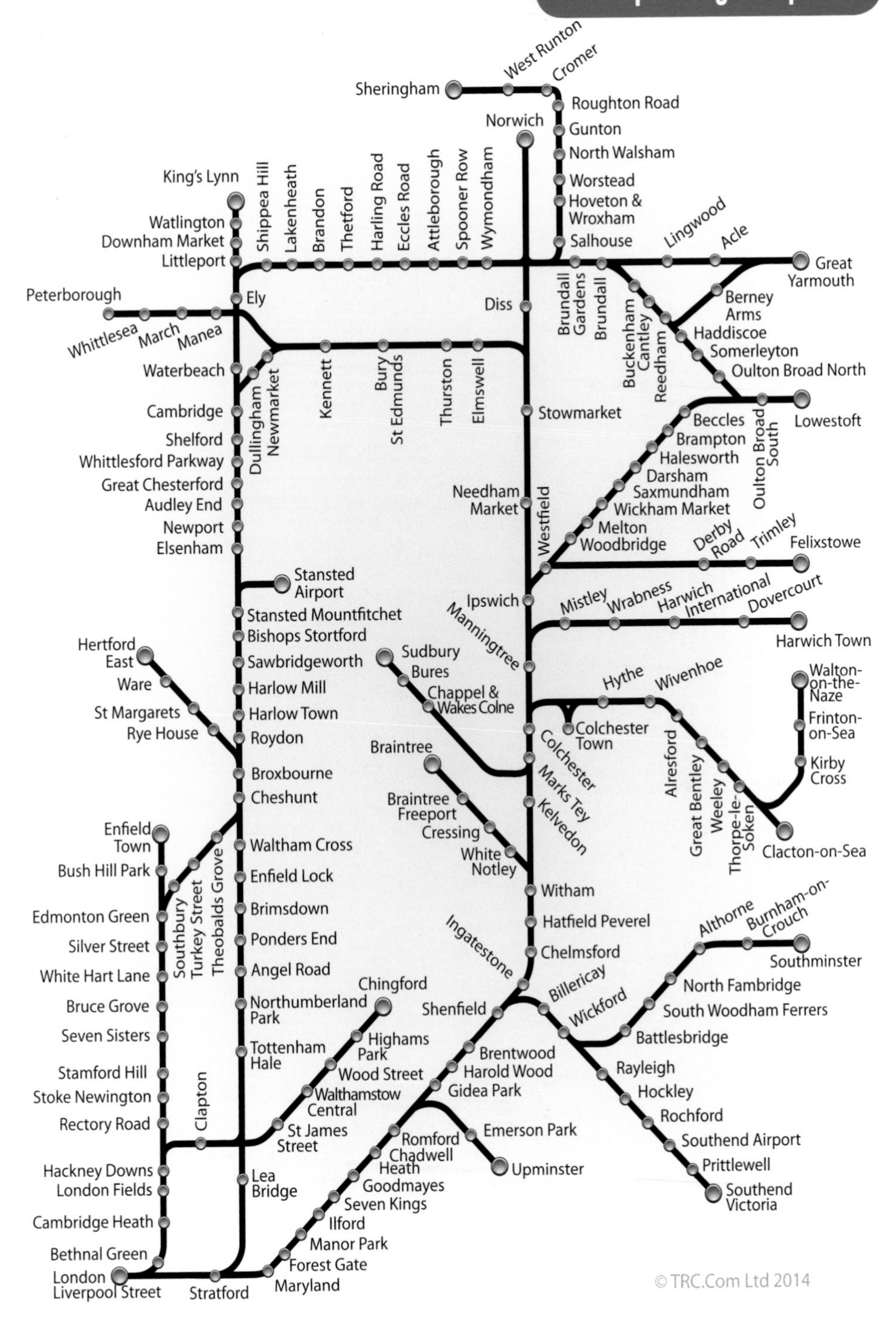

Sheringham
West Runton
Cromer
Roughton Road
Gunton
North Walsham
Worstead
Hoveton & Wroxham
Salhouse
Norwich
King's Lynn
Watlington
Downham Market
Littleport
Shippea Hill
Lakenheath
Brandon
Thetford
Harling Road
Eccles Road
Attleborough
Spooner Row
Wymondham
Brundall Gardens
Brundall
Lingwood
Acle
Great Yarmouth
Buckenham
Cantley
Reedham
Berney Arms
Haddiscoe
Somerleyton
Oulton Broad North
Lowestoft
Oulton Broad South
Peterborough
Whittlesea
March
Manea
Ely
Diss
Waterbeach
Dullingham
Newmarket
Kennett
Bury St Edmunds
Thurston
Elmswell
Stowmarket
Cambridge
Shelford
Whittlesford Parkway
Great Chesterford
Audley End
Newport
Elsenham
Beccles
Brampton
Halesworth
Darsham
Saxmundham
Wickham Market
Melton
Woodbridge
Needham Market
Westfield
Derby Road
Trimley
Felixstowe
Stansted Airport
Stansted Mountfitchet
Bishops Stortford
Sawbridgeworth
Harlow Mill
Harlow Town
Roydon
Broxbourne
Cheshunt
Ipswich
Manningtree
Mistley
Wrabness
Harwich International
Dovercourt
Harwich Town
Hertford East
Ware
St Margarets
Rye House
Sudbury
Bures
Chappel & Wakes Colne
Hythe
Wivenhoe
Colchester Town
Colchester
Walton-on-the-Naze
Frinton-on-Sea
Kirby Cross
Alresford
Great Bentley
Weeley
Thorpe-le-Soken
Clacton-on-Sea
Braintree
Braintree Freeport
Cressing
White Notley
Marks Tey
Kelvedon
Witham
Hatfield Peverel
Chelmsford
Ingatestone
Enfield Town
Bush Hill Park
Edmonton Green
Silver Street
White Hart Lane
Bruce Grove
Seven Sisters
Stamford Hill
Stoke Newington
Rectory Road
Hackney Downs
London Fields
Cambridge Heath
Bethnal Green
London Liverpool Street
Southbury
Turkey Street
Theobalds Grove
Waltham Cross
Enfield Lock
Brimsdown
Ponders End
Angel Road
Northumberland Park
Tottenham Hale
Clapton
Lea Bridge
Stratford
Chingford
Highams Park
Wood Street
Walthamstow Central
St James Street
Shenfield
Billericay
Wickford
Althorne
Burnham-on-Crouch
Southminster
North Fambridge
South Woodham Ferrers
Battlesbridge
Brentwood
Harold Wood
Gidea Park
Romford
Emerson Park
Upminster
Chadwell Heath
Goodmayes
Seven Kings
Ilford
Manor Park
Forest Gate
Maryland
Rayleigh
Hockley
Rochford
Southend Airport
Prittlewell
Southend Victoria
© TRC.Com Ltd 2014

Greater Anglia

Mk 3 Hauled Stock

Vehicle Length: 75ft 0in (22.86m) Width: 8ft 11in (2.71m)
Height: 12ft 9in (3.88m) Bogie Type: BT10

AJ1G - RFM *Seating 24F*

Number	Depot	Livery	Owner
10200 (40519)	NC	ORA	PTR
10203 (40506)	NC	GAR	PTR
10214 (11034)	NC	ORA	PTR
10216 (11041)	NC	ORA	PTR
10223 (11043)	NC	ORA	PTR
10228 (11035)	NC	GAR	PTR
10229 (11059)	NC	AWT	PTR
10247 (10011)	NC	ORA	PTR

AN2G - TSOB *Seating 52S*

Number	Depot	Livery	Owner
10401 (12168)	NC	GAR	PTR
10402 (12010)	NC	ORA	PTR
10403 (12135)	NC	ORA	PTR
10404 (12068)	NC	ORA	PTR
10405 (12137)	NC	ORA	PTR
10406 (12020)	NC	ORA	PTR

AD1G - FO, *FOD *Seating 48F/34F**

Number	Depot	Livery	Owner
11066	NC	ORA	PTR
11067	NC	ORA	PTR
11068	NC	GAR	PTR
11069	NC	ORA	PTR
11070	NC	ORA	PTR
11072*	NC	ORA	PTR
11073*	NC	GAR	PTR
11075	NC	ORA	PTR
11076	NC	ORA	PTR
11077	NC	ORA	PTR
11078*	NC	ORA	PTR
11080	NC	ORA	PTR
11081	NC	ORA	PTR
11082	NC	GAR	PTR
11085*	NC	ORA	PTR
11087*	NC	GAR	PTR
11088*	NC	GAR	PTR
11090*	NC	ORA	PTR
11091*	NC	GAR	PTR
11092	NC	ORA	PTR
11093*	NC	ORA	PTR
11094*	NC	ORA	PTR
11095*	NC	ORA	PTR
11096*	NC	ORA	PTR
11098*	NC	ORA	PTR
11099*	NC	ORA	PTR
11100*	NC	GAR	PTR
11101*	NC	ORA	PTR

AC2G - TSO *Seating 80S*

Number	Depot	Livery	Owner
12005	NC	ORA	PTR
12009	NC	ORA	PTR
12012	NC	ORA	PTR
12013	NC	ORA	PTR
12015	NC	ORA	PTR
12016	NC	ORA	PTR
12019	NC	ORA	PTR
12021	NC	GAR	PTR
12024	NC	ORA	PTR
12026	NC	ORA	PTR
12027	NC	GAR	PTR
12030	NC	ORA	PTR
12031	NC	ORA	PTR
12032	NC	ORA	PTR
12034	NC	ORA	PTR
12035	NC	GAR	PTR
12037	NC	ORA	PTR
12040	NC	ORA	PTR
12041	NC	ORA	PTR
12042	NC	ORA	PTR
12046	NC	ORA	PTR
12049	NC	ORA	PTR
12051	NC	GAR	PTR
12056	NC	ORA	PTR
12057	NC	ORA	PTR
12060	NC	ORA	PTR
12061	NC	ORA	PTR
12062	NC	ORA	PTR
12064	NC	ORA	PTR
12066	NC	ORA	PTR
12067	NC	ORA	PTR
12073	NC	ORA	PTR
12079	NC	ORA	PTR
12081	NC	ORA	PTR
12082	NC	ORA	PTR
12084	NC	GAR	PTR
12089	NC	ORA	PTR
12090	NC	ORA	PTR
12091	NC	ORA	PTR
12093	NC	ORA	PTR
12097	NC	GAR	PTR
12098	NC	ORA	PTR
12099	NC	ORA	PTR
12103	NC	ORA	PTR
12105	NC	ORA	PTR
12107	NC	ORA	PTR
12108	NC	GAR	PTR
12109	NC	ORA	PTR
12110	NC	ORA	PTR
12111	NC	GAR	PTR
12114	NC	GAR	PTR
12115	NC	ORA	PTR
12116	NC	ORA	PTR
12118	NC	GAR	PTR
12120	NC	ORA	PTR
12125	NC	ORA	PTR
12126	NC	ORA	PTR
12129	NC	GAR	PTR
12130	NC	ORA	PTR
12132	NC	GAR	PTR
12137	NC	ORA	PTR
12139	NC	ORA	PTR
12141	NC	ORA	PTR
12143	NC	ORA	PTR
12146	NC	GAR	PTR
12147	NC	ORA	PTR
12148	NC	ORA	PTR
12150	NC	ORA	PTR
12151	NC	ORA	PTR
12153	NC	GAR	PTR
12154	NC	ORA	PTR
12159	NC	ORA	PTR
12164	NC	ORA	PTR
12166	NC	ORA	PTR
12167	NC	ORA	PTR
12170	NC	ORA	PTR
12171	NC	ORA	PTR

NZAH - DVT

Number	Depot	Livery	Owner
82102	NC	ORA	PTR
82103§	NC	ORA	PTR
82105	NC	ORA	PTR
82107	NC	GAR	PTR
82112	NC	ORA	PTR
82114	NC	ORA	PTR
82118	NC	GAR	PTR
82121	NC	ORA	PTR
82127	NC	ORA	PTR
82132	NC	ORA	PTR
82133	NC	ORA	PTR
82136	NC	ORA	PTR
82139	NC	ORA	PTR
82143	NC	GAR	PTR
82152	NC	ORA	PTR

§ Fitted with de-icing equipment

Left: *The vast majority of Greater Anglia Mk3 passenger vehicles, allocated to Norwich, retain their older liveries with Greater Anglia branding; however, a few which have passed through works have been outshopped in an all-white livery with operator branding on the side and blue passenger doors, as demonstrated by vehicle No. 12139 at Ipswich.* **Nathan Williamson**

Class 153

Vehicle Length: 76ft 5in (23.29m)
Height: 12ft 3⅛in (3.75m)
Width: 8ft 10in (2.70m)
Engine: 1 x NT855R5 of 285hp
Horsepower: 285hp (213kW)
Seats (total/car): 72S

Number	Formation DMSL	Depot	Livery	Owner	Operator	Name
153306	52306	NC	AWT	PTR	GAR	
153309	52309	NC	AWT	PTR	GAR	*Gerard Fiennes*
153314	52314	NC	ORA	PTR	GAR	
153322	52322	NC	AWT	PTR	GAR	*Benjamin Britten*
153335	52335	NC	AWT	PTR	GAR	*Michael Palin*

Above: *Some of the Anglia branch lines are operated by a fleet of five Class 153 'bubble-cars', based at Norwich, these vehicles tend to be used on the low-patronage lines. The application of Abellio white livery had extended to four of the vehicles by the end of 2013. No. 153306 (52306) is seen at Ipswich from its original (large) cab end.* **Nathan Williamson**

Class 156

Vehicle Length: 75ft 6in (23.03m)
Height: 12ft 6in (3.81m)
Width: 8ft 11in (2.73m)
Engine: 1 x Cummins NT855R5 of 285hp
Horsepower: 570hp (425kW)
Seats (total/car): 146S, 70/76S

Number	Formation DMSL+DMS	Depot	Livery	Owner	Operator
156402	52402+57402	NC	AWT	PTR	GAR
156407	52407+57407	NC	ADV	PTR	GAR
156409	52409+57409	NC	AWT	PTR	GAR
156412	52412+57412	NC	AWT	PTR	GAR
156416	52416+57416	NC	AWT	PTR	GAR
156417	52417+57417	NC	ADV	PTR	GAR
156418	52418+57418	NC	AWT	PTR	GAR
156419	52419+57419	NC	AWT	PTR	GAR
156422	52422+57422	NC	AWT	PTR	GAR

Name applied

156416	*Saint Edmund*

Right: *Nine Class 156 Metro-Cammell 'express' sets are allocated to Norwich Crown Point for Greater Anglia branch-line use. Owned by Porterbrook, these are in the process of being repainted into white livery with orange passenger doors. Complete with yellow snowplough, No. 156422 is illustrated.* **Nathan Williamson**

Greater Anglia

Class 170/2 *Turbostar*

Vehicle Length: 77ft 6in (23.62m)
Height: 12ft 4½in (3.77m)
Width: 8ft 10in (2.69m)
Engine: 1 x MTU 6R 183TD13H 422hp per vehicle
Horsepower: 1,266hp (944kW)
Seats (total/car): 7F-173S 7F-39S/68S/66S

Number	Formation DMCL+MSL+DMSL	Depot	Livery	Owner	Operator
170201	50201+56201+79201	NC	ORA	PTR	GAR
170202	50202+56202+79202	NC	ORA	PTR	GAR
170203	50203+56203+79203	NC	ORA	PTR	GAR
170204	50204+56204+79204	NC	ORA	PTR	GAR
170205	50205+56205+79205	NC	ORA	PTR	GAR
170206	50206+56206+79206	NC	ORA	PTR	GAR
170207	50207+56207+79207	NC	ORA	PTR	GAR
170208	50208+56208+79208	NC	ADV	PTR	GAR

Vehicle Length: 77ft 6in (23.62m)
Height: 12ft 4½in (3.77m)
Width: 8ft 10in (2.69m)
Engine: 1 x MTU 6R 183TD13H 422hp per vehicle
Horsepower: 844hp (629kW)
Seats (total/car): 9F-110S 57S/9F-53S

Number	Formation DMSL+DMCL	Depot	Livery	Owner	Operator
170270	50270+79270	NC	ORA	PTR	GAR
170271	50271+79271	NC	ANN	PTR	GAR
170272	50272+79272	NC	ANN	PTR	GAR
170273	50273+79273	NC	ANN	PTR	GAR

Left: *Greater Anglia has two fleets of Class 170s based at Norwich for longer-distance routes. Both two- (four sets) and three-car (eight sets), allocated the sub-Class 170/2, are in traffic. The three-car sets are in the One railway livery with Greater Anglia branding, one of the two-car sets sports One railway colours with Greater Anglia branding, with three carrying the original Anglia white and green colours with Greater Anglia branding. Route advertising livery is applied to No. 170208. Set No. 170201 is illustrated at Norwich.* **Nathan Williamson**

Class 315

Vehicle Length: (Driving) 64ft 11½in (19.80m)
(Inter) 65ft 4½in (19.92m)
Height: 11ft 6½in (3.58m)
Width: 9ft 3in (2.82m)
Horsepower: 880hp (656kW)
Seats (total/car): 318S, 74S/86S/84S/74S

Number	Formation DMSO(A)+TSO+PTSO+DMSO(B)	Depot	Livery	Owner	Operator	Name
315801	64461+71281+71389+64462	IL	AWT	EVL	GAR	
315802	64463+71282+71390+64464	IL	AWT	EVL	GAR	
315803	64465+71283+71391+64466	IL	AWT	EVL	GAR	
315804	64467+71284+71392+64468	IL	AWT	EVL	GAR	
315805	64469+71285+71393+64470	IL	AWT	EVL	GAR	
315806	64471+71286+71394+64472	IL	AWT	EVL	GAR	
315807	64473+71287+71395+64474	IL	ORA	EVL	GAR	
315808	64475+71288+71396+64476	IL	AWT	EVL	GAR	
315809	64477+71289+71397+64478	IL	AWT	EVL	GAR	
315810	64479+71290+71398+64480	IL	AWT	EVL	GAR	
315811	64481+71291+71399+64482	IL	ORA	EVL	GAR	
315812	64483+71292+71400+64484	IL	AWT	EVL	GAR	
315813	64485+71293+71401+64486	IL	AWT	EVL	GAR	
315814	64487+71294+71402+64488	IL	AWT	EVL	GAR	
315815	64489+71295+71403+64490	IL	AWT	EVL	GAR	
315816	64491+71296+71404+64492	IL	AWT	EVL	GAR	
315817	64493+71297+71405+64494	IL	ORA	EVL	GAR	*Transport for London*
315818	64495+71298+71406+64496	IL	ORA	EVL	GAR	

315819	64497+71299+71407+64498	IL	ORA	EVL	GAR	
315820	64499+71300+71408+64500	IL	ORA	EVL	GAR	
315821	64501+71301+71409+64502	IL	AWT	EVL	GAR	
315822	64503+71302+71410+64504	IL	AWT	EVL	GAR	
315823	64505+71303+71411+64506	IL	AWT	EVL	GAR	
315824	64507+71304+71412+64508	IL	ORA	EVL	GAR	
315825	64509+71305+71413+64510	IL	ORA	EVL	GAR	
315826	64511+71306+71414+64512	IL	ORA	EVL	GAR	
315827	64513+71307+71415+64514	IL	AWT	EVL	GAR	
315828	64515+71308+71416+64516	IL	AWT	EVL	GAR	
315829	64517+71309+71417+64518	IL	AWT	EVL	GAR	*London Borough of Havering Celebrating 40 Years*
315830	64519+71310+71418+64520	IL	ORA	EVL	GAR	
315831	64521+71311+71419+64522	IL	AWT	EVL	GAR	
315832	64523+71312+71420+64524	IL	AWT	EVL	GAR	
315833	64525+71313+71421+64526	IL	ORA	EVL	GAR	
315834	64527+71314+71422+64528	IL	ORA	EVL	GAR	
315835	64529+71315+71423+64530	IL	ORA	EVL	GAR	
315836	64531+71316+71424+64532	IL	ORA	EVL	GAR	
315837	64533+71317+71425+64534	IL	ORA	EVL	GAR	
315838	64535+71318+71426+64536	IL	ORA	EVL	GAR	
315839	64537+71319+71427+64538	IL	ORA	EVL	GAR	
315840	64539+71320+71428+64540	IL	ORA	EVL	GAR	
315841	64541+71321+71429+64542	IL	ORA	EVL	GAR	
315842	64543+71322+71430+64544	IL	ORA	EVL	GAR	
315843	64545+71323+71431+64546	IL	ORA	EVL	GAR	
315844	64547+71324+71432+64548	IL	ORA	EVL	GAR	
315845	64549+71325+71433+64550	IL	AWT	EVL	GAR	*Herbie Woodward*
315846	64551+71326+71434+64552	IL	ORA	EVL	GAR	
315847	64553+71327+71435+64554	IL	ORA	EVL	GAR	
315848	64555+71328+71436+64556	IL	ORA	EVL	GAR	
315849	64557+71329+71437+64558	IL	ORA	EVL	GAR	
315850	64559+71330+71438+64560	IL	NXU	EVL	GAR	
315851	64561+71331+71439+64562	IL	ORA	EVL	GAR	
315852	64563+71332+71440+64564	IL	ORA	EVL	GAR	
315853	64565+71333+71441+64566	IL	ORA	EVL	GAR	
315854	64567+71334+71442+64568	IL	ORA	EVL	GAR	
315855	64569+71335+71443+64570	IL	AWT	EVL	GAR	
315856	64571+71336+71444+64572	IL	ORA	EVL	GAR	
315857	64573+71337+71445+64574	IL	ORA	EVL	GAR	
315858	64575+71338+71446+64576	IL	ORA	EVL	GAR	
315859	64577+71339+71447+64578	IL	ORA	EVL	GAR	
315860	64579+71340+71448+64580	IL	ORA	EVL	GAR	
315861	64581+71341+71449+64582	IL	ORA	EVL	GAR	

Right: *A fleet of 61 1972-design four-car EMUs presently forms the backbone of metro services operated by Greater Anglia from Liverpool Street to Shenfield. Following the opening of CrossRail many of these local services will be operated by the new through east-west connection and the '315s' are likely to be withdrawn from service. Sets are presently in the process of being repainted from blue to the standard Greater Anglia base white livery with orange doors. Set No. 315832 is illustrated passing Pudding Mill Lane near Stratford.* **CJM**

Greater Anglia

Class 317/5

Vehicle Length: (Driving) 65ft 0¾in (19.83m) (Inter) 65ft 4¼in (19.92m) Height: 12ft 1½in (3.58m) Width: 9ft 3in (2.82m) Horsepower: 1,000hp (746kW) Seats (total/car): 291S, 74S/79S/68S/70S

Number	Former Number	Formation DTSO(A)+MSO+TCO+DTSO(B)	Depot	Livery	Owner	Operator	Name
317501	(317301)	77024+62661+71577+77048	IL	GAR	ANG	GAR	
317502	(317302)	77001+62662+71578+77049	IL	GAR	ANG	GAR	
317503	(317303)	77002+62663+71579+77050	IL	GAR	ANG	GAR	
317504	(317304)	77003+62664+71580+77051	IL	GAR	ANG	GAR	
317505	(317305)	77004+62665+71581+77052	IL	GAR	ANG	GAR	
317506	(317306)	77005+62666+71582+77053	IL	GAR	ANG	GAR	
317507	(317307)	77006+62667+71583+77054	IL	GAR	ANG	GAR	University of Cambridge 800 years 1209-2009
317508	(317311)	77010+62697+71587+77058	IL	GAR	ANG	GAR	
317509	(317312)	77011+62672+71588+77059	IL	GAR	ANG	GAR	
317510	(317313)	77012+62673+71589+77060	IL	GAR	ANG	GAR	
317511	(317315)	77014+62675+71591+77062	IL	NXU	ANG	GAR	
317512	(317316)	77015+62676+71592+77063	IL	NXU	ANG	GAR	
317513	(317317)	77016+62677+71593+77064	IL	GAR	ANG	GAR	
317514	(317318)	77017+62678+71594+77065	IL	GAR	ANG	GAR	
317515	(317320)	77019+62680+71596+77067	IL	GAR	ANG	GAR	

Class 317/6

Vehicle Length: (Driving) 65ft 0¾in (19.83m) (Inter) 65ft 4¼in (19.92m) Height: 12ft 1½in (3.58m) Width: 9ft 3in (2.82m) Horsepower: 1,000hp (746kW) Seats (total/car): 24F/244S, 64S/70S/62S/24F-48S

Number	Former Number	Formation DTSO+MSO+TSO+DTCO	Depot	Livery	Owner	Operator	Name
317649	(317349)	77200+62846+71734+77220	IL	NXU	ANG	GAR	
317650	(317350)	77201+62847+71735+77221	IL	NXU	ANG	GAR	
317651	(317351)	77202+62848+71736+77222	IL	NXU	ANG	GAR	
317652	(317352)	77203+62849+71739+77223	IL	NXU	ANG	GAR	
317653	(317353)	77204+62850+71738+77224	IL	NXU	ANG	GAR	
317654	(317354)	77205+62851+71737+77225	IL	NXU	ANG	GAR	Richard Wells
317655	(317355)	77206+62852+71740+77226	IL	ORA	ANG	GAR	
317656	(317356)	77207+62853+71742+77227	IL	AWT	ANG	GAR	
317657	(317357)	77208+62854+71741+77228	IL	NXU	ANG	GAR	
317658	(317358)	77209+62855+71743+77229	IL	NXU	ANG	GAR	
317659	(317359)	77210+62856+71744+77230	IL	AWT	ANG	GAR	
317660	(317360)	77211+62857+71745+77231	IL	AWT	ANG	GAR	
317661	(317361)	77212+62858+71746+77232	IL	AWT	ANG	GAR	
317662	(317362)	77213+62859+71747+77233	IL	AWT	ANG	GAR	
317663	(317363)	77214+62860+71748+77234	IL	AWT	ANG	GAR	
317664	(317364)	77215+62861+71749+77235	IL	AWT	ANG	GAR	
317665	(317365)	77216+62862+71750+77236	IL	AWT	ANG	GAR	
317666	(317366)	77217+62863+71752+77237	IL	NXU	ANG	GAR	
317667	(317367)	77218+62864+71751+77238	IL	AWT	ANG	GAR	
317668	(317368)	77219+62865+71753+77239	IL	AWT	ANG	GAR	
317669	(317369)	77280+62886+71762+77284	IL	NXU	ANG	GAR	
317670	(317370)	77281+62887+71763+77285	IL	AWT	ANG	GAR	
317671	(317371)	77282+62888+71764+77286	IL	AWT	ANG	GAR	
317672	(317372)	77283+62889+71765+77287	IL	AWT	ANG	GAR	

Class 317/8

Vehicle Length: (Driving) 65ft 0¾in (19.83m) (Inter) 65ft 4¼in (19.92m) Height: 12ft 1½in (3.58m) Width: 9ft 3in (2.82m) Horsepower: 1,000hp (746kW) Seats (total/car): 20F/265S, 74S/79S/20F-42S/70S

Number	Former Number	Formation DTSO(A)+MSO+TCO+DTSO(B)	Depot	Livery	Owner	Operator	Name
317881	(317321)	77020+62681+71597+77068	IL	GAR	ANG	GAR	
317882	(317324)	77023+62684+71600+77071	IL	NXU	ANG	GAR	
317883	(317325)	77000+62685+71601+77072	IL	NXU	ANG	GAR	
317884	(317326)	77025+62686+71602+77073	IL	NXU	ANG	GAR	
317885	(317327)	77026+62687+71603+77074	IL	NXU	ANG	GAR	
317886	(317328)	77027+62688+71604+77075	IL	NXU	ANG	GAR	
317887	(317330)	77043+62704+71606+77077	IL	NXU	ANG	GAR	
317888	(317331)	77030+62691+71607+77078	IL	GAR	ANG	GAR	

317889	(317333)	77032+62693+71609+77080	IL	GAR	ANG	GAR	
317890	(317334)	77033+62694+71610+77081	IL	GAR	ANG	GAR	
317891	(317335)	77034+62695+71611+77082	IL	GAR	ANG	GAR	
317892	(317336)	77035+62696+71612+77083	IL	GAR	ANG	GAR	*Ilford Depot*

Below: *The outer-suburban Anglia services are operated by a fleet of Class 317s based at Ilford and owned by Angel Trains Leasing. Two different body designs are in traffic, phase 1 and phase 2, which mainly affects window and cab-end design. One of the later phase 2 sets, No. 317649 (the original 317349), is illustrated at Stratford painted in Greater Anglia white livery with blue passenger doors.* **CJM**

Class 317/7 No. 317722 is in traffic based at Ilford as a traction and rolling stock development train, fitted with different interior layouts. The set is formed of vehicles 77021+62682+71598+77069.

Class 321/3

Vehicle Length: (Driving) 65ft 0¾in (19.83m) (Inter) 65ft 4¼in (19.92m)
Height: 12ft 4¾in (3.78m)
Width: 9ft 3in (2.82m)
Horsepower: 1,328hp (996kW)
Seats (total/car): 16F/292S, 16F-57S/82S/75S/78S

Number	*Formation DTCO+MSO+TSO+DTSO*	*Depot*	*Livery*	*Owner*	*Operator*	*Name*
321301	78049+62975+71880+77853	IL	GAR	EVL	GAR	
321302	78050+62976+71881+77854	IL	GAR	EVL	GAR	
321303	78051+62977+71882+77855	IL	GAR	EVL	GAR	
321304	78052+62978+71883+77856	IL	GAR	EVL	GAR	
321305	78053+62979+71884+77857	IL	GAR	EVL	GAR	
321306	78054+62980+71885+77858	IL	GAR	EVL	GAR	
321307	78055+62981+71886+77859	IL	GAR	EVL	GAR	
321308	78056+62982+71887+77860	IL	GAR	EVL	GAR	
321309	78057+62983+71888+77861	IL	GAR	EVL	GAR	
321310	78058+62984+71889+77862	IL	NGE	EVL	GAR	
321311	78059+62985+71890+77863	IL	GAR	EVL	GAR	
321312	78060+62986+71891+77864	IL	GAR	EVL	GAR	*Southend-on-Sea*
321313	78061+62987+71892+77865	IL	GAR	EVL	GAR	*University of Essex*
321314	78062+62988+71893+77866	IL	NGE	EVL	GAR	
321315	78063+62989+71894+77867	IL	GAR	EVL	GAR	
321316	78064+62990+71895+77868	IL	GAR	EVL	GAR	
321317	78065+62991+71896+77869	IL	GAR	EVL	GAR	
321318	78066+62992+71897+77870	IL	GAR	EVL	GAR	
321319	78067+62993+71898+77871	IL	GAR	EVL	GAR	
321320	78068+62994+71899+77872	IL	GAR	EVL	GAR	
321321	78069+62995+71900+77873	IL	GAR	EVL	GAR	*NSPCC Essex Full Stop*
321322	78070+62996+71901+77874	IL	GAR	EVL	GAR	
321323	78071+62997+71902+77875	IL	GAR	EVL	GAR	
321324	78072+62998+71903+77876	IL	GAR	EVL	GAR	
321325	78073+62999+71904+77877	IL	GAR	EVL	GAR	
321326	78074+63000+71905+77878	IL	GAR	EVL	GAR	

Greater Anglia

321327	78075+63001+71906+77879	IL	NXU	EVL	GAR	
321328	78076+63002+71907+77880	IL	GAR	EVL	GAR	
321329	78077+63003+71908+77881	IL	GAR	EVL	GAR	
321330	78078+63004+71909+77882	IL	NXU	EVL	GAR	
321331	78079+63005+71910+77883	IL	NXU	EVL	GAR	
321332	78080+63006+71911+77884	IL	NXU	EVL	GAR	
321333	78081+63007+71912+77885	IL	NXU	EVL	GAR	*Amsterdam*
321334	78082+63008+71913+77886	IL	NXU	EVL	GAR	
321335	78083+63009+71914+77887	IL	NXU	EVL	GAR	*Geoffrey Freeman Allen*
321336	78084+63010+71915+77888	IL	NXU	EVL	GAR	
321337	78085+63011+71916+77889	IL	NXU	EVL	GAR	
321338	78086+63012+71917+77890	IL	NXU	EVL	GAR	
321339	78087+63013+71918+77891	IL	NXU	EVL	GAR	
321340	78088+63014+71919+77892	IL	NXU	EVL	GAR	
321341	78089+63015+71920+77893	IL	NXU	EVL	GAR	
321342	78090+63016+71921+77894	IL	NXU	EVL	GAR	*R Barnes*
321343	78091+63017+71922+77895	IL	NXU	EVL	GAR	
321344	78092+63018+71923+77896	IL	NXU	EVL	GAR	
321345	78093+63019+71924+77897	IL	NXU	EVL	GAR	
321346	78094+63020+71925+77898	IL	NGU	EVL	GAR	
321347	78131+63105+71991+78280	IL	NXU	EVL	GAR	
321348	78132+63106+71992+78281	IL	NXU	EVL	GAR	
321349	78133+63107+71993+78282	IL	NGE	EVL	GAR	
321350	78134+63108+71994+78283	IL	NXU	EVL	GAR	*Gurkha*
321351	78135+63109+71995+78284	IL	NXU	EVL	GAR	*London Southend Airport*
321352	78136+63110+71996+78285	IL	NXU	EVL	GAR	
321353	78137+63111+71997+78286	IL	NXU	EVL	GAR	
321354	78138+63112+71998+78287	IL	NXU	EVL	GAR	
321355	78139+63113+71999+78288	IL	NXU	EVL	GAR	
321356	78140+63114+72000+78289	IL	NGU	EVL	GAR	
321357	78141+63115+72001+78290	IL	NGE	EVL	GAR	
321358	78142+63116+72002+78291	IL	NXU	EVL	GAR	
321359	78143+63117+72003+78292	IL	AWT	EVL	GAR	
321360	78144+63118+72004+78293	IL	NXU	EVL	GAR	*Phoenix*
321361	78145+63119+72005+78294	IL	AWT	EVL	GAR	
321362	78146+63120+72006+78295	IL	AWT	EVL	GAR	
321363	78147+63121+72007+78296	IL	AWT	EVL	GAR	
321364	78148+63122+72008+78297	IL	AWT	EVL	GAR	
321365	78149+63123+72009+78298	IL	AWT	EVL	GAR	
321366	78150+63124+72010+78299	IL	AWT	EVL	GAR	

Below: *The core outer-suburban fleet operating for the Greater Anglia franchise is Class 321 sets: 66 Class 321/3s built for the Great Eastern operation and 28 Class 321/4s originally built for use on the southern end of the West Coast. The four-car sets are all based at Ilford and owned by Eversholt Leasing. The majority are painted in base white livery with Greater Anglia branding. Set No. 321338 is seen approaching Stratford from Liverpool Street.* **CJM**

Class 321/4

Vehicle Length: (Driving) 65ft 0¾in (19.83m) (Inter) 65ft 4¼in (19.92m)
Height: 12ft 4¾in (3.78m)
Width: 9ft 3in (2.82m)
Horsepower: 1,328hp (996kW)
Seats (total/car): 16F/283S, 16F-52S/79S/74S/78S

Number	Formation DTCO+MSO+TSO+DTSO	Depot	Livery	Owner	Operator	Name
321421	78115+63083+71969+77963	IL	NXU	EVL	GAR	
321422	78116+63084+71970+77964	IL	NXU	EVL	GAR	
321423	78117+63085+71971+77965	IL	NXU	EVL	GAR	
321424	78118+63086+71972+77966	IL	GAR	EVL	GAR	
321425	78119+63087+71973+77967	IL	AWT	EVL	GAR	
321426	78120+63088+71974+77968	IL	GAR	EVL	GAR	
321427	78121+63089+71975+77969	IL	GAR	EVL	GAR	
321428	78122+63090+71976+77970	IL	AWT	EVL	GAR	*The Essex Commuter*
321429	78123+69031+71977+77971	IL	GAR	EVL	GAR	
321430	78124+63092+71978+77972	IL	GAR	EVL	GAR	
321431	78151+63125+72011+78300	IL	GAR	EVL	GAR	
321432	78152+63126+72012+78301	IL	NXU	EVL	GAR	
321433	78153+63127+72013+78302	IL	NXU	EVL	GAR	
321434	78154+63128+72014+78303	IL	NXU	EVL	GAR	
321435	78155+63129+72015+78304	IL	NXU	EVL	GAR	
321436	78156+63130+72016+78305	IL	NXU	EVL	GAR	
321437	78157+63131+72017+78306	IL	NXU	EVL	GAR	
321438	78158+63132+72018+78307	IL	AWT	EVL	GAR	
321439	78159+63133+72019+78308	IL	AWT	EVL	GAR	
321440	78160+63134+72020+78309	IL	AWT	EVL	GAR	
321441	78161+63135+72021+78310	IL	AWT	EVL	GAR	
321442	78162+63136+72022+78311	IL	AWT	EVL	GAR	
321443	78125+63099+71985+78274	IL	AWT	EVL	GAR	
321444	78126+63100+71986+78275	IL	AWT	EVL	GAR	*Essex Lifeboats*
321445	78127+63101+71987+78276	IL	AWT	EVL	GAR	
321446	78128+63102+71988+78277	IL	AWT	EVL	GAR	*George Mullings*
321447	78129+63103+71989+78278	IL	AWT	EVL	GAR	
321448	78130+63104+71990+78279	IL	ADV	EVL	§	

§ Eversholt development train consisting of two vehicles with Metro interior and two with suburban, seating 246 passengers and allocated to Ilford for demonstration running on Greater Anglia services

Below: *After being displaced from West Coast Main Line duties by the introduction of Class 350 stock, the Class 321s were largely transferred to the Great Eastern network to work alongside the Class 321/3s. Slight detail differences in interior design exist between the two sub-classes. With its DTCO vehicle nearest the camera, set No. 321444 is seen at Stratford.* **CJM**

Greater Anglia

Class 360/1
Desiro

Vehicle Length: 66ft 9in (20.4m)
Height: 12ft 1½in (3.7m)
Width: 9ft 2in (2.79m)
Horsepower: 1,341hp (1,000kW)
Seats (total/car): 16F/265S, 8F-59S/69S/78S/8F-59S

Number	*Formation* DMCO(A)+PTSO+TSO+DMCO(B)	*Depot*	*Livery*	*Owner*	*Operator*
360101	65551+72551+74551+68551	IL	FNA	ANG	GAR
360102	65552+72552+74552+68552	IL	FNA	ANG	GAR
360103	65553+72553+74553+68553	IL	FNA	ANG	GAR
360104	65554+72554+74554+68554	IL	FNA	ANG	GAR
360105	65555+72555+74555+68555	IL	FNA	ANG	GAR
360106	65556+72556+74556+68556	IL	FNA	ANG	GAR
360107	65557+72557+74557+68557	IL	FNA	ANG	GAR
360108	65558+72558+74558+68558	IL	FNA	ANG	GAR
360109	65559+72559+74559+68559	IL	FNA	ANG	GAR
360110	65560+72560+74560+68560	IL	FNA	ANG	GAR
360111	65561+72561+74561+68561	IL	FNA	ANG	GAR
360112	65562+72562+74562+68562	IL	FNA	ANG	GAR
360113	65563+72563+74563+68563	IL	FNA	ANG	GAR
360114	65564+72564+74564+68564	IL	FNA	ANG	GAR
360115	65565+72565+74565+68565	IL	ENA	ANG	GAR
360116	65566+72566+74566+68566	IL	FNA	ANG	GAR
360117	65567+72567+74567+68567	IL	FNA	ANG	GAR
360118	65568+72568+74568+68568	IL	FNA	ANG	GAR
360119	65569+72569+74569+68569	IL	FNA	ANG	GAR
360120	65570+72570+74570+68570	IL	FNA	ANG	GAR
360121	65571+72571+74571+68571	IL	FNA	ANG	GAR

Left: *As part of the modernisation of the privatised railway under First, a fleet of 21 state-of-the art Class 360/1 'Desiro' units was introduced, built by Siemens. The sets were finished in First blue, which later carried National Express and more recently Greater Anglia branding. Set No. 360108 is illustrated. The Class 360s are based at Ilford and owned by Angel Trains.* **CJM**

Class 379
Electrostar

Vehicle Length: (Driving) 66ft 9in (20.40m)
(Inter) 65ft 6in (19.99m)
Height: 12ft 4in (3.77m)
Width: 9ft 2in (2.80m)
Horsepower: 2,010hp (1,500kW)
Seats (total/car): 20F/189S, 60S/62S/43S/20F-24S

Number	*Formation* DMSO(A)+MSO+TSO+DMCO	*Depot*	*Livery*	*Owner*	*Operator*	*Name*
379001	61201+61701+61901+62101	IL	NXU	MAG	GAR	
379002	61202+61702+61902+62102	IL	NXU	MAG	GAR	
379003	61203+61703+61903+62103	IL	NXU	MAG	GAR	
379004	61204+61704+61904+62104	IL	NXU	MAG	GAR	
379005	61205+61705+61905+62105	IL	NXU	MAG	GAR	*Stansted Express*
379006	61206+61706+61906+62106	IL	NXU	MAG	GAR	
379007	61207+61707+61907+62107	IL	NXU	MAG	GAR	
379008	61208+61708+61908+62108	IL	NXU	MAG	GAR	
379009	61209+61709+61909+62109	IL	NXU	MAG	GAR	
379010	61210+61710+61910+62110	IL	NXU	MAG	GAR	
379011	61211+61711+61911+62111	IL	NXU	MAG	GAR	*Ely Cathedral*
379012	61212+61712+61912+62112	IL	NXU	MAG	GAR	*The West Anglian*
379013	61213+61713+61913+62113	IL	NXU	MAG	GAR	
379014	61214+61714+61914+62114	IL	NXU	MAG	GAR	

379015	61215+61715+61915+62115	IL	NXU	MAG	GAR	*City of Cambridge*
379016	61216+61716+61916+62116	IL	NXU	MAG	GAR	
379017	61217+61717+61917+62117	IL	NXU	MAG	GAR	
379018	61218+61718+61918+62118	IL	NXU	MAG	GAR	
379019	61219+61719+61919+62119	IL	NXU	MAG	GAR	
379020	61220+61720+61920+62120	IL	NXU	MAG	GAR	
379021	61221+61721+61921+62121	IL	NXU	MAG	GAR	
379022	61222+61722+61922+62122	IL	NXU	MAG	GAR	
379023	61223+61723+61923+62123	IL	NXU	MAG	GAR	
379024	61224+61724+61924+62124	IL	NXU	MAG	GAR	
379025	61225+61725+61925+62125	IL	NXU	MAG	GAR	*Go Discover*
379026	61226+61726+61926+62126	IL	NXU	MAG	GAR	
379027	61227+61727+61927+62127	IL	NXU	MAG	GAR	
379028	61228+61728+61928+62128	IL	NXU	MAG	GAR	
379029	61229+61729+61929+62129	IL	NXU	MAG	GAR	
379030	61230+61730+61930+62130	IL	NXU	MAG	GAR	

Right and below: *The most modern fleet of EMUs operated by Greater Anglia is a batch of 30 four-car Class 379 'Electrostar' sets built by Bombardier and mainly used on the Liverpool Street to Cambridge and Stansted Airport corridor. The sets are branded both Greater Anglia and Stansted Express. On the right is TSO No. 61925, and below is set No. 379007 arriving at Downham Market.* **Antony Christie / John Binch**

Fleet development: *It was announced in 2013 that a trial fitting of a traction battery system would be tested on a Class 379, to provide restricted traction in the event of power failure or loss.*

Heathrow Express / Heathrow Connect

Address: ✉ 6th Floor, 50 Eastbourne Terrace, Paddington, London, W2 6LX

queries@heathrowexpress.com or queries@heathrowconnect.com

✆ 020 8750 6600

ⓘ www.heathrowexpress.com or www.heathrowconnect.com

Managing Director: Keith Greenfield

Franchise Dates: Private Open Access Operator

Principal Routes: London Paddington - Heathrow Airport

Owned Stations: Heathrow Central, Heathrow Terminal 4, Heathrow Terminal 5

Depots: Old Oak Common HEX (OH)

Parent Company: Heathrow Express - Heathrow Airport Ltd
Heathrow Connect - Heathrow Airport Ltd / First Group

Heathrow Express

Heathrow Airport Terminal 5 — Heathrow Airport Terminals 1-3 — London Paddington

Heathrow Connect

Heathrow Airport Terminal 4 — Heathrow Airport Terminals 1-3 — Hayes — Southall — Hanwell — West Ealing — Ealing Broadway — London Paddington

Shuttle

Below: *The 15-minute-interval service between London Paddington and Heathrow Airport is operated by a fleet of 14 Heathrow Express Class 332 EMUs; nine sets are formed of four cars and five are formed of five carriages. The Heathrow Express operation gets funding from major advertising contracts; at present this is with Vodafone, whose branding is applied. Set No. 332002 leads a Paddington-bound train through West Ealing.* **CJM**

Class 332

Vehicle Length: (Driving) 77ft 10¾in (23.74m)
(Inter) 75ft 11in (23.143m)
Height: 12ft 1½in (3.70m)
Width: 9ft 1in (2.75m)
Horsepower: 1,876hp (1,400kW)
Seats 4-car (total/car): 26F-148S, 26F/56S/44S/48S
5-car (total/car): 26F-204S, 26F/56S/44S/56S/48S

Number	*Formation* DMFO+TSO+PTSO+(TSO)+DMSO	*Depot*	*Livery*	*Owner*	*Operator*
332001	78400+72412+63400+ - +78401	OH	HEX	BAA	HEX
332002	78402+72409+63406+ - +78403	OH	HEX‡	BAA	HEX
332003	78404+72407+63402+ - +78405	OH	HEX	BAA	HEX
332004	78406+72406+63403+ - +78407	OH	HEX‡	BAA	HEX
332005	78408+72411+63404+72417+78409	OH	HEX‡	BAA	HEX
332006	78410+72410+63405+72415+78411	OH	HEX‡	BAA	HEX
332007	78412+72401+63401+72414+78413	OH	HEX‡	BAA	HEX

Vehicle Length: (Driving) 77ft 10¾in (23.74m)
(Inter) 75ft 11in (23.143m)
Height: 12ft 1½in (3.70m)
Width: 9ft 1in (2.75m)
Horsepower: 1,876hp (1,400kW)
Seats 4-car (total/car): 14F-148S, 48S/56S/44S/14F
5-car (total/car): 14F-204S, 48S/56S/44S/56S/14F

Number	*Formation* DMSO+TSO+PTSO+(TSO)+DMFLO	*Depot*	*Livery*	*Owner*	*Operator*
332008	78414+72413+63407+72418+78415	OH	HEX‡	BAA	HEX
332009	78416+72400+63408+72416+78417	OH	HEX‡	BAA	HEX
332010	78418+72402+63409+ - +78419	OH	HEX	BAA	HEX
332011	78420+72403+63410+ - +78421	OH	HEX‡	BAA	HEX
332012	78422+72404+63411+ - +78423	OH	HEX	BAA	HEX
332013	78424+72408+63412+ - +78425	OH	HEX	BAA	HEX
332014	78426+72406+63413+ - +78427	OH	HEX‡	BAA	HEX

‡ First class vehicles carry Vodafone advertising livery

Class 360/2
Desiro

Vehicle Length: 66ft 9in (20.4m)
Height: 12ft 1½in (3.7m)
Width: 9ft 2in (2.79m)
Horsepower: 1,341hp (1,000kW)
Seats (total/car): 340S, 63S/66S/74S/74S/63S
(360205 - 280S using 2+2 seats)

Number	*Formation* DMSO(A)+PTSO+TSO+TSO+DMSO(B)	*Depot*	*Livery*	*Owner*	*Operator*
360201	78431+63421+72431+72421+78441	OH	HEC	BAA	HEC
360202	78432+63422+72432+72422+78442	OH	HEC	BAA	HEC
360203	78433+63423+72433+72423+78443	OH	HEC	BAA	HEC
360204	78434+63424+72434+72424+78444	OH	HEC	BAA	HEC
360205	78435+63425+72435+72425+78445	OH	HEL	BAA	HEC

Below: *The local service between Paddington and Heathrow is operated by Heathrow Connect services, a joint Heathrow Express/ First Group business. Five-car Class 360/2 set No. 360202 is seen approaching West Ealing.* **CJM**

Island Line

Address: ✉ Ryde St Johns Road Station, Ryde, Isle of Wight, PO33 2BA
info@island-line.co.uk
✆ 01983 812591
ⓘ www.island-line.co.uk

Managing Director: Tim Shoveller (South West Trains) **General Manager:** Andy Naylor
Franchise Dates: Part of SWT franchise 2 February 2007 - 3 February 2017
Principal Route: Ryde Pier Head - Shanklin
Owned Stations: All
Depots: Ryde St Johns Road (RY)
Parent Company: Stagecoach

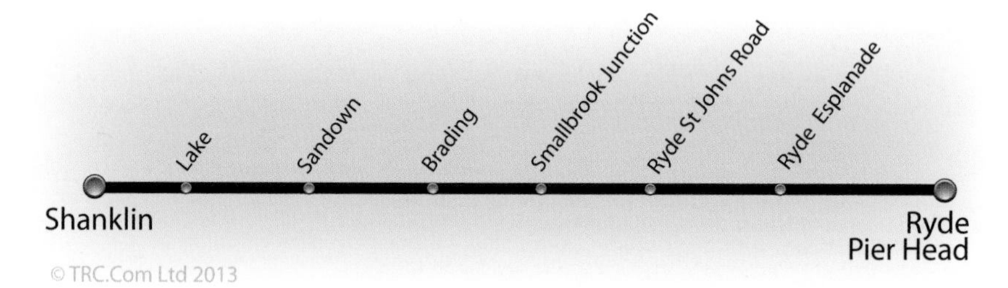

Class 483

Vehicle Length: 52ft 4in (15.95m)
Height: 9ft 5½in (2.88m)
Width: 8ft 8½in (2.65m)
Horsepower: 670hp (500kW)
Seats (total/car): 82S, 40S/42S

Number	Formation DMSO+DMSO	Depot	Livery	Owner	Operator
483002	122+224	RY	LUL	SWT	SIL
483004	124+224	RY	LUL	SWT	SIL
483006	126+226	RY	LUL	SWT	SIL
483007	127+227	RY	LUL	SWT	SIL
483008	128+228	RY	LUL	SWT	SIL
483009	129+229	RY	LUL	SWT	SIL

Below: *Operated by Stagecoach South West Trains, the isolated Isle of Wight line uses the UK's oldest passenger rolling stock, dating back to 1938 when introduced by London Transport. The six remaining two-car sets are allocated to Ryde and operate the service between Ryde Pier Head and Shanklin. Set 483004 is seen at Sandown.* **Ray Humphries**

London Midland

Address: 102 New Street, Birmingham, B2 4JB
comments@londonmidland.com
0844 811 0133
www.londonmidland.com

Managing Director: Patrick Verwer
Franchise Dates: 11 November 2007 - 19 September 2015*
Principal Routes: London Euston - Liverpool Lime Street, West Midlands routes to Stratford, Worcester, Hereford, Shrewsbury, plus Bedford and St Albans Abbey branches
Depots: Northampton (NN)§, Soho (SI), Tyseley (TS), Stourbridge Junction (SJ) § Operated by Siemens
Parent Company: Govia
* Likely extension to July 2017

Class 08

Vehicle Length: 29ft 3in (8.91m)
Height: 12ft 8⅝in (3.87m)
Width: 8ft 6in (2.59m)
Engine: English Electric 6K
Horsepower: 400hp (298kW)
Electrical Equipment: English Electric

Number	*Depot*	*Pool*	*Livery*	*Owner*	*Operator*
08616 (3785)	**TS**	**EJLO**	**LMI**	**LMI**	**LMI**
08805	**SI**	**EJLO**	**BLU**	**LMI**	**LMI**

Names applied

08616 ***Tyseley 100***	**08805** ***Concorde***

Right: *For depot shunting duties at Tyseley and Soho, London Midland operates a fleet of just two Class 08s. No. 08616, which also carries its pre-TOPS identity of 3785, is painted in LM livery and is seen at the depot. No. 08805 used at Soho is painted in rail blue colours.* **Antony Christie**

Class 139

Vehicle Length: 28ft 6in (8.7m)
Width: 7ft 8in (2.4m)
Engine: 1 x MVH420 2.0ltr LPG, flywheel hybrid
Seats (total/car): 18S

Number	*Formation DMS*	*Depot*	*Livery*	*Owner*	*Operator*
139001	**39001**	**SJ**	**LMI**	**LMI**	**LMI**
139002	**39002**	**SJ**	**LMI**	**LMI**	**LMI**

Right: *The Stourbridge Town to Stourbridge Junction 'shuttle' is worked by two Class 139 Parry People Movers operated by Pre Metro Operations on behalf of London Midland. The two Class 139s are captive to the line and have a small servicing shed just beyond Stourbridge Junction station. Each vehicle carries just 19 passengers, they are double-ended and are finished in full London Midland livery. Vehicle No. 139002 is seen at Stourbridge Town.* **John Binch**

London Midland

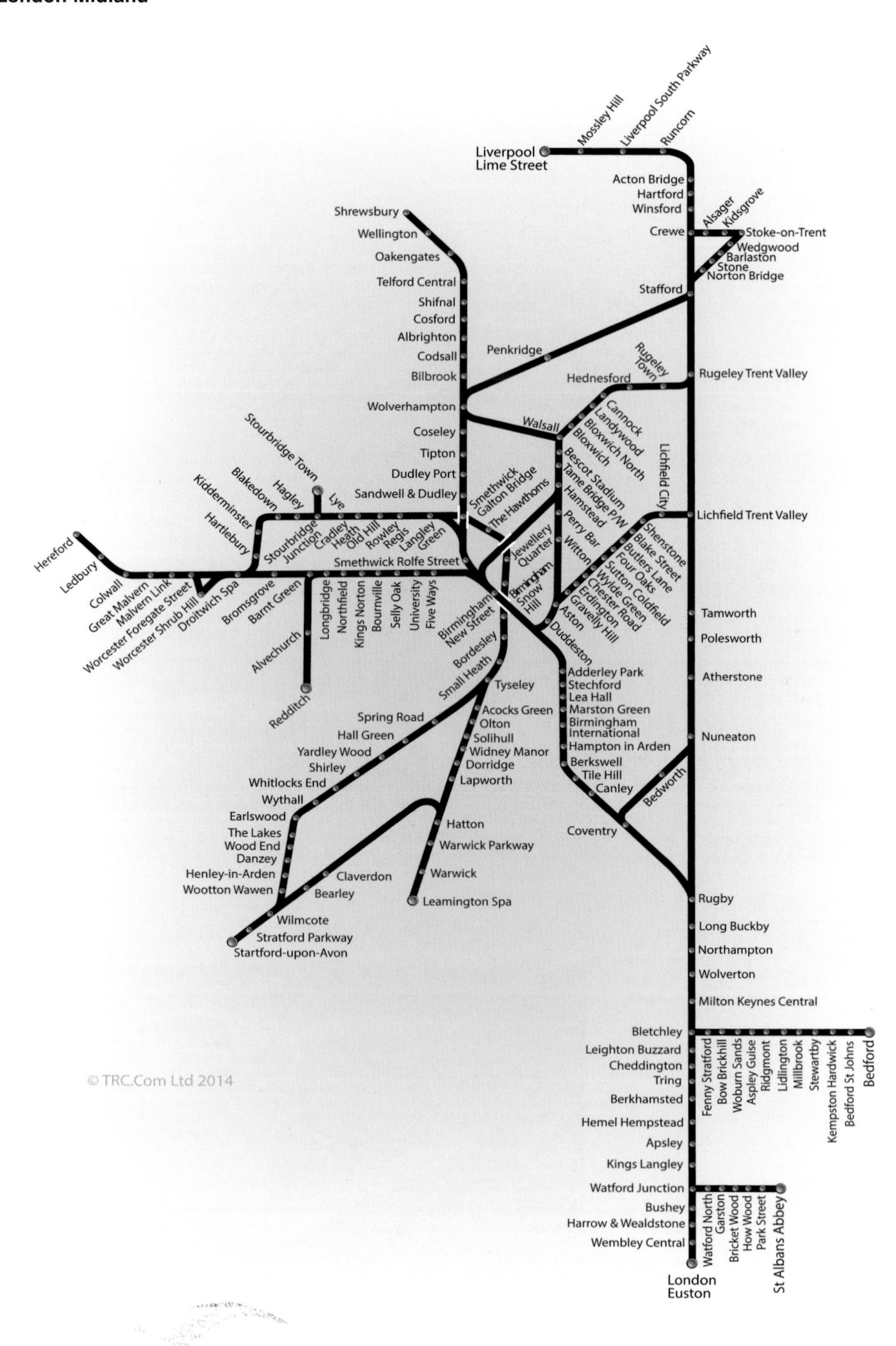

Class 150/1

Vehicle Length: 64ft 9¾in (19.74m)
Height: 12ft 4½in (3.77m)
Width: 9ft 3⅛in (2.82m)
Engine: 1 x NT855R5 of 285hp per vehicle
Horsepower: 855hp (638kW)
Seats (total/car): 148S, 76S/72S

Number	*Formation DMSL+DMS*	*Depot*	*Livery*	*Owner*	*Operator*
150105	**52105+57105**	**TS**	**CTL**	**ANG**	**LMI**
150107	**52107+57107**	**TS**	**LMI**	**ANG**	**LMI**
150109	**52109+57109**	**TS**	**CTL**	**ANG**	**LMI**

Right: *Just three Class 150/1 units remain on the books of London Midland, allocated to Tyseley and used on the Bedford to Bletchley route as well as a handful of fill-in turns between Birmingham and Hereford. All three sets have been facelifted and now sport the latest London Midland livery and standard LM Metro-style seating. Set No. 150105 is seen at Worcester Foregate Street on a Birmingham service with its 57xxx vehicle leading.* **CJM**

Class 153

Vehicle Length: 76ft 5in (23.29m)
Height: 12ft 3⅛in (3.75m)
Width: 8ft 10in (2.70m)
Engine: 1 x NT855R5 of 285hp
Horsepower: 285hp (213kW)
Seats (total/car): 72S

Number	*Formation DMSL*	*Depot*	*Livery*	*Owner*	*Operator*
153334	**52334**	**TS**	**LMI**	**PTR**	**LMI**
153354	**57354**	**TS**	**LMI**	**PTR**	**LMI**
153356	**57356**	**TS**	**LMI**	**PTR**	**LMI**
153364	**57364**	**TS**	**LMI**	**PTR**	**LMI**
153365	**57365**	**TS**	**LMI**	**PTR**	**LMI**
153366	**57366**	**TS**	**LMI**	**PTR**	**LMI**
153371	**57371**	**TS**	**LMI**	**PTR**	**LMI**
153375	**57375**	**TS**	**LMI**	**PTR**	**LMI**

Right: *Eight Class 153 'bubble-cars' are operated by London Midland, allocated to Tyseley and used on lightly used non-electrified routes. All cars carry standard London Midland livery. No. 153371 is viewed at Bletchley while working on the Bedford shuttle service in place on a non-available Class 150. The vehicle is seen from its small cab end.* **John Binch**

Class 170/5
Turbostar

Vehicle Length: 77ft 6in (23.62m)
Height: 12ft 4½in (3.77m)
Width: 8ft 10in (2.69m)
Engine: 1 x MTU 6R 183TD13H 422hp per vehicle
Horsepower: 844hp (629kW)
Seats (total/car): 122S 55S/67S

Number	*Formation DMSL+DMSL*	*Depot*	*Livery*	*Owner*	*Operator*
170501	**50501+79501**	**TS**	**LMI**	**PTR**	**LMI**
170502	**50502+79502**	**TS**	**LMI**	**PTR**	**LMI**
170503	**50503+79503**	**TS**	**LMI**	**PTR**	**LMI**
170504	**50504+79504**	**TS**	**LMI**	**PTR**	**LMI**
170505	**50505+79505**	**TS**	**LMI**	**PTR**	**LMI**
170506	**50506+79506**	**TS**	**LMI**	**PTR**	**LMI**
170507	**50507+79507**	**TS**	**LMI**	**PTR**	**LMI**
170508	**50508+79508**	**TS**	**LMI**	**PTR**	**LMI**

London Midland

170509	50509+79509	TS	LMI	PTR	LMI
170510	50510+79510	TS	LMI	PTR	LMI
170511	50511+79511	TS	LMI	PTR	LMI
170512	50512+79512	TS	LMI	PTR	LMI
170513	50513+79513	TS	LMI	PTR	LMI
170514	50514+79514	TS	LMI	PTR	LMI
170515	50515+79515	TS	LMI	PTR	LMI
170516	50516+79516	TS	LMI	PTR	LMI
170517	50517+79517	TS	LMI	PTR	LMI

Left: *A total of 23 Class 170 'Turbostar' sets are operated by London Midland, 17 two-car sets and six three-car units. Allocated to Tyseley, the sets operate the longer-distance outer-suburban routes. All sets have been internally refurbished and sport full London Midland livery. Two-car set No. 170512 is illustrated at Worcester Foregate Street.* **CJM**

Class 170/6
Turbostar

Vehicle Length: 77ft 6in (23.62m)
Height: 12ft 4½in (3.77m)
Width: 8ft 10in (2.69m)
Engine: 1 x MTU 6R 183TD13H 422hp per vehicle
Horsepower: 1,266hp (944kW)
Seats (total/car): 196S 55S/74S/67S

Number	*Formation DMSL+MS+DMSL*	*Depot*	*Livery*	*Owner*	*Operator*
170630	50630+56630+79630	TS	LMI	PTR	LMI
170631	50631+56631+79631	TS	LMI	PTR	LMI
170632	50632+56632+79632	TS	LMI	PTR	LMI
170633	50633+56633+79633	TS	LMI	PTR	LMI
170634	50634+56634+79634	TS	LMI	PTR	LMI
170635	50635+56635+79635	TS	LMI	PTR	LMI

Class 172/2
Turbostar

Vehicle Length: 73ft 4in (22.37m)
Height: 12ft 4½in (3.77m)
Width: 8ft 8in (2.69m)
Engine: MTU 6H1800 of 360kW
Horsepower: 965hp (720kW)
Seats (total/car): 121S, 53S/68S

Number	*Formation DMS+DMS*	*Depot*	*Livery*	*Owner*	*Operator*
172211	50211+79211	TS	LMI	PTR	LMI
172212	50212+79212	TS	LMI	PTR	LMI
172213	50213+79213	TS	LMI	PTR	LMI
172214	50214+79214	TS	LMI	PTR	LMI
172215	50215+79215	TS	LMI	PTR	LMI
172216	50216+79216	TS	LMI	PTR	LMI
172217	50217+79217	TS	LMI	PTR	LMI
172218	50218+79218	TS	LMI	PTR	LMI
172219	50219+59219	TS	LMI	PTR	LMI
172220	50220+79220	TS	LMI	PTR	LMI
172221	50221+79221	TS	LMI	PTR	LMI
172222	50222+79222	TS	LMI	PTR	LMI

Left: *During 2011-12 funding permitted the replacement of the Class 150 DMU sets in the Birmingham area with new 'Turbostar' Class 172 stock. Two fleets are operated from Tyseley, 12 two-car units classified as 172/2 and 15 three-car sets classified as 172/3. The sets are gangwayed throughout and operate on the Birmingham non-electrified network. Two-car sets seat 121 passengers and three-car sets 193. Three-car set No. 172337 is illustrated at Worcester Foregate Street.* **CJM**

Class 172/3 *Turbostar*

Vehicle Length: (Driving) 73ft 4in (22.37m)
(Inter): 76ft 7in (23.36m)
Height: 12ft 4½in (3.77m)
Width: 8ft 8in (2.69m)
Engine: MTU 6H1800 of 360kW
Horsepower: 1,449hp (1,080kW)
Seats (total/car): 193S, 53S/72S/68S

Number	Formation DMSO+MS+DMSO	Depot	Livery	Owner	Operator
172331	50331+56331+79331	TS	LMI	PTR	LMI
172332	50332+56332+79332	TS	LMI	PTR	LMI
172333	50333+56333+79333	TS	LMI	PTR	LMI
172334	50334+56334+79334	TS	LMI	PTR	LMI
172335	50335+56335+79335	TS	LMI	PTR	LMI
172336	50336+56336+79336	TS	LMI	PTR	LMI
172337	50337+56337+79337	TS	LMI	PTR	LMI
172338	50338+56338+79338	TS	LMI	PTR	LMI
172339	50339+56339+79339	TS	LMI	PTR	LMI
172340	50340+56340+79340	TS	LMI	PTR	LMI
172341	50341+56341+79341	TS	LMI	PTR	LMI
172342	50342+56342+79342	TS	LMI	PTR	LMI
172343	50343+56343+79343	TS	LMI	PTR	LMI
172344	50344+56344+79344	TS	LMI	PTR	LMI
172345	50345+56345+79345	TS	LMI	PTR	LMI

Class 321/4

Vehicle Length: (Driving) 65ft 0¾in (19.83m)
(Inter) 65ft 4¼in (19.92m)
Height: 12ft 4¾in (3.78m)
Width: 9ft 3in (2.82m)
Horsepower: 1,328hp (996kW)
Seats (total/car): 28F/271S, 28F-40S/79S/74S/78S

Number	Formation DMCO+MSO+TSO+DMSO	Depot	Livery	Owner	Operator
321411	78105+63073+71959+77953	NN	LMI	EVL	LMI
321412	78106+63074+71960+77954	NN	LMI	EVL	LMI
321413	78107+63075+71961+77955	NN	LMI	EVL	LMI
321414	78108+63076+71962+77956	NN	LMI	EVL	LMI
321415	78109+63077+71963+77957	NN	LMI	EVL	LMI
321416	78110+63078+71964+77958	NN	LMI	EVL	LMI
321417	78111+63079+71965+77959	NN	LMI	EVL	LMI

Right: *Seven of the original Class 321/4 sets were retained by London Midland after the introduction of Class 350 stock on main West Coast services to cope with traffic growth. The sets are usually only used during the peak periods. Set No. 321417 leads an eight-car formation of '321' stock in this view. The black triangle on the front indicates the first class seating end of the train.* **Nathan Williamson**

Class 323

Vehicle Length: (Driving) 76ft 8¼in (23.37m)
(Inter) 76ft 10¾in (23.44m)
Height: 12ft 4¾in (3.78m)
Width: 9ft 2¼in (2.80m)
Horsepower: 1,565hp (1,168kW)
Seats (total/car): 284S, 98S/88S/98S

Number	Formation DMSO(A)+PTSO+DMSO(B)	Depot	Livery	Owner	Op'r
323201	64001+72201+65001	SI	LMI	PTR	LMI
323202	64002+72202+65002	SI	LMI	PTR	LMI
323203	64003+72203+65003	SI	LMI	PTR	LMI
323204	64004+72204+65004	SI	LMI	PTR	LMI
323205	64005+72205+65005	SI	LMI	PTR	LMI
323206	64006+72206+65006	SI	LMI	PTR	LMI
323207	64007+72207+65007	SI	LMI	PTR	LMI
323208	64008+72208+65008	SI	LMI	PTR	LMI
323209	64009+72209+65009	SI	LMI	PTR	LMI
323210	64010+72210+65010	SI	LMI	PTR	LMI
323211	64011+72211+65011	SI	LMI	PTR	LMI
323212	64012+72212+65012	SI	LMI	PTR	LMI
323213	64013+72213+65013	SI	LMI	PTR	LMI
323214	64014+72214+65014	SI	LMI	PTR	LMI
323215	64015+72215+65015	SI	LMI	PTR	LMI
323216	64016+72216+65016	SI	LMI	PTR	LMI
323217	64017+72217+65017	SI	LMI	PTR	LMI
323218	64018+72218+65018	SI	LMI	PTR	LMI
323219	64019+72219+65019	SI	LMI	PTR	LMI
323220	64020+72220+65020	SI	LMI	PTR	LMI
323221	64021+72221+65021	SI	LMI	PTR	LMI

London Midland

323222	64022+72222+65022	SI	LMI	PTR	LMI
323240	64040+72340+65040	SI	LMI	PTR	LMI
323241	64041+72341+65041	SI	LMI	PTR	LMI
323242	64042+72342+65042	SI	LMI	PTR	LMI
323243	64043+72343+65043	SI	LMI	PTR	LMI

Left: *The London Midland Class 323 EMUs work local services on the Birmingham CrossCity line, the Walsall to Wolverhampton (via Birmingham New Street) and the Birmingham New Street to Coventry routes. Following their C6 overhauls at Wolverton Works in 2008, they have proved very reliable. No. 323209 is seen arriving at Smethwick Rolfe Street. All sets are painted in London Midland livery and sport 2+3 high-density interiors.* **John Binch**

Class 350/1
Desiro

Vehicle Length: 66ft 9in (20.4m)
Height: 12ft 1½in (3.78m)
Width: 9ft 2in (2.7m)
Horsepower: 1,341hp (1,000kW)
Seats (total/car): 24F-209S, 60S/24F-32S/57S/60S

Number	Formation DMSO(A)+TCO+PTSO+DMSO(B)	Depot	Livery	Owner	Operator
350101	63761+66811+66861+63711	NN	LMI	ANG	LMI
350102	63762+66812+66862+63712	NN	LMI	ANG	LMI
350103	63765+66813+66863+63713	NN	LMI	ANG	LMI
350104	63764+66814+66864+63714	NN	LMI	ANG	LMI
350105	63763+66815+66868+63715	NN	LMI	ANG	LMI
350106	63766+66816+66866+63716	NN	LMI	ANG	LMI
350107	63767+66817+66867+63717	NN	LMI	ANG	LMI
350108	63768+66818+66865+63718	NN	LMI	ANG	LMI
350109	63769+66819+66869+63719	NN	LMI	ANG	LMI
350110	63770+66820+66870+63720	NN	LMA	ANG	LMI
350111	63771+66821+66871+63721	NN	LMI	ANG	LMI
350112	63772+66822+66872+63722	NN	LMI	ANG	LMI
350113	63773+66823+66873+63723	NN	LMI	ANG	LMI
350114	63774+66824+66874+63724	NN	LMI	ANG	LMI
350115	63775+66825+66875+63725	NN	LMI	ANG	LMI
350116	63776+66826+66876+63726	NN	LMI	ANG	LMI
350117	63777+66827+66877+63727	NN	LMI	ANG	LMI
350118	63778+66828+66878+63728	NN	LMI	ANG	LMI
350119	63779+66829+66879+63729	NN	LMI	ANG	LMI
350120	63780+66830+66880+63730	NN	LMI	ANG	LMI
350121	63781+66831+66881+63731	NN	LMI	ANG	LMI
350122	63782+66832+66882+63732	NN	LMI	ANG	LMI
350123	63783+66833+66883+63733	NN	LMI	ANG	LMI
350124	63784+66834+66884+63734	NN	LMI	ANG	LMI
350125	63785+66835+66885+63735	NN	LMI	ANG	LMI
350126	63786+66836+66886+63736	NN	LMI	ANG	LMI
350127	63787+66837+66887+63737	NN	LMI	ANG	LMI
350128	63788+66838+66888+63738	NN	LMI	ANG	LMI
350129	63789+66839+66889+63739	NN	LMI	ANG	LMI
350130	63790+66840+66890+63740	NN	LMI	ANG	LMI

Class 350/2
Desiro

Vehicle Length: 66ft 9in (20.4m)
Height: 12ft 1½in (3.78m)
Width: 9ft 2in (2.7m)
Horsepower: 1,341hp (1,000kW)
Seats (total/car): 24F-243S, 70S/24F-42S/61S/70S

Number	Formation DMSO(A)+TCO+PTSO+DMSO(B)	Depot	Livery	Owner	Operator	Name
350231	61431+65231+67531+61531	NN	LMI	PTR	LMI	

350232	61432+65232+67532+61532	NN	LMI	PTR	LMI	*Chad Varah*
350233	61433+65233+67533+61533	NN	LMI	PTR	LMI	
350234	61434+65234+67534+61534	NN	LMI	PTR	LMI	
350235	61435+65235+67535+61535	NN	LMI	PTR	LMI	
350236	61436+65236+67536+61536	NN	LMI	PTR	LMI	
350237	61437+65237+67537+61537	NN	LMI	PTR	LMI	
350238	61438+65238+67538+61538	NN	LMI	PTR	LMI	
350239	61439+65239+67539+61539	NN	LMI	PTR	LMI	
350240	61440+65240+67540+61540	NN	LMI	PTR	LMI	
350241	61441+65241+67541+61541	NN	LMI	PTR	LMI	
350242	61442+65242+67542+61542	NN	LMI	PTR	LMI	
350243	61443+65243+67543+61543	NN	LMI	PTR	LMI	
350244	61444+65244+67544+61544	NN	LMI	PTR	LMI	
350245	61445+65245+67545+61545	NN	LMI	PTR	LMI	
350246	61446+65246+67546+61546	NN	LMI	PTR	LMI	
350247	61447+65247+67547+61547	NN	LMI	PTR	LMI	
350248	61448+65248+67548+61548	NN	LMI	PTR	LMI	
350249	61449+65249+67549+61549	NN	LMI	PTR	LMI	
350250	61450+65250+67550+61550	NN	LMI	PTR	LMI	
350251	61451+65251+67551+61551	NN	LMI	PTR	LMI	
350252	61452+65252+67552+61552	NN	LMI	PTR	LMI	
350253	61453+65253+67553+61553	NN	LMI	PTR	LMI	
350254	61454+65254+67554+61554	NN	LMI	PTR	LMI	
350255	61455+65255+67555+61555	NN	LMI	PTR	LMI	
350256	61456+65256+67556+61556	NN	LMI	PTR	LMI	
350257	61457+65257+67557+61557	NN	LMI	PTR	LMI	
350258	61458+65258+67558+61558	NN	LMI	PTR	LMI	
350259	61459+65259+67559+61559	NN	LMI	PTR	LMI	
350260	61460+65260+67560+61560	NN	LMI	PTR	LMI	
350261	61461+65261+67561+61561	NN	LMI	PTR	LMI	
350262	61462+65262+67562+61562	NN	LMI	PTR	LMI	
350263	61463+65263+67563+61563	NN	LMI	PTR	LMI	
350264	61464+65264+67564+61564	NN	LMI	PTR	LMI	
350265	61465+65265+67565+61565	NN	LMI	PTR	LMI	
350266	61466+65266+67566+61566	NN	LMI	PTR	LMI	
350267	61467+65267+67567+61567	NN	LMI	PTR	LMI	

Right: *Two fleets of Class 350 Siemens 'Desiro' four-car EMUs are operated by London Midland and a further fleet of 10 is on order. All sets operate in a common pool, but some interior seating variations exist between the sub-classes. Class 350/1 sets have a solid yellow corridor door, while 350/2 sets have a lower black panel to the door. Set No. 350119 is illustrated.* **CJM**

Class 350/3
Desiro

Vehicle Length: 66ft 9in (20.4m)
Height: 12ft 1½in (3.78m)
Width: 9ft 2in (2.7m)
Horsepower: 1,341hp (1,000kW)
Seats (total/car): 191S/19F

Number	*Formation* DMSO(A)+TCO+PTSO+DMSO(B)	*Depot*	*Livery*	*Owner*	*Operator*
350301	60141+60511+60651+60151	NN	LMI	ANG	On delivery mid-2014
350302	60142+60512+60652+60152	NN	LMI	ANG	On delivery mid-2014
350303	60143+60513+60653+60153	NN	LMI	ANG	On delivery mid-2014
350304	60144+60514+60654+60154	NN	LMI	ANG	On delivery mid-2014
350305	60145+60515+60655+60155	NN	LMI	ANG	On delivery mid-2014
350306	60146+60516+60656+60156	NN	LMI	ANG	On delivery mid-2014
350307	60147+60517+60657+60157	NN	LMI	ANG	On delivery mid-2014
350308	60148+60518+60658+60158	NN	LMI	ANG	On delivery mid-2014
350309	60149+60519+60659+60159	NN	LMI	ANG	On delivery mid-2014
350310	60150+60520+60660+60160	NN	LMI	ANG	On delivery mid-2014

London Overground

Address: ✉ 125 Finchley Road, London, NW3 6HY
overgroundinfo@tfl.gov.uk
✆ 0845 601 4867
ⓘ www.tfl.gov.uk/overground

Managing Director: Steve Murphy

Principal Routes: Clapham Junction - Willesden, Richmond - Stratford
Gospel Oak - Barking, Euston - Watford
East London Line – Dalston - West Croydon

Depots: Willesden (WN), New Cross Gate (NX)

Parent Company: Transport for London

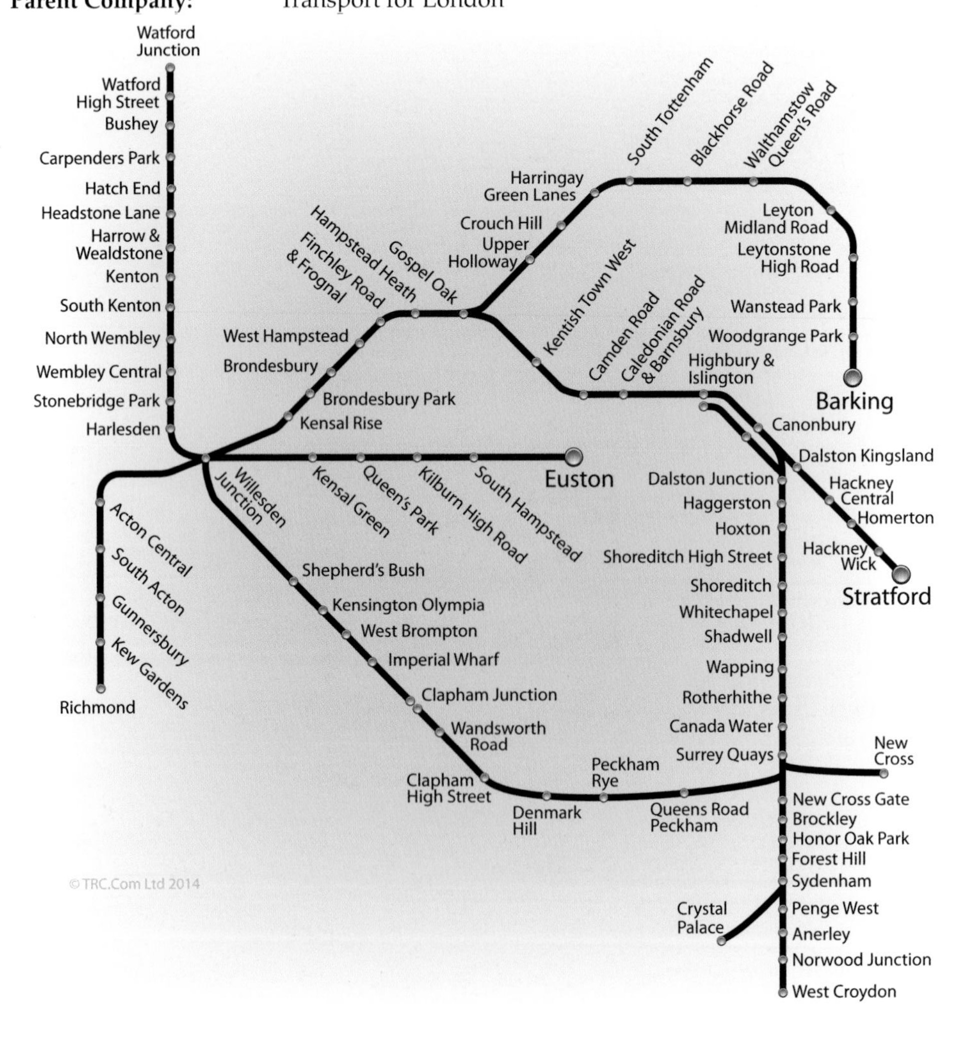

Class 09/0

Vehicle Length: 29ft 3in (8.91m)
Height: 12ft 8⅝in (3.87m)
Width: 8ft 6in (2.59m)
Engine: English Electric 6K
Horsepower: 400hp (298kW)
Electrical Equipment: English Electric

Number	*Depot*	*Pool*	*Livery*	*Owner*	*Operator*
09007	WN	-	GRN	LOG	LOG

Above: *London Overground, a part of Transport for London, operates two depots for its Class 378 fleet, Willesden (the former West Coast loco depot) and a new facility at New Cross Gate. To provide shunting ability at Willesden depot, London Overground operates Class 09 0-6-0 diesel-electric shunting loco No. 09007, which has been restored to 1950s BR green livery, with a red buffer beam, connecting rods and 'wasp' warning ends. The loco is seen outside the north end of Willesden depot.* **Antony Christie**

Class 172/0
Turbostar

Vehicle Length: 73ft 4in (22.37m)
Height: 12ft 4½in (3.77m)
Width: 8ft 8in (2.69m)
Engine: MTU 6H1800R83 of 360kW (483hp)
Horsepower: 965hp (720kW)
Seats (total/car): 124S, 60S/64S

Number	*Formation DMS+DMS*	*Depot*	*Livery*	*Owner*	*Operator*
172001	59311+59411	WN	LOG	ANG	LOG
172002	59312+59412	WN	LOG	ANG	LOG
172003	59313+59413	WN	LOG	ANG	LOG
172004	59314+59414	WN	LOG	ANG	LOG
172005	59315+59415	WN	LOG	ANG	LOG
172006	59316+59416	WN	LOG	ANG	LOG
172007	59317+59417	WN	LOG	ANG	LOG
172008	59318+59418	WN	LOG	ANG	LOG

Right: *To provide power for London Overground's sole non-electrified line between Gospel Oak and Barking, a fleet of Class 172/0 'Turbostar' sets have been placed on the roster. The sets are based at Willesden and work exclusively on that route. Authorisation has now been given to electrify this line, so in the medium-term future these sets will be surplus to London Overground requirements and are likely to be transferred to Chiltern Railways. Set No. 172001 is seen heading for Barking at Crouch Hill.* **CJM**

London Overground

Class 378/1
Capitalstar

Vehicle Length: (Driving) 20.46m, (Inter) 20.14m
Height: 11ft 9in (3.58m)
750V dc sets
Width: 9ft 2in (2.80m)
Horsepower: 2,010hp (1,500kW)
Seats (total/car): 146S, 36S/40S/34S/36S

Number	*Formation* DMSO+MSO+TSO+DMSO	*Depot*	*Livery*	*Owner*	*Operator*
378135	38035+38235+38335+38135	NX	LOG	QWR	LOG
378136	38036+38236+38336+38136	NX	LOG	QWR	LOG
378137	38037+38237+38337+38137	NX	LOG	QWR	LOG
378138	38038+38238+38338+38138	NX	LOG	QWR	LOG
378139	38039+38239+38339+38139	NX	LOG	QWR	LOG
378140	38040+38240+38340+38140	NX	LOG	QWR	LOG
378141	38041+38241+38341+38141	NX	LOG	QWR	LOG
378142	38042+38242+38342+38142	NX	LOG	QWR	LOG
378143	38043+38243+38343+38143	NX	LOG	QWR	LOG
378144	38044+38244+38344+38144	NX	LOG	QWR	LOG
378145	38045+38245+38345+38145	NX	LOG	QWR	LOG
378146	38046+38246+38346+38146	NX	LOG	QWR	LOG
378147	38047+38247+38347+38147	NX	LOG	QWR	LOG
378148	38048+38248+38348+38148	NX	LOG	QWR	LOG
378149	38049+38249+38349+38149	NX	LOG	QWR	LOG
378150	38050+38250+38350+38150	NX	LOG	QWR	LOG
378151	38051+38251+38351+38151	NX	LOG	QWR	LOG
378152	38052+38252+38352+38152	NX	LOG	QWR	LOG
378153	38053+38253+38353+38153	NX	LOG	QWR	LOG
378154	38054+38254+38354+38154	NX	LOG	QWR	LOG

Sets 378150-378154 fitted with de-icing equipment

Ian Brown CBE

Below left: *To date only one cast nameplate has been applied to a London Overground Class 378, that commemorating Ian Brown CBE on set No. 378233. Ian was Managing Director of Transport for London's London Rail operation after spending his entire working life on the railway and the naming was a tribute to what Ian had achieved. Ian is now a Non-Executive Director of CrossRail.* **CJM**

Below: *Two different breeds of Class 378 are in operation. The 20 members of Class 378/1 are fitted for third rail dc operation only and operate on the Highbury & Islington to West Croydon, New Cross and Clapham routes. These sets could be modified for dual voltage operation in the future if needed. Set No. 378148 is seen at Highbury & Islington with a service bound for West Croydon.* **CJM**

Class 378/2
Capitalstar

Vehicle Length: (Driving) 20.46m, (Inter) 20.14m	*Width: 9ft 2in (2.80m)*
Height: 11ft 9in (3.58m)	*Horsepower: 2,010hp (1,500kW)*
Dual voltage - 750V dc third rail and 25kV ac overhead	*Seats (total/car): 146S, 36S/40S/34S/36S*

Sets built as 3-car units as Class 378/0, MSO added and reclassified as 378/2

Number	*Formation* DMSO+MSO+PTSO+DMSO	*Depot*	*Livery*	*Owner*	*Operator*
378201 (378001)	38001+38201+38301+38101	WN	LOG	QWR	LOG
378202 (378002)	38002+38202+38302+38102	WN	LOG	QWR	LOG
378203 (378003)	38003+38203+38303+38103	WN	LOG	QWR	LOG
378204 (378004)	38004+38204+38304+38104	WN	LOG	QWR	LOG
378205 (378005)	38005+38205+38305+38105	WN	LOG	QWR	LOG
378206 (378006)	38006+38206+38306+38106	WN	LOG	QWR	LOG
378207 (378007)	38007+38207+38307+38107	WN	LOG	QWR	LOG
378208 (378008)	38008+38208+38308+38108	WN	LOG	QWR	LOG
378209 (378009)	38009+38209+38309+38109	WN	LOG	QWR	LOG
378210 (378010)	38010+38210+38310+38110	WN	LOG	QWR	LOG
378211 (378011)	38011+38211+38311+38111	WN	LOG	QWR	LOG
378212 (378012)	38012+38212+38312+38112	WN	LOG	QWR	LOG
378213 (378013)	38013+38213+38313+38113	WN	LOG	QWR	LOG
378214 (378014)	38014+38214+38314+38114	WN	LOG	QWR	LOG
378215 (378015)	38015+38215+38315+38115	WN	LOG	QWR	LOG
378216 (378016)	38016+38216+38316+38116	WN	LOG	QWR	LOG
378217 (378017)	38017+38217+38317+38117	WN	LOG	QWR	LOG
378218 (378018)	38018+38218+38318+38118	WN	LOG	QWR	LOG
378219 (378019)	38019+38219+38319+38119	WN	LOG	QWR	LOG
378220 (378020)	38020+38220+38320+38120	WN	LOG	QWR	LOG
378221 (378021)	38021+38221+38321+38121	WN	LOG	QWR	LOG
378222 (378022)	38022+38222+38322+38122	WN	LOG	QWR	LOG
378223 (378023)	38023+38223+38323+38123	WN	LOG	QWR	LOG
378224 (378024)	38024+38224+38324+38124	WN	LOG	QWR	LOG

Sets 378216-378220 fitted with de-icing equipment

Number	*Formation* DMSO+MSO+TSO+DMSO	*Depot*	*Livery*	*Owner*	*Operator*	*Name*
378225	38025+38225+38325+38125	NX	LOG	QWR	LOG	
378226	38026+38226+38326+38126	NX	LOG	QWR	LOG	
378227	38027+38227+38327+38127	NX	LOG	QWR	LOG	
378228	38028+38228+38328+38128	NX	LOG	QWR	LOG	
378229	38029+38229+38329+38129	NX	LOG	QWR	LOG	
378230	38030+38230+38330+38130	NX	LOG	QWR	LOG	
378231	38031+38231+38331+38131	NX	LOG	QWR	LOG	
378232	38032+38232+38332+38132	NX	LOG	QWR	LOG	
378233	38033+38233+38333+38133	NX	LOG	QWR	LOG	*Ian Brown CBE*
378234	38034+38234+38334+38134	NX	LOG	QWR	LOG	
378255	38055+38255+38355+38155	NX	LOG	QWR	LOG	
378256	38056+38256+38356+38156	NX	LOG	QWR	LOG	
378257	38057+38257+38357+38157	NX	LOG	QWR	LOG	

Right: *The 37 Class 378/2 dual voltage sets are identical in internal fittings to the dc sets, but are deployed on the Euston-Watford, Stratford-Richmond and Clapham to Stratford routes, which require dual voltage operation. Running in third rail dc mode, set No. 378212 departs from West Brompton with a service bound for Clapham Junction. A four-car Class 378 has seating for just 146 passengers, but standing room for around 450.* **CJM**

■ All sets to be strengthened to five-car by inserting an additional MSO in 2014-15.

Merseyrail

Address: ✉ Rail House, Lord Nelson Street, Liverpool, L1 1JF
comment@merseyrail.org
✆ 0151 702 2534
ⓘ www.merseyrail.org

Managing Director: Maarten Spaargaren
Franchise Dates: 20 July 2003 - 19 July 2028
Principal Routes: All non-main-line services in Liverpool area
Depots: Birkenhead North (BD)
Parent Company: Serco/Abellio

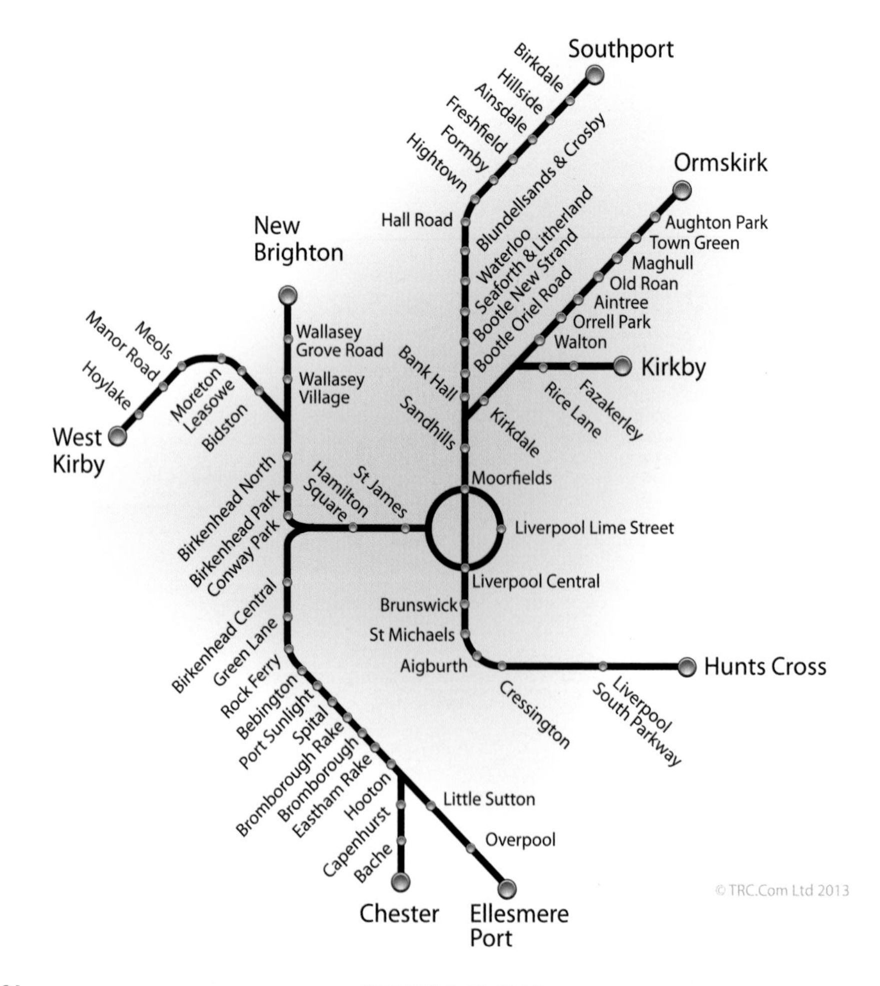

Class 507

Vehicle Length: (Driving) 64ft 11½in (19.80m) (Inter) 65ft 4¼in (19.92m)
Height: 11ft 6½in (3.58m)
Width: 9ft 3in (2.82m)
Horsepower: 880hp (656kW)
Seats (total/car): 186S, 56S/74S/56S

Number	Formation DMSO+TSO+DMSO	Depot	Livery	Owner	Operator	Name
507001	64367+71342+64405	BD	MER	ANG	MER	
507002	64368+71343+64406	BD	ADV§	ANG	MER	
507003	64369+71344+64407	BD	MER	ANG	MER	
507004	64388+71345+64408	BD	MER	ANG	MER	Bob Paisley
507005	64371+71346+64409	BD	MER	ANG	MER	
507006	64372+71347+64410	BD	MER	ANG	MER	
507007	64373+71348+64411	BD	MER	ANG	MER	
507008	64374+71349+64412	BD	MER	ANG	MER	Harold Wilson
507009	64375+71350+64413	BD	MER	ANG	MER	Dixie Dean
507010	64376+71351+64414	BD	MER	ANG	MER	
507011	64377+71352+64415	BD	MER	ANG	MER	
507012	64378+71353+64416	BD	MER	ANG	MER	
507013	64379+71354+64417	BD	MER	ANG	MER	
507014	64380+71355+64418	BD	MER	ANG	MER	
507015	64381+71356+64419	BD	MER	ANG	MER	
507016	64382+71357+64420	BD	MER	ANG	MER	Merseyrail - Celebrating the first ten years 2003-2013
507017	64383+71358+64421	BD	MER	ANG	MER	
507018	64384+71359+64422	BD	MER	ANG	MER	
507019	64385+71360+64423	BD	MER	ANG	MER	
507020	64386+71361+64424	BD	MER	ANG	MER	John Peel
507021	64387+71362+64425	BD	MER	ANG	MER	Red Rum
507023	64389+71364+64427	BD	MER	ANG	MER	Operating Inspector Stuart Mason
507024	64390+71365+64428	BD	MER	ANG	MER	
507025	64391+71366+64429	BD	MER	ANG	MER	
507026	64392+71367+64430	BD	MER	ANG	MER	
507027	64393+71368+64431	BD	MER	ANG	MER	
507028	64394+71369+64432	BD	MER	ANG	MER	
507029	64395+71370+64433	BD	MER	ANG	MER	
507030	64396+71371+64434	BD	MER	ANG	MER	
507031	64397+71372+64435	BD	MER	ANG	MER	
507032	64398+71373+64436	BD	MER	ANG	MER	
507033	64399+71374+64437	BD	MER	ANG	MER	Councillor Jack Spriggs

§ Advertising livery - Hope University

Above: *A fleet of 32 three-car Class 507 sets operates on Merseyrail, based at Birkenhead North. The sets are owned by Angel Trains and are all refurbished with high-back seating and modernised front ends. Sets are painted in silver and yellow livery and operate as a core fleet with the Class 508s throughout the Liverpool electrified area. The pioneer of the fleet, No. 507001, is seen near New Brighton.* **Antony Christie**

Class 508/1

Vehicle Length: (Driving) 64ft 11½in (19.80m) (Inter) 65ft 4¼in (19.92m)
Height: 11ft 6½in (3.58m)
Width: 9ft 3in (2.82m)
Horsepower: 880hp (656kW)
Seats (total/car): 186S, 56S/74S/56S

Number	Formation DMSO+TSO+DMSO	Depot	Livery	Owner	Operator	Name
508103	64651+71485+64694	BD	MER	ANG	MER	
508104	64652+71486+64964	BD	MER	ANG	MER	
508108	64656+71490+64699	BD	MER	ANG	MER	
508110	64658+71492+64701	BD	MER	ANG	MER	
508111	64659+71493+64702	BD	SPL	ANG	MER	*The Beatles*
508112	64660+71494+64703	BD	MER	ANG	MER	
508114	64662+71496+64705	BD	MER	ANG	MER	
508115	64663+71497+64708	BD	MER	ANG	MER	
508117	64665+71499+64908	BD	MER	ANG	MER	
508120	64668+71502+64711	BD	MER	ANG	MER	
508122	64670+71504+64713	BD	MER	ANG	MER	
508123	64671+71505+64714	BD	MER	ANG	MER	
508124	64672+71506+64715	BD	MER	ANG	MER	
508125	64673+71507+64716	BD	MER	ANG	MER	
508126	64674+71508+64717	BD	MER	ANG	MER	
508127	64675+71509+64718	BD	MER	ANG	MER	
508128	64676+71510+64719	BD	MER	ANG	MER	
508130	64678+71512+64721	BD	MER	ANG	MER	
508131	64679+71513+64722	BD	MER	ANG	MER	
508134	64682+71516+64725	BD	MER	ANG	MER	
508136	64684+71518+64727	BD	MER	ANG	MER	
508137	64685+71519+64728	BD	MER	ANG	MER	
508138	64686+71520+64729	BD	MER	ANG	MER	
508139	64687+71521+64730	BD	MER	ANG	MER	
508140	64688+71522+64731	BD	MER	ANG	MER	
508141	64689+71523+64732	BD	MER	ANG	MER	
508143	64691+71525+64734	BD	MER	ANG	MER	

Above: *Originally used on the Southern Region, the Class 508s were quickly transferred to the Mersey network to operate alongside the Class 507s. The three-car sets are identical to the '507s', and all are refurbished with modernised front ends and high-back seating. Set No. 508130 departs from Formby on 24 September 2013.* **John Binch**

Northern Rail

Address: ✉ Northern House, 9 Rougier Street, York, YO1 6HZ
customer.relations@northernrail.org
✆ 0845 000125
ⓘ www.northernrail.org

Managing Director: Alex Hynes

Franchise Dates: 12 December 2004 - 31 March 2014*

Principal Routes: Regional services in Merseyside, Greater Manchester, South/North Yorkshire, Lancashire, Cumbria and the North East

Depots: Newton Heath (NH), Heaton (HT), Longsight (LG), Neville Hill (NL), Allerton (AN)

Parent Company: Serco/Abellio

* Likely extension to February 2016

Class 142

Vehicle Length: 51ft 0½in (15.55m)
Height: 12ft 8in (3.86m)
Width: 9ft 2¼in (2.80m)
Engine: 1 x Cummins LTA10-R per vehicle
Horsepower: 460hp (343kW)
Seats (total/car): 106S, 56S/50S

Number	*Formation DMS+DMSL*	*Depot*	*Livery*	*Owner*	*Operator*
142001	55542+55592	NH	NOU	ANG	NOR
142003	55544+55594	NH	NOR	ANG	NOR
142004	55545+55595	NH	NOR	ANG	NOR
142005	55546+55596	NH	NOR	ANG	NOR
142007	55548+55598	NH	NOR	ANG	NOR
142009	55550+55600	NH	NOU	ANG	NOR
142011	55552+55602	NH	NOR	ANG	NOR
142012	55553+55603	NH	NOR	ANG	NOR
142013	55554+55604	NH	NOR	ANG	NOR
142014	55555+55605	NH	NOR	ANG	NOR
142015	55556+55606	HT	NOR	ANG	NOR
142016	55557+55607	HT	NOR	ANG	NOR
142017	55558+55608	HT	NOR	ANG	NOR
142018	55559+55609	HT	NOR	ANG	NOR
142019	55560+55610	HT	NOR	ANG	NOR
142020	55561+55611	HT	NOR	ANG	NOR
142021	55562+55612	HT	NOR	ANG	NOR
142022	55563+55613	HT	NOR	ANG	NOR
142023	55564+55614	NH	NOR	ANG	NOR
142024	55565+55615	HT	NOR	ANG	NOR
142025	55566+55616	HT	NOR	ANG	NOR
142026	55567+55617	HT	NOR	ANG	NOR
142027	55568+55618	NH	NOR	ANG	NOR
142028	55569+55619	NH	NOR	ANG	NOR
142029	55570+55620	NH	NOU	ANG	NOR
142030	55571+55621	NH	NOU	ANG	NOR
142031	55572+55622	NH	NOR	ANG	NOR
142032	55573+55623	NH	NOR	ANG	NOR
142033	55574+55624	NH	NOR	ANG	NOR
142034	55575+55625	HT	NOR	ANG	NOR
142035	55576+55626	NH	NOR	ANG	NOR
142036	55577+55627	NH	NOR	ANG	NOR
142037	55578+55628	NH	NOR	ANG	NOR
142038	55579+55629	NH	NOR	ANG	NOR
142039	55580+55630	NH	NOR	ANG	NOR
142040	55581+55631	NH	NOR	ANG	NOR
142041	55582+55632	NH	NOR	ANG	NOR
142042(S)	55583+55633	NH	NOR	ANG	NOR
142043	55584+55634	NH	NOR	ANG	NOR
142044	55585+55635	NH	NOR	ANG	NOR
142045	55586+55636	NH	NOR	ANG	NOR
142046	55587+55637	NH	NOR	ANG	NOR
142047	55588+55638	NH	NOR	ANG	NOR
142048	55589+55639	NH	NOR	ANG	NOR
142049	55590+55640	NH	NOR	ANG	NOR
142050	55591+55641	HT	NOR	ANG	NOR
142051	55701+55747	NH	NOR	ANG	NOR
142052	55702+55748	NH	NOR	ANG	NOR
142053	55703+55749	NH	NOR	ANG	NOR
142054	55704+55750	NH	NOR	ANG	NOR
142055	55705+55751	NH	NOR	ANG	NOR
142056	55706+55752	NH	NOR	ANG	NOR
142057	55707+55753	NH	NOR	ANG	NOR
142058	55708+55754	NH	NOR	ANG	NOR
142060	55710+55756	NH	NOR	ANG	NOR
142061	55711+55757	NH	NOR	ANG	NOR
142062	55712+55758	NH	NOR	ANG	NOR
142063	55713+55759	NH	NOU	ANG	NOR
142064	55714+55760	NH	NOU	ANG	NOR
142065	55715+55761	HT	NOR	ANG	NOR
142066	55716+55762	HT	NOR	ANG	NOR
142067	55717+55763	NH	NOR	ANG	NOR
142068	55718+55764	NH	NOU	ANG	NOR
142070	55720+55766	HT	NOR	ANG	NOR
142071	55721+55767	HT	NOR	ANG	NOR
142078	55728+55768	HT	NOR	ANG	NOR
142079	55729+55769	HT	NOR	ANG	NOR
142084	55764+55780	HT	NOR	ANG	NOR
142086	55736+55782	HT	NOR	ANG	NOR
142087	55737+55783	HT	NOR	ANG	NOR
142088	55738+55784	HT	NOR	ANG	NOR
142089	55739+55785	HT	NOR	ANG	NOR
142090	55740+55786	HT	NOR	ANG	NOR
142091	55741+55787	HT	NOR	ANG	NOR
142092	55742+55788	HT	NOR	ANG	NOR
142093	55743+55789	HT	NOR	ANG	NOR
142094	55744+55790	HT	NOR	ANG	NOR
142095	55745+55791	HT	NOR	ANG	NOR
142096	55746+55792	HT	NOR	ANG	NOR

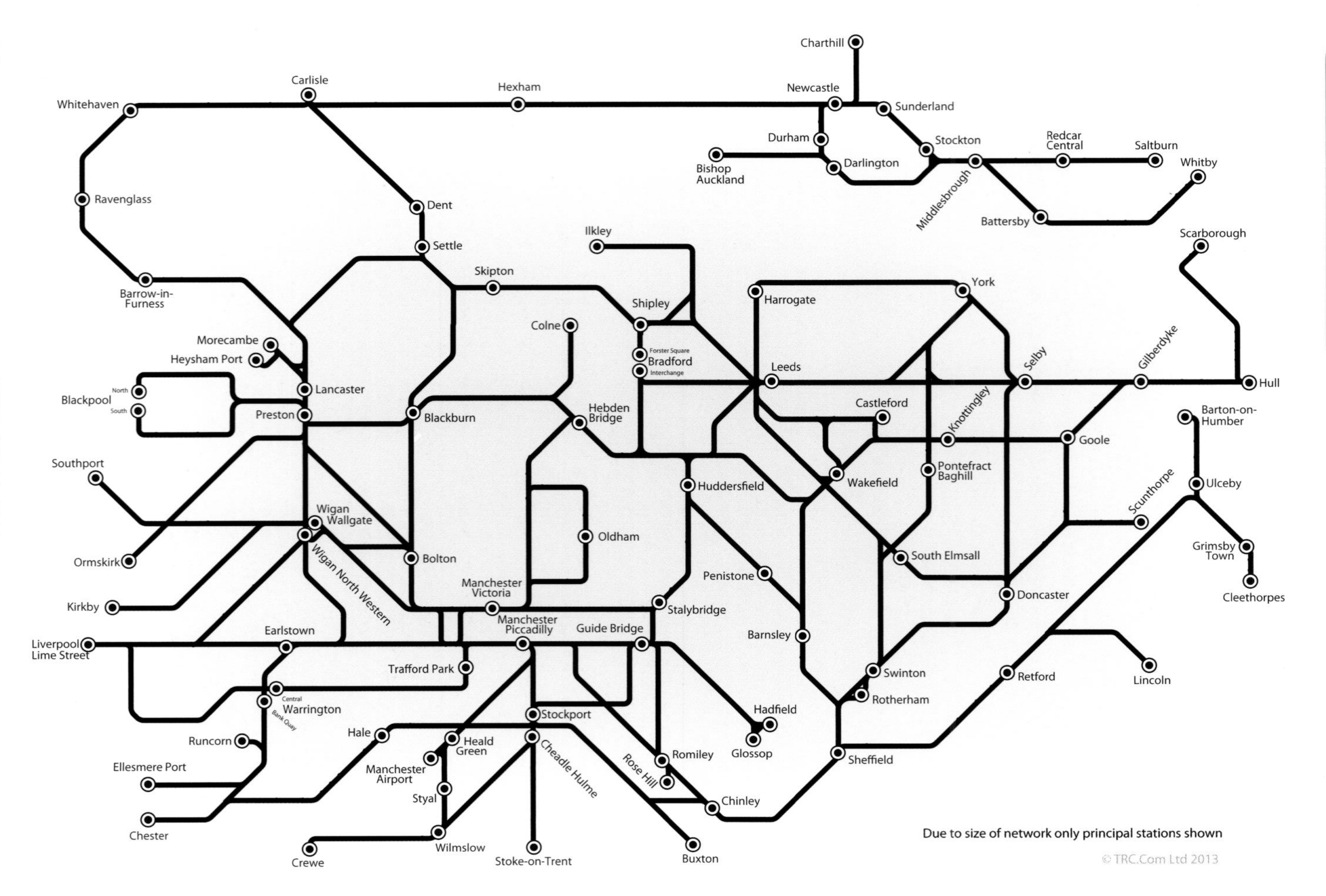

Charthill
Carlisle
Hexham
Newcastle
Whitehaven
Sunderland
Durham
Stockton
Redcar Central
Saltburn
Bishop Auckland
Darlington
Whitby
Ravenglass
Dent
Middlesbrough
Battersby
Ilkley
Scarborough
Settle
Skipton
Barrow-in-Furness
Shipley
Harrogate
York
Colne
Morecambe
Heysham Port
Forster Square
Bradford
Interchange
Leeds
Selby
Gilberdyke
Hull
North
Blackpool
South
Lancaster
Preston
Blackburn
Hebden Bridge
Castleford
Knottingley
Barton-on-Humber
Goole
Southport
Pontefract Baghill
Huddersfield
Wakefield
Ulceby
Scunthorpe
Wigan Wallgate
Wigan North Western
Oldham
Grimsby Town
Ormskirk
Bolton
South Elmsall
Penistone
Cleethorpes
Manchester Victoria
Doncaster
Kirkby
Stalybridge
Manchester Piccadilly
Guide Bridge
Barnsley
Liverpool Lime Street
Earlstown
Trafford Park
Swinton
Retford
Lincoln
Rotherham
Central
Warrington
Bank Quay
Hadfield
Stockport
Runcorn
Hale
Heald Green
Glossop
Romiley
Sheffield
Manchester Airport
Cheadle Hulme
Ellesmere Port
Rose Hill
Styal
Chinley
Chester
Wilmslow
Crewe
Stoke-on-Trent
Buxton
Due to size of network only principal stations shown
© TRC.Com Ltd 2013

Right: *Northern Rail, with 79 two-car Class 142s, is the largest user of the design, with the fleet forming the backbone of local services. The sets, all painted in Northern blue, mauve and grey livery, are allocated to Heaton (Newcastle) and Newton Heath (Manchester) and can be found all over the wandering Northern Rail system. Set No. 142018, with its Driving Motor Standard Lavatory nearest the camera, approaches Doncaster with a service from Sheffield.* **CJM**

Class 144

Vehicle Length: 50ft 2in (15.25m)
Height: 12ft 2½in (3.73m)
Width: 8ft 10½in (2.70m)
Engine: 1 x Cummins LTA10-R per vehicle
Horsepower: 460hp (343kW)
Seats (total/car): 87S, 45S/42S

Number	*Formation DMS+DMSL*	*Depot*	*Livery*	*Owner*	*Operator*
144001	55801+55824	NL	NOR	PTR	NOR
144002	55802+55825	NL	NOR	PTR	NOR
144003	55803+55826	NL	NOR	PTR	NOR
144004	55804+55827	NL	NOR	PTR	NOR
144005	55805+55828	NL	NOR	PTR	NOR
144006	55806+55829	NL	NOR	PTR	NOR
144007	55807+55830	NL	NOR	PTR	NOR
144008	55808+55831	NL	NOR	PTR	NOR
144009	55809+55832	NL	NOR	PTR	NOR
144010	55810+55833	NL	NOR	PTR	NOR
144011	55811+55834	NL	NOR	PTR	NOR
144012	55812+55835	NL	NOR	PTR	NOR
144013	55813+55836	NL	NOR	PTR	NOR

Name applied
144001 ***The Penistone Line Partnership***

Vehicle Length: 50ft 2in (15.25m)
Height: 12ft 2½in (3.73m)
Width: 8ft 10½in (2.70m)
Engine: 1 x Cummins LTA10-R per vehicle
Horsepower: 690hp (515kW)
Seats (total/car): 145S, 45S/58S/42S

Number	*Formation DMS+MS+DMSL*	*Depot*	*Livery*	*Owner*	*Operator*
144014	55814+55850+55837	NL	NOR	PTR	NOR
144015	55815+55851+55838	NL	NOR	PTR	NOR
144016	55816+55852+55839	NL	NOR	PTR	NOR
144017	55817+55853+55840	NL	NOR	PTR	NOR
144018	55818+55854+55841	NL	NOR	PTR	NOR
144019	55819+55855+55842	NL	NOR	PTR	NOR
144020	55820+55856+55843	NL	NOR	PTR	NOR
144021	55821+55857+55844	NL	NOR	PTR	NOR
144022	55822+55858+55845	NL	NOR	PTR	NOR
144023	55823+55859+55846	NL	NOR	PTR	NOR

Below: *Both two- and three-car versions of the BREL/Walter Alexander Class 144s are operated by Northern. Allocated to Leeds Neville Hill, the sets usually operate services in Yorkshire. All sets are painted in Northern Rail livery and have 2+2 seating. Two-car set No. 144006 with its DMSL vehicle on the right is seen at Doncaster.* **CJM**

Northern Rail

Class 150/1

Vehicle Length: 64ft 9¾in (19.74m)
Height: 12ft 4½in (3.77m)
Width: 9ft 3⅛in (2.82m)
Engine: 1 x NT855R5 of 285hp per vehicle
Horsepower: 570hp (425kW)
Seats (total/car): 124S, 59S/65S

Number	Formation DMSL+DMS	Depot	Livery	Owner	Operator
150103§	52103+57103	NH	NOR	ANG	NOR
150110	52110+57110	NH	NOR	ANG	NOR
150111	52111+57111	NH	NOR	ANG	NOR
150112	52112+57112	NH	NOR	ANG	NOR
150113	52113+57113	NH	NOR	ANG	NOR
150114	52114+57114	NH	NOR	ANG	NOR
150115	52115+57115	NH	NOR	ANG	NOR
150116	52116+57116	NH	NOR	ANG	NOR
150117§	52117+57117	NH	NOR	ANG	NOR
150118	52118+57118	NH	NOR	ANG	NOR
150119	52119+57119	NH	NOR	ANG	NOR
150132§	52132+57132	NH	NOR	ANG	NOR
150133	52133+57133	NH	NOR	ANG	NOR
150134	52134+57134	NH	NOR	ANG	NOR
150135	52135+57135	NH	NOR	ANG	NOR
150136	52136+57136	NH	NOR	ANG	NOR
150137	52137+57137	NH	NOR	ANG	NOR
150138	52138+57138	NH	NOR	ANG	NOR
150139	52139+57139	NH	NOR	ANG	NOR
150140	52140+57140	NH	NOR	ANG	NOR
150141	52141+57141	NH	NOR	ANG	NOR
150142	52142+57142	NH	NOR	ANG	NOR
150143	52143+57143	NH	NOR	ANG	NOR
150144	52144+57144	NH	NOR	ANG	NOR
150145	52145+57145	NH	NOR	ANG	NOR
150146	52146+57146	NH	NOR	ANG	NOR
150147	52147+57147	NH	NOR	ANG	NOR
150148	52148+57148	NH	NOR	ANG	NOR
150149	52149+57149	NH	NOR	ANG	NOR
150150	52150+57150	NH	NOR	ANG	NOR

§ Not part of core fleet

Left: *Newton Heath depot, Manchester, is the home to 30 Class 150/1 non-gangwayed sets used for local non-electrified services. Sets are painted in Standard NR colours. No. 150117 arrives at Preston with a local service bound for Blackpool.* **Robin Ralston**

Class 150/2

Vehicle Length: 64ft 9¾in (19.74m)
Height: 12ft 4½in (3.77m)
Width: 9ft 3⅛in (2.82m)
Engine: 1 x NT855R5 of 285hp per vehicle
Horsepower: 570hp (425kW)
Seats (total/car): 132S, 62S/70S

Number	Formation DMSL+DMS	Depot	Livery	Owner	Operator
150201	52201+57201	NH	NOR	ANG	NOR
150203	52203+57203	NH	NOR ¤	ANG	NOR
150204	52204+57204	NH	NOR	ANG	NOR
150205	52205+57205	NH	NOR ¤	ANG	NOR
150206	52206+57206	NH	NOR	ANG	NOR
150207	52207+57207	NH	NOR ¤	ANG	NOR
150210	52210+57210	NH	NOR	ANG	NOR
150211	52211+57211	NH	NOR ¤	ANG	NOR
150214	52214+57214	NH	NOR	ANG	NOR
150215	52215+57215	NH	NOR ¤	ANG	NOR
150218	52218+57218	NH	NOR ¤	ANG	NOR
150220	52220+57220	NH	NOR	ANG	NOR
150222	52222+57222	NH	NOR ¤	ANG	NOR
150223	52223+57223	NH	NOR	ANG	NOR
150224	52224+57224	NH	NOR	ANG	NOR
150225	52225+57225	NH	NOR ¤	ANG	NOR
150226	52226+57226	NH	NOR	ANG	NOR
150228	52228+57228	NH	NOR ¤	PTR	NOR
150268	52268+57268	NH	NOR ¤	PTR	NOR
150269	52269+57269	NH	NOR ¤	PTR	NOR
150270	52270+57270	NH	NOR ¤	PTR	NOR
150271	52271+57271	NH	NOR ¤	PTR	NOR
150272	52272+57272	NH	NOR ¤	PTR	NOR
150273	52273+57273	NH	NOR ¤	PTR	NOR
150274	52274+57274	NH	NOR ¤	PTR	NOR
150275	52275+57275	NH	NOR ¤	PTR	NOR
150276	52276+57276	NH	NOR ¤	PTR	NOR
150277	52277+57277	NH	NOR ¤	PTR	NOR
150285§	52285+57285	NH	ATW	PTR	NOR

§ On loan from Arriva Trains Wales

¤ Advertising liveries
150203 - Yorkshire
150205 - Yorkshire
150207 - Yorkshire
150211 - Yorkshire
150215 - Yorkshire
150218 - Yorkshire
150222 - Yorkshire
150225 - Yorkshire
150228 - Outdoors
150268 - Heritage
150269 - Yorkshire
150270 - City Life
150271 - Arts
150272 - Colne Festival
150273 - Yorkshire
150274 - Events
150275 - Yorkshire
150276 - Sport
150277 - Yorkshire

Above: *A fleet of 29 gangway-fitted Class 150/2s is operated by Northern for medium-distance local services, allocated to Newton Heath. A large number of these sets carry route advertising branding, as shown on set No. 150272 at Manchester Victoria, advertising the Colne Blues Festival.* **Antony Christie**

Class 153

Vehicle Length: 76ft 5in (23.29m)
Height: 12ft 3$^{1}/_{8}$in (3.75m)
Width: 8ft 10in (2.70m)
Engine: 1 x NT855R5 of 285hp
Horsepower: 285hp (213kW)
Seats (total/car): 70S

Number	*Formation* DMSL	*Depot*	*Livery*	*Owner*	*Operator*
153301	52301	NL	NOR	ANG	NOR
153304	52304	NL	NOR	ANG	NOR
153307	52307	NL	NOR	ANG	NOR
153315	52315	NL	NOR	ANG	NOR
153316	52316	NL	NOR	PTR	NOR
153317	52317	NL	NOR	ANG	NOR
153324	52324	NL	NOR	PTR	NOR
153328	52328	NL	NOR	ANG	NOR
153330	52330	NL	NOR	PTR	NOR
153331	52331	NL	NOR	ANG	NOR
153332	52332	NL	NOR	ANG	NOR
153351	57351	NL	NOR	ANG	NOR
153352	57352	NL	NOR	ANG	NOR
153358	57358	NL	NOR	PTR	NOR
153359	57359	NL	NOR	PTR	NOR
153360	57360	NL	NOR	PTR	NOR
153363	57363	NL	NOR	PTR	NOR
153378	57378	NL	NOR	ANG	NOR

Right: *A large fleet of 18 single-car Class 153s is operated by Northern Rail, all based at Leeds Neville Hill and deployed on more lightly used routes and to supplement two-car services to three. The cars carry Northern livery and are leased from both Angel Trains and Porterbrook Leasing. Viewed from its small cab end, No. 153352 is seen at Leeds.* **Ron Cover**

Class 155

Vehicle Length: 76ft 5in (23.29m)
Height: 12ft 3$^{1}/_{8}$in (3.75m)
Width: 8ft 10in (2.70m)
Engine: 1 x NT855R5 of 285hp
Horsepower: 570hp (425kW)
Seats (total/car): 156S, 76S/80S

Number	*Formation* DMSL+DMS	*Depot*	*Livery*	*Owner*	*Operator*
155341	52341+57341	NL	NOR	PTR	NOR
155342	52342+57342	NL	NOR	PTR	NOR
155343	52343+57343	NL	NOR	PTR	NOR
155344	52344+57344	NL	NOR	PTR	NOR
155345	52345+57345	NL	NOR	PTR	NOR
155346	52346+57346	NL	NOR	PTR	NOR
155347	52347+57347	NL	NOR	PTR	NOR

Class 156

Vehicle Length: 75ft 6in (23.03m)
Height: 12ft 6in (3.81m)
Width: 8ft 11in (2.73m)
Engine: 1 x Cummins NT855R5 of 285hp
Horsepower: 570hp (425kW)
Seats (total/car): 146S, 70/76S

Number	*Formation* DMSL+DMS	*Depot*	*Livery*	*Owner*	*Operator*
156420	52420+57420	AN	NOR	PTR	NOR
156421	52421+57421	AN	NOR	PTR	NOR
156423	52423+57423	AN	NOR	PTR	NOR
156424	52424+57424	AN	NOR	PTR	NOR
156425	52425+57425	AN	NOR	PTR	NOR
156426	52426+57426	AN	NOR	PTR	NOR
156427	52427+57427	AN	NOR	PTR	NOR
156428	52428+57428	AN	NOR	PTR	NOR
156429	52429+57429	AN	NOR	PTR	NOR
156438	52438+57438	HT	NOR	ANG	NOR
156440	52440+57440	AN	NOR	PTR	NOR
156441	52441+57441	AN	§	PTR	NOR

Right: *Both Heaton depot in Newcastle and Allerton depot in Liverpool have an allocation of Class 156s, used on longer-distance domestic Northern services. Painted in standard Northern livery, some of these sets are named, using 'stick-on' plates. Set No. 156428 is seen at Manchester Airport with a service bound for Liverpool Lime Street.*
Norman E. Preedy

Northern Rail

156443	52443+57443	HT	NOR	ANG	NOR
156444	52444+57444	HT	NOR	ANG	NOR
156448	52448+57448	HT	NOR	ANG	NOR
156451	52451+57451	HT	NOR	ANG	NOR
156452	52452+57452	AN	NOR	PTR	NOR
156454	52454+57454	HT	NOR	ANG	NOR
156455	52455+57455	AN	NOR	PTR	NOR
156459	52459+57459	AN	NOR	PTR	NOR
156460	52460+57460	AN	NOR	PTR	NOR
156461	52461+57461	AN	NOR	PTR	NOR
156463	52463+57463	HT	NOR	ANG	NOR
156464	52464+57464	AN	SPL	PTR	NOR
156466	52466+57466	AN	NOR	PTR	NOR
156468	52468+57468	AN	NOR	ANG	NOR
156469	52469+57469	HT	NOR	ANG	NOR
156471	52471+57471	AN	NOR	ANG	NOR
156472	52472+57472	AN	NOR	ANG	NOR
156475	52475+57475	HT	NOR	ANG	NOR
156479	52479+57479	AN	NOR	ANG	NOR
156480	52480+57480	HT	NOR	ANG	NOR
156481	52481+57481	AN	NOR	ANG	NOR
156482	52482+57482	AN	NOR	ANG	NOR
156483	52483+57483	AN	NOR	ANG	NOR
156484	52484+57484	HT	NOR	ANG	NOR
156486	52486+57486	AN	NOR	ANG	NOR
156487	52487+57487	AN	NOR	ANG	NOR
156488	52488+57488	AN	NOR	ANG	NOR
156489	52489+57489	AN	NOR	ANG	NOR
156490	52490+57490	HT	NOR	ANG	NOR
156491	52491+57491	AN	NOR	ANG	NOR

§ - Liverpool & Manchester Railway livery

Names applied

156438 *Timothy Hackworth*
156440 *George Bradshaw*
156441 *William Huskisson MP*
156444 *Councillor Bill Cameron*
156459 *Benny Rothman - The Manchester Rambler*
156460 *Driver John Axon GC*
156466 *Gracie Fields*
156464 *Lancashire DalesRail*

Class 158/0

Vehicle Length: 76ft 1¾in (23.21m)
Height: 12ft 6in (3.81m)
Width: 9ft 3¼in (2.82m)
Engine: 1 x Cummins NTA855R of 350hp per vehicle
Horsepower: 1,050hp (783kW)
Seats (total/car): 208S, 68S/70S/70S

Number	*Formation DMSL+MSL+DMSL*	*Depot*	*Livery*	*Owner*	*Operator*
158752	52752+58716+57752	NL	NOR	PTR	NOR
158753	52753+58710+57753	NL	NOR	PTR	NOR
158754	52754+58708+57754	NL	NOR	PTR	NOR
158755	52755+58702+57755	NL	NOR	PTR	NOR
158756	52756+58712+57756	NL	NOR	PTR	NOR
158757	52757+58706+57757	NL	NOR	PTR	NOR
158758	52758+58714+57758	NL	NOR	PTR	NOR
158759	52759+58713+57759	NL	NOR	PTR	NOR

Vehicle Length: 76ft 1¾in (23.21m)
Height: 12ft 6in (3.81m)
Width: 9ft 3¼in (2.82m)
Engine: 1 x Cummins NTA855R of 350hp per vehicle
Horsepower: 700hp (522kW)
Seats (total/car): 138S, 68S/70S

Number	*Formation DMSL+DMSL*	*Depot*	*Livery*	*Owner*	*Operator*
158784	52784+57784	NH	NOR	ANG	NOR
158787	52787+57787	NH	NOR	ANG	NOR
158790	52790+57790	NH	NOR	ANG	NOR
158791	52791+57791	NH	NOR	ANG	NOR
158792	52792+57792	NH	NOR	ANG	NOR
158793	52793+57793	NH	NOR	ANG	NOR
158794	52794+57794	NH	NOR	ANG	NOR
158795	52795+57795	NH	NOR	ANG	NOR
158796	52796+57796	NH	NOR	ANG	NOR
158797	52797+57797	NH	NOR	ANG	NOR

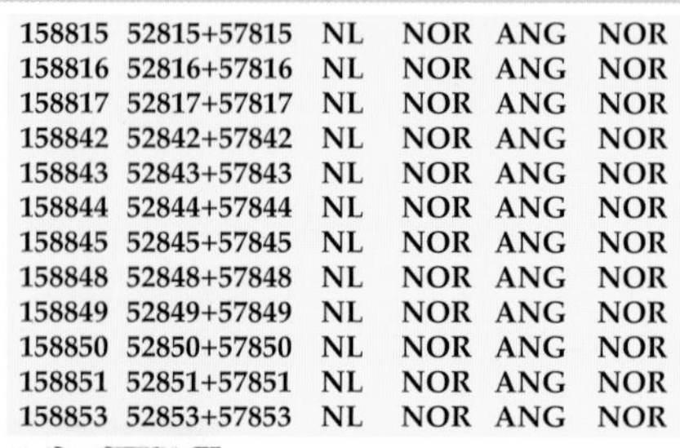

158815	52815+57815	NL	NOR	ANG	NOR
158816	52816+57816	NL	NOR	ANG	NOR
158817	52817+57817	NL	NOR	ANG	NOR
158842	52842+57842	NL	NOR	ANG	NOR
158843	52843+57843	NL	NOR	ANG	NOR
158844	52844+57844	NL	NOR	ANG	NOR
158845	52845+57845	NL	NOR	ANG	NOR
158848	52848+57848	NL	NOR	ANG	NOR
158849	52849+57849	NL	NOR	ANG	NOR
158850	52850+57850	NL	NOR	ANG	NOR
158851	52851+57851	NL	NOR	ANG	NOR
158853	52853+57853	NL	NOR	ANG	NOR

Left: *Northern Rail longer-distance services are operated by a fleet of Class 158s. Eight three-car sets and 37 two-car sets are in operation-allocated to Newton Heath and Neville Hill depots. Some sets carry pictogram branding of routes or events, which is applied in the Northern Rail 'arc' style. Two-car set No. 158796 is seen at Doncaster carrying Yorkshire branding. This set is also named* Fred Trueman - Cricketing Legend. **CJM**

Number	Formation	Depot	Livery	Owner	Operator
158855	52855+57855	NL	NOR	ANG	NOR
158859	52859+57859	NL	NOR	ANG	NOR
158860	52860+57860	NL	NOR	ANG	NOR
158861	52861+57861	NL	SPL§	ANG	NOR
158872	52872+57872	NL	NOR	ANG	NOR

§ Carries Welcome to Yorkshire livery

Class 158/9

Vehicle Length: 76ft 1¾in (23.21m)
Height: 12ft 6in (3.81m)
Width: 9ft 3¼in (2.82m)
Engine: 1 x Cummins NTA855R of 350hp per vehicle
Horsepower: 700hp (522kW)
Seats (total/car): 142S, 70S/72S

Number	Formation DMSL+DMS	Depot	Livery	Owner	Operator
158901	52901+57901	NL	NOR	EVL	NOR
158902	52902+57902	NL	NOR	EVL	NOR
158903	52903+57903	NL	NOR	EVL	NOR
158904	52904+57904	NL	NOR	EVL	NOR
158905	52905+57905	NL	NOR	EVL	NOR
158906	52906+57906	NL	NOR	EVL	NOR
158907	52907+57907	NL	NOR	EVL	NOR
158908	52908+57908	NL	NOR	EVL	NOR
158909	52909+57909	NL	NOR	EVL	NOR
158910	52910+57910	NL	NOR	EVL	NOR

Names applied

158784	*Barbara Castle*
158791	*County of Nottinghamshire*
158796	*Fred Trueman - Cricketing Legend*
158797	*Jane Tomlinson*
158860	*Ian Dewhirst*
158910	*William Wilberforce*

Right: *Ten Class 158/9s are owned by Eversholt Leasing and operated by Northern. These were originally funded by West Yorkshire PTE but now operate as part of the core '158' fleet. Set No. 158901 in Metro Yorkshire pictogram livery is recorded at Doncaster.* **CJM**

Class 321/9

Vehicle Length: (Driving) 65ft 0¾in (19.83m)
(Inter) 65ft 4¼in (19.92m)
Height: 12ft 4¾in (3.78m)
Width: 9ft 3in (2.82m)
Horsepower: 1,328hp (996kW)
Seats (total/car): 293S, 70S/79S/74S/70S

Number	Formation DTCO+MSO+TSO+DTSO	Depot	Livery	Owner	Operator
321901	77990+63153+72128+77993	NL	NOM	EVL	NOR
321902	77991+63154+72129+77994	NL	NOM	EVL	NOR
321903	77992+63155+72130+77995	NL	NOM	EVL	NOR

Right: *Three Class 321 four-car sets were ordered for the modernisation of the Doncaster to Leeds route to replace ageing ex-Network SouthEast EMUs. The sets, now operated by Northern, are in West Yorkshire red livery with blue graphics on the driving cars. Allocated to Leeds Neville Hill, the sets seldom stray off the Leeds-Doncaster route. Set No. 321902 is seen in the north-facing bay at Doncaster.* **CJM**

Class 322

Vehicle Length: (Driving) 65ft 0¾in (19.83m)
(Inter) 65ft 4¼in (19.92m)
Height: 12ft 4¾in (3.78m)
Width: 9ft 3in (2.82m)
Horsepower: 1,328hp (996kW)
Seats (total/car): 291S, 74S/83S/76S/58S

Number	Formation DTSO(A)+MSO+TSO+DTSO(B)	Depot	Livery	Owner	Operator
322481	78163+63137+72023+77985	NL	NOR	EVL	NOR
322482	78164+63138+72024+77986	NL	NOR	EVL	NOR
322483	78165+63139+72025+77987	NL	NOR	EVL	NOR
322484	78166+63140+72026+77988	NL	NOR	EVL	NOR
322485	78167+63141+72027+77989	NL	NOR	EVL	NOR

Northern Rail

Left: *From 2011, Northern Rail has operated the five Class 322 four-car EMUs, that had previously operated in Scotland and prior to that in the North East and the London area on Stansted Airport duties. The sets are now based at Leeds Neville Hill and operate on the Leeds to Doncaster route as well as some Aire Valley duties. Painted in all-over mid-blue livery with Northern branding, set No. 322482 is seen at Doncaster with a Leeds-bound service.* **Nathan Williamson**

Class 323

Vehicle Length: (Driving) 76ft 8¼in (23.37m)
(Inter) 76ft 10¾in (23.44m)
Height: 12ft 4¾in (3.78m)
Width: 9ft 2¼in (2.80m)
Horsepower: 1,565hp (1,168kW)
Seats (total/car) 323223-225: 244S, 82S/80S/82S
323226-239: 284S, 98S/88S/98S

Number	*Formation DMSO(A)+PTSO+DMSO(B)*	*Depot*	*Livery*	*Owner*	*Operator*
323223	64023+72223+65023	LG	NOR	PTR	NOR
323224	64024+72224+65024	LG	NOR	PTR	NOR
323225	64025+72225+65025	LG	FSN	PTR	NOR
323226	64026+72226+65026	LG	FSN	PTR	NOR
323227	64027+72227+65027	LG	FSN	PTR	NOR
323228	64028+72228+65028	LG	NOR	PTR	NOR
323229	64029+72229+65029	LG	NOR	PTR	NOR
323230	64030+72230+65030	LG	FSN	PTR	NOR
323231	64031+72231+65031	LG	NOR	PTR	NOR
323232	64032+72232+65032	LG	NOR	PTR	NOR
323233	64033+72233+65033	LG	NOR	PTR	NOR
323234	64034+72234+65034	LG	NOR	PTR	NOR
323235	64035+72235+65035	LG	NOR	PTR	NOR
323236	64036+72236+65036	LG	NOR	PTR	NOR
323237	64037+72237+65037	LG	NOR	PTR	NOR
323238	64038+72238+65038	LG	FSN	PTR	NOR
323239	64039+72239+65039	LG	FSN	PTR	NOR

Below: *Manchester area electrified local services are in the hands of a fleet of 17 three-car Class 323 units allocated to Manchester Longsight depot. The sets, owned by Porterbrook and painted in Northern livery, are found with two seating configurations. Sets 323223-323225 seat 244 standard class passengers and have extra luggage space for operating Manchester Airport services, while the remainder have seating for 284 passengers. Set No. 323238 is seen approaching Crewe.* **John Wills**

Class 333

Vehicle Length: (Driving) 77ft 10¾in (23.74m) (Inter) 75ft 11in (23.14m)
Height: 12ft 1½in (3.79m)
Width: 9ft 0¼in (2.75m)
Horsepower: 1,877hp (1,400kW)
Seats (total/car): 353S, 90S/73S/100S/90S

Number	*Formation* DMSO(A)+PTSO+TSO+DMSO(B)	*Depot*	*Livery*	*Owner*	*Operator*	*Name*
333001	78451+74461+74477+78452	NL	NOM	ANG	NOR	
333002	78453+74462+74478+78454	NL	NOM	ANG	NOR	
333003	78455+74463+74479+78456	NL	NOM	ANG	NOR	
333004	78457+74464+74480+78458	NL	NOM	ANG	NOR	
333005	78459+74465+74481+78460	NL	NOM	ANG	NOR	
333006	78461+74466+74482+78462	NL	NOM	ANG	NOR	
333007	78463+74467+74483+78464	NL	NOM	ANG	NOR	*Alderman J Arthur Godwin - First Lord Mayor of Bradford 1907*
333008	78465+74468+74484+78466	NL	NOM	ANG	NOR	
333009	78467+74469+74485+78468	NL	NOM	ANG	NOR	
333010	78469+74470+74486+78470	NL	NOM	ANG	NOR	
333011	78471+74471+74487+78472	NL	NOM	ANG	NOR	
333012	78473+74472+74488+78474	NL	NOM	ANG	NOR	
333013	78475+74473+74489+78476	NL	NOM	ANG	NOR	
333014	78477+74474+74490+78478	NL	NOM	ANG	NOR	
333015	78479+74475+74491+78480	NL	NOM	ANG	NOR	
333016	78481+74476+74492+78482	NL	NOM	ANG	NOR	

Above and right: *Following electrification of the Aire Valley lines radiating from Leeds came the ordering of 16 three-car EMUs, built by CAF. The electrification was a great success and passenger growth saw sets strengthened from three to four vehicles. The Class 333s are allocated to Leeds Neville Hill and usually only operate on the Aire Valley lines, with a few rare outings on the Leeds to Doncaster line. In the view above, painted in Northern blue/red livery, set No. 333004 approaches Frizinghall with a service bound for Bradford. On the right is all-red-liveried intermediate vehicle No. 74472 from set No. 333012. Both:* **Antony Christie**

South West Trains

Address: Friars Bridge Court, 41-45 Blackfriars Road, London, SE1 8NZ
customerrelations@swtrains.co.uk
08700 00 5151
www.southwesttrains.co.uk

Managing Director: Tim Shoveller

Franchise Dates: 4 December 1996 - 3 February 2017*

Principal Routes: London Waterloo - Weymouth, Exeter, Portsmouth and suburban services in Surrey, Berkshire, Hampshire

Depots: Wimbledon Park (WD), Bournemouth (BM), Clapham Junction (CJ) [Stabling point], Salisbury (SA), Northam (Siemens Transportation) (NT)

Parent Company: Stagecoach Group

* Likely extension to April 2019

Class 158

Vehicle Length: 76ft 1¾in (23.21m)
Height: 12ft 6in (3.81m)
Width: 9ft 3¼in (2.82m)
Engine: 1 x Cummins NTA855R of 350hp per vehicle
Horsepower: 700hp (522kW)
Seats (total/car): 13F-114S, 13F-44S/70S

Number	*Formation DMSL+DMSL*	*Depot*	*Livery*	*Owner*	*Operator*
158880 (158737)	52737+57737	SA	SWM	PTR	SWT
158881 (158742)	52742+57742	SA	SWM	PTR	SWT
158882 (158743)	52743+57743	SA	SWM	PTR	SWT
158883 (158744)	52744+57744	SA	SWM	PTR	SWT
158884 (158772)	52772+57772	SA	SWM	PTR	SWT
158885 (158775)	52775+57775	SA	SWM	PTR	SWT
158886 (158779)	52779+57779	SA	SWM	PTR	SWT
158887 (158781)	52781+57781	SA	SWM	PTR	SWT
158888 (158802)	52802+57802	SA	SWM	PTR	SWT
158889 (158808)	52808+57808	SA	SWM	PTR	SWT
158890 (158814)	52814+57814	SA	SWM	PTR	SWT

Left: *Salisbury depot has an allocated of 11 two-car Class 158s for deployment on non-electrified South West Trains routes, as well as providing weekday cover for the Brockenhurst to Lymington Pier line, which is electrified. The sets are refurbished and when taken over by SWT were formed into a new numeric group. Sets are painted in South West Trains / Stagecoach main-line white livery. Set No. 158888 (the original 158802) stands at Lymington Pier in summer 2013. The SWT Class 158s seat 13 first and 114 standard class passengers.* **CJM**

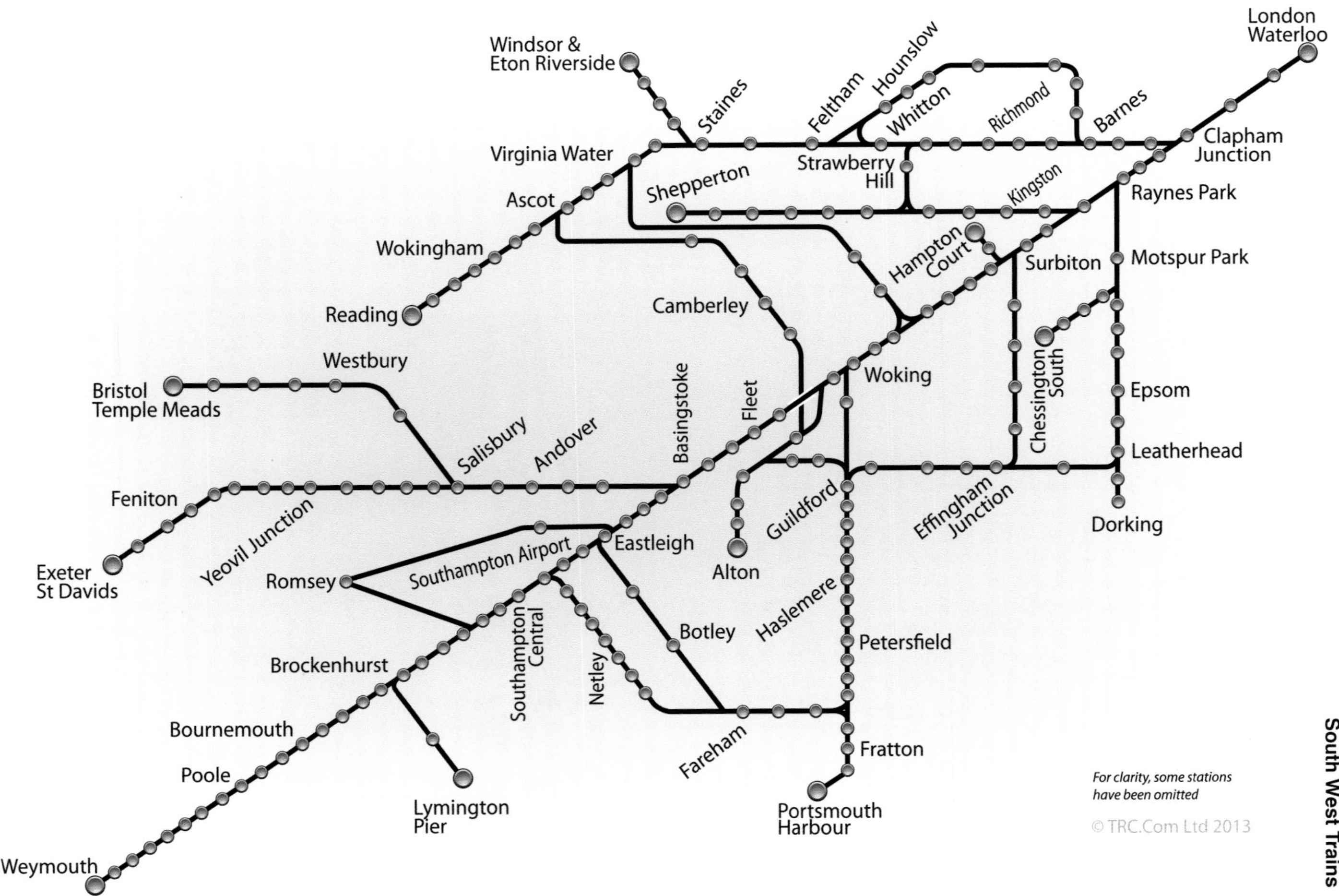
London Waterloo
Clapham Junction
Raynes Park
Motspur Park
Epsom
Leatherhead
Dorking
Barnes
Richmond
Kingston
Surbiton
Chessington South
Hampton Court
Effingham Junction
Whitton
Hounslow
Strawberry Hill
Woking
Petersfield
Fratton
Portsmouth Harbour
Feltham
Guildford
Haslemere
Alton
Fleet
Staines
Shepperton
Camberley
Basingstoke
Eastleigh
Botley
Fareham
Netley
Windsor & Eton Riverside
Virginia Water
Ascot
Andover
Southampton Airport
Southampton Central
Wokingham
Reading
Salisbury
Westbury
Romsey
Brockenhurst
Lymington Pier
Yeovil Junction
Bournemouth
Poole
Bristol Temple Meads
Feniton
Exeter St Davids
Weymouth
For clarity, some stations have been omitted
© TRC.Com Ltd 2013

South West Trains

Class 159/0

Vehicle Length: 76ft 1¾in (23.21m)
Height: 12ft 6in (3.81m)
Width: 9ft 3¼in (2.82m)
Engine: 1 x Cummins NTA855R of 400hp per vehicle
Horsepower: 1,200hp (895kW)
Seats (total/car): 24F-172S, 24F-28S/72S/72S

Number	Formation DMCL+MSL+DMS	Depot	Livery	Owner	Operator	Name
159001	52873+58718+57873	SA	SWM	PTR	SWT	*City of Exeter*
159002	52874+58719+57874	SA	SWM	PTR	SWT	*City of Salisbury*
159003	52875+58720+57875	SA	SWM	PTR	SWT	*Templecombe*
159004	52876+58721+57876	SA	SWM	PTR	SWT	*Basingstoke and Deane*
159005	52877+58722+57877	SA	SWM	PTR	SWT	*West of England Line*
159006	52878+58723+57878	SA	SWM	PTR	SWT	*Seaton Tramway, Seaton-Colyford-Colyton*
159007	52879+58724+57879	SA	SWM	PTR	SWT	
159008	52880+58725+57880	SA	SWM	PTR	SWT	
159009	52881+58726+57881	SA	SWM	PTR	SWT	
159010	52882+58727+57882	SA	SWM	PTR	SWT	
159011	52883+58728+57883	SA	SWM	PTR	SWT	
159012	52884+58729+57884	SA	SWM	PTR	SWT	
159013	52885+58730+57885	SA	SWM	PTR	SWT	
159014	52886+58731+57886	SA	SWM	PTR	SWT	
159015	52887+58732+57887	SA	SWM	PTR	SWT	
159016	52888+58733+57888	SA	SWM	PTR	SWT	
159017	52889+58734+57889	SA	SWM	PTR	SWT	
159018	52890+58735+57890	SA	SWM	PTR	SWT	
159019	52891+58736+57891	SA	SWM	PTR	SWT	
159020	52892+58737+57892	SA	SWM	PTR	SWT	
159021	52893+58738+57893	SA	SWM	PTR	SWT	
159022	52894+58739+57894	SA	SWM	PTR	SWT	

Left: *When Network SouthEast modernised the Waterloo to Exeter route, a fleet of 22 three-car Class 159s was introduced. Based at Salisbury, these sets are now operated by South West Trains and together with the later introduced Class 159/1 fleet are the backbone of Waterloo to Exeter via Salisbury services. The sets were refurbished by SWT and offer a very comfortable interior. Usually the '159s' operate with their first class coach coupled at the London end of formations. Set No. 159017 arrives at Basingstoke.* **Antony Christie**

Class 159/1

Vehicle Length: 76ft 1¾in (23.21m)
Height: 12ft 6in (3.81m)
Width: 9ft 3¼in (2.82m)
Engine: 1 x Cummins NTA855R of 350hp per vehicle
Horsepower: 1,050hp (782kW)
Seats (total/car): 24F-170S, 24F-28S/70S/72S

Number	Formation DMCL+MSL+DMSL	Depot	Livery	Owner	Operator
159101 (158800)	52800+58717+57800	SA	SWM	PTR	SWT
159102 (158803)	52803+58703+57803	SA	SWM	PTR	SWT
159103 (158804)	52804+58704+57804	SA	SWM	PTR	SWT
159104 (158805)	52805+58705+57805	SA	SWM	PTR	SWT
159105 (158807)	52807+58707+57807	SA	SWM	PTR	SWT
159106 (158809)	52809+58709+57809	SA	SWM	PTR	SWT
159107 (158811)	52811+58711+57811	SA	SWM	PTR	SWT
159108 (158801)	52801+58701+57801	SA	SWM	PTR	SWT

Right: *In 2006-07, when SWT improved the frequency of services on the West of England route extra trains were needed, and these came in the form of eight extra three-car sets rebuilt from Class 158 stock and fitted with standard Class 159 interiors. With a snowplough-shaped obstacle deflector plate set No. 159104 passes through Vauxhall forming a Waterloo-Salisbury service with one of the SWT Class 158s coupled on the rear.* **Mark V. Pike**

Class 444
Desiro

Vehicle Length: 77ft 3in (23.57m)
Height: 12ft 1½in (3.7m)
Width: 9ft 2in (2.7m)
Horsepower: 2,682hp (2,000kW)
Seats (total/car): 35F-299S, 35F-24S/47S/76S/76S/76S

Number	Formation DMCO+TSO+TSO+TSRMB+DMSO	Depot	Livery	Owner	Operator	Name
444001	63801+67101+67151+67201+63851	NT	SWM	ANG	SWT	*Naomi House*
444002	63802+67102+67152+67202+63852	NT	SWM	ANG	SWT	
444003	63803+67103+67153+67203+63853	NT	SWM	ANG	SWT	
444004	63804+67104+67154+67204+63854	NT	SWM	ANG	SWT	
444005	63805+67105+67155+67205+63855	NT	SWM	ANG	SWT	
444006	63806+67106+67156+67206+63856	NT	SWM	ANG	SWT	
444007	63807+67107+67157+67207+63857	NT	SWM	ANG	SWT	
444008	63808+67108+67158+67208+63858	NT	SWM	ANG	SWT	
444009	63809+67109+67159+67209+63859	NT	SWM	ANG	SWT	
444010	63810+67110+67160+67210+63860	NT	SWM	ANG	SWT	
444011	63811+67111+67161+67211+63861	NT	SWM	ANG	SWT	
444012	63812+67112+67162+67212+63862	NT	SWM	ANG	SWT	*Destination Weymouth*
444013	63813+67113+67163+67213+63863	NT	SWM	ANG	SWT	
444014	63814+67114+67164+67214+63864	NT	SWM	ANG	SWT	
444015	63815+67115+67165+67215+63865	NT	SWM	ANG	SWT	
444016	63816+67116+67166+67216+63866	NT	SWM	ANG	SWT	
444017	63817+67117+67167+67217+63867	NT	SWM	ANG	SWT	
444018	63818+67118+67168+67218+63868	NT	SWM	ANG	SWT	*The FAB 444*
444019	63819+67119+67169+67219+63869	NT	SWM	ANG	SWT	
444020	63820+67120+67170+67220+63870	NT	SWM	ANG	SWT	
444021	63821+67121+67171+67221+63871	NT	SWM	ANG	SWT	
444022	63822+67122+67172+67222+63872	NT	SWM	ANG	SWT	
444023	63823+67123+67173+67223+63873	NT	SWM	ANG	SWT	
444024	63824+67124+67174+67224+63874	NT	SWM	ANG	SWT	
444025	63825+67125+67175+67225+63875	NT	SWM	ANG	SWT	
444026	63826+67126+67176+67226+63876	NT	SWM	ANG	SWT	
444027	63827+67127+67177+67227+63877	NT	SWM	ANG	SWT	
444028	63828+67128+67178+67228+63878	NT	SWM	ANG	SWT	
444029	63829+67129+67179+67229+63879	NT	SWM	ANG	SWT	
444030	63830+67130+67180+67230+63880	NT	SWM	ANG	SWT	
444031	63831+67131+67181+67231+63881	NT	SWM	ANG	SWT	
444032	63832+67132+67182+67232+63882	NT	SWM	ANG	SWT	
444033	63833+67133+67183+67233+63883	NT	SWM	ANG	SWT	
444034	63834+67134+67184+67234+63884	NT	SWM	ANG	SWT	
444035	63835+67135+67185+67235+63885	NT	SWM	ANG	SWT	
444036	63836+67136+67186+67236+63886	NT	SWM	ANG	SWT	
444037	63837+67137+67187+67237+63887	NT	SWM	ANG	SWT	
444038	63838+67138+67188+67238+63888	NT	SWM	ANG	SWT	*South Western Railway*
444039	63839+67139+67189+67239+63889	NT	SWM	ANG	SWT	
444040	63840+67140+67190+67240+63890	NT	SWM	ANG	SWT	

South West Trains

444041	63841+67141+67191+67241+63891	NT	SWM	ANG	SWT	
444042	63842+67142+67192+67242+63892	NT	SWM	ANG	SWT	
444043	63843+67143+67193+67243+63893	NT	SWM	ANG	SWT	
444044	63844+67144+67194+67244+63894	NT	SWM	ANG	SWT	
444045	63845+67145+67195+67245+63895	NT	SWM	ANG	SWT	

Left: *As part of the post-privatisation modernisation of South West Trains and the replacement of slam-door stock, a fleet of Siemens five-car 'Desiro' sets, classified as 444, was introduced. Allocated to Northam depot near Southampton, the sets operate the main-line services on the Waterloo-Bournemouth/Weymouth and Portsmouth routes, providing a high-quality travelling environment. Set No. 444034 arrives at Dorchester South with a Weymouth-bound service.* **CJM**

Class 450/0
Desiro

Vehicle Length: 66ft 9in (20.4m)
Height: 12ft 1½in (3.7m)
Width: 9ft 2in (2.7m)
Horsepower: 2,682hp (2,000kW)
Seats (total/car): 24F-237S, 70S/24F-36S/61S/70S

Number	Formation DMSO+TCO+TSO+DMSO	Depot	Livery	Owner	Operator	Name
450001	63201+64201+68101+63601	NT	SWO	ANG	SWT	
450002	63202+64202+68102+63602	NT	SWO	ANG	SWT	
450003	63203+64203+68103+63603	NT	SWO	ANG	SWT	
450004	63204+64204+68104+63604	NT	SWO	ANG	SWT	
450005	63205+64205+68205+63605	NT	SWO	ANG	SWT	
450006	63206+64206+68206+63606	NT	SWO	ANG	SWT	
450007	63207+64207+68207+63607	NT	SWO	ANG	SWT	
450008	63208+64208+68108+63608	NT	SWO	ANG	SWT	
450009	63209+64209+68109+63609	NT	SWO	ANG	SWT	
450010	63210+64210+68110+63610	NT	SWO	ANG	SWT	
450011	63211+64211+68111+63611	NT	SWO	ANG	SWT	
450012	63212+64212+68112+63612	NT	SWO	ANG	SWT	
450013	63213+64213+68113+63613	NT	SWO	ANG	SWT	
450014	63214+64214+68114+63614	NT	SWO	ANG	SWT	
450015	63215+64215+68115+63615	NT	SWO	ANG	SWT	*Desiro*
450016	63216+64216+68116+63616	NT	SWO	ANG	SWT	
450017	63217+64217+68117+63617	NT	SWO	ANG	SWT	
450018	63218+64218+68118+63618	NT	SWO	ANG	SWT	
450019	63219+64219+68119+63619	NT	SWO	ANG	SWT	
450020	63220+64220+68120+63620	NT	SWO	ANG	SWT	
450021	63221+64221+68121+63621	NT	SWO	ANG	SWT	
450022	63222+64222+68122+63622	NT	SWO	ANG	SWT	
450023	63223+64223+68123+63623	NT	SWO	ANG	SWT	
450024	63224+64224+68124+63624	NT	SWO	ANG	SWT	
450025	63225+64225+68125+63625	NT	SWO	ANG	SWT	
450026	63226+64226+68126+63626	NT	SWO	ANG	SWT	
450027	63227+64227+68127+63627	NT	SWO	ANG	SWT	
450028	63228+64228+68128+63628	NT	SWO	ANG	SWT	
450029	63229+64229+68129+63629	NT	SWO	ANG	SWT	
450030	63230+64230+68130+63630	NT	SWO	ANG	SWT	
450031	63231+64231+68131+63631	NT	SWO	ANG	SWT	
450032	63232+64232+68132+63632	NT	SWO	ANG	SWT	
450033	63233+64233+68133+63633	NT	SWO	ANG	SWT	
450034	63234+64234+68134+63634	NT	SWO	ANG	SWT	
450035	63235+64235+68135+63635	NT	SWO	ANG	SWT	
450036	63236+64236+68136+63636	NT	SWO	ANG	SWT	

450037	63237+64237+68137+63637	NT	SWO	ANG	SWT	
450038	63238+64238+68138+63638	NT	SWO	ANG	SWT	
450039	63239+64239+68139+63639	NT	SWO	ANG	SWT	
450040	63240+64240+68140+63640	NT	SWO	ANG	SWT	
450041	63241+64241+68141+63641	NT	SWO	ANG	SWT	
450042	63242+64242+68142+63642	NT	SWO	ANG	SWT	*Treloar College*
450071	63271+64271+68171+63671	NT	SWO	ANG	SWT	
450072	63272+64272+68172+63672	NT	SWO	ANG	SWT	
450073	63273+64273+68173+63673	NT	SWO	ANG	SWT	
450074	63274+64274+68174+63674	NT	SWO	ANG	SWT	
450075	63275+64275+68175+63675	NT	SWO	ANG	SWT	
450076	63276+64276+68176+63676	NT	SWO	ANG	SWT	
450077	63277+64277+68177+63677	NT	SWO	ANG	SWT	
450078	63278+64278+68178+63678	NT	SWO	ANG	SWT	
450079	63279+64279+68179+63679	NT	SWO	ANG	SWT	
450080	63280+64280+68180+63680	NT	SWO	ANG	SWT	
450081	63281+64281+68181+63681	NT	SWO	ANG	SWT	
450082	63282+64282+68182+63682	NT	SWO	ANG	SWT	
450083	63283+64283+68183+63683	NT	SWO	ANG	SWT	
450084	63284+64284+68184+63684	NT	SWO	ANG	SWT	
450085	63285+64285+68185+63685	NT	SWO	ANG	SWT	
450086	63286+64286+68186+63686	NT	SWO	ANG	SWT	
450087	63287+64287+68187+63687	NT	SWO	ANG	SWT	
450088	63288+64288+68188+63688	NT	SWO	ANG	SWT	
450089	63289+64289+68189+63689	NT	SWO	ANG	SWT	
450090	63290+64290+68190+63690	NT	SWO	ANG	SWT	
450091	63291+64291+68191+63691	NT	SWO	ANG	SWT	
450092	63292+64292+68192+63692	NT	SWO	ANG	SWT	
450093	63293+64293+68193+63693	NT	SWO	ANG	SWT	
450094	63294+64294+68194+63694	NT	SWO	ANG	SWT	
450095	63295+64295+68195+63695	NT	SWO	ANG	SWT	
450096	63296+64296+68196+63696	NT	SWO	ANG	SWT	
450097	63297+64297+68197+63697	NT	SWO	ANG	SWT	
450098	63298+64298+68198+63698	NT	SWO	ANG	SWT	
450099	63299+64299+68199+63699	NT	SWO	ANG	SWT	
450100	63300+64300+68200+63700	NT	SWO	ANG	SWT	
450101	63701+66851+66801+63751	NT	SWO	ANG	SWT	
450102	63702+66852+66802+63752	NT	SWO	ANG	SWT	
450103	63703+66853+66803+63753	NT	SWO	ANG	SWT	
450104	63704+66854+66804+63754	NT	SWO	ANG	SWT	
450105	63705+66855+66805+63755	NT	SWO	ANG	SWT	
450106	63706+66856+66806+63756	NT	SWO	ANG	SWT	
450107	63707+66857+66807+63757	NT	SWO	ANG	SWT	
450108	63708+66858+66808+63758	NT	SWO	ANG	SWT	
450109	63709+66859+66809+63759	NT	SWO	ANG	SWT	
450110	63710+66860+66810+63750	NT	SWO	ANG	SWT	
450111	63901+66921+66901+63921	NT	SWO	ANG	SWT	
450112	63902+66922+66902+63922	NT	SWO	ANG	SWT	
450113	63903+66923+66903+63923	NT	SWO	ANG	SWT	
450114	63904+66924+66904+63924	NT	SWO	ANG	SWT	*Fairbridge - investing in the Future*
450115	63905+66925+66905+63925	NT	SWO	ANG	SWT	
450116	63906+66926+66906+63926	NT	SWO	ANG	SWT	
450117	63907+66927+66907+63927	NT	SWO	ANG	SWT	
450118	63908+66928+66908+63928	NT	SWO	ANG	SWT	
450119	63909+66929+66909+63929	NT	SWO	ANG	SWT	
450120	63910+66930+66910+63930	NT	SWO	ANG	SWT	
450121	63911+66931+66911+63931	NT	SWO	ANG	SWT	
450122	63912+66932+66912+63932	NT	SWO	ANG	SWT	
450123	63913+66933+66913+63933	NT	SWO	ANG	SWT	
450124	63914+66934+66914+63934	NT	SWO	ANG	SWT	
450125	63915+66935+66915+63935	NT	SWO	ANG	SWT	
450126	63916+66936+66916+63936	NT	SWO	ANG	SWT	
450127	63917+66937+66917+63937	NT	SWO	ANG	SWT	

South West Trains

Above: *A fleet of 127 four-car Class 450 'Desiro' sets form the backbone of South West Trains outer-suburban services. Allocated to Northam near Southampton, the fleet replaced the slam-door stock during South West route modernisation. Set No. 450032 takes the Chertsey line at Virginia Water with a Waterloo to Weybridge via Staines service.* **CJM**

Class 450/5
Desiro

Vehicle Length: 66ft 9in (20.4m)
Height: 12ft 1½in (3.7m)
Width: 9ft 2in (2.7m)
Horsepower: 2,682hp (2,000kW)
Seats (total/car): 240S, 64S/56S/56S/64S
§24F/216S, 64S 24F/32S/56S/54S

Number	Formation DMSO+TSO (§TCO)+TSO+DMSO	Depot	Livery	Owner	Operator
450543§ (450043)	63243+64243+68143+63643	NT	SWO	ANG	SWT
450544§ (450044)	63244+64244+68144+63644	NT	SWO	ANG	SWT
450545 (450045)	63245+64245+68145+63645	NT	SWO	ANG	SWT
450546§ (450046)	63246+64246+68146+63646	NT	SWO	ANG	SWT
450547 (450047)	63247+64247+68147+63647	NT	SWO	ANG	SWT
450548 (450048)	63248+64248+68148+63648	NT	SWO	ANG	SWT
450549 (450049)	63249+64249+68149+63649	NT	SWO	ANG	SWT
450550§ (450050)	63250+64250+68150+63650	NT	SWO	ANG	SWT
450551 (450051)	63251+64251+68151+63651	NT	SWO	ANG	SWT
450552§ (450052)	63252+64252+68152+63652	NT	SWO	ANG	SWT
450553 (450053)	63253+64253+68153+63653	NT	SWO	ANG	SWT
450554 (450054)	63254+64254+68154+63654	NT	SWO	ANG	SWT
450555 (450055)	63255+64255+68155+63655	NT	SWO	ANG	SWT
450556§ (450056)	63256+64256+68156+63656	NT	SWO	ANG	SWT
450557 (450057)	63257+64257+68157+63657	NT	SWO	ANG	SWT
450558§ (450058)	63258+64258+68158+63658	NT	SWO	ANG	SWT
450559§ (450059)	63259+64259+68159+63659	NT	SWO	ANG	SWT
450560§ (450060)	63260+64260+68160+63660	NT	SWO	ANG	SWT
450561§ (450061)	63261+64261+68161+63661	NT	SWO	ANG	SWT
450562§ (450062)	63262+64262+68162+63662	NT	SWO	ANG	SWT
450563§ (450063)	63263+64263+68163+63663	NT	SWO	ANG	SWT
450564§ (450064)	63264+64264+68164+63664	NT	SWO	ANG	SWT
450565§ (450065)	63265+64265+68165+63665	NT	SWO	ANG	SWT
450566§ (450066)	63266+64266+68166+63666	NT	SWO	ANG	SWT
450567§ (450067)	63267+64267+68167+63667	NT	SWO	ANG	SWT
450568§ (450068)	63268+64268+68168+63668	NT	SWO	ANG	SWT
450569 (450069)	63269+64269+68169+63669	NT	SWO	ANG	SWT
450570 (450070)	63270+64270+68170+63670	NT	SWO	ANG	SWT

Right: *A batch of 28 Class 450 sets was modified for standard-class-only occupancy soon after introduction and reclassified as Class 450/5; however, these are currently in the process of being returned to standard format. In addition to the first class area being removed, alterations were also made to the standard class area to increase capacity and thus the sets were deemed as HC or High Capacity units. Class 450/5 No. 450549 is illustrated at Clapham Junction.* **CJM**

Class 455/7

Vehicle Length: (Driving) 65ft 0½in (19.83m)
(Inter) 65ft 4½in (19.92m)
Height: 12ft 1½in (3.79m) [TSO- 11ft 6½in (3.58m)]
Width: 9ft 3¼in (2.82m)
Horsepower: 1,000hp (746kW)
Seats (total/car): 244S, 54S/68S/68S/54S

Number	Formation DMSO(A)+MSO+TSO+DTSO(B)	Depot	Livery	Owner	Operator	Notes
(45)5701	77727+62783+71545+77728	WD	SWS	PTR	SWT	
(45)5702	77729+62784+71547+77730	WD	SWS	PTR	SWT	
(45)5703	77731+62785+71540+77732	WD	SWS	PTR	SWT	
(45)5704	77733+62786+71548+77734	WD	SWS	PTR	SWT	
(45)5705	77735+62787+71565+77736	WD	SWS	PTR	SWT	
(45)5706	77737+62788+71534+77738	WD	SWS	PTR	SWT	
(45)5707	77739+62789+71536+77740	WD	SWS	PTR	SWT	
(45)5708	77741+62790+71560+77742	WD	SWS	PTR	SWT	
(45)5709	77743+62791+71532+77744	WD	SWS	PTR	SWT	
(45)5710	77745+62792+71566+77746	WD	SWS	PTR	SWT	
(45)5711	77747+62793+71542+77748	WD	SWS	PTR	SWT	
(45)5712	77749+62794+71546+77750	WD	SWS	PTR	SWT	
(45)5713	77751+62795+71567+77752	WD	SWS	PTR	SWT	
(45)5714	77753+62796+71539+77754	WD	SWS	PTR	SWT	
(45)5715	77755+62796+71535+77756	WD	SWS	PTR	SWT	
(45)5716	77757+62798+71564+77758	WD	SWS	PTR	SWT	
(45)5717	77759+62799+71528+77760	WD	SWS	PTR	SWT	
(45)5718	77761+62800+71557+77762	WD	SWS	PTR	SWT	
(45)5719	77763+62801+71558+77764	WD	SWS	PTR	SWT	
(45)5720	77765+62802+71568+77766	WD	SWS	PTR	SWT	
(45)5721	77767+62803+71553+77768	WD	SWS	PTR	SWT	
(45)5722	77769+62804+71533+77770	WD	SWS	PTR	SWT	
(45)5723	77771+62805+71526+77772	WD	SWS	PTR	SWT	
(45)5724	77773+62806+71561+77774	WD	SWS	PTR	SWT	
(45)5725	77775+62807+71541+77776	WD	SWS	PTR	SWT	
(45)5726	77777+62608+71556+77778	WD	SWS	PTR	SWT	
(45)5727	77779+62809+71562+77780	WD	SWS	PTR	SWT	
(45)5728	77781+62810+71527+77782	WD	SWS	PTR	SWT	
(45)5729	77783+62811+71550+77784	WD	SWS	PTR	SWT	
(45)5730	77785+62812+71551+77786	WD	SWS	PTR	SWT	
(45)5731	77787+62813+71555+77788	WD	SWS	PTR	SWT	
(45)5732	77789+62814+71552+77790	WD	SWS	PTR	SWT	
(45)5733	77791+62815+71549+77792	WD	SWS	PTR	SWT	
(45)5734	77793+62816+71531+77794	WD	SWS	PTR	SWT	
(45)5735	77795+62817+71563+77796	WD	SWS	PTR	SWT	
(45)5736	77797+62818+71554+77798	WD	SWS	PTR	SWT	
(45)5737	77799+62819+71544+77800	WD	SWS	PTR	SWT	
(45)5738	77801+62820+71529+77802	WD	SWS	PTR	SWT	
(45)5739	77803+62821+71537+77804	WD	SWS	PTR	SWT	
(45)5740	77805+62822+71530+77806	WD	SWS	PTR	SWT	
(45)5741	77807+62823+71559+77808	WD	SWS	PTR	SWT	
(45)5742	77809+62824+71543+77810	WD	SWS	PTR	SWT	
(45)5750*	77811+62825+71538+77812	WD	SWS	PTR	SWT	* Originally numbered (45)5743

South West Trains

Left: *South West Trains local services are operated by three sub-classes of Class 455 four-car EMUs. All have been refurbished and sport high-back seating and a passenger information system. The 43 members of Class 455/7 were built as three-car sets and had one of the original TS vehicles from the Class 508s inserted, which was built to a different body profile. Class 455/7 No. (45)5705 is seen at Clapham Junction with the former '508' coach third from the camera.* **CJM**

Class 455/8

Vehicle Length: (Driving) 65ft 0½in (19.83m)
(Inter) 65ft 4½in (19.92m)
Height: 12ft 1½in (3.79m)
Width: 9ft 3¼in (2.82m)
Horsepower: 1,000hp (746kW)
Seats (total/car): 268S, 50S/84S/84S/50S

Number	*Formation* DMSO(A)+MSO+TSO+DTSO(B)	*Depot*	*Livery*	*Owner*	*Operator*
(45)5847	77671+62755+71683+77672	WD	SWS	PTR	SWT
(45)5848	77673+62756+71684+77674	WD	SWS	PTR	SWT
(45)5849	77675+62757+71685+77676	WD	SWS	PTR	SWT
(45)5850	77677+62758+71686+77678	WD	SWS	PTR	SWT
(45)5851	77679+62759+71687+77680	WD	SWS	PTR	SWT
(45)5852	77681+62760+71688+77682	WD	SWS	PTR	SWT
(45)5853	77683+62761+71689+77684	WD	SWS	PTR	SWT
(45)5854	77685+62762+71690+77686	WD	SWS	PTR	SWT
(45)5855	77687+62763+71691+77688	WD	SWS	PTR	SWT
(45)5856	77689+62764+71692+77690	WD	SWS	PTR	SWT
(45)5857	77691+62765+71693+77692	WD	SWS	PTR	SWT
(45)5858	77693+62766+71694+77694	WD	SWS	PTR	SWT
(45)5859	77695+62767+71695+77696	WD	SWS	PTR	SWT
(45)5860	77697+62768+71696+77698	WD	SWS	PTR	SWT
(45)5861	77699+62769+71697+77700	WD	SWS	PTR	SWT
(45)5862	77701+62770+71698+77702	WD	SWS	PTR	SWT
(45)5863	77703+62771+71699+77704	WD	SWS	PTR	SWT
(45)5864	77705+62772+71700+77706	WD	SWS	PTR	SWT
(45)5865	77707+62773+71701+77708	WD	SWS	PTR	SWT
(45)5866	77709+62774+71702+77710	WD	SWS	PTR	SWT
(45)5867	77711+62775+71703+77712	WD	SWS	PTR	SWT
(45)5868	77713+62776+71704+77714	WD	SWS	PTR	SWT
(45)5869	77715+62777+71705+77716	WD	SWS	PTR	SWT
(45)5870	77717+62778+71706+77718	WD	SWS	PTR	SWT
(45)5871	77719+62779+71707+77720	WD	SWS	PTR	SWT
(45)5872	77721+62780+71708+77722	WD	SWS	PTR	SWT
(45)5873	77723+62781+71709+77724	WD	SWS	PTR	SWT
(45)5874	77725+62782+71710+77726	WD	SWS	PTR	SWT

Left: *The driving car of a Class 455/8 design set shows the early style of roof line, with a central 'blister' and roof-mounted air horns, of a similar style as fitted to the first batch of Class 317s and the Class 210s. The Class 455s retain the old Southern Region tradition of nose-mounted jumper and air connections, rather than using roll-cover boxes for electrical and pneumatic connections.* **CJM**

Class 455/9

Vehicle Length: (Driving) 65ft 0½in (19.83m)
(Inter) 65ft 4½in (19.92m)
Height: 12ft 1½in (3.79m)
Width: 9ft 3¼in (2.82m)
Horsepower: 1,000hp (746kW)
Seats (total/car): 236S, 50S/68S/68S/50S

Number	*Formation* DMSO(A)+MSO+TSO+DTSO(B)	*Depot*	*Livery*	*Owner*	*Operator*
(45)5901	77813+62826+71714+77814	WD	SWS	PTR	SWT
(45)5902	77815+62827+71715+77816	WD	SWS	PTR	SWT
(45)5903	77817+62828+71716+77818	WD	SWS	PTR	SWT
(45)5904	77819+62829+71717+77820	WD	SWS	PTR	SWT
(45)5905	77821+62830+71725+77822	WD	SWS	PTR	SWT
(45)5906	77823+62831+71719+77824	WD	SWS	PTR	SWT
(45)5907	77825+62832+71720+77826	WD	SWS	PTR	SWT
(45)5908	77827+62833+71721+77828	WD	SWS	PTR	SWT
(45)5909	77829+62834+71722+77830	WD	SWS	PTR	SWT
(45)5910	77831+62835+71723+77832	WD	SWS	PTR	SWT
(45)5911	77833+62836+71724+77834	WD	SWS	PTR	SWT
(45)5912	77835+62837+67400+77836	WD	SWS	PTR	SWT
(45)5913	77837+62838+71726+77838	WD	SWS	PTR	SWT
(45)5914	77839+62839+71727+77840	WD	SWS	PTR	SWT
(45)5915	77841+62840+71728+77842	WD	SWS	PTR	SWT
(45)5916	77843+62841+71729+77844	WD	SWS	PTR	SWT
(45)5917	77845+62842+71730+77846	WD	SWS	PTR	SWT
(45)5918	77847+62843+71732+77848	WD	SWS	PTR	SWT
(45)5919	77849+62844+71718+77850	WD	SWS	PTR	SWT
(45)5920	77851+62845+71733+77852	WD	SWS	PTR	SWT

Above: *The final 20 Class 455s delivered from York Works to Wimbledon were classified as 455/9, and had the more pleasing front end and revision to the heating and ventilation system. The SWT Class 455 fleet is set to remain in traffic for many years and in 2013 a major overhaul and upgrade project commenced at Bournemouth depot. Class 455/9 No. (45)5911 is seen departing from Clapham Junction bound for Waterloo.* **CJM**

Class 456

Vehicle Length: (Driving) 65ft 3¼in (19.89m)
Height: 12ft 4½in (3.77m)
Width: 9ft 3in (2.81m)
Horsepower: 500hp (370kW)
Seats (total/car): 152S, 79S/73S

Number	*Formation* DMSO+DTSO	*Depot*	*Livery*	*Owner*	*Operator*
456001	64735+78250	WD	§	PTR	SWT
456002	64736+78251	WD	§	PTR	SWT
456003	64737+78252	WD	§	PTR	SWT
456004	64738+78253	WD	§	PTR	SWT
456005	64739+78254	WD	§	PTR	SWT
456006	64740+78255	WD	§	PTR	SWT
456007	64741+78256	WD	§	PTR	SWT
456008	64742+78257	WD	§	PTR	SWT
456009	64743+78258	WD	§	PTR	SWT
456010	64744+78259	WD	§	PTR	SWT
456011	64745+78260	WD	§	PTR	SWT
456012	64746+78261	WD	§	PTR	SWT
456013	64747+78262	WD	§	PTR	SWT
456014	64748+78263	WD	§	PTR	SWT

South West Trains

456015	64749+78264	WD	§	PTR	SWT
456016	64750+78265	WD	§	PTR	SWT
456017	64751+78266	WD	§	PTR	SWT
456018	64752+78267	WD	§	PTR	SWT
456019	64753+78268	WD	§	PTR	SWT
456020	64754+78269	WD	§	PTR	SWT
456021	64755+78270	WD	§	PTR	SWT
456022	64756+78271	WD	§	PTR	SWT
456023	64757+78272	WD	§	PTR	SWT
456024	64758+78273	WD	§	PTR	SWT

§ In process of transfer from Selhurst to Wimbledon and repainting into SWT livery.

Left: *During the course of 2014, all 24 of the two-car Class 456 sets will transfer from Southern to South West Trains, to be allocated to Wimbledon to allow 10-car formations to operate on suburban routes. The sets are to be refurbished on a par with the Class 455s and painted in South West Trains red suburban livery. It is likely that some Southern green-liveried sets will make an appearance on South Western tracks during the transition period. Here is a drawing of how the 'new' trains will look.* **SWT**

Class 458
Juniper

Vehicle Length: (Driving) 69ft 6in (21.16m) (Inter) 65ft 4in (19.91m)
Height: 12ft 3in (3.73m)
Width: 9ft 2in (2.79m)
Horsepower: 2,172hp (1,620kW)
Seats 4-car sets (total/car): 24F-250S, 12F-63S/49S/75S/12F-63S
5-car sets (total/car): 266S, 60S/52S/42S/52S/60S

4-JOP

Number	*New Number*	*Formation* DMCO(A)+TSO+MSO+(TSO)+DTCO(B)	*Depot*	*Livery*	*Owner*	*Operator*
(45)8001	*(458501)*	67601+74001+74101+(74401)+67701	WD	SWM	PTR	SWT
(45)8002	*(458502)*	67602+74002+74102+(74431)+67702	WD	SWM	PTR	SWT
(45)8003	*(458503)*	67603+74003+74103+(74421)+67703	WD	SWM	PTR	SWT
(45)8004	*(458504)*	67604+74004+74104+(74405)+67704	WD	SWM	PTR	SWT
(45)8005	*(458505)*	67605+74005+74105+(74451)+67705	WD	SWM	PTR	SWT
(45)8006	*(458506)*	67606+74006+74106+(74426)+67706	WD	SWM	PTR	SWT
(45)8007	*(458507)*	67607+74007+74107+(74406)+67707	WD	SWM	PTR	SWT
(45)8008	*(458508)*	67608+74008+74108+(74442)+67708	WD	SWM	PTR	SWT
(45)8009	*(458509)*	67609+74009+74109+(74432)+67709	WD	SWM	PTR	SWT
(45)8010	*(458510)*	67610+74010+74110+(74434)+67710	WD	SWM	PTR	SWT
(45)8011	*(458511)*	67611+74011+74111+(74451)+67711	WD	SWM	PTR	SWT
(45)8012	*(458512)*	67612+74012+74112+(74436)+67712	WD	SWM	PTR	SWT
(45)8013	*(458513)*	67613+74013+74113+(74427)+67713	WD	SWM	PTR	SWT
(45)8014	*(458514)*	67614+74014+74114+(74407)+67714	WD	SWM	PTR	SWT
(45)8015	*(458515)*	67615+74015+74115+(74424)+67715	WD	SWM	PTR	SWT
(45)8016	*(458516)*	67616+74016+74116+(74428)+67716	WD	SWM	PTR	SWT
(45)8017	*(458517)*	67617+74017+74117+(74433)+67717	WD	SWM	PTR	SWT
(45)8018	*(458518)*	67618+74018+74118+(74412)+67718	WD	SWM	PTR	SWT
(45)8019	*(458519)*	67619+74019+74119+(74403)+67719	WD	SWM	PTR	SWT
(45)8020	*(458520)*	67620+74020+74120+(74441)+67720	WD	SWM	PTR	SWT
(45)8021	*(458521)*	67621+74021+74121+(74408)+67721	WD	SWM	PTR	SWT
(45)8022	*(458522)*	67622+74022+74122+(74404)+67722	WD	SWM	PTR	SWT
(45)8023	*(458523)*	67623+74023+74123+(74437)+67723	WD	SWM	PTR	SWT
(45)8024	*(458524)*	67624+74024+74124+(74422)+67724	WD	SWM	PTR	SWT
(45)8025	*(458525)*	67625+74025+74125+(74435)+67725	WD	SWM	PTR	SWT
(45)8026	*(458526)*	67626+74026+74126+(74452)+67726	WD	SWM	PTR	SWT
(45)8027	*(458527)*	67627+74027+74127+(74402)+67727	WD	SWM	PTR	SWT
(45)8028	*(458528)*	67628+74028+74128+(74438)+67728	WD	SWM	PTR	SWT
(45)8029	*(458529)*	67629+74029+74129+(74423)+67729	WD	SWM	PTR	SWT
(45)8030	*(458530)*	67630+74030+74130+(74411)+67730	WD	SWM	PTR	SWT

■ A total of 36 five-car Class 458/5s are currently under conversion from the 30 original Class 458/0 sets, each with one additional TS vehicle, plus six additional sets rebuilt totally from Class 460 stock. All but four of the Class 460 vehicles will be converted. Each 'new' set will be formed of five vehicles, allowing SWT to operate 10-car trains on the outer-suburban routes. The sets have new front ends with modern gangways and sport 2+2 seating. The sets are numbered in the 458501- 458536 series. Sets 8001-30 will be converted in 2014-15.

5-JUP

	DMSO(A)+TSO+MST+TSO+DMSO(B)				
458531	67913+74418+74446+74458+67912	WD	SWO	PTR	SWT

458532	67904+74417+74447+74457+67905	WD	SWO	PTR	SWT
458533	67917+74413+74443+74453+67916	WD	SWO	PTR	SWT
458534	67914+74414+74444+74454+67918	WD	SWO	PTR	SWT
458535	67915+74415+74445+74455+67911	WD	SWO	PTR	SWT
458536	67906+74416+74448+74456+67902	WD	SWO	PTR	SWT

Above: *In the autumn of 2013 the first of the five-car Class 458/5 sets emerged from Wabtec, when five former Class 460 GatX vehicles emerged as set No. 458534, sporting a new '450'-style front end. The set is seen at its home depot of East Wimbledon on 22 October 2013.* **CJM**

Class 73/2

Vehicle Length: 53ft 8in (16.35m)
Height: 12ft 5 5/16in (3.79m)
Width: 8ft 8in (2.64m)

Power: 750V dc third rail or English Electric 6K
Horsepower: electric - 1,600hp (1,193kW)
Horsepower: diesel - 600hp (447kW)
Electrical Equipment: English Electric

Number	*Depot*	*Pool*	*Livery*	*Owner*	*Operator*
73235 (73125)	WD	HYWD	SWO	SWT	SWT

Right: *South West Trains operates one Class 73 at Bournemouth depot for shunting EMU stock as required. No. 73235 still carries South West Trains outer-suburban blue livery and can if required operate over the main line to move stock between depots. The loco is seen inside Bournemouth depot in summer 2013.* **Antony Christie**

New rolling stock: *In 2013 South West Trains announced that it was to order a further 135 new electric multiple unit vehicles for delivery by 2019 to meet the 10-car aspiration and meet customer growth. Rather than SWT extending its 'Desiro' fleet, a fresh tender process has commenced with all major builders invited to tender.*

South Eastern

Address: ✉ Friars Bridge Court, 41-45 Blackfriars Road, London, SE1 8NZ
info@southeasternrailway.co.uk
✆ 08700 000 2222
ⓘ www.southeasternrailway.co.uk

Managing Director: Charles Horton
Franchise Dates: 1 April 2006 - June 2018
Principal Routes: London to Kent and parts of East Sussex, domestic services on HS1
Depots: Slade Green (SG), Ramsgate (RM), Ashford* (AD)
Parent Company: Govia
* Operated by Hitachi

Class 375/3 *Electrostar*

Vehicle Length: (Driving) 66ft 9in (20.3m) (Inter) 65ft 6in (19.96m)
Height: 12ft 4in (3.75m)
Width: 9ft 2in (2.79m)
Horsepower: 1,341hp (1,000kW)
Seats (total/car): 24F-152S, 12F-48S/56S/12F-48S

Number	Formation DMCO(A)+TSO+DMCO(B)	Depot	Livery	Owner	Operator	Name
375301	67921+74351+67931	RM	SET	EVL	SET	
375302	67922+74352+67932	RM	SET	EVL	SET	
375303	67923+74353+67933	RM	SET	EVL	SET	
375304	67924+74354+67934	RM	SET	EVL	SET	*Medway Valley Line 1856-2006*
375305	67925+74355+67935	RM	SET	EVL	SET	
375306	67926+74356+67936	RM	SET	EVL	SET	
375307	67927+74357+67937	RM	SET	EVL	SET	
375308	67928+74358+67938	RM	SET	EVL	SET	
375309	67929+74359+67939	RM	SET	EVL	SET	
375310	67930+74360+67940	RM	SET	EVL	SET	

Class 375/6 *Electrostar*

Vehicle Length: (Driving) 66ft 9in (20.3m) (Inter) 65ft 6in (19.96m)
Height: 12ft 4in (3.75m)
Width: 9ft 2in (2.79m)
Horsepower: 2,012hp (1,500kW)
Seats (total/car): 24F-218S, 12F-48S/66S/56S/12F-48S

Number	Formation DMCO(A)+MSO+TSO+DMCO(B)	Depot	Livery	Owner	Operator	Name
375601	67801+74251+74201+67851	RM	SET	EVL	SET	
375602	67802+74252+74202+67852	RM	SET	EVL	SET	
375603	67803+74253+74203+67853	RM	SET	EVL	SET	
375604	67804+74254+74204+67854	RM	SET	EVL	SET	
375605	67805+74255+74205+67855	RM	SET	EVL	SET	
375606	67806+74256+74206+67856	RM	SET	EVL	SET	
375607	67807+74257+74207+67857	RM	SET	EVL	SET	
375608	67808+74258+74208+67858	RM	SET	EVL	SET	*Bromley Travelwise*
375609	67809+74259+74209+67859	RM	SET	EVL	SET	
375610	67810+74260+74210+67860	RM	SET	EVL	SET	*Royal Tunbridge Wells*
375611	67811+74261+74211+67861	RM	SET	EVL	SET	*Dr William Harvey*
375612	67812+74262+74212+67862	RM	SET	EVL	SET	
375613	67813+74263+74213+67863	RM	SET	EVL	SET	
375614	67814+74264+74214+67864	RM	SET	EVL	SET	
375615	67815+74265+74215+67865	RM	SET	EVL	SET	
375616	67816+74266+74216+67866	RM	SET	EVL	SET	
375617	67817+74267+74217+67867	RM	SET	EVL	SET	
375618	67818+74268+74218+67868	RM	SET	EVL	SET	
375619	67819+74269+74219+67869	RM	SET	EVL	SET	*Driver John Neve*

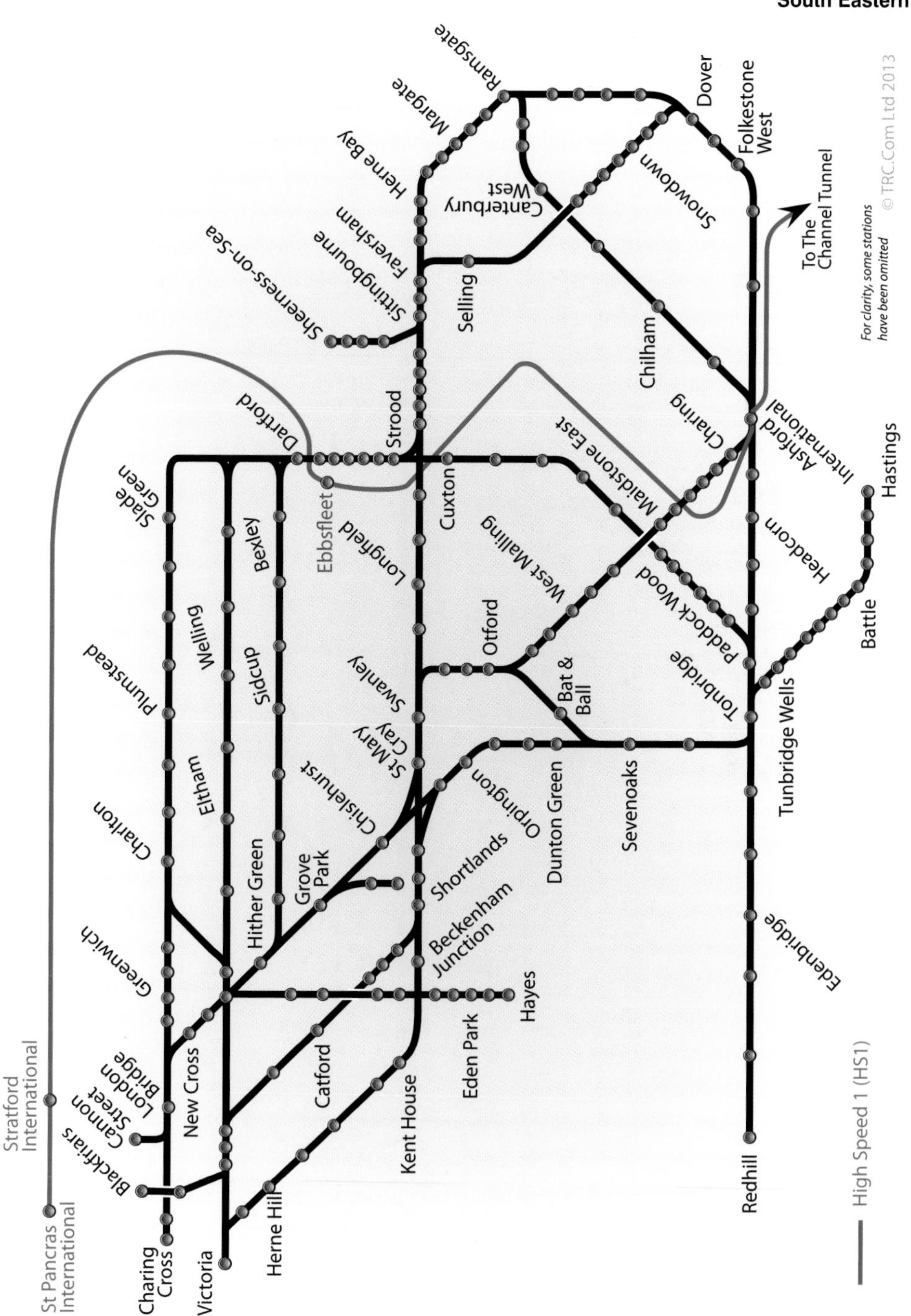
Ramsgate
Margate
Herne Bay
Faversham
Sittingbourne
Sheerness-on-Sea
Dartford
Strood
Slade Green
Bexley
Ebbsfleet
Longfield
Welling
Sidcup
Plumstead
Eltham
Charlton
Hither Green
Grove Park
Greenwich
London Bridge
Cannon Street
Blackfriars
New Cross
Catford
Charing Cross
Victoria
Herne Hill
Kent House
Eden Park
Hayes
Beckenham Junction
Shortlands
Chislehurst
St Mary Cray
Swanley
Orpington
Dunton Green
Sevenoaks
Otford
Bat & Ball
Cuxton
West Malling
Selling
Maidstone East
Canterbury West
Snowdown
Chilham
Charing
Paddock Wood
Tonbridge
Tunbridge Wells
Edenbridge
Redhill
Ashford International
Headcorn
Battle
Hastings
Dover
Folkestone West
To The Channel Tunnel
For clarity, some stations have been omitted
© TRC.Com Ltd 2013
St Pancras International
Stratford International
High Speed 1 (HS1)

South Eastern

Number	Formation	Depot	Livery	Owner	Operator	Name
375620	67820+74270+74220+67870	RM	SET	EVL	SET	
375621	67821+74271+74221+67871	RM	SET	EVL	SET	
375622	67822+74272+74222+67872	RM	SET	EVL	SET	
375623	67823+74273+74223+67873	RM	SET	EVL	SET	*Hospice in the Weald*
375624	67824+74274+74224+67874	RM	SET	EVL	SET	
375625	67825+74275+74225+67875	RM	SET	EVL	SET	
375626	67826+74276+74226+67876	RM	SET	EVL	SET	
375627	67827+74277+74227+67877	RM	SET	EVL	SET	
375628	67828+74278+74228+67878	RM	SET	EVL	SET	
375629	67829+74279+74229+67879	RM	SET	EVL	SET	
375630	67830+74280+74230+67880	RM	SET	EVL	SET	

Class 375/7
Electrostar

Vehicle Length: (Driving) 66ft 9in (20.3m)
(Inter) 65ft 6in (19.96m)
Height: 12ft 4in (3.75m)
Width: 9ft 2in (2.79m)
Horsepower: 2,012hp (1,500kW)
Seats (total/car): 24F-218S, 12F-48S/66S/56S/12F-48S

Number	Formation DMCO(A)+MSO+TSO+DMCO(B)	Depot	Livery	Owner	Operator	Name
375701	67831+74281+74231+67881	RM	SET	EVL	SET	*Kent Air Ambulance Explorer*
375702	67832+74282+74232+67882	RM	SET	EVL	SET	
375703	67833+74283+74233+67883	RM	SET	EVL	SET	
375704	67834+74284+74234+67884	RM	SET	EVL	SET	
375705	67835+74285+74235+67885	RM	SET	EVL	SET	
375706	67836+74286+74236+67886	RM	SET	EVL	SET	
375707	67837+74287+74237+67887	RM	SET	EVL	SET	
375708	67838+74288+74238+67888	RM	SET	EVL	SET	
375709	67839+74289+74239+67889	RM	SET	EVL	SET	
375710	67840+74290+74240+67890	RM	SET	EVL	SET	
375711	67841+74291+74241+67891	RM	SET	EVL	SET	
375712	67842+74292+74242+67892	RM	SET	EVL	SET	
375713	67843+74293+74243+67893	RM	SET	EVL	SET	
375714	67844+74294+74244+67894	RM	SET	EVL	SET	
375715	67845+74295+74245+67895	RM	SET	EVL	SET	

Class 375/8
Electrostar

Vehicle Length: (Driving) 66ft 9in (20.3m)
(Inter) 65ft 6in (19.96m)
Height: 12ft 4in (3.75m)
Width: 9ft 2in (2.79m)
Horsepower: 2,012hp (1,500kW)
Seats (total/car): 24F-218S, 12F-48S/66S/56S/12F-48S

Number	Formation DMCO(A)+MSO+TSO+DMCO(B)	Depot	Livery	Owner	Operator	Name
375801	73301+79001+78201+73701	RM	SET	EVL	SET	
375802	73302+79002+78202+73702	RM	SET	EVL	SET	
375803	73303+79003+78203+73703	RM	SET	EVL	SET	
375804	73304+79004+78204+73704	RM	SET	EVL	SET	
375805	73305+79005+78205+73705	RM	SET	EVL	SET	
375806	73306+79006+78206+73706	RM	SET	EVL	SET	
375807	73307+79007+78207+73707	RM	SET	EVL	SET	
375808	73308+79008+78208+73708	RM	SET	EVL	SET	
375809	73309+79009+78209+73709	RM	SET	EVL	SET	
375810	73310+79010+78210+73710	RM	SET	EVL	SET	
375811	73311+79011+78211+73711	RM	SET	EVL	SET	
375812	73312+79012+78212+73712	RM	SET	EVL	SET	
375813	73313+79013+78213+73713	RM	SET	EVL	SET	
375814	73314+79014+78214+73714	RM	SET	EVL	SET	
375815	73315+79015+78215+73715	RM	SET	EVL	SET	
375816	73316+79016+78216+73716	RM	SET	EVL	SET	
375817	73317+79017+78217+73717	RM	SET	EVL	SET	
375818	73318+79018+78218+73718	RM	SET	EVL	SET	
375819	73319+79019+78219+73719	RM	SET	EVL	SET	
375820	73320+79020+78220+73720	RM	SET	EVL	SET	
375821	73321+79021+78221+73721	RM	SET	EVL	SET	
375822	73322+79022+78222+73722	RM	SET	EVL	SET	
375823	73323+79023+78223+73723	RM	SET	EVL	SET	
375824	73324+79024+78224+73724	RM	SET	EVL	SET	
375825	73325+79025+78225+73725	RM	SET	EVL	SET	

375826	73326+79026+78226+73726	RM	SET	EVL	SET	
375827	73327+79027+78227+73727	RM	SET	EVL	SET	
375828	73328+79028+78228+73728	RM	SET	EVL	SET	
375829	73329+79029+78229+73729	RM	SET	EVL	SET	
375830	73330+79030+78230+73730	RM	SET	EVL	SET	*City of London*

Set 375812 fitted with De-icing equipment

Class 375/9
Electrostar

Vehicle Length: (Driving) 66ft 9in (20.3m)
(Inter) 65ft 6in (19.96m)
Height: 12ft 4in (3.75m)
Width: 9ft 2in (2.79m)
Horsepower: 2,012hp (1,500kW)
Seats (total/car): 24F-250S, 12F-59S/73S/59S/12F-59S

Number	*Formation* DMCO(A)+MSO+TSO+DMCO(B)	*Depot*	*Livery*	*Owner*	*Operator*
375901	73331+79031+79061+73731	RM	SET	EVL	SET
375902	73332+79032+79062+73732	RM	SET	EVL	SET
375903	73333+79033+79063+73733	RM	SET	EVL	SET
375904	73334+79034+79064+73734	RM	SET	EVL	SET
375905	73335+79035+79065+73735	RM	SET	EVL	SET
375906	73336+79036+79066+73736	RM	SET	EVL	SET
375907	73337+79037+79067+73737	RM	SET	EVL	SET
375908	73338+79038+79068+73738	RM	SET	EVL	SET
375909	73339+79039+79069+73739	RM	SET	EVL	SET
375910	73340+79040+79070+73740	RM	SET	EVL	SET
375911	73341+79041+79071+73741	RM	SET	EVL	SET
375912	73342+79042+79072+73742	RM	SET	EVL	SET
375913	73343+79043+79073+73743	RM	SET	EVL	SET
375914	73344+79044+79074+73744	RM	SET	EVL	SET
375915	73345+79045+79075+73745	RM	SET	EVL	SET
375916	73346+79046+79076+73746	RM	SET	EVL	SET
375917	73347+79047+79077+73747	RM	SET	EVL	SET
375918	73348+79048+79078+73748	RM	SET	EVL	SET
375919	73349+79049+79079+73749	RM	SET	EVL	SET
375920	73350+79050+79080+73750	RM	SET	EVL	SET
375921	73351+79051+79081+73751	RM	SET	EVL	SET
375922	73352+79052+79082+73752	RM	SET	EVL	SET
375923	73353+79053+79083+73753	RM	SET	EVL	SET
375924	73354+79054+79084+73754	RM	SET	EVL	SET
375925	73355+79055+79085+73755	RM	SET	EVL	SET
375926	73356+79056+79086+73756	RM	SET	EVL	SET
375927	73357+79057+79087+73757	RM	SET	EVL	SET

Below: *The post-slam-door modernisation of SouthEastern led to five sub-classes of Class 375 'Electrostar' being introduced, with a total fleet of 112 vehicles. All sets are owned by Eversholt Leasing and based at Ramsgate. The sets operate the main-line services. Sets are gangwayed throughout and are of an identical structural design to the Class 377s operated by Southern. High-capacity Class 375/9 No. 375902 is seen departing from Lewisham as empty stock for Charing Cross.* **CJM**

Class 376 *Electrostar*

Vehicle Length: (Driving) 66ft 9in (20.3m)	*Width: 9ft 2in (2.79m)*
(Inter) 65ft 6in (19.96m)	*Horsepower: 2,682hp (2,000kW)*
Height: 12ft 4in (3.75m)	*Seats (total/car): 216S, 36S/48S/48S/48S/36S + 116 perch*

Number	Formation DMSO(A)+MSO+TSO+MSO+DMSO(B)	Depot	Livery	Owner	Operator
376001	61101+63301+64301+63501+61601	SG	SET	EVL	SET
376002	61102+63302+64302+63502+61602	SG	SET	EVL	SET
376003	61103+63303+64303+63503+61603	SG	SET	EVL	SET
376004	61104+63304+64304+63504+61604	SG	SET	EVL	SET
376005	61105+63305+64305+63505+61605	SG	SET	EVL	SET
376006	61106+63306+64306+63506+61606	SG	SET	EVL	SET
376007	61107+63307+64307+63507+61607	SG	SET	EVL	SET
376008	61108+63308+64308+63508+61608	SG	SET	EVL	SET
376009	61109+63309+64309+63509+61609	SG	SET	EVL	SET
376010	61110+63310+64310+63510+61610	SG	SET	EVL	SET
376011	61111+63311+64311+63511+61611	SG	SET	EVL	SET
376012	61112+63312+64312+63512+61612	SG	SET	EVL	SET
376013	61113+63313+64313+63513+61613	SG	SET	EVL	SET
376014	61114+63314+64314+63514+61614	SG	SET	EVL	SET
376015	61115+63315+64315+63515+61615	SG	SET	EVL	SET
376016	61116+63316+64316+63516+61616	SG	SET	EVL	SET
376017	61117+63317+64317+63517+61617	SG	SET	EVL	SET
376018	61118+63318+64318+63518+61618	SG	SET	EVL	SET
376019	61119+63319+64319+63519+61619	SG	SET	EVL	SET
376020	61120+63320+64320+63520+61620	SG	SET	EVL	SET
376021	61121+63321+64321+63521+61621	SG	SET	EVL	SET
376022	61122+63322+64322+63522+61622	SG	SET	EVL	SET
376023	61123+63323+64323+63523+61623	SG	SET	EVL	SET
376024	61124+63324+64324+63524+61624	SG	SET	EVL	SET
376025	61125+63325+64325+63525+61625	SG	SET	EVL	SET
376026	61126+63326+64326+63526+61626	SG	SET	EVL	SET
376027	61127+63327+64327+63527+61627	SG	SET	EVL	SET
376028	61128+63328+64328+63528+61628	SG	SET	EVL	SET
376029	61129+63329+64329+63529+61629	SG	SET	EVL	SET
376030	61130+63330+64330+63530+61630	SG	SET	EVL	SET
376031	61131+63331+64331+63531+61631	SG	SET	EVL	SET
376032	61132+63332+64332+63532+61632	SG	SET	EVL	SET
376033	61133+63333+64333+63533+61633	SG	SET	EVL	SET
376034	61134+63334+64334+63534+61634	SG	SET	EVL	SET
376035	61135+63335+64335+63535+61635	SG	SET	EVL	SET
376036	61136+63336+64336+63536+61636	SG	SET	EVL	SET

Below: *In 2005-06 a fleet of 36 five-car non-gangwayed 'Electrostar' sets was introduced on SouthEastern to operate the heavily used Metro services from Charing Cross and Cannon Street to Kent. The sets were fitted with low-density seating to allow a greater standing space for the huge number of passengers wishing to travel in the peak periods. The front ends were rather bland with an extra window fitted where the gangway would have been installed. Rather that using sliding plug doors, the Class 376s were fitted with sliding pocket doors. All sets are allocated to Slade Green. Set No. 376028 is illustrated arriving at Lewisham with a Charing Cross to Dartford via Sidcup service.* **CJM**

Class 395
Javelin

Vehicle Length: (Driving) 67ft 7in (20.6m)
(Inter) 67ft 6in (20.5m)
Height: 12ft 6in (3.81m)
Width: 9ft 2in (2.79m)
Horsepower: 2,252hp (1,680kW)
Seats (total/car): 340S, 28S/66S/66S/66S/66S/48S

Number	*Formation* DMSO(A)+MSO(A)+MSO(B)+ MSO(C)+MSO(D)+DMSO(B)	*Depot*	*Livery*	*Owner*	*Operator*	*Name*
395001	39011+39012+39013+39014+39015+39016	AD	HS1	EVL	SET	*Dame Kelly Holmes*
395002	39021+39022+39023+39024+39025+39026	AD	HS1	EVL	SET	*Sebastian Coe*
395003	39031+39032+39033+39034+39035+39036	AD	HS1	EVL	SET	*Sir Steve Redgrave*
395004	39041+39042+39043+39044+39045+39046	AD	HS1	EVL	SET	*Sir Chris Hoy*
395005	39051+39052+39053+39054+39055+39056	AD	HS1	EVL	SET	*Dame Tanni Grey-Thompson*
395006	39061+39062+39063+39064+39065+39066	AD	HS1	EVL	SET	*Daley Thompson*
395007	39071+39072+39073+39074+39075+39076	AD	HS1	EVL	SET	*Steve Backley*
395008	39081+39082+39083+39084+39085+39086	AD	HS1	EVL	SET	*Ben Ainslie*
395009	39091+39092+39093+39094+39095+39096	AD	HS1	EVL	SET	*Rebecca Adlington*
395010	39101+39102+39103+39104+39105+39106	AD	HS1	EVL	SET	*Duncan Goodhew*
395011	39111+39112+39113+39114+39115+39116	AD	HS1	EVL	SET	*Katherine Grainger*
395012	39121+39122+39123+39124+39125+39126	AD	HS1	EVL	SET	
395013	39131+39132+39133+39134+39135+39136	AD	HS1	EVL	SET	
395014	39141+39142+39143+39144+39145+39146	AD	HS1	EVL	SET	
395015	39151+39152+39153+39154+39155+39156	AD	HS1	EVL	SET	
395016	39161+39162+39163+39164+39165+39166	AD	HS1	EVL	SET	*Jamie Staff*
395017	39171+39172+39173+39174+39175+39176	AD	HS1	EVL	SET	*Dame Sarah Storey*
395018	39181+39182+39183+39184+39185+39186	AD	HS1	EVL	SET	*Mo Farah*
395019	39191+39192+39193+39194+39195+39196	AD	HS1	EVL	SET	*Jessica Ennis*
395020	39201+39202+39203+39204+39205+39206	AD	HS1	EVL	SET	*Jason Kenny*
395021	39211+39212+39213+39214+39215+39216	AD	HS1	EVL	SET	*Ed Clancy MBE*
395022	39221+39222+39223+39224+39225+39226	AD	HS1	EVL	SET	*Alistair Brownlee*
395023	39231+39232+39233+39234+39235+39236	AD	HS1	EVL	SET	*Ellie Simmonds*
395024	39241+39242+39243+39244+39245+39246	AD	HS1	EVL	SET	*Jonnie Peacock*
395025	39251+39252+39253+39254+39255+39256	AD	HS1	EVL	SET	*Victoria Pendleton*
395026	39261+39262+39263+39264+39265+39266	AD	HS1	EVL	SET	*Marc Woods*
395027	39271+39272+39273+39274+39275+39276	AD	HS1	EVL	SET	*Hannah Cockcroft*
395028	39281+39282+39283+39284+39285+39286	AD	HS1	EVL	SET	*Laura Trott*
395029	39291+39292+39293+39294+39295+39296	AD	HS1	EVL	SET	*David Weir*

Below: *Domestic services over High Speed 1 (HS1) between London St Pancras International and Kent destinations are operated by a fleet of 29 six-car Hitachi-built 'Javelin' sets, which operate over the UK's first high-speed line at speeds of up to 140mph (225km/h). The sets are painted SouthEastern blue and many, following the 2012 Olympic Games, carry bodyside 'Javelin' branding. Set No. 395008* Ben Ainslie *passes Lenham with a Dover to London St Pancras International service.*
Brian Stephenson

South Eastern

Class 465/0
Networker

Vehicle Length: (Driving) 68ft 6½in (20.89m) (Inter) 65ft 9¾in (20.05m)
Height: 12ft 4½in (3.77m)
Width: 9ft 3in (2.81m)
Horsepower: 2,252hp (1,680kW)
Seats (total/car): 348S, 86S/90S/86S/86S

Number	Formation DMSO(A)+TSO+TSO+DMSO(B)	Depot	Livery	Owner	Operator
465001	64759+72028+72029+64809	SG	SET	EVL	SET
465002	64760+72030+72031+64810	SG	SET	EVL	SET
465003	64761+72032+72033+64811	SG	SET	EVL	SET
465004	64762+72034+72035+64812	SG	SET	EVL	SET
465005	64763+72036+72037+64813	SG	SET	EVL	SET
465006	64764+72038+72039+64814	SG	SET	EVL	SET
465007	64765+72040+72041+64815	SG	SET	EVL	SET
465008	64766+72042+72043+64816	SG	SET	EVL	SET
465009	64767+72044+72045+64817	SG	SET	EVL	SET
465010	64768+72046+72047+64818	SG	SET	EVL	SET
465011	64769+72048+72049+64819	SG	SET	EVL	SET
465012	64770+72050+72051+64820	SG	SET	EVL	SET
465013	64771+72052+72053+64821	SG	SET	EVL	SET
465014	64772+72054+72055+64822	SG	SET	EVL	SET
465015	64773+72056+72057+64823	SG	SET	EVL	SET
465016	64774+72058+72059+64824	SG	SET	EVL	SET
465017	64775+72060+72061+64825	SG	SET	EVL	SET
465018	64776+72062+72063+64826	SG	SET	EVL	SET
465019	64777+72064+72065+64827	SG	SET	EVL	SET
465020	64778+72066+72067+64828	SG	SET	EVL	SET
465021	64779+72068+72069+64829	SG	SET	EVL	SET
465022	64780+72070+72071+64830	SG	SET	EVL	SET
465023	64781+72072+72073+64831	SG	SET	EVL	SET
465024	64782+72074+72075+64832	SG	SET	EVL	SET
465025	64783+72076+72077+64833	SG	SET	EVL	SET
465026	64784+72078+72079+64834	SG	SET	EVL	SET
465027	64785+72080+72081+64835	SG	SET	EVL	SET
465028	64786+72082+72083+64836	SG	SET	EVL	SET
465029	64787+72084+72085+64837	SG	SET	EVL	SET
465030	64788+72086+72087+64838	SG	SET	EVL	SET
465031	64789+72088+72089+64839	SG	SET	EVL	SET
465032	64790+72090+72091+64840	SG	SET	EVL	SET
465033	64791+72092+72093+64841	SG	SET	EVL	SET
465034	64792+72094+72095+64842	SG	SET	EVL	SET
465035	64793+72096+72097+64843	SG	SET	EVL	SET
465036	64794+72098+72099+64844	SG	SET	EVL	SET
465037	64795+72100+72101+64845	SG	SET	EVL	SET
465038	64796+72102+72103+64846	SG	SET	EVL	SET
465039	64797+72104+72105+64847	SG	SET	EVL	SET
465040	64798+72106+72107+64848	SG	SET	EVL	SET
465041	64799+72108+72109+64849	SG	SET	EVL	SET
465042	64800+72110+72111+64850	SG	SET	EVL	SET
465043	64801+72112+72113+64851	SG	SET	EVL	SET
465044	64802+72114+72115+64852	SG	SET	EVL	SET
465045	64803+72116+72117+64853	SG	SET	EVL	SET
465046	64804+72118+72119+64854	SG	SET	EVL	SET
465047	64805+72120+72121+64855	SG	SET	EVL	SET
465048	64806+72122+72123+64856	SG	SET	EVL	SET
465049	64807+72124+72125+64857	SG	SET	EVL	SET
465050	64808+72126+72127+64858	SG	SET	EVL	SET

Class 465/1
Networker

Vehicle Length: (Driving) 68ft 6½in (20.89m) (Inter) 65ft 9¾in (20.05m)
Height: 12ft 4½in (3.77m)
Width: 9ft 3in (2.81m)
Horsepower: 2,252hp (1,680kW)
Seats (total/car): 348S, 86S/90S/86S/86S

Number	Formation DMSO(A)+TSO+TSO+DMSO(B)	Depot	Livery	Owner	Operator
465151	65800+72900+72901+65847	SG	SET	EVL	SET
465152	65801+72902+72903+65848	SG	SET	EVL	SET
465153	65802+72904+72905+65849	SG	SET	EVL	SET

465154	65803+72906+72907+65850	SG	SET	EVL	SET
465155	65804+72908+72909+65851	SG	SET	EVL	SET
465156	65805+72910+72911+65852	SG	SET	EVL	SET
465157	65806+72912+72913+65853	SG	SET	EVL	SET
465158	65807+72914+72915+65854	SG	SET	EVL	SET
465159	65808+72916+72917+65855	SG	SET	EVL	SET
465160	65809+72918+72919+65856	SG	SET	EVL	SET
465161	65810+72920+72921+65857	SG	SET	EVL	SET
465162	65811+72922+72923+65858	SG	SET	EVL	SET
465163	65812+72924+72925+65859	SG	SET	EVL	SET
465164	65813+72926+72927+65860	SG	SET	EVL	SET
465165	65814+72928+72929+65861	SG	SET	EVL	SET
465166	65815+72930+72931+65862	SG	SET	EVL	SET
465167	65816+72932+72933+65863	SG	SET	EVL	SET
465168	65817+72934+72935+65864	SG	SET	EVL	SET
465169	65818+72936+72937+65865	SG	SET	EVL	SET
465170	65819+72938+72939+65866	SG	SET	EVL	SET
465171	65820+72940+72941+65867	SG	SET	EVL	SET
465172	65821+72942+72943+65868	SG	SET	EVL	SET
465173	65822+72944+72945+65869	SG	SET	EVL	SET
465174	65823+72946+72947+65870	SG	SET	EVL	SET
465175	65824+72948+72949+65871	SG	SET	EVL	SET
465176	65825+72950+72951+65872	SG	SET	EVL	SET
465177	65826+72952+72952+65873	SG	SET	EVL	SET
465178	65827+72954+72955+65874	SG	SET	EVL	SET
465179	65828+72956+72957+65875	SG	SET	EVL	SET
465180	65829+72958+72959+65876	SG	SET	EVL	SET
465181	65830+72960+72961+65877	SG	SET	EVL	SET
465182	65831+72962+72963+65878	SG	SET	EVL	SET
465183	65832+72964+72965+65879	SG	SET	EVL	SET
465184	65833+72966+72967+65880	SG	SET	EVL	SET
465185	65834+72968+72969+65881	SG	SET	EVL	SET
465186	65835+72970+72971+65882	SG	SET	EVL	SET
465187	65836+72972+72973+65883	SG	SET	EVL	SET
465188	65837+72974+72975+65884	SG	SET	EVL	SET
465189	65838+72976+72977+65885	SG	SET	EVL	SET
465190	65839+72978+72979+65886	SG	SET	EVL	SET
465191	65840+72980+72981+65887	SG	SET	EVL	SET
465192	65841+72982+72983+65888	SG	SET	EVL	SET
465193	65842+72984+72985+65889	SG	SET	EVL	SET
465194	65843+72986+72987+65890	SG	SET	EVL	SET
465195	65844+72988+72989+65891	SG	SET	EVL	SET
465196	65845+72990+72991+65892	SG	SET	EVL	SET
465197	65846+72992+72993+65893	SG	SET	EVL	SET

Below: *The Network SouthEast modernisation of the 'Kent Link' lines saw the introduction of 'Networker' Class 465 sets built by BREL/ABB and Alstom to replacing the aged EPB stock. Four different sub-classes of the four-car design exist, all are allocated to Slade Green and form the backbone of suburban services operated by SouthEastern. Sets have all been facelifted and now sport the latest SouthEastern livery of white and dark blue body, offset by light blue sliding plug passenger doors. ABB-built Class 465/1 No. 465163 is illustrated at Lewisham.* **CJM**

Class 465/2
Networker

Vehicle Length: (Driving) 68ft 6½in (20.89m) (Inter) 65ft 9¾in (20.05m)
Height: 12ft 4½in (3.77m)
Width: 9ft 3in (2.81m)
Horsepower: 2,252hp (1,680kW)
Seats (total/car): 348S, 86S/90S/86S/86S

Number	*Formation* DMSO(A)+TSO+TSO+DMSO(B)	*Depot*	*Livery*	*Owner*	*Operator*
465235	65734+72787+72788+65784	SG	SET	ANG	SET
465236	65735+72789+72790+65785	SG	SET	ANG	SET
465237	65736+72791+72792+65786	SG	SET	ANG	SET
465238	65737+72793+72794+65787	SG	SET	ANG	SET
465239	65738+72795+72796+65788	SG	SET	ANG	SET
465240	65739+72797+72798+65789	SG	SET	ANG	SET
465241	65740+72799+72800+65790	SG	SET	ANG	SET
465242	65741+72801+72802+65791	SG	SET	ANG	SET
465243	65742+72803+72804+65792	SG	SET	ANG	SET
465244	65743+72805+72806+65793	SG	SET	ANG	SET
465245	65744+72807+72808+65794	SG	SET	ANG	SET
465246	65745+72809+72810+65795	SG	SET	ANG	SET
465247	65746+72811+72812+65796	SG	SET	ANG	SET
465248	65747+72813+72814+65797	SG	SET	ANG	SET
465249	65748+72815+72816+65798	SG	SET	ANG	SET
465250	65749+72817+72818+65799	SG	SET	ANG	SET

Class 465/9
Networker

Vehicle Length: (Driving) 68ft 6½in (20.89m) (Inter) 65ft 9¾in (20.05m)
Height: 12ft 4½in (3.77m)
Width: 9ft 3in (2.81m)
Horsepower: 2,252hp (1,680kW)
Seats (total/car): 24F-302S, 12F-68S/76S/90S/12F-68S

Number	*Formation* DMCO(A)+TSO+TSO+DMCO(B)	*Depot*	*Livery*	*Owner*	*Operator*	*Name*
465901 (465201)	65700+72719+72720+65750	SG	SET	ANG	SET	
465902 (465202)	65701+72721+72722+65751	SG	SET	ANG	SET	
465903 (465203)	65702+72723+72724+65752	SG	SET	ANG	SET	*Remembrance*
465904 (465204)	65703+72725+72726+65753	SG	SET	ANG	SET	
465905 (465205)	65704+72727+72728+65754	SG	SET	ANG	SET	
465906 (465206)	65705+72729+72730+65755	SG	SET	ANG	SET	
465907 (465207)	65706+72731+72732+65756	SG	SET	ANG	SET	
465908 (465208)	65707+72733+72734+65757	SG	SET	ANG	SET	
465909 (465209)	65708+72735+72736+65758	SG	SET	ANG	SET	
465910 (465210)	65709+72737+72738+65759	SG	SET	ANG	SET	
465911 (465211)	65710+72739+72740+65760	SG	SET	ANG	SET	
465912 (465212)	65711+72741+72742+65761	SG	SET	ANG	SET	
465913 (465213)	65712+72743+72744+65762	SG	SET	ANG	SET	
465914 (465214)	65713+72745+72746+65763	SG	SET	ANG	SET	
465915 (465215)	65714+72747+72748+65764	SG	SET	ANG	SET	
465916 (465216)	65715+72749+72750+65765	SG	SET	ANG	SET	
465917 (465217)	65716+72751+72752+65766	SG	SET	ANG	SET	
465918 (465218)	65717+72753+72754+65767	SG	SET	ANG	SET	
465919 (465219)	65718+72755+72756+65768	SG	SET	ANG	SET	
465920 (465220)	65719+72757+72758+65769	SG	SET	ANG	SET	
465921 (465221)	65720+72759+72760+65770	SG	SET	ANG	SET	
465922 (465222)	65721+72761+72762+65771	SG	SET	ANG	SET	
465923 (465223)	65722+72763+72764+65772	SG	SET	ANG	SET	
465924 (465224)	65723+72765+72766+65773	SG	SET	ANG	SET	
465925 (465225)	65724+72767+72768+65774	SG	SET	ANG	SET	
465926 (465226)	65725+72769+72770+65775	SG	SET	ANG	SET	
465927 (465227)	65726+72771+72772+65776	SG	SET	ANG	SET	
465928 (465228)	65727+72773+72774+65777	SG	SET	ANG	SET	
465929 (465229)	65728+72775+72776+65778	SG	SET	ANG	SET	
465930 (465230)	65729+72777+72778+65779	SG	SET	ANG	SET	
465931 (465231)	65730+72779+72780+65780	SG	SET	ANG	SET	
465932 (465232)	65731+72781+72782+65781	SG	SET	ANG	SET	
465933 (465233)	65732+72783+72784+65782	SG	SET	ANG	SET	
465934 (465234)	65733+72785+72786+65783	SG	SET	ANG	SET	

Right: *The passenger layout on the Class 465/0, 465/1 and 465/2 sets is the same, with seating for 348 standard class passengers. The 34 modified Class 465/9 sets, upgraded from Class 465/2s, now have first class seating in the driving cars, directly behind the driving position. These sets are used on longer-distance Kent suburban services. One of the early York-built Class 465/0s, No. 465033, is seen at London Bridge with a Cannon Street to Dartford peak-hour service.* **CJM**

Class 466
Networker

Vehicle Length: (Driving) 68ft 6½in (20.89m)
Height: 12ft 4½in (3.77m)
Width: 9ft 3in (2.81m)
Horsepower: 1,126hp (840kW)
Seats (total/car): 168S, 86S/82S

Number	Formation DMSO+DTSO	Depot	Livery	Owner	Operator
466001	64860+78312	SG	SET	ANG	SET
466002	64861+78313	SG	SET	ANG	SET
466003	64862+78314	SG	SET	ANG	SET
466004	64863+78315	SG	SET	ANG	SET
466005	64864+78316	SG	SET	ANG	SET
466006	64865+78317	SG	SET	ANG	SET
466007	64866+78318	SG	SET	ANG	SET
466008	64867+78319	SG	SET	ANG	SET
466009	64868+78320	SG	SET	ANG	SET
466010	64869+78321	SG	SET	ANG	SET
466011	64870+78322	SG	SET	ANG	SET
466012	64871+78323	SG	SET	ANG	SET
466013	64872+78324	SG	SET	ANG	SET
466014	64873+78325	SG	SET	ANG	SET
466015	64874+78326	SG	SET	ANG	SET
466016	64875+78327	SG	SET	ANG	SET
466017	64876+78328	SG	SET	ANG	SET
466018	64877+78329	SG	SET	ANG	SET
466019	64878+78330	SG	SET	ANG	SET
466020	64879+78331	SG	SET	ANG	SET
466021	64880+78332	SG	SET	ANG	SET
466022	64881+78333	SG	SET	ANG	SET
466023	64882+78334	SG	SET	ANG	SET
466024	64883+78335	SG	SET	ANG	SET
466025	64884+78336	SG	SET	ANG	SET
466026	64885+78337	SG	SET	ANG	SET
466027	64886+78338	SG	SET	ANG	SET
466028	64887+78339	SG	SET	ANG	SET
466029	64888+78340	SG	SET	ANG	SET
466030	64889+78341	SG	SET	ANG	SET
466031	64890+78342	SG	SET	ANG	SET
466032	64891+78343	SG	SET	ANG	SET
466033	64892+78344	SG	SET	ANG	SET
466034	64893+78345	SG	SET	ANG	SET
466035	64894+78346	SG	SET	ANG	SET
466036	64895+78347	SG	SET	ANG	SET
466037	64896+78348	SG	SET	ANG	SET
466038	64897+78349	SG	SET	ANG	SET
466039	64898+78350	SG	SET	ANG	SET
466040	64899+78351	SG	SET	ANG	SET
466041	64900+78352	SG	SET	ANG	SET
466042	64901+78353	SG	SET	ANG	SET
466043	64902+78354	SG	SET	ANG	SET

Right: *To allow the operation of 10-car formations of 'Networker' stock, a fleet of 43 two-car Class 466 sets was built by Alstom, formed of a driving motor and a driving trailer vehicle. The sets are now painted in the latest SouthEastern white and blue livery and are allocated to Slade Green. The sets can be found operating on their own for branch line use or in six-, eight- or ten-car formations. Set No. 466008 is shown at Lewisham.* **CJM**

Southern

Address: Go-Ahead House, 26-28 Addiscombe Road, Croydon, CR9 5GA
info@southernrailway.com
08451 272920
www.southernrailway.com

Managing Director: Chris Burchell
Franchise Dates: 1 March 2003 - 25 July 2015
Principal Routes: London Victoria/London Bridge to Brighton, Coastway route, Uckfield/East Grinstead. Services to Surrey/Sussex, and Brighton to Ashford route
Depots: Brighton (BI), Selhurst (SU), Stewarts Lane (SL)
Parent Company: Govia

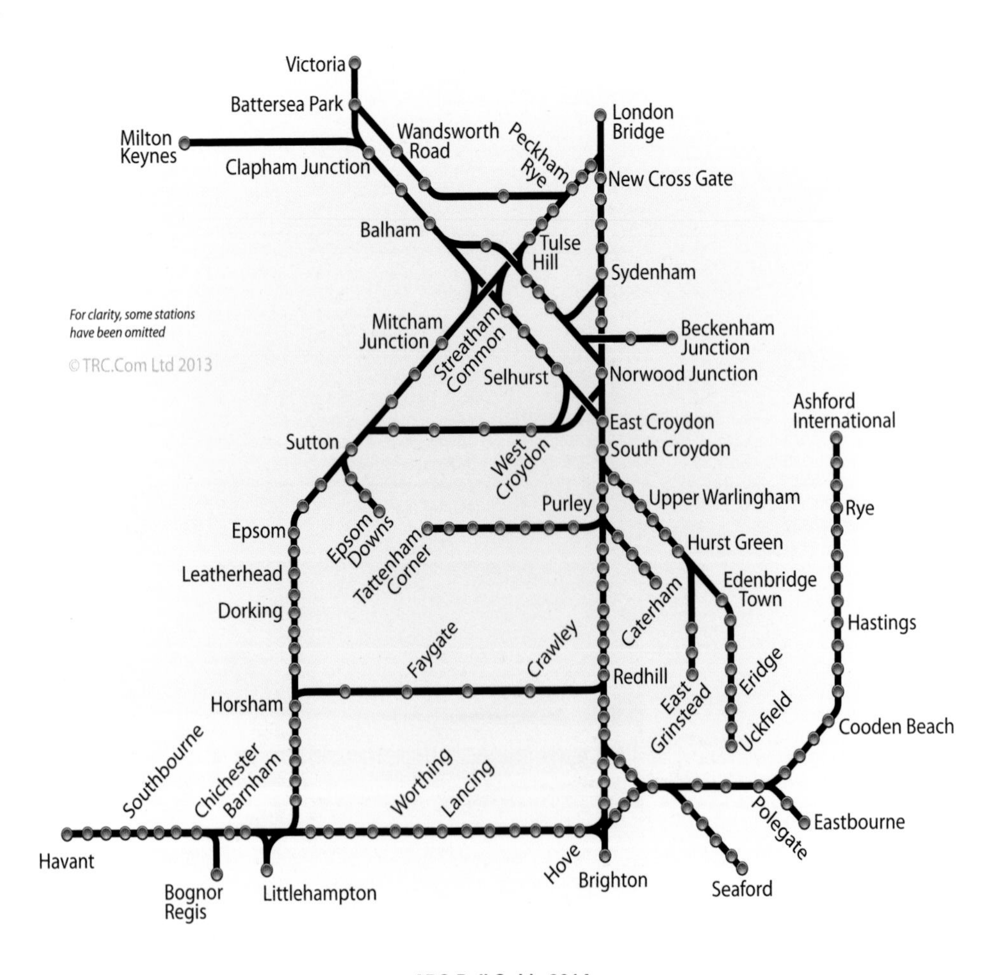

Class 171/7
Turbostar

Vehicle Length: 77ft 6in (23.62m)
Height: 12ft 4½in (3.77m)
Width: 8ft 10in (2.69m)
Engine: 1 x MTU 6R 183TD13H 422hp per vehicle
Horsepower: 844hp (629kW)
Seats (total/car): 9F-107S 9F-43S/64S

Number	Formation DMCL+DMSL	Depot	Livery	Owner	Operator
171721	**50721+79721**	**SU**	**SOU**	**PTR**	**SOU**
171722	**50722+79722**	**SU**	**SOU**	**PTR**	**SOU**
171723	**50723+79723**	**SU**	**SOU**	**PTR**	**SOU**
171724	**50724+79724**	**SU**	**SOU**	**PTR**	**SOU**
171725	**50725+79725**	**SU**	**SOU**	**PTR**	**SOU**
171726	**50726+79726**	**SU**	**SOU**	**PTR**	**SOU**
171727	**50727+79727**	**SU**	**SOU**	**PTR**	**SOU**
171728	**50728+79728**	**SU**	**SOU**	**PTR**	**SOU**
171729	**50729+79729**	**SU**	**SOU**	**PTR**	**SOU**
171730	**50392+79392**	**SU**	**SOU**	**PTR**	**SOU**

171730 Previously numbered 170392

Class 171/8
Turbostar

Vehicle Length: 77ft 6in (23.62m)
Height: 12ft 4½in (3.77m)
Width: 8ft 10in (2.69m)
Engine: 1 x MTU 6R 183TD13H 422hp per vehicle
Horsepower: 1,688hp (1,259kW)
Seats (total/car): 18F-241S 9F-43S/74S/74S/9F-50SS

Number	Formation DMCL(A)+MS+MS+DMCL(B)	Depot	Livery	Owner	Operator
171801	**50801+54801+56801+79801**	**SU**	**SOU**	**PTR**	**SOU**
171802	**50802+54802+56802+79802**	**SU**	**SOU**	**PTR**	**SOU**
171803	**50803+54803+56803+79803**	**SU**	**SOU**	**PTR**	**SOU**
171804	**50804+54804+56804+79804**	**SU**	**SOU**	**PTR**	**SOU**
171805	**50805+54805+56805+79805**	**SU**	**SOU**	**PTR**	**SOU**
171806	**50806+54806+56806+79806**	**SU**	**SOU**	**PTR**	**SOU**

Right: *To replace slam-door DEMU stock on Southern, a fleet of 16 Class 171 'Turbostar' DMUs was built, ten two-car sets and six four-car sets. All are painted in Southern white and green livery and allocated to Selhurst. The sets operate over the few remaining non-electrified sections to Uckfield as well as on the Ashford to Hastings line. Four-car set No. 171802 passes Honor Oak Park in south London with a London Bridge to Uckfield service. A two-car set is attached on the rear.* **CJM**

Class 313/2

Vehicle Length: (Driving) 64ft 11½in (20.75m)
(Inter) 65ft 4½in (19.92m)
Height: 11ft 9in (3.58m)
Width: 9ft 3in (2.82m)
Horsepower: 880hp (656kW)
Seats (total/car): 202S, 66S/70S/66S

Number	Formation DMSO+PTSO+BDMSO	Depot	Livery	Owner	Operator
313201 (313101)	**62529+71213+62593**	**BI**	**SOU**	**BEA**	**SOU**
313202 (313102)	**62530+71214+62594**	**BI**	**SOU**	**BEA**	**SOU**
313203 (313103)	**62531+71215+62595**	**BI**	**SOU**	**BEA**	**SOU**
313204 (313104)	**62532+71216+62596**	**BI**	**SOU**	**BEA**	**SOU**
313205 (313105)	**62533+71217+62597**	**BI**	**SOU**	**BEA**	**SOU**
313206 (313106)	**62534+71218+62598**	**BI**	**SOU**	**BEA**	**SOU**
313207 (313107)	**62535+71219+62599**	**BI**	**SOU**	**BEA**	**SOU**
313208 (313108)	**62536+71220+62600**	**BI**	**SOU**	**BEA**	**SOU**
313209 (313109)	**62537+71221+62601**	**BI**	**SOU**	**BEA**	**SOU**
313210 (313110)	**62538+71222+62602**	**BI**	**SOU**	**BEA**	**SOU**
313211 (313111)	**62539+71223+62603**	**BI**	**SOU**	**BEA**	**SOU**
313212 (313112)	**62540+71224+62604**	**BI**	**SOU**	**BEA**	**SOU**
313213 (313113)	**62541+71225+62605**	**BI**	**SOU**	**BEA**	**SOU**
313214 (313114)	**62542+71226+62606**	**BI**	**SOU**	**BEA**	**SOU**
313215 (313115)	**62543+71227+62607**	**BI**	**SOU**	**BEA**	**SOU**
313216 (313116)	**62544+71228+62608**	**BI**	**SOU**	**BEA**	**SOU**
313217 (313117)	**62545+71229+61609**	**BI**	**SOU**	**BEA**	**SOU**
313219 (313119)	**62547+71231+61611**	**BI**	**SOU**	**BEA**	**SOU**
313220 (313120)	**62548+71232+61612**	**BI**	**SOU**	**BEA**	**SOU**

Left: *Southern, in a quest to modernise its Brighton-based Coastway services, took over a fleet of 19 Class 313s from Transport for London following the delivery of Class 378 stock. The three-car Class 313s were fully refurbished at Doncaster and are now the mainstay of power on the Coastway services radiating from Brighton. The sets have 3+2 seating and carry a mix of Southern white and green livery and route pictogram branding. Set No. 313202 is seen at Fratton on a Portsmouth to Brighton service.* **Antony Christie**

Class 377/1
Electrostar

Vehicle Length: (Driving) 66ft 9in (20.3m) Width: 9ft 2in (2.79m)
(Inter) 65ft 6in (19.96m) Horsepower: 2,012hp (1,500kW)
Height: 12ft 4in (3.75m) Seats (total/car): 24F-210S or 244S 12F-48S(56S)/62S(70S)/52S(62S)/12F-48S(56S)

Number	Formation DMCO(A)+MSO+TSO+DMCO(B)	Depot	Livery	Owner	Operator
377101	78501+77101+78901+78701	BI	SOU	PTR	SOU
377102	78502+77102+78902+78702	BI	SOU	PTR	SOU
377103	78503+77103+78903+78703	BI	SOU	PTR	SOU
377104	78504+77104+78904+78704	BI	SOU	PTR	SOU
377105	78505+77105+78905+78705	BI	SOU	PTR	SOU
377106	78506+77106+78906+78706	BI	SOU	PTR	SOU
377107	78507+77107+78907+78707	BI	SOU	PTR	SOU
377108	78508+77108+78908+78708	BI	SOU	PTR	SOU
377109	78509+77109+78909+78709	BI	SOU	PTR	SOU
377110	78510+77110+78910+78710	BI	SOU	PTR	SOU
377111	78511+77111+78911+78711	BI	SOU	PTR	SOU
377112	78512+77112+78912+78712	BI	SOU	PTR	SOU
377113	78513+77113+78913+78713	BI	SOU	PTR	SOU
377114	78514+77114+78914+78714	BI	SOU	PTR	SOU
377115	78515+77115+78915+78715	BI	SOU	PTR	SOU
377116	78516+77116+78916+78716	BI	SOU	PTR	SOU
377117	78517+77117+78917+78717	BI	SOU	PTR	SOU
377118	78518+77118+78918+78718	BI	SOU	PTR	SOU
377119	78519+77119+78919+78719	BI	SOU	PTR	SOU
377120	78520+77120+78920+78720	BI	SOU	PTR	SOU
377121	78521+77121+78921+78721	BI	SOU	PTR	SOU
377122	78522+77122+78922+78722	BI	SOU	PTR	SOU
377123	78523+77123+78923+78723	BI	SOU	PTR	SOU
377124	78524+77124+78924+78724	BI	SOU	PTR	SOU
377125	78525+77125+78925+78725	BI	SOU	PTR	SOU
377126	78526+77126+78926+78726	BI	SOU	PTR	SOU
377127	78527+77127+78927+78727	BI	SOU	PTR	SOU
377128	78528+77128+78928+78728	BI	SOU	PTR	SOU
377129	78529+77129+78929+78729	BI	SOU	PTR	SOU
377130	78530+77130+78930+78730	BI	SOU	PTR	SOU
377131	78531+77131+78931+78731	BI	SOU	PTR	SOU
377132	78532+77132+78932+78732	BI	SOU	PTR	SOU
377133	78533+77133+78933+78733	BI	SOU	PTR	SOU
377134	78534+77134+78934+78734	BI	SOU	PTR	SOU
377135	78535+77135+78935+78735	BI	SOU	PTR	SOU
377136	78536+77136+78936+78736	BI	SOU	PTR	SOU
377137	78537+77137+78937+78737	BI	SOU	PTR	SOU
377138	78538+77138+78938+78738	BI	SOU	PTR	SOU
377139	78539+77139+78939+78739	BI	SOU	PTR	SOU
377140	78540+77140+78940+78740	BI	SOU	PTR	SOU

377141	78541+77141+78941+78741	BI	SOU	PTR	SOU
377142	78542+77142+78942+78742	BI	SOU	PTR	SOU
377143	78543+77143+78943+78743	BI	SOU	PTR	SOU
377144	78544+77144+78944+78744	BI	SOU	PTR	SOU
377145	78545+77145+78945+78745	BI	SOU	PTR	SOU
377146	78546+77146+78946+78746	BI	SOU	PTR	SOU
377147	78547+77147+78947+78747	BI	SOU	PTR	SOU
377148	78548+77148+78948+78748	BI	SOU	PTR	SOU
377149	78549+77149+78949+78749	BI	SOU	PTR	SOU
377150	78550+77150+78950+78750	BI	SOU	PTR	SOU
377151	78551+77151+78951+78751	BI	SOU	PTR	SOU
377152	78552+77152+78952+78752	BI	SOU	PTR	SOU
377153	78553+77153+78953+78753	BI	SOU	PTR	SOU
377154	78554+77154+78954+78754	BI	SOU	PTR	SOU
377155	78555+77155+78955+78755	BI	SOU	PTR	SOU
377156	78556+77156+78956+78756	BI	SOU	PTR	SOU
377157	78557+77157+78957+78757	BI	SOU	PTR	SOU
377158	78558+77158+78958+78758	BI	SOU	PTR	SOU
377159	78559+77159+78959+78759	BI	SOU	PTR	SOU
377160	78560+77160+78960+78760	BI	SOU	PTR	SOU
377161	78561+77161+78961+78761	BI	SOU	PTR	SOU
377162	78562+77162+78962+78762	SU	SOU	PTR	SOU
377163	78563+77163+78963+78763	SU	SOU	PTR	SOU
377164	78564+77164+78964+78764	SU	SOU	PTR	SOU

Right: *The main-line modernisation of the Central section of the former Southern Region under privatisation led to a huge fleet of ABB/Bombardier 'Electrostar' sets, classified as 377 being constructed. Eventually, eight sub-classes will exist, each having slight variations in equipment, layout and use. A fleet of 64 Class 377/1 sets is allocated to Brighton. This sub-class has two slightly different seating layouts. Class 377/1 No. 377152 passes Honor Oak Park.* **CJM**

Class 377/2
Electrostar

Vehicle Length: (Driving) 66ft 9in (20.3m), (Inter) 65ft 6in (19.96m)
Height: 12ft 4in (3.75m)
Width: 9ft 2in (2.79m)
Horsepower: 2,012hp (1,500kW)
Seats (total/car): 24F-222S, 12F-48S/69S/57S/12F-48S

Number	*Formation* DMCO(A)+MSO+PTSO+DMCO(B)	*Depot*	*Livery*	*Owner*	*Operator*
377201	78571+77171+78971+78771	BI	SOU	PTR	SOU
377202	78572+77172+78972+78772	BI	SOU	PTR	SOU
377203	78573+77173+78973+78773	BI	SOU	PTR	SOU
377204	78574+77174+78974+78774	BI	SOU	PTR	SOU
377205	78575+77175+78975+78775	SU	SOU	PTR	SOU
377206	78576+77176+78976+78776	SU	SOU	PTR	SOU
377207	78577+77177+78977+78777	BI	SOU	PTR	SOU
377208	78578+77178+78978+78778	BI	SOU	PTR	SOU
377209	78579+77179+78979+78779	BI	SOU	PTR	SOU
377210	78580+77180+78980+78780	SU	SOU	PTR	SOU
377211	78581+77181+78981+78781	SU	SOU	PTR	SOU
377212	78582+77182+78982+78782	SU	SOU	PTR	SOU
377213	78583+77183+78983+78783	BI	SOU	PTR	SOU
377214	78584+77184+78984+78784	SU	SOU	PTR	SOU
377215	78585+77185+78985+78785	BI	SOU	PTR	SOU

Southern

Left: *The 15 members of Class 377/2 are dual voltage sets, able to operate from either the 750V dc third rail or from the 25kV ac overhead. The sets are deployed on the Southern cross-London services from Croydon to Milton Keynes via Clapham Junction, Kensington Olympia and Willesden Junction. These sets seat 24 first and 222 standard class passengers. Set No. 377204 is recorded at West Brompton with a Milton Keynes to Croydon service.* **CJM**

Class 377/3
Electrostar

Vehicle Length: (Driving) 66ft 9in (20.3m)
(Inter) 65ft 6in (19.96m)
Height: 12ft 4in (3.75m)
Width: 9ft 2in (2.79m)
Horsepower: 2,012hp (1,500kW)
Seats (total/car): 24F-152S, 12F-48S/56S/12F-48S

Number	*Formation DMCO(A)+TSO+DMCO(B)*	*Depot*	*Livery*	*Owner*	*Operator*
377301 (375311)	**68201+74801+68401**	**SU**	**SOU**	**PTR**	**SOU**
377302 (375312)	**68202+74802+68402**	**SU**	**SOU**	**PTR**	**SOU**
377303 (375313)	**68203+74803+68403**	**SU**	**SOU**	**PTR**	**SOU**
377304 (375314)	**68204+74804+68404**	**SU**	**SOU**	**PTR**	**SOU**
377305 (375315)	**68205+74805+68405**	**SU**	**SOU**	**PTR**	**SOU**
377306 (375316)	**68206+74806+68406**	**SU**	**SOU**	**PTR**	**SOU**
377307 (375317)	**68207+74807+68407**	**SU**	**SOU**	**PTR**	**SOU**
377308 (375318)	**68208+74808+68408**	**SU**	**SOU**	**PTR**	**SOU**
377309 (375319)	**68209+74809+68409**	**SU**	**SOU**	**PTR**	**SOU**
377310 (375320)	**68210+74810+68410**	**SU**	**SOU**	**PTR**	**SOU**
377311 (375321)	**68211+74811+68411**	**SU**	**SOU**	**PTR**	**SOU**
377312 (375322)	**68212+74812+68412**	**SU**	**SOU**	**PTR**	**SOU**

Above: *A fleet of 28 three-car Class 377/3s is in traffic, allocated to Selhurst. These sets when originally introduced were classified as 375, but were changed to Class 377 after installation of Dellner couplings. Carrying 'reduced Co2' branding, set No. 377310 approaches Northam Junction with a Brighton to Southampton service.* **Mark V. Pike**

377313	(375323)	68213+74813+68413	SU	SOU	PTR	SOU
377314	(375324)	68214+74814+68414	SU	SOU	PTR	SOU
377315	(375325)	68215+74815+68415	SU	SOU	PTR	SOU
377316	(375326)	68216+74816+68416	SU	SOU	PTR	SOU
377317	(375327)	68217+74817+68417	SU	SOU	PTR	SOU
377318	(375328)	68218+74818+68418	SU	SOU	PTR	SOU
377319	(375329)	68219+74819+68419	SU	SOU	PTR	SOU
377320	(375330)	68220+74820+68420	SU	SOU	PTR	SOU
377321	(375331)	68221+74821+68421	SU	SOU	PTR	SOU
377322	(375332)	68222+74822+68422	SU	SOU	PTR	SOU
377323	(375333)	68223+74823+68423	SU	SOU	PTR	SOU
377324	(375334)	68224+74824+68424	SU	SOU	PTR	SOU
377325	(375335)	68225+74825+68425	SU	SOU	PTR	SOU
377326	(375336)	68226+74826+68426	SU	SOU	PTR	SOU
377327	(375337)	68227+74827+68427	SU	SOU	PTR	SOU
377328	(375338)	68228+74828+68428	SU	SOU	PTR	SOU

Class 377/4
Electrostar

Vehicle Length: (Driving) 66ft 9in (20.3m)
(Inter) 65ft 6in (19.96m)
Height: 12ft 4in (3.75m)
Width: 9ft 2in (2.79m)
Horsepower: 2,012hp (1,500kW)
Seats (total/car): 20F-221S, 10F-48S/69S/56S/10F-48S

Number	*Formation* DMCO(A)+MSO+TSO+DMCO(B)	*Depot*	*Livery*	*Owner*	*Operator*
377401	73401+78801+78601+73801	BI	SOU	PTR	SOU
377402	73402+78802+78602+73802	BI	SOU	PTR	SOU
377403	73403+78803+78603+73803	BI	SOU	PTR	SOU
377404	73404+78804+78604+73804	BI	SOU	PTR	SOU
377405	73405+78805+78605+73805	BI	SOU	PTR	SOU
377406	73406+78806+78606+73806	BI	SOU	PTR	SOU
377407	73407+78807+78607+73807	BI	SOU	PTR	SOU
377408	73408+78808+78608+73808	BI	SOU	PTR	SOU
377409	73409+78809+78609+73809	BI	SOU	PTR	SOU
377410	73410+78810+78610+73810	BI	SOU	PTR	SOU
377411	73411+78811+78611+73811	BI	SOU	PTR	SOU
377412	73412+78812+78612+73812	BI	SOU	PTR	SOU
377413	73413+78813+78613+73813	BI	SOU	PTR	SOU
377414	73414+78814+78614+73814	BI	SOU	PTR	SOU
377415	73415+78815+78615+73815	BI	SOU	PTR	SOU
377416	73416+78816+78616+73816	SU	SOU	PTR	SOU
377417	73417+78817+78617+73817	BI	SOU	PTR	SOU
377418	73418+78818+78618+73818	BI	SOU	PTR	SOU
377419	73419+78819+78619+73819	BI	SOU	PTR	SOU
377420	73420+78820+78620+73820	BI	SOU	PTR	SOU
377421	73421+78821+78621+73821	BI	SOU	PTR	SOU
377422	73422+78822+78622+73822	BI	SOU	PTR	SOU
377423	73423+78823+78623+73823	BI	SOU	PTR	SOU
377424	73424+78824+78624+73824	BI	SOU	PTR	SOU
377425	73425+78825+78625+73825	BI	SOU	PTR	SOU
377426	73426+78826+78626+73826	BI	SOU	PTR	SOU
377427	73427+78827+78627+73827	BI	SOU	PTR	SOU
377428	73428+78828+78628+73828	BI	SOU	PTR	SOU
377429	73429+78829+78629+73829	SU	SOU	PTR	SOU
377430	73430+78830+78630+73830	BI	SOU	PTR	SOU
377431	73431+78831+78631+73831	BI	SOU	PTR	SOU
377432	73432+78832+78632+73832	BI	SOU	PTR	SOU
377433	73433+78833+78633+73833	BI	SOU	PTR	SOU
377434	73434+78834+78634+73834	BI	SOU	PTR	SOU
377435	73435+78835+78635+73835	BI	SOU	PTR	SOU
377436	73436+78836+78636+73836	BI	SOU	PTR	SOU
377437	73437+78837+78637+73837	BI	SOU	PTR	SOU
377438	73438+78838+78638+73838	BI	SOU	PTR	SOU
377439	73439+78839+78639+73839	BI	SOU	PTR	SOU
377440	73440+78840+78640+73840	BI	SOU	PTR	SOU
377441	73441+78841+78641+73841	BI	SOU	PTR	SOU

Southern

377442	73442+78842+78642+73842	BI	SOU	PTR	SOU
377443	73443+78843+78643+73843	BI	SOU	PTR	SOU
377444	73444+78844+78644+73844	BI	SOU	PTR	SOU
377445	73445+78845+78645+73845	BI	SOU	PTR	SOU
377446	73446+78846+78646+73846	BI	SOU	PTR	SOU
377447	73447+78847+78647+73847	SU	SOU	PTR	SOU
377448	73448+78848+78648+73848	BI	SOU	PTR	SOU
377449	73449+78849+78649+73849	BI	SOU	PTR	SOU
377450	73450+78850+78650+73850	BI	SOU	PTR	SOU
377451	73451+78851+78651+73851	BI	SOU	PTR	SOU
377452	73452+78852+78652+73852	SU	SOU	PTR	SOU
377453	73453+78853+78653+73853	BI	SOU	PTR	SOU
377454	73454+78854+78654+73854	BI	SOU	PTR	SOU
377455	73455+78855+78655+73855	BI	SOU	PTR	SOU
377456	73456+78856+78656+73856	BI	SOU	PTR	SOU
377457	73457+78857+78657+73857	BI	SOU	PTR	SOU
377458	73458+78858+78658+73858	BI	SOU	PTR	SOU
377459	73459+78859+78659+73859	BI	SOU	PTR	SOU
377460	73460+78860+78660+73860	SU	SOU	PTR	SOU
377461	73461+78861+78661+73861	BI	SOU	PTR	SOU
377462	73462+78862+78662+73862	BI	SOU	PTR	SOU
377463	73463+78863+78663+73863	BI	SOU	PTR	SOU
377464	73464+78864+78664+73864	BI	SOU	PTR	SOU
377465	73465+78865+78665+73865	BI	SOU	PTR	SOU
377466	73466+78866+78666+73866	BI	SOU	PTR	SOU
377467	73467+78867+78667+73867	BI	SOU	PTR	SOU
377468	73468+78868+78668+73868	BI	SOU	PTR	SOU
377469	73469+78869+78669+73869	BI	SOU	PTR	SOU
377470	73470+78870+78670+73870	BI	SOU	PTR	SOU
377471	73471+78871+78671+73871	BI	SOU	PTR	SOU
377472	73472+78872+78672+73872	BI	SOU	PTR	SOU
377473	73473+78873+78673+73873	BI	SOU	PTR	SOU
377474	73474+78874+78674+73874	BI	SOU	PTR	SOU
377475	73475+78875+78675+73875	BI	SOU	PTR	SOU

Above: *A fleet of 75 four-car Class 377/4s is in traffic; they are usually deployed on the London to Brighton and South Coast main-line service. Set No. 377419 heads south to Brighton passing Clapham Junction. Note the revised head/marker light assembly on this unit compared to the Class 377/3 illustrated on the previous page.* **CJM**

Class 377/6
Electrostar

Vehicle Length: (Driving) 66ft 9in (20.3m) (Inter) 65ft 6in (19.96m)
Height: 12ft 4in (3.75m)
Width: 9ft 2in (2.79m)
Horsepower: 2,012hp (1,500kW)
Seats (total/car): 298S-60S/64S/46S/66S/62S

Number	*Formation* DMSO(A)+MSO+TSO+MSO+DMSO(B)	*Depot*	*Livery*	*Owner*	*Operator*
377601	70101+70201+70301+70401+70501	BI	SOU	PTR	SOU
377602	70102+70202+70302+70402+70502	BI	SOU	PTR	SOU
377603	70103+70203+70303+70403+70503	BI	SOU	PTR	SOU
377604	70104+70204+70304+70404+70504	BI	SOU	PTR	SOU
377605	70105+70205+70305+70405+70505	BI	SOU	PTR	SOU
377606	70106+70206+70306+70406+70506	BI	SOU	PTR	SOU
377607	70107+70207+70307+70407+70507	BI	SOU	PTR	SOU
377608	70108+70208+70308+70408+70508	BI	SOU	PTR	SOU
377609	70109+70209+70309+70409+70509	BI	SOU	PTR	SOU
377610	70110+70210+70310+70410+70510	BI	SOU	PTR	SOU
377611	70111+70211+70311+70411+70511	BI	SOU	PTR	SOU
377612	70112+70212+70312+70412+70512	BI	SOU	PTR	SOU
377613	70113+70213+70313+70413+70513	BI	SOU	PTR	SOU
377614	70114+70214+70314+70414+70514	BI	SOU	PTR	SOU
377615	70115+70215+70315+70415+70515	BI	SOU	PTR	SOU
377616	70116+70216+70316+70416+70516	BI	SOU	PTR	SOU
377617	70117+70217+70317+70417+70517	BI	SOU	PTR	SOU
377618	70118+70218+70318+70418+70518	BI	SOU	PTR	SOU
377619	70119+70219+70319+70419+70519	BI	SOU	PTR	SOU
377620	70120+70220+70320+70420+70520	BI	SOU	PTR	SOU
377621	70121+70221+70321+70421+70521	BI	SOU	PTR	SOU
377622	70122+70222+70322+70422+70522	BI	SOU	PTR	SOU
377623	70123+70223+70323+70423+70523	BI	SOU	PTR	SOU
377624	70124+70224+70324+70424+70524	BI	SOU	PTR	SOU
377625	70125+70225+70325+70425+70525	BI	SOU	PTR	SOU
377626	70126+70226+70326+70426+70526	BI	SOU	PTR	SOU

Above: *In the autumn of 2013 the first of 26 five-car Class 377/6 sets started to enter traffic from Selhurst on suburban services. The sets will allow the Class 456s to be withdrawn and transferred to South West Trains to permit that company's aspiration of running a 10-car railway on suburban services. Sets Nos. 377609 and 377604 depart from Brockley with the 16.35 London Bridge to West Croydon service on 22 October 2013.* **Antony Christie**

Southern

Class 377/7
Electrostar

Vehicle Length: (Driving) 66ft 9in (20.3m) (Inter) 65ft 6in (19.96m)
Height: 12ft 4in (3.75m)
Dual voltage sets
Width: 9ft 2in (2.79m)
Horsepower: 2,012hp (1,500kW)
Seats (total/car): 298S-60S/64S/46S/662/62S

Number	Formation DMSO(A)+MSO+TSO+MSO+DMSO(B)	Depot	Livery	Owner	Operator
377701	To be advised	BI	SOU	PTR	SOU (delivery 2014)
377702	To be advised	BI	SOU	PTR	SOU (delivery 2014)
377703	To be advised	BI	SOU	PTR	SOU (delivery 2014)
377704	To be advised	BI	SOU	PTR	SOU (delivery 2014)
377705	To be advised	BI	SOU	PTR	SOU (delivery 2014)
377706	To be advised	BI	SOU	PTR	SOU (delivery 2014)
377707	To be advised	BI	SOU	PTR	SOU (delivery 2014)
377708	To be advised	BI	SOU	PTR	SOU (delivery 2014)

Class 377/8
Electrostar

Vehicle Length: (Driving) 66ft 9in (20.3m) (Inter) 65ft 6in (19.96m)
Height: 12ft 4in (3.75m)
Width: 9ft 2in (2.79m)
Horsepower: 2,012hp (1,500kW)
Seats (total/car): To be advised

Number	Formation DMSO(A)+MSO+TSO+DMSO(B)	Depot	Livery	Owner	Operator
377801	To be advised	BI	SOU	PTR	SOU (delivery 2015 for Thameslink)
377802	To be advised	BI	SOU	PTR	SOU (delivery 2015 for Thameslink)
377803	To be advised	BI	SOU	PTR	SOU (delivery 2015 for Thameslink)
377804	To be advised	BI	SOU	PTR	SOU (delivery 2015 for Thameslink)
377805	To be advised	BI	SOU	PTR	SOU (delivery 2015 for Thameslink)
377806	To be advised	BI	SOU	PTR	SOU (delivery 2015 for Thameslink)
377807	To be advised	BI	SOU	PTR	SOU (delivery 2015 for Thameslink)
377808	To be advised	BI	SOU	PTR	SOU (delivery 2015 for Thameslink)
377809	To be advised	BI	SOU	PTR	SOU (delivery 2015 for Thameslink)
377810	To be advised	BI	SOU	PTR	SOU (delivery 2015 for Thameslink)
377811	To be advised	BI	SOU	PTR	SOU (delivery 2015 for Thameslink)
377812	To be advised	BI	SOU	PTR	SOU (delivery 2015 for Thameslink)
377813	To be advised	BI	SOU	PTR	SOU (delivery 2015 for Thameslink)
377814	To be advised	BI	SOU	PTR	SOU (delivery 2015 for Thameslink)
377815	To be advised	BI	SOU	PTR	SOU (delivery 2015 for Thameslink)
377816	To be advised	BI	SOU	PTR	SOU (delivery 2015 for Thameslink)
377817	To be advised	BI	SOU	PTR	SOU (delivery 2015 for Thameslink)
377818	To be advised	BI	SOU	PTR	SOU (delivery 2015 for Thameslink)
377819	To be advised	BI	SOU	PTR	SOU (delivery 2015 for Thameslink)
377820	To be advised	BI	SOU	PTR	SOU (delivery 2015 for Thameslink)
377821	To be advised	BI	SOU	PTR	SOU (delivery 2015 for Thameslink)
377822	To be advised	BI	SOU	PTR	SOU (delivery 2015 for Thameslink)
377823	To be advised	BI	SOU	PTR	SOU (delivery 2015 for Thameslink)
377824	To be advised	BI	SOU	PTR	SOU (delivery 2015 for Thameslink)
377825	To be advised	BI	SOU	PTR	SOU (delivery 2015 for Thameslink)
377826	To be advised	BI	SOU	PTR	SOU (delivery 2015 for Thameslink)
377827	To be advised	BI	SOU	PTR	SOU (delivery 2015 for Thameslink)
377828	To be advised	BI	SOU	PTR	SOU (delivery 2015 for Thameslink)
377829	To be advised	BI	SOU	PTR	SOU (delivery 2015 for Thameslink)

Class 442

Vehicle Length: (Driving) 75ft 11½in (23.15m) (Inter) 75ft 5½in (22.99m)
Height: 12ft 4in (3.81m)
Width: 8ft 11½in (2.73m)
Horsepower: 1,608hp (1,200kW)
Seats (total/car): 24F-318S, 74S/76S/24F-28S/66S/74S

Number	Formation DTSO(A)+TSO+MBC+TSO+DTSO(B)	Depot	Livery	Owner	Operator
442401	77382+71818+62937+71841+77414	SL	SGX	ANG	SOU
442402	77383+71819+62938+71842+77407	SL	SGX	ANG	SOU
442403	77384+71820+62941+71843+77408	SL	SGX	ANG	SOU
442404	77385+71821+62939+71844+77409	SL	SGX	ANG	SOU
442405	77386+71822+62944+71845+77410	SL	SGX	ANG	SOU
442406	77389+71823+62942+71846+77411	SL	SGX	ANG	SOU
442407	77388+71824+62943+71847+77412	SL	SGX	ANG	SOU
442408	77387+71825+62945+71848+77413	SL	SGX	ANG	SOU

442409	77390+71826+62946+71849+77406	SL	SGX	ANG	SOU
442410	77391+71827+62948+71850+77415	SL	SGX	ANG	SOU
442411	77392+71828+62940+71851+77422	SL	SGX	ANG	SOU
442412	77393+71829+62947+71858+77417	SL	SGX	ANG	SOU
442413	77394+71830+62949+71853+77418	SL	SGX	ANG	SOU
442414	77395+71831+62950+71854+77419	SL	SGX	ANG	SOU
442415	77396+71832+62951+71855+77420	SL	SGX	ANG	SOU
442416	77397+71833+62952+71856+77421	SL	SGX	ANG	SOU
442417	77398+71834+62953+71857+77416	SL	SGX	ANG	SOU
442418	77399+71835+62954+71852+77423	SL	SGX	ANG	SOU
442419	77400+71836+62955+71859+77424	SL	SGX	ANG	SOU
442420	77401+71837+62956+71860+77425	SL	SGX	ANG	SOU
442421	77402+71838+62957+71861+77426	SL	SGX	ANG	SOU
442422	77403+71839+62958+71862+77427	SL	SGX	ANG	SOU
442423	77404+71840+62959+71863+77428	SL	SGX	ANG	SOU
442424	77405+71841+62960+71864+77429	SL	SGX	ANG	SOU

Above: *Originally built in the 1980s for the Waterloo-Bournemouth-Weymouth line, the Class 442s were replaced under privatisation by Class 444s, they thus became spare and were taken over by the joint Southern/Gatwick Express franchise and used to replace Class 460 stock on the London Victoria to Gatwick Airport service. The 24 sets are painted in 'express' livery and allocated to Stewarts Lane depot. Set No. 442414 is illustrated from its DMSO(A) vehicle.* **CJM**

Class 455/8

Vehicle Length: (Driving) 65ft 0½in (19.83m)
(Inter) 65ft 4½in (19.92m)
Height: 12ft 1½in (3.79m)
Width: 9ft 3¼in (2.82m)
Horsepower: 1,000hp (746kW)
Seats (total/car): 310S, 74S/78S/84S/74S

Number	*Formation* DTSO(A)+MSO+TSO+DTSO(B)	*Depot*	*Livery*	*Owner*	*Operator*
455801	77627+62709+71657+77580	SU	SOU	EVL	SOU
455802	77581+62710+71664+77582	SU	SOU	EVL	SOU
455803	77583+62711+71639+77584	SU	SOU	EVL	SOU
455804	77585+62712+71640+77586	SU	SOU	EVL	SOU
455805	77587+62713+71641+77588	SU	SOU	EVL	SOU
455806	77589+62714+71642+77590	SU	SOU	EVL	SOU
455807	77591+62715+71643+77592	SU	SOU	EVL	SOU
455808	77637+62716+71644+77594	SU	SOU	EVL	SOU
455809	77623+62717+71648+77602	SU	SOU	EVL	SOU
455810	77597+62718+71646+77598	SU	SOU	EVL	SOU
455811	77599+62719+71647+77600	SU	SOU	EVL	SOU
455812	77595+62720+71645+77626	SU	SOU	EVL	SOU

455813	77603+62721+71649+77604	SU	SOU	EVL	SOU
455814	77605+62722+71650+77606	SU	SOU	EVL	SOU
455815	77607+62723+71651+77608	SU	SOU	EVL	SOU
455816	77609+62724+71652+77633	SU	SOU	EVL	SOU
455817	77611+62725+71653+77612	SU	SOU	EVL	SOU
455818	77613+62726+71654+77632	SU	SOU	EVL	SOU
455819	77615+62727+71637+77616	SU	SOU	EVL	SOU
455820	77617+62728+71656+77618	SU	SOU	EVL	SOU
455821	77619+62729+71655+77620	SU	SOU	EVL	SOU
455822	77621+62730+71658+77622	SU	SOU	EVL	SOU
455823	77601+62731+71659+77596	SU	SOU	EVL	SOU
455824	77593+62732+71660+77624	SU	SOU	EVL	SOU
455825	77579+62733+71661+77628	SU	SOU	EVL	SOU
455826	77630+62734+71662+77629	SU	SOU	EVL	SOU
455827	77610+62735+71663+77614	SU	SOU	EVL	SOU
455828	77631+62736+71638+77634	SU	SOU	EVL	SOU
455829	77635+62737+71665+77636	SU	SOU	EVL	SOU
455830	77625+62743+71666+77638	SU	SOU	EVL	SOU
455831	77639+62739+71667+77640	SU	SOU	EVL	SOU
455832	77641+62740+71668+77642	SU	SOU	EVL	SOU
455833	77643+62741+71669+77644	SU	SOU	EVL	SOU
455834	77645+62742+71670+77646	SU	SOU	EVL	SOU
455835	77647+62738+71671+77648	SU	SOU	EVL	SOU
455836	77649+62744+71672+77650	SU	SOU	EVL	SOU
455837	77651+62745+71673+77652	SU	SOU	EVL	SOU
455838	77653+62746+71674+77654	SU	SOU	EVL	SOU
455839	77655+62747+71675+77656	SU	SOU	EVL	SOU
455840	77657+62748+71676+77658	SU	SOU	EVL	SOU
455841	77659+62749+71677+77660	SU	SOU	EVL	SOU
455842	77661+62750+71678+77662	SU	SOU	EVL	SOU
455843	77663+62751+71679+77664	SU	SOU	EVL	SOU
455844	77665+62752+71680+77666	SU	SOU	EVL	SOU
455845	77667+62753+71681+77668	SU	SOU	EVL	SOU
455846	77669+62754+71682+77670	SU	SOU	EVL	SOU

Left: *Southern's London area Metro services are operated by a fleet of 46 four-car Class 455s, allocated to Selhurst. These once gangway-fitted sets now have the front communicating doors sealed up and the space houses a cab air conditioning system. The sets have 3+2 seating and are finished in Southern white and green livery. Set No. 455819 approaches Clapham Junction with a service to Caterham.* **CJM**

Class 09/0

Vehicle Length: 29ft 3in (8.91m)
Height: 12ft 8⅝in (3.87m)
Width: 8ft 6in (2.59m)
Engine: English Electric 6K
Horsepower: 400hp (298kW)
Electrical Equipment: English Electric

Number	*Depot*	*Pool*	*Livery*	*Owner*	*Operator*	*Name*
09026	BI	HWSU	GRN	SOU	SOU	*Cedric Wares*

Class 73/2

Vehicle Length: 53ft 8in (16.35m)
Height: 12ft 5$^{5}/_{16}$in (3.79m)
Width: 8ft 8in (2.64m)
Power: 750V dc third rail or English Electric 6K
Horsepower: electric - 1,600hp (1,193kW)
Horsepower: diesel - 600hp (447kW)
Electrical Equipment: English Electric

Number	*Depot*	*Pool*	*Livery*	*Owner*	*Operator*
73202 (73137)	SL	MBED	SOU	PTR	SOU

Virgin West Coast

Address: 85 Smallbrook Queensway, Birmingham, B5 4HA
info@virgintrains.co.uk
0845 000 8000
www.virgintrains.co.uk

Lead Executive: Phil Whittingham

Franchise Dates: 12 December 2006 - April 2017

Principal Routes: London Euston - Birmingham, Holyhead, Manchester Liverpool, Glasgow and Edinburgh

Depots: Edge Hill** (LL), Longsight** (MA), Oxley** (OY), Wembley** (WB), Central Rivers (CZ)
** Operated by Alstom

Parent Company: Virgin Group

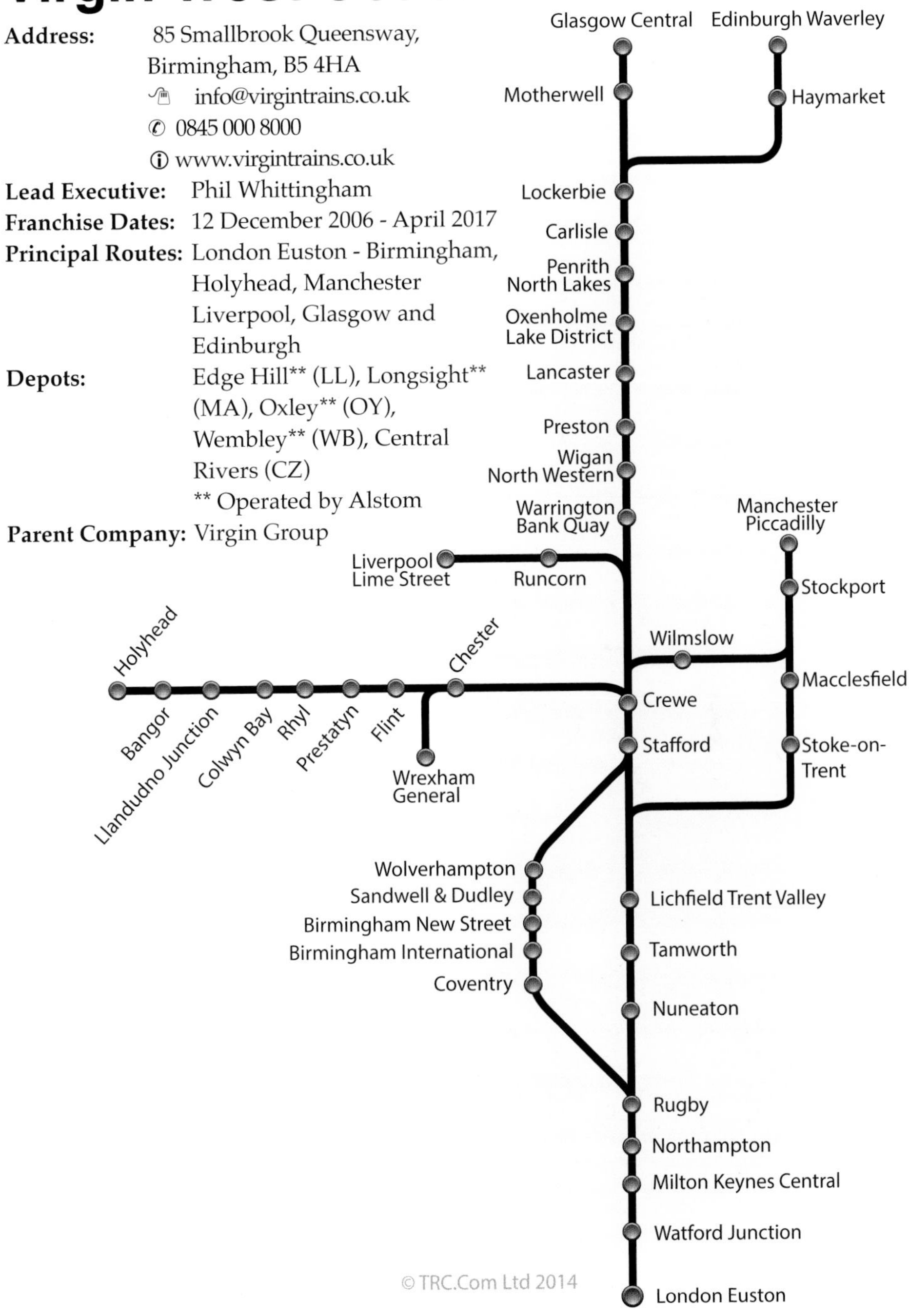

Virgin West Coast

Class 221
Super Voyager

Vehicle Length: 77ft 6in (23.62m)
Height: 12ft 4in (3.75m)
Width: 8ft 11in (2.73m)
Engine: 1 x Cummins 750hp per vehicle
Horsepower: 5-car - 3,750hp (2,796kW). 4-car - 3,000hp (2,237kW)
Seats (total/car): 26F/214S 42S/60S/60S/52S/26F (*not in 4-car set)*

Number	*Formation* DMS+MS+MS+MSRMB+DMF	*Depot*	*Livery*	*Owner*	*Operator*	*Name*
221101	60351+60951+60851+60751+60451	CZ	VWC	HBS	VWC	*Louis Bleriot*
221102	60352+60952+60852+60752+60452	CZ	VWC	HBS	VWC	*John Cabot*
221103	60353+60953+60853+60753+60453	CZ	VWC	HBS	VWC	*Christopher Columbus*
221104	60354+60954+60854+60754+60454	CZ	VWC	HBS	VWC	*Sir John Franklin*
221105	60355+60955+60855+60755+60455	CZ	VWC	HBS	VWC	*William Baffin*
221106	60356+60956+60856+60756+60456	CZ	VWC	HBS	VWC	*William Barents*
221107	60357+60957+60857+60757+60457	CZ	VWC	HBS	VWC	*Sir Martin Frobisher*
221108	60358+60958+60858+60758+60458	CZ	VWC	HBS	VWC	*Sir Ernest Shackleton*
221109	60359+60959+60859+60759+60459	CZ	VWC	HBS	VWC	*Marco Polo*
221110	60360+60960+60860+60760+60460	CZ	VWC	HBS	VWC	*James Cook*
221111	60361+60961+60861+60761+60461	CZ	VWC	HBS	VWC	*Roald Amundsen*
221112	60362+60962+60862+60762+60462	CZ	VWC	HBS	VWC	*Ferdinand Magellan*
221113	60363+60963+60863+60763+60463	CZ	VWC	HBS	VWC	*Sir Walter Raleigh*
221114	60364+60964+60864+60764+60464	CZ	VWC	HBS	VWC	
221115	60365+60965+60865+60765+60465	CZ	VWC¤	HBS	VWC	*Polmadie Depot*
221116	60366+60966+60866+60766+60466	CZ	VWC	HBS	VWC	
221117	60367+60967+60867+60767+60467	CZ	VWC	HBS	VWC	
221118	60368+60968+60868+60768+60468	CZ	VWC	HBS	VWC	
221142	60392+60992+60994ø+60792+60492	CZ	VWC	HBS	VWC	*Bombardier Voyager*
221143	60393+60993+60794+60793+60493	CZ	VWC	HBS	VWC	*Auguste Picard*
221144■	60394+-+-+-+60494	CZ	VWC	HBS	(spare)	

¤ One driving car carries Bombardier branding. **ø** MRSMB vehicle

■ The two spare driving cars from set No. 221144 will be 'rotated' through the VWC Class 221 fleet for extended periods.

Left: *Virgin West Coast operates a fleet of 21 Class 221 'Voyager' sets on its non-electrified routes, as well as some trains that operate exclusively 'under the wires'. The sets are based at Central Rivers, Burton-on-Trent, and are painted in the original Virgin silver and red colours offset by black and white 'zebra' passenger doors. Most of the Virgin 'Voyager' sets retain their originally applied nameplates. No.* 221103 Christopher Columbus *passes South Kenton with a Birmingham New Street to London Euston service.* **CJM**

Left: *In 2013 a start was made to improve the front end valance arrangement on the Class 221 sets, with a re-styled assembly being applied, which slightly alters the front-end and side appearance of the sets. On modified trains, the running numbers are applied higher up the body, making them easier to read. Modified set No. 221111 is seen passing Nuneaton.* **John Binch**

Class 390
Pendolino

Vehicle Length Driving: 75ft 6in (23.01m)
Height: 11ft 6in (3.50m)
Width: 8ft 11in (2.71m)

Horsepower: 6,840hp (5,100kW)
Seats (total/car): 147F/300S, 18F/39F/44F/46F/74S/76S/76S/66S/48S/64S/46S
31 sets are now formed of 11 vehicles 147F/450S

Number	Formation DMRFO+MFO+PTFO+MFO+(TSO+MSO)+TSO+MSO+PTSRMB+MSO+DMSO	Depot	Livery	Owner	Operator	Name
390001	69101+69401+69501+69601+68801+69701+69801+69901+69201	MA	VWC	ANG	VWC	Virgin Pioneer
390002	69102+69402+69502+69602+68802+69702+69802+69902+69202	MA	VWC	ANG	VWC	Virgin Angel
390103	69103+69403+69503+69603+65303+68903+68803+69703+69803+69903+69203	MA	VWC	ANG	VWC	Virgin Hero
390104	69104+69404+69504+69604+65304+68904+68804+69704+69804+69904+69204	MA	VWC	ANG	VWC	Alstom Pendolino
390005	69105+69405+69505+69605+68805+69705+69805+69905+69205	MA	VWC	ANG	VWC	City of Wolverhampton
390006	69106+69406+69506+69606+68806+69706+69806+69906+69206	MA	VWC	ANG	VWC	Tate Liverpool
390107	69107+69407+69507+69607+65307+68907+68807+69707+69807+69907+69207	MA	VWC	ANG	VWC	Virgin Lady (branded Abigail Irozuru)
390008	69108+69408+69508+69608+68808+69708+69808+69908+69208	MA	VWC	ANG	VWC	Virgin King
390009	69109+69409+69509+69609+68809+69709+69809+69909+69209	MA	VWC	ANG	VWC	Treaty of Union
390010	69110+69410+69510+69610+68810+69710+69810+69910+69210	MA	VWC	ANG	VWC	A Decade of Progress
390011	69111+69411+69511+69611+68811+69711+69811+69911+69211	MA	VWC	ANG	VWC	City of Lichfield
390112	69112+69412+69512+69612+65312+68912+68812+69712+69812+69912+69212	MA	VWC	ANG	VWC	Virgin Star
390013	69113+69413+69513+69613+68813+69713+69813+69913+69213	MA	VWC	ANG	VWC	Virgin Spirit
390114	69114+69414+69514+69614+65314+68914+68814+69714+69814+69914+69214	MA	VWC	ANG	VWC	City of Manchester
390115	69115+69415+69515+69615+65315+68915+68815+69715+69815+69915+69215	MA	VWC	ANG	VWC	Virgin Crusader
390016	69116+69416+69516+69616+68816+69716+69816+69916+69216	MA	VWC	ANG	VWC	Virgin Champion
390117§	69117+69417+69517+69617+65317+68917+68817+69717+69817+69917+69217	MA	VWC	ANG	VWC	Virgin Prince
390118	69118+69418+69518+69618+65318+68918+68818+69718+69818+69918+69218	MA	VWC	ANG	VWC	Virgin Princess
390119	69119+69419+69519+69619+65319+68919+68819+69719+69819+69919+69219	MA	VWC	ANG	VWC	Virgin Warrior
390020	69120+69420+69520+69620+68820+69720+69820+69920+69220	MA	VWC	ANG	VWC	Virgin Cavalier
390121	69121+69421+69521+69621+65321+68921+68821+69721+69821+69921+69221	MA	VWC	ANG	VWC	Virgin Dream
390122	69122+69422+69522+69622+65322+68922+68822+69722+69822+69922+69222	MA	VWC	ANG	VWC	Penny the Pendolino
390023	69123+69423+69523+69623+68823+69723+69823+69923+69223	MA	VWC	ANG	VWC	Virgin Glory
390124	69124+69424+69524+69624+65324+68924+68824+69724+69824+69924+69224	MA	VWC	ANG	VWC	Virgin Venturer
390125	69125+69425+69525+69625+65325+68925+68825+69725+69825+69925+69225	MA	VWC	ANG	VWC	Virgin Stagecoach
390126	69126+69426+69526+69626+65326+68926+68826+69726+69826+69926+69226	MA	VWC	ANG	VWC	Virgin Enterprise
390127§	69127+69427+69527+69627+65327+68927+68827+69727+69827+69927+69227	MA	VWC	ANG	VWC	Virgin Buccaneer
390128	69128+69428+69528+69628+65328+68928+68828+69728+69828+69928+69228	MA	VWC	ANG	VWC	City of Preston
390129	69129+69429+69529+69629+65329+68929+68829+69729+69829+69929+69229	MA	VWC	ANG	VWC	City of Stoke-on-Trent
390130	69130+69430+69530+69630+65330+68930+68830+69730+69830+69930+69230	MA	VWC	ANG	VWC	City of Edinburgh
390131§	69131+69431+69531+69631+65331+68931+68831+69731+69831+69931+69231	MA	VWC	ANG	VWC	City of Liverpool
390132	69132+69432+69532+69632+65332+68932+68832+69732+69832+69932+69232	MA	VWC	ANG	VWC	City of Birmingham
390134	69134+69434+69534+69634+65334+68934+68834+69734+69834+69934+69234	MA	VWC	ANG	VWC	City of Carlisle
390035	69135+69435+69535+69635+68835+69735+69835+69935+69235	MA	VWC	ANG	VWC	City of Lancaster
390136	69136+69436+69536+69636+65336+68936+68836+69736+69836+69936+69236	MA	VWC	ANG	VWC	City of Coventry
390137	69137+69437+69537+69637+65337+68937+68837+69737+69837+69937+69237	MA	VWC	ANG	VWC	Virgin Difference
390038	69138+69438+69538+69638+68838+69738+69838+69938+69238	MA	VWC	ANG	VWC	City of London
390039	69139+69439+69539+69639+68839+69739+69839+69939+69239	MA	VWC	ANG	VWC	Virgin Quest
390040	69140+69440+69540+69640+68840+69740+69840+69940+69240	MA	VWC	ANG	VWC	Virgin Pathfinder

Virgin West Coast

390141	69141+69441+69541+69641+65341+68941+68841+69741+69841+69941+69241	MA	VWC	ANG	VWC	*City of Chester*
390042	69142+69442+69542+69642+68842+69742+69842+69942+69242	MA	VWC	ANG	VWC	*City of Bangor / Dinas Bangor*
390043	69143+69443+69543+69643+68843+69743+69843+69943+69243	MA	VWC	ANG	VWC	*Virgin Explorer*
390044	69144+69444+69544+69644+68844+69744+69844+69944+69244	MA	VWC	ANG	VWC	*Virgin Lionheart*
390045	69145+69445+69545+69645+68845+69745+69845+69945+69245	MA	VWC	ANG	VWC	*101 Squadron*
390046	69146+69446+69546+69646+68846+69746+69846+69946+69246	MA	VWC	ANG	VWC	*Virgin Soldiers*
390047	69147+69447+69547+69647+68847+69747+69847+69947+69247	MA	VWC	ANG	VWC	*Clic Sargent*
390148	69148+69448+69548+69648+65348+68948+68848+69748+69848+69948+69248	MA	VWC	ANG	VWC	*Virgin Harrier*
390049	69149+69449+69549+69649+68849+69749+69849+69949+69249	MA	VWC	ANG	VWC	*Virgin Express*
390050	69150+69450+69550+69650+68850+69750+69850+69950+69250	MA	VWC	ANG	VWC	*Virgin Invader*
390151	69151+69451+69551+69651+65351+68951+68851+69751+69851+69951+69251	MA	VWC	ANG	VWC	*Virgin Ambassador*
390152	69152+69452+69552+69652+65352+68952+68852+69752+69852+69952+69252	MA	VWC	ANG	VWC	*Alison Waters*
390153	69153+69453+69553+69653+65353+68953+68853+69753+69853+69953+69253	MA	VWC	ANG	VWC	*Mission Accomplished*
390154	69154+69454+69554+69654+65354+68954+68854+69754+69854+69954+69254	MA	VWC	ANG	VWC	
390155	69155+69455+69555+69655+68355+68955+68855+69755+69855+69955+69255	MA	VWC	ANG	VWC	
390156	69156+69456+69556+69656+68356+68956+68856+69756+69856+69956+69256	MA	VWC	ANG	VWC	*Stockport 170*
390157	69157+69457+69557+69657+68357+68957+68857+69757+69857+69957+69257	MA	VWC	ANG	VWC	*Chad Varah*

Above: *Eleven-car Class 390/1 No. 390104* Alstom Pendolino *is painted in a revised Alstom Pendolino livery, with wider black outline to some of the passenger windows, considerably improving the appearance of the train. The set is seen heading towards London Euston at South Kenton. This set also sports an Alstom logo on the front end.* **CJM**

■ Pendolino set No. 390033 *City of Glasgow*, which was involved in the Grayrigg derailment on 23 February 2007, was withdrawn from service. After spending a period stored at Long Marston, some of the vehicles have now seen further use.

Cars 69133 and 69833 have been rebuilt as static training vehicles for use at the Virgin Trains training school in Crewe.

Nos. 69933 and 69733 are in use at the fire training school in Moreton-in-Marsh.

Vehicle No. 69233 has been broken up.

§ 'Fly the Flag' branding.

Mk3 Hauled Stock

Vehicle Length: 75ft 0in (22.86m)	Width: 8ft 11in (2.71m)
Height: 12ft 9in (3.88m)	Bogie Type: BT10

AJ1G - RFB *Seating 18F*

Number	Depot	Livery	Owner
10212	WB	VWC	PTR
10217 (S)	WB	VWC	PTE

AD1G - FO *Seating 48F*

Number	Depot	Livery	Owner
11007	WB	VWC	PTR
11018	WB	VWC	PTR
11048	WB	VWC	PTR

AC2G - TS0 (*TSOD) *Seating 76/70*S*

Number	Depot	Livery	Owner
12011	WB	VWC	PTR
12078	WB	VWC	PTR
12122*	WB	VWC	PTR
12133	WB	VWC	PTR
12138	WB	VWC	PTR

NL - DVT

Number	Depot	Livery	Owner
82126	WB	VWC	PTR

■ The Virgin West Coast loco-hauled set is operated on an 'as-required' basis to cover for a shortfall in 'Pendolino' stock. Motive power is provided by DBS in the form of a Class 90/0.

Above: *Painted in standard Virgin Trains silver and red livery, with black and white 'zebra' doors, TS No. 12011 is seen at London Euston with a stand-in service.* **Stacey Thew**

Right: *The interior of the loco-hauled stand-in set has been refurbished and retains the original seat style, which is finished in a mix of red and blue moquette. Seating is a mix of group and airline style.* **Nathan Williamson**

Colas Rail Freight

Address: ✉ Dacre House, 19 Dacre Street, London, SW1H 0DJ
enquiries@colasrail.co.uk, ✆ 0207 593 5353, ⓘ www.colasrail.co.uk

Chairman: Charles-Albert Giral

Depots: Washwood Heath (AW), Rugby (RU), Eastleigh Works (ZG)

As we closed for press, Colas completed a deal to obtain four Class 37s Nos. 37116, 37175, 37219 and 37421 from the preservation sector to return to main line operation for new contracts.

Class 47/7

Vehicle Length: 63ft 6in (19.35m)
Height: 12ft 10⅜in (3.91m)
Width: 9ft 2in (2.79m)
Electric Train Heat fitted
Engine: Sulzer 12LDA28C
Horsepower: 2,580hp (1,922kW)
Electrical Equipment: Brush

Number	Depot	Pool	Livery	Owner	Operator	Name
47727 (47569)	ZE	COLO	COL	COL	COL	*Rebecca*
47739 (47594)	ZE	COLO	COL	COL	COL	*Robin of Templecombe 1938-2013*
47749 (47625)	ZE	COLO	COL	COL	COL	*Demelza*

Left: *An operator that has won a number of freight and infrastructure contracts in recent times is Colas Rail Freight. The operator has three Class 47s on its books, all refurbished Class 47/7s. All are painted in the house colours of orange and lime green. Carrying Colas Rail branding No. 47749* Demelza *emerges from Kennaway Tunnel, Dawlish, with an empty rail train from Newton Abbot to Westbury.* **CJM**

Class 56

Vehicle Length: 63ft 6in (19.35m)
Height: 13ft 0in (3.96m)
Width: 9ft 2in (2.79m)
Engine: Ruston Paxman 16RK3CT
Horsepower: 3,250hp (2,420kW)
Electrical Equipment: Brush

Number	Depot	Pool	Livery	Owner	Operator	Notes
56032(S)	RU	COLS	?	COL	-	Awaiting overhaul
56049(S)	RU	COLS	?	COL	-	Awaiting overhaul
56051(S)	RU	COLS	?	COL	-	Awaiting overhaul
56074(S)	RU	COLS	FER	COL	-	Awaiting overhaul
56078(S)	RU	COLS	COL	COL	COL	
56087	RU	COLO	COL	COL	COL	
56090(S)	RU	COLS	?	COL	-	Awaiting overhaul
56094	RU	COLO	COL	COL	COL	
56096	RU	COLS	?	COL	-	Awaiting overhaul
56105	RU	COLO	COL	COL	COL	
56113	RU	COLS	COL	COL	COL	
56302 (56124)	RU	COLO	COL	COL	COL	

Left: *The fleet of Class 56s operated by Colas Rail Freight has expanded over the past year with extra locos being overhauled and returned to front-line service. In the main these locos are used on the heavy log trains that Colas operated to the Kronospan wood processing plant at Chirk in North Wales. No. 56094 pulls a long rake of empty log wagons out of the down loop at Dawlish Warren en route to the Teigngrace log loading facility.* **CJM**

Class 66/8

Vehicle Length: 70ft 0½in (21.34m)
Height: 12ft 10in (3.91m)
Width: 8ft 8¼in (2.65m)
Engine: EMD 12N-710G3B-EC
Horsepower: 3,300hp (2,462kW)
Electrical Equipment: EMD

Number	Depot	Pool	Livery	Owner	Operator	Name
66846 (66573)	RU	COLO	COL	COL	COL	
66847 (66574)	RU	COLO	COL	COL	COL	
66848 (66575)	RU	COLO	COL	COL	COL	
66849 (66576)	RU	COLO	COL	COL	COL	Wylam Dilly
66850 (66577)	RU	COLO	COL	COL	COL	David Maidment OBE www.railwaychildren.org.uk

Above: *The most modern locos operated by Colas in 2013 were a fleet of five Class 66/8s, which were modified from five off-lease Freightliner locos. This fleet operates both timetabled freight services and engineering trains and can be found throughout the country. No. 66846 is seen stabled in Doncaster West yard in April 2013.* **CJM**

Class 70 - PH37ACmi

Vehicle Length: 71ft 2½in (21.71m)
Height: 12ft 10in (3.91m)
Width: 8ft 8in (2.64m)
Engine: GE V16-cyliner PowerHaul 616
Horsepower: 3,700hp (2,750kW)
Electrical Equipment: General Electric

Number	Depot	Pool	Livery	Owner	Operator	Notes
70801 (70099)	(ZE)	COLO	COL	??	COL	
70802	(ZE)	COLO	COL	??	COL	
70803	(ZE)	COLO	COL	??	COL	
70804	(ZE)	COLO	COL	??	COL	
70805	(ZE)	COLO	COL	??	COL	
70806	(ZE)	COLO	COL	??	COL	
70807	(ZE)	COLO	COL	??	COL	On order- delivery Spring 2014
70808	(ZE)	COLO	COL	??	COL	On order- delivery Spring 2014
70809	(ZE)	COLO	COL	??	COL	On order- delivery Spring 2014
70810	(ZE)	COLO	COL	??	COL	On order- delivery Spring 2014

Hauled Stock (NPCCS)

Mk1
Vehicle Length: 64ft 6in (19.65m)
Height: 12ft 9½in (3.89m)
Width: 9ft 3in (2.81m)

Motorail Wagons

Number	Depot	Livery	Operator
96602 (96150)	NV	COL	CF
96603 (96155)	NV	COL	CF
96604 (96156)	NV	COL	CF
96605 (96157)	NV	COL	CF
96606 (96213)	NV	COL	CF
96607 (96215)	NV	COL	CF
96608 (96216)	NV	COL	CF
96609 (96217)	NV	COL	CF

DB Schenker - EWS

Address (UK): ✉ Lakeside Business Park, Caroline Way, Doncaster, DN4 5PN
info@rail.dbschenker.co.uk
✆ 0870 140 5000
ⓘ www.rail.dbschenker.co.uk

Chief Executive: Geoff Spencer

Class 08

Vehicle Length: 29ft 3in (8.91m)
Height: 12ft 8⅝in (3.87m)
Width: 8ft 6in (2.59m)
Engine: English Electric 6K
Horsepower: 400hp (298kW)
Electrical Equipment: English Electric

Number	*Depot*	*Pool*	*Livery*	*Owner*	*Operator*
08405¤	DR	WNYX	EWS	DBS	-
08428	TO	WNYX	EWS	DBS	DBS
08480*	TO	WNYX	EWS	DBS	DBS
08495¤	EH	WSSK	EWS	DBS	DBS
08499(S)	WQ	WSXX	BLU	DBS	PUL
08500(S)	WQ	WNYX	EWS	DBS	-
08567	TO	WNYX	EWS	DBS	DBS
08578¤(S)	TO	WNXX	EWS	DBS	DBS
08580(S)	BS	WNXX	EWS	DBS	-
08593(S)	CE	WNXX	EWS	DBS	-
08605¤	TO	WSSK	EWS	DBS	DBS
08623	TO	WSSL	DBS	DBS	DBS
08630(S)	TO	WNXX	EWS	DBS	-
08632	TO	WSSK	EWS	DBS	DBS
08633¤	CE	WSSK	EWS	DBS	DBS
08653	TO	WNXX	EWS	DBS	-
08676	TO	WSSL	EWS	DBS	
08701¤	TO	WNXX	PCL	DBS	-
08703	CE	WNYX	EWS	DBS	-
08706¤(S)	TO	WNYX	EWS	DBS	-
08709	BS	WNXX	EWS	DBS	-
08711(S)	TE	WNXX	PCL	DBS	-
08714(S)	TO	WSXX	EWS	DBS	-
08735¤	EH	WNYX	EWS	DBS	-
08737	TO	WSSI	EWS	DBS	DBS
08738(S)	TO	WNTS	ECR	DBS	-
08742¤	TO	WSSK	PCL	DBS	DBS
08752	TO	WSSK	EWS	DBS	DBS
08757¤(S)	TO	WNYX	RES	DBS	-
08782	MG	WSSK	BLK	DBS	DBS
08784¤	TO	WNTS	EWS	DBS	-
08799	TO	WNYX	EWS	DBS	-
08802	TO	WSSK	EWS	DBS	DBS
08804¤	TO	WNYX	EWS	DBS	-
08824(S)	WQ	WSXX	BLK	DBS	-
08865	CE	WSSK	EWS	DBS	DBS
08877(S)	WQ	WSXX	BRD	DBS	-
08879¤	TO	WSSK	EWS	DBS	-
08886(S)	BS	WNXX	EWS	DBS	-
08888¤	TO	WSSI	EWS	DBS	DBS
08904(S)	TO	WNYX	EWS	DBS	-
08907	TO	WSSK	DBS	DBS	DBS
08922(S)	TO	WNTS	BRD	DBS	-
08939(S)	TO	WNTS	ECR	DBS	-
08993(S)+	TO	WNTS	EWS	DBS	-
08994(S)+	DR	WNTS	EWS	DBS	DBS
08995+	TO	WSSK	EWS	DBS	DBS

Names applied

08495	*Noel Kirton OBE*
08630	*Bob Brown*
08701	*Type 100*
08799	*Andy Bower / Fred*

+ Named - Toton No. 1, 08993 was previously No. 08592, 08994 was previously No. 08562, 08995 was previously No. 08687.
¤ Remote control fitted.

Left: *Although train locos do most of the yard shunting for DBS these days, a handful of Class 08 and 09 locos still remain on the roster. One location that still uses an '08' is Eastleigh yard, where this view of No. 08495* Noel Kirton OBE *was taken. The loco is seen from its cab end and displays tatty EWS maroon and gold livery.* **Antony Christie**

Class 09/0

Vehicle Length: 29ft 3in (8.91m)
Height: 12ft 8⅝in (3.87m)
Width: 8ft 6in (2.59m)
Engine: English Electric 6K
Horsepower: 400hp (298kW)
Electrical Equipment: English Electric

Number	Depot	Pool	Livery	Owner	Operator
09006(S)	TO	WNXX	EWS	DBS	-

Class 09/1

Vehicle Length: 29ft 3in (8.91m)
Height: 12ft 8⅝in (3.87m)
Width: 8ft 6in (2.59m)
Engine: English Electric 6K
Horsepower: 400hp (298kW)
Electrical Equipment: English Electric

Number		Depot	Pool	Livery	Owner	Operator
09106	(08759)	TO	WSSK	DBS	DBS	DBS

Class 09/2

Vehicle Length: 29ft 3in (8.91m)
Height: 12ft 8⅝in (3.87m)
Width: 8ft 6in (2.59m)
Engine: English Electric 6K
Horsepower: 400hp (298kW)
Electrical Equipment: English Electric

Number		Depot	Pool	Livery	Owner	Operator
09201	(08421)	KY	WSSI	BRD	DBS	DBS

Right: *The higher-speed standard 0-6-0 diesel shunting loco with a maximum speed of 27mph (43.5km/h) was originally designed for use on the Southern Region where trip freights had to fit in with the busy local passenger schedule; these were classified as 09/0. Later when some major refurbishing of Class 08s was undertaken a batch of Class 09/1s and 09/2s emerged, painted in general grey livery. Only one of each Class 09 sub-class remains working for DBS and No. 09201 is illustrated near Knottingley working a trip freight. This example has combination couplers allowing shunting of buck-eye-fitted stock and a portable headlight, required for main-line running.* **Antony Christie**

Class 58

Vehicle Length: 62ft 9½in (19.13m)
Height: 12ft 10in (3.91m)
Width: 9ft 1in (2.72m)
Engine: Ruston Paxman 12RK3ACT
Horsepower: 3,300hp (2,460kW)
Electrical Equipment: Brush

Number	Hire No.	Depot	Pool	Livery	Owner	Location	Operator	Name
58001		-	WNTS	ETF	DBS	France	ETF	
58004§		-	WNTS	TSO	DBS	France	TSO	
58005		-	WNTS	ETF	DBS	France	ETF	
58006§		-	WNTS	ETF	DBS	France	ETF	
58007		-	WNTS	TSO	DBS	France	TSO	
58008(S)		EH	WNTS	MLF	DBS	UK	-	
58009		-	WNTS	TSO	DBS	France	TSO	
58010		-	WNTS	FER	DBS	France	TSO	
58011§		-	WNTS	TSO	DBS	France	TSO	
58012(S)		TO	WNTS	MLG	DBS	UK	-	
58013		-	WNTS	ETF	DBS	France	ETF	
58015	L54	CON/SS	-	CON	DBS/T	Spain	TRN	
58017(S)		EH	WNTS	MLG	DBS	UK	-	
58018		EH	WNTS	TSO	DBS	France	TSO	
58020	L43	CON/SS	-	CON	DBS/T	Spain	TRN	
58021		-	WNTS	TSO	DBS	France	TSO	
58022(S)		CD	WNTS	MLG	DBS	UK	-	
58023(S)		TO	WNTS	MLF	DBS	UK	-	

DB Schenker

58024	L42	CON/SS	-	CON	DBS/T	Spain	TRN	
58025	L41	CON/SS	-	CON	DBS	Spain	CON	
58026§		-	WNTS	TSO	DBS	France	TSO	
58027	L52	CON/SS	-	CON	DBS	Spain	CON	
58029	L44	CON/SS	-	CON	DBS/T	Spain	TRN	
58030	L46	CON/SS	-	CON	DBS/T	Spain	TRN	
58031	L45	CON/SS	-	CON	DBS/T	Spain	TRN	*Cabellero Ferroviaro*
58032		-	WNTS	ETF	DBS	France	ETF	
58033		-	WNTS	TSO	DBS	France	TSO	
58034		-	WNTS	TSO	DBS	France	TSO	
58035		-	WNTS	TSO	DBS	France	TSO	
58036		-	WNTS	ETF	DBS	France	ETF	
58037(S)		EH	WNTS	EWS	DBS	UK	-	
58038	58-038	-	WNTS	ETF	DBS	France	ETF	
58039	58-039	-	WNTS	ETF	DBS	France	ETF	
58040§		-	WNTS	TSO	DBS	France	TSO	
58041	L36	CON/SS	-	CON	DBS/T	Spain	TRN	
58042		-	WNTS	TSO	DBS	France	TSO	
58043	L37	CON/SS	-	CON	DBS/T	Spain	TRN	
58044	58-044	-	WZFF	ETF	DBS	France	ETF	
58046		-	WNTS	TSO	DBS	France	TSO	
58047	L51	CON/SS	-	CON	DBS/T	Spain	TRN	
58048(S)		CE	WNTS	EWS	DBS	UK	-	
50049§		-	WNTS	TSO	DBS	France	ETF	
58050	L53	CON/SS	-	CON	DBS	Spain	CON	

§ Stored at Alizay (Rouen)

Left: *The once 50-strong state-of-the-art Class 58 fleet built for BR Railfreight had a very short operating life and now all are withdrawn from DBS UK use. The majority of locos that remain are stored in either France or Spain and it is doubtful if any will see any further use. The fleet was exported to mainland Europe to assist in the construction of standard-gauge high-speed lines for private construction operators. It is reported that some could be quite easily returned to fully operational condition, while some of the stored locos in the UK are little more than heaps of scrap awaiting disposal. Looking in quite respectable condition, No. 58010 displaying TSO livery is seen 'on shed' at Alizay, near Rouen in France, on the main-line Le Havre, Rouen, Paris St Lazare route.* **Thierry Mazoyer**

Class 59/2

Vehicle Length: 70ft 0½in (21.34m)
Height: 12ft 10in (3.91m)
Width: 8ft 8¼in (2.65m)
Engine: EMD 16-645 E3C
Horsepower: 3,000hp (2,462kW)
Electrical Equipment: EMD

Number	*Depot*	*Pool*	*Livery*	*Owner*	*Operator*	*Name*
59201	TO	WDAK	DBS	DBS	DBS	
59202	TO	WDAK	DBS	DBS	DBS	*Alan Meddows Taylor MD, Mendip Rail Limited*
59203	TO	WDAK	DBS	DBS	DBS	
59204	TO	WDAK	DBS	DBS	DBS	
59205	TO	WDAK	DBS	DBS	DBS	
59206	TO	WDAK	DBS	DBS	DBS	*John F. Yeoman Rail Pioneer*

Above: *The six DBS owned, red-liveried Class 59/2s, which were originally the National Power-owned locomotives, are officially based at Toton but receive maintenance alongside the other Class 59s at Merehead depot in the Mendips. The 59/2s are usually to be found around Westbury and Acton areas powering the many aggregate trains that work in this area. No. 59205 passes South Kenton on 3 July 2013 with a Watford to Acton working.* **CJM**

Class 60

Vehicle Length: 70ft 0½in (21.34m)
Height: 12ft 10⅝in (3.92m)
Width: 8ft 8in (2.64m)
Engine: Mirrlees MB275T
Horsepower: 3,100hp (2,240kW)
Electrical Equipment: Brush

Number	*Depot*	*Pool*	*Livery*	*Owner*	*Operator*	*Name*
60001‡	TO	WNWX	DBS	DBS	DBS	
60003(S)	TO	WNWX	EWS	DBS	-	*Freight Transport Association*
60004(S)	TO	WNTS	EWS	DBS	-	
60005(S)	TO	WNTS	EWS	DBS	-	
60007‡	TO	WFMU	DBS	DBS	-	*The Spirit of Tom Kendell*
60009(S)	TO	WNTS	EWS	DBS	-	
60010‡	TO	WCBI	DBS	DBS	DBS	
60011	TO	WCAK	DBS	DBS	DBS	
60012(S)	TO	WNWX	EWS	DBS	-	
60015‡	TO	WCBK	DBS	DBS	DBS	
60017‡	TO	WCBI	DBS	DBS	DBS	
60018(S)	TO	WNTS	EWS	DBS	-	
60019‡	TO	WCAI	DBS	DBS	DBS	*Port of Grimsby & Immingham*
60020‡	TO	WCBI	DBS	DBS	DBS	
60022(S)	TO	WNTS	EWS	DBS	-	
60024‡	TO	WNWX	DBS	DBS	-	
60025(S)	TO	WNTS	EWS	DBS	-	
60027(S)	TO	WNTS	EWS	DBS	-	
60030(S)	TO	WNTS	EWS	DBS	-	
60032(S)	TO	WNWX	EWS	DBS	-	
60034(S)	TO	WNTS	RFE	DBS	-	*Carnedd Llewelyn*
60035(S)	TO	WCAI	EWS	DBS	-	
60036(S)	TO	WNTS	EWS	DBS	-	*GEFCO*
60037(S)	TO	WNWX	EWS	DBS	-	
60039‡	TO	WFMU	DBS	DBS	DBS	
60040‡	TO	WCAI	DBS	DBS	DBS	*The Territorial Army Centenary*
60043(S)	TO	WNWX	EWS	DBS	-	
60044‡	TO	WNWX	DBS	DBS	-	
60045	TO	WCAI	EWS	DBS	DBS	*The Permanent Way Institution*
60049	TO	WCAK	EWS	DBS	DBS	
60051(S)	TO	WNTS	EWS	DBS	-	
60052(S)	TO	WNTS	EWS	DBS	-	*Glofa Twr - The last deep mine in Wales - Tower Colliery*
60053(S)	TO	WNTS	EWS	DBS	-	
60054‡	TO	WCBI	DBS	DBS	DBS	
60057(S)	TO	WNWX	RFE	DBS	-	*Adam Smith*
60059‡	TO	WCBK	DBS	DBS	DBS	*Swinden Dalesman*
60060(S)	TO	WNWX	RFE	DBS	-	

DB Schenker

60062‡	TO	WNTS	DBS	DBS	DBS	*Stainless Pioneer*
60063‡	TO	WCAI	DBS	DBS	DBS	
60064(S)	TO	WNWX	RFE	DBS	-	*Back Tor*
60065	TO	WCAK	EWS	DBS	DBS	*Spirit of Jaguar*
60066‡	TO	WNTR	ADV	DBS	-	
60067(S)	TO	WNWX	RFE	DBS	-	
60069(S)	TO	WNWX	EWS	DBS	-	*Slioch*
60071	TO	WCBK	DBS	DBS	DBS	*Ribblehead Viaduct*
60072(S)	TO	WNWX	RFE	DBS	-	*Cairn Toul*
60073(S)	TO	WNTS	RFE	DBS	-	*Cairn Gorm*
60074‡	TO	WFMU	DBB	DBS	DBS	*Teenage Spirit*
60077(S)	TO	WNWX	RFE	DBS	-	
60079‡	TO	WFMU	DBS	DBS	DBS	
60083(S)	TO	WNTS	EWS	DBS	-	
60084(S)	TO	WNTS	RFE	DBS	-	*Cross Fell*
60086(S)	TO	WNWX	RFE	DBS	-	
60088(S)	TO	WNWX	MLG	DBS	-	
60090(S)	TO	WNTS	RFE	DBS	-	*Quinag*
60091‡	TO	WCBK	DBS	DBS	DBS	
60092‡	TO	WCBI	DBS	DBS	DBS	
60093(S)	TO	WNTS	EWS	DBS	-	
60094(S)	CD	WNTS	EWS	DBS	-	*Rugby Flyer*
60097(S)	TO	WNTS	EWS	DBS	-	
60099	TO	WFMU	TAT	DBS	DBS	
60100‡	TO	WNTS	DBS	DBS	DBS	
60500(S)*	TO	WNTS	EWS	DBS	-	

* Previously numbered 60016. ‡ Refurbished (Super 60). ADV = Draz biomass livery.

Below: *The DBS Class 60 fleet, which many thought was doomed and would not remain as part of the core fleet, has increased in operational numbers throughout 2013, following further 'Super 60' modifications and refurbishment at DBS Toton depot. A considerable number still remain stored and time will see how many of these return to front line service. In autumn 2013 DBS made available 20 Class 60s for disposal, these being the locos in the worst condition. DBS-liveried No. 60063 passes Gloucester on 10 July 2013 powering the daily 05.07 Robeston to Westerleigh loaded Murco tanks.* **CJM**

Class 66

Vehicle Length: 70ft 0½in (21.34m)
Height: 12ft 10in (3.91m)
Width: 8ft 8¼in (2.65m)
Engine: EMD 12N-710G3B-EC
Horsepower: 3,300hp (2,462kW)
Electrical Equipment: EMD

Number	*Depot*	*Pool*	*Livery*	*Owner*	*Operator*
66001‡	TO	WBAI	DBS	ANG	DBS
66002‡	TO	WNTR	EWS	ANG	DBS
66003	TO	WBAL	EWS	ANG	DBS
66004	TO	WFMU	EWS	ANG	DBS
66005	TO	WBSN	EWS	ANG	DBS
66006(S)	TO	WNWX	EWS	ANG	DBS
66007	TO	WBAI	EWS	ANG	DBS
66008	TO	WSSI	EWS	ANG	DBS
66009	TO	WFMU	EWS	ANG	DBS
66010 ●	AZ	WBEN	EWS	ANG	DBS
66011	TO	WBAI	EWS	ANG	DBS
66012	TO	WNTR	EWS	ANG	DBS
66013 ●	TO	WFMU	EWS	ANG	DBS
66014	TO	WFMS	EWS	ANG	DBS
66015	TO	WBAK	EWS	ANG	DBS
66016	TO	WFMU	EWS	ANG	DBS
66017	TO	WFMS	EWS	ANG	DBS
66018	TO	WBAI	EWS	ANG	DBS
66019	TO	WBAK	EWS	ANG	DBS
66020	TO	WNTR	EWS	ANG	DBS
66021	TO	WBAK	EWS	ANG	DBS
66022 ●	AZ	WBEN	EWS	ANG	DBS
66023	TO	WBAI	EWS	ANG	DBS
66024	TO	WBAL	EWS	ANG	DBS
66025	TO	WFMU	EWS	ANG	DBS
66026 ●	TO	WBEN	EWS	ANG	ECR
66027	TO	WBAI	EWS	ANG	DBS
66028 ●	AZ	WBEN	EWS	ANG	ECR
66029 ●	AZ	WBEN	EWS	ANG	DBS
66030	TO	WBAL	EWS	ANG	DBS
66031 ●	TO	WFMU	EWS	ANG	DBS
66032 ●	TO	WBES	EWS	ANG	ECR
66033 ●	AZ	WBEN	EWS	ANG	DBS
66034	TO	WFMU	EWS	ANG	DBS
66035	TO	WBSN	EWS	ANG	DBS
66036 ●	AZ	WBEN	EWS	ANG	ECR
66037	TO	WNWX	EWS	ANG	DBS
66038 ●	AZ	WBEN	EWS	ANG	ECR
66039	TO	WSSK	EWS	ANG	DBS
66040	TO	WBAI	EWS	ANG	DBS
66041	TO	WBAK	EWS	ANG	DBS
66042 ●	AZ	WFMS	EWS	ANG	ECR
66043	TO	WBAL	EWS	ANG	DBS
66044	TO	WBSN	EWS	ANG	DBS
66045 ●	AZ	WBEN	EWS	ANG	ECR
66046	TO	WFMU	EWS	ANG	DBS
66047	TO	WBSN	EWS	ANG	DBS
66048(S)	TO	WNTS	STO	ANG	-
66049 ●	TO	WBEN	EWS	ANG	ECR
66050	TO	WFMU	EWS	ANG	DBS
66051	TO	WBAK	EWS	ANG	DBS
66052 ●	AZ	WFMS	EWS	ANG	ECR
66053	TO	WFMU	EWS	ANG	DBS
66054	TO	WBAI	EWS	ANG	DBS
66055	TO	WBAL	EWS	ANG	DBS
66056	TO	WBLI	EWS	ANG	DBS
66057	TO	WBLI	EWS	ANG	DBS
66058	TO	WFMU	EWS	ANG	DBS
66059	TO	WBLI	EWS	ANG	DBS
66060	TO	WNTR	EWS	ANG	DBS
66061	TO	WBAI	EWS	ANG	DBS
66062 ●	AZ	WBEN	EWS	ANG	DBS
66063	TO	WFMS	EWS	ANG	DBS
66064 ●	TO	WBEN	EWS	ANG	DBS
66065	TO	WBAI	EWS	ANG	DBS
66066	TO	WBAI	EWS	ANG	DBS
66067	TO	WBAI	EWS	ANG	DBS
66068	TO	WBAK	EWS	ANG	DBS
66069	TO	WBAI	EWS	ANG	DBS
66070	TO	WSSK	EWS	ANG	DBS
66071 ●	AZ	WSSK	EWS	ANG	DBS
66072 ●	AZ	WBEN	EWS	ANG	DBS
66073 ●	AZ	WBEN	EWS	ANG	ECR
66074	TO	WBAL	EWS	ANG	DBS
66075	TO	WBAI	EWS	ANG	DBS
66076	TO	WBAK	EWS	ANG	DBS
66077	TO	WBEN	EWS	ANG	DBS
66078	TO	WBAI	EWS	ANG	DBS
66079	TO	WBAK	EWS	ANG	DBS
66080	TO	WBAI	EWS	ANG	DBS
66081	TO	WBAK	EWS	ANG	DBS
66082	TO	WNWX	EWS	ANG	DBS
66083	TO	WNTR	EWS	ANG	DBS
66084	TO	WBAK	EWS	ANG	DBS
66085	TO	WBAI	EWS	ANG	DBS
66086	TO	WSSK	EWS	ANG	DBS
66087	TO	WBAI	EWS	ANG	DBS
66088	TO	WBAL	EWS	ANG	DBS
66089	TO	WBAI	EWS	ANG	DBS
66090	TO	WBAI	EWS	ANG	DBS
66091	TO	WBAK	EWS	ANG	DBS
66092	TO	WFMU	EWS	ANG	DBS
66093	TO	WBAI	EWS	ANG	DBS
66094	TO	WBAI	EWS	ANG	DBS
66095	TO	WBAK	EWS	ANG	DBS
66096	TO	WNTR	EWS	ANG	DBS
66097	TO	WBAI	DBS	ANG	DBS
66098	TO	WBAK	EWS	ANG	DBS
66099	TO	WBBK	EWS	ANG	DBS
66100	TO	WNTR	EWS	ANG	DBS
66101	TO	WNTR	DBS	ANG	DBS
66102	TO	WFMS	EWS	ANG	DBS
66103	TO	WBAI	EWS	ANG	DBS
66104	TO	WFMU	EWS	ANG	DBS
66105	TO	WFMS	EWS	ANG	DBS
66106	TO	WBBI	EWS	ANG	DBS
66107	TO	WFMU	EWS	ANG	DBS
66108	TO	WBBL	EWS	ANG	DBS
66109	TO	WBAK	EWS	ANG	DBS
66110	TO	WBAK	EWS	ANG	DBS
66111	TO	WNTR	EWS	ANG	DBS
66112	TO	WBBI	EWS	ANG	DBS
66113	TO	WFMU	EWS	ANG	DBS
66114	TO	WBBI	EWS	ANG	DBS
66115	TO	WBAI	EWS	ANG	DBS
66116	TO	WBAK	EWS	ANG	DBS
66117	TO	WBAK	EWS	ANG	DBS
66118	TO	WFMU	DBS	ANG	DBS
66119	TO	WNTR	EWS	ANG	DBS
66120	TO	WSSK	EWS	ANG	DBS
66121	TO	WBAI	EWS	ANG	DBS
66122	TO	WFMU	EWS	ANG	DBS
66123 ●	AZ	WBES	EWS	ANG	DBS

DB Schenker

66124	TO	WBSN	EWS	ANG	DBS
66125	TO	WNTR	EWS	ANG	DBS
66126	TO	WBAK	EWS	ANG	DBS
66127	TO	WBAI	EWS	ANG	DBS
66128	TO	WBAI	EWS	ANG	DBS
66129	TO	WFMS	EWS	ANG	DBS
66130	TO	WBAI	EWS	ANG	DBS
66131	TO	WFMU	EWS	ANG	DBS
66132	TO	WFMU	EWS	ANG	DBS
66133	TO	WBAI	EWS	ANG	DBS
66134	TO	WFMS	EWS	ANG	DBS
66135	TO	WBAK	EWS	ANG	DBS
66136	TO	WBAK	EWS	ANG	DBS
66137	TO	WBAI	EWS	ANG	DBS
66138	TO	WBAL	EWS	ANG	DBS
66139	TO	WBAI	EWS	ANG	DBS
66140	TO	WBAL	EWS	ANG	DBS
66141	TO	WBAK	EWS	ANG	DBS
66142	TO	WBAK	EWS	ANG	DBS
66143	TO	WBAL	EWS	ANG	DBS
66144	TO	WBAI	EWS	ANG	DBS
66145	TO	WNTR	EWS	ANG	DBS
66146 P	PN	WBEP	EWS	ANG	DBS
66147	TO	WBAL	EWS	ANG	DBS
66148	TO	WBAI	EWS	ANG	DBS
66149	TO	WNTR	EWS	ANG	DBS
66150	TO	WBAK	EWS	ANG	DBS
66151	TO	WBAI	EWS	ANG	DBS
66152	TO	WBAI	DBS	ANG	DBS
66153 P	PN	WBEP	EWS	ANG	DBS
66154	TO	WBAI	EWS	ANG	DBS
66155	TO	WBAL	EWS	ANG	DBS
66156	TO	WNTR	EWS	ANG	DBS
66157 P	PN	WBEP	EWS	ANG	DBS
66158	TO	WNTR	EWS	ANG	DBS
66159 P	PN	WBEP	EWS	ANG	DBS
66160	TO	WBAI	EWS	ANG	DBS
66161	TO	WBAK	EWS	ANG	DBS
66162	TO	WBAI	EWS	ANG	DBS
66163 P	PN	WBEP	DBS	ANG	DBS
66164	TO	WFMU	EWS	ANG	DBS
66165	TO	WBAI	EWS	ANG	DBS
66166 P	PN	WBEP	EWS	ANG	DBS
66167	TO	WBAK	EWS	ANG	DBS
66168	TO	WFMU	EWS	ANG	DBS
66169	TO	WBAK	EWS	ANG	DBS
66170	TO	WFMU	EWS	ANG	DBS
66171	TO	WBAK	EWS	ANG	DBS
66172	TO	WBAK	EWS	ANG	DBS
66173 P	PN	WBEP	EWS	ANG	DBS
66174	TO	WNTR	EWS	ANG	DBS
66175	TO	WBAI	EWS	ANG	DBS
66176	TO	WBAK	EWS	ANG	DBS
66177	TO	WBAK	EWS	ANG	DBS
66178 P	PN	WBEP	EWS	ANG	DBS
66179 ●	TO	WBAK	EWS	ANG	ECR
66180 P	PN	WBEP	EWS	ANG	DBS
66181	TO	WBAK	EWS	ANG	DBS
66182	TO	WBAK	EWS	ANG	DBS
66183	TO	WBAK	EWS	ANG	DBS
66184	TO	WNTR	EWS	ANG	DBS
66185	TO	WBAK	DBS	ANG	DBS
66186	TO	WBAI	EWS	ANG	DBS
66187	TO	WFMU	EWS	ANG	DBS
66188	TO	WBAK	EWS	ANG	DBS
66189 P	PN	WBEP	EWS	ANG	DBS
66190 ●	AZ	WBEN	EWS	ANG	ECR
66191 ●	AZ	WBEN	EWS	ANG	DBS
66192	TO	WBAI	EWS	ANG	DBS
66193	TO	WNTR	EWS	ANG	DBS
66194	TO	WBAK	EWS	ANG	DBS
66195 ●	TO	WBEN	EWS	ANG	ECR
66196 P	PN	WBEP	EWS	ANG	DBS
66197	TO	WBAK	EWS	ANG	DBS
66198	TO	WBAK	EWS	ANG	DBS
66199	TO	WBAI	EWS	ANG	DBS
66200	TO	WBAK	EWS	ANG	DBS
66201	TO	WBAI	EWS	ANG	DBS
66202 ●	AZ	WBEN	EWS	ANG	ECR
66203 ●	AZ	WBEN	EWS	ANG	ECR
66204	TO	WBAI	EWS	ANG	DBS
66205 ●	AZ	WBEN	EWS	ANG	ECR
66206	TO	WFMU	EWS	ANG	DBS
66207	TO	WBAI	EWS	ANG	DBS
66208 ●	AZ	WBEN	EWS	ANG	ECR
66209 ●	AZ	WBEN	EWS	ANG	ECR
66210 ●	AZ	WBEN	EWS	ANG	ECR
66211 ●	TO	WBEN	EWS	ANG	ECR
66212 ●	AZ	WBEN	EWS	ANG	ECR
66213	TO	WBAK	EWS	ANG	DBS
66214 ●	AZ	WBEN	EWS	ANG	ECR
66215 ●	AZ	WBEN	EWS	ANG	ECR
66216 ●	AZ	WBEN	EWS	ANG	ECR
66217 ●	AZ	WBEN	EWS	ANG	ECR
66218 ●	AZ	WFMU	EWS	ANG	ECR
66219 ●	AZ	WBEN	EWS	ANG	ECR
66220 P	TO	WBEP	DBS	ANG	DBS
66221	TO	WNTR	EWS	ANG	DBS
66222 ●	AZ	WBEN	EWS	ANG	ECR
66223 ●	AZ	WBEN	EWS	ANG	DBS
66224 ●	AZ	WBEN	EWS	ANG	ECR
66225 ●	AZ	WBEN	EWS	ANG	ECR
66226 ●	AZ	WBEN	EWS	ANG	ECR
66227 P	PN	WBEP	EWS	ANG	DBS
66228 ●	AZ	WBEN	EWS	ANG	ECR
66229 ●	AZ	WBEN	EWS	ANG	ECR
66230	TO	WFMU	EWS	ANG	DBS
66231 ●	AZ	WBEN	EWS	ANG	ECR
66232	TO	WFMU	EWS	ANG	DBS
66233 ●	AZ	WBEN	EWS	ANG	ECR
66234 ●	AZ	WBEN	EWS	ANG	ECR
66235 ●	AZ	WBEN	EWS	ANG	ECR
66236 ●	AZ	WBEN	EWS	ANG	ECR
66237 P	PN	WBEP	EWS	ANG	DBS
66238	TO	WNTR	EWS	ANG	DBS
66239 ●	AZ	WBEN	EWS	ANG	ECR
66240 ●	AZ	WBEN	EWS	ANG	ECR
66241 ●	AZ	WBEN	EWS	ANG	ECR
66242 ●	AZ	WBEN	EWS	ANG	ECR
66243 ●	TO	WBEN	EWS	ANG	ECR
66244 ●	AZ	WBEN	EWS	ANG	ECR
66245 ●	AZ	WBEN	EWS	ANG	DBS
66246 ●	AZ	WBEN	EWS	ANG	ECR
66247 ●	AZ	WBEN	EWS	ANG	ECR
66248 P	PN	WBEP	DBS	ANG	DBS
66249 ●	AZ	WBES	EWS	ANG	DBS
66250	TO	WBAK	EWS	ANG	DBS

‡ Not fitted with combination couplers

Names applied

66002	*Lafarge Quorn*
66048	*James the Engine*
66050	*EWS Energy*
66077	*Benjamin Gimbert GC*
66079	*James Nightall GC*
66152	*Derek Holmes Railway Operator*
66172	*Paul Melleney*
66185	*DP World London Gateway*
66200	*Railway Heritage Committee*
66250	*Robert K. Romak* (not standard nameplate)

● Class 66/0s marked with this symbol are modified and can operate with Euro Cargo Rail in France. Usually around 60 locos are in France at one time, but this figure is reduced in the autumn when a number return to the UK for RHTT operations. Locos working in France operate in the pool WBEN.

P Locomotives marked with a 'P' are operated by DB Schenker in Poland. Only locos from the series 66146-250 can be modified for this contract.

Below: *A total of 76 of the 250 Class 66/0s are modified for use in either France or Poland, leaving just 174 working in the UK. EWS-liveried No. 66174 is seen in charge of an aggregate train at Harringay, departing from Ferme Park yard and heading for Acton on 27 September 2013.* **CJM**

Class 67

Vehicle Length: 64ft 7in (19.68m)
Height: 12ft 9in (3.88m)
Width: 8ft 9in (2.66m)
Engine: EMD 12N-710G3B-EC
Horsepower: 2,980hp (2,223kW)
Electrical Equipment: EMD

Number	Depot	Pool	Livery	Owner	Operator	Name
67001	CE	WAAN	ATW	ANG	DBS/ATW	
67002	CE	WAAN	ATW	ANG	DBS/ATW	
67003	CE	WAAN	ATW	ANG	DBS/ATW	
67004	CE	WABN	EWS	ANG	DBS	
67005	CE	WAAN	ROY	ANG	DBS	*Queen's Messenger*
67006	CE	WAAN	ROY	ANG	DBS	*Royal Sovereign*
67007	CE	WABN	EWS	ANG	DBS	
67008	CE	WAAN	EWS	ANG	DBS	
67009	CE	WFMU	EWS	ANG	DBS	
67010	CE	WNTR	WSR	ANG	DBS/CRW	
67011	CE	WABN	EWS	ANG	DBS	
67012	CE	WAWN	WSR	ANG	DBS/CRW	*A Shropshire Lad*
67013	CE	WNTR	WSR	ANG	DBS/CRW	*Dyfrbont Pontcysyllte*
67014	CE	WAAN	WSR	ANG	DBS/CRW	*Thomas Telford*
67015	CE	WAWN	WSR	ANG	DBS/CRW	*David J. Lloyd*
67016	CE	WAFN	EWS	ANG	DBS	
67017	CE	WAFN	EWS	ANG	DBS	*Arrow*
67018	CE	WAFN	DBS	ANG	DBS	*Keith Heller*
67019	CE	WAAN	EWS	ANG	DBS	
67020	CE	WAAN	EWS	ANG	DBS	
67021	CE	WAAN	EWS	ANG	DBS	
67022	CE	WFMU	EWS	ANG	DBS	
67023	CE	WAAN	EWS	ANG	DBS	
67024	CE	WAAN	EWS	ANG	DBS	
67025	CE	WAAN	EWS	ANG	DBS	*Western Star*
67026	CE	WAAN	ROJ	ANG	DBS	*Diamond Jubilee*
67027	CE	WAAN	EWS	ANG	DBS	*Rising Star*
67028	CE	WAAN	EWS	ANG	DBS	
67029	CE	WAAN	EWE	ANG	DBS	*Royal Diamond*
67030	CE	WABN	EWS	ANG	DBS	

DB Schenker

Left: *Little capacity exists in the Class 67 roster with locos diagrammed for Chiltern, ScotRail and sleeper services every day, plus charter and selected freight operations. The 30-strong fleet is allocated to Crewe but can be found in all parts of the network. Three locos are specially maintained for Royal Train deployment when needed (Nos. 67005, 67006 and 67026). No. 67017 is seen at Haymarket station in Edinburgh in charge of one of the Fife area loco-hauled commuter services.* **Brian Garrett**

Class 90

Vehicle Length: 61ft 6in (18.74m)
Height: 13ft 0¼in (3.96m)
Width: 9ft 0in (2.74m)
Power Collection: 25kV ac overhead
Horsepower: 7,860hp (5,860kW)
Electrical Equipment: GEC

Number		*Depot*	*Pool*	*Livery*	*Owner*	*Operator*	*Name/Notes*
90017		CE	WNTS	EWS	DBS	-	
90018		CE	WEFE	DBS	DBS	DBS	
90019		CE	WEFE	FGS	DBS	DBS	
90020		CE	WEFE	EWS	DBS	DBS	*Collingwood*
90021	(90221)	CE	WEFE	FGS	DBS	-	
90022	(90222)	CE	WNTS	RFE	DBS	-	*Freightconnection*
90023	(90223)	CE	WNTS	EWS	DBS	-	
90024(S)	(90224)	CE	WEFE	FGS	DBS	-	
90025	(90225)	CE	WNTS	FGS	DBS	-	
90026		CE	WEFE	EWS	DBS	DBS	
90027(S)	(90227)	CE	WNTS	RFD	DBS	-	*Allerton T&RS Depot Quality Approved*
90028		CE	WNTR	EWS	DBS	DBS	
90029		CE	WEFE	DBS	DBS	DBS	
90030	(90130)	CE	WNTS	EWS	DBS	-	
90031	(90131)	CE	WNTS	EWS	DBS	-	*The Railway Children Partnership - Working for Street Children Worldwide*
90032	(90132)	CE	WNTS	EWS	DBS	-	
90033	(90233)	CE	WNTS	RFI	DBS	DBS	
90034(S)	(90134)	CE	WNTS	EWS	DBS	-	
90035	(90135)	CE	WEFE	EWS	DBS	DBS	
90036	(90136)	CE	WEFE	DBS	DBS	DBS	
90037	(90137)	CE	WNTS	EWS	DBS	DBS	*Spirit of Dagenham*
90038	(90238)	CE	WNTS	RFI	DBS	-	
90039(S)	(90239)	CE	WEFE	EWS	DBS	-	
90040	(90140)	CE	WNTS	EWS	DBS	DBS	*The Railway Mission*
90050(S)	(90050)	LNWR	WNTS	FLG	DBS	-	(At LNWR Crewe for spares recovery and scrap)

Left: *A fleet of 24 Class 90/0s is on the books of DBS, plus one loco, No. 90050, which is the source of spares at Crewe and previously with Freightliner. At present DBS does not have work for the entire allocation and several are stored at any one time, some locos passing from stored to operational status on a semi-frequent basis. EWS maroon-liveried No. 90028 is seen at Euston after arriving with an overnight ScotRail sleeper service, which Class 90s are booked to operate under the wires on the West Coast Main Line.* **Nathan Williamson**

Class 92

Vehicle Length: 70ft 1in (21.34m)	*Power Collection: 25kV ac overhead / 750V dc third rail*
Height: 13ft 0in (3.95m)	*Horsepower: ac - 6,700hp (5,000kW) / dc 5,360hp (4,000kW)*
Width: 8ft 8in (2.66m)	*Electrical Equipment: Brush*

Number	*Depot*	*Pool*	*Livery*	*Owner*	*Operator*	*Name*
92001■	CE	-	DBS	HBS	*Exported Romania*	*Mircea Eliade*
92002(S)	CE	WNTR	RFE	HBS	-	*H G Wells*
92003	CE	WTHE	RFE	HBS	DBS	*Beethoven*
92004(S)	CE	WNWX	RFE	HBS	-	*Jane Austen*
92005(S)	CE	WNTR	RFE	HBS	-	*Mozart*
92007	CE	WNTR	RFE	HBS	DBS	*Schubert*
92008(S)	CE	WNWX	RFE	HBS	-	*Jules Verne*
92009§(S)	CE	WTHE	DBS	HBS	-	*Marco Polo*
92011	CE	WTAE	RFE	HBS	DBS	*Handel*
92012■	CE	-	DBS	HBS	*Exported Romania*	*Mihai Eminescu*
92013(S)	CE	WNWX	RFE	HBS	-	*Puccini*
92015§	CE	WTHE	DBS	HBS	DBS	*D H Lawrence*
92016§	CE	WTAE	DBS	HBS	DBS	
92017(S)	CE	WNTR	STO	HBS	-	*Bart the Engine*
92019	CE	WTAE	RFE	HBS	DBS	*Wagner*
92022(S)	CE	WNTR	RFE	HBS	-	*Charles Dickens*
92024(S)	CE	WNWX	RFE	HBS	-	*J S Bach*
92025±	-	WNTR	RFE	HBS	*Exported Bulgaria*	*Oscar Wilde*
92026(S)	CE	WNTR	RFE	HBS	-	*Britten*
92027±	-	WTAE	RFE	HBS	*Exported Bulgaria*	*George Eliot*
92029(S)	CE	WNWX	RFE	HBS	-	*Dante*
92030	CE	WTAE	RFE	HBS	DBS	*Ashford*
92031§	CE	WTHE	DBS	HBS	-	
92034±	-	WTEB	RFE	HBS	*Exported Bulgaria*	*Kipling*
92035(S)	CE	WNWX	RFE	HBS	-	*Mendelssohn*
92036§	CE	WTAE	RFE	HBS	DBS	*Bertolt Brecht*
92037	CE	WTAE	RFE	HBS	DBS	*Sullivan*
92039	CE	WTAE	RFE	HBS	DBS	*Johann Strauss*
92041	CE	WNTR	RFE	HBS	DBS	*Vaughan Williams*
92042§	CE	WTHE	DBS	HBS	DBS	

§ Fitted with equipment to allow operation over HS1
± Exported to Bulgaria
■ Exported to Romania and numbered 92012 = 91 53 0472 001-3

Right: *Insufficient work exists to maintain the entire DBS Class 92 fleet in operation and, apart from five exported to Eastern Europe, around a dozen are stored at all times. Painted in Channel Tunnel grey livery with the EWS animal head logo on the side, No. 92030* Ashford *passes West Brompton with a Dollands Moor-bound freight.* **CJM**

Hauled Stock (Passenger)

Mk1	*Height: 12ft 9½in (3.89m)*
Vehicle Length: 64ft 6in (19.65m)	*Width: 9ft 3in (2.81m)*

Mk2	*Height: 12ft 9½in (3.89m)*
Vehicle Length: 66ft 0in (20.11m)	*Width: 9ft 3in (2.81m)*

Mk 3	*Height: 12ft 9in (3.88m)*
Vehicle Length: 75ft 0in (22.86m)	*Width: 8ft 11in (2.71m)*

AD1E - FOT ‡ For sale

Number	*Depot*	*Livery*	*Owner*
3269(S) ‡	EH	MAR	DBR

AD1F - FO ‡ For sale

Number	*Depot*	*Livery*	*Owner*
3292	CE	MAR	DBR
3318	MH	MAR	DBR/FSR
3331	MH	MAR	DBR/FSR
3338(S) ‡	EH	MAR	DBR
3375(S) ‡	EH	MAR	DBR
3388(S)	EH	MAR	DBR

DB Schenker

3399(S)	EH	MAR	DBR
3400	MH	MAR	DBR/FSR
3414(S) ‡	EH	MAR	DBR
3424	MH	MAR	DBR/FSR

AC2B - TSO

Number	*Depot*	*Livery*	*Owner*
5482	TO	BLG	DBR

AC2D - TSO

Number	*Depot*	*Livery*	*Owner*
5631	MH	MAR	AUT
5632	MH	MAR	AUT
5657(S)	MH	MAR	AUT

AC2F - TSO ‡ For sale

Number	*Depot*	*Livery*	*Owner*
5922 ‡	BS	MAR	AUT
5924 ‡	BS	MAR	AUT
5954(S)	EH	MAR	AUT
5959 ‡	BS	MAR	AUT
6036 ‡	BS	MAR	DBR
6110(S)	EH	MAR	DBR
6139(S)	TO	MAR	DBR
6152 ‡	BS	MAR	DBR

AX51 - GEN ‡ For sale

Number	*Depot*	*Livery*	*Owner*
6311(S) (92911) ‡	TO	BLU	DBR

AE2D - BSO

Number	*Depot*	*Livery*	*Owner*
9494	MH	MAR	DBR/FSR

AE2F - BSO

Number	*Depot*	*Livery*	*Owner*
9522	MH	MAR	DBR/FSR
9529(S)	BS	MAR	DBR
9531(S)	BS	MAR	DBR

AJ1G - RFM

Number	*Depot*	*Livery*	*Owner*
10201(S) (40520)	LM	VIR	DBR
10202 (40504)	LM	BLG	DBR/CRW
10211 (40510)	TO	EWE	DBS
10215 (11032)	LM	BLG	DBR/CRW
10222(S) (11063)	BY	BLG	DBR
10226(S) (11015)	LM	VIR	DBR
10233(S) (10013)	LM	VIR	DBR
10235 (10015)	LM	BLG	DBR/CRW
10237(S) (10022)	BY	DRU	DBR
10242(S) (10002)	LM	BLG	DBR
10246 (10114)	CF	BLG	DBR/CRW
10250(S) (10020)	LM	VIR	DBR
10257(S) (10007)	BY	BLG	DBR

AU4G - SLEP

Number	*Depot*	*Livery*	*Owner*
10540(S)	LM	FGW	DBR
10546	TO	EWE	DBS
10554(S)	LM	ICS	DBR (scrap)

AS4G - SLE

Number	*Depot*	*Livery*	*Owner*
10681(S)	LM	-	DBR
10682(S)	LM	ICS	DBR (scrap)
10710(S)	LM	CWR	DBR/CRW
10731(S)	LM	ICS	DBR (scrap)

AD1G - FO

Number	*Depot*	*Livery*	*Owner*
11005(S)	LM	VIR	DBR
11013(S)	LM	DRU	DBR
11019(S)	ZB	DRU	DBR
11027(S)	BY	BLU	DBR
11028(S)	ZB	VIR	DBR
11029	AL	CWR	DBR/CRW
11030(S)	ZB	DRU	DBR
11031	AL	BLG	DBR/CRW
11033(S)	LM	DRU	DBR
11039	TO	EWE	DBS
11044(S)	BY	DRU	DBR
11046(S)	ZB	DRU	DBR
11054(S)	ZB	DRU	DBR
11079(S)	LM	BLG	DBR/CRW
11089	AL	BLG	DBR/CRW
11097(S)	LM	BLG	DBR

AB21 - BSK

Number	*Depot*	*Livery*	*Owner*
35290(S)	CP	CAR	DBR

GK2G - TRSB

Number	*Depot*	*Livery*	*Owner*
40402(S) (40002)	LM	VIR	DBR
40403(S) (40003)	LM	VIR	DBR
40416(S) (40016)	LM	VIR	DBR
40419(S) (40019)	LM	VIR	DBR
40434(S) (40234)	LM	VIR	DBR

Saloon

Number	*Depot*	*Livery*	*Owner*
45020(S)	TO	MAR	DBR

Hauled Stock (NPCCS)

Mk 3 (DVT) *Height: 12ft 9in (3.88m)*
Vehicle Length: 61ft 9in (18.83m) *Width: 8ft 11in (2.71m)*

NZAG - DVT

Number	*Depot*	*Livery*	*Owner*
82106(S)	LM	VIR	DBR
82110(S)	LM	VIR	DBR
82113(S)	LM	VIR	DBR
82116(S)	LM	VIR	DBR
82120(S)	LM	VIR	DBR
82122(S)	LM	VIR	DBR
82123(S)	LM	VIR	DBR
82137(S)	LM	VIR	DBR
82138(S)	LM	VIR	DBR
82141(S)	LM	VIR	DBR
82146	TO	DBE	DBS
82148(S)	LM	VIR	DBR
82150(S)	LM	VIR	DBR

NKA1 - H-GUV

Number	*Depot*	*Livery*	*Owner*
94104 (S) (95104)	TO	RES	DBS
94106 (S) (95106)	MH	RES	DBS

Number	Depot	Livery	Owner
94116 (S) (95116)	TY	RES	DBS
94121 (S) (95121)	TO	RES	DBS
94137 (S) (95137)	MY	RES	DBS
94147 (S) (95147)	MY	RES	DBS
94153 (S) (95153)	WE	RES	DBS
94160 (S) (95160)	MH	RES	DBS
94166 (S) (95166)	BS	RES	DBS
94170 (S) (95170)	BS	RES	DBS
94176 (S) (95176)	MH	RES	DBS
94177 (S) (95177)	TO	RES	DBS
94192 (S) (95352)	MY	RES	DBS
94195 (S) (95355)	BS	RES	DBS
94197 (S) (95357)	BS	RES	DBS
94207 (S) (95367)	TO	RES	DBS
94208 (S) (95368)	TO	RES	DBS
94213 (S) (95373)	MY	RES	DBS
94214 (S) (95374)	MH	RES	DBS
94217 (S) (93131)	MH	RES	DBS
94221 (S) (93905)	MY	RES	DBS
94222 (S) (93474)	MH	RES	DBS
94225 (S) (93849)	MH	RES	DBS
94227 (S) (93585)	TE	RES	DBS
94229 (S) (93720)	MH	RES	DBS

NAA1 - PCV

Number	*Depot*	*Livery*	*Owner*
94302 (S) (75124)	TY	RES	DBS
94303 (S) (75131)	TY	RES	DBS
94304 (S) (75107)	MH	RES	DBS
94306 (S) (75112)	TY	RES	DBS
94308 (S) (75125)	MH	RES	DBS
94310 (S) (75119)	WE	RES	DBS
94311 (S) (75105)	WE	RES	DBS
94313 (S) (75129)	WE	RES	DBS
94316 (S) (75108)	TO	RES	DBS
94317 (S) (75117)	TO	RES	DBS
94322 (S) (75111)	MH	RES	DBS
94323 (S) (75110)	TY	RES	DBS
94326 (S) (75123)	TY	RES	DBS
94332 (S) (75011)	TY	RES	DBS
94333 (S) (75016)	TY	RES	DBS
94334 (S) (75017)	CD	RES	DBS
94335 (S) (75032)	TY	RES	DBS
94336 (S) (75031)	TY	RES	DBS
94340 (S) (75012)	CD	RES	DBS
94343 (S) (75027)	MH	RES	DBS
94344 (S) (75014)	TO	RES	DBS

NBA1, NOA1, NQA, NRA1 - BVHS

Number	*Depot*	*Livery*	*Owner*
94406 (92956)	MH	RES	DBS
94408 (92981)	TY	RES	DBS
94410 (92941)	WE	RES	DBS
94412 (92945)	ML	RES	DBS
94413 (92236)	ML	RES	DBS
94416 (92746)	MY	RES	DBS
94420 (92263)	MH	RES	DBS
94422 (92651)	TO	RES	DBS
94423 (92914)	BS	RES	DBS
94427 (92754)	WE	RES	DBS
94428 (92166)	MY	RES	DBS
94429 (92232)	TE	RES	DBS
94431 (92604)	MH	RES	DBS
94432 (92999)	MY	RES	DBS
94433 (92643)	MH	RES	DBS
94434 (92584)	TY	RES	DBS
94435 (92134)	TO	RES	DBS
94438 (92251)	TO	RES	DBS
94440 (92645)	MY	RES	DBS
94445 (92615)	WE	RES	DBS
94451 (92257)	WE	RES	DBS
94462 (92270)	CD	RES	DBS
94463 (92995)	TY	RES	DBS
94470 (92113)	TO	RES	DBS
94479 (92132)	TO	RES	DBS
94482 (92639)	MH	RES	DBS
94488 (92105)	CD	RES	DBS
94490 (92230)	MH	RES	DBS
94492 (92721)	WE	RES	DBS
94495 (92755)	TY	RES	DBS
94497 (92717)	ML	RES	DBS
94498 (92555)	MH	RES	DBS
94499 (92577)	CD	BLG	DBS
94501 (92725)	TO	RES	DBS
94504 (92748)	TY	RES	DBS
94512 (92582)	TY	RES	DBS
94514 (92122)	MY	RES	DBS
94518 (92258)	MY	RES	DBS
94519 (92916)	ML	RES	DBS
94520 (92917)	TY	RES	DBS
94521 (92917)	CD	RES	DBS
94522 (92907)	TY	RES	DBS
94525 (92229)	TY	RES	DBS
94526 (92518)	TY	RES	DBS
94527 (92728)	TY	RES	DBS
94528 (92252)	ML	RES	DBS
94529 (92267)	CD	RES	DBS
94530 (94409)	MY	RES	DBS
94531 (94456)	TY	RES	DBS
94532 (94489)	LM	RES	DBS
94534 (94430)	MY	RES	DBS
94536 (94491)	MY	RES	DBS
94539 (92302)	MH	RES	DBS
94540 (92860)	TJ	RES	DBS
94541 (92316)	ML	RES	DBS
94542 (92330)	TY	RES	DBS
94543 (92389)	MY	RES	DBS
94544 (92345)	MH	RES	DBS
94545 (92329)	TE	RES	DBS
94546 (92804)	TY	RES	DBS
94547 (92392)	MH	RES	DBS
94548 (92344)	TY	RES	DBS

NAA1 - PCV

Number	*Depot*	*Livery*	*Owner*
95300 (94300)	MH	RES	DBS
95301 (94301)	MH	RES	DBS

NRA1 - BAA

Number	*Depot*	*Livery*	*Owner*
95400 (95203)	MH	EWS	DBS
95410 (95213)	MH	EWS	DBS

DB Schenker

NOA1 - H-GUV

Number	Depot	Livery	Owner
95727 (95127)	WE	RES	DBS
95754 (95154)	TY	RES	DBS
95761 (95161)	WE	RES	DBS
95763 (95163)	BS	RES	DBS

NX5G - NGV

Number	Depot	Livery	Owner
96371(S) (10545)	WB	EPS	DBS
96372(S) (10564)	LM	EPS	DBS
96373(S) (10568)	LM	EPS	DBS
96375(S) (10587)	LM	EPS	DBS

Euro Cargo Rail A part of DB Schenker

Address: ✉ Immeuble la Palacio, 25-29 Place de la Madeleine, Paris, 75008

info@eurocargorail.com, ✆ +33 977 400000, ⓘ www.eurocargorail.com

Class 21

Vehicle Length: (21/5) 48ft 2in (14.70m), (21/6) 46ft 3in (14.13m)
Height: (21/5) 13ft 8in (4.16m), (21/6) 13ft 9in (4.19m)
Width: 8ft 8¼in (2.65m)
Engine: (21/5) Caterpillar 3512B DITA of 2,011hp
Engine: (21/6) MTU 8V 4000 R41L of 1,475hp
Hydraulic Equipment: Voith

Number	Depot	Pool	Livery	Owner	Operator
21544	DM	WLAN	MAR	ANG	ECR
21545	DM	WLAN	MAR	ANG	ECR
21546	DM	WLAN	MAR	ANG	ECR
21547	DM	WLAN	MAR	ANG	ECR
21610	DM	WLAN	MAR	ANG	ECR
21611	DM	WLAN	MAR	ANG	ECR

Class 77 (JT42CWRM)

Vehicle Length: 70ft 0½in (21.34m)
Height: 12ft 10in (3.91m)
Width: 8ft 8¼in (2.65m)
Engine: EMD 12N-710G3B-EC
Horsepower: 3,300hp (2,462kW)
Electrical Equipment: EMD

Number	Depot	Livery	Owner	Opt'r
77001	ND	ELR	DBS	ECR
77002	ND	ELR	DBS	ECR
77003	ND	ELR	DBS	ECR
77004	ND	ELR	DBS	ECR
77005	ND	ELR	DBS	ECR
77006	ND	ELR	DBS	ECR
77007‡	ND	ELR	DBS	ECR
77008	ND	ELR	DBS	ECR
77009	ND	ELR	DBS	ECR
77010	ND	ELR	DBS	ECR
77011	ND	ELR	DBS	ECR
77012	ND	ELR	DBS	ECR
77013	ND	ELR	DBS	ECR
77014	ND	ELR	DBS	ECR
77015	ND	ELR	DBS	ECR
77016	ND	ELR	DBS	ECR
77017	ND	ELR	DBS	ECR
77018	ND	ELR	DBS	ECR
77019	ND	ELR	DBS	ECR
77020‡	ND	ELR	DBS	ECR
77021	ND	ELR	DBS	ECR
77022	ND	ELR	DBS	ECR
77023	ND	ELR	DBS	ECR
77024	ND	ELR	DBS	ECR
77025	ND	ELR	DBS	ECR
77026‡	ND	ELR	DBS	ECR
77027	ND	ELR	DBS	ECR
77028	ND	ELR	DBS	ECR
77029‡	ND	ELR	DBS	ECR
77030	ND	ELR	DBS	ECR
77031‡	ND	ELR	DBS	ECR
77032	ND	ELR	DBS	ECR
77033	ND	ELR	DBS	ECR
77034‡	ND	ELR	DBS	ECR
77035	ND	ELR	DBS	ECR
77036	ND	ELR	DBS	ECR
77037†	ND	ELR	DBS	ECR
77038‡	ND	ELR	DBS	ECR
77039‡	ND	ELR	DBS	ECR
77040	ND	ELR	DBS	ECR
77041‡	ND	ELR	DBS	ECR
77042‡	ND	ELR	DBS	ECR
77043‡	ND	ELR	DBS	ECR
77044‡	ND	ELR	DBS	ECR
77045	ND	ELR	DBS	ECR
77046‡	ND	ELR	DBS	ECR
77047	ND	ELR	DBS	ECR
77048	ND	ELR	DBS	ECR
77049‡	ND	ELR	DBS	ECR
77050‡	ND	ELR	DBS	ECR
77051‡	ND	ELR	DBS	ECR
77052‡	ND	ELR	DBS	ECR
77053‡	ND	ELR	DBS	ECR
77054‡	ND	ELR	DBS	ECR
77055‡	ND	ELR	DBS	ECR
77056‡	ND	ELR	DBS	ECR
77057‡	ND	ELR	DBS	ECR
77058	ND	ELR	DBS	ECR
77059	ND	ELR	DBS	ECR
77060	ND	ELR	DBS	ECR

‡ Working for DBS in Germany, re-classified as Class 247, running in number range 247 007 onwards; final three digits remain the same.
† Working for MEG in Germany as 247-037.

Left: *The Euro Cargo Rail Class 77s can be seen all over France powering a diverse selection of train types. ECR No. 77023 hauls a train of Fiat cars from the Italian plant in Torino to Gevrey (near Dijon, France), from where they will be distributed all over France. The train is seen passing St Jean de la Porte on the picturesque line between Modane and the Italian border and Chambery, in the French Alps on 16 February 2013.* **Frederick Jury**

Direct Rail Services

Address (UK): ✉ Kingmoor Depot, Etterby Road, Carlisle, Cumbria, CA3 9NZ
info@directrailservices.com
✆ 01228 406600
ⓘ www.directrailservices.com

Managing Director: Neil McNicholas
Depots: Carlisle Kingmoor (KM), Crewe Gresty Bridge (CG)

Class 20/3

Vehicle Length: 46ft 9¼in (14.26m)
Height: 12ft 7⅝in (3.84m)
Width: 8ft 9in (2.66m)
Engine: English Electric 8SVT Mk2
Horsepower: 1,000hp (745kW)
Electrical Equipment: English Electric

Number		Depot	Pool	Livery	Owner	Operator	Name
20301	(20047)	KM	XHNC	DRC	DRS	DRS	*Max Joule 1958 - 1999*
20302	(20084)	KM	XHNC	DRC	DRS	DRS	
20303	(20127)	KM	XHNC	DRC	DRS	DRS	
20304	(20120)	KM	XHNC	DRC	DRS	DRS	
20305	(20095)	KM	XHNC	DRC	DRS	DRS	*Gresty Bridge*
20308	(20187)	KM	XHNC	DRC	DRS	DRS	
20309	(20075)	KM	XHNC	DRC	DRS	DRS	
20312(S)	(20042)	KM/CS	XHNC	DRC	DRS	DRS	

Right: *Eight Type 1 Class 20s are still on the books of Direct Rail Services and are deployed mainly on lighter- weight flask trains, sometimes working in multiple with a Class 37. The fleet is very popular with rail enthusiasts and members of the class are frequently requested for charter trains. On 30 August 2013, Nos. 20303 and 20308 pass Dawlish powering the 07.13 Crewe to Kingswear charter.* **CJM**

Class 37/0

Vehicle Length: 61ft 6in (18.74m)
Height: 13ft 0¼in (3.96m)
Width: 8ft 11⅝in (2.73m)
Class 37/4 - Electric Train Heat fitted
Engine: English Electric 12CSVT
Horsepower: 1,750hp (1,304kW)
Electrical Equipment: English Electric

Number	Depot	Pool	Livery	Owner	Operator	Name
37038	KM	XHSS	DRS	DRS	DRS	
37059	KM	XHSS	DRC	DRS	-	
37069	KM	XHSS	DRC	DRS	-	
37194	KM	XHNC	DRC	DRS	DRS	
37218	KM	XHNC	DRC	DRS	DBS	
37259	KM	XHNC	DRU	DRS	DRS	
37261	KM	XHNC	DRC	DRS	DRS	

Class 37/4

Number		Depot	Pool	Livery	Owner	Operator	Name/Notes
37401(S)	(37268)	-	XHHP	EWS	DRS	-	(On Bo'ness Railway on loan from DRS)
37402	(37274)	BH	XHAC	DRC	DBS	DRS	*Stephen Middlemore 23.12.1954 - 8.6.2013*
37405	(37282)	BH	XHAC	DRC	DRS	DRS	
37406(S)	(37295)	KM	XHHP	EWS	DRS	-	*The Saltire Society*
37409	(37270)	KM	XHNC	DRC	DRS	DRS	*Lord Hinton*
37419	(37291)	KM	XHAC	DRC	DRS	DRS	*Carl Haviland 1954-2012*

37422(S)	(37266)	KM	XHHP	DRC	DRS	-	
37423	(37296)	KM	XHND	DRC	DRS	DRS	*Spirit of the Lakes*
37425	(37292)	BH	XHAC	DRC	DRS	DRS	*Sir Robert McAlpine / Concrete Bob*

Class 37/5

Number		Depot	Pool	Livery	Owner	Operator	Name
37503	(37021)	KM	XHSS	EWS	DRS	-	
37510(S)		KM/BH	XHSS	DRC	DRS	-	
37521	(37117)	KM	HXSS	EWS	DRS	-	
37667	(37151)	KM	XHND	DRC	DRS	DRS	*Kingmoor TMD*
37670	(37182)	KM	XHSS	EWS	DRS	-	
37682(S)	(37236)	KM	XHHP	DRC	DRS	-	
37688	(37205)	KM	XHND	DRC	DRS	DRS	
37696	(37129)	KM	XHSS	EWS	DRS	-	

Class 37/6

Number		Depot	Pool	Livery	Owner	Operator	Name
37601	(37501)	KM	XHNC	DRC	DRS	DRS	*Class 37 – 'Fifty'*
37602	(37502)	KM	XHNC	DRC	DRS	DRS	
37603	(37504)	KM	XHND	DRC	DRS	DRS	
37604	(37506)	KM	XHND	DRC	DRS	DRS	
37605	(37507)	KM	XHND	DRC	DRS	DRS	
37606	(37508)	KM	XHNC	DRS	DRS	DRS	
37607	(37511)	KM	XHNC	DRC	DRS	DRS	
37608	(37512)	KM	XHNC	DRC	DRS	DRS	
37609	(37514)	KM	XHNC	DRC	DRS	DRS	
37610	(37687)	KM	XHND	DRC	DRS	DRS	
37611	(37690)	KM	XHNC	DRC	DRS	DRS	
37612	(37691)	KM	XHNC	DRS	DRS	DRS	

Left: *Direct Rail Services operates five sub- classes of Class 37, and each have some technical differences, such as the '37/4s' being fitted with Electric Train Heat and the '37/6s' being former Eurostar UK locos that are now heavily modified. The class operate all types of DRS traffic from flask to intermodal, departmental to charter and passenger. Class 37/6 No. 37608 is shown with its No. 1 end on the right, painted in the latest 'compass' livery style.* **CJM**

Class 37/7

Number		Hire No.	Depot	Pool	Livery	Owner	Operator	Notes
37703(S)	(37067)	L25	BH	XHHP	DRC	DRS	DRS	Used at Daventry as 'super shunter'
37714(S)	(37024)	L26	BH	XHHP	DRC	DRS	DRS	Used at Daventry as 'super shunter'
37716(S)	(37094)	L23	RTC	XHHP	CON	DRS	DRS	Under renovation
37718(S)	(37084)	L22	RTC	XHHP	CON	DRS	DRS	Under renovation

Class 47/4 & 47/7

Vehicle Length: 63ft 6in (19.35m)
Height: 12ft 10⅜in (3.91m)
Width: 9ft 2in (2.79m)
Electric Train Heat fitted
Engine: Sulzer 12LDA28C
Horsepower: 2,580hp (1,922kW)
Electrical Equipment: Brush

Number		Depot	Pool	Livery	Owner	Operator	Name
47501		KM	XHNB	DRC	DRS	DRS	*Craftsman*
47703(S)	(47514)	KM	XHSS	FRB	DRS	-	
47790	(47673)	KM	XHNB	NBP	DRS	DRS	*Galloway Princess*
47802	(47552)	KM	XHAC	DRC	DRS	DRS	*Pride of Cumbria*
47805	(47650)	KM	XHAC	DRC	DRS	DRS	*John Scott 12.5.45 - 22.5.12*
47810	(47247/655)	BH	XHAC	DRC	DRS	DRS	*Peter Bath MBE 1927-2006*

47813	(47129/658)	KM	XHNB	DRC	DRS	DRS	*Solent*
47818	(47240/663)	BH	XHHP	DRC	DRS	DRS	
47828	(47266/629)	BH	XHAC	DRC	DRS	DRS	
47832	(47560)	KM	XHAC	NBP	DRS	DRS	*Solway Princess*
47841	(47622)	KM	XHNC	DRC	DRS	DRS	
47853	(47614)	KM	XHAC	DRC	DRS	DRS	*Rail Express*

Right: *At the start of 2014, 12 Class 47s are operated by Direct Rail Services. They usually operate any passenger charter contracts (together with the Class 57s), as well as taking their turn on freight traffic. Painted in full 'compass' livery, No. 47818 passes Torre with a charter bound for Kingswear. This locomotive retains its electric train supply and a nose-mounted 'green dot' jumper cable.*
Nathan Williamson

Class 57/0

Vehicle Length: 63ft 6in (19.38m)
Height: 12ft 10⅛in (3.91m)
Width: 9ft 2in (2.79m)
Engine: EMD 645-12E3
Horsepower: 2,500hp (1,864kW)
Electrical Equipment: Brush

Number		*Depot*	*Pool*	*Livery*	*Owner*	*Operator*	*Notes*
57002	(47322)	KM	XHCK	DRC	PTR	-	* with Colas branding
57003	(47317)	KM	XHCK	DRC	PTR	DRS	
57004	(47347)	KM	XHCK	DRC	DRS	DRS	
57007	(47332)	KM	XHCK	DRC	PTR	DRS	
57008	(47060)	KM	XHCK	DRC	PTR	DRS	
57009	(47079)	KM	XHCK	DRC	PTR	DRS	
57010	(47231)	KM	XHCK	DRC	PTR	DRS	
57011	(47329)	KM	XHCK	DRC	PTR	DRS	
57012(S)	(47204)	KM	XHSS	DRC	PTR	-	

Class 57/3

Vehicle Length: 63ft 6in (19.38m)
Height: 12ft 10⅛in (3.91m)
Width: 9ft 2in (2.79m)
Engine: EMD 645-12F3B
Horsepower: 2,750hp (2,051kW)
Electrical Equipment: Brush

Number		*Depot*	*Pool*	*Livery*	*Owner*	*Operator*	*Name*
57302	(47827)	KM	XHVT	DRC	PTR	DRS	*Chad Varah*
57304	(47807)	KM	XHVT	DRC	PTR	DRS	*Pride of Cheshire*
57307	(47225)	KM	XHVT	DRA	PBR	DRB	*Lady Penelope*
57308	(47846)	KM	XHVT	DRC	PBR	DRS	*County of Staffordshire*
57309	(47806)	KM	XHVT	DRC	PTR	DRS	*Pride of Crewe*
57311	(47817)	KM	XHVT	DRC	PBR	DRS	*Thunderbird*

Right: *Nine members of Class 57/0 and six members of Class 57/3 are operated by Direct Rail Services. The 57/0s are used on a mix of freight and passenger duties, while the 57/3s are used for passenger and hire to Virgin Trains to provide 'Thunderbird' duties for Class 221 and 390 stock operating on the West Coast route. The locos retain their drop-head Dellner couplers. No. 57309* Pride of Crewe *is seen stabled at London Euston.*
Nathan Williamson

Direct Rail Services

Class 66/3, 66/4

Vehicle Length: 70ft 0½in (21.34m)
Height: 12ft 10in (3.91m)
Width: 8ft 8¼in (2.65m)
Engine: EMD 12N-710G3B-EC
Horsepower: 3,300hp (2,462kW)
Electrical Equipment: EMD

Number	Depot	Pool	Livery	Owner	Operator
66301	KM	XHIM	DRC	BEA	DRS
66302	KM	XHIM	DRC	BEA	DRS
66303	KM	XHIM	DRC	BEA	DRS
66304	KM	XHIM	DRC	BEA	DRS
66305	KM	XHIM	DRC	BEA	DRS
66421	KM	XHIM	DRC	HAL	DRS
66422	KM	XHIM	DRC	HAL	DRS
66423	KM	XHIM	DRC	HAL	DRS
66424	KM	XHIM	DRC	HAL	DRS
66425	KM	XHIM	DRC	HAL	DRS
66426	KM	XHIM	DRC	HAL	DRS
66427	KM	XHIM	DRC	HAL	DRS
66428	KM	XHIM	DRC	HAL	DRS
66429	KM	XHIM	DRC	HAL	DRS
66430	KM	XHIM	DRC	HAL	DRS
66431	KM	XHIM	DRC	HAL	DRS
66432	KM	XHIM	DRC	HAL	DRS
66433	KM	XHIM	DRC	HAL	DRS
66434	KM	XHIM	ADV§	HAL	DRS

§ Malcolm promotional livery

Left: *Five Class 66/3s (previously with Fastline Freight) and 14 Class 66/4s built specifically for DRS are in operation. These are based at Carlisle and principally operate the long-distance container traffic as well as some longer-distance flask operations. All are painted in 'compass-livery'. No. 66428 is illustrated.*
Nathan Williamson

Class 68 'UK Light'

Vehicle Length: 67ft 3in (20.5m)
Height: 12ft 6½in (3.82m)
Speed: 100mph (161km/h)
Engine: Caterpiller C175-16
Horsepower: 3,750hp (2,800kW)
Electrical Equipment: ABB

Number	Depot	Pool	Livery	Owner	Operator
68001	KM	XHVE	DRS	BEA	DRS
68002	KM	XHVE	DRS	BEA	DRS
68003	KM	XHVE	DRS	BEA	DRS
68004	KM	XHVE	DRS	BEA	DRS
68005	KM	XHVE	DRS	BEA	DRS
68006	KM	XHVE	DRS	BEA	DRS
68007	KM	XHVE	DRS	BEA	DRS
68008	KM	XHVE	DRS	BEA	DRS
68009	KM	XHVE	DRS	BEA	DRS
68010	KM	XHVE	DRS	BEA	DRS
68011	KM	XHVE	DRS	BEA	DRS
68012	KM	XHVE	DRS	BEA	DRS
68013	KM	XHVE	DRS	BEA	DRS
68014	KM	XHVE	DRS	BEA	DRS
68015	KM	XHVE	DRS	BEA	DRS

On delivery

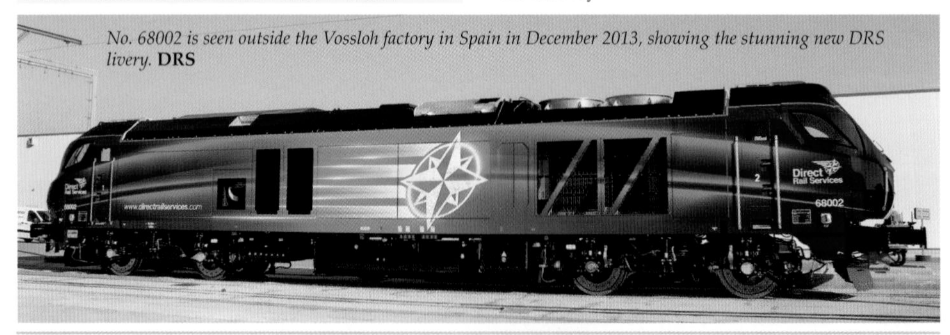

No. 68002 is seen outside the Vossloh factory in Spain in December 2013, showing the stunning new DRS livery. **DRS**

Class 88 'Dual Mode'

Vehicle Length: 67ft 3in (20.5m)
Height: 12ft 6½in (3.82m)
Speed: 100mph (161km/h)
Electric train supply
Engine: Caterpiller
Horsepower: Electro-diesel
Diesel - 938hp (700kW)
Electric - 5,364hp (4,000kW)
Electrical Equipment: ABB

Number	Depot	Pool	Livery	Owner	Operator
88001	KM	XH??	DRS	BEA	On order
88002	KM	XH??	DRS	BEA	On order
88003	KM	XH??	DRS	BEA	On order
88004	KM	XH??	DRS	BEA	On order
88005	KM	XH??	DRS	BEA	On order
88006	KM	XH??	DRS	BEA	On order
88007	KM	XH??	DRS	BEA	On order
88008	KM	XH??	DRS	BEA	On order
88009	KM	XH??	DRS	BEA	On order
88010	KM	XH??	DRS	BEA	On order

Coaching Stock

Number	Type	Depot	Livery	Operator
1254 (3391)	AJ1F/RFO	KM	BLG	DRS
3366	AD1F/FO	KM	BLG	DRS
3374	AD1F/FO	KM	BLG	DRS
5810	AC2E/TSO	KM	DRC	DRS
5919	AC2F/TSO	KM	BLG	DRS
5971	AC2F/TSO	KM	DRC	DRS
5995	AC25/TSO	KM	DRC	DRS
6001	AC2F/TSO	KM	DRC	DRS
6008	AC2F/TSO	KM	DRC	DRS
6046	AC2F/TSO	KM	DRC	DRS
6064	AC2F/TSO	KM	BLG	DRS
6117	AC2F/TSO	KM	DRC	DRS
6122	AC2F/TSO	KM	DRC	DRS
6173	AC2F/TSO	KM	DRS	DRS
9419	AC2E/TSO	KM	DRC	DRS
9428	AE2E/BSO	KM	DRC	DRS
9488	AE2E/BSO	KM	-	-
9506	AE2E/BSO	KM	BLG	DRS
9508	AE2E/BSO	KM	BLG	DRS
9525	AE2E/BSO	KM	DRC	DRS
11006	AD1G/FO	KM	-	DRS
11011	AD1G/FO	KM	-	DRS
12047	AC2G/TSO	KM	-	DRS
12063	AC2G/TSO	KM	-	DRS
12065	AC2G/TSO	KM	-	DRS
12087	AC2G/TSO	KM	-	DRS
12134	AC2G/TSO	KM	-	DRS
17159	AB1D/BFK	KM	DRO	DRS
82101	NZAK/DVT	KM	VIR	DRS

Mk2 — Vehicle Length: 66ft 0in (20.11m); Height: 12ft 9½in (3.89m); Width: 9ft 3in (2.81m)

Mk 3 — Vehicle Length: 75ft 0in (22.86m); Height: 12ft 9in (3.88m); Width: 8ft 11in (2.71m)

NX5G - NGV (Nightstar generators)

Number		Depot	Livery	Owner
96371(S)	(10545)	WB	EPS	DRS
96372(S)	(10564)	LM	EPS	DRS
96373(S)	(10568)	LM	EPS	DRS
96375(S)	(10587)	LM	EPS	DRS

Above: *At the start of 2014 Direct Rail Services did not operate any passenger services, but the company is likely to commence passenger duties during the year. Mk2E TSO No. 5810 in ex-works DRS 'compass'-livery is seen at Eastleigh Works where it was overhauled.* **Antony Christie**

Royal Mail (operations contracted to DBS)

Address: ✉ 148 Old Street, London, EC1V 9HQ

press.office@royalmail.com ✆ 0207 250 2468 ⓘ www.royalmailgroup.com

Class 325

Vehicle Length: (Driving) 65ft 0¾in (19.82m) (Inter) 65ft 4¼in (19.92m); Height: 12ft 4¼in (3.76m); Width: 9ft 2in (2.82m); Horsepower: 1,278hp (990kW); Seats (total/car): None - luggage space

Number	Formation DTPMV+MPMV+TPMV+DTPMV	Depot	Livery	Owner	Operator	Name
325001	68300+68340+68360+68301	CE	RML	RML	DBS	
325002	68302+68341+68361+68303	CE	RML	RML	DBS	Royal Mail North Wales & North West
325003	68304+68342+68362+68305	CE	RML	RML	DBS	
325004	68306+68343+68363+68307	CE	RML	RML	DBS	
325005	68308+68344+68364+68309	CE	RML	RML	DBS	John Grierson
325006	68310+68345+68365+68311	CE	RML	RML	DBS	
325007	68312+68346+68366+68313	CE	RML	RML	DBS	Peter Howarth C.B.E
325008	68314+68347+68367+68315	CE	RML	RML	DBS	
325009	68316+68348+68368+68317	CE	RML	RML	DBS	
325011	68320+68350+68370+68321	CE	RML	RML	DBS	
325012	68322+68351+68371+68323	CE	RML	RML	DBS	
325013	68324+68352+68372+68325	CE	RML	RML	DBS	
325014	68326+68353+68373+68327	CE	RML	RML	DBS	
325015	68328+68354+68374+68329	CE	RML	RML	DBS	
325016	68330+68355+68375+68331	CE	RML	RML	DBS	

Europorte – GB Railfreight (GBRf)

Address: ✉15-25 Artillery Lane, London, E1 7HA

gbrfinfo@gbrailfreight.com

✆ 0207 983 5177

ⓘ www.gbrailfreight.com

Managing Director: John Smith

Depots: Peterborough (PT), Wembley (SV), St Leonards (SE), Coquelles (CQ), Ashford Hitachi (AD)

Class 08/0, 09

Vehicle Length: 29ft 3in (8.91m)
Height: 12ft 8⅝in (3.87m)
Width: 8ft 6in (2.59m)
Engine: English Electric 6K
Horsepower: 400hp (298kW)
Electrical Equipment: English Electric

Number	Depot	Pool	Livery	Owner	Operator
08401	±	GBWM	GRN	HEC	GBR
08925	CF	GBWM	GRN	GBF	GBR
08934	CF	GBWM	GRN	GBF	GBR
09002	§	GBWM	GRN	GBF	GBR
09009	§	GBWM	GRN	GBF	GBR

± Working at Boulby Potash
§ Working at Barton Dock, Trafford Park

Class 20

Vehicle Length: 46ft 9¼in (14.26m)
Height: 12ft 7⅝in (3.84m)
Width: 8ft 9in (2.66m)
Engine: English Electric 8SVT Mk2
Horsepower: 1,000hp (745kW)
Electrical Equipment: English Electric

Number		Depot	Pool	Livery	Owner	Operator
20142		PG	GBEE	SPL	PRI	GBR
20189		PG	GBEE	SPL	201	GBR
20227		PG	GBEE	SPL	PRI	GBR
20901	(20101)	PG	GBEE	GBN	HNR	GBR
20905	(20225)	PG	GBEE	GBN	HNR	GBR

Left: *Five privately owned Class 20s are operating under the GBRf safety case and thus work in one of its pools to fulfill a contract to move new London Underground 'S' stock between Bombardier Derby Works and the Old Dalby Test Track and between Derby Works and the LUL network. The locos operate in pairs at either end of the LU stock, which is flanked by modified bogie fuel tankers acting as coupling adaptors. Two locos sport GBRf livery. No. 20901 in GBRf livery is shown; this loco is owned by the Harry Needle Railroad Co. The other loco here is No. 20107, which is privately owned.* **Antony Christie**

Class 66/7

Vehicle Length: 70ft 0½in (21.34m)
Height: 12ft 10in (3.91m)
Width: 8ft 8¼in (2.65m)
Engine: EMD 12N-710G3B-EC
Horsepower: 3,300hp (2,462kW)
Electrical Equipment: EMD

Number	Depot	Pool	Livery	Owner	Operator	Name/Notes
66701	PG	GBRT	GBR	EVL	GBR	
66702	PG	GBRT	GBR	EVL	GBR	*Blue Lightning*
66703	PG	GBCM	GBR	EVL	GBR	*Doncaster PSB 1981 - 2002*
66704	PG	GBCM	GBR	EVL	GBR	*Colchester Power Signalbox*
66705	PG	GBCM	GBR	EVL	GBR	*Golden Jubilee*
66706	PG	GBCM	GBR	EVL	GBR	*Nene Valley*
66707	PG	GBCM	GBR	EVL	GBR	*Sir Sam Fay / Great Central Railway*
66708	PG	GBRT	GBR	EVL	GBR	*Jayne*
66709	PG	GBRT	MSC	EVL	GBR	*Sorrento*
66710	PG	GBCM	GBR	EVL	GBR	*Phil Packer*
66711	PG	GBCM	GBR	EVL	GBR	

66712	PG	GBCM	GBR	EVL	GBR	*Peterborough Power Signalbox*
66713	PG	GBCM	GBR	EVL	GBR	*Forest City*
66714	PG	GBCM	GBR	EVL	GBR	*Cromer Lifeboat*
66715	PG	GBCM	GBR	EVL	GBR	*Valour*
66716	PG	GBCM	GBN	EVL	GBR	*Locomotive & Carriage Institution Centenary 1911-2011*
66717	PG	GBCM	GBN	EVL	GBR	*Good Old Boy*
66718	PG	GBCM	SPL	EVL	GBR	*Sir Peter Hendy CBE*
66719	PG	GBCM	GBM	EVL	GBR	*Metro-Land*
66720	PG	GBCM	SPL	EVL	GBR	
66721	PG	GBCM	SPL	EVL	GBR	*Harry Beck*
66722	PG	GBCM	GBM	EVL	GBR	*Sir Edward Watkin*
66723	PG	GBSD	GBF	EVL	GBR	*Chinook*
66724	PG	GBSD	GBF	EVL	GBR	*Drax Power Station*
66725	PG	GBSD	GBF	EVL	GBR	*Sunderland*
66726	PG	GBCM	GBF	EVL	GBR	*Sheffield Wednesday*
66727	PG	GBSD	GBF	EVL	GBR	*Andrew Scott CBE*
66728	PG	GBMU	GBN	PTR	GBR	*Institution of Railway Operators*
66729	PG	GBMU	GBN	PTR	GBR	*Derby County*
66730	PG	GBMU	GBF	PTR	GBR	*Whitemoor*
66731	PG	GBMU	GBN	PTR	GBR	*interhubGB*
66732	PG	GBMU	GBN	PTR	GBR	*GBRf The First Decade 1999-2009 John Smith - MD*
66733‡ (66401)	PG	GBFM	BLU	PTR	GBR	

Right: *GBRf has operated Class 66s for many years, and has always had a job to maintain a fleet size suitable to reflect the business of the company, frequently having to hire in other operators' motive power. In 2012 three off-lease European Class 66s were obtained, which were modified for UK use, and in 2013 two further European '66' were secured via Beacon Rail. The three locos obtained in 2012 are now numbered 66747-66749 and finished in all-over grey livery, with an international data panel on the driver's cab side. These three locos were at the end of 2013 operated on North East to Yorkshire coal and biomass flows. No. 66748 is illustrated.* **Antony Christie**

66735‡ (66403)	PG	GBFM	GBN	PTR	GBR	
66736‡ (66404)	PG	GBFM	GBN	PTR	GBR	*Wolverhampton Wanderers*
66737‡ (66405)	PG	GBFM	GBN	PTR	GBR	*Lesia*
66738 (66578)	PG	GBCM	GBN	GBR	GBR	
66739 (66579)	PG	GBCM	GBN	GBR	GBR	*Bluebell Railway*
66740 (66580)	PG	GBCM	GBN	GBR	GBR	
66741 (66581)	PG	GBCM	GBN	GBR	GBR	
66742 (66406, 66841)	PG	GBRT	GBN	PTR	GBR	*Port of Immingham Centenary 1912 - 2012*
66743 (66407, 66842)	PG	GBRT	GBN	PTR	GBR	
66744 (66408, 66843)	PG	GBRT	GBN	PTR	GBR	*Crossrail*
66745 (66409, 66844)	PG	GBRT	GBN	PTR	GBR	*Modern Railways - The First 50 years*
66746 (66410, 66845)	PG	GBRT	GBN	PTR	GBR	
66747	PG	GBNF	GRY		GBR	Former EMD 20078968-004)
66748	PG	GBNF	GRY		GBR	Former EMD 20078968-006
66749	PG	GBNF	GRY		GBR	Former EMD 20078968-007
66750	PG	GBNF	?	BEA	GBR	Being converted from EMD 20038513-001
66751	PG	GBDR	?	BEA	GBR	Being converted from EMD 20038513-004
66752	PG	GB??	GBN	GBR	GBR	On order for delivery in 2014
66753	PG	GB??	GBN	GBR	GBR	On order for delivery in 2014
66754	PG	GB??	GBN	GBR	GBR	On order for delivery in 2014

Europorte – GBRf

66755	PG	GB??	GBN	GBR	GBR	On order for delivery in 2014
66756	PG	GB??	GBN	GBR	GBR	On order for delivery in 2014
66757	PG	GB??	GBN	GBR	GBR	On order for delivery in 2014
66758	PG	GB??	GBN	GBR	GBR	On order for delivery in 2014
66759	PG	GB??	GBN	GBR	GBR	On order for delivery in 2014

‡ Fitted with RETB equipment

■ A further 15 Class 66s have been order from EMD but no operator has yet been specified, GBRf might become the operator of at least some of these.

Class 73

Vehicle Length: 53ft 8in (16.35m)
Height: 12ft 5 5/16in (3.79m)
Width: 8ft 8in (2.64m)
Power: 750V dc third rail or English Electric 6K
Horsepower: electric - 1,600hp (1,193kW)
Horsepower: diesel - 600hp (447kW)
Electrical Equipment: English Electric

Number		Depot	Pool	Livery	Owner	Operator	Name
73109		SE	GBED	BLU	GBR	GBR	
73119		SE	GBED	BLU	GBR	GBR	
73136		SE	GBED	GBU	GBR	GBR	
73141		SE	GBED	GBU	GBR	GBR	*Charlotte*
73204§	(73125)	SE	GBBR	GBR	GBR	GBR	*Janice*
73205	(73124)	SE	GBED	INT	GBR	GBR	*Jeanette*
73206§	(73123)	SE	GBED	GBR	GBR	GBR	*Lisa*
73207	(73122)	SE	GBED	BLL	GBR	GBR	
73208	(73121)	SE	GBED	BLU	GBR	GBR	
73209§	(73120)	SE	GBBR	GBR	GBR	GBR	*Alison*
73212	(73102)	SE	GBED	GBU	GBR	GBR	*Fiona*
73213	(73112)	SE	GBED	GBU	GBR	GBR	*Rhodalyn*

§ To be trial-fitted with new-design MTU R43 4000 V8 power unit set to deliver 1,500hp. Five locos are to be converted by Wabtec (Brush Traction) and renumbered in the series 73901 - 73905. The locos *should* be Nos. 73204/205/206/207/209

Left: *The former Southern Region electro-diesel locos still feature in the GBRf roster, with 11 locos owned by the operator. Based at St Leonards (Hastings), the versatile locos operate over a wide area of third rail electrified and non-electrified routes. A major re-engineering contract is currently being undertaken by Brush, which will see new MTU power units installed and upgraded electrical equipment. No. 73212* Fiona *is seen in full GBRf livery at Eastleigh.* **Brian Garrett**

Class 92

Vehicle Length: 70ft 1in (21.34m)
Height: 13ft 0in (3.95m)
Width: 8ft 8in (2.66m)
Power Collection: 25kV ac overhead / 750V dc third rail
Horsepower: ac - 6,700hp (5,000kW) / dc 5,360hp (4,000kW)
Electrical Equipment: Brush

Number	Depot	Pool	Livery	Owner	Operator	Name
92006(S)	DM	PTXX	SNF	GBR	-	*Louis Armand*
92010(S)	CO	PTXX	EU2	GBR	-	*Moliere*
92014(S)	CE	PTXX	SNF	GBR	-	*Emile Zola*
92018(S)	DM	PTXX	SNF	GBR	-	*Stendhal*
92020(S)	DM	PTXX	EU2	GBR	-	*Milton*
92021(S)	CO	PTXX	EU2	GBR	-	*Purcell*
92023(S)	CE	PTXX	EU2	GBR	-	*Ravel*
92028	CO	GBET	EU2	GBR	GBR	*Saint Saens*
92032	CO	GBET	GBN	GBR	GBR	*I Mech E Railway Division*
92033(S)	DM	PTXX	SNF	GBR	-	*Berlioz*
92038(S)	CE	GBET	EU2	GBR	-	*Voltaire*
92040(S)	CO	PTXX	EU2	GBR	-	*Goethe*
92043	CO	GBET	EU2	GBR	GBR	*Debussy*
92044	CO	GBET	EU2	GBR	GBR	*Couperin*
92045(S)	Brush	PTXX	EU2	GBR	-	*Chaucer*
92046(S)	Brush	PTXX	EU2	GBR	-	*Sweelinck*

Above: *After GBRf was taken over by Europorte, Class 92s were quickly added to the GBRf roster with 16 locos owned by the group, but only a handful are operational. No. 92043 is seen with a container train passing Rugeley Trent Valley.* **Antony Christie**

Coaching Stock

Mk1	*Height: 12ft 9½in (3.89m)*
Vehicle Length: 64ft 6in (19.65m)	*Width: 9ft 3in (2.81m)*

Barrier Vans

AW51

Number	*Depot*	*Livery*	*Owner*
6376 (ADB975973, 1021)	**PG**	**BLU**	**PTR**
6377 (ADB975975, 1042)	**PG**	**BLU**	**PTR**
6378 (ADB975971, 1054)	**PG**	**BLU**	**PTR**
6379 (ADB975972, 1039)	**PG**	**BLU**	**PTR**

Class Di 8

Vehicle Length: 17.38m	*Engine: Caterpillar 3516 DITA*
Height: 4.01m	*Horsepower: 2,100hp (1,566kW)*
Width: 2.95m	*Electrical Equipment: Siemens*

GBRf have purchased 12 former Cargo-Net, Norway, Class Di 8 locos for use within the SSI Lackenby Steelworks in Redcar. The 2,100hp (1,566kW) locos were built in 1996-97 by Mak in Kiel, Germany, as an order for 20 locos. In the UK the fleet, classified by the UIC as 308, will be painted in a joint GBRf/SSI livery.

8.701
8.702
8.703
8.704
8.708
8.711
8.712
8.716
8.717
8.718
8.719
8.720

Industrial 0-6-0DH

DH50-1 Works No. TH278V - 0-6-0DH 50-ton design, built 1978, fitted with a Cummins engine
DH50-2 Works No. TH246V - 0-6-0DH 50-ton design, built 1973

The above two industrial locos are operated by GBRf at the Celsa steel plant in Cardiff.

Right: *Now sporting standard GBRf blue and orange livery, Celsa steel works-operated diesel-hydraulic 0-6-0 shunter No. DH50-1, a product of Thomas Hill, is seen in the yard of the complex with some of its engine compartment doors open.*
Antony Christie

Freightliner

Address: ✉ 3rd Floor, The Podium, 1 Eversholt Street, London, NW1 2FL
pressoffice@freightliner.co.uk
✆ 0207 200 3900
ⓘ www.freightliner.com

Chief Executive: Peter Maybury
Managing Director Intermodal: Adam Cunliffe
Managing Director Heavy Haul: Paul Smart
Depots: Freightliner Diesels (FD), Freightliner Electrics (FE), Freightliner Shunters (FS), Ipswich* (IP), Leeds Midland Road (LD), Southampton Maritime (SZ)
* Stabling point
Parent Company: Arcapita

Class 08/0

Vehicle Length: 29ft 3in (8.91m)
Height: 12ft 8⅝in (3.87m)
Width: 8ft 6in (2.59m)
Engine: English Electric 6K
Horsepower: 400hp (298kW)
Electrical Equipment: English Electric

Number	Depot	Pool	Livery	Owner	Operator
08077(S)	FS/LH	DHLT	FLR	FLR	FLR
08393**	LH				FLR
08530(S)	LH	DFLS	FLR	PTR	FLR
08531	TL	DFLS	FLR	PTR	FLR
08575	SZ	DHLT	FLR	PTR	FLR
08585	FS	DFLS	FLR	PTR	FLR
08624	LH	DFLS	BLU	PTR	FLR
08691 ¤	SZ	DHLT	FLR	FLR	FLR
08785	SZ	DFLS	FLR	PTR	FLR
08891	FD	DFLS	FLR	PTR	FLR

**08393 sold to L H Group Services
¤ 08691 at L H Group Services

Names applied

08585	*Vicky*
08691	*Terri*

Left: *Most shunting work at Freightliner terminals is performed by train locos, but a handful of Class 08s are used at the larger terminals, such as Southampton and Leeds. No. 08575 is seen at Southampton Maritime Terminal with some of its side equipment boxes open.* **Norman E. Preedy**

Class 47/4

Vehicle Length: 63ft 6in (19.35m)
Height: 12ft 10⅜in (3.91m)
Width: 9ft 2in (2.79m)
Electric Train Heat fitted
Engine: Sulzer 12LDA28C
Horsepower: 2,580hp (1,922kW)
Electrical Equipment: Brush

Number		Depot	Pool	Livery	Owner	Operator
47811	(47656)	FD	DFLH	GRN	FLR	FLR (pilot)
47816(S)	(47661)	FD	DFLH	GRN	FLR	-
47830(S)	(47649)	BH	DFLH	GRN	FLR	-

Class 66/4

Vehicle Length: 70ft 0½in (21.34m)
Height: 12ft 10in (3.91m)
Width: 8ft 8¼in (2.65m)
Engine: EMD 12N-710G3B-EC
Horsepower: 3,300hp (2,462kW)
Electrical Equipment: EMD

Number	Depot	Pool	Livery	Owner	Operator	Name
66411	*Exported, working in Poland for Freightliner Poland as 66013FPL*					
66412	*Exported, working in Poland for Freightliner Poland as 66015FPL*					
66413 (S)	LD	DFHG	DRC	CBR	-	

66414	LD	DFIN	TES	HAL	FLT
66415	LD	DFHG	DRC	HAL	FLT
66416	LD	DFIN	DRC	HAL	FLT
66417 *Exported, working in Poland for Freightliner Poland as 66014FPL*					
66418	LD	DFIN	DRC	HAL	FLT
66419	LD	DFHG	DRC	HAL	FLT
66420	LD	DFIN	DRC	HAL	FLT

Class 66/5

Vehicle Length: 70ft 0½in (21.34m)
Height: 12ft 10in (3.91m)
Width: 8ft 8¼in (2.65m)
Engine: EMD 12N-710G3B-EC
Horsepower: 3,300hp (2,462kW)
Electrical Equipment: EMD

Number	*Depot*	*Pool*	*Livery*	*Owner*	*Operator*	*Name*
66501	LD	DFGM	FLR	PTR	FLR	*Japan 2001*
66502	LD	DFGM	FLR	PTR	FLR	*Basford Hall Centenary 2001*
66503	LD	DFGM	FLR	PTR	FLR	*The Railway Magazine*
66504	LD	DFGM	FLP	PTR	FLR	
66505	LD	DFRT	FLR	PTR	FLR	
66506	LD	DFHH	FLR	EVL	FLR	*Crewe Regeneration*
66507	LD	DFHH	FLR	EVL	FLR	
66508	LD	DFRT	FLR	EVL	FLR	
66509	LD	DFHH	FLR	EVL	FLR	
66510	LD	DFRT	FLR	EVL	FLR	
66511	LD	DFRT	FLR	EVL	FLR	
66512	LD	DFHH	FLR	EVL	FLR	
66513	LD	DFHH	FLR	EVL	FLR	
66514	LD	DFRT	FLR	EVL	FLR	
66515	LD	DFGM	FLR	EVL	FLR	
66516	LD	DFGM	FLR	EVL	FLR	
66517	LD	DFGM	FLR	EVL	FLR	
66518	LD	DFRT	FLR	EVL	FLR	
66519	LD	DFHH	FLR	EVL	FLR	
66520	LD	DFRT	FLR	EVL	FLR	
66522	LD	DFRT	FLR	EVL	FLR	*east london express*
66523	LD	DFRT	FLR	EVL	FLR	
66524	LD	DFHH	FLR	EVL	FLR	
66525	LD	DFHH	FLR	EVL	FLR	
66526	LD	DFHH	FLR	PTR	FLR	*Driver Steve Dunn (George)*
66527	LD	DFHH	FLR	EVL	FLR	*Don Raider*
66528	LD	DFHH	FLR	PTR	FLR	
66529	LD	DFHH	FLR	PTR	FLR	
66530	LD	DFGM	FLR	PTR	FLR	
66531	LD	DFHH	FLR	PTR	FLR	
66532	LD	DFGM	FLR	PTR	FLR	*P&O Nedlloyd Atlas*
66533	LD	DFGM	FLR	PTR	FLR	*Hanjin Express / Senator Express*
66534	LD	DFGM	FLR	PTR	FLR	*OOCL Express*
66535	LD	DFHH	FLR	PTR	FLR	
66536	LD	DFHH	FLR	PTR	FLR	
66537	LD	DFGM	FLR	PTR	FLR	
66538	LD	DFIM	FLR	EVL	FLR	
66539	LD	DFHH	FLR	EVL	FLR	
66540	LD	DFIM	FLR	EVL	FLR	*Ruby*
66541	LD	DFIM	FLR	EVL	FLR	
66542	LD	DFIM	FLR	EVL	FLR	
66543	LD	DFIM	FLR	EVL	FLR	
66544	LD	DFHG	FLR	PTR	FLR	
66545	LD	DFHG	FLR	PTR	FLR	
66546	LD	DFHG	FLR	PTR	FLR	
66547	LD	DFHG	FLR	PTR	FLR	
66548	LD	DFHG	FLR	PTR	FLR	
66549	LD	DFHG	FLR	PTR	FLR	
66550	LD	DFHG	FLR	PTR	FLR	
66551	LD	DFHG	FLR	PTR	FLR	
66552	LD	DFHG	FLR	PTR	FLR	*Maltby Raider*
66553	LD	DFHG	FLR	PTR	FLR	

66554	LD	DFHG	FLR	EVL	FLR	
66555	LD	DFHG	FLR	EVL	FLR	
66556	LD	DFHG	FLR	EVL	FLR	
66557	LD	DFHG	FLR	EVL	FLR	
66558	LD	DFIM	FLR	EVL	FLR	
66559	LD	DFIM	FLR	EVL	FLR	
66560	LD	DFHG	FLR	EVL	FLR	
66561	LD	DFHG	FLR	EVL	FLR	
66562	LD	DFHG	FLR	EVL	FLR	
66563	LD	DFHG	FLR	EVL	FLR	
66564	LD	DFIM	FLR	EVL	FLR	
66565	LD	DFIM	FLR	EVL	FLR	
66566	LD	DFIM	FLR	EVL	FLR	
66567	LD	DFIM	FLR	EVL	FLR	
66568	LD	DFIM	FLR	EVL	FLR	
66569	LD	DFIM	FLR	EVL	FLR	
66570	LD	DFIM	FLR	EVL	FLR	
66571	LD	DFIM	FLR	EVL	FLR	
66572	LD	DFIM	FLR	EVL	FLR	
66582	*Exported, working in Poland for Freightliner Poland as 66009FPL*					
66583	*Exported, working in Poland for Freightliner Poland as 66010FPL*					
66584	*Exported, working in Poland for Freightliner Poland as 66011FPL*					
66585	LD	DFHG	FLR	HAL	FLR	*The Drax Flyer*
66586	*Exported, working in Poland for Freightliner Poland as 66008FPL*					
66587	LD	DFFT	FLR	HAL	FLR	
66588	LD	DFIN	FLR	HAL	FLR	
66589	LD	DFIN	FLR	HAL	FLR	
66590	LD	DFIN	FLR	HAL	FLR	
66591	LD	DFIN	FLR	MAG	FLR	
66592	LD	DFIN	FLR	MAG	FLR	*Johnson Stevens Agencies*
66593	LD	DFIN	FLR	MAG	FLR	*3MG Mersey Multimodal Gateway*
66594	LD	DFIN	FLR	MAG	FLR	*NYK Spirit of Kyoto*
66595	LD	DFHG	FLR	BEA	FLR	
66596	LD	DFHG	FLR	BEA	FLR	
66597	LD	DFHG	FLR	BEA	FLR	*Viridor*
66598	LD	DFHG	FLR	BEA	FLR	
66599	LD	DFHG	FLR	BEA	FLR	

Between its Heavy Haul and Intermodal businesses Freightliner operates a fleet of 85 Class 66/5s, all officially based at Leeds Midland Road. A further four are based in Poland. No. 66517 approaches Kensington Olympia with a container train bound for Grain on 1 May 2013. **CJM**

Class 66/6

Number	Depot	Pool	Livery	Owner	Operator	Name
66601	LD	DFHH	FLR	PTR	FLR	*The Hope Valley*
66602	LD	DFHH	FLR	PTR	FLR	
66603	LD	DFHH	FLR	PTR	FLR	
66604	LD	DFHH	FLR	PTR	FLR	
66605	LD	DFHH	FLR	PTR	FLR	
66606	LD	DFHH	FLR	PTR	FLR	
66607	LD	DFHG	FLR	PTR	FLR	
66608	*Exported, working in Poland for Freightliner Poland as 66603FPL*					
66609	*Exported, working in Poland for Freightliner Poland as 66605FPL*					
66610	LD	DFHG	FLR	PTR	FLR	
66611	*Exported, working in Poland for Freightliner Poland as 66604FPL*					
66612	*Exported, working in Poland for Freightliner Poland as 66606FPL*					
66613	LD	DFHG	FLR	PTR	FLR	
66614	LD	DFHG	FLR	PTR	FLR	
66615	LD	DFHG	FLR	PTR	FLR	
66616	LD	DFHG	FLR	PTR	FLR	
66617	LD	DFHG	FLR	PTR	FLR	
66618	LD	DFHG	FLR	PTR	FLR	*Railways Illustrated Annual Photographic Awards - Alan Barnes*
66619	LD	DFHG	FLR	PTR	FLR	*Derek W. Johnson MBE*
66620	LD	DFHG	FLR	PTR	FLR	
66621	LD	DFHG	FLR	PTR	FLR	
66622	LD	DFHG	FLR	PTR	FLR	
66623	LD	DFHG	AIN	EVL	FLR	*Bill Bolsover*
66624	*Exported, working in Poland for Freightliner Poland as 66602FPL*					
66625	*Exported, working in Poland for Freightliner Poland as 66601FPL*					

Above: *Originally 25 increased-adhesion higher-output Class 66/6s were built for use by the Freightliner Heavy Haul business. Six of this batch now operate in Poland for Freightliner Poland and are unlikely to return to the UK. No. 66617 is seen stabled at Cardiff with its cooler group end nearest the camera.* **CJM**

Class 66/9

Number	Depot	Pool	Livery	Owner	Operator	Name
66951	LD	DFHG	FLR	EVL	FLR	
66952	LD	DFHG	FLR	EVL	FLR	
66953	LD	DFHG	FLR	BEA	FLR	
66954	LD	DFIN	FLR	BEA	FLR	
66955	LD	DFIN	FLR	BEA	FLR	
66956	LD	DFHH	FLR	BEA	FLR	
66957	LD	DFIN	FLR	BEA	FLR	*Stephenson Locomotive Society 1909-2009*

Freightliner

Class 70 - PH37ACmi

Vehicle Length: 71ft 2½in (21.71m)
Height: 12ft 10in (3.91m)
Width: 8ft 8in (2.64m)
Engine: GE V16-cyliner PowerHaul 616
Horsepower: 3,700hp (2,750kW)
Electrical Equipment: General Electric

Number	Depot	Pool	Livery	Owner	Operator	Name
70001	LD	DFGI	FLP	MAG	FLR	*PowerHaul*
70002	LD	DFGH	FLP	MAG	FLR	
70003	LD	DFGH	FLP	MAG	FLR	
70004	LD	DFGH	FLP	MAG	FLR	*The Coal Industry Society*
70005	LD	DFGH	FLP	MAG	FLR	
70006	LD	DFGH	FLP	MAG	FLR	
70007	LD	DFGI	FLP	MAG	FLR	
70008	LD	DFGI	FLP	MAG	FLR	
70009	LD	DFGI	FLP	MAG	FLR	
70010	LD	DFGH	FLP	MAG	FLR	
70011	LD	DFGH	FLP	MAG	FLR	
70013	LD	DFGH	FLP	MAG	FLR	
70014	LD	DFGH	FLP	MAG	FLR	
70015	LD	DFGI	FLP	MAG	FLR	
70016	LD	DFGI	FLP	MAG	FLR	
70017	LD	DFGI	FLP	MAG	FLR	
70018	LD	DFGI	FLP	MAG	FLR	
70019	LD	DFGI	FLP	MAG	FLR	
70020	LD	DFGI	FLP	MAG	FLR	

Above: *The fleet of 19 Class 70s built by General Electric often seems to be in trouble with major failures and problems, and in early 2014 it seems unlikely that any further will be built for Freightliner. On 6 June 2013 No. 70008 passes Newport with the daily Wentloog (Cardiff) to Southampton container service. On paper the locos are allocated to Leeds Midland Road depot.* **CJM**

■ Originally 30 locomotives were ordered in 2007 for delivery in 2009-10. Ninteen locos were delivered by February 2012; no further deliveries are due at this stage.

Class 86/5 & 86/6

Vehicle Length: 58ft 6in (17.83m)
Height: 13ft 0⅝in (3.97m)
Width: 8ft 8¼in (2.64m)
Power Collection: 25kV ac overhead
Horsepower: 5,900hp (4,400kW)
Electrical Equipment: GEC

Number		Depot	Pool	Livery	Owner	Operator
86501	(86608/86408)	FE	DFGC	FLR	FLR	FLR
86604	(86404)	FE	DFNC	FLR	FLR	FLR
86605	(86405)	FE	DFNC	FLR	FLR	FLR
86607	(86407)	FE	DFNC	FLR	FLR	FLR
86609	(86409)	FE	DFNC	FLR	PTR	FLR

86610	**(86410)**	**FE**	**DFNC**	**FLR**	**PTR**	**FLR**
86612	**(86412)**	**FE**	**DFNC**	**FLR**	**PTR**	**FLR**
86613	**(86413)**	**FE**	**DFNC**	**FLR**	**PTR**	**FLR**
86614	**(86414)**	**FE**	**DHNC**	**FLR**	**PTR**	**FLR**
86622	**(86422)**	**FE**	**DFNC**	**FLP**	**PTR**	**FLR**
86627	**(86427)**	**FE**	**DFNC**	**FLR**	**PTR**	**FLR**
86628	**(86428)**	**FE**	**DFNC**	**FLR**	**PTR**	**FLR**
86632	**(86432)**	**FE**	**DFNC**	**FLR**	**PTR**	**FLR**
86637	**(86437)**	**FE**	**DFNC**	**FLP**	**PTR**	**FLR**
86638	**(86438)**	**FE**	**DFNC**	**FLR**	**PTR**	**FLR**
86639	**(86439)**	**FE**	**DFNC**	**FLR**	**PTR**	**FLR**

86247 at LNWR Crewe in pool DHLT

Right: *Freightliner Intermodal operates a fleet of 16 Class 86 ac electric locos based at Crewe and used on Intermodal services that operate under the wires. The locos frequently operate in multiple and are fitted with nose-mounted TDM multiple control jumper connections. Nos. 86638 and 86607 are seen passing Lichfield on the West Coast Main Line on 11 July 2013 powering train 4M54, the 10.10 Tilbury to Crewe Basford Hall.* **Antony Christie**

Class 90

Vehicle Length: 61ft 6in (18.74m)
Height: 13ft 0¼in (3.96m)
Width: 9ft 0in (2.74m)
Power Collection: 25kV ac overhead
Horsepower: 7,860hp (5,860kW)
Electrical Equipment: GEC

Number	*Depot*	*Pool*	*Livery*	*Owner*	*Operator*
90016	**CP**	**DFLC**	**FLR**	**PTR**	**FLR**
90041	**CP**	**DFLC**	**FLR**	**PTR**	**FLR**
90042	**CP**	**DFLC**	**FLY**	**PTR**	**FLR**
90043	**CP**	**DFLC**	**FLY**	**PTR**	**FLR**
90044	**CP**	**DFLC**	**FLY**	**PTR**	**FLR**
90045	**CP**	**DFLC**	**FLP**	**PTR**	**FLR**
90046	**CP**	**DFLC**	**FLR**	**PTR**	**FLR**
90047	**CP**	**DFLC**	**FLY**	**PTR**	**FLR**
90048	**CP**	**DFLC**	**FLR**	**PTR**	**FLR**
90049	**CP**	**DFLC**	**FLP**	**PTR**	**FLR**

Name applied

90043 ***Freightliner Coatbridge***

Above: *Ten high-output Class 90s are operated by Freightliner Intermodal, again based at Crewe, and are usually rostered to the longer-distance heavier trains, frequently working through services from the North West to Ipswich with services to the Port of Felixstowe. No. 90049 is seen heading south at South Kenton on 3 July 2013.* **CJM**

Mendip Rail

Address: ✉ Torr Works, East Cranmore, Shepton Mallet, Somerset, BA4 5SQ
info@mendip-rail.co.uk ✆ 01749 880672 ⓘ www.mendip-rail.co.uk

Managing Director: Alan Taylor
Depots: Merehead (MD), Whatley (WH)
Parent Company: Aggregate Industries and Hanson

Class 08

Vehicle Length: 29ft 3in (8.91m)
Height: 12ft 8⅝in (3.87m)
Width: 8ft 6in (2.59m)
Engine: English Electric 6K
Horsepower: 400hp (298kW)
Electrical Equipment: English Electric

Number	Depot	Pool	Livery	Owner	Operator
08643	MD	MBDL	GRN	FOS	MRL
08650	MD	MBDL	MRL	FOS	MRL
08652	WH	MBDL	HAN	HAN	MRL
08731	MD	MBDL	BLU	FOS	MRL
08947	WH	MBDL	BLU	FOS	MRL

Class 59/0 & 59/1

Vehicle Length: 70ft 0½in (21.34m)
Height: 12ft 10in (3.91m)
Width: 8ft 8¼in (2.65m)
Engine: EMD 16-645 E3C
Horsepower: 3,000hp (2,462kW)
Electrical Equipment: EMD

Number	Depot	Pool	Livery	Owner	Operator	Name
59001	MD	XYPO	AGI	FOS	MRL	*Yeoman Endeavour*
59002	MD	XYPO	FOS	FOS	MRL	*Alan J Day*
59003 ■	-	-	HHP	HHP	HHP	*Yeoman Highlander*
59004	MD	XYPO	FOS	FOS	MRL	*Paul A Hammond*
59005	MD	XYPO	AGI	FOS	MRL	*Kenneth J Painter*
59101	MD	XYPA	HAN	HAN	MRL	*Village of Whatley*
59102	MD	XYPA	HAN	HAN	MRL	*Village of Chantry*
59103	MD	XYPA	HAN	HAN	MRL	*Village of Mells*
59104	MD	XYPA	HAN	HAN	MRL	*Village of Great Elm*

Below: *The eight Mendip Rail-operated Class 59s are maintained at Merehead and operate on heavy aggregate trains from Merehead and Whatley Quarries to Westbury and main distribution terminals such as Acton from where feeder services operate to smaller terminals. No. 59002 passes West Brompton on 1 May 2013 heading for Tolworth.* **CJM**

■ Loco No. 59003 *Yeoman Highlander*, originally used by Foster Yeoman in the UK, is now owned and operated by Heavy Haul Power International and based in Germany.

SW1001 'Switcher'

Vehicle Length: 40ft 6in (12.34m)
Height: 14ft 3in (4.34m)
Width: 10ft 0in (3.04m)
Engine: GM 8-645E
Horsepower: 1,000hp (746kW)
Electrical Equipment: EMD

Number	Depot	Pool	Livery	Owner	Operator	Name
44	MD	-	FOS	FOS	MRL	*Western Yeoman II*
120	WH	-	HAN	HAN	MRL	

Eurotunnel

Address (UK): ✉ The Channel Tunnel Group Ltd, Ashford Road, Folkestone, CT18 8XX
info@eurotunnel.com ✆ 01303 282222 ⓘ www.eurotunnel.com

Chairman & CEO: Jacques Gounon
Depot: Coquelles, France (CO)

Shuttle

All locomotives are allocated to the Eurotunnel Maintenance Facility in Coquelles, France, but can be stabled and receive light repair at Cheriton terminal in the UK.

Class 9/0

Vehicle Length: 72ft 2in (22m)
Height: 13ft 9in (4.20m)
Width: 9ft 9in (3.01m)
Power Collection: 25kV ac overhead
Horsepower: 7,720hp (5,760kW)
Electrical Equipment: Brush

Original loco order, many now rebuilt and upgraded to Class 9/8.

9005	*Jessye Norman*	9018	*Wilhelmena Fernandez*	9033	*Montserrat Caballé*
9007	*Dame Joan Sutherland*	9022	*Dame Janet Baker*	9036	*Alain Fondary*
9011	*José Van Dam*	9024	*Gotthard 1882*	9037	*Gabriel Bacquier*
9013	*Maria Callas*	9026	*Furkatunnel 1982*		
9015	*Lötschberg 1913*	9029	*Thomas Allen*		

Class 9/7

Vehicle Length: 72ft 2in (22m)
Height: 13ft 9in (4.20m)
Width: 9ft 9in (3.01m)
Power Collection: 25kV ac overhead
Horsepower: 9,387hp (7,000kW)
Electrical Equipment: Brush

9701	9704	9707	9713 (9103)	9716 (9106)	9719 (9109)	9722 (9112)
9702	9705	9711 (9101)	9714 (9104)	9717 (9107)	9720 (9110)	9723 (9113)
9703	9706	9712 (9102)	9715 (9105)	9718 (9108)	9721 (9111)	

Class 9/8

Rebuilt from Class 9/0 locos; 800 added to original running number on conversion.

Vehicle Length: 72ft 2in (22m)
Height: 13ft 9in (4.20m)
Width: 9ft 9in (3.01m)
Power Collection: 25kV ac overhead
Horsepower: 9,387hp (7,000kW)
Electrical Equipment: Brush

9801	*Lesley Garrett*	9814	*Lucia Popp*	9827	*Barbara Hendricks*
9802	*Stuart Burrows*	9816	*Willard White*	9828	*Dame Kiri Te Kanawa*
9803	*Benjamin Luxon*	9817(S)	*José Carreras*	9831	
9804	*Victoria de Los Angeles*	9819	*Maria Ewing*	9832	*Renata Tebaldi*
9806	*Régine Crespin*	9820	*Nicolai Ghiaurov*	9834	*Mirella Freni*
9808	*Elisabeth Soderstrom*	9821	*Teresa Berganza*	9835	*Nicolai Gedda*
9809	*François Pollet*	9823	*Dame Elisabeth Legge-Schwarzkopf*	9838	*Hildegard Behrens*
9810	*Jean-Philippe Courtis*			9840	
9812	*Luciano Pavarotti*	9825			

Below: *A fleet of 58 Tri-bo shuttle locos are based at Coquelles in France and operate all types of shuttle services for Eurotunnel through the Channel Tunnel between Coquelles (Calais) and Cheriton (Folkestone). Rebuilt Class 9/8 No. 9803, the original 9003, is seen at Coquelles.* **Antony Guppy**

MaK DE1004

Vehicle Length: 54ft 2in (16.50m)
Diesel Engine: MTU 12V396tc
Horsepower: 1,260hp (939.5kW)
Electrical Equipment: BBC

0001 (21901)	0003 (21903)	0005 (21905)	0007 (21907) [6457]
0002 (21902)	0004 (21904)	0006 (21906) [6456]	

Hunslet/Schöma

Diesel Engine: Deutz
Horsepower: 200hp (270kW)
Mechanical Equipment: Hunslet

0031	0033	0035	0037	0039	0041
0032	0034	0036	0038	0040	0042

Network Rail

Address: Kings Place, 90 York Way, London, N1 9AG
enquiries@networkrail.co.uk
Helpline: 08457 114141, Switchboard: 0203 356 9595
www.networkrail.co.uk

Chief Executive: Mark Carne **Director Operations:** Robin Gisby

Depots: Heaton (HT), Barrow Hill (BH), Derby (DF), Rugby (RU), Eastleigh (ZG)

Class 08

Vehicle Length: 29ft 3in (8.91m)
Height: 12ft 8⅝in (3.87m)
Width: 8ft 6in (2.59m)
Engine: English Electric 6K
Horsepower: 400hp (298kW)
Electrical Equipment: English Electric

Number	Depot	Pool	Livery	Owner	Operator
08417	**DF**	**QADD**	**NRL**	**NRL**	**NRL**
08956	**DF**	**QADD**	**BLU**	**NRL**	**NRL**

Class 31/1 & 31/4

Vehicle Length: 56ft 9in (17.29m)
Height: 12ft 7in (3.91m)
Width: 8ft 9in (2.65m)
31/4 Fitted with Electric Train Heat
Engine: English Electric 12SVT
Horsepower: 1,470hp (1,097kW)
Electrical Equipment: Brush

Number	Depot	Pool	Livery	Owner	Operator
31105	**DF**	**QADD**	**NRL**	**NRL**	**NRL**
31233	**DF**	**QADD**	**NRL**	**NRL**	**NRL**
31285	**DF**	**QADD**	**NRL**	**NRL**	**NRL**
31465*	**DF**	**QADD**	**NRL**	**NRL**	**NRL**

* Previously numbered 31565, 31213

Left: *Displaying standard Network Rail high-visibility yellow, Class 31/4 No. 31465 is seen from its No. 1 end at Didcot.* **John Wills**

Below: *The four Network Rail-owned Class 31s are based at the RTC in Derby and can be found operating throughout the National Network on the front or rear of track and infrastructure test trains. One of the Ultrasonic test formations led by a DBSO and powered by No. 31285 on the rear passes westwards through Dawlish.* **CJM**

Class 43

Vehicle Length: 58ft 5in (18.80m)
Height: 12ft 10in (3.90m)
Width: 8ft 11in (2.73m)
Engine: MTU 16V4000 R31R
Horsepower: 2,250hp (1,680kW)
Electrical Equipment: Brush

Number	*Depot*	*Pool*	*Livery*	*Owner*	*Operator*	*Name*
43013	**HT**	**QCAR**	**NRL**	**PTR**	**NRL**	
43014	**HT**	**QCAR**	**NRL**	**PTR**	**NRL**	
43062	**HT**	**QCAR**	**NRL**	**PTR**	**NRL**	***John Armitt***

Right: *The Network Rail-operated 'New Measurement Train' plays a very important part in making sure the track infrastructure is kept in first class condition, regularly traversing the main lines looking at track and overhead power supplies. Three Class 43 power cars are owned by Network Rail, allocated to Heaton depot, Newcastle. No. 43013, plus vehicles 977984, 975814, 977993, 977994, 975984 and, 43014 pass Dawlish on 23 August 2013.* **CJM**

Class 57/3

Vehicle Length: 63ft 6in (19.38m)
Height: 12ft 10⅛in (3.91m)
Width: 9ft 2in (2.79m)
Engine: EMD 645-12F3B
Horsepower: 2,750hp (2,051kW)
Electrical Equipment: Brush

Number	*Depot*	*Pool*	*Livery*	*Owner*	*Operator*	*Name*
57301 (47845)	**ZG**	**QADD**	**NRL**	**PBR**	**NRL**	
57303 (47705)	**ZG**	**QADD**	**NRL**	**PBR**	**NRL**	
57305 (47822)	**ZG**	**QADD**	**NRL**	**PBR**	**NRL**	
57306 (47814)	**ZG**	**QADD**	**NRL**	**PBR**	**NRL**	
57310 (47831)	**ZG**	**QADD**	**NRL**	**PBR**	**NRL**	
57312 (47330) (S)	**ZG**	**QADD**	**NRL**	**PBR**	**NRL**	***Peter Henderson***

57301, 57303 and 57306 fitted with Tightlock couplings, 57310 and 57312 fitted with modified Dellner couplings

Right: *Following the decision by Virgin Trains to rid itself of the Class 57/3 fleet, Network Rail took over six locos from Porterbrook Leasing and modified these for Network Rail use, as either 'Thunderbird' locos or to power RHTT and snow patrol trains. Alterations have also been made to the drop-head couplers with two now sporting Tightlock couplings to fasilitate compatibility with some modern EMUs. All six are based at Eastleigh and sport Network Rail yellow livery. No. 57310 is illustrated.* **Antony Christie**

Class 73/1

Vehicle Length: 53ft 8in (16.35m)
Height: 12ft 5$\frac{5}{16}$in (3.79m)
Width: 8ft 8in (2.64m)
Power: 750V dc third rail or English Electric 6K
Horsepower: electric - 1,600hp (1,193kW)
Horsepower: diesel - 600hp (447kW)
Electrical Equipment: English Electric

Number	*Depot*	*Pool*	*Livery*	*Owner*	*Operator*
73138	**DF**	**QADD**	**NRL**	**NRL**	**NRL**

Right: *At present Network Rail operates just one Class 73, but in the near future two heavily rebuilt Class 73/5s are scheduled to be released from RVEL Derby sporting new power equipment. Network Rail Class 73/1 No. 73138, showing its modified front end passes Clapham Junction.* **Nathan Williamson**

Network Rail

Class 86/9

Vehicle Length: 58ft 6in (17.83m)
Height: 13ft 0⅝in (3.97m)
Width: 8ft 8¼in (2.64m)
Power Collection: 25kV ac overhead
Horsepower: 2,950hp (2,200kW)
Electrical Equipment: GEC

Number		Depot	Pool	Livery	Owner	Operator	Name
86901	(86253)	ZA	QACL	NRL	NRL	NRL	*Chief Engineer*
86902	(86210)	ZA	QACL	NRL	NRL	NRL	*Rail Vehicle Engineering*

Class 97/3 & 37

Vehicle Length: 61ft 6in (18.74m)
Height: 13ft 0¼in (3.96m)
Width: 8ft 11⅝in (2.73m)
Engine: English Electric 12CSVT
Horsepower: 1,750hp (1,304kW)
Electrical Equipment: English Electric

Number		Depot	Pool	Livery	Owner	Operator	Name
37198		BH	MBDL	NRL	NRL	NRL	
97301	(37100)	ZA	QETS	NRL	NRL	NRL	
97302	(37170)	ZA	QETS	NRL	NRL	NRL	
97303	(37178)	ZA	QETS	NRL	NRL	NRL	
97304	(37217)	ZA	QETS	NRL	NRL	NRL	*John Tiley*

Network Rail operates a fleet of five Class 37s. Four are classified as Class 97/3, and one as a Class 37/0. The four Class 97/3s are allocated to Derby and operate test trains as required as well as taking part in the development work of ERTMS equipment on the Cambrian route in Wales. The locos are fitted with full ERTMS cab equipment. No. 97304 John Tiley *is seen stabled at Bristol Temple Meads.* **Nathan Williamson**

Class 313/1

Vehicle Length: (Driving) 64ft 11½in (20.75m)
(Inter) 65ft 4¼in (19.92m)
Height: 11ft 9in (3.58m)
Width: 9ft 3in (2.82m)
Horsepower: 880hp (656kW)
Seats (total/car): 202S, 66S/70S/66S

Great Northern Route - ERTMS development unit

Number	Formation DMSO+PTSO+BDMSO	Depot	Livery	Owner	Operator
313121	62549+71233+61613	HR	YEL	BEA	NRL

Class 950

Vehicle Length: 64ft 9¾in (19.74m)
Height: 12ft 4½in (3.77m)
Width: 9ft 3⅛in (2.82m)
Engine: 1 x NT855R5 of 285hp per vehicle
Horsepower: 570hp (425kW)
Seats (total/car): 124S, 59S/65S

Number	Formation	Depot	Livery	Owner	Operator	Note
950001	999600+999601	ZA	NRL	NRL	NRL	Track assessment train (Class 150 outline)

Right: *On the tail end of the Class 150/1 production programme at York, two specially adapted bodies were assembled for use by the then DM&EE to form a two-car track test train, One vehicle was basically a saloon vehicle, while the other was a full instrumentation coach. Now classified as Class 950, the set traverses the entire Network Rail system looking for track defects. With its instrumentation vehicle nearest the camera the set heads north through Dawlish.* **CJM**

De-Icing Cars

Vehicle Length: 66ft 4in (20.22m)
Height: 12ft 4in (3.75m)
Width: 9ft 2in (2.82m)
Horsepower: 500hp (370kW)
Seats (total/car): None

Number	Vehicle	Depot	Livery	Owner	Operator	Notes
489102	**68501 (977975)**	**TN**	**NRL**	**NRL**	**NRL**	De-icing vehicle modified from Class 489 DMBS
489105	**68504**	**TN**	**NRL**	**NRL**	**GBR**	De-icing vehicle modified from Class 489 DMBS
489106	68505	TN	NRL	NRL	GBR	De-icing vehicle modified from Class 489 DMBS

Hauled Stock

Royal Train

Mk2
Vehicle Length: 66ft 0in (20.11m)
Height: 12ft 9½in (3.89m)
Width: 9ft 3in (2.81m)

Mk 3
Vehicle Length: 75ft 0in (22.86m)
Height: 12ft 9in (3.88m)
Width: 8ft 11in (2.71m)

Number	Type	Depot	Livery	Operator	Use
2903 (11001)	**AT5G**	**ZN**	**ROY**	**NRL/DBS**	**HM The Queen's Saloon**
2904 (12001)	**AT5G**	**ZN**	**ROY**	**NRL/DBS**	**HRH The Duke of Edinburgh's Saloon**
2915 (10735)	**AT5G**	**ZN**	**ROY**	**NRL/DBS**	**Royal Household Sleeping Coach**
2916 (40512)	**AT5G**	**ZN**	**ROY**	**NRL/DBS**	**HRH The Prince of Wales's Dining Coach**
2917 (40514)	**AT5G**	**ZN**	**ROY**	**NRL/DBS**	**Kitchen Car and Royal Household Dining Coach**
2918 (40515)	**AT5G**	**ZN**	**ROY**	**NRL/DBS**	**Royal Household Coach**
2919 (40518)	**AT5G**	**ZN**	**ROY**	**NRL/DBS**	**Royal Household Coach**
2920 (17109)	**AT5B**	**ZN**	**ROY**	**NRL/DBS**	**Generator Coach and Household Sleeping Coach**
2921 (17107)	**AT5B**	**ZN**	**ROY**	**NRL/DBS**	**Brake, Coffin Carrier and Household Accommodation**
2922	**AT5G**	**ZN**	**ROY**	**NRL/DBS**	**HRH The Prince of Wales's Sleeping Coach**
2923	**AT5G**	**ZN**	**ROY**	**NRL/DBS**	**Royal Passenger Saloon**

Below: *Network Rail oversees the operation of the Royal Train, kept at Wolverton Works and made available to the Queen, Prince Philip or Prince Charles as required. Eleven Royal vehicles are registered and trains can be formed of anything from five to eight vehicles depending on requirement. DBS provide the traction and train crew for the train and maintains three Royal Class 67s for use as needed. Led by the Queens Diamond Jubilee-liveried No. 67026* Diamond Jubilee, *the Royal Train heads towards York at Colton Junction.* **Brian Garrett**

Network Rail

Hauled Stock

Number	Type	Depot	Livery	Operator	Use
1205 (6348)	AJIF/RFO	ZA	VIR	NRL	Out of use
1256 (3296)	AJIF/RFO	ZA	NRL	NRL	Special vehicle
5981	AC2F/TSO	ZA	NRL	NRL	Special vehicle
6260 (92116)	AX51/GEN	ZA	RTK	NRL/LUL	Generator (owned by DBS)
6261 (92988)	AX51/GEN	ZA	NRL	NRL	Generator (owned by DBS)
6262 (92928)	AX51/GEN	ZA	NRL	NRL	Generator (owned by DBS)
6263 (92961)	AX51/GEN	ZA	NRL	NRL	Generator (owned by DBS)
6264 (92923)	AX51/GEN	ZA	NRL	NRL	Generator (owned by DBS)
9481	AE2D/BSO	ZA	NRL	NRL	Radio Survey coach
9516	AE2D/BSO	ZA	NRL	NRL	Ultrasonic test car support
9523	AE2D/BSO	ZA	NRL	NRL	Ultrasonic test car support
9701 (9528)	AF2F/DBSO	ZA	NRL	NRL	Remote driving car (Mentor train)
9702 (9510)	AF2F/DBSO	ZA	NRL	NRL	Remote driving car
9703 (9517)	AF2F/DBSO	ZA	NRL	NRL	Remote driving car
9708 (9530)	AF2F/DBSO	ZA	NRL	NRL	Remote driving car (Structure Gauging)
9713	AF2F/DBSO	ZA	NRL	NRL	Remote driving car
9714 (9536)	AF2F/DBSO	ZA	NRL	NRL	Remote driving car
62384	MBS	ZA	NRL	NRL	Structure Gauging test car (SGT2)
72612 (6156)	Mk2f/TSO	ZA	NRL	NRL	Brake force runner
72616 (6007)	Mk2f/TSO	ZA	NRL	NRL	Brake force runner
72630 (6094)	Mk2f/TSO	ZA	NRL	NRL	Brake force runner
72631 (6096)	Mk2f/TSO	ZA	NRL	NRL	Brake force runner
72639 (6070)	Mk2f/TSO	ZA	NRL	NRL	Brake force runner
82111	MK3/DVT	ZA	NRL	NRL	Driving Van Trailer
82115	MK3/DVT	ZA	VIR	NRL	Driving Van Trailer
82124	MK3/DVT	ZA	NRL	NRL	Driving Van Trailer
82129	MK3/DVT	ZA	NRL	NRL	Driving Van Trailer
82145	MK3/DVT	ZA	NRL	NRL	Driving Van Trailer
92114 (81443)	Mk1/BG	ZA	NRL	NRL	Special vehicle
92939 (92039)	Mk1/BG	ZA	INT	NRL	Special vehicle
99666 (3250)	Mk2e/FO	ZA	NRL	NRL	Ultrasonic Test Train
971001 (94150)	Mk1/NKA	BS	NRL	NRL	Tool Van
971002 (94190)	Mk1/NKA	WT	NRL	NRL	Tool Van
971003 (94191)	Mk1/NKA	BS	NRL	NRL	Tool Van
971004 (94168)	Mk1/NKA	WK	NRL	NRL	Tool Van
975025 (60755)	6B Buffet	ZA	GRN	NRL	Control Inspection Saloon *Caroline*
975081 (35313)	Mk1/BSK	ZA	NRL	NRL	Structure Gauging Train
975091 (34615)	Mk1/BSK	ZA	NRL	NRL	Overhead line test coach *Mentor*
975280 (21263)	Mk1/BCK	ZA	NRL	NRL	Staff coach
975464 (35171)	Mk1/BSK	IS	NRL	NRL	Snowblower coach *Ptarmigan*
975486 (34100)	Mk1/BSK	IS	NRL	NRL	Snowblower coach *Polar Bear*
975814 (41000)	HST/TF	EC	NRL	NRL	NMT Conference coach
975984 (40000)	HST/TRUB	EC	NRL	NRL	NMT Lecture coach
977337 (9395)	Mk2/BSO	ZA	NRL	NRL	Track Recording - Staff coach
977868 (5846)	Mk2e/TSO	ZA	NRL	NRL	Radio Survey coach
977869 (5858)	Mk2e/TSO	ZA	NRL	NRL	Radio Survey coach
977969 (14112)	Mk2/BFK	ZA	NRL	NRL	Staff coach (former Royal Saloon 2906)
977974 (5854)	Mk2e/TSO	ZA	NRL	NRL	Laboratory coach (owned by Delta Rail)
977983 (3407)	Mk2f/FO	ZA	NRL	NRL	Hot Box Detection coach
977984 (40501)	HST/TRFK	EC	NRL	NRL	NMT Staff coach
977985 (6019)	Mk2f/TSO	ZA	NRL	NRL	Structure Gauging Train (SGT2)

Left: *Former Southern Region/Network SouthEast MBS No. 62384 from set 1296 (7396) is now one of the main vehicles of the Structure Gauging Train 2 (SGT2). The heavily modified vehicle, rebuilt at Derby, now sports NR yellow livery. The vehicle in ex-works condition with its former brake van at the near end is seen at Paignton.* **Antony Christie**

977986	(3189)	Mk2d/FO	ZA	NRL	NRL	Track Recording coach
977993	(44053)	HST/TGS	EC	NRL	NRL	NMT Overhead Line Test coach
977994	(44087)	HST/TGS	EC	NRL	NRL	NMT Recording coach
977995	(40719)	HST/TRFM	EC	NRL	NRL	NMT Generator coach
977996	(44062)	HST/TGS	EC	NRL	NRL	NMT Battery coach
977997	(72613)	Mk2f/TSO	ZA	NRL	NRL	Radio Survey Test Vehicle (originally TSO 6126)
999508		Saloon	ZA	NRL	NRL	Track Recording coach - UTU3
999550		Mk2	ZA	NRL	NRL	Track Recording coach (purpose-built)
999602	(62483)	Mk1/REP	ZA	NRL	SEC	Ultrasonic Test coach - UTU3
999605	(62482)	Mk1/REP	ZA	NRL	NRL	Ultrasonic Test coach - UTU2
999606	(62356)	Mk1/REP	ZA	NRL	NRL	Ultrasonic Test coach - UTU4

Snowploughs

Independent Drift Ploughs – ZZA

Number	*Allocation*
ADB965203	Tees
ADB965206	Doncaster
ADB965208	Inverness
ADB965209	Bristol Barton H
ADB965210	Tonbridge
ADB965211	March
ADB965217	Slateford
ADB965219	Mossend
ADB965223	Margam
ADB965224	Carlisle
ADB965230	Carlisle
ADB965231	Bristol Barton H
ADB965232	Peterborough
ADB965233	Peterborough
ADB965234	Carlisle
ADB965235	Margam
ADB965236	Tonbridge
ADB965237	March
ADB965240	Inverness
ADB965243	Slateford

Above: *Hopefully not having to be used very often, the fleet of 20 Independent Drift Ploughs is based at main depots throughout the country in pairs and can if needed operate at either end of one or two locomotives. Plough No. 965208 is illustrated at Inverness.* CJM

Beilhack Patrol Ploughs (ex-Class 40 bogies) – ZZA

Number	*Allocation*
ADB965576	Doncaster
ADB965577	Doncaster
ADB965578	Carlisle
ADB965579	Carlisle
ADB965580	Wigan
ADB965581	Wigan
ADB966098	Doncaster
ADB966099	Doncaster

Beilhack Snow Blowers – ZWA

Number	*Allocation*
ADB968500	Rutherglen
ADB968501	Rutherglen

Right: *If weather conditions dictate, two rotary snow blowers built by Beilhack are available to Network Rail; both are based at Rutherglen, but can be made available to operate at any location on the NR network. Snow blower No. 968500 is illustrated inside Inverness depot.* CJM

Network Rail

Track Machines (On-Track Plant)

Plasser & Theurer DTS-62-N – Dynamic Track Stabilliser – ZWA

DR72211	Balfour Beatty	DR72213	Balfour Beatty

Plasser & Theurer 09-16-CSM – Tamper/Liner – ZWA

DR73105(S)	Colas

Plasser & Theurer 09-32-RT – Tamper/Liner – ZWA

DR73108	*Tiger*	Colas

Plasser & Theurer 09-3X – Tamper/Liner – ZWA

DR73109		SB Rail	DR73110	*Peter White*	SB Rail

Plasser & Theurer 09-3X-D-RT – Tamper/Liner ZWA

DR73111	*Reading Panel 1965 - 2005*	Network Rail	DR73116		Network Rail
DR73113		Network Rail	DR73117		Network Rail
DR73114	*Ron Henderson*	Network Rail	DR73118		Network Rail
DR73115		Network Rail			

Left: *Network Rail-owned Plasser & Theurer 09-3X-D-RT tamper and lining machine No. DR73114* Ron Henderson *is seen on the East Coast Main Line near Abbots Ripton.* **Michael J. Collins**

Plasser & Theurer 07-32 – Duomatic Tamper/Liner – ZWA

DR73428	J H Russell	DR73434(S)	Balfour Beatty

Plasser & Theurer 08-16/90 – Tamper/Liner – ZWA

DR73502(S)	Balfour Beatty	DR73503 (S)	Balfour Beatty

Plasser & Theurer 08-32U RT – Plain Line Tamper – ZWA

DR73803	*Alexander Graham Bell*	SBRail

Plasser & Theurer 08-16U RT – Plain Line Tamper – ZWA

DR73804	*James Watt*	SBRail

Plasser & Theurer 08-16(32)U RT – Plain Line Tamper – ZWA

DR73805		Colas	DR73806 *Karine*	Colas

Plasser & Theurer 08-4x4/4S - RT – Switch/Crossing Tamper – ZWA

DR73904	*Thomas Telford*	SBRail	DR73908		Colas
DR73905	*Eddie King*	Colas	DR73909	*Saturn*	Colas
DR73906	*Panther*	Colas	DR73910	*Jupiter*	Colas
DR73907		Colas			

Left: *Painted in Colas Rail orange and yellow livery, Plasser & Theurer 08-4x4/4S switch and crossing tamper No. DR73907 stands in sidings at Plymouth awaiting its next duty.* **Antony Christie**

Plasser & Theurer 08-16/4x4C - RT – Switch/Crossing Tamper – ZWA

DR73911 (S)	*Puma*	Colas	DR73913		Colas
DR73912	*Lynx*	Colas			

Plasser & Theurer 08-4x4S - RT – Switch/Crossing Tamper – ZWA

DR73914	*Robert McAlpine*	SBRail

Plasser & Theurer 08-16/4x4C - RT – Switch/Crossing Tamper – ZWA

DR73915	*William Arrol*	SBRail	DR73916	*First Engineering*	SBRail

Plasser & Theurer 08-4x4S - RT – Switch/Crossing Tamper – ZWA

DR73917	Balfour Beatty	DR93918	Balfour Beatty

Plasser & Theurer 08-16/4x4 C100 - RT – Tamper – ZWA

DR73919	Colas

Plasser & Theurer 08-16/4x4C80 - RT – Tamper – ZWA

DR73920		Colas	DR73922	*John Snowdon*	Colas
DR73921		Colas			

Plasser & Theurer 08-4x4S - RT – Switch/Crossing Tamper – ZWA

DR73923	*Mercury*	Colas

Plasser & Theurer 08-16/4x4C100 - RT – Tamper – ZWA

DR73924	*Atlas*	Colas	DR73927		Balfour Beatty
DR73925	*Europa*	Colas	DR73928		Balfour Beatty
DR73926	*Stephen Keith Blanchard*	Balfour Beatty			

Plasser & Theurer 08-4x4S - RT – Switch/Crossing Tamper – ZWA

DR73929	Colas	DR73930	Colas

Plasser & Theurer 08-16/4x4C100 - RT – Tamper – ZWA

DR73931	Colas

Above: *Colas Rail Plasser & Theurer 06-16/4x4C100-RT tamping machine.* **Mark V. Pike**

Plasser & Theurer 08-4x4/4S - RT – Switch/Crossing Tamper

DR73932	SBRail

Plasser & Theurer 08-16/4x4C100 - RT – Tamper – ZWA

DR73933	SBRail	DR73934	SB Rail

Plasser & Theurer 08-4x4/4S - RT – Switch/Crossing Tamper – ZWA

DR73935	Colas	DR73936	Colas

Network Rail

Above and left: *Plasser & Theurer 08-4x4/4S-RT switch and crossing tamping machine No. DR73935 is shown from both ends is these two illustrations of the Colas Rail machine. In the upper view the vehicle is seen from its short end at Seven Tunnel Junction, while in the view left it is seen from its long end at Newton Abbot.*
Mark V. Pike / Antony Christie

Plasser & Theurer 08-16/4x4C100 - RT – Tamper – ZWA

DR73937		Balfour Beatty
DR73938		Balfour Beatty
DR73939	*Pat Best*	Balfour Beatty

Plasser & Theurer 08-4x4/4S - RT – Switch/Crossing Tamper – ZWA

DR73940	SBRail
DR73941	SBRail
DR73942	Colas

Plasser & Theurer 08-16/4x4C100 - RT – Tamper – ZWA

DR73943	Balfour Beatty
DR73944	Balfour Beatty
DR73945	Balfour Beatty

Plasser & Theurer Euromat 08-4x4/4S – ZWA

DR73946	VolkerRail

Plasser & Theurer 08-4x4/4S - RT – Switch/Crossing Tamper ZWA

DR73947	Colas
DR73948	Colas

Plasser & Theurer 08-16/90 275 – Switch/Crossing Tamper – ZWA

DR75201 (S)	Balfour Beatty
DR75202 (S)	Balfour Beatty

Plasser & Theurer 08-16/90 SP-T – Switch/Crossing Tamper – ZWA

DR75203	MLP Maintenance

Plasser & Theurer 08-275ZW – Switch/Crossing Tamper – ZWY

DR75204	Trackwork

Matisa B45 Tamper – ZWA

DR75301	VolkerRail
DR75302	VolkerRail
DR75303	VolkerRail

Right: *Matisa B45 tamping machine No. DR75303 is operated by VolkerRail and painted in that company's house colours of grey, blue and black. The machine is seen passing through Doncaster station.* **John Wills**

Matisa B41UE Tamper – ZWA

DR75401	VolkerRail	DR75405	VolkerRail	DR75408	Balfour Beatty
DR75402	VolkerRail	DR75406	Colas	DR75409	Balfour Beatty
DR75403	VolkerRail	*Eric Machell*		DR75410	Balfour Beatty
DR75404	VolkerRail	DR75407	Colas	DR75411	Balfour Beatty

Right: *One of the larger Matisa-built tamping machines is No. DR75401, owned by VolkerRail and operated in the Doncaster-Scunthorpe area. It is painted in Volker house colours.* **Antony Christie**

Matisa B66UC Tamper – ZWA

DR75501	Balfour Beatty	DR75502	Balfour Beatty

Plasser & Theurer RM74 – Ballast Cleaner – ZWB

DR76304(S)	Plasser	DR76318(S)	Plasser

Plasser & Theurer RM95RT – Ballast Cleaner – ZWA

DR76323	Network Rail	DR76324	Network Rail

Plasser & Theurer RM900RT Ballast Cleaner – ZWA / ZWQ

DR76501 (HOBC-1)	Network Rail	DR76503 (HOBC-3)	Network Rail
DR76502 (HOBC-2)	Network Rail		

Plasser & Theurer VM80 NR – ZWA

DR76701	(HOBC-3)	Network Rail	DR76710(S)	(HOTRT-2)	Network Rail
DR76702(S)	(HOBC-2)	Network Rail	DR76711(S)	(HOTRT-1)	Network Rail
DR76703(S)	(HOBC-1)	Network Rail			

Matisa D75 Undercutter – ZWA

DR76750	(HRTRT-2)	Network Rail	DR76751	(HRTRT-1)	Network Rail

Plasser & Theurer 09-16 CM NR – ZWA

DR76801	(HOBC-3)	Network Rail

Plasser & Theurer AFM 2000 RT – Rail Finishing Machine – ZWA

DR77001	SBRail	DR77002	SBRail

Network Rail

Plasser & Theurer USP 5000C – Ballast Regulator – ZWA

DR77315(S)	Balfour Beatty	DR77322	Balfour Beatty	DR77336 (S)	Balfour Beatty
DR77316(S)	Balfour Beatty	DR77327	Colas		

Matisa R24S – Ballast Regulator – ZWA

DR77801	VolkerRail	DR77802	VolkerRail

Plasser & Theurer USP 5000RT – Ballast Regulator – ZWA

DR77901		Colas	DR77906	Network Rail
DR77903	*Frank Jones*	Network Rail	DR77907	Network Rail
DR77904		Network Rail	DR77908*	SBRail
DR77905		Network Rail	* Previously DR77902	

Plasser & Theurer Self-Propelled Heavy Duty Twin Jib Crane – YJB

DR78211	Network Rail	DR78216	Balfour Beatty	DR78221	Balfour Beatty
DR78212	Network Rail	DR78217	SB Rail	DR78222	Balfour Beatty
DR78213	VolkerRail	DR78218	Balfour Beatty	DR78223	Balfour Beatty
DR78215	SB Rail	DR78219	SB Rail	DR78224	Balfour Beatty

Cowans Sheldon Self-Propelled Heavy Duty Twin Jib Crane – YJB

DR78226	Colas	DR78231	Network Rail	DR78235	Colas
DR78229	Network Rail	DR78234	Network Rail	DR78237	Network Rail

Left: *A number of engineering work sites require the use of self-propelled twin-jib cranes to lift rail sections and equipment. Two of the Cowans Sheldon self-propelled heavy duty cranes are seen in this view, Colas Rail Nos. DRC78226 and DRC78235, coupled behind the train loco on an engineering train move.* **CJM**

Donelli PD350 Single Line Track Relayer

DR78416	Balfour Beatty	DR78417	Balfour Beatty	DR78490	VolkerRail

Harsco Track Technologies NTC Power Wagon – YJA

DR78701	Balfour Beatty	DR78702	Balfour Beatty

Matisa P95 Track Renewal Train – YJA

DR78801	Network Rail	DR78811	Network Rail	DR78821	Network Rail	DR78831	Network Rail
DR78802	Network Rail	DR78812	Network Rail	DR78822	Network Rail	DR78832	Network Rail

Left: *One of the vehicles from the Matisa P95 Track Renewal Train, No. DR78801, is recorded at Somerton, Somerset. A large number of Network Rail track renewal and ballast train vehicles are based at Taunton.* **Antony Christie**

DR92474	Network Rail	DR92475	Network Rail	DR92476	Network Rail

Sleeper Delivery Train – Generator Wagon – YFA

DR92501	(Stored)	DR92502	(Stored)	DR92503	(Stored)

Twin Jib Rail Recovery Train 'Slinger' – YFA

DR92504 (Stored)
DR92505 (Stored)
DR92506 (Stored)
DR92507 (Stored)
DR92508 (Stored)
DR92509 (Stored)
DR92510 (Stored)
DR92511 (Stored)
DR92512 (Stored)

Single Jib Rail Recovery Train 'Slinger' – YFA

DR92513 (Stored)
DR92514 (Stored)
DR92515 (Stored)
DR92516 (Stored)
DR92517 (Stored)
DR92518 (Stored)

Sleeper Delivery Train – Twin Crane 'Slinger' – YFA

DR92519 (Stored)

Sleeper Delivery Train – Generator Wagon 'Slinger' – YFA

DR92520 (Stored)
DR92521 (Stored)
DR92522 (Stored)
DR92523 (Stored)
DR92524 (Stored)
DR92525 (Stored)

Sleeper Delivery Train – Twin Crane 'Slinger' – YFA

DR92526 (Stored)
DR92527 (Stored)
DR92528 (Stored)
DR92529 (Stored)
DR92530 (Stored)
DR92531 (Stored)
DR92532 (Stored)

Sleeper Delivery Train – Generator Wagon 'Slinger' – YFA

DR92533 (Stored)
DR92534 (Stored)

Sleeper Delivery Train – Twin Crane 'Slinger' – YFA

DR92535 (Stored)
DR92536 (Stored)
DR92537 (Stored)
DR92538 (Stored)
DR92539 (Stored)
DR92540 (Stored)
DR92541 (Stored)
DR92542 (Stored)
DR92543 (Stored)
DR92544 (Stored)
DR92545 (Stored)
DR92546 (Stored)

Sleeper Delivery Train – Generator Wagon 'Slinger' – YFA

DR92547	(Stored)	DR92548	(Stored)	DR92549	(Stored)

Sleeper Delivery Train – Twin Crane 'Slinger' – YFA

DR92550 (Stored)
DR92551 (Stored)
DR92552 (Stored)
DR92553 (Stored)
DR92554 (Stored)
DR92555 (Stored)
DR92556 (Stored)
DR92557 (Stored)
DR92558 (Stored)
DR92559 (Stored)
DR92560 (Stored)
DR92561 (Stored)
DR92562 (Stored)
DR92563 (Stored)
DR92564 (Stored)
DR92565 (Stored)
DR92566 (Stored)
DR92567 (Stored)
DR92568 (Stored)
DR92569 (Stored)
DR92570 (Stored)
DR92571 (Stored)

W H Davis Sleeper Wagons – YXA

DR92601	Network Rail	DR92617	Network Rail	DR92633	Network Rail
DR92602	Network Rail	DR92618	Network Rail	DR92634	Network Rail
DR92603	Network Rail	DR92619	Network Rail	DR92635	Network Rail
DR92604	Network Rail	DR92620	Network Rail	DR92636	Network Rail
DR92605	Network Rail	DR92621	Network Rail	DR92637	Network Rail
DR92606	Network Rail	DR92622	Network Rail	DR92638	Network Rail
DR92607	Network Rail	DR92623	Network Rail	DR92639	Network Rail
DR92608	Network Rail	DR92624	Network Rail	DR92640	Network Rail
DR92609	Network Rail	DR92625	Network Rail	DR92641	Network Rail
DR92610	Network Rail	DR92626	Network Rail	DR92642	Network Rail
DR92611	Network Rail	DR92627	Network Rail	DR92643	Network Rail
DR92612	Network Rail	DR92628	Network Rail	DR92644	Network Rail
DR92613	Network Rail	DR92629	Network Rail	DR92645	Network Rail
DR92614	Network Rail	DR92630	Network Rail	DR92646	Network Rail
DR92615	Network Rail	DR92631	Network Rail	DR92647	Network Rail
DR92616	Network Rail	DR92632	Network Rail	DR92648	Network Rail

Network Rail

DR92649	Network Rail	DR92655	Network Rail	DR92661	Network Rail
DR92650	Network Rail	DR92656	Network Rail	DR92662	Network Rail
DR92651	Network Rail	DR92657	Network Rail	DR92663	Network Rail
DR92652	Network Rail	DR92658	Network Rail	DR92664	Network Rail
DR92653	Network Rail	DR92659	Network Rail	DR92665	Network Rail
DR92654	Network Rail	DR92660	Network Rail		

International Sleeper Wagons – YXA

3170 4629 001 9	*629001*	Network Rail	3170 4629 018 3	*629018*	Network Rail	3170 4629 035 7	*629035* Network Rail
3170 4629 002 7	*629002*	Network Rail	3170 4629 019 1	*629019*	Network Rail	3170 4629 036 5	*629036* Network Rail
3170 4629 003 5	*629003*	Network Rail	3170 4629 020 9	*629020*	Network Rail	3170 4629 037 3	*629037* Network Rail
3170 4629 004 3	*629004*	Network Rail	3170 4629 021 7	*629021*	Network Rail	3170 4629 038 1	*629038* Network Rail
3170 4629 005 0	*629005*	Network Rail	3170 4629 022 5	*629022*	Network Rail	3170 4629 039 9	*629039* Network Rail
3170 4629 006 8	*629006*	Network Rail	3170 4629 023 3	*629023*	Network Rail	3170 4629 040 7	*629040* Network Rail
3170 4629 007 6	*629007*	Network Rail	3170 4629 024 1	*629024*	Network Rail	3170 4629 041 5	*629041* Network Rail
3170 4629 008 4	*629008*	Network Rail	3170 4629 025 8	*629025*	Network Rail	3170 4629 042 3	*629042* Network Rail
3170 4629 009 2	*629009*	Network Rail	3170 4629 026 6	*629026*	Network Rail	3170 4629 043 1	*629043* Network Rail
3170 4629 010 0	*629010*	Network Rail	3170 4629 027 4	*629027*	Network Rail	3170 4629 044 9	*629044* Network Rail
3170 4629 011 8	*629011*	Network Rail	3170 4629 028 2	*629028*	Network Rail	3170 4629 045 6	*629045* Network Rail
3170 4629 012 6	*629012*	Network Rail	3170 4629 029 0	*629029*	Network Rail	3170 4629 046 4	*629046* Network Rail
3170 4629 013 4	*629013*	Network Rail	3170 4629 030 8	*629030*	Network Rail	3170 4629 047 2	*629047* Network Rail
3170 4629 014 2	*629014*	Network Rail	3170 4629 031 6	*629031*	Network Rail	3170 4629 048 0	*629048* Network Rail
3170 4629 015 9	*629015*	Network Rail	3170 4629 032 4	*629032*	Network Rail	3170 4629 049 8	*629049* Network Rail
3170 4629 016 7	*629016*	Network Rail	3170 4629 033 2	*629033*	Network Rail	3170 4629 050 6	*629050* Network Rail
3170 4629 017 5	*629017*	Network Rail	3170 4629 034 0	*629034*	Network Rail		

Left: *Internationally numbered YEA 'Perch' No. 3170-4629-014-2 in a sleeper train consist at Bishopsteignton. Note the handling gantry crane above the sleepers.* **Antony Christie**

Sleeper Delivery Train – Manipulator, Clamp*, Chute§ – JZA

DR93325	Network Rail	DR93383	Network Rail	DR93601*	Network Rail
DR93327	Network Rail	DR93418	Network Rail	DR93603*	Network Rail
DR93334	Network Rail	DR93463	Network Rail	DR93608*	Network Rail
DR93339	Network Rail	DR93465	Network Rail	DR93609*	Network Rail
DR93346	Network Rail	DR93480	Network Rail	DR97501§	Network Rail

W H Davis Flat/Workshop/Barrier Wagons – YSA

DR92701	Network Rail	DR92703	Network Rail	DR92705	Network Rail
DR92702	Network Rail	DR92704	Network Rail	DR92706	Network Rail

Cowans Sheldon 75 tonne Diesel Hydraulic Recovery Crane – ZIA* ZIB¤

ARDC96710¤	Network Rail (BS)	ARDC96714*	Network Rail (MG)
ARDC96713¤	Network Rail (SP)	ARDC96715¤	Network Rail (TO)

Eiv de Brieve DU94BA – TRAMM – ZWA

DR97001	High Speed 1 (HS1)

Windhoff Overhead Line – MPV – YXA

DR97011	High Speed 1 (HS1)	DR97013	High Speed 1 (HS1)
DR97012	High Speed 1 (HS1)	DR97014	High Speed 1 (HS1)

Windhoff Overhead Line – MPV – YXA

DR98001	Network Rail	DR98003	Network Rail	DR98005	Network Rail	DR98007	Network Rail
DR98002	Network Rail	DR98004	Network Rail	DR98006	Network Rail	DR98008	Network Rail

DR98009	Network Rail	DR98010	Network Rail	DR98011	Network Rail	DR98014	Network Rail

DR98003 named *Anthony Wrighton 1944-2011*

Plasser & Theurer General Purpose Machine (GP-TRAMM) – ZWA

DR98215	Balfour Beatty	DR98217	Balfour Beatty	DR98219	Balfour Beatty
DR98216	Balfour Beatty	DR98218	Balfour Beatty	DR98220	Balfour Beatty

Geismar General Purpose Machine (GP-TRAMM)

DR98303	BAR

Geismar VMT860 PL/UM – ZWA

DR98305	Network Rail	DR98306	Network Rail	DR98307(S)	Colas	DR98308(S)	Colas

Rail Head Treatment Train (RHTT) FEA-F

642001	Network Rail	642014	Network Rail	642027	Network Rail	642040	Network Rail
642002	Network Rail	642015	Network Rail	642028	Network Rail	642041	Network Rail
642003	Network Rail	642016	Network Rail	642029	Network Rail	642042	Network Rail
642004	Network Rail	642017	Network Rail	642030	Network Rail	642043	Network Rail
642005	Network Rail	642018	Network Rail	642031	Network Rail	642044	Network Rail
642006	Network Rail	642019	Network Rail	642032	Network Rail	642045	Network Rail
642007	Network Rail	642020	Network Rail	642033	Network Rail	642046	Network Rail
642008	Network Rail	642021	Network Rail	642034	Network Rail	642047	Network Rail
642009	Network Rail	642022	Network Rail	642035	Network Rail	642048	Network Rail
642010	Network Rail	642023	Network Rail	642036	Network Rail	642049	Network Rail
642011	Network Rail	642024	Network Rail	642037	Network Rail	642050	Network Rail
642012	Network Rail	642025	Network Rail	642038	Network Rail		
642013	Network Rail	642026	Network Rail	642039	Network Rail		

Right: *One of the Rail Head Treatment Train vehicles, No. 642010, stabled at Reading and showing two demountable water tanks and an equipment frame in the middle.* **CJM**

Windhoff Multi Purpose Vehicle (MPV) – YXA

DR98901 + DR98951	Network Rail	DR98912 + DR98962	Network Rail	DR98923 + DR98973	Network Rail
DR98902 + DR98952	Network Rail	DR98913 + DR98963	Network Rail	DR98924 + DR98974	Network Rail
DR98903 + DR98953	Network Rail	DR98914 + DR98964	Network Rail	DR98925 + DR98975	Network Rail
DR98904 + DR98954	Network Rail	DR98915 + DR98965	Network Rail	DR98926 + DR98976	Network Rail
DR98905 + DR98955	Network Rail	DR98916 + DR98966	Network Rail	DR98927 + DR98977	Network Rail
DR98906 + DR98956	Network Rail	DR98917 + DR98967	Network Rail	DR98928 + DR98978	Network Rail
DR98907 + DR98957	Network Rail	DR98918 + DR98968	Network Rail	DR98929 + DR98979	Network Rail
DR98908 + DR98958	Network Rail	DR98919 + DR98969	Network Rail	DR98930 + DR98980	Network Rail
DR98909 + DR98959	Network Rail	DR98920 + DR98970	Network Rail	DR98931 + DR98981	Network Rail
DR98910 + DR98960	Network Rail	DR98921 + DR98971	Network Rail	DR98932 + DR98982	Network Rail
DR98911 + DR98961	Network Rail	DR98922 + DR98972	Network Rail		

Right: *A fleet of 32 twin-vehicle Multi-Purpose Vehicles (MPVs) is operated by Network Rail throughout the system and can be fitted with various designs of 'pod' for different work applications, such as rail head cleaning, weed control or general engineering. Nos. DR98929 and DR98979 are seen passing Redhill on RHTT duties.* **CJM**

Network Rail

Rail Wagon – YEA 'Perch'

Number	Owner
DR979001	Network Rail
DR979002	Network Rail
DR979003	Network Rail
DR979004	Network Rail
DR979005	Network Rail
DR979006	Network Rail
DR979007	Network Rail
DR979008	Network Rail
DR979009	Network Rail
DR979010	Network Rail
DR979011	Network Rail
DR979012	Network Rail
DR979013	Network Rail
DR979014	Network Rail
DR979015	Network Rail
DR979016	Network Rail
DR979017	Network Rail
DR979018	Network Rail
DR979019	Network Rail
DR979020	Network Rail
DR979021	Network Rail
DR979022	Network Rail
DR979023	Network Rail
DR979024	Network Rail
DR979025	Network Rail
DR979026	Network Rail
DR979027	Network Rail
DR979028	Network Rail
DR979029	Network Rail
DR979030	Network Rail
DR979031	Network Rail
DR979032	Network Rail
DR979033	Network Rail
DR979034	Network Rail
DR979035	Network Rail
DR979036	Network Rail
DR979037	Network Rail
DR979038	Network Rail
DR979039	Network Rail
DR979040	Network Rail
DR979041	Network Rail
DR979042	Network Rail
DR979043	Network Rail
DR979044	Network Rail
DR979045	Network Rail
DR979046	Network Rail
DR979047	Network Rail
DR979048	Network Rail
DR979049	Network Rail
DR979050	Network Rail
DR979051	Network Rail
DR979052	Network Rail
DR979053	Network Rail
DR979054	Network Rail
DR979055	Network Rail
DR979056	Network Rail
DR979057	Network Rail
DR979058	Network Rail
DR979059	Network Rail
DR979060	Network Rail
DR979061	Network Rail
DR979062	Network Rail
DR979063	Network Rail
DR979064	Network Rail
DR979065	Network Rail
DR979066	Network Rail
DR979067	Network Rail
DR979068	Network Rail
DR979069	Network Rail
DR979070	Network Rail
DR979071	Network Rail
DR979072	Network Rail
DR979073	Network Rail
DR979074	Network Rail
DR979075	Network Rail
DR979076	Network Rail
DR979077	Network Rail
DR979078	Network Rail
DR979079	Network Rail
DR979080	Network Rail
DR979081	Network Rail
DR979082	Network Rail
DR979083	Network Rail
DR979084	Network Rail
DR979085	Network Rail
DR979086	Network Rail
DR979087	Network Rail
DR979088	Network Rail
DR979089	Network Rail
DR979090	Network Rail
DR979091	Network Rail
DR979092	Network Rail
DR979093	Network Rail
DR979094	Network Rail
DR979095	Network Rail
DR979096	Network Rail
DR979097	Network Rail
DR979098	Network Rail
DR979099	Network Rail
DR979100	Network Rail
DR979101	Network Rail
DR979102	Network Rail
DR979103	Network Rail
DR979104	Network Rail
DR979105	Network Rail
DR979106	Network Rail
DR979107	Network Rail
DR979108	Network Rail
DR979109	Network Rail
DR979110	Network Rail
DR979111	Network Rail
DR979112	Network Rail
DR979113	Network Rail
DR979114	Network Rail
DR979115	Network Rail
DR979116	Network Rail
DR979117	Network Rail
DR979118	Network Rail
DR979119	Network Rail
DR979120	Network Rail
DR979121	Network Rail
DR979122	Network Rail
DR979123	Network Rail
DR979124	Network Rail
DR979125	Network Rail
DR979126	Network Rail
DR979127	Network Rail
DR979128	Network Rail
DR979129	Network Rail
DR979130	Network Rail
DR979131	Network Rail
DR979132	Network Rail
DR979133	Network Rail
DR979134	Network Rail

Below: *A brand new 'Perch' engineering wagon is seen awaiting delivery at Doncaster West Yard. The yellow 'racks' on the wagon bed hold the long welded rail sections.* **CJM**

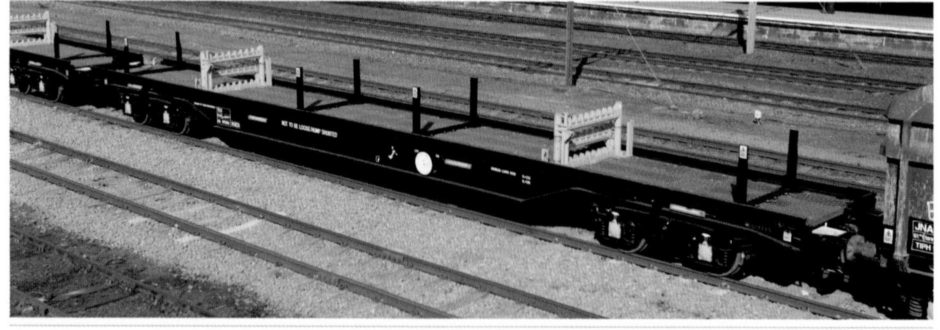

Continuous Welded Rail Clamping Wagon – YEA 'Perch'

Number	Owner
DR979409	Network Rail
DR979412	Network Rail
DR979415	Network Rail

Continuous Welded Rail End of Train Wagon – YEA 'Porpoise'

Number	Owner
DR979505	Network Rail
DR979506	Network Rail
DR979509	Network Rail
DR979511	Network Rail
DR979513	Network Rail
DR979514	Network Rail
DR979515	Network Rail

Continuous Welded Rail 'Chute' Wagon – YEA 'Porpoise'

Number	Owner
DR979500	Network Rail
DR979501	Network Rail
DR979502	Network Rail
DR979503	Network Rail
DR979507	Network Rail
DR979508	Network Rail
DR979510	Network Rail
DR979512	Network Rail

Continuous Welded Rail Gantry Wagon – YEA 'Perch'

DR979604	Network Rail
DR979607	Network Rail
DR979609	Network Rail
DR979611	Network Rail
DR979612	Network Rail
DR979613	Network Rail
DR979614	Network Rail

Plasser & Theurer EM-SAT RT900 Survey Vehicle

DR999800	*Richard Spoors*	Network Rail
DR999801		Network Rail

RailVac Machine - Swedish Rail Vacuum KFA

99-70-9515-001-4 (99709) Railcare, Sweden* * Operated in the UK

Right: *A recent addition to the UK engineering train fleet is the Railcare of Sweden 'RailVac' vehicle 99-70-9515-001-4, which in the UK is often referred to as 99709. The vehicle is loco-hauled, often by Devon & Cornwall Railways to worksites where it uses industrial vacuum technology to collect lineside rubbish. The vehicle is seen stabled at Plymouth during a period of working on the Royal Albert Bridge.* **Nathan Williamson**

Windhoff MPV - High Output Plant System (GW electrification train)

DR 99 70 9131 001	Network Rail
DR 99 70 9131 002	Network Rail
DR 99 70 9131 003	Network Rail
DR 99 70 9131 004	Network Rail
DR 99 70 9131 005	Network Rail
DR 99 70 9131 006	Network Rail
DR 99 70 9131 007	Network Rail
DR 99 70 9131 008	Network Rail
DR 99 70 9131 009	Network Rail
DR 99 70 9131 010	Network Rail
DR 99 70 9131 011	Network Rail
DR 99 70 9131 012	Network Rail
DR 99 70 9131 013	Network Rail
DR 99 70 9131 014	Network Rail
DR 99 70 9131 015	Network Rail
DR 99 70 9131 016	Network Rail
DR 99 70 9131 017	Network Rail
DR 99 70 9131 018	Network Rail
DR 99 70 9131 019	Network Rail
DR 99 70 9131 020	Network Rail
DR 99 70 9131 021	Network Rail
DR 99 70 9131 022	Network Rail
DR 99 70 9131 023	Network Rail

The 23 Windhoff MPV style vehicles for the Great Western route electrification train based at Swindon. The 23 vehicle train can operate to worksites at 60mph and then be split to form several small work trains for the erection of overhead power equipment.

Winter Snow Patrol Train 'Perch'

99709594014-1	IS
977986	IS

Balfour Beatty Rail Services

Address: ✉ 130 Wilton Road, London, SW1V 4LQ
info@bbrail.com
✆ 0207 216 6800
ⓘ www.bbrail.com

Managing Director: Peter Anderson **Depot:** Ashford (AD)

Hauled Stock

Mk1 — *Vehicle Length: 64ft 6in (19.65m)* — *Height: 12ft 9½in (3.89m)* — *Width: 9ft 3in (2.81m)*

Number	*Type*	*Depot*	*Livery*	*Operator*	*Use*
977163 (35487)	Mk1/BSK	AD	BBR	BBR	Staff & Generator coach
977165 (35408)	Mk1/BSK	AD	BBR	BBR	Staff & Generator coach
977166 (35419)	Mk1/BSK	AD	BBR	BBR	Staff & Generator coach
977167 (35400)	Mk1/BSK	AD	BBR	BBR	Staff & Generator coach
977168 (35289)	Mk1/BSK	AD	BBR	BBR	Staff & Generator coach

Alstom Transport

Address: ✉ PO Box 70, Newbold Road, Rugby, Warwickshire, CV21 2WR

info@transport.alstom.com ✆ 01788 577111 ⓘ www.transport.alstom.com

Managing Director: Paul Robinson

Facilities: Following the assembly of the Virgin Trains Class 390 'Pendolino' stock, Alstom closed down its UK production facility at Washwood Heath, Birmingham. However, the company still operates from many specialist sites in mainland Europe and if Alstom wins further new-build contracts in the UK, these will be assembled in Europe.

Depots: Chester (CH), Liverpool - Edge Hill (LL), Manchester - Longsight (MA), Wolverhampton - Oxley (OY), Wembley (WB)

Class 08

Vehicle Length: 29ft 3in (8.91m)
Height: 12ft 8⅝in (3.87m)
Width: 8ft 6in (2.59m)
Engine: English Electric 6K
Horsepower: 400hp (298kW)
Electrical Equipment: English Electric

Number	*Depot*	*Pool*	*Livery*	*Owner*	*Operator*
08451	**AT**	**ATZZ**	**BLK**	**ALS**	**ALS**
08454	**WB**	**ATLO**	**BLK**	**ALS**	**ALS**
08611	**MA**	**ATLO**	**VT1**	**ALS**	**ALS**
08617	**WB**	**ATLO**	**BLK**	**ALS**	**ALS**
08696	**AT**	**ATLO**	**GRN**	**ALS**	**ALS**
08721	**AT**	**ATLO**	**BLU**	**ALS**	**ALS**
08790	**AT**	**ATLO**	**BLU**	**ALS**	**ALS**
08887	**AT**	**ATZZ**	**BLK**	**ALS**	**ALS**

Names applied

08451 ***M A Smith***
08790 ***Starlet***
08721 ***Downside CS***

Bombardier Transportation

Address: ✉ Litchurch Lane, Derby, DE24 8AD

info@bombardier.com ✆ 01332 344666 ⓘ www.bombardier.com

Chief Country Representative: Paul Roberts

Works: Derby (ZD), Crewe (ZC)

Facilities: Bombardier Transportation is one of the largest transport builders in the world, with offices and building facilities in many countries. Its product range extends well beyond rail vehicles and includes aircraft, boats and leisure equipment.

In terms of the UK, two main sites are located in Derby (Litchurch Lane) and Crewe. New-build work is undertaken at the Derby site, which mainly concentrates on electric and diesel multiple unit designs.

Class 08

Vehicle Length: 29ft 3in (8.91m)
Height: 12ft 8⅝in (3.87m)
Width: 8ft 6in (2.59m)
Engine: English Electric 6K
Horsepower: 400hp (298kW)
Electrical Equipment: English Electric

Number	*Depot*	*Pool*	*Livery*	*Owner*	*Operator*	*Name*
08682 (D3849)	**ZD**	**INDL**	**SPL**	**BOM**	**BOM**	***Lionheart***
08846 (No. 3)	**ZD**	**INDL**	**BOM**	**BOM**	**BOM**	

Electro-Motive Diesels (EMD)

Address: ✉ Electro-Motive Diesels Inc, 9301 West 55th Street, LaGrange, Illinois, USA, 60525
Electro-Motive Diesels Inc, Muncie, Indiana, USA

info@emdiesels.com ✆ +1 (800) 255 5355, ⓘ www.emdiesels.com

Facilities: Formerly part of General Motors, Electro-Motive is one of the two largest loco builders in the world. Its main production facility is in Muncie, Indiana, USA. Production from this site took over from the London, Ontario, Canada, plant in 2012.

In terms of the UK, the JT42CWRM or Class 66 were all built at the Canadian facility; however, a new order placed in 2013 by GBRf will see production of the 66 design move to Muncie, Indiana.

EMD is now owned by Progress Rail, which is part of the Caterpillar Group.

General Electric (GE)

Address: ✉ GE Transportation Rail, 2901 East Lake Road, Erie, Pennsylvania, USA, 16531
UK office: Inspira House, Martinfield, Welwyn Garden City, Herts, AL7 1GW
info@getransportation.com ✆ 01707 383700 ⓘ www.getransportation.com

Chief Executive Officer: Lorenzo Simonelli

Facilities: General Electric entered the UK loco arena in recent years, and fulfilled an order for 'PowerHaul' locomotives for Freightliner. GE operates a huge construction facility in Erie, Pennsylvania, USA, where the UK locos were built alongside North American designs.

Hitachi Europe Ltd

Address: ✉ 16 Upper Woburn Place, London, WC1H 0AF
hirofumi.ojima@hitachi-eu.com
✆ 0207 970 2700,
ⓘ www.hitachi-rail.com

Facilities: Hitachi Rail, one of the newer names to the UK rail scene, won the contract to design, build, test and manage the fleet of Class 395 EMUs used for domestic services on HS1. In 2009, the company formed the construction arm of Agility Trains awarded the IEP project to design, build and introduce the next generation of high-speed passenger trains in the UK.

Hitachi is now building construction facilities in the UK at Newton Aycliffe, County Durham.

In 2012, it was announced that the DfT required 596 IEP vehicles for the Great Western franchise and Phase 1 of the East Coast operation, equating to 92 trains. A further 498 vehicles would be needed for the second phase of East Coast, Great Western, West Coast and Cambridge line operations. For the core routes of Phase 1, Great Western will operate a mix of five-car bi-mode and eight-car electric sets on a daily basis plus spare sets, while East Coast will operate 10 five-car electric sets, eight bi-mode sets and 10 nine-car bi-mode sets on a daily basis. This equates to a total of 77 sets being in passenger service every day. 250 vehicles will incorporate one MTU 12V 1600R80L underfloor engine

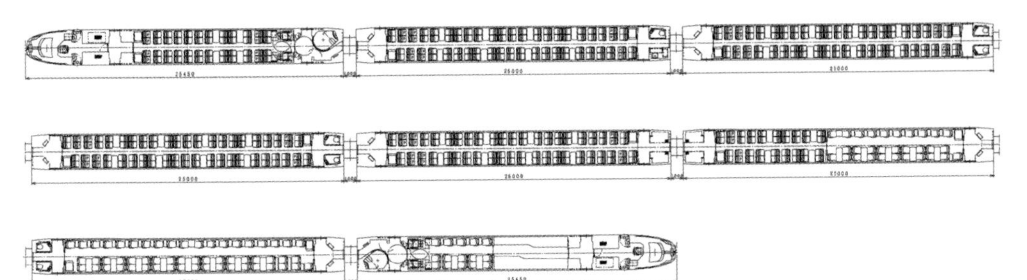

Above: *This drawing of the proposed Hitachi InterCity Express train shows the layout of an eight-car electric and bi-mode set. This set is formed of DPTS with 48 standard class seats, two wheelchair spaces and one disabled access toilet, MS with 88 standard class seats and one toilet, MS with 88 seats and two toilets, TS with 88 seats and two toilets, TS with 88 seats with no toilets, MC with 30 first class and 38 standard class seats with no toilets, MF with 56 first class seats and two toilets, and DF with 15 first class seats, two wheelchair seats, one catering facility and one disabled access toilet.* **DfT**

Arlington Fleet Services

Address: ✉ Eastleigh Rail Works, Campbell Road, Eastleigh, Hampshire, SO50 5AD
info@Arlington-fleet.co.uk ✆ 02380 698789 ⓘ www.arlington-fleet.com

Managing Director: Barry Stephens

Facilities: Arlington Fleet Group offers high-quality rail engineering services to all vehicle owners. The company is based in the former loco / carriage works at Eastleigh.

Depots: Eastleigh (ZG), Shoeburyness (SN)

Class 07

Vehicle Length: 26ft 9½in (8.16m)
Height: 12ft 10in (3.91m)
Width: 8ft 6in (2.59m)
Engine: Paxman 6RPHL MkIII
Horsepower: 275hp (205kW)
Electrical Equipment: AEI

Number	*Depot*	*Pool*	*Livery*	*Owner*	*Operator*
07007 (D2991)	ZG	MBDL	BLU	AFG	AFG

Left: *One of the original Ruston & Hornsby 0-6-0 diesel-electric shunting locos used in Southampton Docks to replace the USA 0-6-0 steam tank locos in the 1960s is still in use at Eastleigh Works. It has been restored for full operation and currently sports 1960s BR rail blue and its TOPS No. 07007.* **Antony Christie**

Ex-DB (Germany) Class 323

Former German shunting locos, built by Gmeinder and now owned by Northumbria Rail and used at Eastleigh Works by Arlington Fleet Services for pilotage.

Number	*Depot*	*Pool*	*Livery*	*Owner*	*Operator*
323-539-7	ZG	-	GRN	NHR	AFS
323-674-2	ZG	-	GRN	NHR	AFS

Left: *In recent times Arlington Fleet Services, the operators of Eastleigh Works, obtained two ex-German Class 323 diesel shunting locomotives for yard and workshop shunting duties. The pair arrived in a poor condition and have received attention at Eastleigh and are now operational. No. 323-539-7 is seen in the works yard in summer 2013.* **Ron Cover**

London & North Western Railway Company (LNWR)

Address: ✉ LNWR Co Ltd, PO Box 111, Crewe, Cheshire, CW1 2FB
allservicedeliverymanagers@lnwr.com ✆ 01270 508000 ⓘ www.lnwr.com

Managing Director: Mark Knowles

Facilities: LNWR is a high-quality engineering company, owned by Arriva and based at Crewe, with outbased facilities at Bristol, Eastleigh, Cambridge and Tyne.

Depot: Crewe (CO), Bristol Barton Hill (BK), Eastleigh (EH), Cambridge (CA), Tyne (TY)

Number	Depot	Pool	Livery	Owner	Operator	Name
08442	EH	MBDL	BRT	LNW	LNW	*Richard J Wenham Eastleigh Depot December 1989 - July 1999*
08516	BK	MBDL	LNW	LNW	LNW	*Rory*
08810	CO	MBDL	LNW	LNW	LNW	
08830	CO	MBDL	BLK	LNW	LNW	
09204	CC	MBDL	BRD	LNW	LNW	

Right: *Although owned by the Harry Needle Railroad Co, No. 08868 is painted in full LNWR two-tone grey livery and is seen stabled outside the Crewe workshops.* **Mark Bearton**

Pullman Group (Colas Rail Freight)

Address: ✉ Train Maintenance Depot, Leckwith Road, Cardiff, CF11 8HP
sales@pullmans.net ✆ 029 2036 8850 ⓘ www.pullmans.net

Managing Director: Colin Robinson

Facilities: Pullman Rail operates from part of the former Canton depot in Cardiff and provides a quality engineering service to all types of rail vehicles.

Depot: Cardiff Canton (CF)

Class 08

Vehicle Length: 29ft 3in (8.91m)
Height: 12ft 8⅝in (3.87m)
Width: 8ft 6in (2.59m)
Engine: English Electric 6K
Horsepower: 400hp (298kW)
Electrical Equipment: English Electric

Number	Depot	Pool	Livery	Owner	Operator
08499	CF	WSXX	BLU	DBS	PUL

Knorr Bremse Rail Services

Address: ✉ Wolverton Works, Stratford Road, Wolverton, Milton Keynes, MK12 5NT
info@railcare.co.uk ✆ 08000 741122 ⓘ www.railcare.co.uk

Managing Director: Colin Love **Depots:** Glasgow (ZH), Wolverton (ZN)

Owner: Knorr Bremse

Class 08

Vehicle Length: 29ft 3in (8.91m)
Height: 12ft 8⅝in (3.87m)
Width: 8ft 6in (2.59m)
Engine: English Electric 6K
Horsepower: 400hp (298kW)
Electrical Equipment: English Electric

Number	Depot	Pool	Livery	Owner	Operator	Name
08568	ZH	RCZH	KBR	KBR	KBR	St Rollox
08629	ZN	RCZN	KBR	KBR	KBR	Wolverton
08649	ZN	RCZN	KBR	KBR	KBR	Bradwell
08730	ZH	RCZH	KBR	KBR	KBR	The Caley

Rail Vehicle Engineering Ltd

Address: ✉ Vehicles Workshop, RTC Business Park, London Road, Derby, DE24 8UP
enquiries@rvel.co.uk ✆ 01332 331210 ⓘ www.rvel.co.uk

Managing Director: Andy Lynch

Depot: Derby (DF)

Class 08

Vehicle Length: 29ft 3in (8.91m)
Height: 12ft 8⅝in (3.87m)
Width: 8ft 6in (2.59m)
Engine: English Electric 6K
Horsepower: 400hp (298kW)
Electrical Equipment: English Electric

Number	Depot	Pool	Livery	Owner	Operator
08536	DF	RVLS	-	RVE	RVE
08697	DF	RVLS	EMT	RVE	RVE

Class 31/1, 31/4

Vehicle Length: 56ft 9in (17.29m)
Height: 12ft 7in (3.91m)
Width: 8ft 9in (2.65m)
Class 31/4 - Fitted with Electric Train Heat
Engine: English Electric 12SVT
Horsepower: 1,470hp (1,097kW)
Electrical Equipment: Brush

Number		Depot	Pool	Livery	Owner	Operator	Name
31106		DF	RVLO	BLU	HJA	RVE	
31422	(31310)	DF	RVLS	INT	RVE	RVE	Cerberus
31459	(31256)	DF	RVLO	BLK	RVE	RVE	Hydra
31468(S)	(31568, 31321)	DF	RVLS	BLK	RVE	RVE	

Left: *RVEL Class 31/1 No. 31106 departs from Maiden Newton with a Weymouth-bound test train. The RVEL locos frequently stand-in for non-available Network Rail locos.* **Mark V. Pike**

Class 73/1

Vehicle Length: 53ft 8in (16.35m)
Height: 12ft 5⁵⁄₁₆in (3.79m)
Width: 8ft 8in (2.64m)
Power: 750V dc third rail or English Electric 6K
Horsepower: electric - 1,600hp (1,193kW)
Horsepower: diesel - 600hp (447kW)
Electrical Equipment: English Electric

Number	Depot	Pool	Livery	Owner	Operator	Notes
73101	DF	RVLO	PUL	RVE	RVE	Super ED project
73104	DF	RVLO	(NRL)	RVE	NRL	Super ED project
73139	DF	RVLO	PUL	RVE	RVE	
73211	DF	RVLO	(NRL)	RVE	NRL	Super ED project (loco 1)

73104/211 to be rebuilt with 2 x Cummins CSK19 750hp engines to provide high-output electro-diesel loco, due in 2013.

Siemens Transportation

Address: ✉ Kings Heath Facility, Heathfield Way, Kings Heath, Northampton, NN5 7QP
enquiries@siemenstransportation.co.uk ✆ 01604 594500
ⓘ www.siemenstransportation.co.uk
✉ Ashby Park, Ashby de la Zouch, Leicestershire, LE65 1JD
uk.mobility@siemens.com ✆ 01530 258000 ⓘ www.siemens.co.uk/mobility

Managing Director UK: Steve Scrimshaw
Depots: Ardwick, Manchester (AK), Kings Heath, Northampton (NN), Northam (NT)
Facilities: Siemens is a provider of UK EMU and DMU rolling stock with various derivatives of its 'Desiro' product line. While having maintenance facilities in the UK, Siemens performs all new-build work in mainland Europe at its Krefeld/Uerdingen factory in Germany. Testing of vehicles is performed in Germany before delivery at the world-famous test track at Wildenrath.

Class 01.5

Number	*Depot*	*Pool*	*Livery*	*Owner*	*Operator*	*Name*
01551 (H016)	**AK**	**MBDL**	**WAB**	**WAB**	**SIE**	***Lancelot***

Barrier Wagons

Number	*Depot*	*Pool*	*Livery*	*Owner*	*Operator*	*Notes*
6321 (96385, 86515)	**NN**	**SIEM**	**BLU**	**SIE**	-	'Desiro' stock barrier wagon
6322 (93686, 86859)	**NN**	**SIEM**	**BLU**	**SIE**	-	'Desiro' stock barrier wagon
6323 (96387, 86973)	**NN**	**SIEM**	**BLU**	**SIE**	-	'Desiro' stock barrier wagon
6324 (96388, 86562)	**CP**	**SIEM**	**BLU**	**SIE**	-	'Desiro' stock barrier wagon
6325 (96389, 86135)	**NN**	**SIEM**	**BLU**	**SIE**	-	'Desiro' stock barrier wagon

Wabtec

Brush Traction, Loughborough

Address: ✉ PO Box 17, Loughborough, Leicestershire, LE11 1HS
sales@brushtraction.com ✆ 01509 617000 ⓘ www.brushtraction.com

Managing Director: John Bidewell
Facilities: The world-famous name of Brush Traction, based in Loughborough, is now part of the Wabtec Group. In recent years the site has been responsible for the majority of UK loco building. The company has been synonymous with loco building for the UK and overseas markets for many years. Although recent main-line loco builds have been awarded overseas, the facilities at the Loughborough plant from which the Class 31, 47, 57, 60 and Eurotunnel Shuttle locos emerged are still available for new-build work. Recently the site has concentrated on re-build operations including the highly successful re-engining of the HST fleet with MTU power units for First Group, East Coast, Grand Central and Network Rail. In 2012-13 the site was undertaking work for General Electric/Freightliner, Arriva and First Group, as well as the re-engining of a Class 73 with an MTU power unit. The site is fully rail connected. In late 2012, Wabtec purchased L H Group Services.

Doncaster

Address: ✉ PO Box 400, Doncaster Works, Hexthorpe Road, Doncaster, DN1 1SL
wabtecrail@wabtec.com ✆ 01302 340700 ⓘ www.wabtecrail.co.uk

Managing Director: John Meehan
Depot: Doncaster (ZB)

Class 08

Vehicle Length: 29ft 3in (8.91m)
Height: 12ft 8⅝in (3.87m)
Width: 8ft 6in (2.59m)
Engine: English Electric 6K
Horsepower: 400hp (298kW)
Electrical Equipment: English Electric

Number	*Depot*	*Pool*	*Livery*	*Owner*	*Operator*	*Name*
08472	**EC**	**HBSH**	**BLK**	**WAB**	**ICE**	

08571	ZB	HBSH	WAB	WAB	ICE	
08596(S)	ZB	HBSH	WAB	WAB	NXE	
08615	ZB	HBSH	WAB	WAB	NXE	
08669	ZB	HBSH	WAB	WAB	WAB	*Bob Machin*
08724	ZB	HBSH	WAB	WAB	WAB	
08764	ZB	MBDL	BLU	WAB	TRN	*Old Tom*
08853	ZB	HBSH	BLU	WAB	WAB	
08871	ZB	MBDL	GRN	WAB	WAB	

Class 60

Vehicle Length: 70ft 0½in (21.34m)
Height: 12ft 10⅝in (3.92m)
Width: 8ft 8in (2.64m)
Engine: Mirrlees MB275T
Horsepower: 3,100hp (2,240kW)
Electrical Equipment: Brush

When *ABC Railguide 2014* closed for press it was anounced that Wabtec had purchased a batch of 20 withdrawn DBS Class 60s. The locos concerned are: 60002, 60013, 60021, 60026, 60028, 60029, 60033, 60038, 60041, 60046, 60047, 60048, 60055, 60056, 60061, 60076, 60085, 60087, 60095, 60096.

Coaching Stock

Vehicle Length: 75ft 0in (22.86m)
Height: 12ft 9in (3.88m)
Width: 8ft 11in (2.71m)
Bogie Type: BT10

NX5G - NGV

Number	*Depot*	*Livery*	*Owner*	
96374(S) (10585)	**ZB**	**EPS**	**WAB**	**Internal user (generator)**

Above: *The present Wabtec Workshops at Doncaster occupy much of the original Doncaster Works site, including the world-famous E2 shop where locos such as* Flying Scotsman *were built as well as the former wagon shop and office complex. E2 shop, which for many years was the main new build area where Class 56s and 58s were built, is now the main locomotive and heavy repair shop, where locos such as the Class 91s from East Coast are overhauled and repainted. The original wagon shops have been adapted and are now equipped to deal with locomotive, multiple unit and wagon work. An ongoing contract in 2013-14 is the total rebuild of the Alstom/South West Trains Class 458 stock from four to five cars incorporating vehicles from the former Class 460 Gatwick Express stock. In this view we see Class 91 No. 91103 nearing completion of a heavy overhaul in E2 shop.* **Derek Porter**

Scotland (previously Brush Barclay)

Address: ✉ Caledonia Works, West Langlands Street, Kilmarnock, Ayrshire, KA1 2QD
sales@brushtraction.com ✆ 01563 523573 ⓘ www.brushtraction.com

Managing Director: John Bidewell

Facilities: The Wabtec site in Scotland concentrates on vehicle overhaul and refurbishment, including EMU, DMU and loco-hauled vehicles as well as HST stock.

Europhoenix Ltd

Address: ✉ 58A High Street, Stony Stratford, Milton Keynes, MK11 1AX
info@europhoenix.eu ✆ 01467 624366 ⓘ www.europhoenix.eu

Facilities: Europhoenix has purchased redundant Class 56, 86 and 87 locos; these are offered to Continental European operators fully refurbished and modified to suit customer needs.

Class 56

Vehicle Length: 63ft 6in (19.35m)
Height: 13ft 0in (3.96m)
Width: 9ft 2in (2.79m)
Engine: Ruston Paxman 16RK3CT
Horsepower: 3,250hp (2,420kW)
Electrical Equipment: Brush

Number	*Owner*	*Location*	*Livery*	*Operator*
56096	EPX	WH	FER	EPX
56101 (92 55 0659 001-5)	EPX	-	BLK	Hire to Floyd (Hungary)
56115 (92 55 0659 002-3)	EPX	-	BLK	Hire to Floyd (Hungary)
56117 (92 55 0659 003-1)	EPX	-	BLK	Hire to Floyd (Hungary)
56301 (56045)	EPX	-	FLF	EPX

Class 86

Vehicle Length: 58ft 6in (17.83m)
Height: 13ft 0⅝in (3.97m)
Width: 8ft 8¼in (2.64m)
Power Collection: 25kV ac overhead
Horsepower: 5,900hp (4,400kW)
Electrical Equipment: GEC

Number	*Location*	*Hire to*
86215	EXP	Floyd (Hungary)
86217	EXP	Floyd (Hungary)
86218	EXP	Floyd (Hungary)
86226	LM	-
86228	EXP	Floyd (Hungary)
86229	LM	-
86231	LM	-
86232	LM	-
86233	EXP	Floyd (Hungary)
86234	LM	-
86235	LM	-
86242	EXP	Floyd (Hungary)
86246	LM	-
86247	LNWR	(Spares)±
86248	EXP	Floyd (Hungary)
86250	EXP	Floyd (Hungary)
86251	LM	-
86424	EXP	Floyd (Hungary) (For spares)

± DHLT pool

Above: *Painted and modified as a Europhoenix demonstrator, Class 86/2 No. 86247 has now been moved to the LNWR works at Crewe where it is providing spare parts for other Class 86s. Note the modified front-end lights and a roof-mounted marker light.* **Mark Bearton**

Class 87

Vehicle Length: 58ft 6in (17.83m)
Height: 13ft 1¼in (3.99m)
Width: 8ft 8¼in (2.64m)
Power Collection: 25kV ac overhead
Horsepower: 7,860hp (5,680kW)
Electrical Equipment: GEC

Number	*Owner*	*Status*	*Location*	*Livery*	*Name*
87009	EPX	Operational	EXP	BUL	
87017	EPX	Operational	EXP	EPX	*Iron Duke*
87023	EPX	Operational	EXP	EPX	*Velocity*
87025	EPX	Stored	EXP	VIR	

(Hire locomotives in Bulgaria working for short line operator Bulmarket)

Porterbrook

Address: ✉ Burdett House, Becket Street, Derby, DE1 1JP
enquiries@porterbrook.co.uk ✆ 01332 262405 ⓘ www.porterbrook.co.uk

Managing Director: Paul Francis

Facilities: Porterbrook Leasing has made available the off-lease Class 87s to mainland European operators, with a significant number being exported to operate in Bulgaria.

Exported

Number	*Present operator*
87003	**BZK Bulgaria**
87004 *Britannia*	**BZK Bulgaria**
87006	**BZK Bulgaria**
87007	**BZK Bulgaria**
87008	**BZK Bulgaria**
87010	**BZK Bulgaria**
87012	**BZK Bulgaria**
87013	**BZK Bulgaria**
87014	**BZK Bulgaria**
87019	**BZK Bulgaria**
87020	**BZK Bulgaria**
87022	**BZK Bulgaria**
87026	**BZK Bulgaria**
87028	**BZK Bulgaria**
87029	**BZK Bulgaria**
87033	**BZK Bulgaria**
87034	**BZK Bulgaria**

Above: *After the introduction of new Class 390 'Pendolino' and Class 220/221 'Voyager' stock on the CrossCountry and West Coast routes under privatisation, the Class 87 fleet of 25kV ac electric locos was surplus to requirements and soon all were returned to their owner Porterbrook which sought a new operator. No UK operators were interested so the company offered the locos overseas with BZK in Bulgaria taking on 17 locos. The locos were shipped in various liveries, including No. 87004 in 1960s BR blue complete with its cast* Britannia *nameplates.* **A. P. Sayer**

Angel Trains

Address: ✉ Portland House, Bressenden Place, London, SW1E 5BH
reception@angeltrains.co.uk ✆ 0207 592 0500 ⓘ www.angeltrains.co.uk
Chief Executive: Malcolm Brown
Owned by: Babcock Brown, AMP Capital and Deutsche Bank

British American Railway Services

Incorporating: RMS Locotec, RT Rail, Dartmoor Railway, Devon & Cornwall Railways, Weardale Railway, Ealing Community Transport and Hanson Rail
Address: ✉ London Riverside, London, SE1 2AQ
President: Ed Ellis
Depots: RMS Wakefield (ZS), Washwood Heath (WH)
UK operation is part of Iowa Pacific Holdings. BARS is also a Train Operating Company.

Class 08

Vehicle Length: 29ft 3in (8.91m)
Height: 12ft 8⅝in (3.87m)
Width: 8ft 6in (2.59m)
Engine: English Electric 6K
Horsepower: 400hp (298kW)
Electrical Equipment: English Electric

Number	Depot	Pool	Livery	Owner	Operator
08308	IS	MRSO	FSR	ECT	FSR
08423	ZS	INDL	RMS	RMS	IND
08523	IS	MRSO	RMS	RMS	FSR
08573	ZB	MRSO	BLK	ECT	BOM
08588	WH	MRSO	BLK	ECT	IND
08613	§	MOLO	BLU	RMS	IND
08622	K	INDL	BLU	RMS	IND
08648	ZB	INDL	YEL	BAR	IND
08750	‡	MRSO	BLK	ECT	IND
08754	NR	MRSO	BLU	ECT	IND
08756	MR	MRSO	GRY	ECT	GBR
08762	ZB	MRSO	BLK	ECT	CEM
08870	ZS	MBDL	BLG	RMS	IND
08873	ZB	MRSO	HUN	ECT	FLR
08885	ZS	INDL	GBR	RMS	GBR
08936	ZS	MBDL	BLU	RMS	IND

§ at Onllwyn, K - Ketton, ‡ - at Weardale

Class 20

Vehicle Length: 46ft 9¼in (14.26m)
Height: 12ft 7⅝in (3.84m)
Width: 8ft 9in (2.66m)
Engine: English Electric 8SVT Mk2
Horsepower: 1,000hp (745kW)
Electrical Equipment: English Electric

Number	Depot	Pool	Livery	Owner	Operator
20189	BH	GBEE	GRN	C20	BAR
20227	BH	GBEE	LUL	C20	BAR

Class 31/1, 31/4 & 31/6

Vehicle Length: 56ft 9in (17.29m)
Height: 12ft 7in (3.91m)
Width: 8ft 9in (2.65m)
31/4 Fitted with Electric Train Heat, 31/6 through wired
Engine: English Electric 12SVT
Horsepower: 1,470hp (1,097kW)
Electrical Equipment: Brush

Number	Depot	Pool	Livery	Owner	Operator
31190	WH	HTLX	GRN	BAR	- (Spot hire)
31452 (31552/279)	WH	HTLX	DCG	ECT	ECT
31454 (31554, 31228)	WH	HTLX	ICS	BAR	Weardale
31601 (31186)	WH	HTLX	DCG	BAR	RVE
31602 (31191)	WH	HTLX	NRL	BAR	RVE

Right: *Displaying Devon & Cornwall Railways green livery with DCR branding, Class 31/6 No. 31601 is seen near Stoke Prior on the Lickey incline hauling two passenger rolling stock barrier coaches. The two Class 31/6s are Class 31s not fitted with electric train supply but fitted with through wiring to allow control over an ETS-fitted loco if either coupled behind or at the remote end of a train.* **John Binch**

Class 56

Vehicle Length: 63ft 6in (19.35m)
Height: 13ft 0in (3.96m)
Width: 9ft 2in (2.79m)
Engine: Ruston Paxman 16RK3CT
Horsepower: 3,250hp (2,420kW)
Electrical Equipment: Brush

Number		Depot	Pool	Livery	Owner	Operator	Name
56091		WH	HTLX	GRY	BAR	BAR	
56103(S)		WH	HTLX	-	BAR	-	
56303	(56125)	WH	HTLX	GRN	BAR	BAR	
56311	(56057)	WH	HTLX	GRY	BAR	BAR	
56312	(56003)	WH	HTLX	DCN	BAR	BAR	*Jeremiah Dixon Son of County Durham Surveyor of the Mason-Dixon Line U.S.A*
(56313) (S)	56128	WH	HTLX	FRB	BAR	-	

Left: *Several Class 56s are on the operating books of Devon & Cornwall Railways, being made available for spot hire or deployment on services operated by DCR. The Class 56s are usually maintained and stabled when not in use at Washwood Heath, Birmingham. Green-liveried DCR-branded No. 56303 is illustrated hauling the RailVac wagon near Tiverton when en route to Plymouth for rail cleaning duties in Devon.* **Antony Christie**

Class 73

Vehicle Length: 53ft 8in (16.35m)
Height: 12ft 5 5/16in (3.79m)
Width: 8ft 8in (2.64m)
Power: 750V dc third rail or English Electric 6K
Horsepower: electric - 1,600hp (1,193kW)
Horsepower: diesel - 600hp (447kW)
Electrical Equipment: English Electric

Number	Depot	Pool	Livery	Owner	Operator	Name
73107	SE	MBED	GRY	RTR	ECT	*Redhill 1844 - 1994*
73201 (73142)	SE	MBED	BLU	PTR	ECT	*Broadlands*

Coaching Stock

Mk2
Vehicle Length: 66ft 0in (20.11m)
Height: 12ft 9 1/2in (3.89m)
Width: 9ft 3in (2.81m)

AF2F - DBSO

Number	Depot	Livery	Owner
9704	EH	-	BAR
9705	RTC	-	BAR
9707	RTC	-	BAR
9709	EH	-	BAR
9710	EH	-	BAR

UK Rail Leasing

Class 56

Vehicle Length: 63ft 6in (19.35m)
Height: 13ft 0in (3.96m)
Width: 9ft 2in (2.79m)
Engine: Ruston Paxman 16RK3CT
Horsepower: 3,250hp (2,420kW)
Electrical Equipment: Brush

Number	Depot	Pool	Livery	Owner	Operator
56007(S)	LR	MBDL	BLU	URL	-
56009(S)	LR	-	BLU	URL	-
56018(S)	P	MBDL		URL	-
56031(S)	LR	MBDL		URL	-
56037(S)	P	WNSO		URL	-
56038(S)	P	-		URL	-
56060(S)	WH	MBDL	-	URL	-
56065(S)	WH	MBDL	-	URL	-
56069(S)	LR	MBDL		URL	-
56077(S)	P	WNSO		URL	- (Spares)
56081(S)	LR	MBDL	-	URL	-
56098(S)	P	MBDL	-	URL	-
56104(S)	P	WNSO		URL	-
56106(S)	LR	MBDL		URL	-

Spot hire locos to be introduced; six from the above list should be returned to traffic. Locos will soon be moving to Leicester depots the new Headquarters for the UK Rail Leasing operation

Electric Traction Limited

Address: ✉ Woodlands, Manse Road, Inverurie, Aberdeenshire, Scotland, AB51 3UJ

Depot: Long Marston (LM)

Electric Traction Ltd provides spot hire of Class 86 and 87 traction, as well as providing engineering and graphic design services to the rail industry.

Class 86

Vehicle Length: 58ft 6in (17.83m)
Height: 13ft 0⁵⁄₈in (3.97m)
Width: 8ft 8¼in (2.64m)
Power Collection: 25kV ac overhead
Horsepower: 5,900hp (4,400kW)
Electrical Equipment: GEC

Number	Depot	Pool	Livery	Owner	Operator	Name
86101	WA	ACAC	BLU	ETL	NRL	*Sir William Stanier FRS*
86401	WA	ETLO	NSE	ETL	ETL	*Northampton Town*
86701 (86205) (S)	WN	EPUK	COL	ETL	-	*Orion*
86702 (86260) (S)	WN	EPUK	ETL	ETL	-	*Cassiopeia*

Right: *Currently used as an ice breaker by Network Rail, the sole surviving member of the prototype Class 86/1 fleet, No. 86101, is painted in rail blue. The loco is seen at Carlisle.* **Murdoch Currie**

Below: *Two Class 86/2s were modified by ETL as Class 86/7s and painted in ETL silver and red livery. Both are currently stored and de-registered from main-line use.* **Antony Guppy**

Class 87

Vehicle Length: 58ft 6in (17.83m)
Height: 13ft 1¼in (3.99m)
Width: 8ft 8¼in (2.64m)
Power Collection: 25kV ac overhead
Horsepower: 7,860hp (5,680kW)
Electrical Equipment: GEC

Number	Depot	Pool	Livery	Owner	Operator	Name
87002	WA	ETLO	BLU	ETL	NRL	*Royal Sovereign*

Eversholt Rail Group (Previously HSBC Rail)

Address: ✉ PO Box 29499, 1 Eversholt Street, London, NW1 2ZF
info@eversholtrail.co.uk ✆ 0207 380 5040 ⓘ www.eversholtrail.co.uk

Chief Operating Officer: Mary Kenny

Harry Needle Railroad Company

Address: ✉ Harry Needle Railway Shed, Barrow Hill Roundhouse, Campbell Drive, Chesterfield, Derbyshire, S43 2PR

Managing Director: Harry Needle

Depot: Barrow Hill (BH)

Harry Needle Railroad Company also operates as a scrap dealer in dismantling locomotives and rolling stock.

Class 01.5

Number	*Depot*	*Pool*	*Livery*	*Owner*	*Operator*	
01552 (TH167V)	BH	HNRL	IND	HNR	IND	
01564 (12088)	-	HNRL	BLK	HNR	IND	Preserved at Aln Valley Railway

Class 08 & 09

Vehicle Length: 29ft 3in (8.91m)
Height: 12ft 8⅝in (3.87m)
Width: 8ft 6in (2.59m)
Engine: English Electric 6K
Horsepower: 400hp (298kW)
Electrical Equipment: English Electric

Number	*Depot*	*Pool*	*Livery*	*Owner*	*Operator*
08389	BH	HNRL	EWS	HNR	BUR
08502	BH	HNRL	NOR	HNR	FLX
08527(S)	BH	HNRL	JAR	HNR	HNR
08685	BH	HNRL	EWS	HNR	HNR
08765	BU	HNRL	EWS	HNR	HNR
08786	BH	HNRL	BRD	HNR	HNR
08818	BH	HNRL	HNR	HNR	IND
08834	BH	HNRL	DRS	HNR	OLD
08868	CP	HNRL	LNW	HNR	LNW
08892	BU	HNRL	DRS	HNR	HNR
08905	BH	HNRL	EWS	HNR	IND
08918	BH	HNRL	EWS	HNR	BUR
08924	BH	HNRL	EWS	HNR	LAF
08929(S)	LM	HNRS	BLK	HNR	-
08943	CZ	MBDL	HNR	HNR	NRM
08954	BU	HNRS	TGG	HNR	BUR
09014	BU	HNRS	EWS	HNR	-
09018	BU	HNRS	HNR	HNR	LAF

Left: *One of the most successful of the private rail companies, offering spot hire of anything from shunting to main-line locomotives, is the Harry Needle Railroad Company, based at Barrow Hill Roundhouse. The company has a large number of ready-to-run locos available and frequently these are painted in customers' own liveries, as demonstrated by Class 08 No. 08834 carrying Direct Rail Services livery.* **Darren Ford**

Class 20

Vehicle Length: 46ft 9¼in (14.26m)
Height: 12ft 7⅝in (3.84m)
Width: 8ft 9in (2.66m)
Engine: English Electric 8SVT Mk2
Horsepower: 1,000hp (745kW)
Electrical Equipment: English Electric

Number	*Depot*	*Pool*	*Livery*	*Owner*	*Operator*
20016(S) ø	BH	HNRS	BLU	HNR	-
20056	BH	HNRL	COR	HNR	TAT
20066	BH	HNRL	TAT	HNR	TAT
20081(S) ø	LM	HNRS	BLU	HNR	-
20088(S) ø	LM	HNRS	RFG	HNR	-
20092(S)	BH	HNRS	LAF	HNR	-
20096	BH	GBEE	BLU	HNR	HNR
20107‡	BH	GBEE	ORG	HNR	HNR
20118	BH	GBEE	GRY	HNR	HNR
20121(S)	WEN	HNRS	BLU	HNR	HNR
20132‡	BH	GBEE	RFG	HNR	HNR
20138(S)	LM	HNRS	RFT	HNR	-
20166	WEN	HNRS	GRN	HNR	HNR
20168	EA	HNRL	WHT	HNR	LAF

‡ Main line certified, **ø** Reported for sale

Number		Depot	Pool	Livery	Owner	Operator	Name/Notes
20311	(20102)	BH	GBEE	ORG	HNR	HNR	
20314 ‡	(20117)	BH	GBEE	ORG	HNR	HNR	‡ Allocated number 92 70 0020314-5
20901	(20101)	BH	GBEE	GBN	HNR	HNR	
20903(S)	(20083)	LM	HNRS	DRS	HNR	-	
20904(S)	(20041)	LM	HNRS	DRS	HNR	-	
20905	(20225)	BH	GBEE	GBN	HNR	HNR	*Roger Whip*
20906	(20219)	LAF	HNRL	WHT	HNR	LAF	(Carries No. 3)

Name applied	
20168	*Sir George Earle*

20056 carries Tata Steel No. 81.
20066 carries Tata Steel No. 82.

Above: *A number of the Harry Needle Railroad-owned Class 20s are main-line certified and regularly operate over Network Rail tracks, especially on spot hire work or for GBRf powering London Underground stock transfer moves between Derby and Old Dalby or between Derby and London with 'A' stock deliveries. Orange-liveried Nos. 20311 and 20314 pass Melton Mowbray with a train of new London Underground 'A' stock.* **Antony Christie**

Class 37/0

Vehicle Length: 61ft 6in (18.74m)
Height: 13ft 0¼in (3.96m)
Width: 8ft 11⅝in (2.73m)
Engine: English Electric 12CSVT
Horsepower: 1,750hp (1,304kW)
Electrical Equipment: English Electric

Number	Depot	Pool	Livery	Owner	Operator/Notes
37029	BH	HNRS	GRN	HNR	HNR *(At Epping & Ongar Railway)*
37057(S)	BH	HNRS	BLU	HNR	- (spares)
37165(S) (37374)	CS	HNRS	CIV	HNR	-

Class 47

Vehicle Length: 63ft 6in (19.35m)
Height: 12ft 10⅜in (3.91m)
Width: 9ft 2in (2.79m)
Electric Train Heat fitted
Engine: Sulzer 12LDA28C
Horsepower: 2,580hp (1,922kW)
Electrical Equipment: Brush

Number	Depot	Pool	Livery	Owner	Opertor
47714 (47511)	OD	HNRL	ANG	HNR	SEC*
47715 (47502)	BH	HNRL	BLK	HNR	HNR
47761 (47038/564)	BH	HNRL	RES	HNR	(Stored)

* Operating at Old Dalby

Nemesis Rail

Address: ✉ Nemesis Rail Ltd, Burton Depot, Burton-on-Trent
enquiries@ nemesisrail.com ✆ 01246 472331 ⓘ www.nemesisrail.com
Formed from the demise of FM Rail
Depot: Burton (BU)

Above: *Nemesis Rail, formed after the demise of FM Rail, rents the former depot at Burton, where the Nemesis loco fleet and locos from private owners receive attention and restoration for either use on light railways or on the main line. The depot has been responsible for the restoration of the three Floyd Class 56s for use in Hungary. The site is also used for storage of locomotives pending sale or disposal. This is a general view of the complex from the north end.* **Antony Christie**

Class 31/1

Vehicle Length: 56ft 9in (17.29m)
Height: 12ft 7in (3.91m)
Width: 8ft 9in (2.65m)
Engine: English Electric 12SVT
Horsepower: 1,470hp (1,097kW)
Electrical Equipment: Brush

Number	*Depot*	*Pool*	*Livery*	*Owner*	*Operator*	*Name*
31128	BU	NRLO	BLU	NEM	NYM	***Charybdis***

Class 33/1

Vehicle Length: 50ft 9in (15.47m)
Height: 12ft 8in (3.86m)
Width: 9ft 3in (2.81m)
Engine: Sulzer 8LDA28A
Horsepower: 1,550hp (1,156kW)
Electrical Equipment: Crompton Parkinson

Number	*Depot*	*Pool*	*Livery*	*Owner*	*Operator*	*Name / Notes*
33103	BU	MBDL	BLU	NEM	WER	***Swordfish*** (at Bluebell Railway)

Class 37/5

Vehicle Length: 61ft 6in (18.74m)
Height: 13ft 0¼in (3.96m)
Width: 8ft 11⅝in (2.73m)
Engine: English Electric 12CSVT
Horsepower: 1,750hp (1,304kW)
Electrical Equipment: English Electric

Number	*Depot*	*Pool*	*Livery*	*Owner*	*Operator*
37679(S) (37123)	BU	MBDL	TGG	NEM	-

Class 45/1

Vehicle Length: 67ft 11in (20.70m)
Height: 12ft 10½in (3.91m)
Width: 9ft 1½in (2.78m)
Engine: Sulzer 12LDA28B
Horsepower: 2,500hp (1,862kW)
Electrical Equipment: Crompton Parkinson

Number	*Depot*	*Pool*	*Livery*	*Owner*	*Operator*	*Name*
45112	BH	MBDL	BLU	NEM	NEM	***Royal Army Ordnance Corps***

Class 47

Vehicle Length: 63ft 6in (19.35m)
Height: 12ft 10⅜in (3.91m)
Width: 9ft 2in (2.79m)
Electric Train Heat fitted to Class 47/4 and 47/7
Engine: Sulzer 12LDA28C
Horsepower: 2,580hp (1,922kW)
Electrical Equipment: Brush

Number	Depot	Pool	Livery	Owner	Operator
47375	BH	MBDL	BLU	NEM	NEM
47488	BH	MBDL	GRN	NEM	NEM
47716	BH	MBDL	RES	NEM	NEM
47744	BH	MBDL	EWS	NEM	NEM

Porterbrook

Address: ✉ Ivatt House, The Point, Pinnacle Way, Pride Park, Derby, DE24 8ZS
enquiries@porterbrook.co.uk ✆ 01332 285050 ⓘ www.porterbrook.co.uk

Managing Director: Paul Francis

Owned by: Antin Infrastructure Partners, Deutsche Bank and OP Trust

Transmart Trains

Address: ✉ Green Farm House, Falfield, Wootton-under-Edge, Gloucestershire, GL12 8DL

Managing Director: Oliver Buxton

Depots: Selhurst (SU), Stewarts Lane (SL) Part of Cambrian Transport

Class 73

Vehicle Length: 53ft 8in (16.35m)
Height: 12ft 5 5/16in (3.79m)
Width: 8ft 8in (2.64m)
Power: 750V dc third rail or English Electric 6K
Horsepower: electric - 1,600hp (1,193kW)
Horsepower: diesel - 600hp (447kW)
Electrical Equipment: English Electric

‡ *At Barry Railway*
• *Not main line certified*

Number	Depot	Pool	Livery	Owner	Operator
73118	‡	-	GRY	TTS	TTS
73133•	BM	-	GRN	TTS	SWT

■ Former Gatwick Express Class 488 vehicles Nos. 72505, 72620, 72621, 72629, 72710 from sets 488206 and 488311 are also owned by Transmart Trains.

Above: *Transmart Trains ED No. 73133 sports a special coupling to allow attachment to the intermediate vehicles of Class 455 stock during refurbishment at Bournemouth depot. The loco is seen at the depot.* **Antony Christie**

Listings provide details of locomotives and stock authorised for operation on the UK National Rail network and that can be seen operating special and charter services.
Preserved locomotives authorised for main-line operation are found in the preserved section.

Bo'ness & Kinneil Railway

Number	Type	Depot	Livery	Operator	Use
464	AO3/BCK	BT	CAL	BOK	Charter train use
1375 (99803)	AO2/TK	BT	CAL	BOK	Charter train use
3096 (99827)	AD11/FO	BT	MAR	BOK	Charter train use
3115	AD11/FO	BT	MAR	BOK	Charter train use
3150	AD11/FO	BT	MAR	BOK	Charter train use
4831 (99824)	AC21/TSO	BT	MAR	BOK	Charter train use
4832 (99823)	AC21/TSO	BT	CHC	BOK	Charter train use
4836 (99831)	AC21/TSO	BT	MAR	BOK	Charter train use
4856 (99829)	AC21/TSO	BT	MAR	BOK	Charter train use
5028 (99830)	AC21/TSO	BT	CAR	BOK	Charter train use
13229 (99826)	AA11/FK	BT	MAR	BOK	Charter train use
13230 (99828)	AA11/FK	BT	MAR	BOK	Charter train use

Flying Scotsman Railway Ltd

Number	Type	Depot	Livery	Operator	Notes/Name
316 (S) (975608)	AO11/PFK	CS	PUL	FSL	Pullman *Magpie*
321 (S)	AO11/PFK	CS	PUL	FSL	Pullman *Swift*
337 (S)	AO11/PSK	CS	PUL	FSL	Pullman Car No. 337

Great Scottish & Western Railway Co

Number	Type	Depot	Livery	Operator	Notes/Name
313 (S) (99964)	AO11/PFK	CS	MAR	GSW	Royal Scotsman - *Finch*
317 (99967)	AO11/PFK	CS	MAR	GSW	Royal Scotsman - *Raven*
319 (99965)	AO11/PFK	CS	MAR	GSW	Royal Scotsman - *Snipe*
324 (99961)	AO11/PFP	CS	MAR	GSW	Royal Scotsman - *Amber*
329 (99962)	AO11/PFP	CS	MAR	GSW	Royal Scotsman - *Pearl*
331 (99963)	AO11/PFP	CS	MAR	GSW	Royal Scotsman - *Topaz*
1999 (99131)	AO10/SAL	CS	MAR	GSW	Royal Scotsman - *Lochaber*

Hastings Diesels Limited

The following vehicles are owned by Hastings Diesels Ltd and kept at St Leonards. Usually a six-car train is formed which is fitted with central door locking and is main-line certified (original class numbers shown in brackets).
60000 (201), 60019 (202), 60116 (202), 60118 (202), 60501 (201), 60528 (202), 60529 (202), 69337 (422 EMU), 70262 (411 EMU).
In autumn 2013, the set **1001** was formed **60116+60529+70262+69337+60501+60118**

Left: *Hastings Diesels Ltd owns a number of former Southern Region former Hastings line DEMU vehicles, together with a couple of former EMU coaches that have been modified to allow operation with DEMU stock. The Hastings unit is authorised for main-line operation and when not in use is kept at St Leonards, Hastings. Painted in BR green with a full yellow warning end, the set is seen at Didcot forming a 'Sussex Coast Express' charter.* **Norman E. Preedy**

Mid-Hants Railway

Number	Type	Depot	Livery	Operator
1105	AJ41/RG	RL	GRN	MHR
21252	AB31/BCK	RL	GRN	MHR

North Yorkshire Moors Railway

Class 08

Vehicle Length: 29ft 3in (8.91m)
Height: 12ft 8⅝in (3.87m)
Width: 8ft 6in (2.59m)
Engine: English Electric 6K
Horsepower: 400hp (298kW)
Electrical Equipment: English Electric

Number	Depot	Pool	Livery	Owner	Operator	Notes
08850	NY	MBDL	BLU	NYM	NYM	Restricted main line use

Class 25

Vehicle Length: 50ft 6in (15.39m)
Height: 12ft 8in (3.86m)
Width: 9ft 1in (2.76m)
Engine: Sulzer 6LDA28B
Horsepower: 1,250hp (932kW)
Electrical Equipment: Brush

Number	Depot	Pool	Livery	Owner	Operator	Name	Notes
25278	NY	MBDL	GRN	NYM	NYM	*Sybilia*	Restricted main line use

Coaching Stock

Number	Type	Depot	Livery	Operator
1823	AN21/RMB	NY	MAR	NYM
3860	AC21/TSO	NY	MAR	NYM
3872	AC21/TSO	NY	CAR	NYM
3948	AC2I/TSO	NY	CAR	NYM
4198	AC21/TSO	NY	CAR	NYM
4252	AC21/TSO	NY	CAR	NYM
4290	AC21/TSO	NY	MAR	NYM
4455	AC21/TSO	NY	CAR	NYM
4786	AC21/TSO	NY	MAR	NYM
4817	AC21/TSO	NY	CHC	NYM
5000	AC21/TSO	NY	MAR	NYM
5029	AC21/TSO	NY	CHC	NYM
9267	AE21/BSO	NY	CHC	NYM
9274	AE21/BSO	NY	CHC	NYM
16156 (7156)	AA31/CK	NY	MAR	NYM
21100	AB31/BCK	NY	CHC	NYM
35089	AB2I/BSK	NY	MAR	NYM

Railfilms Limited / Statesman Rail

Number	Type	Depot	Livery	Operator	Name
84 (99884)	Mk1 Pantry	CS	PUL	RAF	
310 (99107)	AO11/PFL	TS	PUL	RAF	*Pegasus / Trianon Bar*
1211 (3305)	AJ1F/RFB	CS	PUL	RAF	
1659 (16509)	AJ41/RBR	CS	PUL	RAF	
3188	AD1D/FO	CS	PUL	RAF	*Snowdon (ex-Sovereign)*
3231	AD1E/FO	CS	PUL	RAF	*Ben Cruachan (ex-Apollo)*
3312	AD1E/FO	CS	PUL	RAF	*Helvellyn*
3438	AD1F/FO	CS	PUL	RAF	
4362	AC21/SO	BU	-	RAF	*Ben Lomond*
5797	AD2E/TSO	BU	BLG	RAF	
5912	AD2F/TSO	CS	PUL	RAF	
5991	AD2F/TSO	CS	PUL	RAF	
9004	GWR	CS	GWR	RAF	
9005	GWR	SDR	GWR	SDR	
13508	AA1B/FK	BU	MAR	RAF	
17080	AO3/BCK	CS	PUL	RAF	
35511 (17130)	AB5C	Shildon	PUL	RAF	
99993	Mk1 TSO	CS	MAR	RAF	

Ridings Railtours

Number	Type	Depot	Livery	Operator
5520 (S)	AC2C/TSO	SV	PUL	RRS
13581 (S)	AA1D/FK	SV	ICS	RRS
13583 (S)	AA1D/FK	SV	ICS	RRS

Riviera Trains

Class 08

Vehicle Length: 29ft 3in (8.91m)
Height: 12ft 8⅝in (3.87m)
Width: 8ft 6in (2.59m)
Engine: English Electric 6K
Horsepower: 400hp (298kW)
Electrical Equipment: English Electric

Number	Depot	Pool	Livery	Owner	Operator
08507	CP	RTLO	RIV	RIV	RIV
08704	CP	RTLO	BLU	RIV	RIV

Riviera

Class 47

Vehicle Length: 63ft 6in (19.35m)	*Engine: Sulzer 12LDA28C*
Height: 12ft 10⅜in (3.91m)	*Horsepower: 2,580hp (1,922kW)*
Width: 9ft 2in (2.79m)	*Electrical Equipment: Brush*
Electric Train Heat fitted	

Number	*Depot*	*Pool*	*Livery*	*Owner*	*Operator*	*Name*
47769 (47491)	CP	RTLO	VIR	RIV	RIV	
47812 D1916 (47657)	CP	RTLO	GRN	RIV	RIV	
47815 D1748 (47660)	CP	RTLO	GRN	RIV	RIV	*Great Western*
47843 (47623)	CP	RTLO	RIV	RIV	RIV	*Vulcan*
47847 (47577)	CP	RTLO	RIV	RIV	RIV	
47848 (47632)	CP	RTLO	RIV	RIV	RIV	*Titan Star*

One of the principal operators of charter trains in the UK is Riviera Trains, based at Crewe. The company has six main-line certificated Class 47s available for service and a considerable number of Mk1 and Mk2 passenger vehicles. 1960s green-liveried Class 47 No. 47812 (D1916) is seen heading west at Dawlish Warren in the summer of 2013 covering for non-available steam on the 'Torbay Express' from Bristol to Kingswear. **CJM**

Coaching Stock

Number	*Type*	*Depot*	*Livery*	*Operator*	*Notes/Name*
1200 (6459)	AJ1F/RFO	EH	RIV	RIV	Set 04 - The Great Briton - *Amber*
1203 (3291)	AJ1F/RFO	EH	RIV	RIV	
1212 (6453)	AJ1F/RFO	EH	VIR	RIV	Set 05 - The Norfolkman
1250 (3372)	AJ1F/RFO	EH	RIV	RIV	Set 07 - The West Coast Set
1651	AJ41/RBR	EH	RIV	RIV	Set 02 - The Royal Scot Set
1657	AJ41/RBR	EH	CHC	RIV	
1671	AJ41/RBR	EH	CHC	RIV	
1683	AJ41/RBR	BH	BLU	RIV	Set 04 - The Great Briton - *Carol*
1691	AJ41/RBR	CP	CCM	RIV	Set 02 - The Royal Scot Set
1692	AJ41/RBR	CP	CHC	RIV	Set 01 - The British Classic Set
1699	AJ41/RBR	CP	BLU	RIV	Set 04 - The Great Briton
1813	AN21/RMB	CP	CHC	RIV	Set 03
1832	AN21/RMB	EH	CCM	RIV	
1842	AN21/RMB	EH	CCM	RIV	Set 02 - The Royal Scot Set
1863	AN21/RMB	CM	CHC	RIV	Set 01 - The British Classic Set
2834 (21267)	AU51/SLSC	EH	LNR	RIV	
3066 (99566)	AD11/FO	EH	CCM	RIV	Set 02 - The Royal Scot Set
3068 (99568)	AD11/FO	EH	CCM	RIV	Set 02 - The Royal Scot Set
3069 (99540)	AD11/FO	EH	CCM	RIV	Set 02 - The Royal Scot Set
3097	AD11/FO	EH	CCM	RIV	Set 02 - The Royal Scot Set
3098	AD11/FO	EH	CHC	RIV	Set 01 - The British Classic Set
3100	AD11/FO	EH	CHC	RIV	
3107	AD11/FO	EH	CHC	RIV	Set 01 - The British Classic Set
3110 (99124)	AD11/FO	EH	CHC	RIV	Set 01 - The British Classic Set
3112 (99357)	AD11/FO	EH	CHC	RIV	Set 01 - The British Classic Set
3114 (S)	AD11/FO	EH	GRN	RIV	
3119	AD11/FO	EH	CCM	RIV	Set 02 - The Royal Scot Set

3120	AD11/FO	EH	CCM	RIV	Set 03
3121	AD11/FO	EH	CHC	RIV	Set 02 - The Royal Scot Set
3122	AD11/FO	EH	CHC	RIV	Set 01 - The British Classic Set
3123	AD11/FO	EH	CHC	RIV	Set 03
3124 (S)	AD11/FO	EH	GRN	RIV	
3127 (S)	AD11/FO	EH	GRN	RIV	
3133 (S) (99192)	AD11/FO	EH	MAR	RIV	
3140	AD11/FO	EH	CHC	RIV	Set 01 - The British Classic Set
3141 (3608)	AD11/FO	EH	MRN	RIV	Set 03
3144 (3602)	AD11/FO	EH	MRN	RIV	Set 03
3146	AD11/FO	EH	MRN	RIV	Set 03
3147 (3604)	AD11/FO	EH	LNE	RIV	Set 03
3149	AD11/FO	EH	CCM	RIV	Set 02 - The Royal Scot Set
3181 (S)	AD1D/FO	EH	RIV	RIV	*Topaz*
3223 (S)	AD1E/FO	BU	RIV	RIV	*Diamond*
3227	AD1E/FO	EH	RIV	RIV	
3240 (S)	AD1E/FO	BU	RIV	RIV	*Sapphire*
3277	AD1F/FO	EH	ANG	RIV	Set 05 - The Norfolkman
3278	AD1F/FO	EH	RIV	RIV	
3279	AD1F/FO	EH	MAR	RIV	Set 05 - The Norfolkman
3295	AD1F/FO	EH	ANG	RIV	Set 05 - The Norfolkman
3304	AD1F/FO	EH	VIR	RIV	Set 07 - The West Coast Set
3314	AD1F/FO	EH	VIR	RIV	Set 07 - The West Coast Set
3325	AD1F/FO	EH	VIR	RIV	Set 07 - The West Coast Set
3330	AD1F/FO	EH	RIV	RIV	Set 04 - The Great Briton - *Brunel*
3333	AD1F/FO	EH	VIR	RIV	Set 07 - The West Coast Set
3334	AD1F/FO	EH	ANG	RIV	Set 05 - The Norfolkman
3336	AD1F/FO	CD	RIV	RIV	Set 05 - The Norfolkman
3340	AD1F/FO	EH	VIR	RIV	Set 07 - The West Coast Set
3344	AD1F/FO	EH	RIV	RIV	Set 07 - The West Coast Set
3345	ADIF/FO	EH	VIR	RIV	Set 07 - The West Coast Set
3348	AD1F/FO	EH	RIV	RIV	Set 04 - The Great Briton - *Gainsborough*
3356	AD1F/FO	EH	RIV	RIV	Set 04 - The Great Briton - *Tennyson*
3358	AD1F/FO	EH	RIV	RIV	
3364	AD1F/FO	EH	RIV	RIV	Set 04 - The Great Briton - *Shakespeare*
3379	AD1F/FO	EH	ANG	RIV	
3384	AD1F/FO	EH	RIV	RIV	Set 04 - The Great Briton - *Dickens*
3386	AD1F/FO	EH	VIR	RIV	Set 07 - The West Coast Set
3390	AD1F/FO	EH	RIV	RIV	Set 04 - The Great Briton - *Constable*
3397	AD1F/FO	EH	RIV	RIV	Set 04 - The Great Briton - *Wordsworth*
3417	AD1F/FO	EH	ANG	RIV	
3426	AD1F/FO	EH	RIV	RIV	Set 04 - The Great Briton - *Elgar*
4927	AC21/TSO	EH	CHC	RIV	Set 01 - The British Classic Set
4949	AC21/TSO	EH	CHC	RIV	Set 03
4959	AC21/TSO	ZA	CHC	RIV	
4991	AC21/TSO	EH	CHC	RIV	
4996 (99001)	AC21/TSO	CD	MAR	RIV	
4998	AC21/TSO	EH	CHC	RIV	Set 03
5008 (99002)	AC21/TSO	CD	MAN	RIV	
5009	AC21/TSO	EH	CHC	RIV	Set 01 - The British Classic Set
5027 (S)	AC21/TSO	EH	GRN	RIV	
5040	AC21/TSO	EH	CHC	RIV	Set 01 - The British Classic Set
5276	AC2A/TSO	EH	RIV	RIV	Set 02 - The Royal Scot Set
5292	AC2A/TSO	EH	CHC	RIV	Set 02 - The Royal Scot Set
5309 (S)	AC2A/TSO	EH	CHC	RIV	
5341	AC2A/TSO	EH	CCM	RIV	Set 02 - The Royal Scot Set
5350	AC2A/TSO	EH	CHC	RIV	Set 01 - The British Classic Set - *Dawn*
5366	AC2A/TSO	EH	CHC	RIV	Set 02 - The Royal Scot Set
5494 (S)	AC2B/TSO	SV	NSE	RIV	
5647 (S)	AC2D/TSO	EH	RIV	RIV	
5910	AC2F/TSO	EH	VIR	RIV	Set 07 - The West Coast Set
5921	AC2F/TSO	EH	RIV	RIV	Set 05 - The Norfolkman
5929	AC2F/TSO	EH	ANG	RIV	Set 05 - The Norfolkman
5937	AC2F/TSO	EH	VIR	RIV	
5945	AC2F/TSO	EH	VIR	RIV	Set 07 - The West Coast Set
5950	AC2F/TSO	EH	RIV	RIV	
5952 (S)	AC2F/TSO	EH	VIR	RIV	

Riviera

5955 (S)	AC2F/TSO	EH	VIR	RIV	
5961	AC2F/TSO	EH	VIR	RIV	Set 07 - The West Coast Set
5964	AC2F/TSO	EH	ANG	RIV	
5965	AC2F/TSO	CD	ATW	RIV	
5976	AC2F/TSO	CD	ATW	RIV	
5985	AC2F/TSO	EH	ANG	RIV	Set 05 - The Norfolkman
5987	AC2F/TSO	EH	VIR	RIV	Set 07 - The West Coast Set
5997	AC2F/TSO	EH	VIR	RIV	Set 07 - The West Coast Set
5998	AC2F/TSO	EH	ANG	RIV	Set 05 - The Norfolkman
6006	AC2F/TSO	CF	ANG	RIV	Set 05 - The Norfolkman
6024 (S)	AC2F/TSO	EH	VIR	RIV	
6027	AC2F/TSO	EH	RIV	RIV	Set 07 - The West Coast Set
6042	AC2F/TSO	EH	ANG	RIV	Set 05 - The Norfolkman
6051	AC2F/TSO	EH	VIR	RIV	Set 07 - The West Coast Set
6054	AC2F/TSO	EH	VIR	RIV	Set 07 - The West Coast Set
6067 (S)	AC2F/TSO	EH	VIR	RIV	
6137	AC2F/TSO	CD	ATW	RIV	
6141	AC2F/TSO	EH	RIV	RIV	Set 07 - The West Coast Set
6158	AC2F/TSO	EH	VIR	RIV	Set 07 - The West Coast Set
6176 (S)	AC2F/TSO	EH	VIR	RIV	
6177	AC2F/TSO	EH	RIV	RIV	
6183	AC2F/TSO	CD	ATW	RIV	
6310 (81448)	AX51/GEN	EH	CHC	RIV	
6320	AZ5Z/SAL	SK	MRN	RIV	
6720 (6602)	AN1D/RMBF	EH	MRN	RIV	
6722 (6611)	AN1D/RMBF	LM	FSW	RIV	
9504	AC2E/BSO	EH	RIV	RIV	Set 07 - The West Coast Set
9507	AC2E/BSO	EH	VIR	RIV	
9509	AE2E/BSO	CP	ATW	RIV	
9520	AE2F/BSO	EH	RIV	RIV	Set 07 - The West Coast Set
9521	AE2F/BSO	CD	ATW	RIV	
9526	AC2F/BSO	EH	RIV	RIV	
9527	AC2F/BSO	EH	ANG	RIV	
9537	AE2F/BSO	EH	ADV	RIV	
9539	AE2F/BSO	CP	ATW	RIV	
17015 (14015)	AB11/BFK	TM	CHC	RIV	Set 02 - The Royal Scot Set
17056 (S) (14056)	AB1A/BFK	EH	MAR	RIV	
17077 (14077)	AB1A/BFK	EH	RIV	RIV	Set 04 - The Great Briton - *Catherine*
17105 (2905)	AX5B/BFK	EH	RIV	RIV	Set 02 - Staff Couchette
21224	AB31/BCK	EH	MAR	RIV	Directors saloon
21245 (99356)	AB31/BCK	EH	MAR	RIV	Set 03
21269	AB31/BCK	EH	CHC	RIV	
21272 (99129)	AB31/BCK	EH	CHC	RIV	Set 01 - The British Classic Set
35469 (99763)	AB21/BSK	EH	CCM	RIV	Set 03
80041 (1690)	AK51/RK	EH	MAR	RIV	Set 03 - Pride of the Nation
80042 (1646)	AJ41/RK	EH	BLG	RIV	
94538 (94426)	BG	EH	RES	DBS	

Below: *The Riviera Trains passenger fleet is made available to charter operators, with train sets based at both Crewe and Eastleigh. Sets have been carefully formed in like liveries and styles. One of the chocolate and cream-liveried sets contains this buffet car No. 1671, which is seen at Penzance from its kitchen end.* **Antony Christie**

Right: *With its mid-vehicle door removed and plated over. Mk1 TSO No. 4998 is seen in BR branded chocolate and cream livery. This vehicle is fitted with electric train supply and is mounted on cast Commonwealth bogies.* **CJM**

Scottish Railway Preservation Society

Number	*Type*	*Depot*	*Livery*	*Operator*
1859 (99822)	AN21/RMB	BT	MAR	SRP
21241	AB31/BCK	BT	CHC	SRP
35185	AB21/BSK	BT	MAR	SRP

Stratford Class 47 Group

Vehicle Length: 63ft 6in (19.35m)
Height: 12ft 10⅜in (3.91m)
Width: 9ft 2in (2.79m)
Electric Train Heat fitted
Engine: Sulzer 12LDA28C
Horsepower: 2,580hp (1,922kW)
Electrical Equipment: Brush

Number	*Depot*	*Pool*	*Livery*	*Owner*	*Operator*	*Name*
47580 (47732)	MNR	MBDL	LLB	S4G	S4G	*County of Essex*

Right: *Cast nameplate and county emblem, plus 'cockney sparrow' motif on the side of Stratford Class 47 Group's Class 47/4 No. 47580.* **Norman E. Preedy**

Venice Simplon Orient Express (VSOE)

Number	*Name*	*Type*	*Depot*	*Livery*	*Operator*	*Notes*
213 (99535)	*Minerva*	AO40/PFP	SL	PUL	VSO	
239 (S)	*Agatha*	AO40/PFP	SL	PUL	VSO	
243 (99541)	*Lucille*	AO40/PFP	SL	PUL	VSO	
245 (99534)	*Ibis*	AO40/PFK	SL	PUL	VSO	
254 (99536)	*Zena*	AO40/PFP	SL	PUL	VSO	
255 (99539)	*Ione*	AO40/PFK	SL	PUL	VSO	
261 (S)	Car No. 83	AO40/PTP	SL	PUL	VSO	
264 (S)	*Ruth*	AO40/PCK	SL	PUL	VSO	

VSOE

280 (99537)	*Audrey*	AO40/PFK	SL	PUL	VSO	
281 (99546)	*Gwen*	AO40/PFK	SL	PUL	VSO	
283 (S)	*Mona*	AO40/PFK	SL	PUL	VSO	
284 (99543)	*Vera*	AO40/PFK	SL	PUL	VSO	
285 (S)	Car No. 85	AO40/PTP	SL	PUL	VSO	
286 (S)	Car No. 86	AO40/PTP	SL	PUL	VSO	
288 (S)	Car No. 88	AO40/PTB	SL	PUL	VSO	
292 (S)	Car No. 92	AO40/PTB	SL	PUL	VSO	
293 (S)	Car No. 93	AO40/PTB	SL	PUL	VSO	
301 (99530)	*Perseus*	AO41/PFP	SL	PUL	VSO	
302 (99531)	*Phoenix*	AO41/PFP	SL	PUL	VSO	
307 (S)	*Carina*	AO41/PFK	SL	PUL	VSO	
308 (99532)	*Cygnus*	AO41/PFP	SL	PUL	VSO	
325 (2907)		AJ11/RFO	CP	PUL	VSO	
1207 (6422)		AJ11/RFO	CP	-	VSO	
1221 (3371)		AJ11/RFO	CP	-	VSO	
1566		AK51/RKB	CP	VSN	VSO	
1953		AJ41/RBR	CP	VSN	VSO	
3174	*Glamis*	AD1D/FO	CP	VSN	VSO	
3182	*Warwick*	AD1D/FO	CP	VSN	VSO	
3232		AD1E/FO	CD	RIV	CAD	
3247	*Chatsworth*	AD1E/FO	CP	VSN	VSO	
3267	*Belvoir*	AD1E/FO	CP	VSN	VSO	
3273	*Alnwick*	AD1E/FO	CP	VSN	VSO	
3275	*Harlech*	AD1E/FO	CP	VSN	VSO	
6313 (92167)		AX51/GEN	SL	PUL	VSO	
9502		AE2E/BSO	SL	PUL	VSO	
10541 (99968)		AO4G/SSV	CS	MRN	VSO	Royal Scotsman - State Car 5
10556 (99969)		AO4G/SSV	CS	MRN	VSO	Royal Scotsman - Service Car
10569 (S)	*Leviathan*	AU4G/SLEP	CP	PUL	VSO	
10729	*Crewe*	AS4G/SLE	CP	VSN	VSO	
10734 (2914)	*Balmoral*	AS4G/SLE	CP	VSN	VSO	
17167 (14167)		AB1D/BFK	CP	VSN	VSO	
35466 (99545)		AB21/BSK	SL	PUL	VSO	
92904		NBA	CP	PUL	VSO	

Above: *In addition to the luxury Pullman vehicles owned and operated as part of the VSOE, several support vehicles are owned by the company and operate with the train to provide staff accommodation. One such vehicle is former BSK 35466, now running as No. 99545 and used as a staff support vehicle.* **CJM**

Vintage Trains

Class 47

Vehicle Length: 63ft 6in (19.35m)
Height: 12ft 10⅜in (3.91m)
Width: 9ft 2in (2.79m)
Electric Train Heat fitted
Engine: Sulzer 12LDA28C
Horsepower: 2,580hp (1,922kW)
Electrical Equipment: Brush

Number	Depot	Pool	Livery	Owner	Operator
47773 (47541)	TM	MBDL	GRN	VTN	VTN

Coaching Stock

Number	Type	Depot	Livery	Owner	Operator
335 (99361)	AO11/PSK	TM	PUL	VTN	VTN
349 (99349)	AO11/PSP	TM	PUL	VTN	VTN
353 (99353)	AO11/PSP	TM	PUL	VTN	VTN
1201 (6445)	AJ1F/RFO	TM	CHC	VTN	VTN
3351	AD1F/FO	CS	CHC	VTN	VTN
5157	AC2Z/TSO	TM	CHC	VTN	VTN
5177	AC2Z/TSO	TM	CHC	VTN	VTN
5191	AC2Z/TSO	TM	CHC	VTN	VTN
5198	AC2Z/TSO	TM	CHC	VTN	VTN
5212	AC2Z/TSO	TM	CHC	VTN	VTN
5928	AC2F/TSO	TM	CHC	VTN	VTN
9101 (9398)	AH2Z/BSOT	TM	CHC	VTN	VTN
9496	AE2E/BSO	TM	CHC	VTN	VTN
9711	AF2F/DBSO	TM	CHC	VTN	VTN
17018 (99108)	AB11/BFK	TM	CHC	VTN	VTN
17090	AB1A/BFK	TM	CHC	VTN	VTN
96100 (86374)	GUV	TM	BRN	VTN	VTN

West Coast Railway Company

Class 03

Vehicle Length: 26ft 3in (7.92m)
Height: 12ft 7⁷⁄₁₆in (3.72m)
Width: 8ft 6in (2.59m)
Engine: Gardner 8L3
Horsepower: 204hp (149kW)
Mechanical Equipment: Wilson-Drewry

Number	Depot	Pool	Livery	Owner	Operator	Name
03196(S)	CS	MBDL	GRN	WCR	WCR	*Joyce*
D2381(S)	CS	MBDL	BLK	WCR	WCR	

Class 08

Vehicle Length: 29ft 3in (8.91m)
Height: 12ft 8⅝in (3.87m)
Width: 8ft 6in (2.59m)
Engine: English Electric 6K
Horsepower: 400hp (298kW)
Electrical Equipment: English Electric

Number	Depot	Pool	Livery	Owner	Operator	Name
08418	CS	MBDL	EWS	WCR	WCR	
08485	CS	MBDL	BLU	WCR	WCR	
08678(S)	CS	AWCX	GLX	WCR	WCR	*Artila*

Class 33

Vehicle Length: 50ft 9in (15.47m)
Height: 12ft 8in (3.86m)
Width: 33/0, 9ft 3in (2.81m),
33/2 8ft 8in (2.64m)
Engine: Sulzer 8LDA28A
Horsepower: 1,550hp (1,156kW)
Electrical Equipment: Crompton Parkinson

Number	Depot	Pool	Livery	Owner	Operator	Name
33025(S)	CS	AWCX	WCR	WCR	WCR	*Glen Falloch*
33029	CS	AWCA	WCR	WCR	WCR	*Glen Roy*
33207	CS	AWCA	WCR	WCR	WCR	*Jim Martin*

Class 37

Vehicle Length: 61ft 6in (18.74m)
Height: 13ft 0¼in (3.96m)
Width: 8ft 11⅝in (2.73m)
Engine: English Electric 12CSVT
Horsepower: 1,750hp (1,304kW)
Electrical Equipment: English Electric

Number	Depot	Pool	Livery	Owner	Operator	Name
37214 (S)	CS	AWCX	WCR	WCR	WCR	*Loch Laidon*
37516 (S) (37086)	CS	AWCA	WCR	WCR	-	
37517 (S) (37018)	CS	MBDL	LHL	WCR	-	
37518 (37076)	CS	AWCX	ICS	WCR	WCR	*Fort William/An Gearasden*

WCRC

37668 (S) (37257)	**CS**	**AWCX**	**EWS**	**WCR**	**-**	
37669 (S) (37129)	**CS**	**AWCX**	**WCR**	**WCR**	**-**	
37676 (37126)	**CS**	**AWCA**	**WCR**	**WCR**	**WCR**	***Loch Rannoch***
37685 (37234)	**CS**	**AWCA**	**WCR**	**WCR**	**WCR**	***Loch Arkaig***
37706 (37016)	**CS**	**AWCA**	**WCR**	**WCR**	**WCR**	
37710 (S) (37044)	**CS**	**MBDL**	**LHL**	**WCR**	**-**	
37712 (37102)	**CS**	**AWCX**	**WCR**	**WCR**	**WCR**	

37668, 37669 to be fitted with WTRMS for Cambrian Line duties

Class 47

Vehicle Length: 63ft 6in (19.35m)
Height: 12ft 10⅜in (3.91m)
Width: 9ft 2in (2.79m)
Electric Train Heat fitted to Class 47/4, 47/7 and 47/8
Engine: Sulzer 12LDA28C
Horsepower: 2,580hp (1,922kW)
Electrical Equipment: Brush

Number	*Depot*	*Pool*	*Livery*	*Owner*	*Operator*	*Name*
47194 (S)	**CS**	**AWCX**	**TLF**	**WCR**	**-**	
47237	**CS**	**AWCA**	**WCR**	**WCR**	**WCR**	
47245	**CS**	**AWCA**	**WCR**	**WCR**	**WCR**	
47270	**CS**	**AWCA**	**BLU**	**WCR**	**WCR**	***Swift***
47355 (S)	**CS**	**AWCX**	**BLK**	**WCR**	**-**	
47492	**CS**	**AWCX**	**RES**	**WCR**	**WCR**	
47500 (S) (47770)	**CS**	**AWCX**	**WCR**	**WCR**	**-**	
47746 (47605)	**CS**	**AWCX**	**WCR**	**WCR**	**WCR**	
47760 (47562)	**CS**	**AWCA**	**WCR**	**WCR**	**WCR**	
47768 (47490)	**CS**	**AWCX**	**EWS**	**WCR**	**WCR**	
47772 (S) (47537)	**CS**	**AWCX**	**RES**	**WCR**	**-**	
47776 (S) (47578)	**CS**	**AWCX**	**RES**	**WCR**	**-**	
47786 (47821)	**CS**	**AWCA**	**WCR**	**WCR**	**WCR**	***Roy Castle OBE***
47787 (47823)	**CS**	**AWCX**	**WCR**	**WCR**	**WCR**	***Windsor Castle***
47804 (47792)	**CS**	**AWCA**	**WCR**	**WCR**	**WCR**	
47826 (47637)	**CS**	**AWCA**	**WCR**	**WCR**	**WCR**	
47851/D1648 (47639)	**CS**	**AWCA**	**WCR**	**WCR**	**WCR**	
47854 (47674)	**CS**	**AWCA**	**WCR**	**WCR**	**WCR**	***Diamond Jubilee***

Above: *The West Coast Railway Co is another major provider of traction, stock and train crews to the charter and spot hire market. The company has a sizeable fleet of main-line certified locomotives, mostly painted in deep maroon livery. Class 47 No. 47826 is illustrated at Gloucester with its No. 1 end on the right.* **Norman E. Preedy**

Class 57

Vehicle Length: 63ft 6in (19.38m)
Height: 12ft 10⅛in (3.91m)
Width: 9ft 2in (2.79m)
Engine: EMD 645-12E3
Horsepower: 2,500hp (1,860kW)
Electrical Equipment: Brush

Number	*Depot*	*Pool*	*Livery*	*Owner*	*Operator*
57001 (47356)	**CS**	**AWCA**	**WCR**	**WCR**	**WCR**
57005 (47350)	**CS**	**AWCX**	**WCR**	**WCR**	**WCR**
57006 (47187)	**CS**	**AWCA**	**WCR**	**WCR**	**WCR**
57313 (47371)	**CS**	**AWCA**	**BLU**	**WCR**	**ATW**

57314 (47372)	CS	AWCA	WCR	WCR	ATW
57315 (47234)	CS	AWCA	WCR	WCR	ATW
57316 (47290)	CS	AWCA	BLU	WCR	ATW

57601 (47825)	CS	AWCA	WCR	WCR	WCR

Looking very smart in ex-works West Coast Railway maroon, Class 57/6 No. 57601, together with a WCRC Class 47, passes Totnes at the head of a westbound 'Cornish Riviera Express' charter. No. 57601 was the prototype ETH-fitted Class 57 produced in a joint partnership between Porterbrook Leasing and Brush Traction; the project led to the production run of Class 57/6s for First Great Western sleeper services. **Nathan Williamson**

Coaching Stock

Number	*Name*	*Type*	*Depot*	*Livery*	*Operator*	*Notes*
159 (99980)		AO10/SAL	CS	SPL	WCR*	LNWR saloon (ex-Q of Scots)
326 (S) (99402)	*Emerald*	AO11/PFP	CS	PUL	WCR	
347 (99347)	Car No. 347	AO11/PSO	CS	WCR	WCR	
348 (99348)	Car No. 348	AO11/PSP	CS	WCR	WCR	
350 (99350)	Car No. 350	AO11/PSP	CS	GRN	WCR	
352 (99352)	*Amethyst*	AO11/PSP	CS	PUL	WCR	
354 (99354)	*The Hadrian Bar*	AO11/PSP	CS	PUL	WCR	
504 (99678)	*Ullswater*	AP1Z/PFK	CS	PUL	WCR	
506 (99679)	*Windermere*	AP1Z/PFK	CS	PUL	WCR	
546 (S) (99670)	*City of Manchester*	AQ1Z/PFP	CS	PUL	WCR	
548 (99671)	*Grasmere*	AQ1Z/PFP	CS	PUL	WCR	
549 (99672)	*Bassenthwaite*	AQ1Z/PFP	CS	PUL	WCR	
550 (99673)	*Rydal Water*	AQ1Z/PFP	CS	PUL	WCR	
551 (99674)	*Buttermere*	AQ1Z/PFP	CS	PUL	WCR	
552 (99675)	*Ennerdale Water*	AQ1Z/PFP	CS	PUL	WCR	
553 (99676)	*Crummock Water*	AQ1Z/PFP	CS	PUL	WCR	
586 (99677)	*Derwent Water*	AR1Z/PFB	CS	PUL	WCR	
807 (99881)		AO10/SAL	CS	SPL	WCR*	GNR Saloon (ex-Q of Scots)
1644 (S)		AJ41/RBR	CS	ICS	WCR	
1650 (S)		AJ41/RBR	CS	ICS	WCR	
1652 (S)		AJ41/RBR	CS	ICS	WCR	
1655 (S)		AJ41/RBR	CS	ICS	WCR	
1663 (S)		AJ41/RBR	CS	ICS	WCR	
1670 (S)		AJ41/RBR	CS	ICS	WCR	
1730		AJ41/RBR	CS	WCR	WCR	
1800 (5970)		AN2F/RSS	CS	WCR	WCR	
1840		AN21/RMB	CS	WCR	WCR	Set - The Green Train
1860		AN21/RMB	CS	WCR	WCR	
1861 (99132)		AN21/RMB	CS	WCR	WCR	

WCRC

1882 (99311)		AN21/RMB	CS	WCR	WCR	
1961		AJ41/RBR	CS	GRN	WCR	Set - The Green Train
2127 (S)		AO11/SLF	CS	MAR	WCR	
2833 (21270)		AU51/SLSC	CS	WCR	WCR	
3058	*Paula*	AD11/FO	CS	WCR	WCR	
3093 (977594)	*Florence*	AD11/FO	CS	WCR	WCR	
3105 (99121)	*Julia*	AD11/FO	CS	WCR	WCR	
3106 (99122)	*Alexandra*	AD11/FO	CS	WCR	WCR	
3113 (99125)	*Jessica*	AD11/FO	CS	WCR	WCR	
3117 (99127)	*Christina*	AD11/FO	CS	WCR	WCR	
3128 (99371)	*Victoria*	AD11/FO	CS	WCR	WCR	
3130 (99128)	*Pamela*	AD11/FO	CS	WCR	WCR	
3136 (3605)	*Diana*	AD11/FO	CS	WCR	WCR	
3143 (3609)	*Patricia*	AD11/FO	CS	WCR	WCR	
3313		AD1F/FO	CS	WCR	WCR	
3326		AD1F/FO	CS	WCR	WCR	
3350		AD1F/FO	CS	WCR	WCR	
3352		AD1F/FO	CS	WCR	WCR	
3359		AD1F/FO	CS	WCR	WCR	
3360		AD1F/FO	CS	ICS	WCR	
3362		AD1F/FO	CS	ICS	WCR	
3392 (S)		AD1F/FO	CS	BPM	WCR	Blue Pullman vehicle
3395		AD1F/FO	CS	WCR	WCR	
3431		AD1F/FO	CS	WCR	WCR	
3766 (99317)		AC21/SO	CS	WCR	WCR	
4860 (S) (99193)		AC21/TSO	CS	MAR	WCR	
4905		AC21/TSO	CS	WCR	WCR	
4912 (99318)		AC21/TSO	CS	WCR	WCR	
4931 (99329)		AC21/TSO	CS	WCR	WCR	
4932 (S)		AC21/TSO	CS	BLG	WCR	
4940		AC21/TSO	CS	WCR	WCR	
4951		AC21/TSO	CS	WCR	WCR	
4954 (99326)		AC21/TSO	CS	WCR	WCR	
4958		AC21/TSO	CS	WCR	WCR	
4960		AC21/TSO	CS	WCR	WCR	
4973		AC21/TSO	CS	WCR	WCR	
4984		AC21/TSO	CS	WCR	WCR	
4994		AC21/TSO	CS	WCR	WCR	
4997 (S)		AC21/TSO	CS	BLG	WCR	
5032 (99194)		AC21/TSO	CS	WCR	WCR	
5033 (99328)		AC21/TSO	CS	WCR	WCR	
5035 (99195)		AC21/TSO	CS	WCR	WCR	
5044 (99327)		AC21/TSO	CS	WCR	WCR	
5125 (S)		AC2Z/TSO	BH	GRN	WCR	
5171		AC2Z/TSO	CS	MAR	WCR	
5200		AC2Z/TSO	CS	GRN	WCR	
5216		AC2Z/TSO	CS	MAR	WCR	
5222		AC2Z/TSO	CS	MAR	WCR	
5229	*The Green Knight*	AC2Z/SO	CS	MAR	WTN	
5236		AC2Z/SO	CS	MAR	WCR	
5237		AD2Z/SO	CS	MAR	WCR	
5239	*The Red Knight*	AD2Z/SO	CS	MAR	WTN	
5249		AD2Z/SO	CS	GRN	WCR	
5278	*Melisande*	AC2A/TSO	CS	CHC	WTN	
5419		AC2A/TSO	CS	WCR	WTN	
5756 (S)		AC2E/TSO	CS	WCR	WCR	
6000		AC2F/TSO	CS	WCR	WCR	
6012		AC2F/TSO	CS	WCR	WCR	
6014 (S)		AC2F/TSO	CS	ICS	WCR	At Hellifield
6021		AC3F/TSO	CS	WCR	WCR	
6022		AC2F/TSO	CS	WCR	WCR	
6103		AC2F/TSO	CS	WCR	WCR	
6115 (S)		AC2F/TSO	CS	WCR	WCR	
6135 (S)		AC2F/TSO	CS	ICS	WCR	At Hellifield
6312 (92925)		AX51/GEN	CS	WCR	WCR	
6528 (5592)		AG2C/TSOT	CS	WCR	WCR	
6723		AN1D/RMBF	CS	WCR	WCR	
6724		AN1D/RMBF	CS	WCR	WCR	
9104 (S) (9401)		AH2Z/BSOT	CS	WCR	WCR	

9391	*Pendragon*	AE2Z/BSO	CS	PUL	WTN	
9392		AE2Z/BSO	CS	WCR	WCR	Set - The Green Train
9440		AE2C/BSO	SH	WCR	WCR	
9448 (S)		AE2C/BSO	CS	WCR	WCR	
9493		AE2D/BSO	CS	WCR	CWR	Blue Pullman vehicle
13227		AA11/FK	CS	WCR	WCR	
13306 (S)		AA11/FK	CS	WCR	WCR	
13320 (S)		AA11/FK	CS	WCR	WCR	
13321 (99316)		AA11/FK/RBR	CS	WCR	WCR	
13440 (S)		AA1A/FK	CS	GRN	WCR	Set - The Green Train
17102 (99680)		AB1A/BFK	CS	MAB	WCR	
17168 (S) (99319)		AB1D/BFK	CS	WCR	WCR	
18806 (99722)		AA21/SK	CS	WCR	WCR	
18893 (99712)		Kitchen	CS	WCR	WCR	
19208 (99884)	Car No. 84	AA21/SK	CS	WCR	WCR	
21256 (99304)		AB31/BCK	CS	WCR	WCR	
21266		AB31/BCK	CS	WCR	WCR	
34525 (S) (99966)		AR51/GEN	CS	WCR	WCR	
35407 (99886)		AB21/BSK	CS	SPL	WCR	LNWR livery (Q of Scots)
45018 (99052)		AO10/SAL	CS	QOS	WCR	
45026 (S)		SAL	CS	MAR	WCR	LMS Inspection Saloon
96175		GUV	CS	MAR	WCR	Water carrier
99723 (35459)		AB21/BSK	CS	WCR	WCR	

WCR* - Owned by Scottish Highland Railway Co

Right: *The majority of West Coast Railway Co passenger stock has been or is in the process of being outshopped in house colours, which look very smart in good light, but perhaps a little drab in dull light conditions. A recently restored vehicle is former Mk1 BSK No. 35459, which now sports the identity of 99723. This is a 100mph authorised coach mounted on cast Commonwealth bogies.* **Nathan Williamson**

Right: *Mk2F TSO No. 6000 is on the books of West Coast Railway Co and is restored to house livery. The vehicle is seen within a train formation at Totnes.* **Nathan Williamson**

Loco Support Coaches

Most preserved locomotives authorised for main-line operation, either steam or diesel, operate with a support coach conveying owners' representatives, engineering staff and light maintenance equipment. Support coaches can be allocated to a specific locomotive or operate with a pool of locos.

Number	*Type*	*Depot*	*Livery*	*Support Coach for*
14007 (99782) *Mercator*	**AB11/BSK**	**NY**	**MAR**	**61264 or 60163**
17013 (14013) *Botaurus*	**AB11/BFK**	**SH**	**PUL**	**60019**
17019 (14019)	**AB11/BFK**	**CS**	**MAR**	**61994**
17025 (14025)	**AB11/BFK**	**CS**	**MAR**	**45690**
17041 (99141)	**AB1Z/BFK**	**BQ**	**MAR**	**71000**
17096	**AB1B/BFK**	**SL**	**CHC**	**35028**
21096 (99080)	**AB31/BCK**	**NY**	**MAR**	**60007**
21232 (99040)	**AB31/BCK**	**SK**	**MAR**	**46233**
21236 (99120)	**AB31/BCK**	**ZG**	**GRN**	**30828**
21249	**AB21/BCK**	**BH**	**CCM**	**60163**
21268	**AB31/BCK**	**YK**	**MAR**	**6100**
35317	**AD21/BSK**	**BQ**	**GRN**	**30850**
35322 (99035)	**AB21/BSK**	**CS**	**MAR**	**70000 and WCRC traction**
35329	**AB21/BSK**	**RL**	**GRN**	**Mid Hants fleet**
35333 (99180)	**AB21/BSK**	**MI**	**CHC**	**6024**
35449 (99241)	**AB21/BSK**	**BQ**	**MAR**	**45231**
35451	**AB21/BSK**	**MI**	**GRN**	**34046**
35457 (99995)	**AB21/BSK**	**NY**	**MAR**	**60532**
35461 (99720)	**AB21/BSK**	**TM**	**CHC**	**5029**
35463 (99312)	**AB21/BSK**	**CS**	**WCR**	**WCR fleet**
35464	**AB21/BSK**	**PR**	**MAR**	**Swanage Railway**
35465 (99991)	**AB21/BSK**	**BQ**	**CCM**	**Jeremy Hosking / 70000**
35468 (99953)	**AB21/BSK**	**NY**	**MAR**	**NYMR fleet**
35470	**AB21/BSK**	**TM**	**CHC**	**Vintage Trains fleet**
35476 (99041)	**AB21/BSK**	**SK**	**MAR**	**46233**
35486 (99405)	**AB21/BSK**	**--**	**MAR**	**60009 or 61994**
35508	**AB1C/BSK**	**BQ**	**MAR**	**East Lancs fleet**
35517 (17088)	**ABIK/BSKk**	**BQ**	**MAR**	**East Lancs fleet**
35518 (17097)	**AB11/BFK**	**SH**	**GRN**	**34067**
80204 (35297)	**NNX**	**TN**	**MAR**	**61994**
80217 (35299)	**NNX**	**CS**	**MAR**	**WCRC fleet**
80220 (35276)	**NNX**	**NY**	**MAR**	**62005**

Below: *Two steam loco support coaches, BSK No. 35465 which operates with* Britannia *and BCK No. 21249 which operates with A1 No. 60163* Tornado, *both painted in carmine and cream, pass through Kensington Olympia attached to their locomotives together with Bulleid No. 34046* Braunton. *These support vehicles are generally dual braked and dual heated.* **CJM**

Locomotives

No locos were off lease at the time of going to press

Diesel Multiple Units

No DMUs were off lease at the time of going to press

Electric Multiple Units

Number	Class	Owner	Location
317708	317	ANG	KT
317709	317	ANG	IL
317710	317	ANG	KT
317714	317	ANG	KT
317719	317	ANG	IL
317723	317	ANG	IL
317729	317	ANG	IL
317732	317	ANG	IL
508201	508	ANG	ZG
508203	508	ANG	ZG
508207	508	ANG	ZG
508208	508	ANG	ZG
508209	508	ANG	ZG
508210	508	ANG	ZG
508211	508	ANG	ZG
508212	508	-	§

§ Fire training set at Moreton-in -Marsh

■ Cars 64664 and 64707 from 508207 to be converted to EMU translator vehicles for Angel Trains.

Right: *Off-lease Class 508 stock at Eastleigh Works awaiting disposal. These former SouthEastern-operated sets are unlikely to see further use.* **Antony Christie**

Coaching Stock - Passenger

Number	Type	Owner	Location
1209 (6457)	RFO	EVL	ZH
1219 (3418)	RFO	EVL	KT
3229	FO	EVL	KT
3434	FO	EVL	OY
5636	TSO	EVL	PM
5888	TSO	EVL	CS
6121	TSO	EVL	KT
6160	TSO	EVL	LM
6164	TSO	EVL	KT
10204 (40502)	RFM	PTR	3M
10206 (40507)	RFM	PTR	LM
10231 (10016)	RFM	PTR	§
10241 (10009)	RFM	PTR	IL
10253 (10026)	RFM	PTR	LM
10256 (10028)	RFM	PTR	YO¶
10260 (10001)	RFM	PTR	YO¶

¶ Instruction vehicle - Yoker
§ Fire Training School

Number	Type	Owner	Location
10547	SLE	PTR	IS
10661 Concept vehicle at Wolverton			
10667	SLE	-	LM
10682	SLE	PTR	TO
10698	SLE	-	LM
10733	SLE	-	MM
11026	FO	PTR	LM
11074	FO	PTR	LM
12008	TSO	PTR	ZB
12022	TSO	PTR	ZB
12029	TSO	PTR	LM
12036	TSO	PTR	LM
12083	TSO	PTR	LM
12092	TSO	PTR	LM
12095	TSO	PTR	LM
12101	TSO	PTR	LM
12144	TSO	PTR	LM
12156	TSO	PTR	LM
12160	TSO	PTR	LM
12163	TSO	PTR	BN

Coaching Stock - HST

Number	Type	Owner	Location
40417 (40017)	TRSB	DBR	ZK
40419 (40019)	TRSB	DBR	LM
40425 (40025)	TRSB	DBR	ZK

42324 owned by East Midlands Trains now at Birkenshaw Fire Training School

Coaching Stock - NPCCS

Number	Type	Owner	Location
82109	DVT	PTR	ZB
82125	DVT	PTR	LM
82140	DVT	PTR	LM
82149	DVT	PTR	FC
92159 (81534)	BG	EVL	KT
92901 (92001)	BG	EVL	WB
92931 (92031)	BG	EVL	PY
96139 (93751)	GUV	EVL	WB
96181 (93875)	GUV	EVL	LM

Preserved Motive Power

Preserved motive power is listed in this section. Those in a red typeface are authorised for main line operation. For information on preserved steam traction and railway centres, please refer to our sister publication *Railways Restored*, edited by Alan Butcher and published by Ian Allan Publishing.

Locomotives

Main line certified shown in red

Number	*Operator/Base*	*Status*
Prototype Locomotives		
LMS7050	NRM	STC
LMS7051	MID	OPR
LMS7069	GWR	RES
D0226	KWV	OPR
18000	DID	STC
'Deltic'	NRM	STC
Non-Classified		
D2511	KWV	OPR
D2767	BKR	OPR
D2774	STR	RES
DS75	NRS	STC
Class 01		
D2953	PRL	OPR
D2956	ELR	OPR
Class 02		
D2854	PRL	OPR
D2858	MRC	RES
D2860	NRM	OPR
D2866	PRL	RES
D2867	BAT	OPR
D2868	HST	OPR
Class 03		
03018	MFM	RES
03020	LDL	STO
03022	SWI	OPR
D2023	KES	OPR
D2024	KES	STO
03027	PRL	RES
03037	-	OPR
D2041	COL	OPR
D2046	PVR	RES
D2051	NNR	STO
03059	IOW	OPR
03062	ELR	OPR
03063	NNR	OPR
03066	BHR	OPR
03069	GWR	OPR
03072	LHR	OPR
03073	RAC	OPR
03078	TYN	OPR
03079	DER	OPR
03081	MFM	RES
03084	ECC	OPR
03089	MFM	OPR
03090	NRS	OPR
03094	CRT	OPR
03099	PRL	OPR
03112	KES	OPR
03113	PRL	RES
D2117	LHR	OPR
D2118	PRL	RES
03119	EPO	OPR
03120	FHL	OPR
03128	APF	STO
D2133	WSR	OPR
03134	DEE	OPR
D2138	MRC	OPR
D2139	PRL	RES
03141	PRB	RES
03144	WEN	OPR
03145	MOL	OPR
D2148	RIB	OPR
03152	SWI	OPR
03158	LWR	OPR
03162	LAN	OPR
03170	BAT	OPR
D2178	GWI	OPR
03180	PRL	OPR
D2182	GWR	OPR
D2184	COL	OPR
03189	RIB	RES
D2192	PDR	OPR
03197	LDL	RES
D2199	PRL	OPR
03371	ROW	OPR
03399	MFM	OPR
Class 04		
D2203	EMB	OPR
D2205	WSR	STO
D2207	NYM	OPR
D2229	PRL	RES
D2245	BAT	STO
D2246	SDR	OPR
D2271	WSR	STO
D2272	PRL	RES
D2279	EAR	OPR
D2280	NNR	RES
D2284	PRL	OPR
D2298	BRC	OPR
D2302	BHR	OPR
D2310	BAT	OPR
D2324	PRL	STO
D2325	MFM	OPR
D2334	CVR	OPR
D2337	PRL	RES
Class 05		
05001	IOW	OPR
D2578	BHR	OPR
D2587	HST	RES
D2595	RIB	OPR
Class 06		
06003	HST	OPR
Class 07		
07001	HST	OPR
07005	GCR	RES
07010	AVR	OPR
07011	SEL	OPR
07012	APF	RES
07013	ELR	RES
Class 08		
D3000	PRL	RES
D3002	PVR	OPR
D3014	PDR	OPR
08011	CPR	OPR
08012	CRT	OPR
08015	SVR	OPR
08016	PRL	OPR
08021	BRM	OPR
08022	CWR	OPR
08032	MHR	OPR
08046	CRB	OPR
08054	EMB	OPR
08060	CWR	OPR
08064	NRS	OPR
D3101	GCR	OPR
08102	LWR	OPR
08108	KES	OPR
08114	GCR	OPR
08123	CWR	OPR
08133	SVR	OPR
D3255	CVR	STO
08164	ELR	OPR
08168	BAT	OPR
D3261	SWI	RES
08195	LAN	OPR
08220	NHC	STO
08238	DFR	OPR
08266	KWV	OPR
08288	MHR	OPR
08331	MRC	OPR
08359	TSR	OPR
08377	WSR	OPR
08388	NHD	STO
08436	SWN	OPR
08443	BKR	RES
08444	BWR	OPR
08471	SVR	OPR
08473	DFR	STO
08476	SWN	OPR
08479	ELR	OPR
08490	STR	OPR
08528	BAT	OPR
08556	NYM	OPR
08590	MRC	OPR
08598	IND	OPR
08604	DID	OPR
08628	RIB	OPR
08631	MNR	OPR
08635	SVR	RES
08694	GCR	RES
08700	ELR	OPR
08767	NNR	OPR
08769	SVR	OPR
08772	NNR	OPR
08773	EMB	OPR
08780	SOU	OPR
08825	CPR	OPR
08850	NYM	OPR§
D4095	MSR	OPR
08896	SVR	OPR
08911	NRM	OPR
08927	GWR	OPR
08937	DAR	OPR
08944	ELR	OPR

§ Battersby-Whitby only

Class 09

09001	PRL	RES
09004	SPV	OPR
09010	SDR	RES
09012	SVR	OPR
09015	PRI	STO
09017	NRM	OPR
09019	WSR	OPR
09024	PRI	RES
09025	SWI	OPR

Class 10

D3452	BWR	OPR
D3489	SPV	OPR
D4067	GCR	OPR
D4092	BHR	RES

Class 11

12052	CRB	STO
12077	MRC	OPR
12082	MHR	OPR
(Runs as 12049)		
12093	CRB	OPR
12099	SVR	OPR
12131	NNR	OPR

Class 12

15224	SPV	OPR

Class 14

D9500	PRL	RES
D9502	PRL	STO
D9504	NVR	OPR
D9513	EMB	OPR
D9516	WEN	OPR
D9518	WSR	OPR
D9520	NVR	OPR
D9521	DFR	OPR
D9523	DVR	OPR
D9524	EHC	RES
D9525	PRL	OPR
D9526	WSR	OPR
D9529	NVR	OPR
D9531	ELR	RES
D9537	ELR	RES
D9539	RIB	OPR
D9551	SVR	OPR
D9553	GWR	STO
D9555	DFR	OPR

Class 15

D8233	ELR	RES

Class 17

D8568	CPR	RES

Class 20

D8000	NRM	OPR
20001	BAR	OPR
20007	GCR	OPR
20020	BKR	RES
20031	KWV	OPR
20035	CVR	STO
20048	MRC	RES
20057	MRC	RES
20059	BRM	RES
20063	GWR	STO
20069	NNR	OPR
20087	ELR	OPR
20098	GCR	RES
20110	SDR	OPR
20137	GWR	OPR
20154	GCR	OPR
20169	SRC	RES
20177	SVR	STO
20188	SVR	OPR
20205	MRC	RES
20214	LHR	OPR
20228	BIR	OPR

Class 24

24032	NYM	RES
24054	ELR	OPR
24061	NYM	RES
24081	GWR	OPR

Class 25

25035	GCR	OPR
25057	NNR	OPR
25059	KWV	OPR
25067	BAT	OPR
25072	CRB	RES
25083	CRB	RES
25173	EPO	OPR
25185	PDR	OPR
25191	SDR	STO
25235	BKR	RES
25244	EKR	STO
25262	SDR	OPR
25265	GCR	RES
25279	GCR	OPR
25283	DFR	RES
25309	WCR	RES
25313	WEN	RES
25321	MRC	OPR
25322	CVR	RES

Class 26

26001	CRB	OPR
26002	STR	RES
26004	BKR(for sale)	STO
26007	GCR	OPR
26010	LAN	OPR
26011	BHR	RES
26014	CRB	OPR
26024	BKR	OPR
26025	STR	RES
26035	CRB	RES
26038	BKR	RES
26040	MET	RES
26043	GWR	RES

Class 27

27001	BKR	OPR
27005	BKR	STO
27007	MHR	RES
27024	LHR	OPR
27050	STR	RES
27056	GCR	OPR
27059	SVR	RES
27066	DFR	OPR

Class 28

D5705	ELR	RES

Class 31

D5500	NRM	OPR
31101	BAT	RES
31108	MRC	OPR
31119	EMB	OPR
31130	BAT	OPR
31162	EHC	OPR
31163	CPR	OPR
31203	PBR(Nem)	OPR
31206	RST	OPR
31207	NNR	OPR
31210	DFR	RES
31235	MNR	OPR
31255	COL	OPR
31270	PRL	OPR
31271	NVR	OPR
31289	NLR	OPR
31327	STR	OPR
31410	SRC	RES
31414	ECC	OPR
31415	BHR	RES
31418	MRC	RES
31435	EMB	OPR
31438	EPO	OPR
31461	NEM	STO
31463	GCR	OPR
31466	DFR	OPR
31530	MNR	RES

Class 33

33002	SDR	OPR
33008	BAT	RES
33012	SWN	OPR
33018	NEM	RES
33019	BAT	OPR
33021	BRM	RES
33030	BAT	RES
33035	ECC	OPR
33046	MRC	STO
33048	WSR	OPR
33052	KES	OPR
33053	MHR	OPR
33057	WSR	RES
33063	SPV	OPR
33065	SPV	RES
33102	CVR	RES
33108	BHR	RES
33109	ELR	OPR
33110	BWR	RES
33111	SWN	OPR
33116	GCR	OPR
33117	ELR	RES
33201	MRC	OPR
33202	MFM	OPR
33208	MHR	OPR

Class 35

D7017	WSR	OPR
D7018	WSR	RES
D7029	SVR	RES
D7076	ELR	OPR

Class 37

D6700	NRM	OPR
37003	MNR	OPR
37009	GCR	RES
37023	ALY	RES

37025	BKR	RES
37032	NNR	RES
37037	MNR	OPR
37042	EVR	OPR
37075	CVR	OPR
37097	CRB	OPR
37108	RAC	OPR
37109	ELR	OPR
37116	CPR	OPR
37142	BWR	OPR
37146	SRC	RES
37152	PRL	RES
37175	BKR	RES
37188	PRL	RES
37207	PVR	RES
37215	GWR	OPR
37216	PBR	OPR
37219	PBR	OPR
37227	BAT	RES
37240	LAN	OPR
37248	GWR	RES
37250	WED	RES
37254	SPV	OPR
37255	GCR	OPR
37263	DFR	RES
37264	BRM	RES
37275	BHR	OPR
37294	EMB	RES
37308	EHD	RES
37314	MRC	OPR
37324	GWR	OPR
37372	BHR	RES
37403	BKR	RES
37407	CVR	STO
37413	BOK	RES
37418	ELR	RES
37421	PBR	RES
37424	CVR	STO
37674	SRC	RES
37679	NLR	RES
37901	ELR	OPR
37905	BUR	OPR
37906	EUR	OPR

Class 40		
D200	NRM	RES
40012	MRC	OPR
40013	BHR	OPR
40106	WAS	OPR
40118	BRM	RES
40135	ELR	OPR
40145	ELR	OPR

Class 41		
41001	GCN	OPR

Class 42		
D821	SVR	OPR
D832	WSR	OPR

Class 44		
D4	MRC	RES
44008	PRL	OPR

Class 45		
45015	BAT	STO
45041	MRC	OPR
45060	BHR	OPR
45105	BHR	RES
45108	MRC	RES
45118	NLR	RES
45125	GCR	OPR
45132	MHR	RES
45133	MRC	RES
45135	ELR	RES
45149	GWR	RES

Class 46		
46010	GCN	OPR
46035	RAC	STO
46045	MRC	OPR

Class 47		
47004	EMB	OPR
47105	GWR	OPR
47117	GCR	OPR
47192	DAR	OPR
47205	NLR	OPR
47292	GCR	OPR
47306	BWR	OPR
47367	NNR	OPR
47376	GWR	RES
47401	MRC	OPR
47402	ELR	OPR
47417	MRC	RES
47449	LAN	OPR
47484	BHR	RES
47524	CVR	RES
47540	WEN	STO
47596	MNR	RES
47635	BAT	OPR
47640	BAT	OPR
47643	BKR	OPR
47701	DAR	OPR
47712	RAC	OPR
47763	MFM	OPR
47765	GCR	RES
47771	COL	RES
47773	BRM	OPR
47785	ECC	RES
47793	MFM	OPR
47798	NRM	OPR
47799	EVR	RES
47840	WST	OPR

Class 50		
50002	SDR	RES
50007	WAS	RES
50008	ELR	OPR
50015	ELR	OPR
50017	PVR	RES
50019	MNR	OPR
50021	BRM	RES
50026	EHD	RES
50027	MHR	OPR
50029	PRL	STO
50030	PRL	RES
50031	EHD	RES
50033	BRM	STO
50135	EHD	OPR
50042	BWR	OPR
50044	MRC	OPR
50049	SVR (CF)	OPR
50050	YEO	RES

Class 52		
D1010	WSR	OPR
D1013	SVR	OPR
D1015	BRM	OPR
D1023	NRM	OPR
D1041	ELR	STO
D1048	MRC	RES
D1062	SVR	OPR

Class 55		
55002	NRM	RES
55009	BHR	OPR
55015	BHR	RES
55016	BHR	OPR
55019	BHR	OPR
55022	ELR	OPR

Class 56		
56006	BHR	OPR
56097	GCR	OPR

Class 58		
58016	BHR	RES

Class 97		
97650	LWR	OPR
97651	STR	OPR
97654	PRL	OPR

Class 71		
71001	BHR	STO

Class 73		
73001	DFR	OPR
73003	SWI	OPR
73005	SVR	RES
73006	RAC	OPR
73103	THK	STO
73110	GCR	OPR
73114	BAT	OPR
73117	BHR	OPR
73128	PBR	OPR
73129	GWR	OPR
73130	FIN	OPR
73134	BHR	OPR
73140	SPV	OPR
73210	MNR	OPR

Class 76		
E26020	NRM	STC

Class 77		
E27000	MRC	STC
E27001	MSM	STC

Class 81		
81002	BHR	STC

Class 82		
82008	BHR	STC

Class 83		
83012	BHR	STC

Class 84		
84001	BHR	STC

Class 85		
85101	BHR	STC

Class 86		
86213	BHR	OPR
86259	BRM	OPR

Class 87		
87001	NRM	STC
87035	RAC	RES

Class 89		
89001	BHR	STC

London Transport		
12	LUL	OPR

Below: *Restored and main-line certified 'Deltic' No. D9009 is currently in 1960s green livery with a small yellow warning panel.*
Antony Christie

Diesel Units

Number	*Base*
Unclassified	
APT-E	NRS
LEV1	NNR
RB004	TEL
79018	MRC
79612	MRC
79900	ECC
79960	NNR
79962	KWV
79963	NNR
79964	KWV
79976	GCR
79978	COL

Class 100	
56301	MNR

Class 101	
50222	BIR
50256	EKR
50338	BIR
51187	CRT
51188	ECC
51189	KWV
51192	ELR
51205	CRT
51210	WEN
51226	MNR
51228	NNR
51247	WEN
51427	GCR
51432	SWN
51434	MNR
51498	SWN
51499	MNR
51503	MNR
51505	EAR
51511	NYM
51512	CRT
51213	EAR
51803	KWV
53160	MRC
53164	CHS
53170	ECC
53193	GCR
53203	GCR
53204	NYM
53253	MRC
53266	GCR
53321	GCR
53746	WEN
54055	CRT
54062	NNR
54365	EAR
54408	SPV
56343	EKR
56352	ELR
56358	EAR
59117	MNR
59539	NYM

Class 104	
50447	LAN
50454	LAN
50455	TEL
50479	TEL
50494	CVR
50517	CVR
50528	LAN
50531	TEL
50547	CVR
50556	TEL
56182	CVR
59137	CVR
59228	TEL

Class 105	
51485	ELR
56121	ELR
56456	LAN

Class 107	
51990	STR
52005	NVR
52006	AVR
52008	STR
52025	AVR
52030	STR
59791	NVR

Class 108	
50599	EAR
50619	DFR
50632	PBR
50929	KWV
50980	BWR
51562	ELR
51565	KWV
51566	DFR
51567	MRC
51568	KEI
51571	KES
51572	WEN
51907	LAN
51909	MSR
51914	DFR
51919	BVR
51922	ELR
51933	DFR
51941	SVR
51942	PBR
51947	BWR
51950	GWR
51973	MRC
52044	PBR
52048	BVR
52053	KEI
52054	BWR
52062	GWR
52064	SVR
53628	KEI
53645	GCR
53926	GCR
53971	KES
54223	EAR

54270	PBR
54279	LDL
54490	LAN
54504	SWN
56208	SVR
56224	ECC
56271	MSR
56484	MRC
56491	KEI
56492	DFR
56495	KLR
59245	APF
59250	SVR
59387	DFR
59389	GCR

Class 109

50416	LAN
56171	LAN

Class 110

51813	WEN
51842	WEN
52071	LHR
52077	LHR
59701	CVR

Class 111

59575	MRC

Class 114

50015	MRC
50019	MRC
54057	STR
56006	MRC
56015	MRC

Class 115

51655	(BIR)
51663	WSR
51669	SPV
51677	(BIR)
51859	WSR
51880	WSR
51886	BRC
51887	WSR
51899	BRC
59659	SDR
59664	(BIR)
59678	-
59719	SDR
59740	SDR
59761	BRC

Class 116

51131	BAT
51138	GCR
51151	GCR
51321	BAT
59003	PDR
59004	PDR
59444	CHS

Class 117

51339	GWR
51342	EPO
51346	SWN
51347	GWI
51351	PBR
51353	MRC
51356	SWN
51359	NLR
51360	ECC
51363	GWR
51365	GWR
51367	STR
51372	TIT
51381	MFM
51382	GWR
51384	EPO
51388	SWN
51392	SWN
51395	MRC
51397	PBR
51398	MRC
51400	WEN
51401	GWI
51402	STR
51405	GWR
51407	GWR
59486	SWN
59488	PDR
59492	SWN
59494	PDR
59500	WEN
59503	PDR
59506	WSR
59507	PDR
59508	GWI
59509	WEN
59510	GWR
59513	PDR
59514	SWI
59515	YEO
59516	SWN
59517	PDR
59520	PBR
59521	MRC
59522	CHS
59603	CHS

Class 119

51073	ECC
51074	SWI
51104	SWI

Class 120

59276	GCR

Class 121

55019	BRM
55023	CPR
55024	BRM
55028	SWN
55029	RST
55033	COL
54289	ECC
56287	COL

Class 122

55000	SDR
55001	ELR
55003	GWR
55005	BAT
55006	ECC
55009	MNR
55012	SHI

Class 126

51017	BKR
51043	BKR
59404	BKR
79443	BKR

Class 127

51616	GCR
51618	LAN
51622	GCR
55966	MRC
55976	MRC
59609	MRC

Class 140

140001 - 55500/01	KEI

Class 141

141103	WED
141108	COL
141110	WED
141113	MRC

Class 201, 202 & 203

60116	HAD
60118	HAD
60501	HAD
60529	HAD
60750	WPH
201001	HAD

Class 205

60117	PBR
60822	LDL
60828	PBR
60154 X 1101	EKR
60800 X 1101	EKR
70549	ELR
Set 205009	EDR
Set 205025	MHR
Set 205028	DAR
Set 205032	DAR
Set 205033	LDL
Set 205205	EPO

Class 207

60127	SWI
60130 X 207202	ELR
60138	WPH
60142	SPV
60145	SEL
60149	SEL
60616	SPV
60901	SWI
60904 X 207202	ELR
60916	SPV

901001	CVR

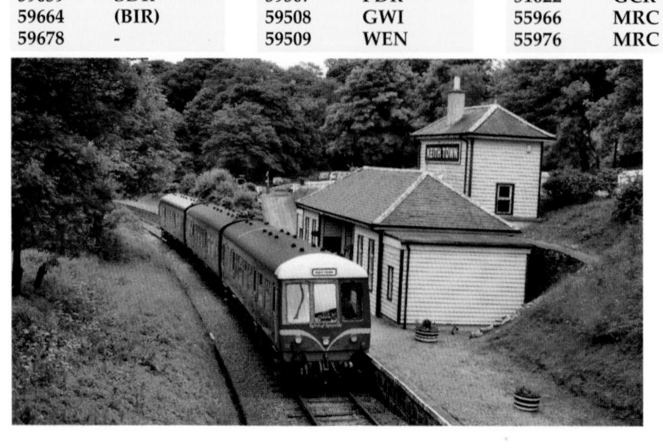

Left: *Preserved on the Keith & Dufftown Railway, Class 108 DMBS No. 53628* Spirit of Speyside *is seen leading a three-car formation at Keith Town.* **Murdock Currie**

Electric Units

Unclassified	
28249	NRM
29666	MRC
29670	MRC
79998	DEE
79999	DEE

BEL	
85	SOU
87	KEI
91	RAM

BIL	
10656 (2090)	NRS
12123 (2090)	NRS

COR	
10096	EKR
11161	EKR
11179	NRM
11201	BLU
11825	EKR

DD	
13004	NIR

Class 302	
75033	MFM
75250	MFM

Class 303	
303023/032	BKR

Class 306	
306017	EAR

Class 307	
75023	ERM

Class 308	
75881	ERM

Class 309	
309616	COV
309624	COV

Class 405 (SUB)	
S8143S	NRM
4732	COV

Class 411/412 (CEP)	
61742	DAR
61743	DAR
61798	EVR
61799	EVR
61804	EVR
61805	EVR
70229	EVR
70257	GCR
70273	DFR
70284	NIR
70292	SMP
70296	NIR
70354	EVR
70527	WRN
70531	SMP
70539	EVR
70576	SNI
70607	EVR
Set 1198	PBR
Set 7105	EKR

Class 414 (HAP)	
61275	NRM
61287 (4311)	COV
75395	NRM
75407 (4311)	COV

Class 415 (EPB)	
14351 (5176)	NIR
14352 (5176)	NIR
15345	COV
15396 (5176)	NIR

Class 416 (EPB)	
65302	FIN
65304	FIN
65373 (5759)	EKR
77558 (5759)	EKR
14573 (6307)	COV
16117 (6307)	COV
65321 (5791)	COV
77112 (5793)	COV

Class 419 (MLV)	
68001	EKR
68002	EKR
68003	EVR
68004	MNR
68005	EVR
68008	EKR
68009	EKR

Class 421 (CIG)	
62364	DFR
62378	DFR
62887	LWR
69339	GCR
76726	DFR
76740	DFR
76797	DFR
76811	DFR
76812	DAR
Set 1496	DAR
Set 1497	MNR
Set 1498	EPO
Set 1399	PBR

Class 422 (BEP)	
69304	NIR
69310	DAR
69318	COL
69332	DAR
69333	LDL
69337	HAD

Class 423 (VEP)	
(42)3417	BLU
76398 (3905)	DAR
76875	NRM

Class 457	
67300	COV

Class 488	
72501	ECC
72617	ECC

Class 489	
68500	ECC
68506	ECC

Class 501	
61183	COV
75186	COV

Class 502	
28361	TEB
29896	TEB

Class 503	
28690	COV
29298	COV
29720	COV

Class 504	
65451	ELR
77172	ELR

Right: *Preserved Class 423 4-VEP No. 3417, the original 7717 and introduced for the 1967 Bournemouth electrification, is now preserved by South West Trains and is often stored at one of the operator's depots. In this view the operational set is stabled in Clapham Junction yard. The set is restored to 1960s BR blue.* **CJM**

Ex-BR Industrial Locos

Over the years a number of former BR locomotives have, after withdrawal from normal duties, taken up use for industrial operators. The list below represents those which are understood to still be in existence in late 2012. Some locos operated at preservation sites are deemed to be 'industrial' but these are grouped in the preserved section.

Class 03

03179 *Clive*	First Capital Connect, Hornsey Depot

Class 08

08202	The Potter Group, Ely
08375	Tata Steel, Shotton
08411	LH Group, Burton – owned by Classic Traction
08441	Colne Valley Railway
08445	Daventry International Railfreight Terminal (DIRFT) – at LH Group, Burton
08447	John G. Russell Transit, Hillington, Glasgow
08460	Colne Valley Railway
08484 *Captain Nathaniel Darell*	Felixstowe Dock & Railway
08503	Barry Island Railway
08511	Freightliner Tilbury
08535	Corus, Shotton Works
08598	Chasewater Light Railway
08600	LH Group Services, Barton-under-Needwood
08613	Hanson Traction, Washwood Heath
08622 (H028) (7)	Hanson, Ketton
08643	Aggregate Industries, Whatley
08648	P D Ports, Teesport No. 20
08652	Hanson Aggregates, Whatley Quarry
08670	Colas, Cardiff Canton
08683	Electro-Motive, Longport
08699	Weardale Railway
08728	St Modwen Storage, Long Marston
08731	Aggregate Industries, Merehead
08743 *Bryan Turner*	LH Group Services, Barton-under-Needwood
08774 *Arthur Vernon Dawson*	AV Dawson, Middlesbrough
08787	Hanson Aggregates, Machen
08807	AV Dawson, Middlesbrough
08809	Corus, Shotton (at Washwood Heath 12/10)
08818 *Molly*	Faber Prest Ports, Flixborough Wharf
08823 (D3991)	Daventry International Railfreight Terminal
08847	Stored at Norwich Crown Point (Cotswold Rail - for sale)
08870 (H024)	Castle Cement, Ketton
08872	European Metal Reprocessing, Attercliffe
08873	Freightliner Terminal, Southampton
08903 *John W. Antill*	SembCorp Utilities Teesside, Wilton
08912	AV Dawson, Middlesbrough
08913	LH Group Services, Barton-under-Needwood
08915	Stephenson Railway Museum
08933	Aggregate Industries, Merehead
08936	Corus, Shotton Works
08937 *Bluebell Mel*	Aggregate Industries, Meldon Quarry
08947	Aggregate Industries, Knights Rail Services, Eastleigh

Class 09

09022	Boston Docks Co
09023	European Metal Reprocessing, Kingsbury

Class 11

12088	Butterwell

Class 14

D9529 (14029)	Aggregate Industries, Bardon Quarry

These lists give details of former UK diesel and electric locos exported for further use overseas and understood to still be operational.

Class 03

D2013	Italy
D2032	Italy
D2033	Italy
D2036	Italy

Class 04

D2216	Italy
D2232	Italy
D2289	Italy
D2295	Italy

Class 08

D3047	Lamco Liberia
D3092	Lamco Liberia
D3094	Lamco Liberia
D3098	Lamco Liberia
D3100	Lamco Liberia

Class 10

D3639	Conakry (Guinea)
D3649	Conakry (Guinea)

Class 14

D9534	Bruges

Class 56

56101	Floyd, Hungary 92 55 0659-001-5
56115	Floyd, Hungary 92 55 0659-002-3
56117	Floyd, Hungary 92 55 0659-003-1

Class 58

58001	ETF France
58004	TSO France
58005	ETF France
58006	ETF France
58007	TSO France
58009	TSO France
58010	TSO France
58011	TSO France
58013	ETF France
58015	Transfesa, Spain
58018	TSO France
58020	Transfesa, Spain
58021	TSO France
58024	Transfesa, Spain
58025	Continental Rail, Spain
58026	TSO France
58027	Continental Rail, Spain
58029	Transfesa, Spain
58030	Transfesa, Spain
58031	Transfesa, Spain
58032	ETF France
58033	TSO France
58034	TSO France
58035	TSO France
58036	ETF France
58038	ETF France
58039	ETF France
58040	TSO France
58041	Transfesa, Spain
58042	TSO France
58043	Transfesa, Spain
58044	ETF France
58046	TSO France
58047	Transfesa, Spain
58049	ETF France
58050	Continental Rail, Spain

Class 59

59003	HHPI, Germany

Class 66

66010	ECR, France
66022	ECR, France
66026	ECR, France
66032	ECR, France
66036	ECR, France
66038	ECR, France
66042	ECR, France
66045	ECR, France
66049	ECR, France
66052	ECR, France
66064	ECR, France
66072	ECR, France
66073	ECR, France
66123	ECR, France
66146	ECR, Poland
66153	ECR, Poland
66157	ECR, Poland
66159	ECR, Poland
66163	ECR, Poland
66166	ECR, Poland
66173	ECR, Poland
66178	ECR, Poland
66179	ECR, France
66180	ECR, Poland
66189	ECR, Poland
66190	ECR, France
66195	ECR, France
66196	ECR, Poland
66202	ECR, France
66203	ECR, France
66205	ECR, France
66208	ECR, France
66209	ECR, France
66210	ECR, France
66211	ECR, France
66212	ECR, France
66214	ECR, France
66215	ECR, France
66216	ECR, France
66217	ECR, France
66218	ECR, France
66219	ECR, France
66220	ECR, Poland
66222	ECR, France
66223	ECR, France
66224	ECR, France
66225	ECR, France
66226	ECR, France
66228	ECR, France
66229	ECR, France
66231	ECR, France
66233	ECR, France
66234	ECR, France
66235	ECR, France
66236	ECR, France
66237	ECR, Poland
66240	ECR, France
66241	ECR, France
66242	ECR, France
66244	ECR, France
66246	ECR, France
66247	ECR, France
66248	ECR, Poland
66411	Freightliner PL, As 66013FPL
66412	Freightliner PL, As 660xxFPL
66417	Freightliner PL, As 66014FPL
66582	Freightliner PL, As 66009FPL
66583	Freightliner PL, As 66010FPL
66584	Freightliner PL, As 66011FPL
66586	Freightliner PL, As 66008FPL
66608	Freightliner PL, As 66603FPL
66609	Freightliner PL, As 66605FPL
66611	Freightliner PL, As 66604FPL
66612	Freightliner PL, As 66606FPL
66624	Freightliner PL, As 66602FPL
66625	Freightliner PL, As 66601FPL

Class 86

86215	Floyd, Hungary 91 55 0450-005-8
86217	Floyd, Hungary 91 55 0450-006-?
86218	Floyd, Hungary 91 55 0450-004-1
86228	Floyd, Hungary 91 55 0450-007-
86233	Bulgaria (spares)
86232	Floyd, Hungary 91 55 0450-003-3
86242	Floyd, Hungary 91 55 0450-008-
86248	Floyd, Hungary 91 55 0450-001-7
86250	Floyd, Hungary 91 55 0450-002-5
86424	Floyd, Hungary (spares)

Class 87

87003	BZK Bulgaria
87004	BZK Bulgaria
87006	BZK Bulgaria
87007	BZK Bulgaria
87008	BZK Bulgaria
87009	BUL Bulgaria
87010	BZK Bulgaria
87012	BZK Bulgaria
87013	BZK Bulgaria
87014	BZK Bulgaria (spares)
87017	BUL Bulgaria
87019	BZK Bulgaria
87020	BZK Bulgaria
87022	BZK Bulgaria
87023	BUL Bulgaria
87025	BUL Bulgaria
87026	BZK Bulgaria
87028	BZK Bulgaria
87029	BZK Bulgaria
87033	BZK Bulgaria
87034	BZK Bulgaria

Class 92

92001	DBS Bulgaria
92012	DBS Romania 472-001-3
92025	DBS Bulgaria
92027	DBS Bulgaria
92034	DBS Bulgaria

A number of preserved modern traction locomotives have been allocated five-digit Class 89 TOPS numbers to allow their operation either under power or dead over the National Network. The numbers allocated are shown below; not all locos may currently be authorised for use on Network Rail metals.

The first two digits are the class, the third is the power type, while the final two digits are the final two of the original running number. If two locos clash with the same number, the second to be registered will have 1 added to the number.

Class 89 TOPS No.	BR No.	Type	Name
89100	20050	Class 20	-
89101	20001	Class 20	-
89110	20110	Class 20	-
89127	20227	Class 20	-
89166	20166	Class 20	-
89188	20188	Class 20	-
89200	31018	Class 31	-
89204	26004	Class 26	-
89210	27059	Class 27	-
89212	LT 12	Met Loco	*Sarah Siddons*
89223	25173	Class 25	-
89233	25283	Class 25	-
89247	27001	Class 27	-
89254	24054	Class 24	-
89259	25309	Class 25	-
89261	24061	Class 24	-
89262	25262	Class 25	-
89280	31162	Class 31	-
89317	D7017	Class 35	-
89376	D7076	Class 35	-
89400	E27000	Class 77	*Electra*
89401	47401	Class 47	*North Eastern*
89402	50002	Class 50	*Superb*
89403	71001	Class 71	-
89404	44004	Class 44	*Great Gable*
89405	47105	Class 47	-
89407	50007	Class 50	*Sir Edward Elgar*
89408	50008	Class 50	*Thunderer*
89412	40012	Class 40	*Aureol*
89413	D1013	Class 52	*Western Ranger*
89415	50015	Class 50	*Valiant*
89416	D1015	Class 52	*Western Champion*
89417	50017	Class 50	*Royal Oak*
89420	45108	Class 45	-
89421:1	D821	Class 42	*Greyhound*
89421:2	50021	Class 50	*Rodney*
89423	45125	Class 45	-
89424	D1023	Class 52	*Western Fusilier*
89427	50027	Class 50	*Lion*
89431	50031	Class 50	*Hood*
89432	D832	Class 42	*Onslaught*
89435	40135	Class 40	-
89440	45133	Class 45	-
89441	D1041	Class 52	*Western Prince*
89442	47192	Class 47	-
89443	50042	Class 50	*Triumph*
89444	50044	Class 50	*Exeter*
89445	40145	Class 40	-
89448	D1048	Class 52	*Western Lady*
89449	50049	Class 50	*Defiance*
89453	45041	Class 45	*Royal Tank Regiment*
89460	45060	Class 45	*Sherwood Forester*
89462	D1062	Class 52	*Western Courier*
89466	47449	Class 47	-
89472	46035	Class 46	*Ixion*
89500	55022	Class 55	*Royal Scots Grey*
89502	55002	Class 55	*The King's Own Yorkshire Light Infantry*
89503	81002	Class 81	-
89509	55009	Class 55	*Alycidon*
89515	55015	Class 55	*Tulyar*
89516	55016	Class 55	*Gordon Highlander*
89519	55019	Class 55	*Royal Highland Fusilier*
89523	DP1	Proto	*Deltic*
89535	83012	Class 83	-
89561	85101	Class 85	-

Below: *Preserved and main-line certified 'Deltic' No. 55022 (D9000) is seen near Tring.* **Mark V. Pike**

Several preserved steam locomotives have been allocated five-digit TOPS numbers to allow their operation over the National Network. The numbers allocated are shown below; not all locos may currently be authorised for use on Network Rail metals.

TOPS No.	Railway No.	Type	Name
98150	1450	GWR 14xx	
98166	1466	GWR 14xx	
98186	686	0-6-0T	*Lady Armaghdale*
98212	41312	LMS 2MT	
98219	55189	CR 0-4-4T	
98221	46521	LMS 2MT	
98238	1638	GWR 16xx	
98240	3440	GWR 34xx	*City of Truro*
98241	46441	LMS 2MT	
98243	46443	LMS 2MT	
98253	30053	SR M7	
98254	58926	LNWR 2F	
98273	65243	NBR J36	*Maude*
98315	7715	GWR 57xx	
98321	69621	GER N7	*A. J. Hill*
98372	30072	SR USA	
98400	41000	LMS 4P	
98406	43106	LMS 4MT	
98414	75014	BR 4MT	
98425	7325	GWR 7321	
98426	31625	SR U	
98427	44027	LMS 4F	
98435	80135	BR 4MT	
98455	4555	GWR 45xx	
98457	9600	GWR 8750	
98460	7760	GWR 57xx	
98466	9466	GWR 94xx	
98469	75069	BR 4MT	
98472	5572	GWR 4575	
98476	76079	BR 4MT	
98478	68078	WD 4F	
98479	80079	BR 4MT	
98480	80080	BR 4MT	
98482	3882	0-6-0ST	*Barbara*
98488	4588	GWR 4575	
98494	65894	LNER J27	
98498	80098	BR 4MT	
98500	45000	LMS 5MT	
98502	7802	GWR 78xx	*Bradley Manor*
98505	45305	LMS 5MT	*Alderman A E Draper*
98507	45407	LMS 5MT	*Lancashire Fusilier*
98510	45110	LMS 5MT	
98512	7812	GWR 78xx	*Erlestoke Manor*
98519	7819	GWR 78xx	*Hinton Manor*
98525	45025	LMS 5MT	
98526	30925	SR V	*Cheltenham*
98529	73129	BR 5MT	
98530	4930	GWR 49xx	*Hagley Hall*
98531	45231	LMS 5MT	*Sherwood Forester*
98532	44932	LMS 5MT	
98536	4936	GWR 49xx	*Kinlet Hall*
98549	4965	GWR 49xx	*Rood Ashton Hall*
98553	4953	GWR 49xx	*Pitchford Hall*
98560	6960	GWR 6959	*Raveningham Hall*
98564	61264	LNER B1	
98565	42765	LMS 5MT	
98567	44767	LMS 5MT	*George Stephenson*
98568	42968	LMS 5MT	
98571	44871	LMS 5MT	
98572	5972	GWR 49xx	*Olton Hall*
98577	30777	SR N15	*Sir Lamiel*
98596	73096	BR 5MT	
98598	6998	GWR 6959	*Burton Agnes Hall*
98605	62005	LNER K1	
98628	30828	SR S15	
98641	30841	SR S15	
98642	61994	LNER K4	*The Great Marquess*
98690	45690	LMS 6P5F	*Leander*
98693	45593	LMS 6P5F	*Kolhapur*
98696	45596	LMS 6P5F	*Bahamas*
98699	45699	LMS 6P5F	*Galatea*
98700	70000	BR 7P	*Britannia*
98701	34101	SR WC	*Hartland*
98709	53809	SDJR 7F	
98713	70013	BR 7P	*Oliver Cromwell*
98715	46115	LMS 7P	*Scots Guardsman*
98716	34016	SR WC	*Bodmin*
98727	34027	SR WC	*Taw Valley*
98728	5029	GWR 4073	*Nunney Castle*
98729	7029	GWR 4073	*Clun Castle*
98750	30850	SR LN	*Lord Nelson*
98751	5051	GWR 4073	*Earl Bathurst*
98767	34067	SR BB	*Tangmere*
98771	60800	LNER V2	*Green Arrow*
98772	34072	SR BB	*257 Squadron*
98780	5080	GWR 4073	*Defiant*
98792	34092	SR WC	*City of Wells*
98800	6000	GWR 60xx	*King George V*
98801	46201	LMS 8P	*Princess Elizabeth*
98802	71000	BR 8P	*Duke of Gloucester*
98803	46203	LMS 8P	*Princess Margaret Rose*
98805	35005	SR MN	*Canadian Pacific*
98809	60009	LNER A4	*Union of South Africa*
98824	6024	GWR 60xx	*King Edward I*
98828	35028	SR MN	*Clan Line*
98829	46229	LMS 8P	*Duchess of Hamilton*
98832	60532	LNER A2	*Blue Peter*
98834	46233	LMS 8P	*Duchess of Sutherland*
98851	48151	LMS 8F	
98857	2857	GWR 28xx	
98863	60163	LNER A1	*Tornado*
98868	60022	LNER A4	*Mallard*
98872	60103	LNER A3	*Flying Scotsman*
98873	48773	LMS 8F	
98898	60007	LNER A4	*Sir Nigel Gresley*
98920	92220	BR 9F	*Evening Star*

Above: *TOPS No. 98713 - 70013* Oliver Cromwell *- is seen on Dainton bank on 8 September 2013.* **Antony Christie**

Coupling Codes & Couplings

With the introduction of modern traction from the 1950s a number of different methods of multiple operation were introduced, covering the different control principles of locomotives, for example those using electro-pneumatic or electro-magnetic systems.

Six main systems are in operation today:

Blue Star ★ using the electro-pneumatic system and fitted to Classes 20, 25, 31, 33, 37, 40 and 73.

Green Spot ● a unique system installed on some Class 47s operated by the freight sector.

Orange Square ■ an English Electric system used only on the Class 50s.

Red Diamond ♦ a 1970s system developed for the modern freight locos of Classes 56 and 58.

In addition to the above coded systems, the American-developed main-line locos of Classes 59, 66, 67 and 70 use the US standard AAR (Association of American Railroads) system. Direct Rail Services (DRS) have also developed a unique system which is installed on some of the company's Class 20, 37, 47 and 57 locos.

A number of locomotives have either been built with or modified to incorporate Time Division Multiplex (TDM) remote operation equipment, which uses coach lighting type Railway Clearing House (RCH) nose-end jumper cables.

Some of the surviving first generation DMMU sets carry a **Blue Square** ■ multiple operation system.

Details of the main coupling systems in operation in the UK are included in the accompanying illustrations.

Above: *Class 59 and 66 front-end layout (non-DB-S operated). 1-Coupling hook, 2-Coupling shackle, 3-Air brake pipe (red), 4-Main reservoir pipe (yellow), 5-Buffer, 6-Association of American Railroads (AAR) jumper socket. No. 66726 illustrated.* **CJM**

Above: *Standard coupling arrangement to be found on many classes of UK loco. 1-Electric Train Supply (ETS) jumper socket, 2-Main reservoir air pipe (yellow), 3-Vacuum brake pipe, 4-Coupling hook and shackle, 5-Air brake pipe (red), 6-Electric Train Supply (ETS) jumper cable. Loco No. 47580 illustrated.* **CJM**

Above: *The unique front-end layout of the Royal Mail Class 325. 1-Brake pipe (red), 2-Main reservoir pipe (yellow), 3-Electric Train Supply (ETS) socket, 4-Time Division Multiplex (TDM) jumper socket, 5-Drop head buck-eye coupling, 6-Electric Train Supply (ETS) cable.* **CJM**

Above: *Following the introduction of Virgin Trains 'Voyager' and 'Pendolino' stock, a fleet of 16 Class 57/3s was introduced with drop-head Dellner couplers and cabling to provide 'hotel power'. The coupling is seen in this illustration in the raised position. 1-Electric Train Supply (ETS) jumper socket, 2-Main reservoir pipe (yellow), 3-Air brake pipe (red), 4-Coupling hook, 5-Dellner coupling face, 6-Electric Train Supply (ETS) jumper cable.* **CJM**

Above: *With the birth of modern multiple unit trains came the Bergische Stahl Industrie (BSI) automatic coupling, first seen in the UK on the Tyne & Wear Metro vehicles in 1978. The modern generation of UK DMUs now concentrate on the Compact BSI coupler with a CK2 coupling interface. The couplers are engaged by the compression of the two coupling faces, which completes a physical connection and also opens a watertight cover to an electrical connection box. The full train air connection is made during the coupling compression process. The coupling is completed by the driver pressing a 'couple' button in the driving cab. 1-Emergency air connection, 2-Coupling face, 3-Electric connection (behind plate), 4-Air connection. The coupling shown is on a Class 166.* **CJM**

Above: *The Tightlock coupler is a derivative of the Association of American Railroads (AAR) Type H coupler, later under the control of American Public Transportation Association (APTA). A modified Type H coupler was introduced in the UK from the early 1970s and has become a standard fitting on many of the later BR and several post-privatisation EMUs. The UK Tightlock design can be supplied with or without an electrical connection box and with or without a pneumatic connection. This view shows a fully automated version as fitted to the 'Networker' fleet. Attachment is achieved by driving the two vehicles together, which physically connects the vehicles, while a 'roll-cover' box opens to connect electric and pneumatic services. 1-Emergency air connector, 2-Manual release handle, 3-Semi-rotary electric/pneumatic cover, 4-Physical coupler.* **CJM**

Above: *The BR Southern Region-designed Class 455 and 456 units have a semi-automatic Tightlock used for physical connections, while air and electrical connections are made by waist-height flexible pipes. 1-Main reservoir pipe (yellow), 2-Control jumper, 3-Tightlock coupler, 4-Couple/Uncouple drum switch, 5-Manual release handle, 6-Control jumper receptacle.* **CJM**

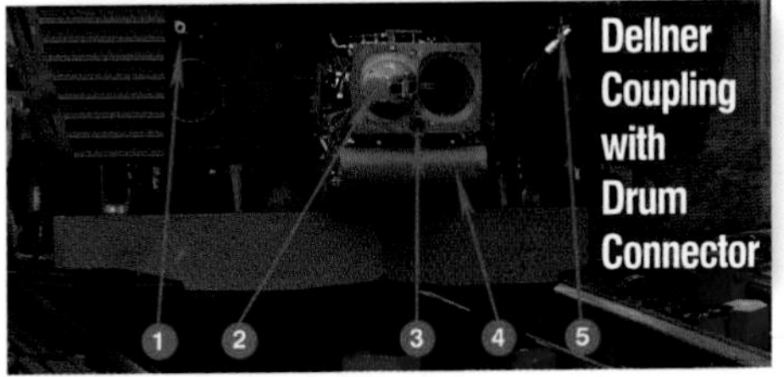

Above: *Dellner couplers have become the standard in the UK and much of Europe; these are fully automatic and come in various forms. 1-Emergency air supply, 2-Dellner coupling plate, 3-Pneumatic connection, 4-Roll-cover to electrical connections, 5-Air supply. Coupling of Class 360 illustrated.* **CJM**

Above: *A large number of different designs of Dellner couplers exist on UK rolling stock. Some feature full automatic operation including pneumatic and electrical connections, while others only provide physical coupling. This view shows a pair of 'Voyager' units coupled together with Dellner couplers. The electrical connection box is above the physical coupler. After trains are 'pushed' together the driver operates a 'couple' button in the cab to complete the attachment. Uncoupling is achieved by the driver pressing an 'uncouple' button and driving the trains apart.* **CJM**

Left: *The Virgin Trains 'Pendolino' stock uses Dellner couplers with a rotary covered electrical connector plate above. These couplers are supplemented by electric train supply connections either side to provide 'hotel power' to Class 390 sets from attached Class 57 locos. 1-Electric Train Supply (ETS) socket, 2-Emergency air connector, 3-Electrical connector plate under semi-rotary cover, 4-Dellner physical coupler, 5-Pneumatic connections. In normal use the Dellner coupler on 'Pendolino' stock is covered by a front fairing.* **CJM**

Above: *Under the front-end fairing of the Eurostar Class 373 stock a standard Scharfenberg coupler is located for assistance purposes and shunting. No electrical provision is made and the couplers are seldom used. 1-Scharfenberg coupling face, 2-Pneumatic connections, 3-Manual uncoupling handle.* **CJM**

Above: *In as-installed condition and having never been coupled to another set, a Class 380 Scharfenberg coupler is viewed, showing the auto opening electrical connection box above. 1-Electrical connection box, 2-Coupling face plate, 3-Pneumatic connection.* **CJM**

Above: *If High Speed Trains are required to be coupled to conventional hook couplings an adaptor coupling is carried on the HST for this purpose. It has to be first attached to the front of the HST by opening the front panel and attaching the aluminium bar to a coupling lug. The other end is then at the right level and length to attach to a standard loco hook coupling without the loco's buffers touching the HST's bodywork. Standard air connection is provided. Locos fitted with swing-head or combination couplers cannot be used to assist HST stock. A Class 59/1 is seen attached to HST power car No. 43150 in this view at Westbury.* **Greg Welsh**

Right: *All DBS Class 66s (except 66001/002) and all Class 67s are fitted with swing-head combination couplers allowing attachment to other like-fitted locos or rolling stock using a knuckle coupling. Two Class 66s are seen here attached using the swing-head coupler. Note that the buffers do not touch and that all traction and braking forces are transmitted through the coupler. Standard buffer beam air connections are provided on one main reservoir and one brake pipe. The auto coupler can be disconnected by using the white uncoupling handle seen on the left.* **Antony Christie**

Transport for London
London Underground

Address: ✉ Floor 11, Windsor House, 50 Victoria Street, London, SW1H 0TL
pressoffice@tfl.gov.uk
✆ 0845 604 4141
ⓘ www.tfl.gov.uk

Managing Director: Peter Austin

Operations: The London Underground system, now operated by Transport for London (TfL), operates services on 10 lines in and around the capital and uses a mix of surface and tunnel stock.

Bakerloo Line	Tube Line. Operates services between Elephant & Castle and Harrow & Wealdstone. **Rolling Stock:** 1972 Mk2, livery - red, white and blue, allocated to Stonebridge Park. Scheduled for replacement in 2018.
Central Line	Tube Line. Operates services between West Ruislip/Ealing and Epping. **Rolling Stock:** 1992, livery - red, white and blue, allocated to Hainault.
Circle Line	Sub-Surface Line. Operates circle network in Central London and the branch from Edgware Road to Hammersmith. **Rolling Stock:** 'A' stock, introduced 2013-14, livery - red, white and blue, allocated to Hammersmith.
District Line	Sub-Surface Line. Operates services between Wimbledon, Richmond, Ealing, Edgware Road, Kensington Olympia and Upminster. **Rolling Stock:** 'D' and 'S' stock, livery - red, white and blue, allocated to Ealing Common and Upminster.
Jubilee Line	Tube Line. Operates services between Stanmore and Stratford. **Rolling Stock:** 1996, livery - red, white and blue, allocated to Wembley Park.
Metropolitan Line	Sub-Surface Line. Operates services from Amersham, Chesham, Watford and Uxbridge to Aldgate. **Rolling Stock:** 'S' stock, livery - red, white and blue, allocated to Wembley Park.
Northern Line	Tube Line. Operates services between Morden and Edgware, Mill Hill East and High Barnet. **Rolling Stock:** 1995 stock, livery - red, white and blue, allocated to Morden.
Piccadilly Line	Tube Line. Operates services between Heathrow Airport / Uxbridge and Cockfosters. **Rolling Stock:** 1973 stock, livery - red, white and blue, allocated to Northfields and Cockfosters. Stock due for replacement in 2014.
Victoria Line	Tube Line. Operates services between Brixton and Walthamstow Central **Rolling Stock:** 2009 stock, livery - red, white and blue, allocated to Northumberland Park.
Waterloo & City Line	Tube Line. Operates services between Waterloo and Bank. **Rolling Stock:** 1992 stock, livery - red, white and blue, allocated to Waterloo.

Above: *The Bakerloo Line, which operates through central London from Elephant & Castle in the south to Harrow & Wealdstone in the north, is operated by 1972 Mk2 stock, painted in standard London Underground white, blue and red livery. A southbound train is seen approaching Willesden Junction Low Level.* **CJM**

Below: *A rake of the new 'S' stock, currently being introduced on London Underground Metropolitan, Circle and District lines, departs from Paddington on a Circle Line service bound for Hammersmith.* **CJM**

For space reasons, we are unable in this publication to provide vehicle numbers for London Underground stock.

Blackpool Tramway

Address: ✉ Blackpool Transport, Rigby Road, Blackpool, FY1 5DD
✉ jean.cox@blackpooltransport.com
✆ 01253 473001 ⓘ www.blackpooltrams.info

Blackpool Tramway is operated by Blackpool Transport.

Operations: Blackpool Tramway operates frequent services between Fleetwood and Starr Gate.

Flexity 2

Train Length: 105ft 9in (32.23m)
Width: 8ft 8in (2.65m)
Power Supply: 600V dc overhead
Seating: 74 + 148 standing
Horsepower: 4 x 160hp (120kW) three phase TMs
Electrical Equipment: Bombardier

001	003	005	007	009	011	013	015
002	004	006	008	010	012	014	016

Left: *Interior layout of Flexity 2 tram stock as used on the Blackpool system.* **CJM**

Transport for London Docklands Light Railway

Contact details as London Underground.

Operations: The Docklands Light Railway operates between Bank and Tower Gateway and Woolwich Arsenal, Beckton and Stratford, as well as a Lewisham to Stratford service.

Class B90 (twin)

Train Length: 94ft 5in (28.80m)
Width: 8ft 7in (2.65m)
Power Supply: 750V dc third rail
Seating: 52 + 4 tip-up
Horsepower: 375hp (280kW)
Electrical Equipment: Brush

22	25	28	31	34	37	40	43
23	26	29	32	35	38	41	44
24	27	30	33	36	39	42	

Class B92 (twin)

Train Length: 94ft 5in (28.80m)
Width: 8ft 7in (2.65m)
Power Supply: 750V dc third rail
Seating: 54 + 4 tip-up
Horsepower: 375hp (280kW)
Electrical Equipment: Brush

45	51	57	63	69	75	81	87
46	52	58	64	70	76	82	88
47	53	59	65	71	77	83	89
48	54	60	66	72	78	84	90
49	55	61	67	73	79	85	91
50	56	62	68	74	80	86	

Class B2K (twin)

Train Length: 94ft 5in (28.80m)
Width: 8ft 7in (2.65m)
Power Supply: 750V dc third rail
Seating: 52 + 4 tip-up
Horsepower: 375hp (280kW)
Electrical Equipment: Brush

01	03	05	07	09	11	13	15	92	94	96	98
02	04	06	08	10	12	14	16	93	95	97	99

Class B07 (twin)

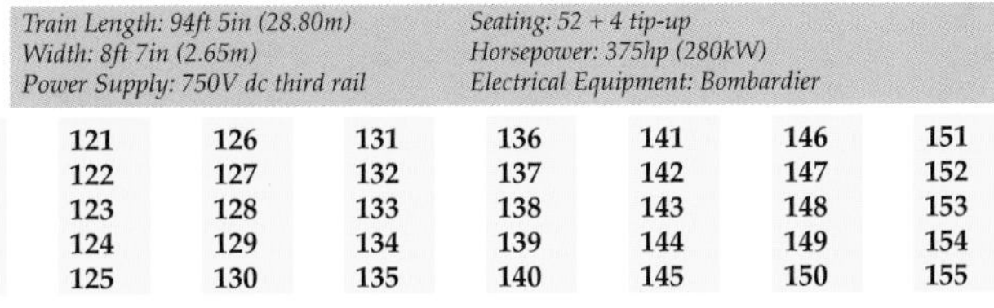

Train Length: 94ft 5in (28.80m)
Width: 8ft 7in (2.65m)
Power Supply: 750V dc third rail
Seating: 52 + 4 tip-up
Horsepower: 375hp (280kW)
Electrical Equipment: Bombardier

101	106	111	116	121	126	131	136	141	146	151
102	107	112	117	122	127	132	137	142	147	152
103	108	113	118	123	128	133	138	143	148	153
104	109	114	119	124	129	134	139	144	149	154
105	110	115	120	125	130	135	140	145	150	155

Right: *One of the recently introduced B07 Docklands units, No. 105, departs from Poplar with a service bound for Stratford.* **CJM**

Transport for London Croydon Tramlink

Contact details as London Underground.

Operations: The Croydon Tramlink operates between Croydon and Wimbledon, New Addington, Beckenham and Elmers End.

CR4000 stock

Train Length: 98ft 9in (30.1m)
Width: 8ft 7in (2.65m)
Power Supply: 750V dc overhead
Seating: 70
Horsepower: 643hp (480kW)
Electrical Equipment: Bombardier

2530	2533	2536	2539	2542	2545	2548	2551
2531	2534	2537	2540	2543	2546	2549	2552
2532	2535	2538	2541	2544	2547	2550	2553

Stadler Variobahn

Train Length: 106ft 2½in (32.37m)
Width: 8ft 7in (2.65m)
Power Supply: 750V dc overhead
Seating: 70
Horsepower: 650hp (483kW)
Electrical Equipment: Stadler

2554	2555	2556	2557	2558	2559

Name applied

2535	***Stephen Parascandolo 1980-2007***

Right: *Six of the new Stadler Variobahn trams are now in operation on the Croydon network, allocated the numbers 2554 to 2559. No. 2559 is seen departing from Arena station.* **Murdoch Currie**

Manchester Metrolink

Address: ✉ Greater Manchester PTE, 2 Piccadilly Gardens, Manchester, M1 3BG
RATP Metrolink, Metrolink House, Queens Road, Manchester, M8 ORY
customerservices@metrolink.co.uk
✆ 0161 205 2000 ⓘ www.metrolink.co.uk

Metrolink is operated for GMPTE by Metrolink RATP Dev UK Ltd.

Operations: Manchester Metrolink operates a street and dedicated track tram system around Manchester. Services operate from the city centre to Bury, Altrincham, Eccles via MediaCity UK and St Werburgh's Road.

T-68 Six-axle stock

Train Length: 95ft 1in (29m)
Width: 8ft 7in (2.65m)
Power Supply: 750V dc overhead
Seating: 82 + 4 tip-up
Horsepower: 697hp (520kW)
Electrical Equipment: Firema

1002	1012	1016	1023
1003	1013	1017	1024
1007	1014	1021	1025
1009	1015	1022	1026

T-68 Six-axle stock

Train Length: 95ft 1in (29m)
Width: 8ft 7in (2.65m)
Power Supply: 750V dc overhead
Seating: 82 + 4 tip-up
Horsepower: 697hp (520kW)
Electrical Equipment: Ansaldo

2001	2002	2003	2004	2005	2006

M5000 stock

Train Length: 93ft 1in (28.4m)
Width: 8ft 7in (2.65m)
Power Supply: 750V dc overhead
Seating: 52 + 8 tip-up
Horsepower: 643hp (480kW)
Electrical Equipment: Bombardier

3001	3012	3023	3034	3045	3056	3067
3002	3013	3024	3035	3046	3057	3068
3003	3014	3025	3036	3047	3058	3069
3004	3015	3026	3037	3048	3059	3070
3005	3016	3027	3038	3049	3060	3071
3006	3017	3028	3039	3050	3061	3072
3007	3018	3029	3040	3051	3062	3073
3008	3019	3030	3041	3052	3063	3074
3009	3020	3031	3042	3053	3064	
3010	3021	3032	3043	3054	3064	
3011	3022	3033	3044	3055	3066	

Names carried

3009	*50th Anniversary Coronation Street 1960-2010*
3020	*Lancashire Fusilier*

Left: *M5000 two-vehicle tram No. 3001 is seen at Piccadilly Gardens, Manchester, with a service for East Didsbury.* **Antony Christie**

Nottingham Express Transit

Address: ✉ Transdev Tram UK Ltd, Garrick House, 74 Chiswick High Road, London, W4 1SY
Nottingham City Transport Ltd, Lower Parliament Street, Nottingham, NG1 1GG
info@thetram.net ✆ 0115 942 7777 ⓘ www.thetram.net

Operations: Nottingham Express Transit (NET) operate trams between Hucknall and Nottingham.

Incentro AT6/5

Train Length: 108ft 3in (29m)
Width: 7ft 9in (2.4m)
Power Supply: 750V dc overhead
Seating: 54 + 4 tip-up
Horsepower: 697hp (520kW)
Electrical Equipment: Bombardier

No.	Name
201	
202	*DH Lawrence*
203	*Bendigo Thompson*
204	*Erica Beardsmore*
205	*Lord Byron*
206	*Angela Alcock*
207	*Mavis Worthington*
208	*Dinah Minton*
209	*Sid Standard*
210	*Sir Jesse Boot*
211	*Robin Hood*
212	*William Booth*
213	*Mary Potter*
214	*Dennis McCarthy*
215	*Brian Clough*

Right: *Nottingham tram No. 214 is seen at Station Street, Nottingham.* **John Binch**

■ 22 new Alstom-built Citadis trams are currently on delivery to Nottingham Express Transit as Nos. 216-237.

Midland Metro

Address: ✉ Travel West Midlands, PO Box 3565, Birmingham, B1 3JR
info@travelmetro.co.uk ✆ 0121 254 7272 ⓘ www.travelmetro.co.uk

Operations: Midland Metro operates trams between Birmingham Snow Hill and Wolverhampton.

T-69 Six-axle stock

Train Length: 108ft 3in (29m)
Width: 7ft 9in (2.4m)
Power Supply: 750V dc overhead
Seating: 54 + 4 tip-up
Horsepower: 697hp (520kW)
Electrical Equipment: Bombardier

No.	Name
01(S)	*Sir Frank Whittle*
02	
03	*Ray Lewis*
04	
05	*Sister Dora*
06	*Alan Garner*
07	*Billy Wright*
08	*Joseph Chamberlain*
09	*Jeff Astle*
10	*John Stanley Webb*
11	*Theresa Stewart*
12	
13	*Anthony Nolan*
14	*Jim Eames*
15	*Agenoria*
16	*Gerwyn John*

Right: *Midland Metro tram No. 11 is seen at Jewellery Quarter on 23 August 2013 painted in historic blue and cream livery to mark the 60th anniversary of the closure of the Birmingham tram system.* **John Binch**

Sheffield Super Tram

Address: ✉ Stagecoach Supertram, Nunnery Depot, Woodburn Road, Sheffield, S9 3LS
enquiries@supertram.com
✆ 0114 272 8282
ⓘ www.supertram.com

Operations: Sheffield Super Tram operates services within Sheffield city centre and to Herdings Park, Halfway, Meadowhall Interchange, Middlewood and Malin Bridge.

Six-axle stock

Train Length: 113ft 6in (34.75m)
Width: 8ft 7in (2.65m)
Power Supply: 750V dc overhead
Seating: 80 + 6 tip-up
Horsepower: 800hp (596kW)
Electrical Equipment: Siemens

101	105	109	113	117	121	125
102	106	110	114	118	122	
103	107	111	115	119	123	
104	108	112	116	120	124	

Left: *Sheffield three-section tram No. 103, painted in Stagecoach blue, orange and red livery, at Sheffield Hallam on 26 February 2013.*
Antony Christie

Tyne & Wear Metro

Address: ✉ Tyne & Wear Passenger Transport Executive (NEXUS), Nexus House, 33 St James Boulevard, Newcastle upon Tyne, NE1 4AX
enquiries@nexus.co.uk
✆ 0191 203 3333
ⓘ www.nexus.org.uk

Operations: Tyne & Wear Metro operates tram services within Newcastle city centre and to Whitley Bay, Newcastle Airport, South Shields, Sunderland and South Hylton.

Six-axle stock

Train Length: 91ft 3in (27.80m)
Width: 8ft 7in (2.65m)
Power Supply: 1500V dc overhead
Seating: 68 tip-up
Horsepower: 500hp (374kW)
Electrical Equipment: Siemens

4001	4011	4021	4031	4041	4051	4061
4002	4012	4022	4032	4042	4052	4062
4003	4013	4023	4033	4043	4053	4063
4004	4014	4024	4034	4044	4054	4064
4005	4015	4025	4035	4045	4055	4065
4006	4016	4026	4036	4046	4056	4066
4007	4017	4027	4037	4047	4057	4067
4008	4018	4028	4038	4048	4058	4068
4009	4019	4029	4039	4049	4059	4069
4010	4020	4030	4040	4050	4060	4070

4071	4074	4077	4080	4083	4086	4089
4072	4075	4078	4081	4084	4087	4090
4073	4076	4079	4082	4085	4088	

Names applied

4026	*George Stephenson*
4041	*Harry Cowans*
4060	*Thomas Bewick*
4064	*Michael Campbell*
4065	*Dame Catherine Cookson*
4073	*Danny Marshall*
4077	*Robert Stephenson*
4078	*Ellen Wilkinson*

Right: *A pair of black and yellow-liveried Tyne & Wear Metro light rail vehicles, led by No. 4061, arrives at North Shields on 6 June 2012.* **Antony Christie**

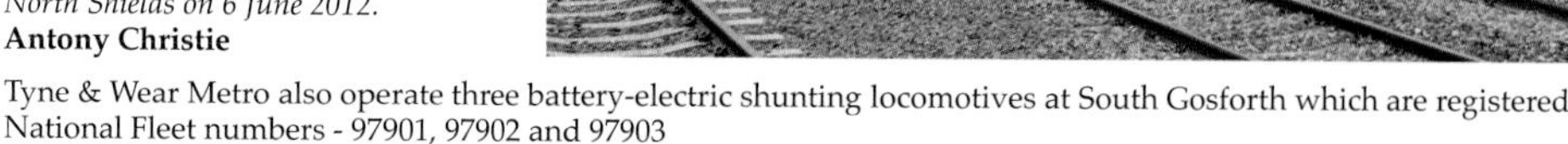

Tyne & Wear Metro also operate three battery-electric shunting locomotives at South Gosforth which are registered National Fleet numbers - 97901, 97902 and 97903

Glasgow Subway

Address: ✉ SPT, Consort House, 12 West George Street, Glasgow, G2 1HN
enquiry@spt.co.uk
✆ 0141 332 6811
ⓘ www.spt.co.uk

Glasgow Subway is operated by Strathclyde Partnership for Transport (SPT).
Operations: Circular network around Glasgow city centre.

Single Power Cars

Length: 42ft 2in (12.81m)
Width: 7ft 7in (2.34m)
Power Supply: 600V dc third rail
Seating: 36S
Horsepower: 190hp (142.4kW)
Electrical Equipment: GEC

101	105	109	113	117	121	125	129	133
102	106	110	114	118	122	126	130	
103	107	111	115	119	123	127	131	
104	108	112	116	120	124	128	132	

Trailer Cars

Length: 41ft 6in (12.70m)
Width: 7ft 7in (2.34m)
Seating: 40S

201	202	203	204	205	206	207	208

Right: *Painted in the latest Glasgow SPT orange and brown livery, a three-car set is seen at Govan on 20 July 2013 formed of vehicles 109, 123 and 114.* **Murdoch Currie**

Livery Codes

ABL	Arriva Trains - blue
AGI	Aggregate Industries - green, silver and green
AIN	Aggregate Industries blue
ALS	Alstom Transportation
ANG	Anglia - mid blue
ANN	Anglia - turquoise/white with Greater Anglia branding
ATE	Arriva Trains Executive - turquoise/cream with branding
ATT	Arriva Trains Wales - Welsh Government
ATW	Arriva Trains Wales - turquoise/cream
AWT	Abellio - white Greater Anglia
AXC	Arriva Cross Country - brown, silver, pink
BBR	Balfour Beatty Rail - blue/white
BLG	Blue and grey
BLK	Black
BLL	BR rail blue with large logo
BLU	Blue
BLW	Carillion Rail - blue/white
BOM	Bombardier Transportation
BPM	Blue Pullman - Nankin blue and white
BRD	BR Departmental mid grey
BRT	BR Trainload two-tone grey
C2C	c2c - blue/pink
CAL	Caledonian Railway
CAR	Carmine and Cream
CEN	Central Trains - blue and two-tone green
CHC	Chocolate and Cream
CIV	BR Civil Engineers - grey and yellow
COL	Colas - orange, lime green and black
CON	Continental Rail - light/mid blue
COR	Corus Steel - light blue or yellow
COX	Connex - white and yellow
CRG	Chilton Railways - grey
CRW	Chilton Railways - white/blue
CTL	Central Trains - blue, green with yellow doors
CWR	Cotswold Rail - silver with branding
DBB	DB Schenker - light blue
DBM	DB Schenker - maroon
DBS	DB Schenker - red
DCG	Devon & Cornwall Railways - green
DCN	Devon & Cornwall Railways - grey
DRC	Direct Rail Services - blue 'Compass' branding
DRO	Direct Rail Services - Ocean Liner blue
DRS	Direct Rail Services - blue
DRU	Direct Rail Services - unbranded blue
ECG	East Coast - grey
ECR	European Cargo Rail - grey
ECS	East Coast - silver
ECW	East Coast - white
ECT	East Coast - branded National Express livery
EMT	East Midlands Trains, white, blue, swirl cab ends
EPS	European Passenger Services
EPX	Europhoenix - red/silver
ETF	ETF Rail - yellow with green band
EU2	Eurotunnel - Europorte2
EUS	Eurostar - white, yellow and blue
EWE	DBS Executive
EWS	English Welsh Scottish - red with gold band
FCC	First Capital Connect, First Group Urban Lights - mauve/blue with pink, blue and white lower branding
FER	Fertis - grey with branding
FGB	First Great Western - blue
FGF	First Group - GBRf (Barbie)
FGL	First Great Western - local lines
FGS	First Group ScotRail with EWS branding
FGT	First Great Western, Thames/London area branding
FGW	First Great Western - as FST with FGW branding
FHT	First Hull Trains - as FST with Hull Trains branding
FLG	Freightliner - green unbranded
FLP	Freightliner - green/yellow - PowerHaul
FLR	Freightliner - green/yellow - original
FLU	Freightliner - green/yellow - unbranded
FLY	Freightliner - grey
FNA	First livery with National Express East Anglia branding
FOS	Foster Yeoman
FSN	Northern branded First Group
FSP	First ScotRail Strathclyde - carmine and cream (some with turquoise band)
FSR	First ScotRail - as FST with FSR branding
FSS	First ScotRail - blue with white Saltire branding
FST	First Group - dark blue, pink and white swirl
FSW	First Group - green and white with gold branding
FTP	First TransPennine - as FST with FTP branding
GAT	Gatwick Express - white, mid-grey and red with red doors
GBE	GB Railfreight - Europorte branding
GBF	GB Railfreight - swirl
GBM	GB Railfreight Metronet
GBN	GB Railfreight/Eurotunnel new livery
GBR	GB Railfreight - blue
GBU	GB Railfreight swirl (no First branding)
GLX	Glaxochem - grey, blue and black
GNE	Great North Eastern Railway - blue
GRN	Green
GRY	Grey
GSW	Great Scottish & Western Railway - maroon
GTL	Grand Central Railway - black
GTO	Grand Central Railway - black with orange
GWG	First Great Western - green
GWR	Great Western Railway - green
HAN	Hanson
HEC	Heathrow Connect - grey, orange
HEL	Heathrow Connect - Terminal 4 'Link'
HEX	Heathrow Express - silver, grey
HNR	Harry Needle Railroad - yellow/grey
HS1	High Speed 1 - blue with powder blue doors
HUN	Hunslet
IND	Industrial colours of operator

INT	InterCity - two-tone grey off-set with red and white body band
JAR	Jarvis - maroon
KBR	Knorr Bremse Rail - blue, white, green
LAF	Lafarge Aggregates - green/white
LHL	Loadhaul Freight - black and orange
LLB	Large Logo Blue
LMI	London Midland - grey, green and black
LNE	LNER tourist green/cream
LOG	London Overground - white and blue with orange doors
LUL	London Underground red
MAB	Statesman Pullman - maroon/beige
MAI	MainTrain - blue with branding
MAL	Malcolm Rail
MAR	Maroon
MER	Merseyrail - silver and yellow
MLF	Mainline Freight - aircraft blue
MLG	Mainline Freight - branded double grey
MML	Midland Main Line - turquoise/white
MSC	Mediterranean Shipping Company
NBP	Northern Belle Pullman - cream/umber
NE2	National Express with c2c branding
NGE	First Great Eastern - grey/blue with cab end swirl, branded National Express
NOM	Northern Rail - blue Metro branded
NOR	Northern - blue, purple, grey
NOU	Northern unbranded
NRL	Network Rail - yellow with branding
NSE	Network SouthEast - red, white and blue
NUB	Northern Rail blue - unbranded ScotRail
NWT	North West Trains - dark blue
GAR	National Express East Anglia (now Abellio)
NXE	National Express East Coast
NXG	National Express East Coast branding on GNER blue livery
NXS	National Express brand on Silverlink
NXU	National Express unbranded white/grey
ONE	One Anglia mid-blue (now Abellio)
ORA	One Railway with Greater Anglia branding
ORG	HNRC orange
PCL	BR Parcels - red/grey
PTR	Porterbrook
PUL	Pullman - umber/cream
QOS	Queen of Scots Pullman
REG	Regional Railways - blue, white
RES	Rail express systems - red and graphite
RFD	Railfreight Distribution
RFE	Railfreight grey with EWS branding
RFG	Railfreight grey
RFI	Railfreight International
RFP	Railfreight with Petroleum branding
RFT	BR Railfreight - grey, red and yellow, with large logo and numbers
RIV	Riviera Trains - maroon
RML	Royal Mail Limited - red
ROJ	Royal Diamond Jubilee
ROY	Royal Train - claret
RTB	Railtrack - blue
RTK	Railtrack - grey/brown
SCE	Stagecoach - white with East Midlands branding
SCT	ScotRail Caledonian Sleeper - mauve/ white
SEC	Serco
SET	South Eastern Trains - white with branding
SGK	Southern Gatwick Express - blue, white and red with swirl ends
SIL	Silver
SKL	Silverlink London Overground, SLK with London Overground branding
SLF	Silverlink, with First Great Western branding
SLK	Silverlink - mauve, green and white
SNF	Railfreight grey with SNCF branding
SNT	SNCF domestic on Eurostar - silver, white and yellow
SOU	Southern - white, black and green
SPL	Special livery
STN	Stansted Express
STO	Stobart Rail
SWM	South West Trains - main line white and blue
SWO	South West Trains - outer suburban blue
SWS	South West Trains - suburban red
SWT	South West Trains - blue, red, grey
TAT	Tata Steel - blue
TES	Tesco
TEX	TransPennine Express - As FST with TPE brand
TGG	Transrail Grey with 'T' branding
THM	Thameslink - blue, white, yellow
TLF	Trainload Freight - grey
TLL	Trainload grey with Loadhaul branding
TLP	Thameslink promotional multi-coloured stripes
TPD	Trans Pennine/Central Trains logo
TSO	Travaux du Sud Ouest - yellow
TTG	Two-tone grey
VIR	Virgin - red/grey
VSN	VSOE Northern
VT1	Virgin - red/grey unbranded
VWC	Virgin West Coast - silver, red, white and black
WAB	Wabtec Rail - black
WAG	West Anglia Great Northern - purple
WCR	West Coast Railway - maroon
WES	Wessex Trains - maroon
WET	Wessex Trains - silver, maroon/pink doors
WEX	Wessex Rail Engineering
WHT	White
YEL	Yellow

Operational Pool Codes

ATLO	West Coast Traincare - Locomotives
ATTB	West Coast Traincare - Class 57/3 with Dellner
ATZZ	West Coast Traincare - Locos for disposal
AWCX	West Coast Railway - Stored locos
CDJD	Serco Railtest - Shunting locos
COLO	Colas Rail - Operational locomotives
COLS	Colas Rail - Stored locomotives
DFFT	Freightliner - Restricted duties
DFGC	Freightliner - Class 86/5 trials locomotive
DFGH	Freightliner - Heavy Haul Class 70
DFGI	Freightliner - Intermodal Class 70
DFGM	Freightliner - Intermodal Class 66/5
DFHG	Freightliner - Heavy Haul Class 66/5 & 66/6
DFHH	Freightliner - Heavy Haul Class 66/5 & 66/6
DFIM	Freightliner - Intermodal Class 66/5
DFIN	Freightliner - Intermodal - low emission
DFLC	Freightliner - Class 90
DFLS	Freightliner - Class 08
DFNC	Freightliner - Class 86/6
DFRT	Freightliner - Class 66 Infrastructure contracts
DFTZ	Freightliner - Stored Class 66
DHLT	Freightliner - Awaiting repairs
EFOO	First Great Western - Class 57
EFPC	First Great Western - HST power cars
EFSH	First Great Western - Class 08
EHPC	CrossCountry Trains - HST power cars
EJLO	London Midland - Class 08
EMPC	East Midlands Trains - HST power cars
EMSL	East Midlands Trains - Class 08
EPXX	Europhoenix - Class 86
GBBR	Europorte/GBRf - Class 73/9
GBCM	Europorte/GBRf - Class 66 commercial contracts
GBED	Europorte/GBRf - Class 73/1, 73/2
GBET	Europorte/GBRf - Class 92
GBFM	Europorte/GBRf - Class 66 modified with RETB
GBMU	Europorte/GBRf - Class 66 modified for MU
GBRT	Europorte/GBRf - Class 66 Infrastructure
GBSD	Europorte/GBRf - Class 66 RETB
GBWM	Europorte/GBRf - Class 08
GBZZ	Europorte/GBRf - Stored locomotives
GCHP	Grand Central - HST power cars
GPSS	Eurostar UK - Class 08
HNRL	Harry Needle Railroad - Class 08, 20 hire locos
HNRS	Harry Needle Railroad - Stored locomotives
HTCX	Hanson Traction - Class 56
IANA	National Express East Anglia - Class 90
IECA	National Express East Coast - Class 91
IECP	National Express East Coast - HST power cars
INDL	Industrial (unofficial code)
MBDL	Private operators - Diesel traction
MBED	Private operators - Class 73
MRSO	Mainline Rail - Class 08
PTXX	Eurotunnel - Europorte2 Class 92
QACL	Network Rail - Class 86 load banks
QADD	Network Rail - Class 31
QCAR	Network Rail - HST power cars
QETS	Network Rail - Class 97/3
RCZH	Railcare Springburn - Class 08
RCZN	Railcare Wolverton - Class 08
RFSH	Wabtec Rail Doncaster - Class 08
RVLO	Rail Vehicle Engineering Derby - Locos
RVLS	Rail Vehicle Engineering Derby - Stored locos
SIEM	Siemens Transportation - Barriers
TTLS	Traditional Traction - Locomotives
WAAN	DB Schenker - Class 67
WABN	DB Schenker - Class 67 RETB fitted
WATN	DB Schenker - Class 67 hire to Arriva T W
WBAI	DB Schenker - Class 66 Industrial
WBAK	DB Schenker - Class 66 Construction
WBAM	DB Schenker - Class 66 Energy
WBAN	DB Schenker - Class 66 Network
WBBI	DB Schenker - Class 66 Industrial RETB fitted
WBBM	DB Schenker - Class 66 Energy RETB fitted
WBBN	DB Schenker - Class 66 Network RETB fitted
WBEI	DB Schenker - Class 66 Euro in the UK
WBEN	DB Schenker - Class 66 Euro Cargo Rail
WBEP	DB Schenker - Class 66 Poland
WBES	DB Schenker - Class 66 ECR RHTT
WBLI	DB Schenker - Class 66 Industrial auto coupler
WCAI	DB Schenker - Class 60 Industrial 990 gal fuel
WCAK	DB Schenker - Class 60 Construction 990 gal fuel
WCAM	DB Schenker - Class 60 Energy 990 gal fuel
WCBI	DB Schenker - Class 60 Industrial 1150 gal fuel
WCBK	DB Schenker - Class 60 Construct'n 1150 gal fuel
WDAI	DB Schenker - Class 59/2 Industrial
WDAK	DB Schenker - Class 59/2 Construction
WEFE	DB Schenker - Class 90
WFMS	DB Schenker - Class 60 Fleet Management
WFMU	DB Schenker - Fleet Management
WKBN	DB Schenker - Class 37 Network RETB fitted
WLAN	DB Schenker - Euro Cargo Rail Class 21
WNTR	DB Schenker - Stored locos - reserve
WNTS	DB Schenker - Stored locos - serviceable
WNXX	DB Schenker - Stored locos - unserviceable
WNYX	DB Schenker - Stored locos - parts recovery
WNZX	DB Schenker - Awaiting disposal
WRLN	DB Schenker - Class 08, 09 - North London
WSEN	DB Schenker - Euro Cargo Rail - Class 08
WSSA	DB Schenker - Class 08, 09 - Axiom Rail
WSSI	DB Schenker - Class 08, 09 Industrial
WSSL	DB Schenker - Class 08, 09 Logistics
WSSM	DB Schenker - Class 08, 09 Energy
WSSK	DB Schenker - Class 08, 09 Network/Const'n
WSXX	DB Schenker - Class 08, 09 Stored
WTAE	DB Schenker - Class 92 Network
WTHE	DB Schenker - Class 92 HS1 authorised
WZFF	DB Schenker - Class 58 France
WZGF	DB Schenker - Class 56, 92 France
WZTS	DB Schenker - Class 08, 56, 58 Stored (hire pool)
XHAC	Direct Rail Services - Class 47
XHCK	Direct Rail Services - Class 57
XHNB	Direct Rail Services - Northern Belle
XHND	Direct Rail Services - Class 37 Network Rail
XHHP	Direct Rail Services - Holding Pool
XHIM	Direct Rail Services - Class 66 - Intermodal
XHNC	Direct Rail Services - Nuclear Traffic
XHSS	Direct Rail Services - Stored
XHVT	Direct Rail Services - Class 57 Thunderbird
XYPA	Mendip Rail - Hanson Group
XYPO	Mendip Rail - Foster Yeoman (Aggregate Inds)

■ Pools are given only for locomotive groups which are included in this book. Pool codes for multiple units are not included.

Preserved site codes

ACL	AC Locomotive Group
ALY	Allelys, Studley
APF	Appleby-Frodingham RPS
AVR	Avon Valley Railway
BAT	Battlefield Line
BEL	5Bel Trust Barrow Hill
BHR	Barrow Hill Roundhouse
BIR	Barry Island Railway
BKR	Bo'ness & Kinneil Railway
BLU	Bluebell Railway
BRC	Buckinghamshire Railway Centre
BRM	Birmingham Railway Museum, Tyseley
BVR	Bridgend Valleys Railway
BWR	Bodmin & Wenford Railway
CAN	Canton (Pullman Rail)
CHS	Chasewater Railway
COL	Colne Valley Railway
COV	Coventry Electric Railway Museum
CPR	Chinnor & Princes Risborough Railway
CRB	Caledonian Railway, Brechin
CRT	Cambrian Railway Trust
CVR	Churnet Valley Railway
CWR	Cholsey & Wallingford Railway
DAR	Dartmoor Railway
DEE	Royal Deeside Railway
DER	Derwent Valley Railway
DFR	Dean Forest Railway
DID	Didcot Railway Centre
EAR	East Anglian Railway Museum
ECC	Ecclesbourne Valley Railway
EDR	Eden Valley Railway
EHC	Elsecar Heritage Centre
EHD	Eastleigh DBS Depot
EKR	East Kent Railway
ELR	East Lancashire Railway
EMB	Embsay Steam Railway
EPO	Epping Ongar Railway
FHL	Fawley Hall (Private)
FIN	Finmere Station, Oxfordshire
GCN	Great Central Railway (North)
GCR	Great Central Railway
GKR	Graham Kirk Rail
GWI	Gwili Railway
GWR	Gloucestershire Warwickshire Railway
HAD	Hastings Diesels
IOW	Isle of Wight Railway
KEI	Keith & Dufftown Railway
KES	Kent & East Sussex Railway
KIN	MoD Kineton
KWV	Keighley & Worth Valley Railway
LAN	Llangollen Railway
LDL	Lavender Line
LHG	L H Group Services, Burton
LHR	Lakeside & Haverthwaite Railway
LNW	London & North Western, Crewe
LWR	Lincolnshire Wolds Railway
MET	Methill (Private)
MFM	Mangapps Farm Railway Museum
MHR	Mid Hants Railway
MID	Middleton Railway
MLM	Motorail - Long Marston
MNF	Mid-Norfolk Railway
MOR	Moreton-on-Lugg
MRC	Middleton Railway Centre
MSM	Museum of Science & Industry, Manchester
MSR	Midsomer Norton
NHD	Newton Heath Depot
NIR	Northamptonshire Ironstone Railway
NLR	Northampton & Lamport Railway
NNR	North Norfolk Railway
NRM	National Railway Museum, York
NRS	National Railway Museum, Shildon
NYM	North Yorkshire Moors Railway
PBR	Pontypool & Blaenavon Railway
PDR	Paignton & Dartmouth Railway
PRL	Peak Rail
PVR	Plym Valley Railway
RAC	Railway Age, Crewe
RAM	Rampart, Derby
RIB	Ribble Steam Railway
RIP	Rippingdale Station
ROW	Rowley Mill
RST	Rushden Station Transport Museum
SEL	St Leonards Railway Engineering
SLN	Stewarts Lane Depot
SNI	Snibston Railway
SPV	Spa Valley Railway
SRC	Stainmore Railway Co
STR	Strathspey Railway
SVR	Severn Valley Railway
SWI	Swindon & Cricklade Railway
SWN	Swanage Railway
TEB	Friends of 502 Group, Tebay
TEL	Telford Horsehay Steam Trust
THK	Throckmorton Airfield
TIT	Titley Junction
TSR	Telford Steam Railway
TYN	North Tyneside Railway
VOG	Vale of Glamorgan Railway
WAS	Washwood Heath
WCR	West Coast Railway Co
WED	Weardale Railway
WEN	Wensleydale Railway
WPH	Walthamstow Pump House
WSR	West Somerset Railway
XXX	Private unspecified site
YEO	Yeovil Railway Centre

Status

	Status
OPR	Operational
OPR	Operational Main Line certified
RES	Under restoration
STC	Static exhibit
STO	Stored

Depot Codes

Code	Facility	Name	Operator
AB	SD	Aberdeen Guild Street	DBS
AC	CSD	Aberdeen Clayhills	ICE
AD	EMUD	Ashford Hitachi	HIT/SET
AF	T&RSMD	Ashford Chart Leacon	BOM
AH	MoD	Ashchurch	MoD
AK	DMUD	Ardwick	SIE/FTP
AL	DMUD	Aylesbury	CRW
AN	TMD/WRD	Allerton, Liverpool	DBS/NOR
AP	TMD	Ashford Rail Plant	BBR
AS	Store	Allelys	ALL
AT	TMD	Various sites	ALS
AW	SD	Washwood Heath	Hanson
AY	SD	Ayr	DBS
AZ	TMD	Ashford	BBR
AZ	TMD	Alizay (France)	ECR (DBS)
BA	TMD	Crewe Basford Hall	FLR, DBS
BC	MoD	Bicester	MoD
BD	T&RSMD	Birkenhead North	MER
BF	EMUD	Bedford Cauldwell Walk	FCC
BG	SD	Hull Botanic Gardens	NOR
BH	Eng	Barrow Hill Roundhouse	BHE
BI	EMUD	Brighton	SOU
BK	T&RSMD	Barton Hill	LNWR
BM	T&RSMD	Bournemouth	SWT
BN	T&RSMD	Bounds Green	ICE
BO	T&RSMD	Burton	Nemesis
BP	SD	Blackpool CS	NOR
BQ	TMD	Bury	ELR
BR	SD	Bristol Kingsland Road	NRL, FLR
BS	TMD	Bescot	DBS
BT	TMD	Bo'ness	BOK
BW	SD	Barrow-in-Furness	NOR
BZ	T&RSMD	St Blazey	DBS
CA	SD	Cambridge Coldhams Ln	AXI
CB	STORE	Crewe Brook Sidings	DBS
CC	T&RSMD	Clacton	GAR
CD	SD	Crewe Diesel	RIV, DBS
CE	IEMD	Crewe Electric	DBS
CF	DMUD	Cardiff Canton	PUL, ATW
CG	TMD	Crewe Gresty Bridge	DRS
CH	DMUD	Chester	ALS, ATW
CJ	SD	Clapham Junction	SWT
CK	DMUD	Corkerhill	FSR
CL	Store	Carlisle Upperby	DBS
CM	SD	Camden	LMI
CO	IEMD	Coquelles (France)	EUR
CP	CARMD	Crewe Carriage Shed	LNW
CQ	T&RSMD	Crewe Railway Age	CHC
CR	SD	Colchester	GAR
CS	T&RSMD	Carnforth	WCR
CT	SD	Cleethorpes	FTP
CW	MoD	Caerwent	MoD
CX	Store	Cardiff Tidal	DBS
CY	Store	Crewe Coal/South Yards	DRS
CZ	TMD	Central Rivers	BOM
DD	SD	Doncaster Wood Yard	DBS
DF	T&RSMD	Rail Vehicle Engineering	RVE
DI	Pres	Didcot Railway Centre	GWS
DM	TMD	Dollands Moor	DBS
DO	Store	Donnington Railfreight	-
DR	TMD	Doncaster Carr	DBS
DT	SD	Didcot Triangle	DBS
DV	SD	Dover	SET
DW	SD	Doncaster West Yard	NRL, WAB
DY	T&RSMD	Derby Etches Park	EMT
EA	SD	Earles Sidings	DBS
EC	T&RSMD	Craigentinny (Edinburgh)	ICE
ED	DMUD	Eastfield	FSR
EF	MPVD	Effingham Junction	AMS
EH	SD	Eastleigh	DBS
EM	EMUD	East Ham	c2c
EN	CARMD	Euston Downside	NRL
EU	SD	Euston Station Sidings	VWC
EZ	DMUD	Exeter	FGW
FB	Store	Ferrybridge	DBS
FC*		Fire College (Moreton-in-Marsh)	
FD	Mobile	Diesel loco	FLR
FE	Mobile	Electric loco	FLR
FF	TRSMD	Forest - Brussels	SNCB, NMBS, EUS
FH	TRACK	Frodingham	GRP
FN	Hire	France	ECR
FP	CSD	Ferme Park	ICE
FR	EMUD	Fratton	SWT
FS	Mobile	Diesel Shunter	FLR
FW	SD	Fort William	DBS
FX	TMD	Felixstowe	FDH
GI	EMUD	Gillingham	SET
GL	TMD	Gloucester	CWR, ADV
GP	SD	Grove Park	SET
GW	EMUD	Glasgow Shields	FSR
HA	TMD	Haymarket	FSR
HD	SD	Holyhead	ATW
HE	EMUD	Hornsey	FCC
HF	SD	Hereford	DBS
HG	Store	Hither Green	DBS
HI	TM	Hitchin	BBR
HJ	SD	Hoo Junction	DBS
HM	SD/WRD	Healey Mills	DBS
HT	T&RSMD	Heaton	NOR, GTL
HY	SD	Oxford Hinksey Yard	NRL
IL	T&RSMD	Ilford	GAR
IM	SD	Immingham	DBS
IP	SD	Ipswich	FLR
IS	TMD	Inverness	FSR
KC	Store	Carlisle Currock WRD	DBS
KD	SD	Kingmoor Yard	DRS
KK	EMUD	Kirkdale	MER
KM	TMD	Carlisle Kingmoor	DRS
KR	T&RSMD	Kidderminster	SVR
KT	MoD	Kineton	MoD
KY	SD/WRD	Knottingley	DBS
LA	T&RSMD	Laira	FGW
LB	Eng	Loughborough	BTL
LD	TMD	Leeds Midland Road	FLR
LE	T&RSMD	Landore	FGW
LG	T&RSMD	Longsight Electric	ALT
LH	Eng	LH Group	LHG
LL	CSD	Liverpool Edge Hill	ALS
LM	Store	Long Marston	MLS
LO	T&RSMD	Longsight Diesel	NOR

LP*	Eng	EMD Longport	EMD
LR	Eng	Leicester	EMD
LT	MoD	Longtown	MoD
LU	MoD	Ludgershall	MoD
LY	T&RSMD	Le Landy - Paris	SNCF, EUS
MA	CARMD	Manchester International	ALS
MD	TMD	Merehead	MRL
MG	TMD	Margam	DBS
MH	SD	Millerhill	DBS
ML	SD	Motherwell	DRS
MM	Store	Moreton-in-Marsh	-
MN	DMUD	Machynlleth	ATW
MQ	Store	Meldon Quarry	BAR
MR	SD	March	GBR
MW	MoD	Marchwood Military Port	MoD
MY	SD/Store	Mossend Yard	DBS, FLR
NB	SD	New Brighton	MER
NC	T&RSMD	Norwich Crown Point	GAR
ND	Works	NedTrans, Tilburg	NDZ
NG	T&RSMD	New Cross Gate	LOL
NH	DMUD	Newton Heath	NOR
NL	T&RSMD	Neville Hill (Leeds)	EMT, ICE
NM	SD	Nottingham Eastcroft	EMT
NN	EMUD	Northampton, Kings Heath	SIE, LMI
NT	EMUD	Northam	SIE, SWT
NY	T&RSMD	Grosmont	NYM
OD	Eng	Old Dalby	ALS
OH	EMUD	Old Oak Common Electric	SIE
ON	SD	Orpington	SET
OO	HSTMD	Old Oak Common HST	FGW
OX	CSD	Oxford Carriage Sidings	FGW
OY	CARMD	Oxley	ALS
PB	SD	Peterborough	DBS
PC	TRSMD	Polmadie	ALS
PE	SD	Peterborough Nene	FCC
PF	SD	Peak Forest	DBS
PH	SD	Perth	FSR
PM	TRSMD	St Philip's Marsh (Bristol)	FGW
PN	SD	Preston Station	NOR
PN	TMD	Poznan (Poland)	ECR (DBS)
PQ	SD	Harwich Parkeston Quay	DBS
PT	SD	Peterborough	GBR
PY	MoD	Shoeburyness (Pigs Bay)	MoD, KRS
PZ	TRSMD	Penzance (Long Rock)	FGW
RE	EMUD	Ramsgate	SET
RG	DMUD	Reading	FGW
RH	SD	Redhill	DBS
RL	TRSMD	Ropley	MHR
RO	SD	Rotherham Steel	DBS
RU	TMD	Rugby Rail Plant	GRP
RY	EMUD	Ryde	SWT
SA	DMUD	Salisbury	SWT
SB	TMD	Shrewsbury	NOR
SE	TRSMD	St Leonards	SLR
SG	EMUD	Slade Green	SET
SH	CARMD	Southall Railway Centre	WCR
SI	EMUD	Soho	LMI
SJ	TRSMD	Stourbridge Junction	LMI
SK	TRSMD	Swanwick	MRC
SL	TRSMD	Stewarts Lane	DBS, VSO, SOU
SM	SD	Sheffield Station	NOR
SN	SD	Shoeburyness	c2c
SO*		Southend	
SP	CRDC	Springs Branch	DBS
SQ	SD	Stockport	NOR
ST	SD	Southport	MER
SU	TRSMD	Selhurst	SOU
SX	SD	Shrewsbury	ATW
SZ	TMD	Southampton Maritime	FLR
TB	SD	Three Bridges	DBS
TE	TMD	Thornaby/Tees Yard	DBS
TF	SD	Orient Way	GAR
TG	SD	Tonbridge	GBR
TI	TRSMD	Temple Mills	EUS
TJ	TMD	Tavistock Junction	COL
TM	SD	Tyseley Loco Works	BRM
TN	SD	Taunton Fairwater	NRL, FLR
TO	TMD	Toton	DBS
TS	DMUD	Tyseley	LMI
TT	Store	Toton Training Compound	DBS
TY	Store	Tyne Yard	DBS
VI	SD	Victoria	SET
VR	SD	Aberystwyth	ATW
VZ	EMUD	Strawberry Hill	SIE, SWT
WA	SD	Warrington Arpley	DBS
WB	TRSMD	Wembley	ALS
WD	EMUD	East Wimbledon	SWT
WE	SD	Willesden Brent	DBS
WF	SD	Wansford	NVR
WH	Eng	Whatley	MRL
WK	SD	West Kirby	MER
WN	EMUD	Willesden	LOG
WO	TMD	Wolsingham	WER
WP	SD	Worksop	DBS
WS	SD	Worcester	LMI
WW	SD	West Worthing	SOU
WY	SD/CSD	Westbury Yard	DBS
WZ*	TRSMD	Washwood Heath	HAN
XW	TMD	Crofton	BOM
XX	-	Exported	-
YK	DMUD	Siemens York	SIE, FTP
YL	TMD	York Leeman Road	JAR, FLF
YM	Store	National Railway Museum	NRM
YN	SD	York North Yard	DBS
YO	SD	Yoker	FSR
ZA	Eng	RTC Derby	SER, NRL, AEA
ZB	Eng	Doncaster	WAB
ZC	Eng	Crewe	BOM
ZD	Eng	Derby Litchurch Lane	BOM
ZE	Eng	Washwood Heath	COL
ZG	Eng	Eastleigh Works	KRS
ZH	Eng	Glasgow	RCL
ZI	Eng	Ilford	BOM
ZK	Eng	Kilmarnock	BTL
ZL	Eng	Cardiff Canton	PUL
ZN	Eng	Wolverton	RCL
ZS	Eng	Locotech Wakefield	BAR
ZW	Eng	Stoke-on-Trent (Marcroft)	AXI
WZ		Warsaw (Poland)	DBS
3M*		3M Industries, Bracknell	

* Unofficial code

Operator Codes

AFG	Arlington Fleet Group
ALL	Allelys Heavy Haul
ALS	Alstom
AMS	Amec Spie Rail
ATW	Arriva Trains Wales
AXC	Arriva Cross Country
AXI	Axiom Rail
BAR	British American Railway Services
BBR	Balfour Beatty
BHE	Barrow Hill Roundhouse
BOK	Bo'ness & Kinneil
BOM	Bombardier
BRM	Birmingham Railway Museum
BTL	Brush Traction Limited
C2C	c2c Rail
CAR	Carillion
CHS	Crewe Heritage Centre
COL	Colas Rail
CON	Continental Rail (Spain)
COR	Corus Steel
CRW	Chiltern Railways
DBA	DB Arriva
DBR	DB Regio
DBS	DB Schenker West
DRS	Direct Rail Services
ECR	Euro Cargo Rail (DBS)
ELR	East Lancashire Railway
EMT	East Midlands Trains
ETF	ETF Freight (France)
ETL	Electric Traction Ltd
EU2	Eurotunnel Europorte2
EUR	Eurotunnel
EUS	Eurostar
FCC	First Capital Connect
FDH	Felixstowe Dock & Harbour
FGW	First Great Western
FHT	First Hull Trains
FLR	Freightliner
FSL	Flying Scotsman Railway Ltd
FSR	First ScotRail
FTP	First TransPennine
GBR	GB Railfreight
GRP	Grant Rail Plant
GTL	Grand Central Railway
GWS	Great Western Society
HEC	Heathrow Connect
HEX	Heathrow Express
HIT	Hitachi
HNR	Harry Needle Railroad
ICE	Inter City East Coast
IND	Industrial operator
IRY	Ian Riley
JHS	Jeremy Hoskins
KBR	Knorr Bremse Rail
KRS	Knights Rail Services
LAF	Lafarge Aggregates
LMI	London Midland
LNW	L&NWR Railway Co
LOG	London Overground
LUL	London Underground Ltd
MER	Merseyrail
MHR	Mid Hants Railway
MoD	Ministry of Defence
MRC	Midland Railway Centre
MRL	Mendip Rail Ltd
MRS	Motorail Logistics
NDZ	NedTrains
NOR	Northern Rail
NOT	Northumbria Rail
NRL	Network Rail
NRM	National Railway Museum
NVR	Nene Valley Railway
NYM	North Yorkshire Moors Railway
OLD	Old Dalby Test Track
POB	Port of Boston
PUL	Pullman Group
RAF	Railfilms Ltd
RCL	Railcare Ltd
RIV	Riviera Trains
RRS	Ridings Railtours
RVE	Rail Vehicle Engineering
S4G	Stratford 47 Group
SET	SouthEastern Trains
SIE	Siemens
SIL	Stagecoach Island Line
SLR	St Leonards Rail Engineering
SNB	Société Nationale des Chemins de fer Belges
SNF	Société Nationale des Chemins de fer Français
SOU	Southern
SRP	Scottish Railway Preservation Society
SVR	Severn Valley Railway
SWT	South West Trains
TRN	Transfesa
TSO	Travaux du Sud Ouest (France)
TTS	Transmart Trains
VSO	Venice Simplon Orient Express
VTN	Vintage Trains
VWC	Virgin West Coast
WAB	Wabtec
WCR	West Coast Railway Co

Below: *Arriva Trains Wales three-car Class 175/1 No. 175108 stands at Swansea High Street station with a service from Manchester to Carmarthan on 24 July 2013.* **CJM**

Owner Codes

201	20189 Ltd (Michael Owen)
AEA	AEA Rail Technology
ALS	Alstom
ANG	Angel Trains
ATW	Arriva Trains Wales
AUT	Arriva UK Trains
BAA	British Airports Authority
BCC	Bridgend County Council
BEA	Beacon Rail
BOM	Bombardier
BOT	Bank of Tokyo (Mitsubishi)
BTM	BTMU Capital Corporation
C20	Class 20 Locomotive Ltd
CBR	CB Rail
CCC	Cardiff County Council
COL	Colas Rail
CRW	Chiltern Railways
CWR	Cotswold Rail
DBR	DB Regio
DBS	DB Schenker West
DBS/T	DB Schenker/Transfesa
DRS	Direct Rail Services
ECR	Euro Cargo Rail (DBS)
ECT	ECT Main Line Rail
EMT	East Midlands Trains
ETL	Electric Traction Ltd
EU2	Eurotunnel Europorte2
EUR	Eurotunnel
EUS	Eurostar
EVL	Eversholt Leasing
FGP	First Group
FLF	Fastline Freight
FLR	Freightliner
FOS	Foster Yeoman
GBR	GB Railfreight
GTL	Grand Central Railway Ltd
HAN	Hanson Traction
HEC	Hunslet Engine Co
HBS	Halifax-Bank of Scotland
HJA	Howard Johnson Associates
HNR	Harry Needle Railroad
IRY	Ian Riley
JAR	Jarvis
KBR	Knorr Bremse Rail
KRS	Knights Rail Services
MAG	Macquarie Group
NRL	Network Rail
NYM	North Yorkshire Moors Railway
PTR	Porterbrook
QWR	QW Rail Leasing
RCL	Railcare Limited
RIV	Riviera Trains
RML	Royal Mail
RMS	RMS Locotech
RTR	RT Rail
RVE	Rail Vehicle Engineering
S4G	Stratford Class 47 Group
SEC	Serco
SIE	Siemens
SNB	Société Nationale des Chemins de fer Belges
SNF	Société Nationale des Chemins de fer Français
SOU	Southern (Govia)
SWT	South West Trains (Stagecoach)
TTS	Transmart Trains
URL	UK Rail Leasing
VTN	Vintage Trains
WAB	Wabtec
WCR	West Coast Railway Co
WYP	West Yorkshire PTE

Below: *In stunning evening light on 8 May 2013, DRS Class 37/6s Nos. 37612 and 37608 pass Salterbeck between Harrington and Workington on the Cumbrian coast route powering train 6C46, the 19.36 Sellafield to Carlisle Kingmoor formed of two flask wagons.* **Nathan Williamson**

Station three-letter Codes

Abbey Wood	ABW
Aber	ABE
Abercynon	ACY
Aberdare	ABA
Aberdeen	ABD
Aberdour	AUR
Aberdovey	AVY
Abererch	ABH
Abergavenny	AGV
Abergele & Pensarn	AGL
Aberystwyth	AYW
Accrington	ACR
Achanalt	AAT
Achnasheen	ACN
Achnashellach	ACH
Acklington	ACK
Acle	ACL
Acocks Green	ACG
Acton Bridge	ACB
Acton Central	ACC
Acton Main Line	AML
Adderley Park	ADD
Addiewell	ADW
Addlestone	ASN
Adisham	ADM
Adlington (Cheshire)	ADC
Adlington (Lancs)	ADL
Adwick	AWK
Aigburth	AIG
Ainsdale	ANS
Aintree	AIN
Airbles	AIR
Airdrie	ADR
Albany Park	AYP
Albrighton	ALB
Alderley Edge	ALD
Aldermaston	AMT
Aldershot	AHT
Aldrington	AGT
Alexandra Palace	AAP
Alexandra Parade	AXP
Alexandria	ALX
Alfreton	ALF
Allens West	ALW
Alloa	ALO
Alness	ASS
Alnmouth	ALM
Alresford	ALR
Alsager	ASG
Althorne	ALN
Althorpe	ALP
Altnabreac	ABC
Alton	AON
Altrincham	ALT
Alvechurch	ALV
Ambergate	AMB
Amberley	AMY
Amersham	AMR
Ammanford	AMF
Ancaster	ANC
Anderston	AND
Andover	ADV
Anerley	ANZ
Angel Road	AGR
Angmering	ANG
Annan	ANN
Anniesland	ANL
Ansdell & Fairhaven	AFV
Appleby	APP
Appledore (Kent)	APD
Appleford	APF
Appley Bridge	APB
Apsley	APS
Arbroath	ARB
Ardgay	ARD
Ardlui	AUI
Ardrossan Harbour	ADS
Ardrossan South Beach	ASB
Ardrossan Town	ADN
Ardwick	ADK
Argyle Street	AGS
Arisaig	ARG
Arlesey	ARL
Armathwaite	AWT
Arnside	ARN
Arram	ARR
Arrochar & Tarbet	ART
Arundel	ARU
Ascot	ACT
Ascott-u-Wychwood	AUW
Ash	ASH
Ash Vale	AHV
Ashburys	ABY
Ashchurch	ASC
Ashfield	ASF
Ashford International	AFK
Ashford (Eurostar)	ASI
Ashford (Surrey)	AFS
Ashley	ASY
Ashtead	AHD
Ashton-under-Lyne	AHN
Ashurst	AHS
Ashurst New Forest	ANF
Ashwell & Morden	AWM
Askam	ASK
Aslockton	ALK
Aspatria	ASP
Aspley Guise	APG
Aston	AST
Atherstone	ATH
Atherton	ATN
Attadale	ATT
Attenborough	ATB
Attleborough	ATL
Auchinleck	AUK
Audley End	AUD
Aughton Park	AUG
Aviemore	AVM
Avoncliff	AVF
Avonmouth	AVN
Axminster	AXM
Aylesbury	AYS
Aylesbury Parkway	AVP
Aylesford	AYL
Aylesham	AYH
Ayr	AYR
Bache	BAC
Baglan	BAJ
Bagshot	BAG
Baildon	BLD
Baillieston	BIO
Balcombe	BAB
Baldock	BDK
Balham	BAL
Balloch	BHC
Balmossie	BSI
Bamber Bridge	BMB
Bamford	BAM
Banavie	BNV
Banbury	BAN
Bangor (Gwynedd)	BNG
Bank Hall	BAH
Banstead	BAD
Barassie	BSS
Barbican	ZBB
Bardon Mill	BLL
Bare Lane	BAR
Bargeddie	BGI
Bargoed	BGD
Barking	BKG
Barking Underground	ZBK
Barlaston	BRT
Barming	BMG
Barmouth	BRM
Barnehurst	BNH
Barnes	BNS
Barnes Bridge	BNI
Barnetby	BTB
Barnham	BAA
Barnhill	BNL
Barnsley	BNY
Barnstaple	BNP
Barnt Green	BTG
Barrhead	BRR
Barrhill	BRL
Barrow Haven	BAV
Barrow upon Soar	BWS
Barrow-in-Furness	BIF
Barry	BRY
Barry Docks	BYD
Barry Island	BYI
Barry Links	BYL
Barton-on-Humber	BAU
Basildon	BSO
Basingstoke	BSK
Bat & Ball	BBL
Bath Spa	BTH
Bathgate	BHG
Batley	BTL
Battersby	BTT
Battersea Park	BAK
Battle	BAT
Battlesbridge	BLB
Bayford	BAY
Beaconsfield	BCF
Bearley	BER
Bearsden	BRN
Bearsted	BSD
Beasdale	BSL
Beaulieu Road	BEU
Beauly	BEL
Bebington	BEB
Beccles	BCC
Beckenham Hill	BEC
Beckenham Junction	BKJ
Bedford	BDM
Bedford St Johns	BSJ
Bedhampton	BDH
Bedminster	BMT
Bedworth	BEH
Bedwyn	BDW
Beeston	BEE
Bekesbourne	BKS
Belle Vue	BLV
Bellgrove	BLG
Bellingham	BGM
Bellshill	BLH
Belmont	BLM
Belper	BLP
Beltring	BEG
Belvedere	BVD
Bempton	BEM
Ben Rhydding	BEY
Benfleet	BEF
Bentham	BEN
Bentley	BTY
Bentley (South Yorks)	BYK
Bere Alston	BAS
Bere Ferrers	BFE
Berkhamsted	BKM
Berkswell	BKW
Berney Arms	BYA
Berry Brow	BBW
Berrylands	BRS
Berwick	BRK
Berwick-upon-Tweed	BWK
Bescar Lane	BES
Bescot Stadium	BSC
Betchworth	BTO
Bethnal Green	BET
Betws-y-Coed	BYC
Beverley	BEV
Bexhill	BEX
Bexley	BXY
Bexleyheath	BXH
Bicester North	BCS
Bicester Town	BIT
Bickley	BKL
Bidston	BID
Biggleswade	BIW
Bilbrook	BBK
Billericay	BIC
Billingham	BIL
Billingshurst	BIG
Bingham	BIN
Bingley	BIY
Birchgrove	BCG
Birchington-on-Sea	BCH
Birchwood	BWD
Birkbeck	BIK
Birkdale	BDL
Birkenhead Central	BKC
Birkenhead North	BKN
Birkenhead Park	BKP
Birmingham Int	BHI
Birmingham Moor St	BMO
Birmingham New St	BHM
Birmingham Snow Hill	BSW
Bishop Auckland	BIA
Bishopbriggs	BBG
Bishops Stortford	BIS
Bishopstone	BIP
Bishopton	BPT
Bitterne	BTE
Blackburn	BBN
Blackheath	BKH
Blackhorse Road	BHO
Blackpool North	BPN
Blackpool P Beach	BPB
Blackpool South	BPS
Blackrod	BLK
Blackwater	BAW
Blaenau Ffestiniog	BFF
Blair Atholl	BLA
Blairhill	BAI
Blake Street	BKT
Blakedown	BKD
Blantyre	BLT
Blaydon	BLO
Bleasby	BSB
Bletchley	BLY
Bloxwich	BLX
Bloxwich North	BWN
Blundellsands & Crosby	BLN
Blythe Bridge	BYB
Bodmin Parkway	BOD
Bodorgan	BOR
Bognor Regis	BOG
Bogston	BGS
Bolton	BON
Bolton-on-Dearne	BTD
Bookham	BKA

Bootle	BOC
Bootle New Strand	BNW
Bootle Oriel Road	BOT
Bordesley	BBS
Borough Green	BRG
Borth	BRH
Bosham	BOH
Boston	BSN
Botley	BOE
Bottesford	BTF
Bourne End	BNE
Bournemouth	BMH
Bournville	BRV
Bow Brickhill	BWB
Bowes Park	BOP
Bowling	BWG
Boxhill & Westhumble	BXW
Bracknell	BCE
Bradford Forster Sq	BDQ
Bradford Interchange	BDI
Bradford-on-Avon	BOA
Brading	BDN
Braintree	BTR
Braintree Freeport	BTP
Bramhall	BML
Bramley	BLE
Bramley (Hants)	BMY
Brampton (Cumbria)	BMP
Brampton (Suffolk)	BRP
Branchton	BCN
Brandon	BND
Branksome	BSM
Braystones	BYS
Bredbury	BDY
Breich	BRC
Brentford	BFD
Brentwood	BRE
Bricket Wood	BWO
Bridge of Allan	BEA
Bridge of Orchy	BRO
Bridgend	BGN
Bridgeton	BDG
Bridgwater	BWT
Bridlington	BDT
Brierfield	BRF
Brigg	BGG
Brighouse	BGH
Brighton	BTN
Brimsdown	BMD
Brinnington	BNT
Bristol Parkway	BPW
Bristol Temple Meads	BRI
Brithdir	BHD
British Steel Redcar	RBS
Briton Ferry	BNF
Brixton	BRX
Broad Green	BGE
Broadbottom	BDB
Broadstairs	BSR
Brockenhurst	BCU
Brockholes	BHS
Brockley	BCY
Brockley Whins	BNR
Bromborough	BOM
Bromborough Rake	BMR
Bromley Cross	BMC
Bromley North	BMN
Bromley South	BMS
Bromsgrove	BMV
Brondesbury	BSY
Brondesbury Park	BSP
Brookmans Park	BPK
Brookwood	BKO
Broome	BME
Broomfleet	BMF
Brora	BRA
Brough	BUH
Broughty Ferry	BYF
Broxbourne	BXB
Bruce Grove	BCV
Brundall	BDA
Brundall Gardens	BGA
Brunstane	BSU
Brunswick	BRW
Bruton	BRU
Bryn	BYN
Buckenham	BUC
Buckley	BCK
Bucknell	BUK
Bugle	BGL
Builth Road	BHR
Bulwell	BLW
Bures	BUE
Burgess Hill	BUG
Burley Park	BUY
Burley-in-Wharfedale	BUW
Burnage	BNA
Burneside	BUD
Burnham	BNM
Burnham-on-Crouch	BUU
Burnley Barracks	BUB
Burnley Central	BNC
Burnley Manchester Rd	BYM
Burnside	BUI
Burntisland	BTS
Burscough Bridge	BCB
Burscough Junction	BCJ
Bursledon	BUO
Burton Joyce	BUJ
Burton-on-Trent	BUT
Bury St Edmunds	BSE
Busby	BUS
Bush Hill Park	BHK
Bushey	BSH
Butlers Lane	BUL
Buxted	BXD
Buxton	BUX
Byfleet & New Haw	BFN
Bynea	BYE
Cadoxton	CAD
Caergwrle	CGW
Caerphilly	CPH
Caersws	CWS
Caldicot	CDT
Caledonian Rd & Bby	CIR
Calstock	CSK
Cam & Dursley	CDU
Camberley	CAM
Camborne	CBN
Cambridge	CBG
Cambridge Heath	CBH
Cambuslang	CBL
Camden Road	CMD
Camelon	CMO
Canley	CNL
Cannock	CAO
Canonbury	CNN
Canterbury East	CBE
Canterbury West	CBW
Cantley	CNY
Capenhurst	CPU
Carbis Bay	CBB
Cardenden	CDD
Cardiff Bay	CDB
Cardiff Central	CDF
Cardiff Queen Street	CDQ
Cardonald	CDO
Cardross	CDR
Carfin	CRF
Cark & Cartmel	CAK
Carlisle	CAR
Carlton	CTO
Carluke	CLU
Carmarthen	CMN
Carmyle	CML
Carnforth	CNF
Carnoustie	CAN
Carntyne	CAY
Carpenders Park	CPK
Carrbridge	CAG
Carshalton	CSH
Carshalton Beeches	CSB
Carstairs	CRS
Cartsdyke	CDY
Castle Bar Park	CBP
Castle Cary	CLC
Castleford	CFD
Castleton	CAS
Castleton Moor	CSM
Caterham	CAT
Catford	CTF
Catford Bridge	CFB
Cathays	CYS
Cathcart	CCT
Cattal	CTL
Causeland	CAU
Cefn-y-Bedd	CYB
Chadwell Heath	CTH
Chafford Hundred	CFH
Chalfont & Latimer	CFO
Chalkwell	CHW
Chandlers Ford	CFR
Chapel-en-le-Frith	CEF
Chapelton	CPN
Chapeltown	CLN
Chappel & Wakes Colne	CWC
Charing	CHG
Charing Cross (FSR)	CHC
Charlbury	CBY
Charlton	CTN
Chartham	CRT
Chassen Road	CSR
Chatelherault	CTE
Chatham	CTM
Chathill	CHT
Cheadle Hulme	CHU
Cheam	CHE
Cheddington	CED
Chelford	CEL
Chelmsford	CHM
Chelsfield	CLD
Cheltenham Spa	CNM
Chepstow	CPW
Cherry Tree	CYT
Chertsey	CHY
Cheshunt	CHN
Chessington North	CSN
Chessington South	CSS
Chester	CTR
Chester Road	CRD
Chesterfield	CHD
Chester-le-Street	CLS
Chestfield & Swalecliffe	CSW
Chetnole	CNO
Chichester	CCH
Chilham	CIL
Chilworth	CHL
Chingford	CHI
Chinley	CLY
Chippenham	CPM
Chipstead	CHP
Chirk	CRK
Chislehurst	CIT
Chiswick	CHK
Cholsey	CHO
Chorley	CRL
Chorleywood	CLW
Christchurch	CHR
Christs Hospital	CHH
Church & Oswaldtwistle	CTW
Church Fenton	CHF
Church Stretton	CTT
Cilmeri	CIM
City Thameslink	CTK
Clacton on Sea	CLT
Clandon	CLA
Clapham High Street	CLP
Clapham Junction	CLJ
Clapham (Yorkshire)	CPY
Clapton	CPT
Clarbeston Road	CLR
Clarkston	CKS
Claverdon	CLV
Claygate	CLG
Cleethorpes	CLE
Cleland	CEA
Clifton	CLI
Clifton Down	CFN
Clitheroe	CLH
Clock House	CLK
Clunderwen	CUW
Clydebank	CYK
Coatbridge Central	CBC
Coatbridge Sunnyside	CBS
Coatdyke	COA
Cobham & Stoke d'A'n	CSD
Codsall	CSL
Cogan	CGN
Colchester	COL
Colchester Town	CET
Coleshill Parkway	CEH
Collingham	CLM
Collington	CLL
Colne	CNE
Colwall	CWL
Colwyn Bay	CWB
Combe	CME
Commondale	COM
Congleton	CNG
Conisbrough	CNS
Connel Ferry	CON
Cononley	CEY
Conway Park	CNP
Conwy	CNW
Cooden Beach	COB
Cookham	COO
Cooksbridge	CBR
Coombe Halt	COE
Copplestone	COP
Corbridge	CRB
Corby	COR
Corkerhill	CKH
Corkickle	CKL
Corpach	CPA
Corrour	CRR
Coryton	COY
Coseley	CSY
Cosford	COS
Cosham	CSA
Cottingham	CGM
Cottingley	COT
Coulsdon South	CDS
Coventry	COV
Cowden	CWN
Cowdenbeath	COW
Cradley Heath	CRA
Craigendoran	CGD
Cramlington	CRM
Craven Arms	CRV
Crawley	CRW

Crayford	CRY
Crediton	CDI
Cressing	CES
Cressington	CSG
Creswell	CWD
Crewe	CRE
Crewkerne	CKN
Crews Hill	CWH
Crianlarich	CNR
Criccieth	CCC
Cricklewood	CRI
Croftfoot	CFF
Crofton Park	CFT
Cromer	CMR
Cromford	CMF
Crookston	CKT
Cross Gates	CRG
Crossflatts	CFL
Crosshill	COI
Crosskeys	CKY
Crossmyloof	CMY
Croston	CSO
Crouch Hill	CRH
Crowborough	COH
Crowhurst	CWU
Crowle	CWE
Crowthorne	CRN
Croy	CRO
Crystal Palace	CYP
Cuddington	CUD
Cuffley	CUF
Culham	CUM
Culrain	CUA
Cumbernauld	CUB
Cupar	CUP
Curriehill	CUH
Cuxton	CUX
Cwmbach	CMH
Cwmbran	CWM
Cynghordy	CYN
Dagenham Dock	DDK
Daisy Hill	DSY
Dalgety Bay	DAG
Dalmally	DAL
Dalmarnock	DAK
Dalmeny	DAM
Dalmuir	DMR
Dalreoch	DLR
Dalry	DLY
Dalston	DLS
Dalston Kingsland	DLK
Dalton	DLT
Dalwhinnie	DLW
Danby	DNY
Danescourt	DCT
Danzey	DZY
Darlington	DAR
Darnall	DAN
Darsham	DSM
Dartford	DFD
Darton	DRT
Darwen	DWN
Datchet	DAT
Davenport	DVN
Dawlish	DWL
Dawlish Warren	DWW
Deal	DEA
Dean	DEN
Dean Lane	DNN
Deansgate	DGT
Deganwy	DGY
Deighton	DHN
Delamere	DLM
Denby Dale	DBD
Denham	DNM
Denham Golf Club	DGC
Denmark Hill	DMK
Dent	DNT
Denton	DTN
Deptford	DEP
Derby	DBY
Derby Road	DBR
Derker	DKR
Devonport	DPT
Dewsbury	DEW
Didcot Parkway	DID
Digby & Sowton	DIG
Dilton Marsh	DMH
Dinas Powys	DNS
Dinas Rhondda	DMG
Dingle Road	DGL
Dingwall	DIN
Dinsdale	DND
Dinting	DTG
Disley	DSL
Diss	DIS
Dockyard	DOC
Dodworth	DOD
Dolau	DOL
Doleham	DLH
Dolgarrog	DLG
Dolwyddelan	DWD
Doncaster	DON
Dorchester South	DCH
Dorchester West	DCW
Dore	DOR
Dorking	DKG
Dorking Deepdene	DPD
Dorking West	DKT
Dormans	DMS
Dorridge	DDG
Dove Holes	DVH
Dover Priory	DVP
Dovercourt	DVC
Dovey Junction	DVY
Downham Market	DOW
Drayton Green	DRG
Drayton Park	DYP
Drem	DRM
Driffield	DRF
Drigg	DRI
Droitwich Spa	DTW
Dronfield	DRO
Drumchapel	DMC
Drumfrochar	DFR
Drumgelloch	DRU
Drumry	DMY
Dublin Ferryport	DFP
Dublin Port - Stena	DPS
Duddeston	DUD
Dudley Port	DDP
Duffield	DFI
Duirinish	DRN
Duke Street	DST
Dullingham	DUL
Dumbarton Central	DBC
Dumbarton East	DBE
Dumbreck	DUM
Dumfries	DMF
Dumpton Park	DMP
Dunbar	DUN
Dunblane	DBL
Duncraig	DCG
Dundee	DEE
Dunfermline Q'n Margaret	DFL
Dunfermline Town	DFE
Dunkeld & Birnam	DKD
Dunlop	DNL
Dunrobin Castle	DNO
Dunston	DOT
Dunton Green	DNG
Durham	DHM
Durrington-on-Sea	DUR
Dyce	DYC
Dyffryn Ardudwy	DYF
Eaglescliffe	EAG
Ealing Broadway	EAL
Earlestown	ERL
Earley	EAR
Earlsfield	EAD
Earlswood (Surrey)	ELD
Earlswood (Midlands)	EWD
East Boldon	EBL
East Croydon	ECR
East Didsbury	EDY
East Dulwich	EDW
East Farleigh	EFL
East Garforth	EGF
East Grinstead	EGR
East Kilbride	EKL
East Malling	EML
East Midlands Parkway	EMD
East Tilbury	ETL
East Worthing	EWR
Eastbourne	EBN
Eastbrook	EBK
Easterhouse	EST
Eastham Rake	ERA
Eastleigh	ESL
Eastrington	EGN
Ebbw Vale Parkway	EBV
Eccles	ECC
Eccles Road	ECS
Eccleston Park	ECL
Edale	EDL
Eden Park	EDN
Edenbridge	EBR
Edenbridge Town	EBT
Edge Hill	EDG
Edinburgh Park	EDP
Edinburgh Waverley	EDB
Edmonton Green	EDR
Effingham Junction	EFF
Eggesford	EGG
Egham	EGH
Egton	EGT
Elephant & Castle	EPH
Elgin	ELG
Ellesmere Port	ELP
Elmers End	ELE
Elmstead Woods	ESD
Elmswell	ESW
Elsecar	ELR
Elsenham	ESM
Elstree & Borehamwood	ELS
Eltham	ELW
Elton & Orston	ELO
Ely	ELY
Emerson Park	EMP
Emsworth	EMS
Enfield Chase	ENC
Enfield Lock	ENL
Enfield Town	ENF
Entwistle	ENT
Epsom	EPS
Epsom Downs	EPD
Erdington	ERD
Eridge	ERI
Erith	ERH
Esher	ESH
Essex Road	EXR
Etchingham	ETC
Euxton Balshaw Lane	EBA
Evesham	EVE
Ewell East	EWE
Ewell West	EWW
Exeter Central	EXC
Exeter St Davids	EXD
Exeter St Thomas	EXT
Exhibition Centre	EXG
Exmouth	EXM
Exton	EXN
Eynsford	EYN
Failsworth	FLS
Fairbourne	FRB
Fairfield	FRF
Fairlie	FRL
Fairwater	FRW
Falconwood	FCN
Falkirk Grahamston	FKG
Falkirk High	FKK
Falls of Cruachan	FOC
Falmer	FMR
Falmouth Docks	FAL
Falmouth Town	FMT
Fareham	FRM
Farnborough (Main)	FNB
Farnborough North	FNN
Farncombe	FNC
Farnham	FNH
Farningham Road	FNR
Farnworth	FNW
Farringdon	ZFD
Fauldhouse	FLD
Faversham	FAV
Faygate	FGT
Fazakerley	FAZ
Fearn	FRN
Featherstone	FEA
Fellgate	FEG
Felixstowe	FLX
Feltham	FEL
Feniton	FNT
Fenny Stratford	FEN
Fernhill	FER
Ferriby	FRY
Ferryside	FYS
Ffairfach	FFA
Filey	FIL
Filton Abbey Wood	FIT
Finchley Rd & Frognal	FNY
Finsbury Park	FPK
Finstock	FIN
Fishbourne (Sussex)	FSB
Fishersgate	FSG
Fishguard Harbour	FGH
Fiskerton	FSK
Fitzwilliam	FZW
Five Ways	FWY
Fleet	FLE
Flimby	FLM
Flint	FLN
Flitwick	FLT
Flixton	FLI
Flowery Field	FLF
Folkestone Central	FKC
Folkestone West	FKW
Ford	FOD
Forest Gate	FOG
Forest Hill	FOH
Formby	FBY
Forres	FOR
Forsinard	FRS
Fort Matilda	FTM
Fort William	FTW
Four Oaks	FOK
Foxfield	FOX
Foxton	FXN
Frant	FRT
Fratton	FTN
Freshfield	FRE
Freshford	FFD
Frimley	FML
Frinton on Sea	FRI

Frizinghall	FZH
Frodsham	FRD
Frome	FRO
Fulwell	FLW
Furness Vale	FNV
Furze Platt	FZP
Gainsborough Central	GNB
Gainsborough Lea Rd	GBL
Garelochhead	GCH
Garforth	GRF
Gargrave	GGV
Garrowhill	GAR
Garscadden	GRS
Garsdale	GSD
Garston (Hertfordshire)	GSN
Garswood	GSW
Gartcosh	GRH
Garth (Bridgend)	GMG
Garth (Powys)	GTH
Garve	GVE
Gathurst	GST
Gatley	GTY
Gatwick Airport	GTW
Georgemas Junction	GGJ
Gerrards Cross	GER
Gidea Park	GDP
Giffnock	GFN
Giggleswick	GIG
Gilberdyke	GBD
Gilfach Fargoed	GFF
Gillingham (Dorset)	GIL
Gillingham (Kent)	GLM
Gilshochill	GSC
Gipsy Hill	GIP
Girvan	GIR
Glaisdale	GLS
Glan Conwy	GCW
Glasgow Central	GLC
Glasgow Queen Street	GLQ
Glasshoughton	GLH
Glazebrook	GLZ
Gleneagles	GLE
Glenfinnan	GLF
Glengarnock	GLG
Glenrothes with Thornton	GLT
Glossop	GLO
Gloucester	GCR
Glynde	GLY
Gobowen	GOB
Godalming	GOD
Godley	GDL
Godstone	GDN
Goldthorpe	GOE
Golf Street	GOF
Golspie	GOL
Gomshall	GOM
Goodmayes	GMY
Goole	GOO
Goostrey	GTR
Gordon Hill	GDH
Goring & Streatley	GOR
Goring-by-Sea	GBS
Gorton	GTO
Gospel Oak	GPO
Gourock	GRK
Gowerton	GWN
Goxhill	GOX
Grange Park	GPK
Grange-Over-Sands	GOS
Grangetown	GTN
Grantham	GRA
Grateley	GRT
Gravelly Hill	GVH
Gravesend	GRV
Grays	GRY
Great Ayton	GTA
Great Bentley	GRB
Great Chesterford	GRC
Great Coates	GCT
Great Malvern	GMV
Great Missenden	GMN
Great Yarmouth	GYM
Green Lane	GNL
Green Road	GNR
Greenbank	GBK
Greenfaulds	GRL
Greenfield	GNF
Greenford	GFD
Greenhithe for Bluewater	GNH
Greenock Central	GKC
Greenock West	GKW
Greenwich	GNW
Gretna Green	GEA
Grimsby Docks	GMD
Grimsby Town	GMB
Grindleford	GRN
Grosmont	GMT
Grove Park	GRP
Guide Bridge	GUI
Guildford	GLD
Guiseley	GSY
Gunnersbury	GUN
Gunnislake	GSL
Gunton	GNT
Gwersyllt	GWE
Gypsy Lane	GYP
Habrough	HAB
Hackbridge	HCB
Hackney Central	HKC
Hackney Downs	HAC
Hackney Wick	HKW
Haddenham & T Parkway	HDM
Haddiscoe	HAD
Hadfield	HDF
Hadley Wood	HDW
Hag Fold	HGF
Hagley	HAG
Hairmyres	HMY
Hale	HAL
Halesworth	HAS
Halewood	HED
Halifax	HFX
Hall Green	HLG
Hall-i'-th'-Wood	HID
Hall Road	HLR
Halling	HAI
Haltwhistle	HWH
Ham Street	HMT
Hamble	HME
Hamilton Central	HNC
Hamilton Square	BKQ
Hamilton West	HNW
Hammerton	HMM
Hampden Park	HMD
Hampstead Heath	HDH
Hampton	HMP
Hampton Court	HMC
Hampton Wick	HMW
Hampton-in-Arden	HIA
Hamstead	HSD
Hamworthy	HAM
Hanborough	HND
Handforth	HTH
Hanwell	HAN
Hapton	HPN
Harlech	HRL
Harlesden	HDN
Harling Road	HRD
Harlington	HLN
Harlow Mill	HWM
Harlow Town	HWN
Harold Wood	HRO
Harpenden	HPD
Harrietsham	HRM
Harringay	HGY
Harringay Green Lanes	HRY
Harrington	HRR
Harrogate	HGT
Harrow & Wealdstone	HRW
Harrow-on-the-Hill	HOH
Hartford	HTF
Hartlebury	HBY
Hartlepool	HPL
Hartwood	HTW
Harwich International	HPQ
Harwich Town	HWC
Haslemere	HSL
Hassocks	HSK
Hastings	HGS
Hatch End	HTE
Hatfield	HAT
Hatfield & Stainforth	HFS
Hatfield Peverel	HAP
Hathersage	HSG
Hattersley	HTY
Hatton	HTN
Havant	HAV
Havenhouse	HVN
Haverfordwest	HVF
Hawarden	HWD
Hawarden Bridge	HWB
Hawkhead	HKH
Haydon Bridge	HDB
Haydons Road	HYR
Hayes & Harlington	HAY
Hayes (Kent)	HYS
Hayle	HYL
Haymarket	HYM
Haywards Heath	HHE
Hazel Grove	HAZ
Headcorne	HCN
Headingley	HDY
Headstone Lane	HDL
Heald Green	HDG
Healing	HLI
Heath High Level	HHL
Heath Low Level	HLL
Heathrow Airport T123	HXX
Heathrow Airport T4	HAF
Heathrow Terminal 5	HWV
Heaton Chapel	HTC
Hebden Bridge	HBD
Heckington	HEC
Hedge End	HDE
Hednesford	HNF
Heighington	HEI
Helensburgh Central	HLC
Helensburgh Upper	HLU
Hellifield	HLD
Helmsdale	HMS
Helsby	HSB
Hemel Hempstead	HML
Hendon	HEN
Hengoed	HNG
Henley-in-Arden	HNL
Henley-on-Thames	HOT
Hensall	HEL
Hereford	HFD
Herne Bay	HNB
Herne Hill	HNH
Hersham	HER
Hertford East	HFE
Hertford North	HFN
Hessle	HES
Heswall	HSW
Hever	HEV
Heworth	HEW
Hexham	HEX
Heyford	HYD
Heysham Port	HHB
High Brooms	HIB
High St (Glasgow)	HST
High Street Kensington	ZHS
High Wycombe	HWY
Higham	HGM
Highams Park	HIP
Highbridge & Burnham	HIG
Highbury & Islington	HHY
Hightown	HTO
Hildenborough	HLB
Hillfoot	HLF
Hillington East	HLE
Hillington West	HLW
Hillside	HIL
Hilsea	HLS
Hinchley Wood	HYW
Hinckley	HNK
Hindley	HIN
Hinton Admiral	HNA
Hitchin	HIT
Hither Green	HGR
Hockley	HOC
Hollingbourne	HBN
Hollinwood	HOD
Holmes Chapel	HCH
Holmwood	HLM
Holton Heath	HOL
Holyhead	HHD
Holytown	HLY
Homerton	HMN
Honeybourne	HYB
Honiton	HON
Honley	HOY
Honor Oak Park	HPA
Hook	HOK
Hooton	HOO
Hope (Derbyshire)	HOP
Hope (Flintshire)	HPE
Hopton Heath	HPT
Horley	HOR
Hornbeam Park	HBP
Hornsey	HRN
Horsforth	HRS
Horsham	HRH
Horsley	HSY
Horton-in-Ribblesdale	HIR
Horwich Parkway	HWI
Hoscar	HSC
Hough Green	HGN
Hounslow	HOU
Hove	HOV
Hoveton & Wroxham	HXM
How Wood	HWW
Howden	HOW
Howwood (Renfrew)	HOZ
Hoylake	HYK
Hubberts Bridge	HBB
Hucknall	HKN
Huddersfield	HUD
Hull Paragon	HUL
Humphrey Park	HUP
Huncoat	HCT
Hungerford	HGD
Hunmanby	HUB
Huntingdon	HUN
Huntly	HNT
Hunts Cross	HNX
Hurst Green	HUR
Hutton Cranswick	HUT
Huyton	HUY
Hyde Central	HYC
Hyde North	HYT
Hykeham	HKM
Hyndland	HYN

Hythe	HYH
IBM	IBM
Ifield	IFI
Ilford	IFD
Ilkley	ILK
Imperial Wharf	IMW
Ince	INC
Ince & Elton	INE
Ingatestone	INT
Insch	INS
Invergordon	IGD
Invergowrie	ING
Inverkeithing	INK
Inverkip	INP
Inverness	INV
Invershin	INH
Inverurie	INR
Ipswich	IPS
Irlam	IRL
Irvine	IRV
Isleworth	ISL
Islip	ISP
Iver	IVR
Ivybridge	IVY
Jewellery Quarter	JEQ
Johnston	JOH
Johnstone	JHN
Jordanhill	JOR
Kearsley	KSL
Kearsney	KSN
Keighley	KEI
Keith	KEH
Kelvedon	KEL
Kelvindale	KVD
Kemble	KEM
Kempston Hardwick	KMH
Kempton Park	KMP
Kemsing	KMS
Kemsley	KML
Kendal	KEN
Kenley	KLY
Kennett	KNE
Kennishead	KNS
Kensal Green	KNL
Kensal Rise	KNR
Kensington Olympia	KPA
Kent House	KTH
Kentish Town	KTN
Kentish Town West	KTW
Kenton	KNT
Kents Bank	KBK
Kettering	KET
Kew Bridge	KWB
Kew Gardens	KWG
Keyham	KEY
Keynsham	KYN
Kidbrooke	KDB
Kidderminster	KID
Kidsgrove	KDG
Kidwelly	KWL
Kilburn High Road	KBN
Kildale	KLD
Kildonan	KIL
Kilgetty	KGT
Kilmarnock	KMK
Kilmaurs	KLM
Kilpatrick	KPT
Kilwinning	KWN
Kinbrace	KBC
Kingham	KGM
Kinghorn	KGH
Kings Langley	KGL
King's Lynn	KLN
Kings Norton	KNN
Kings Nympton	KGN
Kings Park	KGP
Kings Sutton	KGS
Kingsknowe	KGE
Kingston	KNG
Kingswood	KND
Kingussie	KIN
Kintbury	KIT
Kirby Cross	KBX
Kirk Sandall	KKS
Kirkby	KIR
Kirkby-in-Ashfield	KKB
Kirkby Stephen	KSW
Kirkby-in-Furness	KBF
Kirkcaldy	KDY
Kirkconnel	KRK
Kirkdale	KKD
Kirkham & Wesham	KKM
Kirkhill	KKH
Kirknewton	KKN
Kirkwood	KWD
Kirton Lindsey	KTL
Kiveton Bridge	KIV
Kiveton Park	KVP
Knaresborough	KNA
Knebworth	KBW
Knighton	KNI
Knockholt	KCK
Knottingley	KNO
Knucklas	KNU
Knutsford	KNF
Kyle of Lochalsh	KYL
Ladybank	LDY
Ladywell	LAD
Laindon	LAI
Lairg	LRG
Lake	LKE
Lakenheath	LAK
Lamphey	LAM
Lanark	LNK
Lancaster	LAN
Lancing	LAC
Landywood	LAW
Langbank	LGB
Langho	LHO
Langley	LNY
Langley Green	LGG
Langley Mill	LGM
Langside	LGS
Langwathby	LGW
Langwith-Whaley Thorns	LAG
Lapford	LAP
Lapworth	LPW
Larbert	LBT
Largs	LAR
Larkhall	LRH
Lawrence Hill	LWH
Layton	LAY
Lazonby & Kirkoswald	LZB
Lea Green	LEG
Lea Hall	LEH
Leagrave	LEA
Lealholm	LHM
Leamington Spa	LMS
Leasowe	LSW
Leatherhead	LHD
Ledbury	LED
Lee	LEE
Leeds	LDS
Leicester	LEI
Leigh (Kent)	LIH
Leigh-on-Sea	LES
Leighton Buzzard	LBZ
Lelant	LEL
Lelant Saltings	LTS
Lenham	LEN
Lenzie	LNZ
Leominster	LEO
Letchworth Garden City	LET
Leuchars (St Andrews)	LEU
Levenshulme	LVM
Lewes	LWS
Lewisham	LEW
Leyland	LEY
Leyton Midland Road	LEM
Leytonstone High Road	LER
Lichfield City	LIC
Lichfield Trent Valley	LTV
Lidlington	LID
Limehouse	LHS
Lincoln Central	LCN
Lingfield	LFD
Lingwood	LGD
Linlithgow	LIN
Liphook	LIP
Liskeard	LSK
Liss	LIS
Lisvane & Thornhill	LVT
Little Kimble	LTK
Little Sutton	LTT
Littleborough	LTL
Littlehampton	LIT
Littlehaven	LVN
Littleport	LTP
Liverpool Central	LVC
Liverpool James Street	LVJ
Liverpool Lime Street	LIV
Liverpool South Parkway	LPY
Livingston North	LSN
Livingston South	LVG
Llanaber	LLA
Llanbedr	LBR
Llanbister Road	LLT
Llanbradach	LNB
Llandaf	LLN
Llandanwg	LDN
Llandecwyn	LLC
Llandeilo	LLL
Llandovery	LLV
Llandrindod	LLO
Llandudno	LLD
Llandudno Junction	LLJ
Llandybie	LLI
Llanelli	LLE
Llanfairfechan	LLF
Llanfairpwll	LPG
Llangadog	LLG
Llangammarch	LLM
Llangennech	LLH
Llangynllo	LGO
Llanharan	LLR
Llanhilleth	LTH
Llanishen	LLS
Llanrwst	LWR
Llansamlet	LAS
Llantwit Major	LWM
Llanwrda	LNR
Llanwrtyd	LNW
Llwyngwril	LLW
Llwynypia	LLY
Loch Awe	LHA
Loch Eil Outward Bound	LHE
Lochailort	LCL
Locheilside	LCS
Lochgelly	LCG
Lochluichart	LCC
Lochwinnoch	LHW
Lockerbie	LOC
Lockwood	LCK
London Blackfriars	BFR
London Bridge	LBG
London Cannon Street	CST
London Charing Cross	CHX
London Euston	EUS
London Fenchurch St	FST
London Fields	LOF
London King's Cross	KGX
London Liverpool St	LST
London Marylebone	MYB
London Paddington	PAD
London Road (Brighton)	LRB
London Road (Guildford)	LRD
London St Pancras	STP
London Victoria	VIC
London Waterloo	WAT
London Waterloo East	WAE
Long Buckby	LBK
Long Eaton	LGE
Long Preston	LPR
Longbeck	LGK
Longbridge	LOB
Longcross	LNG
Longfield	LGF
Longniddry	LND
Longport	LPT
Longton	LGN
Looe	LOO
Lostock	LOT
Lostock Gralam	LTG
Lostock Hall	LOH
Lostwithiel	LOS
Loughborough	LBO
Loughborough Junction	LGJ
Lowdham	LOW
Lower Sydenham	LSY
Lowestoft	LWT
Ludlow	LUD
Luton	LUT
Luton Airport Parkway	LTN
Luxulyan	LUX
Lydney	LYD
Lye	LYE
Lymington Pier	LYP
Lymington Town	LYT
Lympstone Commando	LYC
Lympstone Village	LYM
Lytham	LTM
Macclesfield	MAC
Machynlleth	MCN
Maesteg	MST
Maesteg (Ewenny Rd)	MEW
Maghull	MAG
Maiden Newton	MDN
Maidenhead	MAI
Maidstone Barracks	MDB
Maidstone East	MDE
Maidstone West	MDW
Malden Manor	MAL
Mallaig	MLG
Malton	MLT
Malvern Link	MVL
Manchester Airport	MIA
Manchester Oxford Rd	MCO
Manchester Piccadilly	MAN
Manchester United FC	MUF
Manchester Victoria	MCV
Manea	MNE
Manningtree	MNG
Manor Park	MNP
Manor Road	MNR
Manorbier	MRB
Manors	MAS
Mansfield	MFT
Mansfield Woodhouse	MSW
March	MCH
Marden	MRN

Margate	MAR
Market Harborough	MHR
Market Rasen	MKR
Markinch	MNC
Marks Tey	MKT
Marlow	MLW
Marple	MPL
Marsden	MSN
Marske	MSK
Marston Green	MGN
Martin Mill	MTM
Martins Heron	MAO
Marton	MTO
Maryhill	MYH
Maryland	MYL
Maryport	MRY
Matlock	MAT
Matlock Bath	MTB
Mauldeth Road	MAU
Maxwell Park	MAX
Maybole	MAY
Maze Hill	MZH
Meadowhall	MHS
Meldreth	MEL
Melksham	MKM
Melton	MES
Melton Mowbray	MMO
Menheniot	MEN
Menston	MNN
Meols	MEO
Meols Cop	MEC
Meopham	MEP
Merrytown	MEY
Merstham	MHM
Merthyr Tydfil	MER
Merthyr Vale	MEV
Metheringham	MGM
MetroCentre	MCE
Mexborough	MEX
Micheldever	MIC
Micklefield	MIK
Middlesbrough	MBR
Middlewood	MDL
Midgham	MDG
Milford Haven	MFH
Milford (Surrey)	MLF
Mill Hill Broadway	MIL
Mill Hill (Lancashire)	MLH
Millbrook (Bedfordshire)	MLB
Millbrook (Hants)	MBK
Milliken Park	MIN
Millom	MLM
Mills Hill	MIH
Milngavie	MLN
Milnrow	MLR
Milton Keynes Central	MKC
Minffordd	MFF
Minster	MSR
Mirfield	MIR
Mistley	MIS
Mitcham Eastfields	MTC
Mitcham Junction	MIJ
Mobberley	MOB
Monifieth	MON
Monks Risborough	MRS
Montpelier	MTP
Montrose	MTS
Moorfields	MRF
Moorgate	ZMG
Moorside	MSD
Moorthorpe	MRP
Morar	MRR
Morchard Road	MRD
Morden South	MDS
Morecambe	MCM
Moreton (Dorset)	MTN
Moreton (Merseyside)	MRT
Moreton-in-Marsh	MIM
Morfa Mawddach	MFA
Morley	MLY
Morpeth	MPT
Mortimer	MOR
Mortlake	MTL
Moses Gate	MSS
Moss Side	MOS
Mossley	MSL
Mossley Hill	MSH
Mosspark	MPK
Moston	MSO
Motherwell	MTH
Motspur Park	MOT
Mottingham	MTG
Mottisfont & Dunbridge	DBG
Mouldsworth	MLD
Moulsecoomb	MCB
Mount Florida	MFL
Mount Vernon	MTV
Mountain Ash	MTA
Muir of Ord	MOO
Muirend	MUI
Musselburgh	MUB
Mytholmroyd	MYT
Nafferton	NFN
Nailsea & Backwell	NLS
Nairn	NRN
Nantwich	NAN
Narberth	NAR
Narborough	NBR
Navigation Road	NVR
Neath	NTH
Needham Market	NMT
Neilston	NEI
Nelson	NEL
Neston	NES
Netherfield	NET
Nethertown	NRT
Netley	NTL
New Barnet	NBA
New Beckenham	NBC
New Brighton	NBN
New Clee	NCE
New Cross	NWX
New Cross Gate	NXG
New Cumnock	NCK
New Eltham	NEH
New Hey	NHY
New Holland	NHL
New Hythe	NHE
New Lane	NLN
New Malden	NEM
New Mills Central	NMC
New Mills Newtown	NMN
New Milton	NWM
New Pudsey	NPD
New Southgate	NSG
Newark Castle	NCT
Newark North Gate	NNG
Newbridge	NBE
Newbury	NBY
Newbury Racecourse	NRC
Newcastle	NCL
Newcraighall	NEW
Newhaven Harbour	NVH
Newhaven Town	NVN
Newington	NGT
Newmarket	NMK
Newport (Essex)	NWE
Newport (S. Wales)	NWP
Newquay	NQY
Newstead	NSD
Newton Abbot	NTA
Newton Aycliffe	NAY
Newton for Hyde	NWN
Newton (Lanarks)	NTN
Newton St Cyres	NTC
Newton-le-Willows	NLW
Newtonmore	NWR
Newton-on-Ayr	NOA
Newtown (Powys)	NWT
Ninian Park	NNP
Nitshill	NIT
Norbiton	NBT
Norbury	NRB
Normans Bay	NSB
Normanton	NOR
North Berwick	NBW
North Camp	NCM
North Dulwich	NDL
North Fambridge	NFA
North Llanrwst	NLR
North Queensferry	NQU
North Road	NRD
North Sheen	NSH
North Walsham	NWA
North Wembley	NWB
Northallerton	NTR
Northampton	NMP
Northfield	NFD
Northfleet	NFL
Northolt Park	NLT
Northumberland Park	NUM
Northwich	NWI
Norton Bridge	NTB
Norwich	NRW
Norwood Junction	NWD
Nottingham	NOT
Nuneaton	NUN
Nunhead	NHD
Nunthorpe	NNT
Nutbourne	NUT
Nutfield	NUF
Oakengates	OKN
Oakham	OKM
Oakleigh Park	OKL
Oban	OBN
Ockendon	OCK
Ockley	OLY
Old Hill	OHL
Old Roan	ORA
Old Street	OLD
Oldfield Park	OLF
Oldham Mumps	OLM
Oldham Werneth	OLW
Olton	OLT
Ore	ORE
Ormskirk	OMS
Orpington	ORP
Orrell	ORR
Orrell Park	OPK
Otford	OTF
Oulton Broad North	OUN
Oulton Broad South	OUS
Outwood	OUT
Overpool	OVE
Overton	OVR
Oxenholme Lake District	OXN
Oxford	OXF
Oxshott	OXS
Oxted	OXT
Paddock Wood	PDW
Padgate	PDG
Paignton	PGN
Paisley Canal	PCN
Paisley Gilmour Street	PYG
Paisley St James	PYJ
Palmers Green	PAL
Pangbourne	PAN
Pannal	PNL
Pantyffynnon	PTF
Par	PAR
Parbold	PBL
Park Street	PKT
Parkstone (Dorset)	PKS
Parson Street	PSN
Partick	PTK
Parton	PRN
Patchway	PWY
Patricroft	PAT
Patterton	PTT
Peartree	PEA
Peckham Rye	PMR
Pegswood	PEG
Pemberton	PEM
Pembrey & Burry Port	PBY
Pembroke	PMB
Pembroke Dock	PMD
Penally	PNA
Penarth	PEN
Pencoed	PCD
Pengam	PGM
Penge East	PNE
Penge West	PNW
Penhelig	PHG
Penistone	PNS
Penkridge	PKG
Penmaenmawr	PMW
Penmere	PNM
Penrhiwceiber	PER
Penrhyndeudraeth	PRH
Penrith	PNR
Penryn	PYN
Pensarn (Gwynedd)	PES
Penshurst	PHR
Pentre-Bach	PTB
Pen-y-Bont	PNY
Penychain	BPC
Penyffordd	PNF
Penzance	PNZ
Perranwell	PRW
Perry Barr	PRY
Pershore	PSH
Perth	PTH
Peterborough	PBO
Petersfield	PTR
Petts Wood	PET
Pevensey & Westham	PEV
Pevensey Bay	PEB
Pewsey	PEW
Pilning	PIL
Pinhoe	PIN
Pitlochry	PIT
Pitsea	PSE
Pleasington	PLS
Plockton	PLK
Pluckley	PLC
Plumley	PLM
Plumpton	PMP
Plumstead	PLU
Plymouth	PLY
Pokesdown	POK
Polegate	PLG
Polesworth	PSW
Pollokshaws East	PWE
Pollokshaws West	PWW
Pollokshields East	PLE
Pollokshields West	PLW
Polmont	PMT
Polsloe Bridge	POL
Ponders End	PON
Pontarddulais	PTD

Pontefract Baghill	PFR
Pontefract Monkhill	PFM
Pontefract Tanshelf	POT
Pontlottyn	PLT
Pontyclun	PYC
Pont-y-Pant	PYP
Pontypool & New Inn	PPL
Pontypridd	PPD
Poole	POO
Poppleton	POP
Port Glasgow	PTG
Port Sunlight	PSL
Port Talbot Parkway	PTA
Portchester	PTC
Porth	POR
Porthmadog	PTM
Portlethen	PLN
Portslade	PLD
Portsmouth & Southsea	PMS
Portsmouth Arms	PMA
Portsmouth Harbour	PMH
Possilpark & Parkhouse	PPK
Potters Bar	PBR
Poulton-le-Fylde	PFY
Poynton	PYT
Prees	PRS
Prescot	PSC
Prestatyn	PRT
Prestbury	PRB
Preston	PRE
Preston Park	PRP
Prestonpans	PST
Prestwick Int Airport	PRA
Prestwick Town	PTW
Priesthill & Darnley	PTL
Princes Risborough	PRR
Prittlewell	PRL
Prudhoe	PRU
Pulborough	PUL
Purfleet	PFL
Purley	PUR
Purley Oaks	PUO
Putney	PUT
Pwllheli	PWL
Pyle	PYL
Quakers Yard	QYD
Queenborough	QBR
Queens Park (Glasgow)	QPK
Queens Park (London)	QPW
Queens Road, Peckham	QRP
Queenstown Road	QRB
Quintrell Downs	QUI
Radcliffe (Notts)	RDF
Radlett	RDT
Radley	RAD
Radyr	RDR
Rainford	RNF
Rainham (Essex)	RNM
Rainham (Kent)	RAI
Rainhill	RNH
Ramsgate	RAM
Ramsgreave & Wilpshire	RGW
Rannoch	RAN
Rauceby	RAU
Ravenglass for Eskdale	RAV
Ravensbourne	RVB
Ravensthorpe	RVN
Rawcliffe	RWC
Rayleigh	RLG
Raynes Park	RAY
Reading	RDG
Reading West	RDW
Rectory Road	REC
Redbridge	RDB
Redcar Central	RCC
Redcar East	RCE
Reddish North	RDN
Reddish South	RDS
Redditch	RDC
Redhill	RDH
Redland	RDA
Redruth	RED
Reedham (Norfolk)	REE
Reedham (Surrey)	RHM
Reigate	REI
Renton	RTN
Retford	RET
Rhiwbina	RHI
Rhoose Cardiff Int Airport	RIA
Rhosneigr	RHO
Rhyl	RHL
Rhymney	RHY
Ribblehead	RHD
Rice Lane	RIL
Richmond	RMD
Rickmansworth	RIC
Riddlesdown	RDD
Ridgmont	RID
Riding Mill	RDM
Risca & Pontymister	RCA
Rishton	RIS
Robertsbridge	RBR
Roby	ROB
Rochdale	RCD
Roche	ROC
Rochester	RTR
Rochford	RFD
Rock Ferry	RFY
Rogart	ROG
Rogerstone	ROR
Rolleston	ROL
Roman Bridge	RMB
Romford	RMF
Romiley	RML
Romsey	ROM
Roose	ROO
Rose Grove	RSG
Rose Hill Marple	RSH
Rosyth	ROS
Rotherham Central	RMC
Roughton Road	RNR
Rowlands Castle	RLN
Rowley Regis	ROW
Roy Bridge	RYB
Roydon	RYN
Royston	RYS
Ruabon	RUA
Rufford	RUF
Rugby	RUG
Rugeley Town	RGT
Rugeley Trent Valley	RGL
Runcorn	RUN
Runcorn East	RUE
Ruskington	RKT
Ruswarp	RUS
Rutherglen	RUT
Ryde St Johns Road	RYR
Ryde Esplanade	RYD
Ryde Pier Head	RYP
Ryder Brow	RRB
Rye	RYE
Rye House	RYH
Salford Central	SFD
Salford Crescent	SLD
Salfords	SAF
Salhouse	SAH
Salisbury	SAL
Saltaire	SAE
Saltash	STS
Saltburn	SLB
Saltcoats	SLT
Saltmarshe	SAM
Salwick	SLW
Sandal & Agbrigg	SNA
Sandbach	SDB
Sanderstead	SNR
Sandhills	SDL
Sandhurst	SND
Sandling	SDG
Sandown	SAN
Sandplace	SDP
Sandwell & Dudley	SAD
Sandwich	SDW
Sandy	SDY
Sankey for Penketh	SNK
Sanquhar	SQH
Sarn	SRR
Saundersfoot	SDF
Saunderton	SDR
Sawbridgeworth	SAW
Saxilby	SXY
Saxmundham	SAX
Scarborough	SCA
Scotscalder	SCT
Scotstounhill	SCH
Scunthorpe	SCU
Seaburn	SEB
Sea Mills	SML
Seaford	SEF
Seaforth & Litherland	SFL
Seaham	SEA
Seamer	SEM
Seascale	SSC
Seaton Carew	SEC
Seer Green & Jordans	SRG
Selby	SBY
Selhurst	SRS
Sellafield	SEL
Selling	SEG
Selly Oak	SLY
Settle	SET
Seven Kings	SVK
Seven Sisters	SVS
Sevenoaks	SEV
Severn Beach	SVB
Severn Tunnel Junction	STJ
Shalford	SFR
Shanklin	SHN
Shaw & Crompton	SHA
Shawford	SHW
Shawlands	SHL
Sheerness-on-Sea	SSS
Sheffield	SHF
Shelford	SED
Shenfield	SNF
Shenstone	SEN
Shepherd's Bush	SPB
Shepherds Well	SPH
Shepley	SPY
Shepperton	SHP
Shepreth	STH
Sherborne	SHE
Sherburn-in-Elmet	SIE
Sheringham	SHM
Shettleston	SLS
Shieldmuir	SDM
Shifnal	SFN
Shildon	SHD
Shiplake	SHI
Shipley	SHY
Shippea Hill	SPP
Shipton	SIP
Shirebrook	SHB
Shirehampton	SHH
Shireoaks	SRO
Shirley	SRL
Shoeburyness	SRY
Sholing	SHO
Shoreham (Kent)	SEH
Shoreham-by-Sea	SSE
Shortlands	SRT
Shotton	SHT
Shotts	SHS
Shrewsbury	SHR
Sidcup	SID
Sileby	SIL
Silecroft	SIC
Silkstone Common	SLK
Silver Street	SLV
Silverdale	SVR
Singer	SIN
Sittingbourne	SIT
Skegness	SKG
Skewen	SKE
Skipton	SKI
Slade Green	SGR
Slaithwaite	SWT
Slateford	SLA
Sleaford	SLR
Sleights	SLH
Slough	SLO
Small Heath	SMA
Smallbrook Junction	SAB
Smethwick Galton Bridge	SGB
Smethwick Rolfe Street	SMR
Smitham	SMI
Smithy Bridge	SMB
Snaith	SNI
Snodland	SDA
Snowdown	SWO
Sole Street	SOR
Solihull	SOL
Somerleyton	SYT
South Acton	SAT
South Bank	SBK
South Bermondsey	SBM
South Croydon	SCY
South Elmsall	SES
South Greenford	SGN
South Gyle	SGL
South Hampstead	SOH
South Kenton	SOK
South Merton	SMO
South Milford	SOM
South Ruislip	SRU
South Tottenham	STO
South Wigston	SWS
South Woodham Ferrers	SOF
Southall	STL
Southampton Airport	SOA
Southampton Central	SOU
Southbourne	SOB
Southbury	SBU
Southease	SEE
Southend Central	SOC
Southend East	SOE
Southend Victoria	SOV
Southminster	SMN
Southport	SOP
Southwick	SWK
Sowerby Bridge	SOW
Spalding	SPA
Spean Bridge	SBR
Spital	SPI
Spondon	SPO
Spooner Row	SPN
Spring Road	SRI
Springburn	SPR
Springfield	SPF
Squires Gate	SQU
St Albans	SAC
St Albans Abbey	SAA
St Andrews Road	SAR
St Annes-on-the-Sea	SAS

St Austell	SAU	Strood	SOO	Three Oaks	TOK	Wakefield Kirkgate	WKK
St Bees	SBS	Stroud	STD	Thurgarton	THU	Wakefield Westgate	WKF
St Budeaux Ferry Road	SBF	Sturry	STU	Thurnscoe	THC	Walkden	WKD
St Budeaux Victoria Rd	SBV	Styal	SYA	Thurso	THS	Wallasey Grove Road	WLG
St Columb Road	SCR	Sudbury	SUY	Thurston	TRS	Wallasey Village	WLV
St Denys	SDN	Sudbury & Harrow Road	SUD	Tilbury Town	TIL	Wallington	WLT
St Erth	SER	Sudbury Hill Harrow	SDH	Tile Hill	THL	Wallyford	WAF
St Germans	SGM	Sugar Loaf	SUG	Tilehurst	TLH	Walmer	WAM
St Helens Central	SNH	Summerston	SUM	Tipton	TIP	Walsall	WSL
St Helens Junction	SHJ	Sunbury	SUU	Tir-Phil	TIR	Walsden	WDN
St Helier	SIH	Sunderland	SUN	Tisbury	TIS	Waltham Cross	WLC
St Ives (Cornwall)	SIV	Sundridge Park	SUP	Tiverton Parkway	TVP	Walthamstow Central	WHC
St James Park	SJP	Sunningdale	SNG	Todmorden	TOD	Walthamstow Queen's Rd	WMW
St James Street	SJS	Sunnymeads	SNY	Tolworth	TOL	Walton (Merseyside)	WAO
St Johns	SAJ	Surbiton	SUR	Ton Pentre	TPN	Walton-on-the-Naze	WON
St Keyne	SKN	Sutton Coldfield	SUT	Tonbridge	TON	Walton-on-Thames	WAL
St Leonards Warrior Sq	SLQ	Sutton Common	SUC	Tondu	TDU	Wanborough	WAN
St Margarets (London)	SMG	Sutton Parkway	SPK	Tonfanau	TNF	Wandsworth Common	WSW
St Margarets (Herts)	SMT	Sutton (Surrey)	SUO	Tonypandy	TNP	Wandsworth Road	WWR
St Mary Cray	SMY	Swale	SWL	Tooting	TOO	Wandsworth Town	WNT
St Michaels	STM	Swanley	SAY	Topsham	TOP	Wanstead Park	WNP
St Neots	SNO	Swanscombe	SWM	Torquay	TQY	Warblington	WBL
St Pancras International	SPX	Swansea	SWA	Torre	TRR	Ware	WAR
St Peter's	STZ	Swanwick	SNW	Totnes	TOT	Wareham	WRM
Stadium of Light	STI	Sway	SWY	Tottenham Hale	TOM	Wargrave	WGV
Stafford	STA	Swaythling	SWG	Totton	TTN	Warminster	WMN
Staines	SNS	Swinderby	SWD	Town Green	TWN	Warnham	WNH
Stallingborough	SLL	Swindon	SWI	Trafford Park	TRA	Warrington Bank Quay	WBQ
Stalybridge	SYB	Swineshead	SWE	Trefforest	TRF	Warrington Central	WAC
Stamford	SMD	Swinton (Gr Manchester)	SNN	Trefforest Estate	TRE	Warwick	WRW
Stamford Hill	SMH	Swinton (Yorks)	SWN	Trehafod	TRH	Warwick Parkway	WRP
Stanford-le-Hope	SFO	Sydenham	SYD	Treherbert	TRB	Water Orton	WTO
Stanlow & Thornton	SNT	Sydenham Hill	SYH	Treorchy	TRY	Waterbeach	WBC
Stansted Airport	SSD	Syon Lane	SYL	Trimley	TRM	Wateringbury	WTR
Stansted Mountfitchet	SST	Syston	SYS	Tring	TRI	Waterloo (Merseyside)	WLO
Staplehurst	SPU	Tackley	TAC	Troed-y-rhiw	TRD	Watford High Street	WFH
Stapleton Road	SRD	Tadworth	TAD	Troon	TRN	Watford Junction	WFJ
Starbeck	SBE	Taffs Well	TAF	Trowbridge	TRO	Watford North	WFN
Starcross	SCS	Tain	TAI	Truro	TRU	Watlington	WTG
Staveley (Cumbria)	SVL	Talsarnau	TAL	Tulloch	TUL	Watton-at-Stone	WAS
Stechford	SCF	Talybont	TLB	Tulse Hill	TUH	Waun-Gron Park	WNG
Steeton & Silsden	SON	Tal-y-Cafn	TLC	Tunbridge Wells	TBW	Wavertree Tech Park	WAV
Stepps	SPS	Tame Bridge Parkway	TAB	Turkey Street	TUR	Wedgwood	WED
Stevenage	SVG	Tamworth	TAM	Tutbury & Hatton	TUT	Weeley	WEE
Stevenston	STV	Taplow	TAP	Twickenham	TWI	Weeton	WET
Stewartby	SWR	Tattenham Corner	TAT	Twyford	TWY	Welham Green	WMG
Stewarton	STT	Taunton	TAU	Ty Croes	TYC	Welling	WLI
Stirling	STG	Taynuilt	TAY	Ty Glas	TGS	Wellingborough	WEL
Stockport	SPT	Teddington	TED	Tygwyn	TYG	Wellington (Shropshire)	WLN
Stocksfield	SKS	Teesside Airport	TEA	Tyndrum Lower	TYL	Welshpool	WLP
Stocksmoor	SSM	Teignmouth	TGM	Tyseley	TYS	Welwyn Garden City	WGC
Stockton	STK	Telford Central	TFC	Tywyn	TYW	Welwyn North	WLW
Stoke Mandeville	SKM	Templecombe	TMC	Uckfield	UCK	Wem	WEM
Stoke Newington	SKW	Tenby	TEN	Uddingston	UDD	Wembley Central	WMB
Stoke-on-Trent	SOT	Teynham	TEY	Ulceby	ULC	Wembley Stadium	WCX
Stone	SNE	Thames Ditton	THD	Ulleskelf	ULL	Wemyss Bay	WMS
Stone Crossing	SCG	Thatcham	THA	Ulverston	ULV	Wendover	WND
Stonebridge Park	SBP	Thatto Heath	THH	Umberleigh	UMB	Wennington	WNN
Stonegate	SOG	The Hawthorns	THW	University	UNI	West Allerton	WSA
Stonehaven	STN	The Lakes	TLK	Uphall	UHA	West Brompton	WBP
Stonehouse	SHU	Theale	THE	Upholland	UPL	West Byfleet	WBY
Stoneleigh	SNL	Theobalds Grove	TEO	Upminster	UPM	West Calder	WCL
Stourbridge Junction	SBJ	Thetford	TTF	Upper Halliford	UPH	West Croydon	WCY
Stourbridge Town	SBT	Thirsk	THI	Upper Holloway	UHL	West Drayton	WDT
Stowmarket	SMK	Thornaby	TBY	Upper Tyndrum	UTY	West Dulwich	WDU
Stranraer	STR	Thorne North	TNN	Upper Warlingham	UWL	West Ealing	WEA
Stratford (London)	SRA	Thorne South	TNS	Upton	UPT	West Ham	WEH
Stratford-upon-Avon	SAV	Thornford	THO	Upwey	UPW	West Hampstead	WHD
Strathcarron	STC	Thornliebank	THB	Urmston	URM	West Hampstead T'link	WHP
Strawberry Hill	STW	Thornton Abbey	TNA	Uttoxeter	UTT	West Horndon	WHR
Streatham	STE	Thornton Heath	TTH	Valley	VAL	West Kilbride	WKB
Streatham Common	SRC	Thorntonhall	THT	Vauxhall	VXH	West Kirby	WKI
Streatham Hill	SRH	Thorpe Bay	TPB	Virginia Water	VIR	West Malling	WMA
Streethouse	SHC	Thorpe Culvert	TPC	Waddon	WDO	West Norwood	WNW
Strines	SRN	Thorpe-le-Soken	TLS	Wadhurst	WAD	West Ruislip	WRU
Stromeferry	STF	Three Bridges	TBD	Wainfleet	WFL	West Runton	WRN

West St Leonards	WLD
West Sutton	WSU
West Wickham	WWI
West Worthing	WWO
Westbury (Wilts)	WSB
Westcliff	WCF
Westcombe Park	WCB
Westenhanger	WHA
Wester Hailes	WTA
Westerfield	WFI
Westerton	WES
Westgate-on-Sea	WGA
Westhoughton	WHG
Weston Milton	WNM
Weston-super-Mare	WSM
Wetheral	WRL
Weybridge	WYB
Weymouth	WEY
Whaley Bridge	WBR
Whalley	WHE
Whatstandwell	WTS
Whifflet	WFF
Whimple	WHM
Whinhill	WNL
Whiston	WHN
Whitby	WTB
Whitchurch (Cardiff)	WHT
Whitchurch (Hants)	WCH
Whitchurch (Shropshire)	WTC
White Hart Lane	WHL
White Notley	WNY
Whitecraigs	WCR
Whitehaven	WTH
Whitland	WTL
Whitley Bridge	WBD
Whitlocks End	WTE
Whitstable	WHI
Whittlesea	WLE
Whittlesford Parkway	WLF
Whitton	WTN
Whitwell	WWL
Whyteleafe	WHY
Whyteleafe South	WHS
Wick	WCK
Wickford	WIC
Wickham Market	WCM
Widdrington	WDD
Widnes	WID
Widney Manor	WMR
Wigan North Western	WGN
Wigan Wallgate	WGW
Wigton	WGT
Wildmill	WMI
Willesden Junction	WIJ
Williamwood	WLM
Willington	WIL
Wilmcote	WMC
Wilmslow	WML
Wilnecote	WNE
Wimbledon	WIM
Wimbledon Chase	WBO
Winchelsea	WSE
Winchester	WIN
Winchfield	WNF
Winchmore Hill	WIH
Windermere	WDM
Windsor & Eton Central	WNC
Windsor & Eton Riverside	WNR
Winnersh	WNS
Winnersh Triangle	WTI
Winsford	WSF
Wishaw	WSH
Witham	WTM
Witley	WTY
Witton	WTT
Wivelsfield	WVF
Wivenhoe	WIV
Woburn Sands	WOB
Woking	WOK
Wokingham	WKM
Woldingham	WOH
Wolverhampton	WVH
Wolverton	WOL
Wombwell	WOM
Wood End	WDE
Wood Street	WST
Woodbridge	WDB
Woodgrange Park	WGR
Woodhall	WDL
Woodhouse	WDH
Woodlesford	WDS
Woodley	WLY
Woodmansterne	WME
Woodsmoor	WSR
Wool	WOO
Woolston	WLS
Woolwich Arsenal	WWA
Woolwich Dockyard	WWD
Wootton Wawen	WWW
Worcester Foregate St	WOF
Worcester Park	WCP
Worcester Shrub Hill	WOS
Workington	WKG
Worksop	WRK
Worle	WOR
Worplesdon	WPL
Worstead	WRT
Worthing	WRH
Wrabness	WRB
Wraysbury	WRY
Wrenbury	WRE
Wressle	WRS
Wrexham Central	WXC
Wrexham General	WRX
Wye	WYE
Wylam	WYM
Wylde Green	WYL
Wymondham	WMD
Wythall	WYT
Yalding	YAL
Yardley Wood	YRD
Yarm	YRM
Yate	YAE
Yatton	YAT
Yeoford	YEO
Yeovil Junction	YVJ
Yeovil Pen Mill	YVP
Yetminster	YET
Ynyswen	YNW
Yoker	YOK
York	YRK
Yorton	YRT
Ystrad Mynach	YSM
Ystrad Rhondda	YSR

Left: *DRS Class 20s Nos. 20303 and 20308 stand at the flask transfer crane at Bridgwater on 28 August 2013 waiting to shunt the Hinkley Point flask before its return to Crewe forming train 6M67, the 11.51 departure.* **Brian Garrett**

DMU and EMU Vehicle Codes

BDMSO	Battery Driving Motor Standard Open
DM	Driving Motor
DMBO	Driving Motor Brake Open
DMBS	Driving Motor Brake Standard
DMCL	Driving Motor Composite Lavatory
DMCO	Driving Motor Composite Open
DMF	Driving Motor First
DMFLO	Driving Motor First Luggage Open
DMRFO	Driving Motor Restaurant First Open
DMS	Driving Motor Standard
DMSL	Driving Motor Standard Lavatory
DMSO	Driving Motor Standard Open
DTCO	Driving Trailer Composite Open
DTPMV	Driving Trailer Parcels Mail Van
DTSO	Driving Trailer Standard Open
MBC	Motor Brake Composite
MBSO	Motor Brake Standard Open
MC	Motor Composite
MFL	Motor First Lavatory
MPMV	Motor Parcels Mail Van
MS	Motor Standard
MSL	Motor Standard Lavatory
MSLRB	Motor Standard Lavatory Restaurant Buffet
MSO	Motor Standard Open
MSRMB	Motor Standard Restaurant Micro Buffet
PTSO	Pantograph Trailer Standard Open
RB	Restaurant Buffet
TBFO	Trailer Brake First Open
TCO	Trailer Composite Open
TFO	Trailer First Open
TPMV	Trailer Parcels Mail Van
TSO	Trailer Standard Open
TSRMB	Trailer Standard Restaurant Micro Buffet

(A) - A Car
(B) - B Car

This cross number checklist indicates in which section of the ABC Rail Guide 2014 full details of rolling stock can be found.

Number Cross-Link Codes

3MP 3M Productions
AEA Abellio East Anglia
AFG Arlington Fleet Group
ALS Alstom
ATW Arriva Trains Wales
AXC Arriva CrossCountry
BAR British American Railway
BOK Bo'ness & Kinneil Railway
BOM Bombardier Transportation
C2C c2c Railway
COL Colas
CRW Chiltern Railways
DBR DB Regio
DBS DB Schenker
DRS Direct Rail Services
ECR Euro Cargo Rail
EMT East Midlands Trains
EPX Europhoenix Ltd
ETL Electric Traction Ltd
EUR Eurotunnel
EUR Europorte2
EUS Eurostar UK
EXP Exported
FCC First Capital Connect
FGW First Great Western
FHT First Hull Trains
FLR Freightliner
FSL Flying Scotsman Railway Ltd
FSR First ScotRail
FTP First TransPennine
GBR GB Railfreight
GSW Great Scottish & Western Rly
GTL Grand Central Railway
HAN Hanson Traction
HEC Heathrow Connect
HEX Heathrow Express
HNR Harry Needle Railroad Co
ICE InterCity East Coast
IND Industrial
JHS Jeremy Hoskins
LMI London Midland
LNW London North Western
LOG London Overground
MER Merseyrail
MHR Mid Hants Railway
MRL Mendip Rail Ltd
NEM Nemesis Rail
NOR Northern
NRL Network Rail Limited
NYM North Yorkshire Moors Railway
OLS Off Lease
PRE Preserved
PUL Pullman Rail
RAF Railfilms
RCL Railcare
RIV Riviera
RRS Ridings Railtours
RVE Rail Vehicle Engineering
S47 Stratford Class 47 Group
SEC Serco Railtest
SET SouthEastern Trains
SIE Siemens
SIL Stagecoach Island Line
SNF SNCF (French Railways)
SOU Southern
SRP Scottish Railway Preservation Soc
SUP Support Coaches
SWT South West Trains
TTS Transmart Trains
VSO Venice Simplon Orient Express
VTN Vintage Trains
VWC Virgin West Coast
WAB Wabtec
WCR West Coast Railway

Locomotives – Diesel & Electric

❑ D0226 PRE

❑ D4 PRE

❑ 12 PRE

❑ 44 MRL
❑ 120 MRL

❑ D200 PRE

❑ D821 PRE
❑ D832 PRE

❑ D1010 PRE
❑ D1013 PRE
❑ D1015 PRE
❑ D1023 PRE
❑ D1041 PRE
❑ D1048 PRE
❑ D1062 PRE

❑ D2023 PRE
❑ D2024 PRE
❑ D2041 PRE
❑ D2046 PRE
❑ D2051 PRE
❑ D2117 PRE
❑ D2118 PRE
❑ D2133 PRE
❑ D2138 PRE
❑ D2139 PRE
❑ D2148 PRE
❑ D2178 PRE
❑ D2182 PRE
❑ D2184 PRE
❑ D2192 PRE
❑ D2199 PRE

❑ D2203 PRE
❑ D2205 PRE
❑ D2207 PRE
❑ D2229 PRE
❑ D2245 PRE
❑ D2246 PRE
❑ D2271 PRE
❑ D2272 PRE
❑ D2279 PRE
❑ D2280 PRE
❑ D2284 PRE
❑ D2298 PRE
❑ D2302 PRE
❑ D2310 PRE
❑ D2324 PRE
❑ D2325 PRE
❑ D2334 PRE
❑ D2337 PRE

❑ D2511 PRE
❑ D2578 PRE
❑ D2587 PRE
❑ D2595 PRE
❑ D2767 PRE
❑ D2774 PRE
❑ D2854 PRE
❑ D2858 PRE
❑ D2860 PRE
❑ D2866 PRE
❑ D2867 PRE
❑ D2868 PRE

❑ D2953 PRE
❑ D2956 PRE

❑ D3000 PRE
❑ D3002 PRE
❑ D3014 PRE
❑ D3101 PRE
❑ D3255 PRE
❑ D3261 PRE
❑ D3452 PRE
❑ D3489 PRE

❑ D4067 PRE
❑ D4092 PRE
❑ D4095 PRE

❑ D5500 PRE

❑ D5705 PRE

❑ D6700 PRE

❑ D7017 PRE
❑ D7018 PRE
❑ D7029 PRE
❑ D7076 PRE
❑ D8000 PRE

❑ D8233 PRE

❑ D8568 PRE

❑ D9500 PRE
❑ D9502 PRE
❑ D9504 PRE
❑ D9513 PRE
❑ D9516 PRE
❑ D9518 PRE
❑ D9520 PRE
❑ D9521 PRE
❑ D9523 PRE
❑ D9524 PRE
❑ D9525 PRE
❑ D9526 PRE
❑ D9529 PRE
❑ D9531 PRE
❑ D9537 PRE
❑ D9539 PRE
❑ D9551 PRE
❑ D9553 PRE
❑ D9555 PRE

❑ DELTIC PRE

❑ DS75 PRE

❑ LMS7050 PRE
❑ LMS7051 PRE
❑ LMS7069 PRE
❑ E5001 PRE

❑ E26020 PRE
❑ E27000 PRE
❑ E27001 PRE

❑ 9005 EUR
❑ 9007 EUR
❑ 9011 EUR
❑ 9013 EUR
❑ 9015 EUR
❑ 9018 EUR
❑ 9022 EUR
❑ 9024 EUR
❑ 9026 EUR
❑ 9029 EUR
❑ 9033 EUR
❑ 9036 EUR
❑ 9037 EUR

❑ 9701 EUR
❑ 9702 EUR
❑ 9703 EUR
❑ 9704 EUR
❑ 9705 EUR
❑ 9706 EUR
❑ 9707 EUR
❑ 9711 EUR
❑ 9712 EUR
❑ 9713 EUR
❑ 9714 EUR
❑ 9715 EUR
❑ 9716 EUR

Number	Operator
❑ 9717	EUR
❑ 9718	EUR
❑ 9719	EUR
❑ 9720	EUR
❑ 9721	EUR
❑ 9722	EUR
❑ 9723	EUR
❑ 9801	EUR
❑ 9802	EUR
❑ 9803	EUR
❑ 9804	EUR
❑ 9806	EUR
❑ 9808	EUR
❑ 9809	EUR
❑ 9810	EUR
❑ 9812	EUR
❑ 9814	EUR
❑ 9816	EUR
❑ 9817	EUR
❑ 9819	EUR
❑ 9820	EUR
❑ 9821	EUR
❑ 9823	EUR
❑ 9825	EUR
❑ 9827	EUR
❑ 9828	EUR
❑ 9831	EUR
❑ 9832	EUR
❑ 9834	EUR
❑ 9835	EUR
❑ 9838	EUR
❑ 9840	EUR
❑ 01509	CRW
❑ 01551	SIE
❑ 01552	HNR
❑ 01564	HNR
❑ 03018	PRE
❑ 03020	PRE
❑ 03022	PRE
❑ 03027	PRE
❑ 03037	PRE
❑ 03059	PRE
❑ 03062	PRE
❑ 03063	PRE
❑ 03066	PRE
❑ 03069	PRE
❑ 03072	PRE
❑ 03073	PRE
❑ 03078	PRE
❑ 03079	PRE
❑ 03081	PRE
❑ 03084	PRE
❑ 03089	PRE
❑ 03090	PRE
❑ 03094	PRE
❑ 03099	PRE
❑ 03112	PRE
❑ 03113	PRE
❑ 03119	PRE
❑ 03120	PRE
❑ 03128	PRE
❑ 03134	PRE
❑ 03141	PRE
❑ 03144	PRE
❑ 03145	PRE
❑ 03152	PRE
❑ 03158	PRE
❑ 03162	PRE
❑ 03170	PRE
❑ 03179	IND
❑ 03189	PRE
❑ 03196	WCR
❑ 03197	PRE
❑ 03180	PRE
❑ 03371	PRE
❑ 03381	WCR
❑ 03399	PRE
❑ 05001	PRE
❑ 06003	PRE
❑ 07001	PRE
❑ 07005	PRE
❑ 07007	AFG
❑ 07010	PRE
❑ 07011	PRE
❑ 07012	PRE
❑ 07013	PRE
❑ 08011	PRE
❑ 08012	PRE
❑ 08015	PRE
❑ 08016	PRE
❑ 08021	PRE
❑ 08022	PRE
❑ 08032	PRE
❑ 08046	PRE
❑ 08054	PRE
❑ 08060	PRE
❑ 08064	PRE
❑ 08077	FLR
❑ 08102	PRE
❑ 08108	PRE
❑ 08114	PRE
❑ 08123	PRE
❑ 08133	PRE
❑ 08164	PRE
❑ 08168	PRE
❑ 08195	PRE
❑ 08202	IND
❑ 08220	PRE
❑ 08238	PRE
❑ 08266	PRE
❑ 08288	PRE
❑ 08308	BAR
❑ 08331	PRE
❑ 08359	PRE
❑ 08375	IND
❑ 08377	PRE
❑ 08388	PRE
❑ 08389	HNR
❑ 08393	FLR
❑ 08401	GBR
❑ 08405	DBS
❑ 08410	FGW
❑ 08411	IND
❑ 08417	NRL
❑ 08418	WCR
❑ 08423	BAR
❑ 08428	DBS
❑ 08436	PRE
❑ 08441	IND
❑ 08442	LNW
❑ 08443	PRE
❑ 08444	PRE
❑ 08445	IND
❑ 08447	IND
❑ 08451	ALS
❑ 08454	ALS
❑ 08460	IND
❑ 08471	PRE
❑ 08472	WAB
❑ 08473	PRE
❑ 08476	PRE
❑ 08479	PRE
❑ 08480	DBS
❑ 08483	FGW
❑ 08484	IND
❑ 08485	WCR
❑ 08490	PRE
❑ 08495	DBS
❑ 08499	PUL
❑ 08500	DBS
❑ 08502	HNR
❑ 08503	IND
❑ 08507	RIV
❑ 08511	IND
❑ 08516	LNW
❑ 08523	BAR
❑ 08525	EMT
❑ 08527	HNR
❑ 08528	PRE
❑ 08530	FLR
❑ 08531	FLR
❑ 08535	IND
❑ 08536	RVE
❑ 08556	PRE
❑ 08567	DBS
❑ 08568	KBR
❑ 08571	WAB
❑ 08573	BAR
❑ 08575	FLR
❑ 08578	DBS
❑ 08580	DBS
❑ 08585	FLR
❑ 08588	BAR
❑ 08590	PRE
❑ 08593	DBS
❑ 08596	WAB
❑ 08598	IND
❑ 08600	IND
❑ 08604	PRE
❑ 08605	DBS
❑ 08611	ALS
❑ 08613	BAR
❑ 08615	WAB
❑ 08616	LMI
❑ 08617	ALS
❑ 08622	BAR
❑ 08623	DBS
❑ 08624	FLR
❑ 08629	KBR
❑ 08628	PRE
❑ 08630	DBS
❑ 08631	PRE
❑ 08632	DBS
❑ 08633	DBS
❑ 08635	PRE
❑ 08641	FGW
❑ 08643	MRL
❑ 08644	FGW
❑ 08645	FGW
❑ 08648	BAR
❑ 08649	KBR
❑ 08650	MRL
❑ 08652	MRL
❑ 08653	DBS
❑ 08663	FGW
❑ 08669	WAB
❑ 08670	IND
❑ 08676	DBS
❑ 08678	WCR
❑ 08682	BOM
❑ 08683	IND
❑ 08685	HNR
❑ 08690	EMT
❑ 08691	FLR
❑ 08694	PRE
❑ 08696	ALS
❑ 08697	RVE
❑ 08699	IND
❑ 08700	PRE
❑ 08701	DBS
❑ 08703	DBS
❑ 08704	RIV
❑ 08706	DBS
❑ 08709	DBS
❑ 08711	DBS
❑ 08714	DBS
❑ 08721	ALS
❑ 08724	WAB
❑ 08728	IND
❑ 08730	KBR
❑ 08731	MRL
❑ 08735	DBS
❑ 08737	DBS
❑ 08738	DBS
❑ 08742	DBS
❑ 08743	IND
❑ 08750	BAR
❑ 08752	DBS
❑ 08754	BAR
❑ 08756	BAR
❑ 08757	DBS
❑ 08762	BAR
❑ 08764	WAB
❑ 08765	HNR
❑ 08767	PRE
❑ 08769	PRE
❑ 08772	PRE
❑ 08773	PRE
❑ 08774	IND
❑ 08780	PRE
❑ 08782	DBS
❑ 08784	DBS
❑ 08785	FLR
❑ 08786	HNR
❑ 08787	IND
❑ 08790	ALS
❑ 08795	FGW
❑ 08799	DBS
❑ 08802	DBS
❑ 08804	DBS
❑ 08805	LMI
❑ 08807	IND
❑ 08809	IND
❑ 08810	LNW
❑ 08818	HNR
❑ 08822	FGW
❑ 08823	IND
❑ 08824	DBS
❑ 08825	PRE
❑ 08830	LNW
❑ 08834	HNR
❑ 08836	FGW
❑ 08846	BOM
❑ 08847	IND
❑ 08850	NYM
❑ 08853	WAB
❑ 08865	DBS
❑ 08868	HNR
❑ 08870	BAR
❑ 08871	WAB
❑ 08872	IND
❑ 08873	BAR
❑ 08877	DBS
❑ 08879	DBS
❑ 08881	PRE
❑ 08885	BAR
❑ 08886	DBS
❑ 08887	ALS
❑ 08888	DBS
❑ 08891	FLR
❑ 08892	HNR
❑ 08896	PRE
❑ 08899	EMT
❑ 08903	IND
❑ 08904	DBS
❑ 08905	HNR
❑ 08907	DBS
❑ 08908	EMT
❑ 08911	PRE
❑ 08912	IND
❑ 08913	IND
❑ 08915	IND
❑ 08918	HNR
❑ 08922	DBS
❑ 08924	HNR
❑ 08925	GBR
❑ 08927	PRE
❑ 08929	HNR

❑ 08933 IND
❑ 08934 GBR
❑ 08936 BAR
❑ 08937 PRE
❑ 08939 DBS
❑ 08943 HNR
❑ 08944 PRE
❑ 08947 MRL
❑ 08948 EUS
❑ 08950 EMT
❑ 08954 HNR
❑ 08956 NRL
❑ 08993 DBS
❑ 08994 DBS
❑ 08995 DBS

❑ 09001 PRE
❑ 09002 GBR
❑ 09004 PRE
❑ 09006 DBS
❑ 09007 LOG
❑ 09009 GBR
❑ 09010 PRE
❑ 09012 PRE
❑ 09014 HNR
❑ 09015 PRE
❑ 09017 PRE
❑ 09018 HNR
❑ 09019 PRE
❑ 09022 IND
❑ 09023 IND
❑ 09024 PRE
❑ 09025 PRE
❑ 09026 SOU
❑ 09106 DBS
❑ 09201 DBS
❑ 09204 LNW

❑ 12052 PRE
❑ 12077 PRE
❑ 12082 PRE
❑ 12088 IND
❑ 12093 PRE
❑ 12099 PRE
❑ 12131 PRE

❑ 15224 PRE

❑ 18000 PRE

❑ 20001 PRE
❑ 20007 PRE
❑ 20016 HNR
❑ 20020 PRE
❑ 20031 PRE
❑ 20035 PRE
❑ 20048 PRE
❑ 20056 HNR
❑ 20057 PRE
❑ 20059 PRE
❑ 20063 PRE
❑ 20066 HNR
❑ 20069 PRE
❑ 20081 HNR
❑ 20087 PRE
❑ 20088 HNR
❑ 20092 HNR
❑ 20096 HNR
❑ 20098 PRE
❑ 20107 HNR
❑ 20110 PRE
❑ 20118 HNR
❑ 20121 HNR
❑ 20132 HNR
❑ 20137 PRE
❑ 20138 HNR
❑ 20142 GBR
❑ 20154 PRE
❑ 20166 PRE
❑ 20168 HNR
❑ 20169 PRE
❑ 20177 PRE
❑ 20188 PRE
❑ 20189 GBR
❑ 20205 PRE
❑ 20214 PRE
❑ 20227 GBR
❑ 20228 PRE
❑ 20301 DRS
❑ 20302 DRS
❑ 20303 DRS
❑ 20304 DRS
❑ 20305 DRS
❑ 20308 DRS
❑ 20309 DRS
❑ 20311 HNR
❑ 20312 DRS
❑ 20314 HNR
❑ 20901 GBR
❑ 20903 HNR
❑ 20904 HNR
❑ 20905 GBR
❑ 20906 HNR

❑ 21544 ECR
❑ 21545 ECR
❑ 21546 ECR
❑ 21547 ECR
❑ 21610 ECR
❑ 21611 ECR

❑ 21901 EUR
❑ 21902 EUR
❑ 21903 EUR
❑ 21904 EUR
❑ 21905 EUR

❑ 24032 PRE
❑ 24054 PRE
❑ 24061 PRE
❑ 24081 PRE

❑ 25035 PRE
❑ 25057 PRE
❑ 25059 PRE
❑ 25067 PRE
❑ 25072 PRE
❑ 25083 PRE
❑ 25173 PRE
❑ 25185 PRE
❑ 25191 PRE
❑ 25235 PRE
❑ 25244 PRE
❑ 25262 PRE
❑ 25265 PRE
❑ 25278 NYM
❑ 25279 PRE
❑ 25283 PRE
❑ 25309 PRE
❑ 25313 PRE
❑ 25321 PRE
❑ 25322 PRE

❑ 26001 PRE
❑ 26002 PRE
❑ 26004 PRE
❑ 26007 PRE
❑ 26010 PRE
❑ 26011 PRE
❑ 26014 PRE
❑ 26024 PRE
❑ 26025 PRE
❑ 26035 PRE
❑ 26038 PRE
❑ 26040 PRE
❑ 26043 PRE

❑ 27001 PRE
❑ 27005 PRE
❑ 27007 PRE
❑ 27024 PRE
❑ 27050 PRE
❑ 27056 PRE
❑ 27059 PRE
❑ 27066 PRE

❑ 31101 PRE
❑ 31105 NRL
❑ 31106 RVE
❑ 31108 PRE
❑ 31119 PRE
❑ 31128 NEM
❑ 31130 PRE
❑ 31162 PRE
❑ 31163 PRE
❑ 31190 BAR
❑ 31203 PRE
❑ 31206 PRE
❑ 31207 PRE
❑ 31210 PRE
❑ 31233 NRL
❑ 31235 PRE
❑ 31255 PRE
❑ 31270 PRE
❑ 31271 PRE
❑ 31285 NRL
❑ 31289 PRE
❑ 31327 PRE
❑ 31410 PRE
❑ 31414 PRE
❑ 31415 PRE
❑ 31418 PRE
❑ 31422 RVE
❑ 31435 PRE
❑ 31438 PRE
❑ 31452 BAR
❑ 31454 BAR
❑ 31459 RVE
❑ 31461 PRE
❑ 31463 PRE
❑ 31465 NRL
❑ 31466 PRE
❑ 31468 RVE
❑ 31530 PRE
❑ 31601 BAR
❑ 31602 BAR

❑ 33002 PRE
❑ 33008 PRE
❑ 33012 PRE
❑ 33018 PRE
❑ 33019 PRE
❑ 33021 PRE
❑ 33025 WCR
❑ 33029 WCR
❑ 33030 PRE
❑ 33035 PRE
❑ 33046 PRE
❑ 33048 PRE
❑ 33052 PRE
❑ 33053 PRE
❑ 33057 PRE
❑ 33063 PRE
❑ 33065 PRE
❑ 33102 PRE
❑ 33103 NEM
❑ 33108 PRE
❑ 33109 PRE
❑ 33110 PRE
❑ 33111 PRE
❑ 33116 PRE
❑ 33117 PRE
❑ 33201 PRE
❑ 33202 PRE
❑ 33207 WCR
❑ 33208 PRE

❑ 37003 PRE
❑ 37009 PRE
❑ 37023 PRE
❑ 37025 PRE
❑ 37029 HNR
❑ 37032 PRE
❑ 37037 PRE
❑ 37038 DRS
❑ 37042 PRE
❑ 37057 HNR
❑ 37059 DRS
❑ 37069 DRS
❑ 37075 PRE
❑ 37097 PRE
❑ 37108 PRE
❑ 37109 PRE
❑ 37116 PRE
❑ 37142 PRE
❑ 37146 PRE
❑ 37152 PRE
❑ 37165 HNR
❑ 37175 PRE
❑ 37188 PRE
❑ 37194 DRS
❑ 37198 NRL
❑ 37207 PRE
❑ 37214 WCR
❑ 37215 PRE
❑ 37216 PRE
❑ 37218 DRS
❑ 37219 PRE
❑ 37227 PRE
❑ 37240 PRE
❑ 37248 PRE
❑ 37250 PRE
❑ 37254 PRE
❑ 37255 PRE
❑ 37259 DRS
❑ 37261 DRS
❑ 37263 PRE
❑ 37264 PRE
❑ 37275 PRE
❑ 37294 PRE
❑ 37308 PRE
❑ 37314 PRE
❑ 37324 PRE
❑ 37372 PRE
❑ 37401 DRS
❑ 37402 DRS
❑ 37403 PRE
❑ 37405 DRS
❑ 37406 DRS
❑ 37407 PRE
❑ 37409 DRS
❑ 37413 PRE
❑ 37418 PRE
❑ 37419 DRS
❑ 37421 PRE
❑ 37422 DRS
❑ 37423 DRS
❑ 37424 PRE
❑ 37425 DRS
❑ 37502 FLR
❑ 37503 DRS
❑ 37510 DRS
❑ 37516 WCR
❑ 37517 WCR
❑ 37518 WCR
❑ 37521 DRS
❑ 37601 DRS
❑ 37602 DRS
❑ 37603 DRS
❑ 37604 DRS
❑ 37605 DRS
❑ 37606 DRS
❑ 37607 DRS
❑ 37608 DRS
❑ 37609 DRS

❑ 37610 DRS
❑ 37611 DRS
❑ 37612 DRS
❑ 37667 DRS
❑ 37668 WCR
❑ 37669 WCR
❑ 37670 DRS
❑ 37674 PRE
❑ 37676 WCR
❑ 37679 NEM
❑ 37682 DRS
❑ 37685 WCR
❑ 37688 DRS
❑ 37696 DRS
❑ 37703 DRS
❑ 37706 WCR
❑ 37710 WCR
❑ 37712 WCR
❑ 37714 DRS
❑ 37716 DRS
❑ 37718 DRS
❑ 37901 PRE
❑ 37905 PRE
❑ 37906 PRE

❑ 40012 PRE
❑ 40013 PRE
❑ 40106 PRE
❑ 40118 PRE
❑ 40135 PRE
❑ 40145 PRE

❑ 41001 PRE

❑ 43002 FGW
❑ 43003 FGW
❑ 43004 FGW
❑ 43005 FGW
❑ 43009 FGW
❑ 43010 FGW
❑ 43012 FGW
❑ 43013 NRL
❑ 43014 NRL
❑ 43015 FGW
❑ 43016 FGW
❑ 43017 FGW
❑ 43018 FGW
❑ 43020 FGW
❑ 43021 FGW
❑ 43022 FGW
❑ 43023 FGW
❑ 43024 FGW
❑ 43025 FGW
❑ 43026 FGW
❑ 43027 FGW
❑ 43028 FGW
❑ 43029 FGW
❑ 43030 FGW
❑ 43031 FGW
❑ 43032 FGW
❑ 43033 FGW
❑ 43034 FGW
❑ 43035 FGW
❑ 43036 FGW
❑ 43037 FGW
❑ 43040 FGW
❑ 43041 FGW
❑ 43042 FGW
❑ 43043 EMT
❑ 43044 EMT
❑ 43045 EMT
❑ 43046 EMT
❑ 43047 EMT
❑ 43048 EMT
❑ 43049 EMT
❑ 43050 EMT
❑ 43052 EMT
❑ 43053 FGW
❑ 43054 EMT
❑ 43055 EMT
❑ 43056 FGW
❑ 43058 EMT
❑ 43059 EMT
❑ 43060 EMT
❑ 43061 EMT
❑ 43062 NRL
❑ 43063 FGW
❑ 43064 EMT
❑ 43066 EMT
❑ 43069 FGW
❑ 43070 FGW
❑ 43071 FGW
❑ 43073 EMT
❑ 43075 EMT
❑ 43076 EMT
❑ 43078 FGW
❑ 43079 FGW
❑ 43081 EMT
❑ 43082 EMT
❑ 43083 EMT
❑ 43086 FGW
❑ 43087 FGW
❑ 43088 FGW
❑ 43089 EMT
❑ 43091 FGW
❑ 43092 FGW
❑ 43093 FGW
❑ 43094 FGW
❑ 43097 FGW
❑ 43098 FGW
❑ 43122 FGW
❑ 43124 FGW
❑ 43125 FGW
❑ 43126 FGW
❑ 43127 FGW
❑ 43128 FGW
❑ 43129 FGW
❑ 43130 FGW
❑ 43131 FGW
❑ 43132 FGW
❑ 43133 FGW
❑ 43134 FGW
❑ 43135 FGW
❑ 43136 FGW
❑ 43137 FGW
❑ 43138 FGW
❑ 43139 FGW
❑ 43140 FGW
❑ 43141 FGW
❑ 43142 FGW
❑ 43143 FGW
❑ 43144 FGW
❑ 43145 FGW
❑ 43146 FGW
❑ 43147 FGW
❑ 43148 FGW
❑ 43149 FGW
❑ 43150 FGW
❑ 43151 FGW
❑ 43152 FGW
❑ 43153 FGW
❑ 43154 FGW
❑ 43155 FGW
❑ 43156 FGW
❑ 43158 FGW
❑ 43159 FGW
❑ 43160 FGW
❑ 43161 FGW
❑ 43162 FGW
❑ 43163 FGW
❑ 43164 FGW
❑ 43165 FGW
❑ 43168 FGW
❑ 43169 FGW
❑ 43170 FGW
❑ 43171 FGW
❑ 43172 FGW
❑ 43174 FGW
❑ 43175 FGW
❑ 43176 FGW
❑ 43177 FGW
❑ 43179 FGW
❑ 43180 FGW
❑ 43181 FGW
❑ 43182 FGW
❑ 43183 FGW
❑ 43185 FGW
❑ 43186 FGW
❑ 43187 FGW
❑ 43188 FGW
❑ 43189 FGW
❑ 43190 FGW
❑ 43191 FGW
❑ 43192 FGW
❑ 43193 FGW
❑ 43194 FGW
❑ 43195 FGW
❑ 43196 FGW
❑ 43197 FGW
❑ 43198 FGW
❑ 43206 ICE
❑ 43207 AXC
❑ 43208 ICE
❑ 43238 ICE
❑ 43239 ICE
❑ 43251 ICE
❑ 43257 ICE
❑ 43272 ICE
❑ 43274 ICE
❑ 43277 ICE
❑ 43285 AXC
❑ 43290 ICE
❑ 43295 ICE
❑ 43296 ICE
❑ 43299 ICE
❑ 43300 ICE
❑ 43301 AXC
❑ 43302 ICE
❑ 43303 AXC
❑ 43304 AXC
❑ 43305 ICE
❑ 43306 ICE
❑ 43307 ICE
❑ 43308 ICE
❑ 43309 ICE
❑ 43310 ICE
❑ 43311 ICE
❑ 43312 ICE
❑ 43313 ICE
❑ 43314 ICE
❑ 43315 ICE
❑ 43316 ICE
❑ 43317 ICE
❑ 43318 ICE
❑ 43319 ICE
❑ 43320 ICE
❑ 43321 AXC
❑ 43357 AXC
❑ 43366 AXC
❑ 43367 ICE
❑ 43378 AXC
❑ 43384 AXC
❑ 43423 GTL
❑ 43465 GTL
❑ 43467 GTL
❑ 43468 GTL
❑ 43480 GTL
❑ 43484 GTL

❑ 44008 PRE

❑ 45015 PRE
❑ 45041 PRE
❑ 45060 PRE
❑ 45105 PRE
❑ 45108 PRE
❑ 45112 NEM
❑ 45118 PRE
❑ 45125 PRE
❑ 45132 PRE
❑ 45133 PRE
❑ 45135 PRE
❑ 45149 PRE

❑ 46010 PRE
❑ 46035 PRE
❑ 46045 PRE

❑ 47004 PRE
❑ 47105 PRE
❑ 47117 PRE
❑ 47192 PRE
❑ 47194 WCR
❑ 47205 PRE
❑ 47237 WCR
❑ 47245 WCR
❑ 47270 WCR
❑ 47292 PRE
❑ 47306 PRE
❑ 47355 WCR
❑ 47367 PRE
❑ 47375 NEM
❑ 47376 PRE
❑ 47401 PRE
❑ 47402 PRE
❑ 47417 PRE
❑ 47449 PRE
❑ 47484 PRE
❑ 47488 NEM
❑ 47492 WCR
❑ 47500 WCR
❑ 47501 DRS
❑ 47524 PRE
❑ 47526 WCR
❑ 47540 PRE
❑ 47580 S4L
❑ 47596 PRE
❑ 47635 PRE
❑ 47640 PRE
❑ 47643 PRE
❑ 47701 PRE
❑ 47703 DRS
❑ 47712 PRE
❑ 47714 HNR
❑ 47715 HNR
❑ 47716 NEM
❑ 47727 COL
❑ 47739 COL
❑ 47744 NEM
❑ 47746 WCR
❑ 47749 COL
❑ 47760 WCR
❑ 47761 HNR
❑ 47763 PRE
❑ 47765 PRE
❑ 47768 WCR
❑ 47769 RIV
❑ 47771 PRE
❑ 47772 WCR
❑ 47773 VTN
❑ 47776 WCR
❑ 47785 PRE
❑ 47786 WCR
❑ 47787 WCR
❑ 47790 DRS
❑ 47793 PRE
❑ 47798 PRE
❑ 47799 PRE
❑ 47802 DRS
❑ 47804 WCR
❑ 47805 DRS
❑ 47810 DRS
❑ 47811 FLR
❑ 47812 RIV
❑ 47813 DRS

Number	Operator
❑ 47815	RIV
❑ 47816	FLR
❑ 47818	DRS
❑ 47826	WCR
❑ 47828	DRS
❑ 47830	FLR
❑ 47832	DRS
❑ 47840	PRE
❑ 47841	DRS
❑ 47843	RIV
❑ 47847	RIV
❑ 47848	RIV
❑ 47851	WCR
❑ 47853	DRS
❑ 47854	WCR
❑ 50002	PRE
❑ 50007	PRE
❑ 50008	PRE
❑ 50015	PRE
❑ 50017	PRE
❑ 50019	PRE
❑ 50021	PRE
❑ 50026	PRE
❑ 50027	PRE
❑ 50029	PRE
❑ 50030	PRE
❑ 50031	PRE
❑ 50033	PRE
❑ 50135	PRE
❑ 50042	PRE
❑ 50044	PRE
❑ 50049	PRE
❑ 50050	PRE
❑ 55002	PRE
❑ 55009	PRE
❑ 55015	PRE
❑ 55016	PRE
❑ 55019	PRE
❑ 55022	PRE
❑ 56006	PRE
❑ 56007	URL
❑ 56009	URL
❑ 56018	URL
❑ 56031	URL
❑ 56037	URL
❑ 56038	URL
❑ 56049	COL
❑ 56051	COL
❑ 56060	URL
❑ 56065	URL
❑ 56069	URL
❑ 56077	URL
❑ 56078	COL
❑ 56081	URL
❑ 56087	COL
❑ 56091	BAR
❑ 56090	COL
❑ 56094	COL
❑ 56096	EPX
❑ 56097	PRE
❑ 56098	URL
❑ 56101	EXP
❑ 56103	BAR
❑ 56104	URL
❑ 56105	COL
❑ 56106	URL
❑ 56113	COL
❑ 56115	EXP
❑ 56117	EXP
❑ 56301	EPX
❑ 56302	COL
❑ 56303	BAR
❑ 56311	BAR
❑ 56312	BAR
❑ 56313	BAR
❑ 57001	WCR
❑ 57002	DRS
❑ 57003	DRS
❑ 57004	DRS
❑ 57005	WCR
❑ 57006	WCR
❑ 57007	DRS
❑ 57008	DRS
❑ 57009	DRS
❑ 57010	DRS
❑ 57011	DRS
❑ 57012	DRS
❑ 57301	NRL
❑ 57302	DRS
❑ 57303	NRL
❑ 57304	DRS
❑ 57305	NRL
❑ 57306	NRL
❑ 57307	DRS
❑ 57308	DRS
❑ 57309	DRS
❑ 57310	NRL
❑ 57311	DRS
❑ 57312	NRL
❑ 57313	WCR
❑ 57314	WCR
❑ 57315	WCR
❑ 57316	WCR
❑ 57601	WCR
❑ 57602	FGW
❑ 57603	FGW
❑ 57604	FGW
❑ 57605	FGW
❑ 58001	DBS
❑ 58004	DBS
❑ 58005	DBS
❑ 58006	DBS
❑ 58007	DBS
❑ 58008	DBS
❑ 58009	DBS
❑ 58010	DBS
❑ 58011	DBS
❑ 58012	DBS
❑ 58013	DBS
❑ 58015	DBS
❑ 58016	PRE
❑ 58017	DBS
❑ 58018	DBS
❑ 58020	DBS
❑ 58021	DBS
❑ 58022	DBS
❑ 58023	DBS
❑ 58024	DBS
❑ 58025	DBS
❑ 58026	DBS
❑ 58027	DBS
❑ 58029	DBS
❑ 58030	DBS
❑ 58031	DBS
❑ 58032	DBS
❑ 58033	DBS
❑ 58034	DBS
❑ 58035	DBS
❑ 58036	DBS
❑ 58037	DBS
❑ 58038	DBS
❑ 58039	DBS
❑ 58040	DBS
❑ 58041	DBS
❑ 58042	DBS
❑ 58043	DBS
❑ 58044	DBS
❑ 58046	DBS
❑ 58047	DBS
❑ 58048	DBS
❑ 58049	DBS
❑ 58050	DBS
❑ 59001	MRL
❑ 59002	MRL
❑ 59003	EXP
❑ 59004	MRL
❑ 59005	MRL
❑ 59101	MRL
❑ 59102	MRL
❑ 59103	MRL
❑ 59104	MRL
❑ 59201	DBS
❑ 59202	DBS
❑ 59203	DBS
❑ 59204	DBS
❑ 59205	DBS
❑ 59206	DBS
❑ 60001	DBS
❑ 60002	WAB
❑ 60003	DBS
❑ 60004	DBS
❑ 60005	DBS
❑ 60007	DBS
❑ 60009	DBS
❑ 60010	DBS
❑ 60011	DBS
❑ 60012	DBS
❑ 60013	WAB
❑ 60015	DBS
❑ 60017	DBS
❑ 60018	DBS
❑ 60019	DBS
❑ 60020	DBS
❑ 60021	WAB
❑ 60022	DBS
❑ 60024	DBS
❑ 60025	DBS
❑ 60026	WAB
❑ 60027	DBS
❑ 60028	WAB
❑ 60029	WAB
❑ 60030	DBS
❑ 60032	DBS
❑ 60033	WAB
❑ 60034	DBS
❑ 60035	DBS
❑ 60036	DBS
❑ 60037	DBS
❑ 60038	WAB
❑ 60039	DBS
❑ 60040	DBS
❑ 60041	WAB
❑ 60043	DBS
❑ 60044	DBS
❑ 60045	DBS
❑ 60046	WAB
❑ 60047	WAB
❑ 60048	WAB
❑ 60049	DBS
❑ 60051	DBS
❑ 60052	DBS
❑ 60053	DBS
❑ 60054	DBS
❑ 60055	WAB
❑ 60056	DBS
❑ 60057	DBS
❑ 60059	DBS
❑ 60060	DBS
❑ 60061	WAB
❑ 60062	DBS
❑ 60063	DBS
❑ 60064	DBS
❑ 60065	DBS
❑ 60066	DBS
❑ 60067	DBS
❑ 60069	DBS
❑ 60071	DBS
❑ 60072	DBS
❑ 60073	DBS
❑ 60074	DBS
❑ 60076	WAB
❑ 60077	DBS
❑ 60079	DBS
❑ 60083	DBS
❑ 60084	DBS
❑ 60085	WAB
❑ 60086	DBS
❑ 60087	WAB
❑ 60088	DBS
❑ 60090	DBS
❑ 60091	DBS
❑ 60092	DBS
❑ 60093	DBS
❑ 60094	DBS
❑ 60095	WAB
❑ 60096	WAB
❑ 60097	DBS
❑ 60099	DBS
❑ 60100	DBS
❑ 60500	DBS
❑ 66001	DBS
❑ 66002	DBS
❑ 66003	DBS
❑ 66004	DBS
❑ 66005	DBS
❑ 66006	DBS
❑ 66007	DBS
❑ 66008	DBS
❑ 66009	DBS
❑ 66010	DBS
❑ 66011	DBS
❑ 66012	DBS
❑ 66013	DBS
❑ 66014	DBS
❑ 66015	DBS
❑ 66016	DBS
❑ 66017	DBS
❑ 66018	DBS
❑ 66019	DBS
❑ 66020	DBS
❑ 66021	DBS
❑ 66022	DBS
❑ 66023	DBS
❑ 66024	DBS
❑ 66025	DBS
❑ 66026	DBS
❑ 66027	DBS
❑ 66028	DBS
❑ 66029	DBS
❑ 66030	DBS
❑ 66031	DBS
❑ 66032	DBS
❑ 66033	DBS
❑ 66034	DBS
❑ 66035	DBS
❑ 66036	DBS
❑ 66037	DBS
❑ 66038	DBS
❑ 66039	DBS
❑ 66040	DBS
❑ 66041	DBS
❑ 66042	DBS
❑ 66043	DBS
❑ 66044	DBS
❑ 66045	DBS
❑ 66046	DBS
❑ 66047	DBS
❑ 66048	DBS
❑ 66049	DBS
❑ 66050	DBS
❑ 66051	DBS
❑ 66052	DBS
❑ 66053	DBS
❑ 66054	DBS
❑ 66055	DBS

Number	Operator
❑ 66056	DBS
❑ 66057	DBS
❑ 66058	DBS
❑ 66059	DBS
❑ 66060	DBS
❑ 66061	DBS
❑ 66062	DBS
❑ 66063	DBS
❑ 66064	DBS
❑ 66065	DBS
❑ 66066	DBS
❑ 66067	DBS
❑ 66068	DBS
❑ 66069	DBS
❑ 66070	DBS
❑ 66071	DBS
❑ 66072	DBS
❑ 66073	DBS
❑ 66074	DBS
❑ 66075	DBS
❑ 66076	DBS
❑ 66077	DBS
❑ 66078	DBS
❑ 66079	DBS
❑ 66080	DBS
❑ 66081	DBS
❑ 66082	DBS
❑ 66083	DBS
❑ 66084	DBS
❑ 66085	DBS
❑ 66086	DBS
❑ 66087	DBS
❑ 66088	DBS
❑ 66089	DBS
❑ 66090	DBS
❑ 66091	DBS
❑ 66092	DBS
❑ 66093	DBS
❑ 66094	DBS
❑ 66095	DBS
❑ 66096	DBS
❑ 66097	DBS
❑ 66098	DBS
❑ 66099	DBS
❑ 66100	DBS
❑ 66101	DBS
❑ 66102	DBS
❑ 66103	DBS
❑ 66104	DBS
❑ 66105	DBS
❑ 66106	DBS
❑ 66107	DBS
❑ 66108	DBS
❑ 66109	DBS
❑ 66110	DBS
❑ 66111	DBS
❑ 66112	DBS
❑ 66113	DBS
❑ 66114	DBS
❑ 66115	DBS
❑ 66116	DBS
❑ 66117	DBS
❑ 66118	DBS
❑ 66119	DBS
❑ 66120	DBS
❑ 66121	DBS
❑ 66122	DBS
❑ 66123	DBS
❑ 66124	DBS
❑ 66125	DBS
❑ 66126	DBS
❑ 66127	DBS
❑ 66128	DBS
❑ 66129	DBS
❑ 66130	DBS
❑ 66131	DBS
❑ 66132	DBS
❑ 66133	DBS
❑ 66134	DBS
❑ 66135	DBS
❑ 66136	DBS
❑ 66137	DBS
❑ 66138	DBS
❑ 66139	DBS
❑ 66140	DBS
❑ 66141	DBS
❑ 66142	DBS
❑ 66143	DBS
❑ 66144	DBS
❑ 66145	DBS
❑ 66146	DBS
❑ 66147	DBS
❑ 66148	DBS
❑ 66149	DBS
❑ 66150	DBS
❑ 66151	DBS
❑ 66152	DBS
❑ 66153	DBS
❑ 66154	DBS
❑ 66155	DBS
❑ 66156	DBS
❑ 66157	DBS
❑ 66158	DBS
❑ 66159	DBS
❑ 66160	DBS
❑ 66161	DBS
❑ 66162	DBS
❑ 66163	DBS
❑ 66164	DBS
❑ 66165	DBS
❑ 66166	DBS
❑ 66167	DBS
❑ 66168	DBS
❑ 66169	DBS
❑ 66170	DBS
❑ 66171	DBS
❑ 66172	DBS
❑ 66173	DBS
❑ 66174	DBS
❑ 66175	DBS
❑ 66176	DBS
❑ 66177	DBS
❑ 66178	DBS
❑ 66179	DBS
❑ 66180	DBS
❑ 66181	DBS
❑ 66182	DBS
❑ 66183	DBS
❑ 66184	DBS
❑ 66185	DBS
❑ 66186	DBS
❑ 66187	DBS
❑ 66188	DBS
❑ 66189	DBS
❑ 66190	DBS
❑ 66191	DBS
❑ 66192	DBS
❑ 66193	DBS
❑ 66194	DBS
❑ 66195	DBS
❑ 66196	DBS
❑ 66197	DBS
❑ 66198	DBS
❑ 66199	DBS
❑ 66200	DBS
❑ 66201	DBS
❑ 66202	DBS
❑ 66203	DBS
❑ 66204	DBS
❑ 66205	DBS
❑ 66206	DBS
❑ 66207	DBS
❑ 66208	DBS
❑ 66209	DBS
❑ 66210	DBS
❑ 66211	DBS
❑ 66212	DBS
❑ 66213	DBS
❑ 66214	DBS
❑ 66215	DBS
❑ 66216	DBS
❑ 66217	DBS
❑ 66218	DBS
❑ 66219	DBS
❑ 66220	DBS
❑ 66221	DBS
❑ 66222	DBS
❑ 66223	DBS
❑ 66224	DBS
❑ 66225	DBS
❑ 66226	DBS
❑ 66227	DBS
❑ 66228	DBS
❑ 66229	DBS
❑ 66230	DBS
❑ 66231	DBS
❑ 66232	DBS
❑ 66233	DBS
❑ 66234	DBS
❑ 66235	DBS
❑ 66236	DBS
❑ 66237	DBS
❑ 66238	DBS
❑ 66239	DBS
❑ 66240	DBS
❑ 66241	DBS
❑ 66242	DBS
❑ 66243	DBS
❑ 66244	DBS
❑ 66245	DBS
❑ 66246	DBS
❑ 66247	DBS
❑ 66248	DBS
❑ 66249	DBS
❑ 66250	DBS
❑ 66301	DRS
❑ 66302	DRS
❑ 66303	DRS
❑ 66304	DRS
❑ 66305	DRS
❑ 66411	EXP
❑ 66412	EXP
❑ 66413	FLR
❑ 66414	FLR
❑ 66415	FLR
❑ 66416	FLR
❑ 66417	EXP
❑ 66418	FLR
❑ 66419	FLR
❑ 66420	FLR
❑ 66421	DRS
❑ 66422	DRS
❑ 66423	DRS
❑ 66424	DRS
❑ 66425	DRS
❑ 66426	DRS
❑ 66427	DRS
❑ 66428	DRS
❑ 66429	DRS
❑ 66430	DRS
❑ 66431	DRS
❑ 66432	DRS
❑ 66433	DRS
❑ 66434	DRS
❑ 66501	FLR
❑ 66502	FLR
❑ 66503	FLR
❑ 66504	FLR
❑ 66505	FLR
❑ 66506	FLR
❑ 66507	FLR
❑ 66508	FLR
❑ 66509	FLR
❑ 66510	FLR
❑ 66511	FLR
❑ 66512	FLR
❑ 66513	FLR
❑ 66514	FLR
❑ 66515	FLR
❑ 66516	FLR
❑ 66517	FLR
❑ 66518	FLR
❑ 66519	FLR
❑ 66520	FLR
❑ 66522	FLR
❑ 66523	FLR
❑ 66524	FLR
❑ 66525	FLR
❑ 66526	FLR
❑ 66527	FLR
❑ 66528	FLR
❑ 66529	FLR
❑ 66530	FLR
❑ 66531	FLR
❑ 66532	FLR
❑ 66533	FLR
❑ 66534	FLR
❑ 66535	FLR
❑ 66536	FLR
❑ 66537	FLR
❑ 66538	FLR
❑ 66539	FLR
❑ 66540	FLR
❑ 66541	FLR
❑ 66542	FLR
❑ 66543	FLR
❑ 66544	FLR
❑ 66545	FLR
❑ 66546	FLR
❑ 66547	FLR
❑ 66548	FLR
❑ 66549	FLR
❑ 66550	FLR
❑ 66551	FLR
❑ 66552	FLR
❑ 66553	FLR
❑ 66554	FLR
❑ 66555	FLR
❑ 66556	FLR
❑ 66557	FLR
❑ 66558	FLR
❑ 66559	FLR
❑ 66560	FLR
❑ 66561	FLR
❑ 66562	FLR
❑ 66563	FLR
❑ 66564	FLR
❑ 66565	FLR
❑ 66566	FLR
❑ 66567	FLR
❑ 66568	FLR
❑ 66569	FLR
❑ 66570	FLR
❑ 66571	FLR
❑ 66572	FLR
❑ 66582	EXP
❑ 66583	EXP
❑ 66584	EXP
❑ 66585	FLR
❑ 66586	EXP
❑ 66587	FLR
❑ 66588	FLR
❑ 66589	FLR
❑ 66590	FLR
❑ 66591	FLR
❑ 66592	FLR
❑ 66593	FLR
❑ 66594	FLR
❑ 66595	FLR
❑ 66596	FLR
❑ 66597	FLR
❑ 66598	FLR

❑ 66599 FLR

❑ 66601 FLR
❑ 66602 FLR
❑ 66603 FLR
❑ 66604 FLR
❑ 66605 FLR
❑ 66606 FLR
❑ 66607 FLR
❑ 66608 EXP
❑ 66609 EXP
❑ 66610 FLR
❑ 66611 EXP
❑ 66612 EXP
❑ 66613 FLR
❑ 66614 FLR
❑ 66615 FLR
❑ 66616 FLR
❑ 66617 FLR
❑ 66618 FLR
❑ 66619 FLR
❑ 66620 FLR
❑ 66621 FLR
❑ 66622 FLR
❑ 66623 FLR
❑ 66624 EXP
❑ 66625 EXP

❑ 66701 GBR
❑ 66702 GBR
❑ 66703 GBR
❑ 66704 GBR
❑ 66705 GBR
❑ 66706 GBR
❑ 66707 GBR
❑ 66708 GBR
❑ 66709 GBR
❑ 66710 GBR
❑ 66711 GBR
❑ 66712 GBR
❑ 66713 GBR
❑ 66714 GBR
❑ 66715 GBR
❑ 66716 GBR
❑ 66717 GBR
❑ 66718 GBR
❑ 66719 GBR
❑ 66720 GBR
❑ 66721 GBR
❑ 66722 GBR
❑ 66723 GBR
❑ 66724 GBR
❑ 66725 GBR
❑ 66726 GBR
❑ 66727 GBR
❑ 66728 GBR
❑ 66729 GBR
❑ 66730 GBR
❑ 66731 GBR
❑ 66732 GBR
❑ 66733 GBR
❑ 66735 GBR
❑ 66736 GBR
❑ 66737 GBR
❑ 66738 GBR
❑ 66739 GBR
❑ 66740 GBR
❑ 66741 GBR
❑ 66742 GBR
❑ 66743 GBR
❑ 66744 GBR
❑ 66745 GBR
❑ 66746 GBR
❑ 66747 GBR
❑ 66748 GBR
❑ 66749 GBR
❑ 66750 GBR
❑ 66751 GBR
❑ 66752 GBR
❑ 66753 GBR
❑ 66754 GBR
❑ 66755 GBR
❑ 66756 GBR
❑ 66757 GBR
❑ 66758 GBR
❑ 66759 GBR

❑ 66846 COL
❑ 66847 COL
❑ 66848 COL
❑ 66849 COL
❑ 66850 COL

❑ 66951 FLR
❑ 66952 FLR
❑ 66953 FLR
❑ 66954 FLR
❑ 66955 FLR
❑ 66956 FLR
❑ 66957 FLR

❑ 67001 ATW
❑ 67002 ATW
❑ 67003 ATW
❑ 67004 DBS
❑ 67005 DBS
❑ 67006 DBS
❑ 67007 DBS
❑ 67008 DBS
❑ 67009 DBS
❑ 67010 CRW
❑ 67011 DBS
❑ 67012 CRW
❑ 67013 CRW
❑ 67014 CRW
❑ 67015 CRW
❑ 67016 DBS
❑ 67017 DBS
❑ 67018 DBS
❑ 67019 DBS
❑ 67020 DBS
❑ 67021 DBS
❑ 67022 DBS
❑ 67023 DBS
❑ 67024 DBS
❑ 67025 DBS
❑ 67026 DBS
❑ 67027 DBS
❑ 67028 DBS
❑ 67029 DBS
❑ 67030 DBS

❑ 68001 DRS
❑ 68002 DRS
❑ 68003 DRS
❑ 68004 DRS
❑ 68005 DRS
❑ 68006 DRS
❑ 68007 DRS
❑ 68008 DRS
❑ 68009 DRS
❑ 68010 DRS
❑ 68011 DRS
❑ 68012 DRS
❑ 68013 DRS
❑ 68014 DRS
❑ 68015 DRS
❑ 68016 DRS

❑ 70001 FLR
❑ 70002 FLR
❑ 70003 FLR
❑ 70004 FLR
❑ 70005 FLR
❑ 70006 FLR
❑ 70007 FLR
❑ 70008 FLR
❑ 70009 FLR
❑ 70010 FLR
❑ 70011 FLR
❑ 70013 FLR
❑ 70014 FLR
❑ 70015 FLR
❑ 70016 FLR
❑ 70017 FLR
❑ 70018 FLR
❑ 70019 FLR
❑ 70020 FLR

❑ 70801 COL
❑ 70802 COL
❑ 70803 COL
❑ 70804 COL
❑ 70805 COL
❑ 70806 COL
❑ 70807 COL
❑ 70808 COL
❑ 70809 COL
❑ 70810 COL

❑ 73001 PRE
❑ 73003 PRE
❑ 73005 PRE
❑ 73006 PRE

❑ 73101 RVE
❑ 73103 PRE
❑ 73104 RVE
❑ 73107 BAR
❑ 73109 201
❑ 73110 PRE
❑ 73114 PRE
❑ 73117 PRE
❑ 73118 TTS
❑ 73119 GBR
❑ 73128 PRE
❑ 73129 PRE
❑ 73130 PRE
❑ 73133 TTS
❑ 73134 PRE
❑ 73136 GBR
❑ 73138 NRL
❑ 73139 RVE
❑ 73140 PRE
❑ 73141 GBR

❑ 73201 BAR
❑ 73202 SOU
❑ 73204 GBR
❑ 73205 GBR
❑ 73206 GBR
❑ 73207 GBR
❑ 73208 GBR
❑ 73209 GBR
❑ 73210 PRE
❑ 73211 RVL
❑ 73212 GBR
❑ 73213 GBR
❑ 73235 SWT

❑ 73901 GBR
❑ 73902 GBR

❑ 77001 ECR
❑ 77002 ECR
❑ 77003 ECR
❑ 77004 ECR
❑ 77005 ECR
❑ 77006 ECR
❑ 77007 ECR
❑ 77008 ECR
❑ 77009 ECR
❑ 77010 ECR
❑ 77011 ECR
❑ 77012 ECR
❑ 77013 ECR
❑ 77014 ECR
❑ 77015 ECR
❑ 77016 ECR
❑ 77017 ECR
❑ 77018 ECR
❑ 77019 ECR
❑ 77020 ECR
❑ 77021 ECR
❑ 77022 ECR
❑ 77023 ECR
❑ 77024 ECR
❑ 77025 ECR
❑ 77026 ECR
❑ 77027 ECR
❑ 77028 ECR
❑ 77029 ECR
❑ 77030 ECR
❑ 77031 ECR
❑ 77032 ECR
❑ 77033 ECR
❑ 77034 ECR
❑ 77035 ECR
❑ 77036 ECR
❑ 77037 ECR
❑ 77038 ECR
❑ 77039 ECR
❑ 77040 ECR
❑ 77041 ECR
❑ 77042 ECR
❑ 77043 ECR
❑ 77044 ECR
❑ 77045 ECR
❑ 77046 ECR
❑ 77047 ECR
❑ 77048 ECR
❑ 77049 ECR
❑ 77050 ECR
❑ 77051 ECR
❑ 77052 ECR
❑ 77053 ECR
❑ 77054 ECR
❑ 77055 ECR
❑ 77056 ECR
❑ 77057 ECR
❑ 77058 ECR
❑ 77059 ECR
❑ 77060 ECR

❑ 81002 PRE

❑ 82008 PRE

❑ 83012 PRE

❑ 84001 PRE

❑ 85101 PRE

❑ 86101 ETL
❑ 86213 PRE
❑ 86215 EXP
❑ 86217 EXP
❑ 86218 EXP
❑ 86226 EPX
❑ 86228 EXP
❑ 86229 EPX
❑ 86231 EPX
❑ 86232 EPX
❑ 86233 EXP
❑ 86234 EPX
❑ 86235 EPX
❑ 86242 EXP
❑ 86246 EPX
❑ 86247 EPX
❑ 86248 EXP
❑ 86250 EXP
❑ 86251 EPX
❑ 86259 PRE
❑ 86401 ETL

❑ 86424 EXP
❑ 86501 FLR
❑ 86604 FLR
❑ 86605 FLR
❑ 86607 FLR
❑ 86609 FLR
❑ 86610 FLR
❑ 86612 FLR
❑ 86613 FLR
❑ 86614 FLR
❑ 86622 FLR
❑ 86627 FLR
❑ 86628 FLR
❑ 86632 FLR
❑ 86637 FLR
❑ 86638 FLR
❑ 86639 FLR
❑ 86701 ETL
❑ 86702 ETL
❑ 86901 NRL
❑ 86902 NRL

❑ 87001 PRE
❑ 87002 ETL
❑ 87003 EXP
❑ 87004 EXP
❑ 87006 EXP
❑ 87007 EXP
❑ 87008 EXP
❑ 87009 EXP
❑ 87010 EXP
❑ 87012 EXP
❑ 87013 EXP
❑ 87014 EXP
❑ 87017 EXP
❑ 87019 EXP
❑ 87020 EXP
❑ 87022 EXP
❑ 87023 EXP
❑ 87025 EXP
❑ 87026 EXP
❑ 87028 EXP
❑ 87029 EXP
❑ 87033 EXP
❑ 87034 EXP
❑ 87035 PRE

❑ 88001 DRS
❑ 88002 DRS
❑ 88003 DRS
❑ 88004 DRS
❑ 88005 DRS
❑ 88006 DRS
❑ 88007 DRS
❑ 88008 DRS
❑ 88009 DRS
❑ 88010 DRS

❑ 89001 PRE

❑ 90001 AEA
❑ 90002 AEA
❑ 90003 AEA
❑ 90004 AEA
❑ 90005 AEA
❑ 90006 AEA
❑ 90007 AEA
❑ 90008 AEA
❑ 90009 AEA
❑ 90010 AEA
❑ 90011 AEA
❑ 90012 AEA
❑ 90013 AEA
❑ 90014 AEA
❑ 90015 AEA
❑ 90016 FLR
❑ 90017 DBS
❑ 90018 DBS
❑ 90019 DBS
❑ 90020 DBS
❑ 90021 DBS
❑ 90022 DBS
❑ 90023 DBS
❑ 90024 DBS
❑ 90025 DBS
❑ 90026 DBS
❑ 90027 DBS
❑ 90028 DBS
❑ 90029 DBS
❑ 90030 DBS
❑ 90031 DBS
❑ 90032 DBS
❑ 90033 DBS
❑ 90034 DBS
❑ 90035 DBS
❑ 90036 DBS
❑ 90037 DBS
❑ 90038 DBS
❑ 90039 DBS
❑ 90040 DBS
❑ 90041 FLR
❑ 90042 FLR
❑ 90043 FLR
❑ 90044 FLR
❑ 90045 FLR
❑ 90046 FLR
❑ 90047 FLR
❑ 90048 FLR
❑ 90049 FLR
❑ 90050 DBS

❑ 91101 ICE
❑ 91102 ICE
❑ 91103 ICE
❑ 91104 ICE
❑ 91105 ICE
❑ 91106 ICE
❑ 91107 ICE
❑ 91108 ICE
❑ 91109 ICE
❑ 91110 ICE
❑ 91111 ICE
❑ 91112 ICE
❑ 91113 ICE
❑ 91114 ICE
❑ 91115 ICE
❑ 91116 ICE
❑ 91117 ICE
❑ 91118 ICE
❑ 91119 ICE
❑ 91120 ICE
❑ 91121 ICE
❑ 91122 ICE
❑ 91124 ICE
❑ 91125 ICE
❑ 91126 ICE
❑ 91127 ICE
❑ 91128 ICE
❑ 91129 ICE
❑ 91130 ICE
❑ 91131 ICE
❑ 91132 ICE

❑ 92001 EXP
❑ 92002 DBS
❑ 92003 DBS
❑ 92004 DBS
❑ 92005 DBS
❑ 92006 GBR
❑ 92007 DBS
❑ 92008 DBS
❑ 92009 DBS
❑ 92010 GRB
❑ 92011 DBS
❑ 92012 EXP
❑ 92013 DBS
❑ 92014 GBR
❑ 92015 DBS
❑ 92016 DBS
❑ 92017 DBS
❑ 92018 GBR
❑ 92019 DBS
❑ 92020 GBR
❑ 92021 GBR
❑ 92022 DBS
❑ 92023 GBR
❑ 92024 DBS
❑ 92025 EXP
❑ 92026 DBS
❑ 92027 EXP
❑ 92028 GBR
❑ 92029 DBS
❑ 92030 DBS
❑ 92031 DBS
❑ 92032 GBR
❑ 92033 GBR
❑ 92034 EXP
❑ 92035 DBS
❑ 92036 DBS
❑ 92037 DBS
❑ 92038 GBR
❑ 92039 DBS
❑ 92040 GBR
❑ 92041 DBS
❑ 92042 DBS
❑ 92043 GBR
❑ 92044 GBR
❑ 92045 GBR
❑ 92046 GBR

❑ 97301 NRL
❑ 97302 NRL
❑ 97303 NRL
❑ 97304 NRL

❑ 97650 PRE
❑ 97651 PRE
❑ 97654 PRE

❑ 323 539-7 AFG
❑ 323 674-2 AFG

❑ DH50-1 GBR
❑ DH50-2 GBR

❑ 8.701 GBR
❑ 8.702 GBR
❑ 8.703 GBR
❑ 8.704 GBR
❑ 8.708 GBR
❑ 8.711 GBR
❑ 8.712 GBR
❑ 8.716 GBR
❑ 8.717 GBR
❑ 8.718 GBR
❑ 8.719 GBR
❑ 8.720 GBR

Diesel Multiple Units

❑ APT-E PRE
❑ LEV1 PRE

❑ RB004 PRE

❑ 50015 PRE
❑ 50019 PRE
❑ 50222 PRE
❑ 50256 PRE
❑ 50338 PRE
❑ 50416 PRE
❑ 50447 PRE
❑ 50454 PRE
❑ 50455 PRE
❑ 50479 PRE
❑ 50494 PRE
❑ 50517 PRE
❑ 50528 PRE
❑ 50531 PRE
❑ 50547 PRE
❑ 50556 PRE
❑ 50599 PRE
❑ 50619 PRE
❑ 50632 PRE
❑ 50929 PRE
❑ 50980 PRE

❑ 51017 PRE
❑ 51043 PRE
❑ 51073 PRE
❑ 51074 PRE
❑ 51104 PRE
❑ 51131 PRE
❑ 51138 PRE
❑ 51151 PRE
❑ 51187 PRE
❑ 51188 PRE
❑ 51189 PRE
❑ 51192 PRE
❑ 51205 PRE
❑ 51210 PRE
❑ 51226 PRE
❑ 51228 PRE
❑ 51247 PRE
❑ 51321 PRE
❑ 51339 PRE
❑ 51342 PRE
❑ 51346 PRE
❑ 51347 PRE
❑ 51351 PRE
❑ 51353 PRE
❑ 51356 PRE
❑ 51359 PRE
❑ 51360 PRE
❑ 51363 PRE
❑ 51365 PRE
❑ 51367 PRE
❑ 51372 PRE
❑ 51381 PRE
❑ 51382 PRE
❑ 51384 PRE
❑ 51388 PRE
❑ 51392 PRE
❑ 51395 PRE
❑ 51397 PRE
❑ 51398 PRE
❑ 51400 PRE
❑ 51401 PRE
❑ 51402 PRE
❑ 51405 PRE
❑ 51407 PRE
❑ 51427 PRE
❑ 51432 PRE
❑ 51434 PRE
❑ 51485 PRE
❑ 51498 PRE
❑ 51499 PRE
❑ 51503 PRE
❑ 51505 PRE
❑ 51511 PRE
❑ 51512 PRE
❑ 51513 PRE
❑ 51562 PRE
❑ 51565 PRE
❑ 51566 PRE
❑ 51567 PRE
❑ 51568 PRE
❑ 51571 PRE
❑ 51572 PRE
❑ 51604 PRE
❑ 51616 PRE
❑ 51618 PRE
❑ 51622 PRE
❑ 51655 PRE
❑ 51663 PRE
❑ 51669 PRE

Number	Operator
❑ 51677	PRE
❑ 51803	PRE
❑ 51813	PRE
❑ 51842	PRE
❑ 51859	PRE
❑ 51880	PRE
❑ 51886	PRE
❑ 51887	PRE
❑ 51899	PRE
❑ 51907	PRE
❑ 51909	PRE
❑ 51914	PRE
❑ 51919	PRE
❑ 51922	PRE
❑ 51933	PRE
❑ 51941	PRE
❑ 51942	PRE
❑ 51947	PRE
❑ 51950	PRE
❑ 51973	PRE
❑ 51990	PRE
❑ 52005	PRE
❑ 52006	PRE
❑ 52008	PRE
❑ 52025	PRE
❑ 52030	PRE
❑ 52044	PRE
❑ 52048	PRE
❑ 52053	PRE
❑ 52054	PRE
❑ 52062	PRE
❑ 52064	PRE
❑ 52071	PRE
❑ 52077	PRE
❑ 53160	PRE
❑ 53164	PRE
❑ 53170	PRE
❑ 53193	PRE
❑ 53203	PRE
❑ 53204	PRE
❑ 53253	PRE
❑ 53266	PRE
❑ 53321	PRE
❑ 53628	PRE
❑ 53645	PRE
❑ 53746	PRE
❑ 53926	PRE
❑ 53971	PRE
❑ 54055	PRE
❑ 54057	PRE
❑ 54062	PRE
❑ 54223	PRE
❑ 54270	PRE
❑ 54279	PRE
❑ 54289	PRE
❑ 54365	PRE
❑ 54408	PRE
❑ 54490	PRE
❑ 54504	PRE
❑ 55000	PRE
❑ 55001	PRE
❑ 55003	PRE
❑ 55005	PRE
❑ 55006	PRE
❑ 55009	PRE
❑ 55012	PRE
❑ 55020	CRW
❑ 55023	PRE
❑ 55028	PRE
❑ 55029	PRE
❑ 55032	CRW
❑ 55033	PRE
❑ 55034	CRW
❑ 55966	PRE
❑ 55976	PRE
❑ 56006	PRE
❑ 56015	PRE
❑ 56121	PRE
❑ 56171	PRE
❑ 56182	PRE
❑ 56208	PRE
❑ 56224	PRE
❑ 56271	PRE
❑ 56287	PRE
❑ 56301	PRE
❑ 56343	PRE
❑ 56352	PRE
❑ 56358	PRE
❑ 56456	PRE
❑ 56484	PRE
❑ 56491	PRE
❑ 56492	PRE
❑ 56495	PRE
❑ 59003	PRE
❑ 59004	PRE
❑ 59117	PRE
❑ 59137	PRE
❑ 59228	PRE
❑ 59245	PRE
❑ 59250	PRE
❑ 59276	PRE
❑ 59387	PRE
❑ 59389	PRE
❑ 59404	PRE
❑ 59444	PRE
❑ 59486	PRE
❑ 59488	PRE
❑ 59492	PRE
❑ 59494	PRE
❑ 59500	PRE
❑ 59503	PRE
❑ 59506	PRE
❑ 59507	PRE
❑ 59508	PRE
❑ 59509	PRE
❑ 59510	PRE
❑ 59513	PRE
❑ 59514	PRE
❑ 59515	PRE
❑ 59516	PRE
❑ 59517	PRE
❑ 59520	PRE
❑ 59521	PRE
❑ 59522	PRE
❑ 59539	PRE
❑ 59575	PRE
❑ 59603	PRE
❑ 59609	PRE
❑ 59659	PRE
❑ 59664	PRE
❑ 59678	PRE
❑ 59701	PRE
❑ 59719	PRE
❑ 59740	PRE
❑ 59761	PRE
❑ 59791	PRE
❑ 60000	HDL
❑ 60019	HDL
❑ 60116	HDL
❑ 60117	PRE
❑ 60118	HDL
❑ 60127	PRE
❑ 60130	PRE
❑ 60138	PRE
❑ 60142	PRE
❑ 60145	PRE
❑ 60149	PRE
❑ 60154	PRE
❑ 60501	HDL
❑ 60528	HDL
❑ 60529	HDL
❑ 60616	PRE
❑ 60750	PRE
❑ 60800	PRE
❑ 60822	PRE
❑ 60828	PRE
❑ 60901	PRE
❑ 60904	PRE
❑ 60916	PRE
❑ 69337	HDL
❑ 70262	HDL
❑ 70549	PRE
❑ 79018	PRE
❑ 79443	PRE
❑ 79612	PRE
❑ 79900	PRE
❑ 79960	PRE
❑ 79962	PRE
❑ 79963	PRE
❑ 79964	PRE
❑ 79976	PRE
❑ 79978	PRE
❑ 121019	PRE
❑ 121020	CRW
❑ 121024	PRE
❑ 121032	CRW
❑ 121034	CRW
❑ 139001	LMI
❑ 139002	LMI
❑ 140001	PRE
❑ 141103	PRE
❑ 141108	PRE
❑ 141110	PRE
❑ 141113	PRE
❑ 142001	NOR
❑ 142002	ATW
❑ 142003	NOR
❑ 142004	NOR
❑ 142005	NOR
❑ 142006	ATW
❑ 142007	NOR
❑ 142009	NOR
❑ 142010	ATW
❑ 142011	NOR
❑ 142012	NOR
❑ 142013	NOR
❑ 142014	NOR
❑ 142015	NOR
❑ 142016	NOR
❑ 142017	NOR
❑ 142018	NOR
❑ 142019	NOR
❑ 142020	NOR
❑ 142021	NOR
❑ 142022	NOR
❑ 142023	NOR
❑ 142024	NOR
❑ 142025	NOR
❑ 142026	NOR
❑ 142027	NOR
❑ 142028	NOR
❑ 142029	NOR
❑ 142030	NOR
❑ 142031	NOR
❑ 142032	NOR
❑ 142033	NOR
❑ 142034	NOR
❑ 142035	NOR
❑ 142036	NOR
❑ 142037	NOR
❑ 142038	NOR
❑ 142039	NOR
❑ 142040	NOR
❑ 142041	NOR
❑ 142042	NOR
❑ 142043	NOR
❑ 142044	NOR
❑ 142045	NOR
❑ 142046	NOR
❑ 142047	NOR
❑ 142048	NOR
❑ 142049	NOR
❑ 142050	NOR
❑ 142051	NOR
❑ 142052	NOR
❑ 142053	NOR
❑ 142054	NOR
❑ 142055	NOR
❑ 142056	NOR
❑ 142057	NOR
❑ 142058	NOR
❑ 142060	NOR
❑ 142061	NOR
❑ 142062	NOR
❑ 142063	NOR
❑ 142064	NOR
❑ 142065	NOR
❑ 142066	NOR
❑ 142067	NOR
❑ 142068	NOR
❑ 142069	ATW
❑ 142070	NOR
❑ 142071	NOR
❑ 142072	ATW
❑ 142073	ATW
❑ 142074	ATW
❑ 142075	ATW
❑ 142076	ATW
❑ 142077	ATW
❑ 142078	NOR
❑ 142079	NOR
❑ 142080	ATW
❑ 142081	ATW
❑ 142082	ATW
❑ 142083	ATW
❑ 142084	NOR
❑ 142085	ATW
❑ 142086	NOR
❑ 142087	NOR
❑ 142088	NOR
❑ 142089	NOR
❑ 142090	NOR
❑ 142091	NOR
❑ 142092	NOR
❑ 142093	NOR
❑ 142094	NOR
❑ 142095	NOR
❑ 142096	NOR
❑ 143601	ATW
❑ 143602	ATW
❑ 143603	FGW
❑ 143604	ATW
❑ 143605	ATW
❑ 143606	ATW
❑ 143607	ATW
❑ 143608	ATW
❑ 143609	ATW
❑ 143610	ATW
❑ 143611	FGW
❑ 143612	FGW
❑ 143614	ATW
❑ 143616	ATW
❑ 143617	FGW
❑ 143618	FGW
❑ 143619	FGW
❑ 143620	FGW
❑ 143621	FGW
❑ 143622	ATW
❑ 143623	ATW
❑ 143624	ATW

❑ 143625 ATW

❑ 144001 NOR
❑ 144002 NOR
❑ 144003 NOR
❑ 144004 NOR
❑ 144005 NOR
❑ 144006 NOR
❑ 144007 NOR
❑ 144008 NOR
❑ 144009 NOR
❑ 144010 NOR
❑ 144011 NOR
❑ 144012 NOR
❑ 144013 NOR
❑ 144014 NOR
❑ 144015 NOR
❑ 144016 NOR
❑ 144017 NOR
❑ 144018 NOR
❑ 144019 NOR
❑ 144020 NOR
❑ 144021 NOR
❑ 144022 NOR
❑ 144023 NOR

❑ 150001 FGW
❑ 150002 FGW

❑ 150101 FGW
❑ 150102 FGW
❑ 150103 NOR
❑ 150104 FGW
❑ 150105 LMI
❑ 150106 FGW
❑ 150107 LMI
❑ 150108 FGW
❑ 150109 LMI
❑ 150110 NOR
❑ 150111 NOR
❑ 150112 NOR
❑ 150113 NOR
❑ 150114 NOR
❑ 150115 NOR
❑ 150116 NOR
❑ 150117 NOR
❑ 150118 NOR
❑ 150119 NOR
❑ 150120 FGW
❑ 150122 FGW
❑ 150123 FGW
❑ 150124 FGW
❑ 150125 FGW
❑ 150126 FGW
❑ 150128 FGW
❑ 150129 FGW
❑ 150130 FGW
❑ 150131 FGW
❑ 150132 NOR
❑ 150133 NOR
❑ 150134 NOR
❑ 150135 NOR
❑ 150136 NOR
❑ 150137 NOR
❑ 150138 NOR
❑ 150139 NOR
❑ 150140 NOR
❑ 150141 NOR
❑ 150142 NOR
❑ 150143 NOR
❑ 150144 NOR
❑ 150145 NOR
❑ 150146 NOR
❑ 150147 NOR
❑ 150148 NOR
❑ 150149 NOR
❑ 150150 NOR

❑ 150201 NOR
❑ 150202 FGW
❑ 150203 NOR
❑ 150205 NOR
❑ 150207 NOR
❑ 150208 ATW
❑ 150210 NOR
❑ 150211 NOR
❑ 150213 ATW
❑ 150214 NOR
❑ 150215 NOR
❑ 150216 FGW
❑ 150217 ATW
❑ 150218 NOR
❑ 150219 FGW
❑ 150220 NOR
❑ 150221 FGW
❑ 150222 NOR
❑ 150223 NOR
❑ 150224 NOR
❑ 150225 NOR
❑ 150226 NOR
❑ 150227 ATW
❑ 150228 NOR
❑ 150229 ATW
❑ 150230 ATW
❑ 150231 ATW
❑ 150232 FGW
❑ 150233 FGW
❑ 150234 FGW
❑ 150235 ATW
❑ 150236 ATW
❑ 150237 ATW
❑ 150238 FGW
❑ 150239 FGW
❑ 150240 ATW
❑ 150241 ATW
❑ 150242 ATW
❑ 150243 FGW
❑ 150244 FGW
❑ 150245 ATW
❑ 150246 FGW
❑ 150247 FGW
❑ 150248 FGW
❑ 150249 FGW
❑ 150250 ATW
❑ 150251 ATW
❑ 150252 ATW
❑ 150253 ATW
❑ 150254 ATW
❑ 150255 ATW
❑ 150256 ATW
❑ 150257 ATW
❑ 150258 ATW
❑ 150259 ATW
❑ 150260 ATW
❑ 150261 FGW
❑ 150262 ATW
❑ 150263 FGW
❑ 150264 ATW
❑ 150265 FGW
❑ 150266 FGW
❑ 150267 ATW
❑ 150268 NOR
❑ 150269 NOR
❑ 150270 NOR
❑ 150271 NOR
❑ 150272 NOR
❑ 150273 NOR
❑ 150274 NOR
❑ 150275 NOR
❑ 150276 NOR
❑ 150277 NOR
❑ 150278 ATW
❑ 150279 ATW
❑ 150280 ATW
❑ 150281 ATW
❑ 150282 ATW
❑ 150283 ATW
❑ 150284 ATW
❑ 150285 ATW

❑ 150921 FGW
❑ 150927 FGW

❑ 153301 NOR
❑ 153302 EMT
❑ 153303 ATW
❑ 153304 NOR
❑ 153305 FGW
❑ 153306 AEA
❑ 153307 NOR
❑ 153308 EMT
❑ 153309 AEA
❑ 153310 EMT
❑ 153311 EMT
❑ 153312 ATW
❑ 153313 EMT
❑ 153314 AEA
❑ 153315 NOR
❑ 153316 NOR
❑ 153317 NOR
❑ 153318 FGW
❑ 153319 EMT
❑ 153320 ATW
❑ 153321 EMT
❑ 153322 AEA
❑ 153323 ATW
❑ 153324 NOR
❑ 153325 FGW
❑ 153326 EMT
❑ 153327 ATW
❑ 153328 NOR
❑ 153329 FGW
❑ 153330 NOR
❑ 153331 NOR
❑ 153332 NOR
❑ 153333 FGW
❑ 153334 LMI
❑ 153335 AEA
❑ 153351 NOR
❑ 153352 NOR
❑ 153353 ATW
❑ 153354 LMI
❑ 153355 EMT
❑ 153356 LMI
❑ 153357 EMT
❑ 153358 NOR
❑ 153359 NOR
❑ 153360 NOR
❑ 153361 FGW
❑ 153362 ATW
❑ 153363 NOR
❑ 153364 LMI
❑ 153365 LMI
❑ 153366 LMI
❑ 153367 ATW
❑ 153368 FGW
❑ 153369 FGW
❑ 153370 FGW
❑ 153371 LMI
❑ 153372 FGW
❑ 153373 FGW
❑ 153374 EMT
❑ 153375 LMI
❑ 153376 EMT
❑ 153377 FGW
❑ 153378 NOR
❑ 153379 EMT
❑ 153380 FGW
❑ 153381 EMT
❑ 153382 FGW
❑ 153383 EMT
❑ 153384 EMT
❑ 153385 EMT

❑ 155341 NOR
❑ 155342 NOR
❑ 155343 NOR
❑ 155344 NOR
❑ 155345 NOR
❑ 155346 NOR
❑ 155347 NOR

❑ 156401 EMT
❑ 156402 AEA
❑ 156403 EMT
❑ 156404 EMT
❑ 156405 EMT
❑ 156406 EMT
❑ 156407 AEA
❑ 156408 EMT
❑ 156409 AEA
❑ 156410 EMT
❑ 156411 EMT
❑ 156412 AEA
❑ 156413 EMT
❑ 156414 EMT
❑ 156415 EMT
❑ 156416 AEA
❑ 156417 AEA
❑ 156418 AEA
❑ 156419 AEA
❑ 156420 NOR
❑ 156421 NOR
❑ 156422 AEA
❑ 156423 NOR
❑ 156424 NOR
❑ 156425 NOR
❑ 156426 NOR
❑ 156427 NOR
❑ 156428 NOR
❑ 156429 NOR
❑ 156430 FSR
❑ 156431 FSR
❑ 156432 FSR
❑ 156433 FSR
❑ 156434 FSR
❑ 156435 FSR
❑ 156436 FSR
❑ 156437 FSR
❑ 156438 NOR
❑ 156439 FSR
❑ 156440 NOR
❑ 156441 NOR
❑ 156442 FSR
❑ 156443 NOR
❑ 156444 NOR
❑ 156445 FSR
❑ 156446 FSR
❑ 156447 FSR
❑ 156448 NOR
❑ 156449 FSR
❑ 156450 FSR
❑ 156451 NOR
❑ 156452 NOR
❑ 156453 FSR
❑ 156454 NOR
❑ 156455 NOR
❑ 156456 FSR
❑ 156457 FSR
❑ 156458 FSR
❑ 156459 NOR
❑ 156460 NOR
❑ 156461 NOR
❑ 156462 FSR
❑ 156463 NOR
❑ 156464 NOR
❑ 156465 FSR
❑ 156466 NOR
❑ 156467 FSR
❑ 156468 NOR
❑ 156469 NOR
❑ 156470 EMT
❑ 156471 NOR
❑ 156472 NOR
❑ 156473 EMT

❑ 156474 FSR
❑ 156475 NOR
❑ 156476 FSR
❑ 156477 FSR
❑ 156478 FSR
❑ 156479 NOR
❑ 156480 NOR
❑ 156481 NOR
❑ 156482 NOR
❑ 156483 NOR
❑ 156484 NOR
❑ 156485 FSR
❑ 156486 NOR
❑ 156487 NOR
❑ 156488 NOR
❑ 156489 NOR
❑ 156490 NOR
❑ 156491 NOR
❑ 156492 FSR
❑ 156493 FSR
❑ 156494 FSR
❑ 156495 FSR
❑ 156496 FSR
❑ 156497 EMT
❑ 156498 EMT
❑ 156499 FSR
❑ 156500 FSR
❑ 156501 FSR
❑ 156502 FSR
❑ 156503 FSR
❑ 156504 FSR
❑ 156505 FSR
❑ 156506 FSR
❑ 156507 FSR
❑ 156508 FSR
❑ 156509 FSR
❑ 156510 FSR
❑ 156511 FSR
❑ 156512 FSR
❑ 156513 FSR
❑ 156514 FSR

❑ 158701 FSR
❑ 158702 FSR
❑ 158703 FSR
❑ 158704 FSR
❑ 158705 FSR
❑ 158706 FSR
❑ 158707 FSR
❑ 158708 FSR
❑ 158709 FSR
❑ 158710 FSR
❑ 158711 FSR
❑ 158712 FSR
❑ 158713 FSR
❑ 158714 FSR
❑ 158715 FSR
❑ 158716 FSR
❑ 158717 FSR
❑ 158718 FSR
❑ 158719 FSR
❑ 158720 FSR
❑ 158721 FSR
❑ 158722 FSR
❑ 158723 FSR
❑ 158724 FSR
❑ 158725 FSR
❑ 158726 FSR
❑ 158727 FSR
❑ 158728 FSR
❑ 158729 FSR
❑ 158730 FSR
❑ 158731 FSR
❑ 158732 FSR
❑ 158733 FSR
❑ 158734 FSR
❑ 158735 FSR
❑ 158736 FSR
❑ 158737 FSR
❑ 158738 FSR
❑ 158739 FSR
❑ 158740 FSR
❑ 158741 FSR
❑ 158752 NOR
❑ 158753 NOR
❑ 158754 NOR
❑ 158755 NOR
❑ 158756 NOR
❑ 158757 NOR
❑ 158758 NOR
❑ 158759 NOR
❑ 158763 FGW
❑ 158766 FGW
❑ 158770 EMT
❑ 158773 EMT
❑ 158774 EMT
❑ 158777 EMT
❑ 158780 EMT
❑ 158782 FSR
❑ 158783 EMT
❑ 158784 NOR
❑ 158785 EMT
❑ 158786 FSR
❑ 158787 NOR
❑ 158788 EMT
❑ 158789 FSR
❑ 158790 NOR
❑ 158791 NOR
❑ 158792 NOR
❑ 158793 NOR
❑ 158794 NOR
❑ 158795 NOR
❑ 158796 NOR
❑ 158797 NOR
❑ 158798 FGW
❑ 158799 EMT

❑ 158806 EMT
❑ 158810 EMT
❑ 158812 EMT
❑ 158813 EMT
❑ 158815 NOR
❑ 158816 NOR
❑ 158817 NOR
❑ 158818 ATW
❑ 158819 ATW
❑ 158820 ATW
❑ 158821 ATW
❑ 158822 ATW
❑ 158823 ATW
❑ 158824 ATW
❑ 158825 ATW
❑ 158826 ATW
❑ 158827 ATW
❑ 158828 ATW
❑ 158829 ATW
❑ 158830 ATW
❑ 158831 ATW
❑ 158832 ATW
❑ 158833 ATW
❑ 158834 ATW
❑ 158835 ATW
❑ 158836 ATW
❑ 158837 ATW
❑ 158838 ATW
❑ 158839 ATW
❑ 158840 ATW
❑ 158841 ATW
❑ 158842 NOR
❑ 158843 NOR
❑ 158844 NOR
❑ 158845 NOR
❑ 158846 EMT
❑ 158847 EMT
❑ 158848 NOR
❑ 158849 NOR
❑ 158850 NOR
❑ 158851 NOR
❑ 158852 EMT
❑ 158853 NOR
❑ 158854 EMT
❑ 158855 NOR
❑ 158856 EMT
❑ 158857 EMT
❑ 158858 EMT
❑ 158859 NOR
❑ 158860 NOR
❑ 158861 NOR
❑ 158862 EMT
❑ 158863 EMT
❑ 158864 EMT
❑ 158865 EMT
❑ 158866 EMT
❑ 158867 FSR
❑ 158868 FSR
❑ 158869 FSR
❑ 158870 FSR
❑ 158871 FSR
❑ 158872 NOR
❑ 158880 SWT
❑ 158881 SWT
❑ 158882 SWT
❑ 158883 SWT
❑ 158884 SWT
❑ 158885 SWT
❑ 158886 SWT
❑ 158887 SWT
❑ 158888 SWT
❑ 158889 SWT
❑ 158890 SWT
❑ 158901 NOR
❑ 158902 NOR
❑ 158903 NOR
❑ 158904 NOR
❑ 158905 NOR
❑ 158906 NOR
❑ 158907 NOR
❑ 158908 NOR
❑ 158909 NOR
❑ 158910 NOR
❑ 158950 FGW
❑ 158951 FGW
❑ 158952 FGW
❑ 158953 FGW
❑ 158954 FGW
❑ 158955 FGW
❑ 158956 FGW
❑ 158957 FGW
❑ 158958 FGW
❑ 158959 FGW
❑ 158960 FGW
❑ 158961 FGW

❑ 159001 SWT
❑ 159002 SWT
❑ 159003 SWT
❑ 159004 SWT
❑ 159005 SWT
❑ 159006 SWT
❑ 159007 SWT
❑ 159008 SWT
❑ 159009 SWT
❑ 159010 SWT
❑ 159011 SWT
❑ 159012 SWT
❑ 159013 SWT
❑ 159014 SWT
❑ 159015 SWT
❑ 159016 SWT
❑ 159017 SWT
❑ 159018 SWT
❑ 159019 SWT
❑ 159020 SWT
❑ 159021 SWT
❑ 159022 SWT

❑ 159101 SWT
❑ 159102 SWT
❑ 159103 SWT
❑ 159104 SWT
❑ 159105 SWT
❑ 159106 SWT
❑ 159107 SWT
❑ 159108 SWT

❑ 165001 CRW
❑ 165002 CRW
❑ 165003 CRW
❑ 165004 CRW
❑ 165005 CRW
❑ 165006 CRW
❑ 165007 CRW
❑ 165008 CRW
❑ 165009 CRW
❑ 165010 CRW
❑ 165011 CRW
❑ 165012 CRW
❑ 165013 CRW
❑ 165014 CRW
❑ 165015 CRW
❑ 165016 CRW
❑ 165017 CRW
❑ 165018 CRW
❑ 165019 CRW
❑ 165020 CRW
❑ 165021 CRW
❑ 165022 CRW
❑ 165023 CRW
❑ 165024 CRW
❑ 165025 CRW
❑ 165026 CRW
❑ 165027 CRW
❑ 165028 CRW
❑ 165029 CRW
❑ 165030 CRW
❑ 165031 CRW
❑ 165032 CRW
❑ 165033 CRW
❑ 165034 CRW
❑ 165035 CRW
❑ 165036 CRW
❑ 165037 CRW
❑ 165038 CRW
❑ 165039 CRW

❑ 165101 FGW
❑ 165102 FGW
❑ 165103 FGW
❑ 165104 FGW
❑ 165105 FGW
❑ 165106 FGW
❑ 165107 FGW
❑ 165108 FGW
❑ 165109 FGW
❑ 165110 FGW
❑ 165111 FGW
❑ 165112 FGW
❑ 165113 FGW
❑ 165114 FGW
❑ 165116 FGW
❑ 165117 FGW
❑ 165118 FGW
❑ 165119 FGW
❑ 165120 FGW
❑ 165121 FGW
❑ 165122 FGW
❑ 165123 FGW
❑ 165124 FGW
❑ 165125 FGW
❑ 165126 FGW
❑ 165127 FGW
❑ 165128 FGW
❑ 165129 FGW
❑ 165130 FGW
❑ 165131 FGW

❑ 165132 FGW
❑ 165133 FGW
❑ 165134 FGW
❑ 165135 FGW
❑ 165136 FGW
❑ 165137 FGW

❑ 166201 FGW
❑ 166202 FGW
❑ 166203 FGW
❑ 166204 FGW
❑ 166205 FGW
❑ 166206 FGW
❑ 166207 FGW
❑ 166208 FGW
❑ 166209 FGW
❑ 166210 FGW
❑ 166211 FGW
❑ 166212 FGW
❑ 166213 FGW
❑ 166214 FGW
❑ 166215 FGW
❑ 166216 FGW
❑ 166217 FGW
❑ 166218 FGW
❑ 166219 FGW
❑ 166220 FGW
❑ 166221 FGW

❑ 168001 CRW
❑ 168002 CRW
❑ 168003 CRW
❑ 168004 CRW
❑ 168005 CRW

❑ 168106 CRW
❑ 168107 CRW
❑ 168108 CRW
❑ 168109 CRW
❑ 168110 CRW
❑ 168111 CRW
❑ 168112 CRW
❑ 168113 CRW

❑ 168214 CRW
❑ 168215 CRW
❑ 168216 CRW
❑ 168217 CRW
❑ 168218 CRW
❑ 168219 CRW

❑ 170101 AXC
❑ 170102 AXC
❑ 170103 AXC
❑ 170104 AXC
❑ 170105 AXC
❑ 170106 AXC
❑ 170107 AXC
❑ 170108 AXC
❑ 170109 AXC
❑ 170110 AXC
❑ 170111 AXC
❑ 170112 AXC
❑ 170113 AXC
❑ 170114 AXC
❑ 170115 AXC
❑ 170116 AXC
❑ 170117 AXC
❑ 170201 AEA
❑ 170202 AEA
❑ 170203 AEA
❑ 170204 AEA
❑ 170205 AEA
❑ 170206 AEA
❑ 170207 AEA
❑ 170208 AEA
❑ 170270 AEA
❑ 170271 AEA
❑ 170272 AEA
❑ 170273 AEA
❑ 170301 FTP
❑ 170302 FTP
❑ 170303 FTP
❑ 170304 FTP
❑ 170305 FTP
❑ 170306 FTP
❑ 170307 FTP
❑ 170308 FTP
❑ 170309 FTP
❑ 170393 FSR
❑ 170394 FSR
❑ 170395 FSR
❑ 170396 FSR
❑ 170397 AXC
❑ 170398 AXC
❑ 170401 FSR
❑ 170402 FSR
❑ 170403 FSR
❑ 170404 FSR
❑ 170405 FSR
❑ 170406 FSR
❑ 170407 FSR
❑ 170408 FSR
❑ 170409 FSR
❑ 170410 FSR
❑ 170411 FSR
❑ 170412 FSR
❑ 170413 FSR
❑ 170414 FSR
❑ 170415 FSR
❑ 170416 FSR
❑ 170417 FSR
❑ 170418 FSR
❑ 170419 FSR
❑ 170420 FSR
❑ 170421 FSR
❑ 170422 FSR
❑ 170423 FSR
❑ 170424 FSR
❑ 170425 FSR
❑ 170426 FSR
❑ 170427 FSR
❑ 170428 FSR
❑ 170429 FSR
❑ 170430 FSR
❑ 170431 FSR
❑ 170432 FSR
❑ 170433 FSR
❑ 170434 FSR
❑ 170450 FSR
❑ 170451 FSR
❑ 170452 FSR
❑ 170453 FSR
❑ 170454 FSR
❑ 170455 FSR
❑ 170456 FSR
❑ 170457 FSR
❑ 170458 FSR
❑ 170459 FSR
❑ 170460 FSR
❑ 170461 FSR
❑ 170470 FSR
❑ 170471 FSR
❑ 170472 FSR
❑ 170473 FSR
❑ 170474 FSR
❑ 170475 FSR
❑ 170476 FSR
❑ 170477 FSR
❑ 170478 FSR
❑ 170501 LMI
❑ 170502 LMI
❑ 170503 LMI
❑ 170504 LMI
❑ 170505 LMI
❑ 170506 LMI
❑ 170507 LMI
❑ 170508 LMI
❑ 170509 LMI
❑ 170510 LMI
❑ 170511 LMI
❑ 170512 LMI
❑ 170513 LMI
❑ 170514 LMI
❑ 170515 LMI
❑ 170516 LMI
❑ 170517 LMI
❑ 170518 AXC
❑ 170519 AXC
❑ 170520 AXC
❑ 170521 AXC
❑ 170522 AXC
❑ 170523 AXC
❑ 170630 LMI
❑ 170631 LMI
❑ 170632 LMI
❑ 170633 LMI
❑ 170634 LMI
❑ 170635 LMI
❑ 170636 AXC
❑ 170637 AXC
❑ 170638 AXC
❑ 170639 AXC

❑ 171721 SOU
❑ 171722 SOU
❑ 171723 SOU
❑ 171724 SOU
❑ 171725 SOU
❑ 171726 SOU
❑ 171727 SOU
❑ 171728 SOU
❑ 171729 SOU
❑ 171730 SOU
❑ 171801 SOU
❑ 171802 SOU
❑ 171803 SOU
❑ 171804 SOU
❑ 171805 SOU
❑ 171806 SOU
❑ 172001 LOG
❑ 172002 LOG
❑ 172003 LOG
❑ 172004 LOG
❑ 172005 LOG
❑ 172006 LOG
❑ 172007 LOG
❑ 172008 LOG

❑ 172101 CRW
❑ 172102 CRW
❑ 172103 CRW
❑ 172104 CRW

❑ 172211 LMI
❑ 172212 LMI
❑ 172213 LMI
❑ 172214 LMI
❑ 172215 LMI
❑ 172216 LMI
❑ 172217 LMI
❑ 172218 LMI
❑ 172219 LMI
❑ 172220 LMI
❑ 172221 LMI
❑ 172222 LMI

❑ 172331 LMI
❑ 172332 LMI
❑ 172333 LMI
❑ 172334 LMI
❑ 172335 LMI
❑ 172336 LMI
❑ 172337 LMI
❑ 172338 LMI
❑ 172339 LMI
❑ 172340 LMI
❑ 172341 LMI
❑ 172342 LMI
❑ 172343 LMI
❑ 172344 LMI
❑ 172345 LMI

❑ 175001 ATW
❑ 175002 ATW
❑ 175003 ATW
❑ 175004 ATW
❑ 175005 ATW
❑ 175006 ATW
❑ 175007 ATW
❑ 175008 ATW
❑ 175009 ATW
❑ 175010 ATW
❑ 175011 ATW

❑ 175101 ATW
❑ 175102 ATW
❑ 175103 ATW
❑ 175104 ATW
❑ 175105 ATW
❑ 175106 ATW
❑ 175107 ATW
❑ 175108 ATW
❑ 175109 ATW
❑ 175110 ATW
❑ 175111 ATW
❑ 175112 ATW
❑ 175113 ATW
❑ 175114 ATW
❑ 175115 ATW
❑ 175116 ATW

❑ 180101 GTL
❑ 180102 FGW
❑ 180103 FGW
❑ 180104 FGW
❑ 180105 GTL
❑ 180106 FGW
❑ 180107 GTL
❑ 180108 FGW
❑ 180109 FHT
❑ 180110 FHT
❑ 180111 FHT
❑ 180112 GTL
❑ 180113 FHT
❑ 180114 GTL

❑ 185101 FTP
❑ 185102 FTP
❑ 185103 FTP
❑ 185104 FTP
❑ 185105 FTP
❑ 185106 FTP
❑ 185107 FTP
❑ 185108 FTP
❑ 185109 FTP
❑ 185110 FTP
❑ 185111 FTP
❑ 185112 FTP
❑ 185113 FTP
❑ 185114 FTP
❑ 185115 FTP
❑ 185116 FTP
❑ 185117 FTP
❑ 185118 FTP
❑ 185119 FTP
❑ 185120 FTP
❑ 185121 FTP
❑ 185122 FTP
❑ 185123 FTP
❑ 185124 FTP
❑ 185125 FTP
❑ 185126 FTP
❑ 185127 FTP
❑ 185128 FTP

❑ 185129 FTP
❑ 185130 FTP
❑ 185131 FTP
❑ 185132 FTP
❑ 185133 FTP
❑ 185134 FTP
❑ 185135 FTP
❑ 185136 FTP
❑ 185137 FTP
❑ 185138 FTP
❑ 185139 FTP
❑ 185140 FTP
❑ 185141 FTP
❑ 185142 FTP
❑ 185143 FTP
❑ 185144 FTP
❑ 185145 FTP
❑ 185146 FTP
❑ 185147 FTP
❑ 185148 FTP
❑ 185149 FTP
❑ 185150 FTP
❑ 185151 FTP

❑ 202202 PRE

❑ 205009 PRE
❑ 205025 PRE
❑ 205028 PRE
❑ 205032 PRE
❑ 205033 PRE
❑ 205101 PRE
❑ 205205 PRE

❑ 220001 AXC
❑ 220002 AXC
❑ 220003 AXC
❑ 220004 AXC
❑ 220005 AXC
❑ 220006 AXC
❑ 220007 AXC
❑ 220008 AXC
❑ 220009 AXC
❑ 220010 AXC
❑ 220011 AXC
❑ 220012 AXC
❑ 220013 AXC
❑ 220014 AXC
❑ 220015 AXC
❑ 220016 AXC
❑ 220017 AXC
❑ 220018 AXC
❑ 220019 AXC
❑ 220020 AXC
❑ 220021 AXC
❑ 220022 AXC
❑ 220023 AXC
❑ 220024 AXC
❑ 220025 AXC
❑ 220026 AXC
❑ 220027 AXC
❑ 220028 AXC
❑ 220029 AXC
❑ 220030 AXC
❑ 220031 AXC
❑ 220032 AXC
❑ 220033 AXC
❑ 220034 AXC

❑ 221101 VWC
❑ 221102 VWC
❑ 221103 VWC
❑ 221104 VWC
❑ 221105 VWC
❑ 221106 VWC
❑ 221107 VWC
❑ 221108 VWC
❑ 221109 VWC
❑ 221110 VWC
❑ 221111 VWC
❑ 221112 VWC
❑ 221113 VWC
❑ 221114 VWC
❑ 221115 VWC
❑ 221116 VWC
❑ 221117 VWC
❑ 221118 VWC
❑ 221119 AXC
❑ 221120 AXC
❑ 221121 AXC
❑ 221122 AXC
❑ 221123 AXC
❑ 221124 AXC
❑ 221125 AXC
❑ 221126 AXC
❑ 221127 AXC
❑ 221128 AXC
❑ 221129 AXC
❑ 221130 AXC
❑ 221131 AXC
❑ 221132 AXC
❑ 221133 AXC
❑ 221134 AXC
❑ 221135 AXC
❑ 221136 AXC
❑ 221137 AXC
❑ 221138 AXC
❑ 221139 AXC
❑ 221140 AXC
❑ 221141 AXC
❑ 221142 VWC
❑ 221143 VWC
❑ 221144 VWC

❑ 222001 EMT
❑ 222002 EMT
❑ 222003 EMT
❑ 222004 EMT
❑ 222005 EMT
❑ 222006 EMT
❑ 222007 EMT
❑ 222008 EMT
❑ 222009 EMT
❑ 222010 EMT
❑ 222011 EMT
❑ 222012 EMT
❑ 222013 EMT
❑ 222014 EMT
❑ 222015 EMT
❑ 222016 EMT
❑ 222017 EMT
❑ 222018 EMT
❑ 222019 EMT
❑ 222020 EMT
❑ 222021 EMT
❑ 222022 EMT
❑ 222023 EMT

❑ 222101 EMT
❑ 222102 EMT
❑ 222103 EMT
❑ 222104 EMT

Electric Multiple Units

❑ 85 PRE
❑ 87 PRE
❑ 91 PRE
❑ 2090 PRE
❑ 4732 PRE
❑ 5176 PRE
❑ 5759 PRE
❑ 5791 PRE
❑ 5793 PRE
❑ 6307 PRE
❑ 7105 PRE
❑ 8143 PRE

❑ 10096 PRE
❑ 11161 PRE
❑ 11179 PRE
❑ 11201 PRE
❑ 11825 PRE

❑ 13004 PRE

❑ 15345 PRE

❑ 28249 PRE
❑ 28361 PRE
❑ 28690 PRE
❑ 29298 PRE
❑ 29666 PRE
❑ 29670 PRE
❑ 29720 PRE
❑ 29896 PRE

❑ 61183 PRE
❑ 61275 PRE
❑ 61287 PRE
❑ 61742 PRE
❑ 61743 PRE
❑ 61798 PRE
❑ 61799 PRE
❑ 61804 PRE
❑ 61805 PRE

❑ 62364 PRE
❑ 62384 NRL
❑ 62378 PRE
❑ 62887 PRE
❑ 65302 PRE
❑ 65304 PRE
❑ 65451 PRE

❑ 67300 PRE

❑ 68001 PRE
❑ 68002 PRE
❑ 68003 PRE
❑ 68004 PRE
❑ 68005 PRE
❑ 68008 PRE
❑ 68009 PRE
❑ 68500 PRE
❑ 68506 PRE

❑ 69304 PRE
❑ 69310 PRE
❑ 69318 PRE
❑ 69332 PRE
❑ 69333 PRE
❑ 69337 PRE
❑ 69339 PRE

❑ 70229 PRE
❑ 70257 PRE
❑ 70273 PRE
❑ 70284 PRE
❑ 70292 PRE
❑ 70296 PRE
❑ 70354 PRE
❑ 70527 PRE
❑ 70531 PRE
❑ 70539 PRE
❑ 70576 PRE
❑ 70607 PRE

❑ 72501 PRE
❑ 72617 PRE

❑ 75023 PRE
❑ 75033 PRE
❑ 75186 PRE
❑ 75250 PRE
❑ 75395 PRE
❑ 75407 PRE
❑ 75881 PRE

❑ 76726 PRE
❑ 76740 PRE
❑ 76746 PRE
❑ 76797 PRE
❑ 76811 PRE
❑ 76812 PRE
❑ 76875 PRE

❑ 76398 PRE

❑ 77172 PRE

❑ 79998 PRE
❑ 79999 PRE

❑ 303032 PRE

❑ 306017 PRE
❑ 309616 PRE
❑ 309624 PRE

❑ 313018 FCC
❑ 313024 FCC
❑ 313025 FCC
❑ 313026 FCC
❑ 313027 FCC
❑ 313028 FCC
❑ 313029 FCC
❑ 313030 FCC
❑ 313031 FCC
❑ 313032 FCC
❑ 313033 FCC
❑ 313035 FCC
❑ 313036 FCC
❑ 313037 FCC
❑ 313038 FCC
❑ 313039 FCC
❑ 313040 FCC
❑ 313041 FCC
❑ 313042 FCC
❑ 313043 FCC
❑ 313044 FCC
❑ 313045 FCC
❑ 313046 FCC
❑ 313047 FCC
❑ 313048 FCC
❑ 313049 FCC
❑ 313050 FCC
❑ 313051 FCC
❑ 313052 FCC
❑ 313053 FCC
❑ 313054 FCC
❑ 313055 FCC
❑ 313056 FCC
❑ 313057 FCC
❑ 313058 FCC
❑ 313059 FCC
❑ 313060 FCC
❑ 313061 FCC
❑ 313062 FCC
❑ 313063 FCC
❑ 313064 FCC
❑ 313121 NRL
❑ 313122 FCC
❑ 313123 FCC
❑ 313134 FCC
❑ 313201 SOU
❑ 313202 SOU
❑ 313203 SOU
❑ 313204 SOU
❑ 313205 SOU
❑ 313206 SOU
❑ 313207 SOU
❑ 313208 SOU
❑ 313209 SOU
❑ 313210 SOU

- ❑ 313211 SOU
- ❑ 313212 SOU
- ❑ 313213 SOU
- ❑ 313214 SOU
- ❑ 313215 SOU
- ❑ 313216 SOU
- ❑ 313217 SOU
- ❑ 313219 SOU
- ❑ 313220 SOU

- ❑ 314201 FSR
- ❑ 314202 FSR
- ❑ 314203 FSR
- ❑ 314204 FSR
- ❑ 314205 FSR
- ❑ 314206 FSR
- ❑ 314207 FSR
- ❑ 314208 FSR
- ❑ 314209 FSR
- ❑ 314210 FSR
- ❑ 314211 FSR
- ❑ 314212 FSR
- ❑ 314213 FSR
- ❑ 314214 FSR
- ❑ 314215 FSR
- ❑ 314216 FSR

- ❑ 315801 AEA
- ❑ 315802 AEA
- ❑ 315803 AEA
- ❑ 315804 AEA
- ❑ 315805 AEA
- ❑ 315806 AEA
- ❑ 315807 AEA
- ❑ 315808 AEA
- ❑ 315809 AEA
- ❑ 315810 AEA
- ❑ 315811 AEA
- ❑ 315812 AEA
- ❑ 315813 AEA
- ❑ 315814 AEA
- ❑ 315815 AEA
- ❑ 315816 AEA
- ❑ 315817 AEA
- ❑ 315818 AEA
- ❑ 315819 AEA
- ❑ 315820 AEA
- ❑ 315821 AEA
- ❑ 315822 AEA
- ❑ 315823 AEA
- ❑ 315824 AEA
- ❑ 315825 AEA
- ❑ 315826 AEA
- ❑ 315827 AEA
- ❑ 315828 AEA
- ❑ 315829 AEA
- ❑ 315830 AEA
- ❑ 315831 AEA
- ❑ 315832 AEA
- ❑ 315833 AEA
- ❑ 315834 AEA
- ❑ 315835 AEA
- ❑ 315836 AEA
- ❑ 315837 AEA
- ❑ 315838 AEA
- ❑ 315839 AEA
- ❑ 315840 AEA
- ❑ 315841 AEA
- ❑ 315842 AEA
- ❑ 315843 AEA
- ❑ 315844 AEA
- ❑ 315845 AEA
- ❑ 315846 AEA
- ❑ 315847 AEA
- ❑ 315848 AEA
- ❑ 315849 AEA
- ❑ 315850 AEA
- ❑ 315851 AEA
- ❑ 315852 AEA
- ❑ 315853 AEA
- ❑ 315854 AEA
- ❑ 315855 AEA
- ❑ 315856 AEA
- ❑ 315857 AEA
- ❑ 315858 AEA
- ❑ 315859 AEA
- ❑ 315860 AEA
- ❑ 315861 AEA

- ❑ 317337 FCC
- ❑ 317338 FCC
- ❑ 317339 FCC
- ❑ 317340 FCC
- ❑ 317341 FCC
- ❑ 317342 FCC
- ❑ 317343 FCC
- ❑ 317344 FCC
- ❑ 317345 FCC
- ❑ 317346 FCC
- ❑ 317347 FCC
- ❑ 317348 FCC

- ❑ 317501 AEA
- ❑ 317502 AEA
- ❑ 317503 AEA
- ❑ 317504 AEA
- ❑ 317505 AEA
- ❑ 317506 AEA
- ❑ 317507 AEA
- ❑ 317508 AEA
- ❑ 317509 AEA
- ❑ 317510 AEA
- ❑ 317511 AEA
- ❑ 317512 AEA
- ❑ 317513 AEA
- ❑ 317514 AEA
- ❑ 317515 AEA

- ❑ 317649 AEA
- ❑ 317650 AEA
- ❑ 317651 AEA
- ❑ 317652 AEA
- ❑ 317653 AEA
- ❑ 317654 AEA
- ❑ 317655 AEA
- ❑ 317656 AEA
- ❑ 317657 AEA
- ❑ 317658 AEA
- ❑ 317659 AEA
- ❑ 317660 AEA
- ❑ 317661 AEA
- ❑ 317662 AEA
- ❑ 317663 AEA
- ❑ 317664 AEA
- ❑ 317665 AEA
- ❑ 317666 AEA
- ❑ 317667 AEA
- ❑ 317668 AEA
- ❑ 317669 AEA
- ❑ 317670 AEA
- ❑ 317671 AEA
- ❑ 317672 AEA
- ❑ 317708 OLS

- ❑ 317709 OLS
- ❑ 317710 OLS
- ❑ 317714 OLS
- ❑ 317719 OLS
- ❑ 317722 OLS
- ❑ 317723 OLS
- ❑ 317729 OLS
- ❑ 317732 OLS

- ❑ 317881 AEA
- ❑ 317882 AEA
- ❑ 317883 AEA
- ❑ 317884 AEA
- ❑ 317885 AEA
- ❑ 317886 AEA
- ❑ 317887 AEA
- ❑ 317888 AEA
- ❑ 317889 AEA
- ❑ 317890 AEA
- ❑ 317891 AEA
- ❑ 317892 AEA

- ❑ 318250 FSR
- ❑ 318251 FSR
- ❑ 318252 FSR
- ❑ 318253 FSR
- ❑ 318254 FSR
- ❑ 318255 FSR
- ❑ 318256 FSR
- ❑ 318257 FSR
- ❑ 318258 FSR
- ❑ 318259 FSR
- ❑ 318260 FSR
- ❑ 318261 FSR
- ❑ 318262 FSR
- ❑ 318263 FSR
- ❑ 318264 FSR
- ❑ 318265 FSR
- ❑ 318266 FSR
- ❑ 318267 FSR
- ❑ 318268 FSR
- ❑ 318269 FSR
- ❑ 318270 FSR

- ❑ 319001 FCC
- ❑ 319002 FCC
- ❑ 319003 FCC
- ❑ 319004 FCC
- ❑ 319005 FCC
- ❑ 319006 FCC
- ❑ 319007 FCC
- ❑ 319008 FCC
- ❑ 319009 FCC
- ❑ 319010 FCC
- ❑ 319011 FCC
- ❑ 319012 FCC
- ❑ 319013 FCC
- ❑ 319214 FCC
- ❑ 319215 FCC
- ❑ 319216 FCC
- ❑ 319217 FCC
- ❑ 319218 FCC
- ❑ 319219 FCC
- ❑ 319220 FCC

- ❑ 319361 FCC
- ❑ 319362 FCC
- ❑ 319363 FCC
- ❑ 319364 FCC
- ❑ 319365 FCC
- ❑ 319366 FCC
- ❑ 319367 FCC
- ❑ 319368 FCC
- ❑ 319369 FCC
- ❑ 319370 FCC
- ❑ 319371 FCC
- ❑ 319372 FCC
- ❑ 319373 FCC
- ❑ 319374 FCC
- ❑ 319375 FCC
- ❑ 319376 FCC
- ❑ 319377 FCC
- ❑ 319378 FCC
- ❑ 319379 FCC
- ❑ 319380 FCC
- ❑ 319381 FCC
- ❑ 319382 FCC
- ❑ 319383 FCC
- ❑ 319384 FCC
- ❑ 319385 FCC
- ❑ 319386 FCC

- ❑ 319421 FCC
- ❑ 319422 FCC
- ❑ 319423 FCC
- ❑ 319424 FCC
- ❑ 319425 FCC
- ❑ 319426 FCC
- ❑ 319427 FCC
- ❑ 319428 FCC
- ❑ 319429 FCC
- ❑ 319430 FCC
- ❑ 319431 FCC
- ❑ 319432 FCC
- ❑ 319433 FCC
- ❑ 319434 FCC
- ❑ 319435 FCC
- ❑ 319436 FCC
- ❑ 319437 FCC
- ❑ 319438 FCC
- ❑ 319439 FCC
- ❑ 319440 FCC
- ❑ 319441 FCC
- ❑ 319442 FCC
- ❑ 319443 FCC
- ❑ 319444 FCC
- ❑ 319445 FCC
- ❑ 319446 FCC
- ❑ 319447 FCC
- ❑ 319448 FCC
- ❑ 319449 FCC
- ❑ 319450 FCC
- ❑ 319451 FCC
- ❑ 319452 FCC
- ❑ 319453 FCC
- ❑ 319454 FCC
- ❑ 319455 FCC
- ❑ 319456 FCC
- ❑ 319457 FCC
- ❑ 319458 FCC
- ❑ 319459 FCC
- ❑ 319460 FCC

- ❑ 320301 FSR
- ❑ 320302 FSR
- ❑ 320303 FSR
- ❑ 320304 FSR
- ❑ 320305 FSR
- ❑ 320306 FSR
- ❑ 320307 FSR
- ❑ 320308 FSR
- ❑ 320309 FSR
- ❑ 320310 FSR
- ❑ 320311 FSR
- ❑ 320312 FSR
- ❑ 320313 FSR
- ❑ 320314 FSR
- ❑ 320315 FSR
- ❑ 320316 FSR
- ❑ 320317 FSR
- ❑ 320318 FSR
- ❑ 320319 FSR
- ❑ 320320 FSR
- ❑ 320321 FSR
- ❑ 320322 FSR

- ❑ 321301 AEA
- ❑ 321302 AEA
- ❑ 321303 AEA
- ❑ 321304 AEA
- ❑ 321305 AEA
- ❑ 321306 AEA
- ❑ 321307 AEA
- ❑ 321308 AEA
- ❑ 321309 AEA
- ❑ 321310 AEA
- ❑ 321311 AEA
- ❑ 321312 AEA
- ❑ 321313 AEA
- ❑ 321314 AEA
- ❑ 321315 AEA

❑ 321316 AEA
❑ 321317 AEA
❑ 321318 AEA
❑ 321319 AEA
❑ 321320 AEA
❑ 321321 AEA
❑ 321322 AEA
❑ 321323 AEA
❑ 321324 AEA
❑ 321325 AEA
❑ 321326 AEA
❑ 321327 AEA
❑ 321328 AEA
❑ 321329 AEA
❑ 321330 AEA
❑ 321331 AEA
❑ 321332 AEA
❑ 321333 AEA
❑ 321334 AEA
❑ 321335 AEA
❑ 321336 AEA
❑ 321337 AEA
❑ 321338 AEA
❑ 321339 AEA
❑ 321340 AEA
❑ 321341 AEA
❑ 321342 AEA
❑ 321343 AEA
❑ 321344 AEA
❑ 321345 AEA
❑ 321346 AEA
❑ 321347 AEA
❑ 321348 AEA
❑ 321349 AEA
❑ 321350 AEA
❑ 321351 AEA
❑ 321352 AEA
❑ 321353 AEA
❑ 321354 AEA
❑ 321355 AEA
❑ 321356 AEA
❑ 321357 AEA
❑ 321358 AEA
❑ 321359 AEA
❑ 321360 AEA
❑ 321361 AEA
❑ 321362 AEA
❑ 321363 AEA
❑ 321364 AEA
❑ 321365 AEA
❑ 321366 AEA

❑ 321401 FCC
❑ 321402 FCC
❑ 321403 FCC
❑ 321404 FCC
❑ 321405 FCC
❑ 321406 FCC
❑ 321407 FCC
❑ 321408 FCC
❑ 321409 FCC
❑ 321410 FCC
❑ 321411 LMI
❑ 321412 LMI
❑ 321413 LMI
❑ 321414 LMI
❑ 321415 LMI
❑ 321416 LMI
❑ 321417 LMI
❑ 321418 FCC
❑ 321419 FCC
❑ 321420 FCC
❑ 321421 AEA
❑ 321422 AEA
❑ 321423 AEA
❑ 321424 AEA
❑ 321425 AEA
❑ 321426 AEA
❑ 321427 AEA
❑ 321428 AEA
❑ 321429 AEA
❑ 321430 AEA
❑ 321431 AEA
❑ 321432 AEA
❑ 321433 AEA
❑ 321434 AEA
❑ 321435 AEA
❑ 321436 AEA
❑ 321437 AEA
❑ 321438 AEA
❑ 321439 AEA
❑ 321440 AEA
❑ 321441 AEA
❑ 321442 AEA
❑ 321443 AEA
❑ 321444 AEA
❑ 321445 AEA
❑ 321446 AEA
❑ 321447 AEA
❑ 321448 AEA

❑ 321901 NOR
❑ 321902 NOR
❑ 321903 NOR

❑ 322481 NOR
❑ 322482 NOR
❑ 322483 NOR
❑ 322484 NOR
❑ 322485 NOR

❑ 323201 LMI
❑ 323202 LMI
❑ 323203 LMI
❑ 323204 LMI
❑ 323205 LMI
❑ 323206 LMI
❑ 323207 LMI
❑ 323208 LMI
❑ 323209 LMI
❑ 323210 LMI
❑ 323211 LMI
❑ 323212 LMI
❑ 323213 LMI
❑ 323214 LMI
❑ 323215 LMI
❑ 323216 LMI
❑ 323217 LMI
❑ 323218 LMI
❑ 323219 LMI
❑ 323220 LMI
❑ 323221 LMI
❑ 323222 LMI
❑ 323223 NOR
❑ 323224 NOR
❑ 323225 NOR
❑ 323226 NOR
❑ 323227 NOR
❑ 323228 NOR
❑ 323229 NOR
❑ 323230 NOR
❑ 323231 NOR
❑ 323232 NOR
❑ 323233 NOR
❑ 323234 NOR
❑ 323235 NOR
❑ 323236 NOR
❑ 323237 NOR
❑ 323238 NOR
❑ 323239 NOR
❑ 323240 LMI
❑ 323241 LMI
❑ 323242 LMI
❑ 323243 LMI

❑ 325001 DBS
❑ 325002 DBS
❑ 325003 DBS
❑ 325004 DBS
❑ 325005 DBS
❑ 325006 DBS
❑ 325007 DBS
❑ 325008 DBS
❑ 325009 DBS
❑ 325011 DBS
❑ 325012 DBS
❑ 325013 DBS
❑ 325014 DBS
❑ 325015 DBS
❑ 325016 DBS

❑ 332001 HEX
❑ 332002 HEX
❑ 332003 HEX
❑ 332004 HEX
❑ 332005 HEX
❑ 332006 HEX
❑ 332007 HEX
❑ 332008 HEX
❑ 332009 HEX
❑ 332010 HEX
❑ 332011 HEX
❑ 332012 HEX
❑ 332013 HEX
❑ 332014 HEX

❑ 333001 NOR
❑ 333002 NOR
❑ 333003 NOR
❑ 333004 NOR
❑ 333005 NOR
❑ 333006 NOR
❑ 333007 NOR
❑ 333008 NOR
❑ 333009 NOR
❑ 333010 NOR
❑ 333011 NOR
❑ 333012 NOR
❑ 333013 NOR
❑ 333014 NOR
❑ 333015 NOR
❑ 333016 NOR

❑ 334001 FSR
❑ 334002 FSR
❑ 334003 FSR
❑ 334004 FSR
❑ 334005 FSR
❑ 334006 FSR
❑ 334007 FSR
❑ 334008 FSR
❑ 334009 FSR
❑ 334010 FSR
❑ 334011 FSR
❑ 334012 FSR
❑ 334013 FSR
❑ 334014 FSR
❑ 334015 FSR
❑ 334016 FSR
❑ 334017 FSR
❑ 334018 FSR
❑ 334019 FSR
❑ 334020 FSR
❑ 334021 FSR
❑ 334022 FSR
❑ 334023 FSR
❑ 334024 FSR
❑ 334025 FSR
❑ 334026 FSR
❑ 334027 FSR
❑ 334028 FSR
❑ 334029 FSR
❑ 334030 FSR
❑ 334031 FSR
❑ 334032 FSR
❑ 334033 FSR
❑ 334034 FSR
❑ 334035 FSR
❑ 334036 FSR
❑ 334037 FSR
❑ 334038 FSR
❑ 334039 FSR
❑ 334040 FSR

❑ 350101 LMI
❑ 350102 LMI
❑ 350103 LMI
❑ 350104 LMI
❑ 350105 LMI
❑ 350106 LMI
❑ 350107 LMI
❑ 350108 LMI
❑ 350109 LMI
❑ 350110 LMI
❑ 350111 LMI
❑ 350112 LMI
❑ 350113 LMI
❑ 350114 LMI
❑ 350115 LMI
❑ 350116 LMI
❑ 350117 LMI
❑ 350118 LMI
❑ 350119 LMI
❑ 350120 LMI
❑ 350121 LMI
❑ 350122 LMI
❑ 350123 LMI
❑ 350124 LMI
❑ 350125 LMI
❑ 350126 LMI
❑ 350127 LMI
❑ 350128 LMI
❑ 350129 LMI
❑ 350130 LMI

❑ 350231 LMI
❑ 350232 LMI
❑ 350233 LMI
❑ 350234 LMI
❑ 350235 LMI
❑ 350236 LMI
❑ 350237 LMI
❑ 350238 LMI
❑ 350239 LMI
❑ 350240 LMI
❑ 350241 LMI
❑ 350242 LMI
❑ 350243 LMI
❑ 350244 LMI
❑ 350245 LMI
❑ 350246 LMI
❑ 350247 LMI
❑ 350248 LMI
❑ 350249 LMI
❑ 350250 LMI
❑ 350251 LMI
❑ 350252 LMI
❑ 350253 LMI
❑ 350254 LMI
❑ 350255 LMI
❑ 350256 LMI
❑ 350257 LMI
❑ 350258 LMI
❑ 350259 LMI
❑ 350260 LMI
❑ 350261 LMI
❑ 350262 LMI
❑ 350263 LMI
❑ 350264 LMI
❑ 350265 LMI
❑ 350266 LMI
❑ 350267 LMI

❑ 350301 LMI
❑ 350302 LMI

❑ 350303 LMI
❑ 350304 LMI
❑ 350305 LMI
❑ 350306 LMI
❑ 350307 LMI
❑ 350308 LMI
❑ 350309 LMI
❑ 350310 LMI

❑ 350401 FTP
❑ 350402 FTP
❑ 350403 FTP
❑ 350404 FTP
❑ 350405 FTP
❑ 350406 FTP
❑ 350407 FTP
❑ 350408 FTP
❑ 350409 FTP
❑ 350410 FTP

❑ 357001 C2C
❑ 357002 C2C
❑ 357003 C2C
❑ 357004 C2C
❑ 357005 C2C
❑ 357006 C2C
❑ 357007 C2C
❑ 357008 C2C
❑ 357009 C2C
❑ 357010 C2C
❑ 357011 C2C
❑ 357012 C2C
❑ 357013 C2C
❑ 357014 C2C
❑ 357015 C2C
❑ 357016 C2C
❑ 357017 C2C
❑ 357018 C2C
❑ 357019 C2C
❑ 357020 C2C
❑ 357021 C2C
❑ 357022 C2C
❑ 357023 C2C
❑ 357024 C2C
❑ 357025 C2C
❑ 357026 C2C
❑ 357027 C2C
❑ 357028 C2C
❑ 357029 C2C
❑ 357030 C2C
❑ 357031 C2C
❑ 357032 C2C
❑ 357033 C2C
❑ 357034 C2C
❑ 357035 C2C
❑ 357036 C2C
❑ 357037 C2C
❑ 357038 C2C
❑ 357039 C2C
❑ 357040 C2C
❑ 357041 C2C
❑ 357042 C2C
❑ 357043 C2C
❑ 357044 C2C
❑ 357045 C2C
❑ 357046 C2C

❑ 357201 C2C
❑ 357202 C2C
❑ 357203 C2C
❑ 357204 C2C
❑ 357205 C2C
❑ 357206 C2C
❑ 357207 C2C
❑ 357208 C2C
❑ 357209 C2C
❑ 357210 C2C
❑ 357211 C2C
❑ 357212 C2C
❑ 357213 C2C
❑ 357214 C2C
❑ 357215 C2C
❑ 357216 C2C
❑ 357217 C2C
❑ 357218 C2C
❑ 357219 C2C
❑ 357220 C2C
❑ 357221 C2C
❑ 357222 C2C
❑ 357223 C2C
❑ 357224 C2C
❑ 357225 C2C
❑ 357226 C2C
❑ 357227 C2C
❑ 357228 C2C

❑ 360101 AEA
❑ 360102 AEA
❑ 360103 AEA
❑ 360104 AEA
❑ 360105 AEA
❑ 360106 AEA
❑ 360107 AEA
❑ 360108 AEA
❑ 360109 AEA
❑ 360110 AEA
❑ 360111 AEA
❑ 360112 AEA
❑ 360113 AEA
❑ 360114 AEA
❑ 360115 AEA
❑ 360116 AEA
❑ 360117 AEA
❑ 360118 AEA
❑ 360119 AEA
❑ 360120 AEA
❑ 360121 AEA

❑ 360201 HEC
❑ 360202 HEC
❑ 360203 HEC
❑ 360204 HEC
❑ 360205 HEC

❑ 365501 FCC
❑ 365502 FCC
❑ 365503 FCC
❑ 365504 FCC
❑ 365505 FCC
❑ 365506 FCC
❑ 365507 FCC
❑ 365508 FCC
❑ 365509 FCC
❑ 365510 FCC
❑ 365511 FCC
❑ 365512 FCC
❑ 365513 FCC
❑ 365514 FCC
❑ 365515 FCC
❑ 365516 FCC
❑ 365517 FCC
❑ 365518 FCC
❑ 365519 FCC
❑ 365520 FCC
❑ 365521 FCC
❑ 365522 FCC
❑ 365523 FCC
❑ 365524 FCC
❑ 365525 FCC
❑ 365527 FCC
❑ 365528 FCC
❑ 365529 FCC
❑ 365530 FCC
❑ 365531 FCC
❑ 365532 FCC
❑ 365533 FCC
❑ 365534 FCC
❑ 365535 FCC
❑ 365536 FCC
❑ 365537 FCC
❑ 365538 FCC
❑ 365539 FCC
❑ 365540 FCC
❑ 365541 FCC

❑ 373001 EUS
❑ 373002 EUS
❑ 373003 EUS
❑ 373004 EUS
❑ 373005 EUS
❑ 373006 EUS
❑ 373007 EUS
❑ 373008 EUS
❑ 373009 EUS
❑ 373010 EUS
❑ 373011 EUS
❑ 373012 EUS
❑ 373013 EUS
❑ 373014 EUS
❑ 373015 EUS
❑ 373016 EUS
❑ 373017 EUS
❑ 373018 EUS
❑ 373019 EUS
❑ 373020 EUS
❑ 373021 EUS
❑ 373022 EUS
❑ 373101 EUS
❑ 373102 EUS
❑ 373103 EUS
❑ 373104 EUS
❑ 373105 EUS
❑ 373106 EUS
❑ 373107 EUS
❑ 373108 EUS
❑ 373201 EUS
❑ 373202 EUS
❑ 373203 EUS
❑ 373204 EUS
❑ 373205 EUS
❑ 373206 EUS
❑ 373207 EUS
❑ 373208 EUS
❑ 373209 EUS
❑ 373210 EUS
❑ 373211 EUS
❑ 373212 EUS
❑ 373213 EUS
❑ 373214 EUS
❑ 373215 EUS
❑ 373216 EUS
❑ 373217 EUS
❑ 373218 EUS
❑ 373219 EUS
❑ 373220 EUS
❑ 373221 EUS
❑ 373222 EUS
❑ 373223 EUS
❑ 373224 EUS
❑ 373225 EUS
❑ 373226 EUS
❑ 373227 EUS
❑ 373228 EUS
❑ 373229 EUS
❑ 373230 EUS
❑ 373231 EUS
❑ 373232 EUS
❑ 373301 EUS
❑ 373302 EUS
❑ 373303 EUS
❑ 373304 EUS
❑ 373305 EUS
❑ 373306 EUS
❑ 373307 EUS
❑ 373308 EUS
❑ 373309 EUS
❑ 373310 EUS
❑ 373311 EUS
❑ 373312 EUS
❑ 373313 EUS
❑ 373314 EUS
❑ 373999 EUS

❑ 374001 EUS
❑ 374002 EUS
❑ 374003 EUS
❑ 374004 EUS
❑ 374005 EUS
❑ 374006 EUS
❑ 374007 EUS
❑ 374008 EUS
❑ 374009 EUS
❑ 374010 EUS
❑ 374011 EUS
❑ 374012 EUS
❑ 374013 EUS
❑ 374014 EUS
❑ 374015 EUS
❑ 374016 EUS
❑ 374017 EUS
❑ 374018 EUS
❑ 374019 EUS
❑ 374020 EUS

❑ 375301 SET
❑ 375302 SET
❑ 375303 SET
❑ 375304 SET
❑ 375305 SET
❑ 375306 SET
❑ 375307 SET
❑ 375308 SET
❑ 375309 SET
❑ 375310 SET

❑ 375601 SET
❑ 375602 SET
❑ 375603 SET
❑ 375604 SET
❑ 375605 SET
❑ 375606 SET
❑ 375607 SET
❑ 375608 SET
❑ 375609 SET
❑ 375610 SET
❑ 375611 SET
❑ 375612 SET
❑ 375613 SET
❑ 375614 SET
❑ 375615 SET
❑ 375616 SET
❑ 375617 SET
❑ 375618 SET
❑ 375619 SET
❑ 375620 SET
❑ 375621 SET
❑ 375622 SET
❑ 375623 SET
❑ 375624 SET
❑ 375625 SET
❑ 375626 SET
❑ 375627 SET
❑ 375628 SET
❑ 375629 SET
❑ 375630 SET

❑ 375701 SET
❑ 375702 SET
❑ 375703 SET
❑ 375704 SET
❑ 375705 SET
❑ 375706 SET
❑ 375707 SET
❑ 375708 SET
❑ 375709 SET

❑ 375710 SET
❑ 375711 SET
❑ 375712 SET
❑ 375713 SET
❑ 375714 SET
❑ 375715 SET

❑ 375801 SET
❑ 375802 SET
❑ 375803 SET
❑ 375804 SET
❑ 375805 SET
❑ 375806 SET
❑ 375807 SET
❑ 375808 SET
❑ 375809 SET
❑ 375810 SET
❑ 375811 SET
❑ 375812 SET
❑ 375813 SET
❑ 375814 SET
❑ 375815 SET
❑ 375816 SET
❑ 375817 SET
❑ 375818 SET
❑ 375819 SET
❑ 375820 SET
❑ 375821 SET
❑ 375822 SET
❑ 375823 SET
❑ 375824 SET
❑ 375825 SET
❑ 375826 SET
❑ 375827 SET
❑ 375828 SET
❑ 375829 SET
❑ 375830 SET

❑ 375901 SET
❑ 375902 SET
❑ 375903 SET
❑ 375904 SET
❑ 375905 SET
❑ 375906 SET
❑ 375907 SET
❑ 375908 SET
❑ 375909 SET
❑ 375910 SET
❑ 375911 SET
❑ 375912 SET
❑ 375913 SET
❑ 375914 SET
❑ 375915 SET
❑ 375916 SET
❑ 375917 SET
❑ 375918 SET
❑ 375919 SET
❑ 375920 SET
❑ 375921 SET
❑ 375922 SET
❑ 375923 SET
❑ 375924 SET
❑ 375925 SET
❑ 375926 SET
❑ 375927 SET

❑ 376001 SET
❑ 376002 SET
❑ 376003 SET
❑ 376004 SET
❑ 376005 SET
❑ 376006 SET
❑ 376007 SET
❑ 376008 SET
❑ 376009 SET
❑ 376010 SET
❑ 376011 SET
❑ 376012 SET
❑ 376013 SET
❑ 376014 SET
❑ 376015 SET
❑ 376016 SET
❑ 376017 SET
❑ 376018 SET
❑ 376019 SET
❑ 376020 SET
❑ 376021 SET
❑ 376022 SET
❑ 376023 SET
❑ 376024 SET
❑ 376025 SET
❑ 376026 SET
❑ 376027 SET
❑ 376028 SET
❑ 376029 SET
❑ 376030 SET
❑ 376031 SET
❑ 376032 SET
❑ 376033 SET
❑ 376034 SET
❑ 376035 SET
❑ 376036 SET

❑ 377101 SOU
❑ 377102 SOU
❑ 377103 SOU
❑ 377104 SOU
❑ 377105 SOU
❑ 377106 SOU
❑ 377107 SOU
❑ 377108 SOU
❑ 377109 SOU
❑ 377110 SOU
❑ 377111 SOU
❑ 377112 SOU
❑ 377113 SOU
❑ 377114 SOU
❑ 377115 SOU
❑ 377116 SOU
❑ 377117 SOU
❑ 377118 SOU
❑ 377119 SOU
❑ 377120 SOU
❑ 377121 SOU
❑ 377122 SOU
❑ 377123 SOU
❑ 377124 SOU
❑ 377125 SOU
❑ 377126 SOU
❑ 377127 SOU
❑ 377128 SOU
❑ 377129 SOU
❑ 377130 SOU
❑ 377131 SOU
❑ 377132 SOU
❑ 377133 SOU
❑ 377134 SOU
❑ 377135 SOU
❑ 377136 SOU
❑ 377137 SOU
❑ 377138 SOU
❑ 377139 SOU
❑ 377140 SOU
❑ 377141 SOU
❑ 377142 SOU
❑ 377143 SOU
❑ 377144 SOU
❑ 377145 SOU
❑ 377146 SOU
❑ 377147 SOU
❑ 377148 SOU
❑ 377149 SOU
❑ 377150 SOU
❑ 377151 SOU
❑ 377152 SOU
❑ 377153 SOU
❑ 377154 SOU
❑ 377155 SOU
❑ 377156 SOU
❑ 377157 SOU
❑ 377158 SOU
❑ 377159 SOU
❑ 377160 SOU
❑ 377161 SOU
❑ 377162 SOU
❑ 377163 SOU
❑ 377164 SOU

❑ 377201 SOU
❑ 377202 SOU
❑ 377203 SOU
❑ 377204 SOU
❑ 377205 SOU
❑ 377206 SOU
❑ 377207 SOU
❑ 377208 SOU
❑ 377209 SOU
❑ 377210 SOU
❑ 377211 SOU
❑ 377212 SOU
❑ 377213 SOU
❑ 377214 SOU
❑ 377215 SOU

❑ 377301 SOU
❑ 377302 SOU
❑ 377303 SOU
❑ 377304 SOU
❑ 377305 SOU
❑ 377306 SOU
❑ 377307 SOU
❑ 377308 SOU
❑ 377309 SOU
❑ 377310 SOU
❑ 377311 SOU
❑ 377312 SOU
❑ 377313 SOU
❑ 377314 SOU
❑ 377315 SOU
❑ 377316 SOU
❑ 377317 SOU
❑ 377318 SOU
❑ 377319 SOU
❑ 377320 SOU
❑ 377321 SOU
❑ 377322 SOU
❑ 377323 SOU
❑ 377324 SOU
❑ 377325 SOU
❑ 377326 SOU
❑ 377327 SOU
❑ 377328 SOU

❑ 377401 SOU
❑ 377402 SOU
❑ 377403 SOU
❑ 377404 SOU
❑ 377405 SOU
❑ 377406 SOU
❑ 377407 SOU
❑ 377408 SOU
❑ 377409 SOU
❑ 377410 SOU
❑ 377411 SOU
❑ 377412 SOU
❑ 377413 SOU
❑ 377414 SOU
❑ 377415 SOU
❑ 377416 SOU
❑ 377417 SOU
❑ 377418 SOU
❑ 377419 SOU
❑ 377420 SOU
❑ 377421 SOU
❑ 377422 SOU
❑ 377423 SOU
❑ 377424 SOU
❑ 377425 SOU
❑ 377426 SOU
❑ 377427 SOU
❑ 377428 SOU
❑ 377429 SOU
❑ 377430 SOU
❑ 377431 SOU
❑ 377432 SOU
❑ 377433 SOU
❑ 377434 SOU
❑ 377435 SOU
❑ 377436 SOU
❑ 377437 SOU
❑ 377438 SOU
❑ 377439 SOU
❑ 377440 SOU
❑ 377441 SOU
❑ 377442 SOU
❑ 377443 SOU
❑ 377444 SOU
❑ 377445 SOU
❑ 377446 SOU
❑ 377447 SOU
❑ 377448 SOU
❑ 377449 SOU
❑ 377450 SOU
❑ 377451 SOU
❑ 377452 SOU
❑ 377453 SOU
❑ 377454 SOU
❑ 377455 SOU
❑ 377456 SOU
❑ 377457 SOU
❑ 377458 SOU
❑ 377459 SOU
❑ 377460 SOU
❑ 377461 SOU
❑ 377462 SOU
❑ 377463 SOU
❑ 377464 SOU
❑ 377465 SOU
❑ 377466 SOU
❑ 377467 SOU
❑ 377468 SOU
❑ 377469 SOU
❑ 377470 SOU
❑ 377471 SOU
❑ 377472 SOU
❑ 377473 SOU
❑ 377474 SOU
❑ 377475 SOU

❑ 377501 FCC
❑ 377502 FCC
❑ 377503 FCC
❑ 377504 FCC
❑ 377505 FCC
❑ 377506 FCC
❑ 377507 FCC
❑ 377508 FCC
❑ 377509 FCC
❑ 377510 FCC
❑ 377511 FCC
❑ 377512 FCC
❑ 377513 FCC
❑ 377514 FCC
❑ 377515 FCC
❑ 377516 FCC
❑ 377517 FCC
❑ 377518 FCC
❑ 377519 FCC
❑ 377520 FCC
❑ 377521 FCC
❑ 377522 FCC
❑ 377523 FCC

❑ 377601 SOU
❑ 377602 SOU

❑ 377603 SOU
❑ 377604 SOU
❑ 377605 SOU
❑ 377606 SOU
❑ 377607 SOU
❑ 377608 SOU
❑ 377609 SOU
❑ 377610 SOU
❑ 377611 SOU
❑ 377612 SOU
❑ 377613 SOU
❑ 377614 SOU
❑ 377615 SOU
❑ 377616 SOU
❑ 377617 SOU
❑ 377618 SOU
❑ 377619 SOU
❑ 377620 SOU
❑ 377621 SOU
❑ 377622 SOU
❑ 377623 SOU
❑ 377624 SOU
❑ 377625 SOU
❑ 377626 SOU

❑ 377701 SOU
❑ 377702 SOU
❑ 377703 SOU
❑ 377704 SOU
❑ 377705 SOU
❑ 377706 SOU
❑ 377707 SOU
❑ 377708 SOU

❑ 377801 SOU
❑ 377802 SOU
❑ 377803 SOU
❑ 377804 SOU
❑ 377805 SOU
❑ 377806 SOU
❑ 377807 SOU
❑ 377808 SOU
❑ 377809 SOU
❑ 377810 SOU
❑ 377811 SOU
❑ 377812 SOU
❑ 377813 SOU
❑ 377814 SOU
❑ 377815 SOU
❑ 377816 SOU
❑ 377817 SOU
❑ 377818 SOU
❑ 377819 SOU
❑ 377820 SOU
❑ 377821 SOU
❑ 377822 SOU
❑ 377823 SOU
❑ 377824 SOU
❑ 377825 SOU
❑ 377826 SOU
❑ 377827 SOU
❑ 377828 SOU
❑ 377829 SOU

❑ 378135 LOG
❑ 378136 LOG
❑ 378137 LOG
❑ 378138 LOG
❑ 378139 LOG
❑ 378140 LOG
❑ 378141 LOG
❑ 378142 LOG
❑ 378143 LOG
❑ 378144 LOG
❑ 378145 LOG
❑ 378146 LOG
❑ 378147 LOG
❑ 378148 LOG
❑ 378149 LOG
❑ 378150 LOG
❑ 378151 LOG
❑ 378152 LOG
❑ 378153 LOG
❑ 378154 LOG

❑ 378201 LOG
❑ 378202 LOG
❑ 378203 LOG
❑ 378204 LOG
❑ 378205 LOG
❑ 378206 LOG
❑ 378207 LOG
❑ 378208 LOG
❑ 378209 LOG
❑ 378210 LOG
❑ 378211 LOG
❑ 378212 LOG
❑ 378213 LOG
❑ 378214 LOG
❑ 378215 LOG
❑ 378216 LOG
❑ 378217 LOG
❑ 378218 LOG
❑ 378219 LOG
❑ 378220 LOG
❑ 378221 LOG
❑ 378222 LOG
❑ 378223 LOG
❑ 378224 LOG
❑ 378225 LOG
❑ 378226 LOG
❑ 378227 LOG
❑ 378228 LOG
❑ 378229 LOG
❑ 378230 LOG
❑ 378231 LOG
❑ 378232 LOG
❑ 378233 LOG
❑ 378234 LOG
❑ 378255 LOG
❑ 378256 LOG
❑ 378257 LOG

❑ 379001 AEA
❑ 379002 AEA
❑ 379003 AEA
❑ 379004 AEA
❑ 379005 AEA
❑ 379006 AEA
❑ 379007 AEA
❑ 379008 AEA
❑ 379009 AEA
❑ 379010 AEA
❑ 379011 AEA
❑ 379012 AEA
❑ 379013 AEA
❑ 379014 AEA
❑ 379015 AEA
❑ 379016 AEA
❑ 379017 AEA
❑ 379018 AEA
❑ 379019 AEA
❑ 379020 AEA
❑ 379021 AEA
❑ 379022 AEA
❑ 379023 AEA
❑ 379024 AEA
❑ 379025 AEA
❑ 379026 AEA
❑ 379027 AEA
❑ 379028 AEA
❑ 379029 AEA
❑ 379030 AEA

❑ 380001 FSR
❑ 380002 FSR
❑ 380003 FSR
❑ 380004 FSR
❑ 380005 FSR
❑ 380006 FSR
❑ 380007 FSR
❑ 380008 FSR
❑ 380009 FSR
❑ 380010 FSR
❑ 380011 FSR
❑ 380012 FSR
❑ 380013 FSR
❑ 380014 FSR
❑ 380015 FSR
❑ 380016 FSR
❑ 380017 FSR
❑ 380018 FSR
❑ 380019 FSR
❑ 380020 FSR
❑ 380021 FSR
❑ 380022 FSR

❑ 380101 FSR
❑ 380102 FSR
❑ 380103 FSR
❑ 380104 FSR
❑ 380105 FSR
❑ 380106 FSR
❑ 380107 FSR
❑ 380108 FSR
❑ 380109 FSR
❑ 380110 FSR
❑ 380111 FSR
❑ 380112 FSR
❑ 380113 FSR
❑ 380114 FSR
❑ 380115 FSR
❑ 380116 FSR

❑ 390001 VWC
❑ 390002 VWC
❑ 390103 VWC
❑ 390104 VWC
❑ 390005 VWC
❑ 390006 VWC
❑ 390107 VWC
❑ 390008 VWC
❑ 390009 VWC
❑ 390010 VWC
❑ 390011 VWC
❑ 390112 VWC
❑ 390013 VWC
❑ 390114 VWC
❑ 390115 VWC
❑ 390016 VWC
❑ 390117 VWC
❑ 390118 VWC
❑ 390119 VWC
❑ 390020 VWC
❑ 390121 VWC
❑ 390122 VWC
❑ 390023 VWC
❑ 390124 VWC
❑ 390125 VWC
❑ 390126 VWC
❑ 390127 VWC
❑ 390128 VWC
❑ 390129 VWC
❑ 390130 VWC
❑ 390131 VWC
❑ 390132 VWC
❑ 390134 VWC
❑ 390035 VWC
❑ 390136 VWC
❑ 390137 VWC
❑ 390038 VWC
❑ 390039 VWC
❑ 390040 VWC
❑ 390141 VWC
❑ 390042 VWC
❑ 390043 VWC
❑ 390044 VWC
❑ 390045 VWC
❑ 390046 VWC
❑ 390047 VWC
❑ 390148 VWC
❑ 390049 VWC
❑ 390050 VWC
❑ 390151 VWC
❑ 390152 VWC
❑ 390153 VWC
❑ 390154 VWC
❑ 390155 VWC
❑ 390156 VWC
❑ 390157 VWC

❑ 395001 SET
❑ 395002 SET
❑ 395003 SET
❑ 395004 SET
❑ 395005 SET
❑ 395006 SET
❑ 395007 SET
❑ 395008 SET
❑ 395009 SET
❑ 395010 SET
❑ 395011 SET
❑ 395012 SET
❑ 395013 SET
❑ 395014 SET
❑ 395015 SET
❑ 395016 SET
❑ 395017 SET
❑ 395018 SET
❑ 395019 SET
❑ 395020 SET
❑ 395021 SET
❑ 395022 SET
❑ 395023 SET
❑ 395024 SET
❑ 395025 SET
❑ 395026 SET
❑ 395027 SET
❑ 395028 SET
❑ 395029 SET

❑ 411198 PRE

❑ 421399 PRE
❑ 421496 PRE
❑ 421497 PRE
❑ 421498 PRE

❑ 432417 PRE

❑ 442401 SOU
❑ 442402 SOU
❑ 442403 SOU
❑ 442404 SOU
❑ 442405 SOU
❑ 442406 SOU
❑ 442407 SOU
❑ 442408 SOU
❑ 442409 SOU
❑ 442410 SOU
❑ 442411 SOU
❑ 442412 SOU
❑ 442413 SOU
❑ 442414 SOU
❑ 442415 SOU
❑ 442416 SOU
❑ 442417 SOU
❑ 442418 SOU
❑ 442419 SOU
❑ 442420 SOU
❑ 442421 SOU
❑ 442422 SOU
❑ 442423 SOU
❑ 442424 SOU

❑ 444001 SWT

❑ 444002 SWT
❑ 444003 SWT
❑ 444004 SWT
❑ 444005 SWT
❑ 444006 SWT
❑ 444007 SWT
❑ 444008 SWT
❑ 444009 SWT
❑ 444010 SWT
❑ 444011 SWT
❑ 444012 SWT
❑ 444013 SWT
❑ 444014 SWT
❑ 444015 SWT
❑ 444016 SWT
❑ 444017 SWT
❑ 444018 SWT
❑ 444019 SWT
❑ 444020 SWT
❑ 444021 SWT
❑ 444022 SWT
❑ 444023 SWT
❑ 444024 SWT
❑ 444025 SWT
❑ 444026 SWT
❑ 444027 SWT
❑ 444028 SWT
❑ 444029 SWT
❑ 444030 SWT
❑ 444031 SWT
❑ 444032 SWT
❑ 444033 SWT
❑ 444034 SWT
❑ 444035 SWT
❑ 444036 SWT
❑ 444037 SWT
❑ 444038 SWT
❑ 444039 SWT
❑ 444040 SWT
❑ 444041 SWT
❑ 444042 SWT
❑ 444043 SWT
❑ 444044 SWT
❑ 444045 SWT

❑ 450001 SWT
❑ 450002 SWT
❑ 450003 SWT
❑ 450004 SWT
❑ 450005 SWT
❑ 450006 SWT
❑ 450007 SWT
❑ 450008 SWT
❑ 450009 SWT
❑ 450010 SWT
❑ 450011 SWT
❑ 450012 SWT
❑ 450013 SWT
❑ 450014 SWT
❑ 450015 SWT
❑ 450016 SWT
❑ 450017 SWT
❑ 450018 SWT
❑ 450019 SWT
❑ 450020 SWT
❑ 450021 SWT
❑ 450022 SWT
❑ 450023 SWT
❑ 450024 SWT
❑ 450025 SWT
❑ 450026 SWT
❑ 450027 SWT
❑ 450028 SWT
❑ 450029 SWT
❑ 450030 SWT
❑ 450031 SWT
❑ 450032 SWT
❑ 450033 SWT
❑ 450034 SWT
❑ 450035 SWT
❑ 450036 SWT
❑ 450037 SWT
❑ 450038 SWT
❑ 450039 SWT
❑ 450040 SWT
❑ 450041 SWT
❑ 450042 SWT
❑ 450071 SWT
❑ 450072 SWT
❑ 450073 SWT
❑ 450074 SWT
❑ 450075 SWT
❑ 450076 SWT
❑ 450077 SWT
❑ 450078 SWT
❑ 450079 SWT
❑ 450080 SWT
❑ 450081 SWT
❑ 450082 SWT
❑ 450083 SWT
❑ 450084 SWT
❑ 450085 SWT
❑ 450086 SWT
❑ 450087 SWT
❑ 450088 SWT
❑ 450089 SWT
❑ 450090 SWT
❑ 450091 SWT
❑ 450092 SWT
❑ 450093 SWT
❑ 450094 SWT
❑ 450095 SWT
❑ 450096 SWT
❑ 450097 SWT
❑ 450098 SWT
❑ 450099 SWT
❑ 450100 SWT
❑ 450101 SWT
❑ 450102 SWT
❑ 450103 SWT
❑ 450104 SWT
❑ 450105 SWT
❑ 450106 SWT
❑ 450107 SWT
❑ 450108 SWT
❑ 450109 SWT
❑ 450110 SWT
❑ 450111 SWT
❑ 450112 SWT
❑ 450113 SWT
❑ 450114 SWT
❑ 450115 SWT
❑ 450116 SWT
❑ 450117 SWT
❑ 450118 SWT
❑ 450119 SWT
❑ 450120 SWT
❑ 450121 SWT
❑ 450122 SWT
❑ 450123 SWT
❑ 450124 SWT
❑ 450125 SWT
❑ 450126 SWT
❑ 450127 SWT

❑ 450543 SWT
❑ 450544 SWT
❑ 450545 SWT
❑ 450546 SWT
❑ 450547 SWT
❑ 450548 SWT
❑ 450549 SWT
❑ 450550 SWT
❑ 450551 SWT
❑ 450552 SWT
❑ 450553 SWT
❑ 450554 SWT
❑ 450555 SWT
❑ 450556 SWT
❑ 450557 SWT
❑ 450558 SWT
❑ 450559 SWT
❑ 450560 SWT
❑ 450561 SWT
❑ 450562 SWT
❑ 450563 SWT
❑ 450564 SWT
❑ 450565 SWT
❑ 450566 SWT
❑ 450567 SWT
❑ 450568 SWT
❑ 450569 SWT
❑ 450570 SWT

❑ 455701 SWT
❑ 455702 SWT
❑ 455703 SWT
❑ 455704 SWT
❑ 455705 SWT
❑ 455706 SWT
❑ 455707 SWT
❑ 455708 SWT
❑ 455709 SWT
❑ 455710 SWT
❑ 455711 SWT
❑ 455712 SWT
❑ 455713 SWT
❑ 455714 SWT
❑ 455715 SWT
❑ 455716 SWT
❑ 455717 SWT
❑ 455718 SWT
❑ 455719 SWT
❑ 455720 SWT
❑ 455721 SWT
❑ 455722 SWT
❑ 455723 SWT
❑ 455724 SWT
❑ 455725 SWT
❑ 455726 SWT
❑ 455727 SWT
❑ 455728 SWT
❑ 455729 SWT
❑ 455730 SWT
❑ 455731 SWT
❑ 455732 SWT
❑ 455733 SWT
❑ 455734 SWT
❑ 455735 SWT
❑ 455736 SWT
❑ 455737 SWT
❑ 455738 SWT
❑ 455739 SWT
❑ 455740 SWT
❑ 455741 SWT
❑ 455742 SWT
❑ 455750 SWT

❑ 455801 SOU
❑ 455802 SOU
❑ 455803 SOU
❑ 455804 SOU
❑ 455805 SOU
❑ 455806 SOU
❑ 455807 SOU
❑ 455808 SOU
❑ 455809 SOU
❑ 455810 SOU
❑ 455811 SOU
❑ 455812 SOU
❑ 455813 SOU
❑ 455814 SOU
❑ 455815 SOU
❑ 455816 SOU
❑ 455817 SOU
❑ 455818 SOU
❑ 455819 SOU
❑ 455820 SOU
❑ 455821 SOU
❑ 455822 SOU
❑ 455823 SOU
❑ 455824 SOU
❑ 455825 SOU
❑ 455826 SOU
❑ 455827 SOU
❑ 455828 SOU
❑ 455829 SOU
❑ 455830 SOU
❑ 455831 SOU
❑ 455832 SOU
❑ 455833 SOU
❑ 455834 SOU
❑ 455835 SOU
❑ 455836 SOU
❑ 455837 SOU
❑ 455838 SOU
❑ 455839 SOU
❑ 455840 SOU
❑ 455841 SOU
❑ 455842 SOU
❑ 455843 SOU
❑ 455844 SOU
❑ 455845 SOU
❑ 455846 SOU
❑ 455847 SWT
❑ 455848 SWT
❑ 455849 SWT
❑ 455850 SWT
❑ 455851 SWT
❑ 455852 SWT
❑ 455853 SWT
❑ 455854 SWT
❑ 455855 SWT
❑ 455856 SWT
❑ 455857 SWT
❑ 455858 SWT
❑ 455859 SWT
❑ 455860 SWT
❑ 455861 SWT
❑ 455862 SWT
❑ 455863 SWT
❑ 455864 SWT
❑ 455865 SWT
❑ 455866 SWT
❑ 455867 SWT
❑ 455868 SWT
❑ 455869 SWT
❑ 455870 SWT
❑ 455871 SWT
❑ 455872 SWT
❑ 455873 SWT
❑ 455874 SWT

❑ 455901 SWT
❑ 455902 SWT
❑ 455903 SWT
❑ 455904 SWT
❑ 455905 SWT
❑ 455906 SWT
❑ 455907 SWT
❑ 455908 SWT
❑ 455909 SWT
❑ 455910 SWT
❑ 455911 SWT
❑ 455912 SWT
❑ 455913 SWT
❑ 455914 SWT
❑ 455915 SWT
❑ 455916 SWT
❑ 455917 SWT
❑ 455918 SWT
❑ 455919 SWT
❑ 455920 SWT

❑ 456001 SWT

❑ 456002 SWT
❑ 456003 SWT
❑ 456004 SWT
❑ 456005 SWT
❑ 456006 SWT
❑ 456007 SWT
❑ 456008 SWT
❑ 456009 SWT
❑ 456010 SWT
❑ 456011 SWT
❑ 456012 SWT
❑ 456013 SWT
❑ 456014 SWT
❑ 456015 SWT
❑ 456016 SWT
❑ 456017 SWT
❑ 456018 SWT
❑ 456019 SWT
❑ 456020 SWT
❑ 456021 SWT
❑ 456022 SWT
❑ 456023 SWT
❑ 456024 SWT

❑ 458001 SWT
❑ 458002 SWT
❑ 458003 SWT
❑ 458004 SWT
❑ 458005 SWT
❑ 458006 SWT
❑ 458007 SWT
❑ 458008 SWT
❑ 458009 SWT
❑ 458010 SWT
❑ 458011 SWT
❑ 458012 SWT
❑ 458013 SWT
❑ 458014 SWT
❑ 458015 SWT
❑ 458016 SWT
❑ 458017 SWT
❑ 458018 SWT
❑ 458019 SWT
❑ 458020 SWT
❑ 458021 SWT
❑ 458022 SWT
❑ 458023 SWT
❑ 458024 SWT
❑ 458025 SWT
❑ 458026 SWT
❑ 458027 SWT
❑ 458028 SWT
❑ 458029 SWT
❑ 458030 SWT

❑ 458531 SWT
❑ 458532 SWT
❑ 458533 SWT
❑ 458534 SWT
❑ 458535 SWT
❑ 458536 SWT

❑ 465001 SET
❑ 465002 SET
❑ 465003 SET
❑ 465004 SET
❑ 465005 SET
❑ 465006 SET
❑ 465007 SET
❑ 465008 SET
❑ 465009 SET
❑ 465010 SET
❑ 465011 SET
❑ 465012 SET
❑ 465013 SET
❑ 465014 SET
❑ 465015 SET
❑ 465016 SET
❑ 465017 SET
❑ 465018 SET
❑ 465019 SET
❑ 465020 SET
❑ 465021 SET
❑ 465022 SET
❑ 465023 SET
❑ 465024 SET
❑ 465025 SET
❑ 465026 SET
❑ 465027 SET
❑ 465028 SET
❑ 465029 SET
❑ 465030 SET
❑ 465031 SET
❑ 465032 SET
❑ 465033 SET
❑ 465034 SET
❑ 465035 SET
❑ 465036 SET
❑ 465037 SET
❑ 465038 SET
❑ 465039 SET
❑ 465040 SET
❑ 465041 SET
❑ 465042 SET
❑ 465043 SET
❑ 465044 SET
❑ 465045 SET
❑ 465046 SET
❑ 465047 SET
❑ 465048 SET
❑ 465049 SET
❑ 465050 SET

❑ 465151 SET
❑ 465152 SET
❑ 465153 SET
❑ 465154 SET
❑ 465155 SET
❑ 465156 SET
❑ 465157 SET
❑ 465158 SET
❑ 465159 SET
❑ 465160 SET
❑ 465161 SET
❑ 465162 SET
❑ 465163 SET
❑ 465164 SET
❑ 465165 SET
❑ 465166 SET
❑ 465167 SET
❑ 465168 SET
❑ 465169 SET
❑ 465170 SET
❑ 465171 SET
❑ 465172 SET
❑ 465173 SET
❑ 465174 SET
❑ 465175 SET
❑ 465176 SET
❑ 465177 SET
❑ 465178 SET
❑ 465179 SET
❑ 465180 SET
❑ 465181 SET
❑ 465182 SET
❑ 465183 SET
❑ 465184 SET
❑ 465185 SET
❑ 465186 SET
❑ 465187 SET
❑ 465188 SET
❑ 465189 SET
❑ 465190 SET
❑ 465191 SET
❑ 465192 SET
❑ 465193 SET
❑ 465194 SET
❑ 465195 SET
❑ 465196 SET
❑ 465197 SET

❑ 465235 SET
❑ 465236 SET
❑ 465237 SET
❑ 465238 SET
❑ 465239 SET
❑ 465240 SET
❑ 465241 SET
❑ 465242 SET
❑ 465243 SET
❑ 465244 SET
❑ 465245 SET
❑ 465246 SET
❑ 465247 SET
❑ 465248 SET
❑ 465249 SET
❑ 465250 SET

❑ 465901 SET
❑ 465902 SET
❑ 465903 SET
❑ 465904 SET
❑ 465905 SET
❑ 465906 SET
❑ 465907 SET
❑ 465908 SET
❑ 465909 SET
❑ 465910 SET
❑ 465911 SET
❑ 465912 SET
❑ 465913 SET
❑ 465914 SET
❑ 465915 SET
❑ 465916 SET
❑ 465917 SET
❑ 465918 SET
❑ 465919 SET
❑ 465920 SET
❑ 465921 SET
❑ 465922 SET
❑ 465923 SET
❑ 465924 SET
❑ 465925 SET
❑ 465926 SET
❑ 465927 SET
❑ 465928 SET
❑ 465929 SET
❑ 465930 SET
❑ 465931 SET
❑ 465932 SET
❑ 465933 SET
❑ 465934 SET

❑ 466001 SET
❑ 466002 SET
❑ 466003 SET
❑ 466004 SET
❑ 466005 SET
❑ 466006 SET
❑ 466007 SET
❑ 466008 SET
❑ 466009 SET
❑ 466010 SET
❑ 466011 SET
❑ 466012 SET
❑ 466013 SET
❑ 466014 SET
❑ 466015 SET
❑ 466016 SET
❑ 466017 SET
❑ 466018 SET
❑ 466019 SET
❑ 466020 SET
❑ 466021 SET
❑ 466022 SET
❑ 466023 SET
❑ 466024 SET
❑ 466025 SET
❑ 466026 SET
❑ 466027 SET
❑ 466028 SET
❑ 466029 SET
❑ 466030 SET
❑ 466031 SET
❑ 466032 SET
❑ 466033 SET
❑ 466034 SET
❑ 466035 SET
❑ 466036 SET
❑ 466037 SET
❑ 466038 SET
❑ 466039 SET
❑ 466040 SET
❑ 466041 SET
❑ 466042 SET
❑ 466043 SET

❑ 483002 SIL
❑ 483004 SIL
❑ 483006 SIL
❑ 483007 SIL
❑ 483008 SIL
❑ 483009 SIL

❑ 489102 NRL
❑ 489105 NRL
❑ 489106 NRL

❑ 507001 MER
❑ 507002 MER
❑ 507003 MER
❑ 507004 MER
❑ 507005 MER
❑ 507006 MER
❑ 507007 MER
❑ 507008 MER
❑ 507009 MER
❑ 507010 MER
❑ 507011 MER
❑ 507012 MER
❑ 507013 MER
❑ 507014 MER
❑ 507015 MER
❑ 507016 MER
❑ 507017 MER
❑ 507018 MER
❑ 507019 MER
❑ 507020 MER
❑ 507021 MER
❑ 507023 MER
❑ 507024 MER
❑ 507025 MER
❑ 507026 MER
❑ 507027 MER
❑ 507028 MER
❑ 507029 MER
❑ 507030 MER
❑ 507031 MER
❑ 507032 MER
❑ 507033 MER

❑ 508103 MER
❑ 508104 MER
❑ 508108 MER
❑ 508110 MER
❑ 508111 MER
❑ 508112 MER
❑ 508114 MER
❑ 508115 MER
❑ 508117 MER
❑ 508120 MER
❑ 508122 MER
❑ 508123 MER
❑ 508124 MER
❑ 508125 MER

❑ 508126 MER
❑ 508127 MER
❑ 508128 MER
❑ 508130 MER
❑ 508131 MER
❑ 508134 MER
❑ 508136 MER
❑ 508137 MER
❑ 508138 MER
❑ 508139 MER
❑ 508140 MER
❑ 508141 MER
❑ 508143 MER
❑ 508201 OLS
❑ 508203 OLS
❑ 508207 OLS
❑ 508208 OLS
❑ 508209 OLS
❑ 508210 OLS
❑ 508211 OLS
❑ 508212 OLS

❑ 901001 PRE

Coaching Stock

❑ 84 RAF
❑ 159 WCR

❑ 213 VSO
❑ 239 VSO
❑ 243 VSO
❑ 245 VSO
❑ 254 VSO
❑ 255 VSO
❑ 261 VSO
❑ 264 VSO
❑ 280 VSO
❑ 281 VSO
❑ 283 VSO
❑ 284 VSO
❑ 285 VSO
❑ 286 VSO
❑ 288 VSO
❑ 292 VSO
❑ 293 VSO
❑ 301 VSO
❑ 302 VSO
❑ 307 VSO
❑ 308 VSO
❑ 310 RAF
❑ 313 GSW
❑ 316 FSL
❑ 317 GSW
❑ 319 GSW
❑ 321 FSL
❑ 324 GSW
❑ 325 VSO
❑ 326 WCR
❑ 329 GSW
❑ 331 GSW
❑ 335 VTN
❑ 337 FSL
❑ 347 WCR
❑ 348 WCR
❑ 349 VTN
❑ 350 WCR
❑ 352 WCR
❑ 353 VTN
❑ 354 WCR
❑ 464 BOK
❑ 504 WCR
❑ 506 WCR
❑ 546 WCR
❑ 548 WCR
❑ 549 WCR
❑ 550 WCR
❑ 551 WCR
❑ 552 WCR
❑ 553 WCR
❑ 586 WCR
❑ 807 WCR

❑ 1105 MHR

❑ 1200 RIV
❑ 1201 VTN
❑ 1203 RIV
❑ 1205 NRL
❑ 1207 VSO
❑ 1209 OLS
❑ 1211 RAF
❑ 1212 RIV
❑ 1219 OLS
❑ 1221 VSO
❑ 1250 RIV
❑ 1254 DRS
❑ 1256 NRL
❑ 1375 BOK
❑ 1566 VSO
❑ 1644 WCR
❑ 1650 WCR
❑ 1651 RIV
❑ 1652 WCR
❑ 1655 WCR
❑ 1657 RIV
❑ 1659 RAF
❑ 1663 WCR
❑ 1670 WCR
❑ 1671 RIV
❑ 1683 RIV
❑ 1691 RIV
❑ 1692 RIV
❑ 1699 RIV
❑ 1730 WCR
❑ 1800 WCR
❑ 1813 RIV
❑ 1823 NYM
❑ 1832 RIV
❑ 1840 WCR
❑ 1842 RIV
❑ 1859 SRP
❑ 1860 WCR
❑ 1861 WCR
❑ 1863 RIV
❑ 1882 WCR
❑ 1953 VSO
❑ 1961 WCR
❑ 1999 GSW

❑ 2127 WCR
❑ 2833 WCR
❑ 2834 RIV

❑ 2903 NRL
❑ 2904 NRL
❑ 2915 NRL
❑ 2916 NRL
❑ 2917 NRL
❑ 2918 NRL
❑ 2919 NRL
❑ 2920 NRL
❑ 2921 NRL
❑ 2922 NRL
❑ 2923 NRL

❑ 3058 WCR
❑ 3066 RIV
❑ 3068 RIV
❑ 3069 RIV
❑ 3093 WCR
❑ 3096 BOK
❑ 3097 RIV
❑ 3098 RIV
❑ 3100 RIV
❑ 3105 WCR
❑ 3106 WCR
❑ 3107 RIV
❑ 3110 RIV
❑ 3112 RIV
❑ 3113 WCR
❑ 3114 RIV
❑ 3115 BOK
❑ 3117 WCR
❑ 3119 RIV
❑ 3120 RIV
❑ 3121 RIV
❑ 3122 RIV
❑ 3123 RIV
❑ 3124 RIV
❑ 3127 RIV
❑ 3128 WCR
❑ 3130 WCR
❑ 3133 RIV
❑ 3136 WCR
❑ 3140 RIV
❑ 3141 RIV
❑ 3143 WCR
❑ 3144 RIV
❑ 3146 RIV
❑ 3147 RIV
❑ 3149 RIV
❑ 3150 BOK
❑ 3174 VSO
❑ 3181 RIV
❑ 3182 VSO
❑ 3188 RAF
❑ 3223 RIV
❑ 3227 RIV
❑ 3229 OLS
❑ 3231 RAF
❑ 3232 VSO
❑ 3240 RIV
❑ 3247 VSO
❑ 3267 VSO
❑ 3269 DBS
❑ 3273 VSO
❑ 3275 VSO
❑ 3277 RIV
❑ 3278 RIV
❑ 3279 RIV
❑ 3292 DBS
❑ 3295 RIV
❑ 3304 RIV
❑ 3312 RAF
❑ 3313 WCR
❑ 3314 RIV
❑ 3318 DBR
❑ 3325 RIV
❑ 3326 WCR
❑ 3330 RIV
❑ 3331 DBR
❑ 3333 RIV
❑ 3334 RIV
❑ 3336 RIV
❑ 3338 DBS
❑ 3340 RIV
❑ 3344 RIV
❑ 3345 RIV
❑ 3348 RIV
❑ 3350 WCR
❑ 3351 VTN
❑ 3352 WCR
❑ 3356 RIV
❑ 3358 RIV
❑ 3359 WCR
❑ 3360 WCR
❑ 3362 WCR
❑ 3364 RIV
❑ 3366 DRS
❑ 3374 DRS
❑ 3375 DBS
❑ 3379 RIV
❑ 3384 RIV
❑ 3386 RIV
❑ 3388 DBS
❑ 3390 RIV
❑ 3392 WCR
❑ 3395 WCR
❑ 3397 RIV
❑ 3399 DBS
❑ 3400 DBS
❑ 3414 DBS
❑ 3417 RIV
❑ 3424 DBS
❑ 3426 RIV
❑ 3431 WCR
❑ 3434 OLS
❑ 3438 RAF
❑ 3766 WCR
❑ 3860 NYM
❑ 3872 NYM
❑ 3948 NYM
❑ 4198 NYM
❑ 4252 NYM
❑ 4290 NYM
❑ 4362 RAF
❑ 4455 NYM
❑ 4786 NYM
❑ 4817 NYM
❑ 4831 BOK
❑ 4832 BOK
❑ 4836 BOK
❑ 4856 BOK
❑ 4860 WCR
❑ 4905 WCR
❑ 4912 WCR
❑ 4927 RIV
❑ 4931 WCR
❑ 4932 WCR
❑ 4940 WCR
❑ 4949 RIV
❑ 4951 WCR
❑ 4954 WCR
❑ 4958 WCR
❑ 4959 RIV
❑ 4960 WCR
❑ 4973 WCR
❑ 4984 WCR
❑ 4991 RIV
❑ 4994 WCR
❑ 4996 RIV
❑ 4997 WCR
❑ 4998 RIV

❑ 5000 NYM
❑ 5008 RIV
❑ 5009 RIV
❑ 5027 RIV
❑ 5028 BOK
❑ 5029 NYM
❑ 5032 WCR
❑ 5033 WCR
❑ 5035 WCR
❑ 5040 RIV
❑ 5044 WCR
❑ 5125 WCR
❑ 5157 VTN
❑ 5171 WCR
❑ 5177 VTN
❑ 5191 VTN
❑ 5198 VTN
❑ 5200 WCR
❑ 5212 VTN
❑ 5216 WCR
❑ 5229 WCR
❑ 5236 WCR
❑ 5237 WCR
❑ 5239 WCR
❑ 5249 WCR
❑ 5276 RIV
❑ 5278 WCR
❑ 5292 RIV
❑ 5309 RIV
❑ 5322 RIV
❑ 5341 RIV

Number	Operator
❑ 5350	RIV
❑ 5366	RIV
❑ 5419	WCR
❑ 5482	DBS
❑ 5494	RIV
❑ 5520	RRS
❑ 5631	DBS
❑ 5632	DBS
❑ 5636	OLS
❑ 5647	RIV
❑ 5657	DBS
❑ 5756	WCR
❑ 5797	RAF
❑ 5810	DRS
❑ 5888	OLS
❑ 5910	RIV
❑ 5912	RAF
❑ 5919	DRS
❑ 5921	RIV
❑ 5922	DBS
❑ 5924	DBS
❑ 5928	VTN
❑ 5929	RIV
❑ 5937	RIV
❑ 5945	RIV
❑ 5946	RIV
❑ 5950	RIV
❑ 5952	RIV
❑ 5954	DBS
❑ 5955	RIV
❑ 5959	DBS
❑ 5961	RIV
❑ 5964	RIV
❑ 5965	RIV
❑ 5971	DRS
❑ 5976	RIV
❑ 5981	NRL
❑ 5985	RIV
❑ 5987	RIV
❑ 5991	RAF
❑ 5995	DRS
❑ 5997	RIV
❑ 5998	RIV
❑ 6000	WCR
❑ 6001	DRS
❑ 6006	RIV
❑ 6008	DRS
❑ 6012	WCR
❑ 6014	WCR
❑ 6021	WCR
❑ 6022	WCR
❑ 6024	RIV
❑ 6027	RIV
❑ 6036	DBR
❑ 6042	RIV
❑ 6046	DRS
❑ 6051	RIV
❑ 6054	RIV
❑ 6064	DRS
❑ 6067	RIV
❑ 6103	WCR
❑ 6110	DBR
❑ 6115	WCR
❑ 6117	DRS
❑ 6121	OLS
❑ 6122	DRS
❑ 6135	WCR
❑ 6137	RIV
❑ 6139	DBR
❑ 6141	RIV
❑ 6152	DBR
❑ 6158	RIV
❑ 6160	OLS
❑ 6164	OLS
❑ 6173	DRS
❑ 6176	RIV
❑ 6177	RIV
❑ 6183	RIV
❑ 6310	RIV
❑ 6311	DBR
❑ 6312	WCR
❑ 6313	VSO
❑ 6320	RIV
❑ 6528	WCR
❑ 6700	FSR
❑ 6701	FSR
❑ 6702	FSR
❑ 6703	FSR
❑ 6704	FSR
❑ 6705	FSR
❑ 6706	FSR
❑ 6707	FSR
❑ 6708	FSR
❑ 6720	RIV
❑ 6722	RIV
❑ 6723	WCR
❑ 6724	WCR
❑ 9004	RAF
❑ 9005	RAF
❑ 9101	VTN
❑ 9104	WCR
❑ 9267	NYM
❑ 9274	NYM
❑ 9391	WCR
❑ 9392	WCR
❑ 9419	DRS
❑ 9428	DRS
❑ 9440	WCR
❑ 9448	WCR
❑ 9481	NRL
❑ 9488	DRS
❑ 9493	WCR
❑ 9494	DBR
❑ 9496	VTN
❑ 9502	VSO
❑ 9504	RIV
❑ 9506	DRS
❑ 9507	RIV
❑ 9508	DRS
❑ 9509	RIV
❑ 9516	NRL
❑ 9520	RIV
❑ 9521	RIV
❑ 9522	DBR
❑ 9523	NRL
❑ 9525	DRS
❑ 9526	RIV
❑ 9527	RIV
❑ 9529	DBR
❑ 9531	DBR
❑ 9537	RIV
❑ 9539	RIV
❑ 9704	BAR
❑ 9705	BAR
❑ 9707	BAR
❑ 9709	BAR
❑ 9710	BAR
❑ 9711	VTN
❑ 9713	NRL
❑ 9800	FSR
❑ 9801	FSR
❑ 9802	FSR
❑ 9803	FSR
❑ 9804	FSR
❑ 9805	FSR
❑ 9806	FSR
❑ 9807	FSR
❑ 9808	FSR
❑ 9809	FSR
❑ 9810	FSR
❑ 10200	AEA
❑ 10201	DBR
❑ 10202	DBR
❑ 10203	AEA
❑ 10204	3MP
❑ 10206	OLS
❑ 10211	DBS
❑ 10212	VWC
❑ 10214	AEA
❑ 10215	DBS
❑ 10216	AEA
❑ 10217	VWC
❑ 10219	FGW
❑ 10222	DBS
❑ 10223	AEA
❑ 10225	FGW
❑ 10226	DBS
❑ 10228	AEA
❑ 10229	AEA
❑ 10231	OLS
❑ 10232	FGW
❑ 10233	DBS
❑ 10235	DBR
❑ 10237	DBS
❑ 10241	OLS
❑ 10242	DBR
❑ 10246	DBR
❑ 10247	AEA
❑ 10249	ATW
❑ 10250	DBS
❑ 10253	OLS
❑ 10256	OLS
❑ 10257	DBS
❑ 10259	ATW
❑ 10260	OLS
❑ 10271	DBR
❑ 10272	DBR
❑ 10273	DBR
❑ 10274	DBR
❑ 10300	ICE
❑ 10301	ICE
❑ 10302	ICE
❑ 10303	ICE
❑ 10304	ICE
❑ 10305	ICE
❑ 10306	ICE
❑ 10307	ICE
❑ 10308	ICE
❑ 10309	ICE
❑ 10310	ICE
❑ 10311	ICE
❑ 10312	ICE
❑ 10313	ICE
❑ 10315	ICE
❑ 10317	ICE
❑ 10318	ICE
❑ 10319	ICE
❑ 10320	ICE
❑ 10321	ICE
❑ 10323	ICE
❑ 10324	ICE
❑ 10325	ICE
❑ 10326	ICE
❑ 10328	ICE
❑ 10329	ICE
❑ 10330	ICE
❑ 10331	ICE
❑ 10332	ICE
❑ 10333	ICE
❑ 10401	AEA
❑ 10402	AEA
❑ 10403	AEA
❑ 10404	AEA
❑ 10405	AEA
❑ 10406	AEA
❑ 10501	FSR
❑ 10502	FSR
❑ 10504	FSR
❑ 10506	FSR
❑ 10507	FSR
❑ 10508	FSR
❑ 10513	FSR
❑ 10516	FSR
❑ 10519	FSR
❑ 10520	FSR
❑ 10522	FSR
❑ 10523	FSR
❑ 10526	FSR
❑ 10527	FSR
❑ 10529	FSR
❑ 10531	FSR
❑ 10532	FGW
❑ 10534	FGW
❑ 10540	DBR
❑ 10541	VSO
❑ 10542	FSR
❑ 10543	FSR
❑ 10544	FSR
❑ 10546	DBR
❑ 10547	OLS
❑ 10548	FSR
❑ 10551	FSR
❑ 10553	FSR
❑ 10554	DBR
❑ 10556	VSO
❑ 10561	FSR
❑ 10562	FSR
❑ 10563	FGW
❑ 10565	FSR
❑ 10569	VSO
❑ 10580	FSR
❑ 10584	FGW
❑ 10589	FGW
❑ 10590	FGW
❑ 10594	FGW
❑ 10596	FGW
❑ 10597	FSR
❑ 10598	FSR
❑ 10600	FSR
❑ 10601	FGW
❑ 10605	FSR
❑ 10607	FSR
❑ 10610	FSR
❑ 10612	FGW
❑ 10613	FSR
❑ 10614	FSR
❑ 10616	FGW
❑ 10617	FSR
❑ 10648	FSR
❑ 10650	FSR
❑ 10661	OLS
❑ 10666	FSR
❑ 10667	OLS
❑ 10675	FSR
❑ 10680	FSR
❑ 10681	DBR
❑ 10682	OLS
❑ 10683	FSR
❑ 10688	FSR
❑ 10689	FSR
❑ 10690	FSR
❑ 10693	FSR
❑ 10698	OLS
❑ 10699	FSR
❑ 10703	FSR
❑ 10706	FSR
❑ 10710	DBR
❑ 10714	FSR
❑ 10718	FSR
❑ 10719	FSR
❑ 10722	FSR
❑ 10723	FSR
❑ 10729	VSO
❑ 10731	DBR
❑ 10733	OLS
❑ 10734	VSO
❑ 11005	DBR
❑ 11006	DRS
❑ 11007	VWC
❑ 11011	OLS
❑ 11013	DBR

❑ 11018 VWC
❑ 11019 DBR
❑ 11021 DRS
❑ 11026 OLS
❑ 11027 DBR
❑ 11028 DBR
❑ 11029 DBR
❑ 11030 DBR
❑ 11031 DBS
❑ 11033 DBR
❑ 11039 DBS
❑ 11044 DBR
❑ 11046 DBR
❑ 11048 VWC
❑ 11054 DBR
❑ 11066 AEA
❑ 11067 AEA
❑ 11068 AEA
❑ 11069 AEA
❑ 11070 AEA
❑ 11072 AEA
❑ 11073 AEA
❑ 11074 OLS
❑ 11075 AEA
❑ 11076 AEA
❑ 11077 AEA
❑ 11078 AEA
❑ 11079 DBR
❑ 11080 AEA
❑ 11081 AEA
❑ 11082 AEA
❑ 11085 AEA
❑ 11087 AEA
❑ 11088 AEA
❑ 11089 DBR
❑ 11090 AEA
❑ 11091 AEA
❑ 11092 AEA
❑ 11093 AEA
❑ 11094 AEA
❑ 11095 AEA
❑ 11096 AEA
❑ 11097 DBR
❑ 11098 AEA
❑ 11099 AEA
❑ 11100 AEA
❑ 11101 AEA
❑ 11201 ICE
❑ 11219 ICE
❑ 11229 ICE
❑ 11237 ICE
❑ 11241 ICE
❑ 11244 ICE
❑ 11273 ICE
❑ 11277 ICE
❑ 11278 ICE
❑ 11279 ICE
❑ 11280 ICE
❑ 11281 ICE
❑ 11282 ICE
❑ 11283 ICE
❑ 11284 ICE
❑ 11285 ICE
❑ 11286 ICE
❑ 11287 ICE
❑ 11288 ICE
❑ 11289 ICE
❑ 11290 ICE
❑ 11291 ICE
❑ 11292 ICE
❑ 11293 ICE
❑ 11294 ICE
❑ 11295 ICE
❑ 11298 ICE
❑ 11299 ICE
❑ 11301 ICE
❑ 11302 ICE
❑ 11303 ICE
❑ 11304 ICE
❑ 11305 ICE
❑ 11306 ICE
❑ 11307 ICE
❑ 11308 ICE
❑ 11309 ICE
❑ 11310 ICE
❑ 11311 ICE
❑ 11312 ICE
❑ 11313 ICE
❑ 11314 ICE
❑ 11315 ICE
❑ 11316 ICE
❑ 11317 ICE
❑ 11318 ICE
❑ 11319 ICE
❑ 11320 ICE
❑ 11321 ICE
❑ 11322 ICE
❑ 11323 ICE
❑ 11324 ICE
❑ 11325 ICE
❑ 11326 ICE
❑ 11327 ICE
❑ 11328 ICE
❑ 11329 ICE
❑ 11330 ICE
❑ 11401 ICE
❑ 11402 ICE
❑ 11403 ICE
❑ 11404 ICE
❑ 11405 ICE
❑ 11406 ICE
❑ 11407 ICE
❑ 11408 ICE
❑ 11409 ICE
❑ 11410 ICE
❑ 11411 ICE
❑ 11412 ICE
❑ 11413 ICE
❑ 11414 ICE
❑ 11415 ICE
❑ 11416 ICE
❑ 11417 ICE
❑ 11418 ICE
❑ 11419 ICE
❑ 11420 ICE
❑ 11421 ICE
❑ 11422 ICE
❑ 11423 ICE
❑ 11424 ICE
❑ 11425 ICE
❑ 11426 ICE
❑ 11427 ICE
❑ 11428 ICE
❑ 11429 ICE
❑ 11430 ICE
❑ 11998 ICE
❑ 11999 ICE

❑ 12005 AEA
❑ 12008 OLS
❑ 12009 AEA
❑ 12011 VWC
❑ 12012 AEA
❑ 12013 AEA
❑ 12015 AEA
❑ 12016 AEA
❑ 12019 AEA
❑ 12021 AEA
❑ 12022 OLS
❑ 12024 AEA
❑ 12026 AEA
❑ 12027 AEA
❑ 12029 OLS
❑ 12030 AEA
❑ 12031 AEA
❑ 12032 AEA
❑ 12034 AEA
❑ 12035 AEA
❑ 12036 OLS
❑ 12037 AEA
❑ 12040 AEA
❑ 12041 AEA
❑ 12042 AEA
❑ 12046 AEA
❑ 12047 DRS
❑ 12049 AEA
❑ 12051 AEA
❑ 12056 AEA
❑ 12057 AEA
❑ 12060 AEA
❑ 12061 AEA
❑ 12062 AEA
❑ 12063 DRS
❑ 12064 AEA
❑ 12065 DRS
❑ 12066 AEA
❑ 12067 AEA
❑ 12073 AEA
❑ 12078 VWC
❑ 12079 AEA
❑ 12081 AEA
❑ 12082 AEA
❑ 12083 OLS
❑ 12084 AEA
❑ 12087 DRS
❑ 12089 AEA
❑ 12090 AEA
❑ 12091 AEA
❑ 12092 OLS
❑ 12093 AEA
❑ 12095 OLS
❑ 12097 AEA
❑ 12098 AEA
❑ 12099 AEA
❑ 12100 FGW
❑ 12101 OLS
❑ 12103 AEA
❑ 12105 AEA
❑ 12107 AEA
❑ 12108 AEA
❑ 12109 AEA
❑ 12110 AEA
❑ 12111 AEA
❑ 12114 AEA
❑ 12115 AEA
❑ 12116 AEA
❑ 12118 AEA
❑ 12120 AEA
❑ 12122 VWC
❑ 12125 AEA
❑ 12126 AEA
❑ 12129 AEA
❑ 12130 AEA
❑ 12132 AEA
❑ 12133 VWC
❑ 12134 DRS
❑ 12137 AEA
❑ 12138 VWC
❑ 12139 AEA
❑ 12141 AEA
❑ 12142 FGW
❑ 12143 AEA
❑ 12144 OLS
❑ 12146 AEA
❑ 12147 AEA
❑ 12148 AEA
❑ 12150 AEA
❑ 12151 AEA
❑ 12153 AEA
❑ 12154 AEA
❑ 12156 OLS
❑ 12159 AEA
❑ 12160 OLS
❑ 12161 FGW
❑ 12163 OLS
❑ 12164 AEA
❑ 12166 AEA
❑ 12167 AEA
❑ 12170 AEA
❑ 12171 AEA
❑ 12176 ATW
❑ 12177 ATW
❑ 12178 ATW
❑ 12179 ATW
❑ 12180 ATW
❑ 12181 ATW

❑ 12200 ICE
❑ 12201 ICE
❑ 12202 ICE
❑ 12203 ICE
❑ 12204 ICE
❑ 12205 ICE
❑ 12207 ICE
❑ 12208 ICE
❑ 12209 ICE
❑ 12210 ICE
❑ 12211 ICE
❑ 12212 ICE
❑ 12213 ICE
❑ 12214 ICE
❑ 12215 ICE
❑ 12216 ICE
❑ 12217 ICE
❑ 12218 ICE
❑ 12219 ICE
❑ 12220 ICE
❑ 12222 ICE
❑ 12223 ICE
❑ 12224 ICE
❑ 12225 ICE
❑ 12226 ICE
❑ 12227 ICE
❑ 12228 ICE
❑ 12229 ICE
❑ 12230 ICE
❑ 12231 ICE
❑ 12232 ICE

❑ 12300 ICE
❑ 12301 ICE
❑ 12302 ICE
❑ 12303 ICE
❑ 12304 ICE
❑ 12305 ICE
❑ 12307 ICE
❑ 12308 ICE
❑ 12309 ICE
❑ 12310 ICE
❑ 12311 ICE
❑ 12312 ICE
❑ 12313 ICE
❑ 12315 ICE
❑ 12316 ICE
❑ 12317 ICE
❑ 12318 ICE
❑ 12319 ICE
❑ 12320 ICE
❑ 12321 ICE
❑ 12322 ICE
❑ 12323 ICE
❑ 12324 ICE
❑ 12325 ICE
❑ 12326 ICE
❑ 12327 ICE
❑ 12328 ICE
❑ 12329 ICE
❑ 12330 ICE
❑ 12331 ICE
❑ 12400 ICE
❑ 12401 ICE
❑ 12402 ICE
❑ 12403 ICE
❑ 12404 ICE
❑ 12405 ICE

Number	Operator
❑ 12406	ICE
❑ 12407	ICE
❑ 12409	ICE
❑ 12410	ICE
❑ 12411	ICE
❑ 12414	ICE
❑ 12415	ICE
❑ 12417	ICE
❑ 12419	ICE
❑ 12420	ICE
❑ 12421	ICE
❑ 12422	ICE
❑ 12423	ICE
❑ 12424	ICE
❑ 12425	ICE
❑ 12426	ICE
❑ 12427	ICE
❑ 12428	ICE
❑ 12429	ICE
❑ 12430	ICE
❑ 12431	ICE
❑ 12432	ICE
❑ 12433	ICE
❑ 12434	ICE
❑ 12436	ICE
❑ 12437	ICE
❑ 12438	ICE
❑ 12439	ICE
❑ 12440	ICE
❑ 12441	ICE
❑ 12442	ICE
❑ 12443	ICE
❑ 12444	ICE
❑ 12445	ICE
❑ 12446	ICE
❑ 12447	ICE
❑ 12448	ICE
❑ 12449	ICE
❑ 12450	ICE
❑ 12452	ICE
❑ 12453	ICE
❑ 12454	ICE
❑ 12455	ICE
❑ 12456	ICE
❑ 12457	ICE
❑ 12458	ICE
❑ 12459	ICE
❑ 12460	ICE
❑ 12461	ICE
❑ 12462	ICE
❑ 12463	ICE
❑ 12464	ICE
❑ 12465	ICE
❑ 12466	ICE
❑ 12467	ICE
❑ 12468	ICE
❑ 12469	ICE
❑ 12470	ICE
❑ 12471	ICE
❑ 12472	ICE
❑ 12473	ICE
❑ 12474	ICE
❑ 12476	ICE
❑ 12477	ICE
❑ 12478	ICE
❑ 12480	ICE
❑ 12481	ICE
❑ 12483	ICE
❑ 12484	ICE
❑ 12485	ICE
❑ 12486	ICE
❑ 12488	ICE
❑ 12489	ICE
❑ 12513	ICE
❑ 12514	ICE
❑ 12515	ICE
❑ 12518	ICE
❑ 12519	ICE
❑ 12520	ICE
❑ 12522	ICE
❑ 12526	ICE
❑ 12533	ICE
❑ 12534	ICE
❑ 12538	ICE
❑ 12602	DBR
❑ 12603	DBR
❑ 12604	DBR
❑ 12605	DBR
❑ 12606	DBR
❑ 12607	DBR
❑ 12608	DBR
❑ 12609	DBR
❑ 12612	DBR
❑ 12613	DBR
❑ 12614	DBR
❑ 12615	DBR
❑ 12616	DBR
❑ 12617	DBR
❑ 12618	DBR
❑ 12619	DBR
❑ 12621	DBR
❑ 12623	DBR
❑ 12625	DBR
❑ 12627	DBR
❑ 13227	WCR
❑ 13229	BOK
❑ 13230	BOK
❑ 13306	WCR
❑ 13320	WCR
❑ 13321	WCR
❑ 13440	WCR
❑ 13508	RAF
❑ 13581	RRS
❑ 13583	RRS
❑ 14007	SUP
❑ 16156	NYM
❑ 17013	SUP
❑ 17015	RIV
❑ 17018	VTN
❑ 17019	SUP
❑ 17025	SUP
❑ 17041	SUP
❑ 17056	RIV
❑ 17077	RIV
❑ 17080	RAF
❑ 17090	VTN
❑ 17096	SUP
❑ 17102	WCR
❑ 17105	RIV
❑ 17159	DRS
❑ 17167	VSO
❑ 17168	WCR
❑ 17173	FGW
❑ 17174	FGW
❑ 17175	FGW
❑ 18806	WCR
❑ 18893	WCR
❑ 19208	WCR
❑ 21096	SUP
❑ 21100	NYM
❑ 21224	RIV
❑ 21232	SUP
❑ 21236	SUP
❑ 21241	SRP
❑ 21245	RIV
❑ 21249	SUP
❑ 21252	MHR
❑ 21256	WCR
❑ 21266	WCR
❑ 21268	SUP
❑ 21269	RIV
❑ 21272	RIV
❑ 34525	WCR
❑ 35089	NYM
❑ 35185	SRP
❑ 35290	DBR
❑ 35317	SUP
❑ 35322	SUP
❑ 35329	SUP
❑ 35333	SUP
❑ 35407	WCR
❑ 35449	SUP
❑ 35451	SUP
❑ 35457	SUP
❑ 35461	SUP
❑ 35463	SUP
❑ 35464	SUP
❑ 35465	SUP
❑ 35466	VSO
❑ 35468	SUP
❑ 35469	RIV
❑ 35470	SUP
❑ 35476	SUP
❑ 35486	SUP
❑ 35508	SUP
❑ 35511	RAF
❑ 35517	SUP
❑ 35518	SUP
❑ 40101	FGW
❑ 40102	FGW
❑ 40103	FGW
❑ 40104	FGW
❑ 40105	FGW
❑ 40106	FGW
❑ 40107	FGW
❑ 40108	FGW
❑ 40109	FGW
❑ 40110	FGW
❑ 40111	FGW
❑ 40112	FGW
❑ 40113	FGW
❑ 40114	FGW
❑ 40115	FGW
❑ 40116	FGW
❑ 40117	FGW
❑ 40118	FGW
❑ 40119	FGW
❑ 40204	FGW
❑ 40205	FGW
❑ 40207	FGW
❑ 40210	FGW
❑ 40221	FGW
❑ 40231	FGW
❑ 40402	DBR
❑ 40403	DBR
❑ 40416	DBR
❑ 40417	OLS
❑ 40419	OLS
❑ 40424	GTL
❑ 40425	OLS
❑ 40426	GTL
❑ 40433	GTL
❑ 40434	DBR
❑ 40700	EMT
❑ 40701	ICE
❑ 40702	ICE
❑ 40703	FGW
❑ 40704	ICE
❑ 40705	ICE
❑ 40706	ICE
❑ 40708	ICE
❑ 40710	FGW
❑ 40711	ICE
❑ 40713	FGW
❑ 40715	FGW
❑ 40716	FGW
❑ 40718	FGW
❑ 40720	ICE
❑ 40721	FGW
❑ 40722	FGW
❑ 40727	FGW
❑ 40728	EMT
❑ 40730	EMT
❑ 40732	ICE
❑ 40733	FGW
❑ 40734	FGW
❑ 40735	ICE
❑ 40737	ICE
❑ 40739	FGW
❑ 40740	ICE
❑ 40741	EMT
❑ 40742	ICE
❑ 40743	FGW
❑ 40746	EMT
❑ 40748	ICE
❑ 40749	EMT
❑ 40750	ICE
❑ 40751	EMT
❑ 40752	FGW
❑ 40753	EMT
❑ 40754	EMT
❑ 40755	FGW
❑ 40756	EMT
❑ 40757	FGW
❑ 40801	FGW
❑ 40802	FGW
❑ 40803	FGW
❑ 40805	ICE
❑ 40806	FGW
❑ 40807	FGW
❑ 40808	FGW
❑ 40809	FGW
❑ 40810	FGW
❑ 40811	FGW
❑ 40900	FGW
❑ 40901	FGW
❑ 40902	FGW
❑ 40903	FGW
❑ 40904	FGW
❑ 41003	FGW
❑ 41004	FGW
❑ 41005	FGW
❑ 41006	FGW
❑ 41007	FGW
❑ 41008	FGW
❑ 41009	FGW
❑ 41010	FGW
❑ 41011	FGW
❑ 41012	FGW
❑ 41015	FGW
❑ 41016	FGW
❑ 41017	FGW
❑ 41018	FGW
❑ 41019	FGW
❑ 41020	FGW
❑ 41021	FGW
❑ 41022	FGW
❑ 41023	FGW
❑ 41024	FGW
❑ 41026	AXC
❑ 41027	FGW
❑ 41028	FGW
❑ 41029	FGW
❑ 41030	FGW
❑ 41031	FGW
❑ 41032	FGW
❑ 41033	FGW
❑ 41034	FGW
❑ 41035	AXC
❑ 41037	FGW
❑ 41038	FGW
❑ 41039	ICE
❑ 41040	ICE

Number	Operator
❑ 41041	EMT
❑ 41043	ICE
❑ 41044	ICE
❑ 41045	FGW
❑ 41046	EMT
❑ 41051	FGW
❑ 41052	FGW
❑ 41055	FGW
❑ 41056	FGW
❑ 41057	EMT
❑ 41058	ICE
❑ 41059	FGW
❑ 41061	EMT
❑ 41062	ICE
❑ 41063	EMT
❑ 41064	EMT
❑ 41065	FGW
❑ 41066	ICE
❑ 41067	EMT
❑ 41068	EMT
❑ 41069	EMT
❑ 41070	EMT
❑ 41071	EMT
❑ 41072	EMT
❑ 41075	EMT
❑ 41076	EMT
❑ 41077	EMT
❑ 41079	EMT
❑ 41081	FGW
❑ 41083	ICE
❑ 41084	EMT
❑ 41085	FGW
❑ 41086	FGW
❑ 41087	ICE
❑ 41088	ICE
❑ 41089	FGW
❑ 41090	ICE
❑ 41091	ICE
❑ 41092	ICE
❑ 41093	FGW
❑ 41094	FGW
❑ 41095	ICE
❑ 41096	FGW
❑ 41097	ICE
❑ 41098	ICE
❑ 41099	ICE
❑ 41100	ICE
❑ 41101	FGW
❑ 41102	FGW
❑ 41103	FGW
❑ 41104	FGW
❑ 41105	FGW
❑ 41106	FGW
❑ 41108	FGW
❑ 41109	FGW
❑ 41110	FGW
❑ 41111	EMT
❑ 41112	EMT
❑ 41113	EMT
❑ 41114	FGW
❑ 41115	ICE
❑ 41116	FGW
❑ 41117	EMT
❑ 41118	ICE
❑ 41119	FGW
❑ 41120	ICE
❑ 41121	FGW
❑ 41122	FGW
❑ 41123	FGW
❑ 41124	FGW
❑ 41125	FGW
❑ 41126	FGW
❑ 41127	FGW
❑ 41128	FGW
❑ 41129	FGW
❑ 41130	FGW
❑ 41131	FGW
❑ 41132	FGW
❑ 41133	FGW
❑ 41134	FGW
❑ 41135	FGW
❑ 41136	FGW
❑ 41137	FGW
❑ 41138	FGW
❑ 41139	FGW
❑ 41140	FGW
❑ 41141	FGW
❑ 41142	FGW
❑ 41143	FGW
❑ 41144	FGW
❑ 41145	FGW
❑ 41146	FGW
❑ 41147	FGW
❑ 41148	FGW
❑ 41149	FGW
❑ 41150	ICE
❑ 41151	ICE
❑ 41152	ICE
❑ 41154	ICE
❑ 41155	FGW
❑ 41156	EMT
❑ 41157	FGW
❑ 41158	FGW
❑ 41159	ICE
❑ 41160	FGW
❑ 41161	FGW
❑ 41162	FGW
❑ 41163	FGW
❑ 41164	ICE
❑ 41165	ICE
❑ 41166	FGW
❑ 41167	FGW
❑ 41168	FGW
❑ 41169	FGW
❑ 41170	ICE
❑ 41176	FGW
❑ 41179	FGW
❑ 41180	FGW
❑ 41181	FGW
❑ 41182	FGW
❑ 41183	FGW
❑ 41184	FGW
❑ 41185	ICE
❑ 41186	FGW
❑ 41187	FGW
❑ 41189	FGW
❑ 41190	ICE
❑ 41191	FGW
❑ 41192	FGW
❑ 41193	AXC
❑ 41194	AXC
❑ 41195	AXC
❑ 41201	GTL
❑ 41202	GTL
❑ 41203	GTL
❑ 41204	GTL
❑ 41205	GTL
❑ 41206	GTL
❑ 42003	FGW
❑ 42004	FGW
❑ 42005	FGW
❑ 42006	FGW
❑ 42007	FGW
❑ 42008	FGW
❑ 42009	FGW
❑ 42010	FGW
❑ 42012	FGW
❑ 42013	FGW
❑ 42014	FGW
❑ 42015	FGW
❑ 42016	FGW
❑ 42019	FGW
❑ 42021	FGW
❑ 42023	FGW
❑ 42024	FGW
❑ 42025	FGW
❑ 42026	FGW
❑ 42027	FGW
❑ 42028	FGW
❑ 42029	FGW
❑ 42030	FGW
❑ 42031	FGW
❑ 42032	FGW
❑ 42033	FGW
❑ 42034	FGW
❑ 42035	FGW
❑ 42036	AXC
❑ 42037	AXC
❑ 42038	AXC
❑ 42039	FGW
❑ 42040	FGW
❑ 42041	FGW
❑ 42042	FGW
❑ 42043	FGW
❑ 42044	FGW
❑ 42045	FGW
❑ 42046	FGW
❑ 42047	FGW
❑ 42048	FGW
❑ 42049	FGW
❑ 42050	FGW
❑ 42051	AXC
❑ 42052	AXC
❑ 42053	AXC
❑ 42054	FGW
❑ 42055	FGW
❑ 42056	FGW
❑ 42057	ICE
❑ 42058	ICE
❑ 42059	ICE
❑ 42060	FGW
❑ 42061	FGW
❑ 42062	FGW
❑ 42063	ICE
❑ 42064	ICE
❑ 42065	ICE
❑ 42066	FGW
❑ 42067	FGW
❑ 42068	FGW
❑ 42069	FGW
❑ 42070	FGW
❑ 42071	FGW
❑ 42072	FGW
❑ 42073	FGW
❑ 42074	FGW
❑ 42075	FGW
❑ 42076	FGW
❑ 42077	FGW
❑ 42078	FGW
❑ 42079	FGW
❑ 42080	FGW
❑ 42081	FGW
❑ 42083	FGW
❑ 42085	FGW
❑ 42087	FGW
❑ 42089	FGW
❑ 42091	ICE
❑ 42092	FGW
❑ 42093	FGW
❑ 42094	FGW
❑ 42095	FGW
❑ 42096	FGW
❑ 42097	AXC
❑ 42098	FGW
❑ 42099	FGW
❑ 42100	EMT
❑ 42101	FGW
❑ 42102	FGW
❑ 42103	FGW
❑ 42105	FGW
❑ 42106	ICE
❑ 42107	FGW
❑ 42108	FGW
❑ 42109	ICE
❑ 42110	ICE
❑ 42111	EMT
❑ 42112	EMT
❑ 42113	EMT
❑ 42115	FGW
❑ 42116	ICE
❑ 42117	ICE
❑ 42118	FGW
❑ 42119	EMT
❑ 42120	EMT
❑ 42121	EMT
❑ 42123	ICE
❑ 42124	EMT
❑ 42125	ICE
❑ 42126	FGW
❑ 42127	ICE
❑ 42128	ICE
❑ 42129	FGW
❑ 42130	ICE
❑ 42131	EMT
❑ 42132	EMT
❑ 42133	EMT
❑ 42134	ICE
❑ 42135	EMT
❑ 42136	EMT
❑ 42137	EMT
❑ 42138	FGW
❑ 42139	EMT
❑ 42140	EMT
❑ 42141	EMT
❑ 42143	FGW
❑ 42144	FGW
❑ 42145	FGW
❑ 42146	ICE
❑ 42147	ICE
❑ 42148	EMT
❑ 42149	EMT
❑ 42150	ICE
❑ 42151	EMT
❑ 42152	EMT
❑ 42153	EMT
❑ 42154	ICE
❑ 42155	EMT
❑ 42156	EMT
❑ 42157	EMT
❑ 42158	ICE
❑ 42159	ICE
❑ 42160	ICE
❑ 42161	ICE
❑ 42163	ICE
❑ 42164	EMT
❑ 42165	EMT
❑ 42166	FGW
❑ 42167	FGW
❑ 42168	FGW
❑ 42169	FGW
❑ 42171	ICE
❑ 42172	ICE
❑ 42173	FGW
❑ 42174	FGW
❑ 42175	FGW
❑ 42176	FGW
❑ 42177	FGW
❑ 42178	FGW
❑ 42179	ICE
❑ 42180	ICE
❑ 42181	ICE
❑ 42182	ICE
❑ 42183	FGW
❑ 42184	FGW
❑ 42185	FGW
❑ 42186	ICE
❑ 42188	ICE
❑ 42189	ICE
❑ 42190	ICE
❑ 42191	ICE
❑ 42192	ICE
❑ 42193	ICE
❑ 42194	EMT
❑ 42195	FGW

❑ 42196 FGW
❑ 42197 FGW
❑ 42198 ICE
❑ 42199 ICE
❑ 42200 FGW
❑ 42201 FGW
❑ 42202 FGW
❑ 42203 FGW
❑ 42204 FGW
❑ 42205 ICE
❑ 42206 FGW
❑ 42207 FGW
❑ 42208 FGW
❑ 42209 FGW
❑ 42210 ICE
❑ 42211 FGW
❑ 42212 FGW
❑ 42213 FGW
❑ 42214 FGW
❑ 42215 ICE
❑ 42216 FGW
❑ 42217 FGW
❑ 42218 FGW
❑ 42219 ICE
❑ 42220 EMT
❑ 42221 FGW
❑ 42222 FGW
❑ 42224 FGW
❑ 42225 EMT
❑ 42226 ICE
❑ 42227 EMT
❑ 42228 ICE
❑ 42229 EMT
❑ 42230 EMT
❑ 42231 FGW
❑ 42232 FGW
❑ 42233 FGW
❑ 42234 AXC
❑ 42235 ICE
❑ 42236 FGW
❑ 42237 ICE
❑ 42238 ICE
❑ 42239 ICE
❑ 42240 ICE
❑ 42241 ICE
❑ 42242 ICE
❑ 42243 ICE
❑ 42244 ICE
❑ 42245 FGW
❑ 42247 FGW
❑ 42250 FGW
❑ 42251 FGW
❑ 42252 FGW
❑ 42253 FGW
❑ 42255 FGW
❑ 42256 FGW
❑ 42257 FGW
❑ 42258 FGW
❑ 42259 FGW
❑ 42260 FGW
❑ 42261 FGW
❑ 42263 FGW
❑ 42264 FGW

❑ 42265 FGW
❑ 42266 FGW
❑ 42267 FGW
❑ 42268 FGW
❑ 42269 FGW
❑ 42271 FGW
❑ 42272 FGW
❑ 42273 FGW
❑ 42275 FGW
❑ 42276 FGW
❑ 42277 FGW
❑ 42279 FGW
❑ 42280 FGW
❑ 42281 FGW
❑ 42283 FGW
❑ 42284 FGW
❑ 42285 FGW
❑ 42286 ICE
❑ 42287 FGW
❑ 42288 FGW
❑ 42289 FGW
❑ 42290 AXC
❑ 42291 FGW
❑ 42292 FGW
❑ 42293 FGW
❑ 42294 FGW
❑ 42295 FGW
❑ 42296 FGW
❑ 42297 FGW
❑ 42299 FGW
❑ 42300 FGW
❑ 42301 FGW
❑ 42302 FGW
❑ 42303 FGW
❑ 42304 FGW
❑ 42305 FGW
❑ 42306 ICE
❑ 42307 ICE
❑ 42308 FGW
❑ 42310 FGW
❑ 42315 FGW
❑ 42317 FGW
❑ 42319 FGW
❑ 42321 FGW
❑ 42322 ICE
❑ 42323 ICE
❑ 42325 FGW
❑ 42326 ICE
❑ 42327 EMT
❑ 42328 EMT
❑ 42329 EMT
❑ 42330 ICE
❑ 42331 EMT
❑ 42332 FGW
❑ 42333 FGW
❑ 42335 ICE
❑ 42337 EMT
❑ 42339 EMT
❑ 42340 ICE
❑ 42341 EMT
❑ 42342 AXC
❑ 42343 FGW
❑ 42344 FGW

❑ 42345 FGW
❑ 42346 FGW
❑ 42347 FGW
❑ 42348 FGW
❑ 42349 FGW
❑ 42350 FGW
❑ 42351 FGW
❑ 42352 ICE
❑ 42353 FGW
❑ 42354 ICE
❑ 42355 ICE
❑ 42356 FGW
❑ 42357 ICE
❑ 42360 FGW
❑ 42361 FGW
❑ 42362 FGW
❑ 42363 ICE
❑ 42364 FGW
❑ 42365 FGW
❑ 42366 AXC
❑ 42367 AXC
❑ 42368 AXC
❑ 42369 AXC
❑ 42370 AXC
❑ 42371 AXC
❑ 42372 AXC
❑ 42373 AXC
❑ 42374 AXC
❑ 42375 AXC
❑ 42376 AXC
❑ 42377 AXC
❑ 42378 AXC
❑ 42379 AXC
❑ 42380 AXC
❑ 42381 FGW
❑ 42382 FGW
❑ 42383 FGW
❑ 42384 EMT
❑ 42385 FGW

❑ 42401 GTL
❑ 42402 GTL
❑ 42403 GTL
❑ 42404 GTL
❑ 42405 GTL
❑ 42406 GTL
❑ 42407 GTL
❑ 42408 GTL
❑ 42409 GTL

❑ 42501 FGW
❑ 42502 FGW
❑ 42503 FGW
❑ 42504 FGW
❑ 42505 FGW
❑ 42506 FGW
❑ 42507 FGW
❑ 42508 FGW
❑ 42509 FGW
❑ 42510 FGW
❑ 42511 FGW
❑ 42512 FGW
❑ 42513 FGW

❑ 42514 FGW
❑ 42515 FGW
❑ 42516 FGW
❑ 42517 FGW
❑ 42518 FGW
❑ 42519 FGW
❑ 42520 FGW

❑ 44000 FGW
❑ 44001 FGW
❑ 44002 FGW
❑ 44003 FGW
❑ 44004 FGW
❑ 44005 FGW
❑ 44007 FGW
❑ 44008 FGW
❑ 44009 FGW
❑ 44010 FGW
❑ 44011 FGW
❑ 44012 AXC
❑ 44013 FGW
❑ 44014 FGW
❑ 44015 FGW
❑ 44016 FGW
❑ 44017 AXC
❑ 44018 FGW
❑ 44019 ICE
❑ 44020 FGW
❑ 44021 AXC
❑ 44022 FGW
❑ 44023 FGW
❑ 44024 FGW
❑ 44025 FGW
❑ 44026 FGW
❑ 44027 EMT
❑ 44028 FGW
❑ 44029 FGW
❑ 44030 FGW
❑ 44031 ICE
❑ 44032 FGW
❑ 44033 FGW
❑ 44034 FGW
❑ 44035 FGW
❑ 44036 FGW
❑ 44037 FGW
❑ 44038 FGW
❑ 44039 FGW
❑ 44040 FGW
❑ 44041 EMT
❑ 44042 FGW
❑ 44043 FGW
❑ 44044 EMT
❑ 44045 ICE
❑ 44046 EMT
❑ 44047 EMT
❑ 44048 EMT
❑ 44049 FGW
❑ 44050 ICE
❑ 44051 EMT
❑ 44052 AXC
❑ 44054 EMT
❑ 44055 FGW
❑ 44056 ICE

❑ 44057 ICE
❑ 44058 ICE
❑ 44059 FGW
❑ 44060 FGW
❑ 44061 ICE
❑ 44063 ICE
❑ 44064 FGW
❑ 44065 GTL
❑ 44066 FGW
❑ 44067 FGW
❑ 44068 FGW
❑ 44069 FGW
❑ 44070 EMT
❑ 44071 EMT
❑ 44072 AXC
❑ 44073 ICE
❑ 44074 FGW
❑ 44075 ICE
❑ 44076 FGW
❑ 44077 ICE
❑ 44078 FGW
❑ 44079 FGW
❑ 44080 ICE
❑ 44081 FGW
❑ 44083 FGW
❑ 44085 EMT
❑ 44086 FGW
❑ 44088 GTL
❑ 44089 GTL
❑ 44090 FGW
❑ 44091 FGW
❑ 44093 FGW
❑ 44094 ICE
❑ 44097 FGW
❑ 44098 ICE
❑ 44100 FGW
❑ 44101 FGW

❑ 45001 AXC
❑ 45002 AXC
❑ 45003 AXC
❑ 45004 AXC
❑ 45005 AXC
❑ 45018 WCR
❑ 45020 DBR
❑ 45026 WCR

❑ 80041 RIV
❑ 80042 RIV

❑ 99035 SUP
❑ 99040 SUP
❑ 99041 SUP
❑ 99080 SUP
❑ 99108 VTN
❑ 99120 SUP
❑ 99121 WCR
❑ 99125 WCR
❑ 99127 WCR
❑ 99128 WCR
❑ 99132 WCR
❑ 99193 WCR
❑ 99194 WCR

❑ 99195 WCR
❑ 99241 SUP
❑ 99304 WCR
❑ 99311 WCR
❑ 99312 SUP
❑ 99316 WCR
❑ 99317 WCR
❑ 99318 WCR
❑ 99319 WCR
❑ 99326 WCR
❑ 99327 WCR
❑ 99328 WCR
❑ 99329 WCR
❑ 99348 WCR
❑ 99349 VTN
❑ 99350 WCR
❑ 99353 VTN
❑ 99354 WCR
❑ 99361 VTN
❑ 99371 WCR
❑ 99402 WCR
❑ 99405 SUP
❑ 99530 VSO
❑ 99531 VSO
❑ 99532 VSO
❑ 99534 VSO
❑ 99535 VSO
❑ 99536 VSO
❑ 99537 VSO
❑ 99539 VSO
❑ 99541 VSO
❑ 99543 VSO
❑ 99545 VSO
❑ 99546 VSO
❑ 99678 WCR
❑ 99679 WCR
❑ 99670 WCR
❑ 99671 WCR
❑ 99672 WCR
❑ 99673 WCR
❑ 99674 WCR
❑ 99675 WCR
❑ 99676 WCR
❑ 99677 WCR
❑ 99680 WCR
❑ 99706 WCR
❑ 99710 WCR
❑ 99712 WCR
❑ 99713 WCR
❑ 99717 WCR
❑ 99718 WCR
❑ 99721 WCR
❑ 99722 WCR
❑ 99723 WCR
❑ 99782 SUP
❑ 99792 SUP
❑ 99884 WCR
❑ 99953 SUP
❑ 99966 WCR
❑ 99968 VSO
❑ 99969 VSO

❑ 99991 SUP
❑ 99993 RAF
❑ 99995 SUP

NPCCS Stock

❑ 6260 NRL
❑ 6261 NRL
❑ 6262 NRL
❑ 6263 NRL
❑ 6264 NRL
❑ 6321 SIE
❑ 6322 SIE
❑ 6323 SIE
❑ 6324 SIE
❑ 6325 SIE
❑ 6330 FGW
❑ 6336 FGW
❑ 6338 FGW
❑ 6340 ICE
❑ 6344 ICE
❑ 6346 ICE
❑ 6348 FGW
❑ 6352 ICE
❑ 6353 ICE
❑ 6354 ICE
❑ 6355 ICE
❑ 6358 ICE
❑ 6359 ICE
❑ 6376 GBR
❑ 6377 GBR
❑ 6378 GBR
❑ 6379 GBR
❑ 6392 EMT
❑ 6395 EMT
❑ 6397 EMT
❑ 6398 EMT
❑ 6399 EMT

❑ 9393 ICE
❑ 9394 ICE

❑ 9701 NRL
❑ 9702 NRL
❑ 9703 NRL
❑ 9708 NRL
❑ 9713 NRL
❑ 9714 NRL

❑ 72612 NRL
❑ 72616 NRL
❑ 72630 NRL
❑ 72631 NRL
❑ 72639 NRL

❑ 80204 SUP
❑ 80217 SUP
❑ 80220 SUP

❑ 82101 DRS
❑ 82102 AEA
❑ 82103 AEA
❑ 82105 AEA
❑ 82106 DBR
❑ 82107 AEA
❑ 82109 OLS
❑ 82110 DBR
❑ 82111 NRL
❑ 82112 AEA
❑ 82113 DBR
❑ 82114 AEA
❑ 82115 NRL
❑ 82116 DBR
❑ 82118 AEA
❑ 82120 DBR
❑ 82121 AEA
❑ 82122 DBR
❑ 82123 DBR
❑ 82124 NRL
❑ 82125 OLS
❑ 82126 VWC
❑ 82127 AEA
❑ 82129 NRL
❑ 82132 AEA
❑ 82133 AEA
❑ 82136 AEA
❑ 82137 DBR
❑ 82138 DBR
❑ 82139 AEA
❑ 82140 OLS
❑ 82141 DBR
❑ 82143 AEA
❑ 82145 NRL
❑ 82146 DBS
❑ 82148 DBR
❑ 82149 OLS
❑ 82150 DBR
❑ 82152 AEA

❑ 82200 ICE
❑ 82201 ICE
❑ 82202 ICE
❑ 82203 ICE
❑ 82204 ICE
❑ 82205 ICE
❑ 82206 ICE
❑ 82207 ICE
❑ 82208 ICE
❑ 82209 ICE
❑ 82210 ICE
❑ 82211 ICE
❑ 82212 ICE
❑ 82213 ICE
❑ 82214 ICE
❑ 82215 ICE
❑ 82216 ICE
❑ 82217 ICE
❑ 82218 ICE
❑ 82219 ICE
❑ 82220 ICE
❑ 82222 ICE
❑ 82223 ICE
❑ 82224 ICE
❑ 82225 ICE
❑ 82226 ICE
❑ 82227 ICE
❑ 82228 ICE
❑ 82229 ICE
❑ 82230 ICE
❑ 82231 ICE

❑ 82301 CRW
❑ 82302 CRW
❑ 82303 CRW
❑ 82304 CRW
❑ 82305 CRW
❑ 82306 ATW
❑ 82307 ATW
❑ 82308 CRW
❑ 82309 DBR

❑ 92114 NRL
❑ 92159 OLS

❑ 92901 OLS
❑ 92904 VSO
❑ 92931 OLS
❑ 92939 NRL
❑ 94104 DBS
❑ 94106 DBS
❑ 94116 DBS
❑ 94121 DBS
❑ 94137 DBS
❑ 94147 DBS
❑ 94153 DBS
❑ 94160 DBS
❑ 94166 DBS
❑ 94170 DBS
❑ 94176 DBS
❑ 94177 DBS
❑ 94192 DBS
❑ 94195 DBS
❑ 94197 DBS
❑ 94207 DBS
❑ 94208 DBS
❑ 94213 DBS
❑ 94214 DBS
❑ 94217 DBS
❑ 94221 DBS
❑ 94222 DBS
❑ 94225 DBS
❑ 94227 DBS
❑ 94229 DBS
❑ 94302 DBS
❑ 94303 DBS
❑ 94304 DBS
❑ 94306 DBS
❑ 94308 DBS
❑ 94310 DBS
❑ 94311 DBS
❑ 94313 DBS
❑ 94316 DBS
❑ 94317 DBS
❑ 94322 DBS
❑ 94323 DBS
❑ 94326 DBS
❑ 94332 DBS
❑ 94333 DBS
❑ 94334 DBS
❑ 94335 DBS
❑ 94336 DBS
❑ 94340 DBS
❑ 94343 DBS
❑ 94344 DBS
❑ 94406 DBS
❑ 94408 DBS
❑ 94410 DBS
❑ 94412 DBS
❑ 94413 DBS
❑ 94416 DBS
❑ 94420 DBS
❑ 94422 DBS
❑ 94423 DBS
❑ 94427 DBS
❑ 94428 DBS
❑ 94429 DBS
❑ 94431 DBS
❑ 94432 DBS
❑ 94433 DBS
❑ 94434 DBS
❑ 94435 DBS
❑ 94438 DBS
❑ 94440 DBS
❑ 94445 DBS
❑ 94451 DBS
❑ 94462 DBS
❑ 94463 DBS
❑ 94470 DBS
❑ 94479 DBS
❑ 94482 DBS
❑ 94488 DBS
❑ 94490 DBS
❑ 94492 DBS
❑ 94495 DBS
❑ 94497 DBS
❑ 94498 DBS
❑ 94499 DBS
❑ 94501 DBS
❑ 94504 DBS
❑ 94512 DBS
❑ 94514 DBS
❑ 94518 DBS
❑ 94519 DBS
❑ 94520 DBS
❑ 94521 DBS
❑ 94522 DBS
❑ 94525 DBS
❑ 94526 DBS
❑ 94527 DBS
❑ 94528 DBS
❑ 94529 DBS
❑ 94530 DBS
❑ 94531 DBS
❑ 94532 DBS
❑ 94534 DBS
❑ 94536 DBS
❑ 94538 RIV
❑ 94539 DBS
❑ 94540 DBS
❑ 94541 DBS
❑ 94542 DBS
❑ 94543 DBS
❑ 94544 DBS
❑ 94545 DBS

❑ 94546 DBS
❑ 94547 DBS
❑ 94548 DBS
❑ 95300 DBS
❑ 95301 DBS
❑ 95400 DBS
❑ 95410 DBS
❑ 95727 DBS
❑ 95754 DBS
❑ 95761 DBS
❑ 95763 DBS
❑ 96100 VTN
❑ 96139 OLS
❑ 96175 WCR
❑ 96181 OLS
❑ 96371 DRS
❑ 96372 DRS
❑ 96373 DRS
❑ 96374 WAB
❑ 96375 DRS
❑ 96602 COL
❑ 96603 COL
❑ 96604 COL
❑ 96605 COL
❑ 96606 COL
❑ 96607 COL
❑ 96608 COL
❑ 96609 COL

❑ 99666 NRL

❑ 99993 RAF

Service Stock

❑ 950001 NRL
❑ 960014 CRW
❑ 960301 CRW

❑ 971001 NRL
❑ 971002 NRL
❑ 971003 NRL
❑ 971004 NRL

❑ 975025 NRL
❑ 975081 NRL
❑ 975091 NRL
❑ 975280 NRL
❑ 975464 NRL
❑ 975486 NRL
❑ 975814 NRL
❑ 975984 NRL

❑ 977337 NRL
❑ 977868 NRL
❑ 977869 NRL
❑ 977969 NRL
❑ 977974 NRL
❑ 977983 NRL
❑ 977984 NRL
❑ 977985 NRL
❑ 977986 NRL
❑ 977993 NRL
❑ 977994 NRL
❑ 977995 NRL
❑ 977996 PRE
❑ 977997 NRL

❑ 999508 NRL
❑ 999550 NRL
❑ 999602 NRL
❑ 999605 NRL
❑ 999606 NRL

Below: *Three-car First Great Western Class 158/9 No. 158956, formed of set No. 158768 plus car No. 57748 from set 158748, arrives at Bristol Temple Meads on 26 November 2013 with a morning Cardiff to Portsmouth Harbour service. The proper two-car set of these three-car formations can be split from the third vehicle and operate on its own if required.* **CJM**